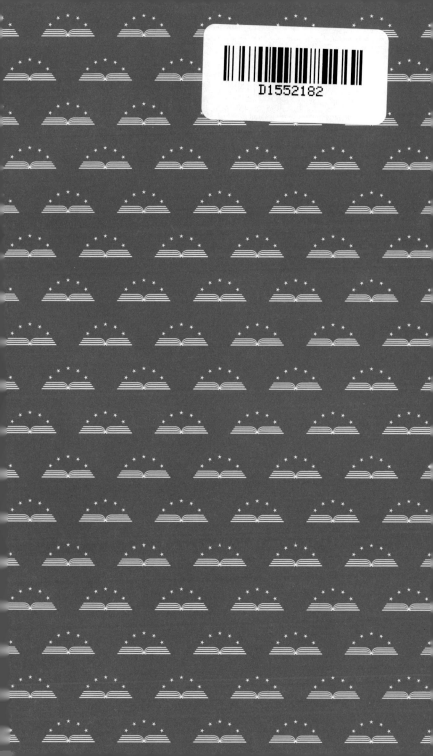

Library of America, a nonprofit organization,
champions our nation's cultural heritage
by publishing America's greatest writing in
authoritative new editions and providing resources
for readers to explore this rich, living legacy.

JONATHAN SCHELL

JONATHAN SCHELL

THE FATE OF THE EARTH
THE ABOLITION
THE UNCONQUERABLE WORLD

Martin J. Sherwin, *editor*

THE LIBRARY OF AMERICA

Jonathan Schell:
The Fate of the Earth, The Abolition, The Unconquerable World
is published and kept in print with a gift from

THE GOULD FAMILY FOUNDATION

to the Guardians of American Letters Fund
established by the Library of America
to ensure that every volume in the series
will be permanently available.

Contents

THE FATE OF THE EARTH

*I dedicate this book
with love to my sister, Suzy.*

Contents

I. A REPUBLIC OF INSECTS
AND GRASS

SINCE JULY 16, 1945, when the first atomic bomb was detonated, at the Trinity test site, near Alamogordo, New Mexico, mankind has lived with nuclear weapons in its midst. Each year, the number of bombs has grown, until now there are some fifty thousand warheads in the world, possessing the explosive yield of roughly twenty billion tons of TNT, or one million six hundred thousand times the yield of the bomb that was dropped by the United States on the city of Hiroshima, in Japan, less than a month after the Trinity explosion. These bombs were built as "weapons" for "war," but their significance greatly transcends war and all its causes and outcomes. They grew out of history, yet they threaten to end history. They were made by men, yet they threaten to annihilate man. They are a pit into which the whole world can fall—a nemesis of all human intentions, actions, and hopes. Only life itself, which they threaten to swallow up, can give the measure of their significance. Yet in spite of the immeasurable importance of nuclear weapons, the world has declined, on the whole, to think about them very much. We have thus far failed to fashion, or to discover within ourselves, an emotional or intellectual or political response to them. This peculiar failure of response, in which hundreds of millions of people acknowledge the presence of an immediate, unremitting threat to their existence and to the existence of the world they live in but do nothing about it—a failure in which both self-interest and fellow-feeling seem to have died—has itself been such a striking phenomenon that it has to be regarded as an extremely important part of the nuclear predicament as this has existed so far. Only very recently have there been signs, in Europe and in the United States, that public opinion has been stirring awake, and that ordinary people may be beginning to ask themselves how they should respond to the nuclear peril.

In what follows, I shall offer some thoughts on the origin and the significance of this predicament, on why we have so long resisted attempts to think about it (we even call a nuclear

5

holocaust "unthinkable") or deal with it, and on the shape and magnitude of the choice that it forces upon us. But first I wish to describe the consequences for the world, insofar as these can be known, of a full-scale nuclear holocaust at the current level of global armament. We have lived in the shadow of nuclear arms for more than thirty-six years, so it does not seem too soon for us to familiarize ourselves with them—to acquaint ourselves with such matters as the "thermal pulse," the "blast wave," and the "three stages of radiation sickness." A description of a full-scale holocaust seems to be made necessary by the simple but basic rule that in order to discuss something one should first know what it is. A considerable number of excellent studies concentrating on various aspects of the damage that can be done by nuclear arms do exist, many of them written only in the last few years. These include a report entitled "The Effects of Nuclear War," which was published in 1979 by the Congressional Office of Technology Assessment, and which deals chiefly with the consequences of a holocaust for the societies of the United States and the Soviet Union; the latest (1977) edition of the indispensable classic textbook "The Effects of Nuclear Weapons," which is edited by Samuel Glasstone and Philip J. Dolan (hereafter I shall refer to it as "Glasstone") and was published jointly by the Department of Defense and the Energy Research and Development Administration, and which makes use of the government's findings from the bombing of Hiroshima and Nagasaki and from the American nuclear-test program to describe the characteristics and the destructive effects of nuclear explosions of all kinds; "Hiroshima and Nagasaki," a comprehensive study, carried out by a group of distinguished Japanese scientists and published here in 1981, of the consequences of the bombing of those two cities; "Long-Term Worldwide Effects of Multiple Nuclear-Weapons Detonations," a report on the global ecological consequences of a nuclear holocaust which was published in 1975 by the National Academy of Sciences (hereafter referred to as the N.A.S. report); a report of research conducted in 1974 and 1975 for the Department of Transportation's Climatic Impact Assessment Program on the consequences of man-made perturbances—including the explosion of nuclear weapons—of the earth's atmosphere; and "Survival of Food Crops and Livestock in the Event of Nuclear

War," proceedings of a 1970 symposium held at Brookhaven National Laboratory, on Long Island, and sponsored by the Office of Civil Defense, the Atomic Energy Commission, and the Department of Agriculture, at which the effects of radiation from fallout on both domesticated and natural ecosystems were discussed. Drawing on these and other printed sources, and also on interviews that I conducted recently with a number of scientists, I have attempted to piece together an account of the principal consequences of a full-scale holocaust. Such an account, which in its nature must be both technical and gruesome, cannot be other than hateful to dwell on, yet it may be only by descending into this hell in imagination now that we can hope to escape descending into it in reality at some later time. The knowledge we thus gain cannot in itself protect us from nuclear annihilation, but without it we cannot begin to take the measures that can actually protect us—or, for that matter, even begin to think in an appropriate way about our plight.

The widespread belief that a nuclear holocaust would in some sense bring about the end of the world has been reflected in the pronouncements of both American and Soviet leaders in the years since the invention of nuclear weapons. For example, President Dwight Eisenhower wrote in a letter in 1956 that one day both sides would have to "meet at the conference table with the understanding that the era of armaments has ended, and the human race must conform its actions to this truth or die." More recently—at a press conference in 1974—Secretary of State Henry Kissinger said that "the accumulation of nuclear arms has to be constrained if mankind is not to destroy itself." And President Jimmy Carter said in his farewell address a year ago that after a nuclear holocaust "the survivors, if any, would live in despair amid the poisoned ruins of a civilization that had committed suicide." Soviet leaders have been no less categorical in their remarks. In late 1981, for example, the Soviet government printed a booklet in which it stated, "The Soviet Union holds that nuclear war would be a universal disaster, and that it would most probably mean the end of civilization. It may lead to the destruction of all mankind." In these and other statements, examples of which could be multiplied indefinitely, Soviet and American leaders have acknowledged the supreme importance of the nuclear peril. However, they have not been precise about what level of catastrophe they were speaking of, and a variety of different outcomes, including the annihilation of the belligerent nations, the destruction of "human civilization," the extinction of mankind, and the extinction of life on earth, have been mentioned, in loose rhetorical fashion, more or less interchangeably. No doubt, the leaders have been vague in part because of the difficulty of making reliable predictions about an event that has no precedent. Yet it seems important to arrive, on the basis of available information, at some judgment concerning the likelihood of these outcomes, for they are not the same. Nor, presumably, would the appropriate political response to all of them be the same. The annihilation of the belligerent nations would be a catastrophe beyond anything in history, but it would not be the end of the world. The destruction of human civilization, even without the biological destruction of the human species, may perhaps rightly be called the end of the world, since it would be the end of that sum of cultural achievements and human relationships which constitutes what many people mean when they speak of "the world." The biological destruction of mankind would, of course, be the end of the world in a stricter sense. As for the destruction of all life on the planet, it would be not merely a human but a planetary end—the death of the earth. And although the annihilation of other forms of life could hardly be of concern to human beings once they themselves had been annihilated, this more comprehensive, planetary termination is nevertheless full of sorrowful meaning for us as we reflect on the possibility now, while we still exist. We not only live on the earth but also are of the earth, and the thought of its death, or even of its mutilation, touches a deep chord in our nature. Finally, it must be noted that a number of observers have, especially in recent years, denied that a holocaust would obliterate even the societies directly attacked. If this were so, then nuclear weapons, while remaining fearsome, would be qualitatively no different from other weapons of war, and the greater part of the nuclear predicament would melt away. (In the discussions of some analysts, nuclear attacks are made to sound almost beneficial. For example, one official of the Office of Civil Defense wrote a few years back that although it might be "verging on the macabre" to say so, "a nuclear war could alleviate some of the factors leading to today's ecological disturbances that are due to current high-population concentrations and heavy industrial production." According to a different, less sanguine view of things, this observation and other cheerful asides of the kind which crop up from time to time in the literature go well over the verge of the macabre.)

Anyone who inquires into the effects of a nuclear holocaust is bound to be assailed by powerful and conflicting emotions. Preëminent among these, almost certainly, will be an overwhelming revulsion at the tremendous scene of devastation, suffering, and death which is opened to view. And accompanying the revulsion there may be a sense of helplessness and defeat, brought about by an awareness of the incapacity of the human soul to take in so much horror. A nuclear holocaust, widely regarded as "unthinkable" but never as undoable, appears to confront us with an action that we can perform but cannot quite conceive. Following upon these first responses, there may come a recoil, and a decision, whether conscious or unconscious, not to think any longer about the possibility of a nuclear holocaust. (Since a holocaust is a wholly prospective rather than a present calamity, the act of thinking about it is voluntary, and the choice of not thinking about it is always available.) When one tries to face the nuclear predicament, one feels sick, whereas when one pushes it out of mind, as apparently one must do most of the time in order to carry on with life, one feels well again. But this feeling of well-being is based on a denial of the most important reality of our time, and therefore is itself a kind of sickness. A society that systematically shuts its eyes to an urgent peril to its physical survival and fails to take any steps to save itself cannot be called psychologically well. In effect, whether we think about nuclear weapons or avoid thinking about them, their presence among us makes us sick, and there seems to be little of a purely mental or emotional nature that we can do about it.

A part of our quandary may lie in the fact that even a denial of the reality stems from what is, in a sense, a refusal to accept nuclear annihilation; that is, a refusal to accept even in imagination what Dr. Robert Jay Lifton, the author of pioneering studies of the psychology of the nuclear predicament, has appropriately called an "immersion in death." As such, the denial may have intermixed in it something that is valuable and worthy of respect. Like active revulsion and protest against nuclear weapons, a denial of their reality may spring—in part, at least—from a love of life, and since a love of life may ultimately be all that we have to pit against our doom, we cannot afford thoughtlessly to tear aside any of its manifestations. Because denial is a form of self-protection, if only against anguishing thoughts and feelings, and because it contains something useful, and perhaps even, in its way, necessary to life, anyone who invites people to draw aside the veil and look at the peril face to face is at risk of trespassing on inhibitions that are a part of our humanity. I hope in these reflections to proceed with the utmost possible respect for all forms of refusal to accept the unnatural and horrifying prospect of a nuclear holocaust.

When men split the nucleus of the atom, they unleashed into terrestrial nature a basic energy of the cosmos—the energy latent in mass—which had never before been active in any major way on earth. Until then, this energy had been kept largely within the nucleus by a force known to physicists as the strong force, which is the glue that holds the nucleus of an atom together, and is by far the strongest of the four basic forces that determine the behavior of all matter in the universe. The strong force and what is called the weak force are chiefly responsible for the static properties of nuclei. The two others, which, being outside the nucleus, had until the explosion of nuclear weapons been responsible for virtually all life and motion on earth since the earth's formation, four and a half billion years ago, are the electromagnetic force, which is responsible for, among other things, all chemical bonds, and the gravitational force, which is a force of attraction between masses. It is largely because strong-force reactions, in which the energy in mass is released, were almost entirely excluded from terrestrial affairs (one of the few exceptions is a spontaneous nuclear chain reaction that once broke out in a West African uranium deposit) and because weak-force reactions (manifested in the decay of radioactive materials) were inconspicuous enough to go mostly unnoticed that the two great conservation laws of nineteenth-century physics—the law of the conservation of energy and the law of the conservation of mass—appeared to physicists of that time to hold true. Nineteenth-century science believed that mass and energy constituted separate, closed systems, in which the amount of each remained forever constant, no matter what transformations each might undergo. It was not until twentieth-century physicists, pursuing their investigations into the realms of the irreducibly small and the unexceedably large, examined the properties of energy, mass, time, and space in the subatomic realm and the cosmic realm that mass and energy were discovered to be interchangeable entities. The new relationship was governed by Albert Einstein's laws of relativity and by quantum theory, and these—not to go deeply into theoretical matters—can be described as general physical laws of the universe, of which the Newtonian laws proved to be limiting cases. (It is because the limits included almost all the middle-sized phenomena readily available to human inspection that the need for more encompassing laws was not felt until our century.)

Broadly speaking, Newtonian physics emerged as a human-scale or earthly-scale physics, valid for velocities and sizes commonly encountered by human senses, while relativity together with quantum theory was recognized as a universal physics, valid for all phenomena. (Something of the uncanny quality of modern physics' violation of common sense—by, for instance, the concept of "curved space"—inheres in the seemingly ungraspable, and therefore "unreal," power of nuclear weapons, whose construction is based on the new principles.) Likewise, the laws of conservation of mass and energy held, to a high degree of approximation, for most then observable earthly energies, masses, and velocities but broke down for the energies, masses, and velocities in the subatomic realm. Einstein noted, "It turned out that the inertia of a system necessarily depends on its energy content, and this led straight to the notion that inert mass is simply latent energy. The principle of the conservation of mass lost its independence and became fused with that of the conservation of energy." Of mass in its slow-moving, relatively unenergetic terrestrial state, Einstein remarked, "It is as though a man who is fabulously rich [i.e., mass] should never spend or give away a cent [i.e., of its energy]; no one could tell how rich he was," and on that ground Einstein excused his nineteenth-century predecessors for failing to notice what he called the "tremendous energy" in mass. By comparison with the forms of energy active on earth during its first four and a half billion years, the amount of energy latent in mass was indeed tremendous. The rate of conversion of mass into energy is given by Einstein's formula $E = mc^2$, or energy equals mass times the speed of light squared—a formula that has won what is, considering the fateful importance it has assumed for the survival of human life, a well-justified place in popular folklore. Since the speed of light is over a hundred and eight-six thousand miles per second—the greatest velocity attainable by anything in the universe—the value in energy obtained from the transformation of even small quantities of mass is extremely high. For example, the amount of mass expended in the destruction of Hiroshima was about a gram—or one-thirtieth of an ounce. (The bomb itself, a complex machine, weighed four tons.) It would have required twelve thousand five hundred tons of TNT to release the same amount of energy. You might say that the energy yielded by application of the universal physics of the twentieth century exceeds the energy yielded by that of the terrestrial, or planetary, physics of the nineteenth century as the cosmos exceeds the earth. Yet it was within the earth's comparatively tiny, frail ecosphere that mankind released the newly tapped cosmic energy. In view of this scientific background, President Harry Truman was speaking to the point when, in his announcement that the United States had dropped an atomic bomb on Hiroshima, he told the world that "the basic power of the universe" had been harnessed for war by the United States, and added that "the force from which the sun draws its powers has been loosed against those who brought war to the Far East." The huge—the monstrous—disproportion between "the basic power of the universe" and the merely terrestrial creatures by which and against which it was aimed in anger defined the dread predicament that the world has tried, and failed, to come to terms with ever since.

It was fortunate for earthly life that it grew up sheltered from strong-force reactions and from the nuclear energies that they release; in fact, it is doubtful whether life could have developed at all on earth if it had somehow been conditioned by continuous strong-force reactions. These release enormous bursts of energy themselves, but they also set the stage for the protracted release of energy by the other nuclear force—the weak force—in the form of nuclear radiation. When an atomic nucleus is split, releasing energy, various unstable isotopes are produced, and these new nuclei, acting under the influence of the weak force, decay, emitting radioactivity into the environment. Most of the radioactivity that occurs naturally on earth is emitted by radioactive isotopes created in strong-force reactions that occurred before the formation of the earth—in early supernovae or at the beginning of the universe, when atoms were taking shape—and by new unstable isotopes that are the products of this radioactivity. (A smaller amount of radioactivity is being continually created by the bombardment of the earth with cosmic rays.) The original radioactive isotopes are like clocks that were wound up once and have been running down ever since. Their numbers have been decreasing as their nuclei have decayed and become stable, with each species dwindling at a precise and different rate. Left to itself, the planet's supply of radioactivity would, over billions of years, have gradually declined. But when man began to split the nuclei of atoms, in bombs and in nuclear reactors, he began to create fresh batches of radioactive materials and these, like new clocks set ticking, emitted new radiation as they also began to dwindle away toward stability. (Testing in the atmosphere was banned by treaty in 1963—France and China did not concur and have since held atmospheric tests—but before that it increased the background radiation of the earth. As a result, the present annual per-capita radiation dose in the United States is four and a half per cent above the natural background level for this country.) In general magnitude, the energy of radioactive emissions greatly overmatches the strength of the chemical bonds that hold living things together. The vulnerability to radioactivity of genetic material, in particular, is well known. It is perhaps not surprising that when cosmic energies are turned loose on a small planet overwhelming destruction is the result. Einstein was only one among many far-seeing people to express an understanding of this fundamental mismatch of strengths when he stated, in 1950, as he contemplated the likely detonation of a hydrogen—or thermonuclear—bomb (the first one was actually exploded, by the United States, in the fall of

1952), that "radioactive poisoning of the atmosphere and hence annihilation of any life on earth has been brought within the range of technical possibilities."

The path of scientific discovery from Einstein's formulation, in 1905, for the conversion of mass into energy to the actual release by man of nuclear energy—a path in which the principles of quantum mechanics had to be developed and the basic structure of matter had to be unfolded—took several decades to travel. As late as the early nineteen-thirties, many of the best-qualified scientists had no notion that the nucleus of the atom could be fissioned. But in 1938 two Austrian physicists, Lise Meitner and Otto Frisch, correctly interpreting the results of some earlier experiments, announced that if uranium atoms were bombarded with neutrons they would split—of fission— into nearly equal parts, forming new elements and releasing some of their mass as energy, the amount being calculable by Einstein's renowned equation. The next step in obtaining usable energy from matter would be to bring about a chain reaction of fissioning uranium atoms, and this was undertaken in 1939 by the United States government, first under the auspices of an Advisory Committee on Uranium and later by the secret, multi-billion-dollar program known as the Manhattan Project, whose aim was to build an atomic bomb for use by the Allies in the Second World War. When a uranium nucleus is split, it releases several neutrons at high velocity. In a chain reaction, the neutrons released split other nuclei, which, in turn, release other neutrons, and these neutrons split still further nuclei, and so on—in a series that ends only when the available material is used up or dispersed. In some substances, such as uranium-235 or plutonium-239, a spontaneous chain reaction will start when enough of the material—a quantity known as a critical mass—is assembled in one place. But a chain reaction does not necessarily make a bomb. For an explosion to occur, the reaction has to go on long enough for explosive energies to build up before the immensely rapid expansion of the fissionable material brought about by the energy released in the chain reaction terminates the reaction. The required prolongation can be produced by sudden compression of the fissionable material to a very high density. Then the neutrons, flying about among the more

tightly packed atoms, will spawn a larger number of "generations" of fissioned nuclei before the chain reaction is halted by
dispersion. Since the number of fissions increases exponentially
with each new generation, a huge amount of energy is created
very rapidly in the late generations of the reaction. According
to Glasstone, the release of energy equivalent to one hundred
thousand tons of TNT would require the creation of fifty-eight
generations before the reaction ended, and ninety-nine and
nine-tenths per cent of the energy would be released in the
last seven generations. Since each generation would require
no more than a hundred-millionth of a second, this energy
would be released in less than a tenth of a millionth of a second.
("Clearly," Glasstone remarks, "most of the fission energy is
released in an extremely short period.")

    In a fission reaction, energy is released in an expenditure
of mass. Each atom contains a balance of forces and energies.
Within the nucleus, the "tremendous energy" latent in mass
is kept out of general circulation by the binding action of the
strong force, holding the particles of the nucleus—its protons
and neutrons—together. The strong force, however, is opposed
by positive electrical charges that are carried by the protons in
the nucleus and tend to drive the protons apart. The nuclei of
the heaviest atoms, such as uranium and plutonium, are the
least tightly bound together, because they contain the largest
numbers of protons, and so the electrical repulsion is greatest
in them. (In fact, the presence of the disintegrative pressure
of the electrical force within nuclei, which increases with the
number of protons, forms an upper limit to the size of nuclei;
there is a point beyond which they cannot cohere for any length
of time.) Because of the relative weakness of the binding force
in the heaviest nuclei, they are the best for fissioning. When the
nucleus of an atom of uranium-235 is struck by a neutron, the
binding grip of the strong force is loosed, electrical repulsion
takes over, the nucleus divides, and its fragments are driven
apart with an energy of motion which, in obedience to Einstein's equation, is equal to the amount of the mass lost times
the speed of light squared.

    Energy can also be released by fusion, which is the basis for
the hydrogen bomb. To cause fusion, nuclei must be driven
against one another with such velocity that the electrical

repulsion between their respective protons is overcome and the strong force can act to bind them together into new nuclei. The best nuclei for fusion are the lightest—those of hydrogen and its isotopes and the elements nearest them in mass, because, having the fewest protons, they have the smallest amount of electrical repulsion to overcome. Dr. Henry Kendall, who teaches physics at the Massachusetts Institute of Technology and guides research in particle physics there, and who, as chairman of the Union of Concerned Scientists, has for many years devoted much of his time and attention to the nuclear question in all its aspects, recently described to me what happens in a fusion reaction. "Let a small rounded depression—or 'well,' to use the proper physical term—in a level board stand for a nucleus, and let a much smaller steel ball stand for a particle," he said. "If you roll the ball along the board at the well, it will travel down one side of the well, up the other, and out again. On the other hand, if you start the ball rolling at a point partway down one side of the well, it will rise to an equal height on the other side, then return to its starting point, and, barring other influences, continue to oscillate like that forever. This is a good representation of the bound state of the particle in the nucleus. The problem of fusion is to introduce the steel ball into the well from the outside and have it remain there in the bound state instead of shooting out the other side. It can do this only by somehow *giving up* energy. In fusion, we give the name 'binding energy' to the amount that must be given up for the outside particle to become bound in the well. A good example of this loss of energy occurs in the fusion of deuterium and tritium, two isotopes of hydrogen. The tritium nucleus contains one proton and two neutrons, and the deuterium nucleus contains one proton and one neutron, for a total of five particles. In the fusion of these isotopes, four of the particles—two neutrons and two protons—hang together very tightly, and are able to swat out the remaining neutron with incredible violence, thus getting rid of the necessary amount of energy. And this is the energy that a fusion reaction releases. Once the four other particles have done that, they can run around in their hole undisturbed. But in order for this or any fusion reaction to take place the nuclei have to be driven very close together. Only then can the strong force reach out its

stubby but powerful arms in the giant handshake that fuses
the nuclei together and unleashes the explosive energy of the
hydrogen bomb."

Fission and fusion can occur in a great many forms, but in
all of them mass is lost, the grip of the strong force is tight-
ened on the products of the reaction, and energy is released.
A typical hydrogen bomb is a four-stage device. In the first
stage, a conventional explosion is set off; in the second stage,
the conventional explosion initiates a fission reaction, which
is, in fact, an atomic bomb; in the third stage, the heat from
the atomic bomb initiates a fusion reaction; and in the fourth
stage neutrons from the fusion reaction initiate additional
fission, on a scale vastly greater than the first, in a surrounding
blanket of fissionable material. In my conversation with Dr.
Kendall, he described the explosion of an average hydrogen
bomb to me in somewhat more detail. "The trigger," he said,
"consists of a carefully fashioned, subcritical, spherical piece
of plutonium, with a neutron-initiator device in its interior
and a high-explosive jacket surrounding it. Things begin when
detonators all over the sphere of the high-explosive jacket go
off—as nearly simultaneously as the design permits. Now the
high-explosive jacket explodes and sends a shock wave travelling
inward in a shrinking concentric sphere, and gaining in force
and temperature as it proceeds. When its leading edge reaches
the plutonium core, there is an abrupt jump in pressure, which
squeezes the plutonium in on all sides with great precision.
The pressure makes the plutonium go from subcritical to
supercritical. At this point, the neutron initiator fires, and the
chain reaction begins. The trick is to compress the plutonium
as much as possible as quickly as possible because then more
generations of nuclei will be fissioned, and more energy will be
released, before the explosion, in effect, blows itself out. When
that happens, all the energy from the plutonium trigger will have
been released, and particles whose atomic identity has been lost
will be boiling and surging in an expanded sphere whose temperature exceeds stellar levels. In all the universe, temperatures
of equal heat are to be found only in such transient phenomena
as exploding supernovae. Now the fusion—otherwise known
as the thermonuclear reaction, because of the extreme heat
needed to initiate it—can begin. The fusion fuels—lithium and

isotopes of hydrogen—fly around with such velocity that they can simply coast right into one another, spitting out nuclear particles as they fuse. This is not a chain reaction, but again the explosion is stopped by the expansion caused by its own heat. By the time that happens, however, the last stage—the fissioning, by neutrons released both by the fission trigger and by the fusion reaction, of the surrounding blanket of material, which might be uranium-238—is under way. There is basically no limit to the size or yield of a thermonuclear weapon. The only limits on a bomb's destructive effect are the earth's capacity to absorb the blast."

Whereas most conventional bombs produce only one destructive effect—the shock wave—nuclear weapons produce many destructive effects. At the moment of the explosion, when the temperature of the weapon material, instantly gasified, is at the superstellar level, the pressure is millions of times the normal atmospheric pressure. Immediately, radiation, consisting mainly of gamma rays, which are a very high-energy form of electromagnetic radiation, begins to stream outward into the environment. This is called the "initial nuclear radiation," and is the first of the destructive effects of a nuclear explosion. In an air burst of a one-megaton bomb—a bomb with the explosive yield of a million tons of TNT, which is a medium-sized weapon in present-day nuclear arsenals—the initial nuclear radiation can kill unprotected human beings in an area of some six square miles. Virtually simultaneously with the initial nuclear radiation, in a second destructive effect of the explosion, an electromagnetic pulse is generated by the intense gamma radiation acting on the air. In a high-altitude detonation, the pulse can knock out electrical equipment over a wide area by inducing a powerful surge of voltage through various conductors, such as antennas, overhead power lines, pipes, and railroad tracks. The Defense Department's Civil Preparedness Agency reported in 1977 that a single multi-kiloton nuclear weapon detonated one hundred and twenty-five miles over Omaha, Nebraska, could generate an electromagnetic pulse strong enough to damage solid-state electrical circuits throughout the entire continental United States and in parts of Canada and Mexico, and thus threaten to bring the economies of these countries to a halt. When the fusion and fission reactions have blown themselves out, a fireball takes shape. As it expands, energy is absorbed in the form of X rays by the surrounding air, and then the air re-radiates a portion of that energy into the environment in the form of the thermal pulse—a wave of blinding light and intense heat—which is the third of the destructive effects of a nuclear explosion. (If the burst is low enough, the fireball touches the ground, vaporizing or incinerating almost everything within it.) The thermal pulse of a one-megaton bomb lasts for about ten seconds and can cause second-degree burns in exposed human beings at a distance of nine and a half miles, or in an area of more than two hundred and eighty square miles, and that of a twenty-megaton bomb (a large weapon by modern standards) lasts for about twenty seconds and can produce the same consequences at a distance of twenty-eight miles, or in an area of two thousand four hundred and sixty square miles. As the fireball expands, it also sends out a blast wave in all directions, and this is the fourth destructive effect of the explosion. The blast wave of an air-burst one-megaton bomb can flatten or severely damage all but the strongest buildings within a radius of four and a half miles, and that of a twenty-megaton bomb can do the same within a radius of twelve miles. As the fireball burns, it rises, condensing water from the surrounding atmosphere to form the characteristic mushroom cloud. If the bomb has been set off on the ground or close enough to it so that the fireball touches the surface, in a so-called ground burst, a crater will be formed, and tons of dust and debris will be fused with the intensely radioactive fission products and sucked up into the mushroom cloud. This mixture will return to earth as radioactive fallout, most of it in the form of fine ash, in the fifth destructive effect of the explosion. Depending upon the composition of the surface, from forty to seventy per cent of this fallout—often called the "early" or "local" fallout—descends to earth within about a day of the explosion, in the vicinity of the blast and downwind from it, exposing human beings to radiation disease, an illness that is fatal when exposure is intense. Air bursts may also produce local fallout, but in much smaller quantities. The lethal range of the local fallout depends on a number of circumstances, including the weather, but under average conditions a one-megaton ground burst would, according to the report by the Office of Technology Assessment, lethally contaminate over a thousand square miles. (A lethal dose, by convention, is considered to be the amount of radiation that, if delivered over a short period of time, would kill half the able-bodied young adult population.)

The initial nuclear radiation, the electromagnetic pulse, the thermal pulse, the blast wave, and the local fallout may be described as the local primary effects of nuclear weapons. Naturally, when many bombs are exploded the scope of these effects is increased accordingly. But in addition these primary effects produce innumerable secondary effects on societies and natural environments, some of which may be even more harmful than the primary ones. To give just one example, nuclear weapons, by flattening and setting fire to huge, heavily built-up areas, generate mass fires, and in some cases these may kill more people than the original thermal pulses and blast waves. Moreover, there are—quite distinct from both the local primary effects of individual bombs and their secondary effects—global primary effects, which do not become significant unless thousands of bombs are detonated all around the earth. And these global primary effects produce innumerable secondary effects of their own throughout the ecosystem of the earth as a whole. For a full-scale holocaust is more than the sum of its local parts; it is also a powerful direct blow to the ecosphere. In that sense, a holocaust is to the earth what a single bomb is to a city. Three grave direct global effects have been discovered so far. The first is the "delayed," or "worldwide," fallout. In detonations greater than one hundred kilotons, part of the fallout does not fall to the ground in the vicinity of the explosion but rises high into the troposphere and into the stratosphere, circulates around the earth, and then, over months or years, descends, contaminating the whole surface of the globe—although with doses of radiation far weaker than those delivered by the local fallout. Nuclear-fission products comprise some three hundred radioactive isotopes, and though some of them decay to relatively harmless levels of radioactivity within a few hours, minutes, or even seconds, others persist to emit radiation for up to millions of years. The short-lived isotopes are the ones most responsible for the lethal effects of the local fallout, and the long-lived ones are responsible for the contamination of the earth by stratospheric fallout. The energy released by all fallout from a thermonuclear explosion is about five per cent of the total. By convention, this energy is not calculated in the stated yield of a weapon, yet in a ten-thousand-megaton attack the equivalent of five hundred megatons of explosive energy, or forty thousand times the yield of the Hiroshima bomb, would be released in the form of radioactivity. This release may be considered a protracted afterburst, which is dispersed into the land, air, and sea, and into the tissues, bones, roots, stems, and leaves of living things, and goes on detonating there almost indefinitely after the explosion. The second of the global effects that have been discovered so far is the lofting, from ground bursts, of millions of tons of dust into the stratosphere; this is likely to produce general cooling of the earth's surface. The third of the global effects is a predicted partial destruction of the layer of ozone that surrounds the entire earth in the stratosphere. A nuclear fireball, by burning nitrogen in the air, produces large quantities of oxides of nitrogen. These are carried by the heat of the blast into the stratosphere, where, through a series of chemical reactions, they bring about a depletion of the ozone layer. Such a depletion may persist for years. The 1975 N.A.S. report has estimated that in a holocaust in which ten thousand megatons were detonated in the Northern Hemisphere the reduction of ozone in this hemisphere could be as high as seventy per cent and in the Southern Hemisphere as high as forty per cent, and that it could take as long as thirty years for the ozone level to return to normal. The ozone layer is crucial to life on earth, because it shields the surface of the earth from lethal levels of ultraviolet radiation, which is present in sunlight. Glasstone remarks, simply, "If it were not for the absorption of much of the solar ultraviolet radiation by the ozone, life as currently known could not exist except possibly in the ocean." Without the ozone shield, sunlight, the life-giver, would become a life-extinguisher. In judging the global effects of a holocaust, therefore, the primary question is not how many people would be irradiated, burned, or crushed to death by the immediate effects of the bombs but how well the ecosphere, regarded as a single living entity, on which all forms of life depend for their continued existence, would hold up. The issue is the habitability of the earth, and it is in this context, not in the context of the direct slaughter of hundreds of millions of people by the local effects, that the question of human survival arises.

Usually, people wait for things to occur before trying to describe them. (Futurology has never been a very respectable field of inquiry.) But since we cannot afford under any circumstances to let a holocaust occur, we are forced in this one case to become the historians of the future—to chronicle and commit to memory an event that we have never experienced and must never experience. This unique endeavor, in which foresight is asked to perform a task usually reserved for hindsight, raises a host of special difficulties. There is a categorical difference, often overlooked, between trying to describe an event that has already happened (whether it is Napoleon's invasion of Russia or the pollution of the environment by acid rain) and trying to describe one that has yet to happen—and one, in addition, for which there is no precedent, or even near-precedent, in history. Lacking experience to guide our thoughts and impress itself on our feelings, we resort to speculation. But speculation, however brilliantly it may be carried out, is at best only a poor substitute for experience. Experience gives us facts, whereas in pure speculation we are thrown back on theory, which has never been a very reliable guide to future events. Moreover, experience engraves its lessons in our hearts through suffering and the other consequences that it has for our lives; but speculation leaves our lives untouched, and so gives us leeway to reject its conclusions, no matter how well argued they may be. (In the world of strategic theory, in particular, where strategists labor to simulate actual situations on the far side of the nuclear abyss, so that generals and statesmen can prepare to make their decisions in case the worst happens, there is sometimes an unfortunate tendency to mistake pure ratiocination for reality, and to pretend to a knowledge of the future that it is not given to human beings to have.) Our knowledge of the local primary effects of the bombs, which is based both on the physical principles that made their construction possible and on experience gathered from the bombs of Hiroshima and Nagasaki and from testing, is quite solid. And our knowledge of the extent of the local primary effects of many weapons used together, which is obtained simply by using the multiplication table, is also solid: knowing that the thermal pulse of a twenty-megaton bomb can give people at least second-degree burns in an area of two thousand four hundred and sixty square miles, we can easily figure out that the pulses of a hundred twenty-megaton bombs can give people at least second-degree burns in an area of two hundred and forty-six thousand square miles. Nevertheless, it may be that our knowledge even of the primary effects is still incomplete, for during our test program new ones kept being discovered. One example is the electromagnetic pulse, whose importance was not recognized until around 1960, when, after more than a decade of tests, scientists realized that this effect accounted for unexpected electrical failures that had been occurring all along in equipment around the test sites. And it is only in recent years that the Defense Department has been trying to take account strategically of this startling capacity of just one bomb to put the technical equipment of a whole continent out of action.

When we proceed from the local effects of single explosions to the effects of thousands of them on societies and environments, the picture clouds considerably, because then we go beyond both the certainties of physics and our slender base of experience, and speculatively encounter the full complexity of human affairs and of the biosphere. Looked at in its entirety, a nuclear holocaust can be said to assail human life at three levels: the level of individual life, the level of human society, and the level of the natural environment—including the environment of the earth as a whole. At none of these levels can the destructiveness of nuclear weapons be measured in terms of firepower alone. At each level, life has both considerable recuperative powers, which might restore it even after devastating injury, and points of exceptional vulnerability, which leave it open to sudden, wholesale, and permanent collapse, even when comparatively little violence has been applied. Just as a machine may break down if one small part is removed, and a person may die if a single artery or vein is blocked, a modern technological society may come to a standstill if its fuel supply is cut off, and an ecosystem may collapse if its ozone shield is depleted. Nuclear weapons thus do not only kill directly, with their tremendous violence, but also kill indirectly, by breaking down the man-made and the natural systems on which individual lives collectively depend. Human beings require constant provision and care, supplied both by their societies and by the natural environment, and if these are suddenly removed people will die just as surely as if they had been struck by a bullet. Nuclear weapons are unique in that they attack the support systems of life at every level. And these systems, of course, are not isolated from each other but are parts of a single whole: ecological collapse, if it goes far enough, will bring about social collapse, and social collapse will bring about individual deaths. Furthermore, the destructive consequences of a nuclear attack are immeasurably compounded by the likelihood that all or most of the bombs will be detonated within the space of a few hours, in a single huge concussion. Normally, a locality devastated by a catastrophe, whether natural or man-made, will sooner or later receive help from untouched outside areas, as Hiroshima and Nagasaki did after they were bombed; but a nuclear holocaust would devastate the "outside" areas as well, leaving the victims to fend for themselves in a shattered society and natural environment. And what is true for each city is also true for the earth as a whole: a devastated earth can hardly expect "outside" help. The earth is the largest of the support systems for life, and the impairment of the earth is the largest of the perils posed by nuclear weapons.

The incredible complexity of all these effects, acting, interacting, and interacting again, precludes confident detailed representation of the events in a holocaust. We deal inevitably with approximations, probabilities, even guesses. However, it is important to point out that our uncertainty pertains not to *whether* the effects will interact, multiplying their destructive power as they do so, but only to *how*. It follows that our almost built-in bias, determined by the limitations of the human mind in judging future events, is to underestimate the harm. To fear interactive consequences that we cannot predict, or even imagine, may not be impossible, but it is very difficult. Let us consider, for example, some of the possible ways in which a person in a targeted country might die. He might be incinerated by the fireball or the thermal pulse. He might be lethally irradiated by the initial nuclear radiation. He might be crushed to death or hurled to his death by the blast wave or its debris. He might be lethally irradiated by the local fallout. He might be burned to death in a firestorm. He might be injured by one or another of these effects and then die of his wounds before he was able to make his way out of the devastated zone in which

he found himself. He might die of starvation, because the economy had collapsed and no food was being grown or delivered,
or because existing local crops had been killed by radiation, or
because the local ecosystem had been ruined, or because the
ecosphere of the earth as a whole was collapsing. He might
die of cold, for lack of heat and clothing, or of exposure, for
lack of shelter. He might be killed by people seeking food or
shelter that he had obtained. He might die of an illness spread
in an epidemic. He might be killed by exposure to the sun if
he stayed outside too long following serious ozone depletion.
Or he might be killed by any combination of these perils. But
while there is almost no end to the ways to die in and after
a holocaust, each person has only one life to lose: someone
who has been killed by the thermal pulse can't be killed again
in an epidemic. Therefore, anyone who wishes to describe a
holocaust is always at risk of depicting scenes of devastation
that in reality would never take place, because the people in
them would already have been killed off in some earlier scene of
devastation. The task is made all the more confusing by the fact
that causes of death and destruction do not exist side by side in
the world but often encompass one another, in widening rings.
Thus, if it turned out that a holocaust rendered the earth uninhabitable by human beings, then all the more immediate forms
of death would be nothing more than redundant preliminaries,
leading up to the extinction of the whole species by a hostile
environment. Or if a continental ecosystem was so thoroughly
destroyed by a direct attack that it could no longer sustain a
significant human population, the more immediate causes of
death would again decline in importance. In much the same
way, if an airplane is hit by gunfire, and thereby caused to crash,
dooming all the passengers, it makes little difference whether
the shots also killed a few of the passengers in advance of the
crash. On the other hand, if the larger consequences, which are
less predictable than the local ones, failed to occur, then the
local ones would have their full importance again.

Faced with uncertainties of this kind, some analysts of nuclear
destruction have resorted to fiction, assigning to the imagination the work that investigation is unable to do. But then the
results are just what one would expect: fiction. An approach
more appropriate to our intellectual circumstances would be

to acknowledge a high degree of uncertainty as an intrinsic and extremely important part of dealing with a possible holocaust. A nuclear holocaust is an event that is obscure because it is future, and uncertainty, while it has to be recognized in all calculations of future events, has a special place in calculations of a nuclear holocaust, because a holocaust is something that we aspire to keep in the future forever, and never to permit into the present. You might say that uncertainty, like the thermal pulses or the blast waves, is one of the features of a holocaust. Our procedure, then, should be not to insist on a precision that is beyond our grasp but to inquire into the rough probabilities of various results insofar as we can judge them, and then to ask ourselves what our political responsibilities are in the light of these probabilities. This embrace of investigative modesty—this acceptance of our limited ability to predict the consequences of a holocaust—would itself be a token of our reluctance to extinguish ourselves.

There are two further aspects of a holocaust which, though they do not further obscure the factual picture, nevertheless vex our understanding of this event. The first is that although in imagination we can try to survey the whole prospective scene of destruction, inquiring into how many would live and how many would die and how far the collapse of the environment would go under attacks of different sizes, and piling up statistics on how many square miles would be lethally contaminated, or what percentage of the population would receive first-, second-, or third-degree burns, or be trapped in the rubble of its burning houses, or be irradiated to death, no one actually experiencing a holocaust would have any such overview. The news of other parts necessary to put together that picture would be one of the things that were immediately lost, and each surviving person, his vision drastically foreshortened by the collapse of his world, and his impressions clouded by his pain, shock, bewilderment, and grief, would see only as far as whatever scene of chaos and agony happened to lie at hand. For it would not be only such abstractions as "industry" and "society" and "the environment" that would be destroyed in a nuclear holocaust; it would also be, over and over again, the small collections of cherished things, known landscapes, and beloved people that made up the immediate contents of individual lives.

The other obstacle to our understanding is that when we

strain to picture what the scene would be like after a holocaust we tend to forget that for most people, and perhaps for all, it wouldn't be *like* anything, because they would be dead. To depict the scene as it would appear to the living is to that extent a falsification, and the greater the number killed, the greater the falsification. The right vantage point from which to view a holocaust is that of a corpse, but from that vantage point, of course, there is nothing to report.

The specific train of events that might lead up to an attack is, obviously, among the unpredictables, but a few general possibilities can be outlined. One would be a wholly accidental attack, triggered by human error or mechanical failure. On three occasions in the last couple of years, American nuclear forces were placed on the early stages of alert: twice because of the malfunctioning of a computer chip in the North American Air Defense Command's warning system, and once when a test tape depicting a missile attack was inadvertently inserted in the system. The greatest danger in computer-generated misinformation and other mechanical errors may be that one error might start a chain reaction of escalating responses between command centers, leading, eventually, to an attack. If in the midst of a crisis Country A was misled by its computers into thinking that Country B was getting ready to attack, and went on alert, Country B might notice this and go on alert in response. Then Country A, observing the now indubitably real alert of Country B, might conclude that its computers had been right after all, and increase its alert. This move would then be noticed by Country B, which would, in turn, increase its alert, and so on, until either the mistake was straightened out or an attack was launched. A holocaust might also be touched off by conventional or nuclear hostilities between smaller powers, which could draw in the superpowers. Another possibility would be a deliberate, unprovoked preëmptive strike by one side against the other. Most observers regard an attack of this kind as exceedingly unlikely in either direction, but the logic of present nuclear strategy drives both sides to prepare to respond to one, for the central tenet of nuclear strategy is that each side will refrain from launching an all-out first strike against the other only if it knows that even after it has done so the other side will retain forces sufficient to launch an utterly devastating counterblow. What is more likely, in the opinion of many, is a preëmptive strike launched in the midst of an international crisis. Neither quite planned (in the sense of being a cold-blooded, premeditated strike, out of the blue) nor quite accidental (in the sense of being caused by technical failure), such an attack would be precipitated by a combination on one side or both sides of belligerency, reckless actions, miscalculation, and fear of a first strike by the other side. Each side's possible fear of a first strike by the other side has become an element of increasing danger in recent years. Modern weapons, such as the Soviet SS-18 and SS-19 and the improved American Minuteman III missile and planned MX missile, have a greatly increased ability to destroy enemy missiles in their silos, thus adding to the incentive on both sides to strike first. The peril is that in a crisis either side, fearful of losing the preëmptive advantage, would go ahead and order a first strike.

It was during an international crisis—the Cuban missile crisis, in 1962—that the world apparently came as close as it has yet come to a nuclear holocaust. On that occasion, and perhaps on that occasion alone, a dread of nuclear doom became palpable not only in the councils of power but among ordinary people around the world. At the height of the crisis, it is reported, President John Kennedy believed that the odds on the occurrence of a holocaust were between one out of three and even. In the memoir "Thirteen Days," Robert Kennedy, the President's brother, who was Attorney General at the time, and who advised the President in the crisis, offered a recollection of the moments of greatest peril. President Kennedy had ordered a blockade of all shipping to Cuba, where, American intelligence had found, the Soviet Union was emplacing missiles capable of carrying nuclear warheads. Missile crews in the United States had been placed on maximum alert. Now, at a few minutes after ten o'clock on the morning of October 24th, two Russian ships, accompanied by a Russian submarine, had approached to within a few miles of the blockade. Robert Kennedy wrote in his memoir:

> I think these few minutes were the time of gravest concern for the President. Was the world on the brink of a holocaust? Was it our error? A mistake? Was there something further that should

have been done? Or not done? His hand went up to his face and covered his mouth. He opened and closed his fist. His face seemed drawn, his eyes pained, almost gray. We stared at each other across the table. For a few fleeting seconds, it was almost as though no one else was there and he was no longer the President.

Inexplicably, I thought of when he was ill and almost died; when he lost his child; when we learned that our oldest brother had been killed; of personal times of strain and hurt. . . . We had come to the time of final decision. . . . I felt we were on the edge of a precipice with no way off. This time, the moment was now—not next week—not tomorrow, "so we can have another meeting and decide"; not in eight hours, "so we can send another message to Khrushchev and perhaps he will finally understand." No, none of that was possible. One thousand miles away in the vast expanse of the Atlantic Ocean the final decisions were going to be made in the next few minutes. President Kennedy had initiated the course of events, but he no longer had control over them.

Any number of future crises that would lead to an attack can be pictured, but I would like to mention one possible category that seems particularly dangerous. In the theory of nuclear deterrence, each side would ideally deter attacks at every level of violence with a deterrent force at the same level. Thus, conventional attacks would be deterred with conventional forces, tactical attacks would be deterred with tactical forces, and strategic attacks would be deterred with strategic forces. The theoretical advantage of matching forces in this fashion would be that the opening moves in hypothetical hostilities would not automatically lead to escalation—for example, by leading the side weaker in conventional forces to respond to a conventional attack with nuclear weapons. However, the facts of geography make such ideal deterrent symmetry impracticable. The Soviet Union's proximity both to Western Europe and to the Middle East gives it a heavy conventional preponderance in those parts of the world. Therefore, throughout the postwar period it has been American policy to deter a Soviet conventional attack in Europe with tactical nuclear arms. And in January of 1980 President Carter, in effect, extended the policy to include protection of the nations around the Persian Gulf. In his State of the Union address for 1980, Carter said, "An attempt by any outside force to gain control of the Persian Gulf region will be regarded as an assault on the vital interests of the United States of America. And such an assault will be repelled by any means necessary, including military force." Since the United States clearly lacked the conventional power to repel a Soviet attack in a region near the borders of the Soviet Union, "any means" could refer to nothing but nuclear arms. The threat was spelled out explicitly shortly after the speech, in a story in the New York *Times*—thought to be a leak from the Administration—about a 1979 Defense Department "study," which, according to the *Times*, said that American conventional forces could not stop a Soviet thrust into northern Iran, and that "to prevail in an Iranian scenario, we might have to threaten or make use of tactical nuclear weapons." The words of this study put the world on notice that the use of nuclear arms not only was contemplated in past crises but will continue to be contemplated in future ones.

It is possible to picture a nuclear attack of any shape or size. An attack might use all the weapons at the attacker's disposal or any portion of them. It might be aimed at military targets, at industry, at the population, or at all or some combination of these. The attack might be mainly air-burst, and would increase the range of severe damage from the blast waves, or it might be mainly ground-burst, to destroy hard targets such as land-based nuclear missiles or command-and-control centers, or to deliver the largest possible amount of fallout, or it might combine air bursts and ground bursts in any proportion. It could be launched in the daytime or at night, in summer or in winter, with warning or without warning. The sequence of events once hostilities had begun also lies open. For example, it seems quite possible that the leaders of a nation that had just suffered a nuclear attack would be sparing in their response, tailoring it to political objectives rather than to the vengeful aim of wiping out the society whose leaders had launched the attack. On the other hand, they might retaliate with all the forces at their disposal, as they say they will do. Then again, the two sides might expend their forces gradually, in a series of ad-hoc "exchanges," launched in an atmosphere of misinformation and intellectual and moral disorientation. The state of mind of the decision-makers might be one of calm rationality, of hatred, of shock, of hysteria, or even of outright insanity. They might follow coldly reasoned scenarios of destruction to the letter, and exterminate one another in that way. Or, for all we are able to know now, having at first hardened their "resolve" to follow the scenarios through to the end, they might suddenly reverse themselves, and proceed to the negotiating table after only incompletely destroying one another. Lacking any experience of what decisions human beings make under full-scale nuclear attack, we simply do not know what they would do.

Not surprisingly, predictions of the course of an attack are subject to intellectual fashion (there being nothing in the way of experience to guide them). In the nineteen-sixties, for example, it was widely believed that the most important attack to deter was an all-out one, but in the last few years the idea that a "limited nuclear war" might be fought has come into vogue. (The concept of limited nuclear war also had an earlier vogue, in the late nineteen-fifties, when some strategists were seeking an alternative to Secretary of State John Foster Dulles's strategy of "massive retaliation.") The premise of the limited-war theory is that nuclear hostilities can be halted at some new equilibrium in the balance of forces, before all-out attacks have been launched. In particular, it has been argued recently by nuclear theorists that the Soviet Union is now able to launch a devastating first strike at American bombers and land-based missiles, leaving the United States in the unfavorable position of having to choose between using its less accurate submarine-based missiles to directly attack Soviet society—and thus risk a direct attack on its own society in return—and doing nothing. Rather than initiate the annihilation of both societies, it is argued, American leaders might acquiesce in the Soviet first strike. But there is something dreamlike and fantastic in this concept of a wholly one-way nuclear strike, which, while leaving intact the power of the assaulted country to devastate the society of the aggressor, would somehow allow the aggressor to dictate terms. What seems to have been forgotten is that, unless one assumes that the adversary has gone insane (in which case not even the most foolproof scenarios can save us), military actions are taken with some aim in mind—for example, the aim of conquering a particular territory. This imagined first strike would in itself achieve nothing, and the moment the Soviet Union might try to achieve some actual advantage—for example, by marching into the Middle East to seize its oil fields—two or three nuclear weapons from among the thousands remaining in American arsenals would suffice to put a quick end to the undertaking. Or if the United States retaliated with only ten bombs on Soviet cities, holding back the rest, the Soviet Union would suffer unprecedented losses while gaining nothing. In other words, in this scenario—and, indeed, in any number of other scenarios for "limited nuclear war" which could be mentioned—strategic theory seems to have taken on a weird life of its own, in which the weapons are pictured as having their own quarrel to settle, irrespective of mere human purposes. In general, in the theoretically sophisticated but often humanly deficient world of nuclear strategic theory it is likely to be overlooked that the outbreak of nuclear hostilities in itself assumes the collapse of every usual restraint of reason and humanity. Once the mass killing of a nuclear holocaust had begun, the scruples, and even the reckonings of self-interest, that normally keep the actions of nations within certain bounds would by definition have been trampled down, and would probably offer little further protection for anybody. In the unimaginable mental and spiritual climate of the world at that point it is hard to imagine what force could be counted on to hold the world back from all-out destruction.

However, it would be misleading to suggest that once one nuclear weapon had been used it would be inevitable for all of them to be used. Rather, the point is that once a catastrophe that we now find "unthinkable" actually commenced, people would act in ways that are unforeseeable by theorists—or, for that matter, by the future actors themselves. Predictions about the size and form of a nuclear holocaust are really predictions about human decisions, and these are notoriously incalculable in advance—especially when the decisions in question are going to be made in the midst of unimaginable mayhem. Secretary of Defense Robert McNamara probably said the last word on this subject when he remarked before the House Armed Services Committee in 1963, in regard to a possible defense of Europe, that once the first tactical nuclear weapon had been used the world would have been launched into "a vast unknown." Therefore, in picturing a Soviet attack on the United States I shall not venture any predictions concerning the shape and size of the attack, since to do so, it seems to me, would be to pretend to a kind of knowledge that we are incapable of. Instead, I shall simply choose two basic assumptions—using the word to mean not predictions but postulates. The first assumption is that most of the Soviet strategic forces are used in the attack, and the second is that the attack is aimed at military facilities, industry, and the population centers of the United States. I have chosen these assumptions not because I "predict" an attack of this kind, which is the most damaging of the attacks that appear to have a likely chance of occurring, but because, in the absence of any basis for confident prediction, and, in particular, of any reliable assurance that an attack would remain "limited," they are the only assumptions that represent the full measure of our peril. At the very least, they are not farfetched. The first assumption is supported by many statements by leaders on both sides. The Soviet government, which, of course, is one of the actors concerned, has frequently stated the view that nuclear hostilities cannot be limited, and Secretary of Defense Harold Brown also said, in 1977, that a nuclear conflict probably could not be limited. Concerning the second assumption, the significant point is that the fundamental logic of the strategy of both sides is, in McNamara's words, to hold not just the military forces of the other side hostage but also its "society as a whole." Just how the strategists on both sides achieve this is unknown, but it seems unwarranted to suppose that there will be much relief for either population in the merciful sentiments of targeters.

A further set of assumptions that influence one's judgment of the consequences of a holocaust concerns the possibility of civil defense. These assumptions also depend in part on certain circumstances that are unknowable in advance, such as whether the attack occurs in the daytime or at night, but they also depend on circumstances that are more or less built into the situation, and can therefore be predicted. The two main components of a conceivable civil defense against nuclear attack are evacuation and sheltering. In a protracted crisis, a country might seek to protect its population by evacuating its cities and towns before any attack had actually been launched; but, for a variety of reasons, such a strategy seems impracticable or useless. To begin with, an enemy that was bent on attacking one's population might retarget its missiles against people in the places to which they had fled. Also, during the days of evacuation people would be more vulnerable to attack than they were even in their cities. (Probably the worst assumption regarding evacuation would be that the attack came while evacuation was under way.) A further disadvantage of a policy of evacuation is that it would offer the foe a means of utterly disrupting the society by threats alone, since an evacuated society would be one that had stopped functioning for any other purpose. Shelters appear to be no more promising than evacuation. The Soviet missiles closest to the United States, which are stationed on submarines several hundred miles from our shores, can deliver their warheads on coastal targets about ten minutes after they are fired, and on inland targets a few minutes later. The intercontinental ballistic missiles, which are all launched from within the Soviet Union, would arrive fifteen or twenty minutes after that. The bombers would arrive in several hours. But, according to the Arms Control and Disarmament Agency, it requires fifteen minutes after missiles have been launched for the earliest warnings to be given to the population. Even assuming—very optimistically, I think—that it would take only another fifteen minutes or so for any significant number of people to become aware of the warnings and go to shelters, a surprise attack would indeed catch the great majority of people by surprise.

For most people, however, the lack of any opportunity to proceed to shelters would be without importance in any case, since shelters, even if they existed, would be of no use. It is now commonly acknowledged that economically feasible shelters cannot provide protection against the blast, heat, intense radiation, and mass fires that would probably occur in densely populated regions of the country—that such shelters could save lives only in places that were subjected to nothing worse than modest amounts of fallout. Furthermore, there is a very serious question whether many people would survive in the long run even if they did manage to save themselves in the short run by sealing themselves up in shelters for several weeks or months. Finally, it seems worth mentioning that, whatever the potential value of shelters might be, most existing ones either are situated in places where they are useless (in large cities, for example) or lack some or all of the following necessary equipment for an effective shelter: adequate shielding from radiation; air filters that would screen out radioactive particles; food and water to last as long as several months; an independent heating system, in places where winters are severe; medical supplies for the injured, sick, and dying, who might be in the majority in the shelters; radiation counters to measure levels of radiation outdoors, so that people could know when it was safe to leave the shelter and could determine whether food and drink were contaminated; and a burial system wholly contained within the shelter, in which to bury those who died of their injuries or illness during the shelter period.

Systems setting up evacuation procedures and shelters are often presented as humanitarian measures that would save lives in the event of a nuclear attack. In the last analysis, however, the civil-defense issue is a strategic, not a humanitarian, question. It is fundamental to the nuclear strategy of both the Soviet Union and the United States that each preserve the capacity to devastate the population of the other after itself absorbing the largest first strike that is within the other's capacity. Therefore, any serious attempt by either side to make its population safe from nuclear attack—assuming for the moment that this could be done—would be extremely likely to call forth a strategic countermove by the other side, probably taking the form of increased armament. Since the extraordinary power of modern weapons makes such compensation quite easy, it is safe to assume that for the foreseeable future the population of each side is going to remain exactly as vulnerable as the other side wants it to be.

The yardsticks by which one can measure the destruction that will be caused by weapons of different sizes are provided by the bombings of Hiroshima and Nagasaki and American nuclear tests in which the effects of hydrogen bombs with up to sixteen hundred times the explosive yield of the Hiroshima bomb were determined. The data gathered from these experiences make it a straightforward matter to work out the distances from the explosion at which different intensities of the various effects of a bomb are likely to occur. In the back of the Glasstone book, the reader will find a small dial computer that places all this information at his fingertips. Thus, if one would like to know how deep a crater a twenty-megaton ground burst will leave in wet soil one has only to set a pointer at twenty megatons and look in a small window showing crater size to find that the depth would be six hundred feet—a hold deep enough to bury a fair-sized skyscraper. Yet this small circular computer, on which the downfall of every city on earth is distilled into a few lines and figures, can, of course, tell us nothing of the human reality of nuclear destruction. Part of the horror of thinking about a holocaust lies in the fact that it leads us to supplant the human world with a statistical world; we seek a human truth and come up with a handful of figures. The only source that gives us a glimpse of that human truth is the testimony of the survivors of the Hiroshima and Nagasaki bombings. Because the bombing of Hiroshima has been more thoroughly investigated than the bombing of Nagasaki, and therefore more information about it is available, I shall restrict myself to a brief description of that catastrophe.

On August 6, 1945, at 8:16 A.M., a fission bomb with a yield of twelve and a half kilotons was detonated about nineteen hundred feet above the central section of Hiroshima. By present-day standards, the bomb was a small one, and in to-day's arsenals it would be classed among the merely tactical weapons. Nevertheless, it was large enough to transform a city of some three hundred and forty thousand people into hell in the space of a few seconds. "It is no exaggeration," the authors of "Hiroshima and Nagasaki" tell us, "to say that the whole city was ruined instantaneously." In that instant, tens of thousands of people were burned, blasted, and crushed to death. Other tens of thousands suffered injuries of every description or were doomed to die of radiation sickness. The center of the city was flattened, and every part of the city was damaged. The trunks of bamboo trees as far away as five miles from ground zero—the point on the ground directly under the center of the explosion—were charred. Almost half the trees within a mile and a quarter were knocked down. Windows nearly seventeen miles away were broken. Half an hour after the blast, fires set by the thermal pulse and by the collapse of the buildings began to coalesce into a firestorm, which lasted for six hours. Starting about 9 A.M. and lasting until late afternoon, a "black rain" generated by the bomb (otherwise, the day was fair) fell on the western portions of the city, carrying radioactive fallout from the blast to the ground. For four hours at midday, a violent whirlwind, born of the strange meteorological conditions produced by the explosion, further devastated the city. The number of people who were killed outright or who died of their injuries over the next three months is estimated to be a hundred and thirty thousand. Sixty-eight per cent of the buildings in the city were either completely destroyed or damaged beyond repair, and the center of the city was turned into a flat, rubble-strewn plain dotted with the ruins of a few of the sturdier buildings.

In the minutes after the detonation, the day grew dark, as heavy clouds of dust and smoke filled the air. A whole city had fallen in a moment, and in and under its ruins were its people. Among those still living, most were injured, and of these most were burned or had in some way been battered or had suffered both kinds of injury. Those within a mile and a quarter of ground zero had also been subjected to intense nuclear radiation, often in lethal doses. When people revived enough from their unconsciousness or shock to see what was happening around them, they found that where a second before there had been a city getting ready to go about its daily business on a peaceful, warm August morning, now there was a heap of debris and corpses and a stunned mass of injured humanity. But at first, as they awakened and tried to find their bearings in the gathering darkness, many felt cut off and alone. In a recent volume of recollections by survivors called "Unforgettable Fire," in which the effects of the bombing are rendered in drawings as well as in words, Mrs. Haruko Ogasawara, a young girl on that August morning, recalls that she was at first knocked unconscious. She goes on to write:

> How many seconds or minutes had passed I could not tell, but, regaining consciousness, I found myself lying on the ground covered with pieces of wood. When I stood up in a frantic effort to look around, there was darkness. Terribly frightened, I thought I was alone in a world of death, and groped for any light. My fear was so great I did not think anyone would truly understand. When I came to my senses, I found my clothes in shreds, and I was without my wooden sandals.

Soon cries of pain and cries for help from the wounded filled the air. Survivors heard the voices of their families and their friends calling out in the gloom. Mrs. Ogasawara writes:

> Suddenly, I wondered what had happened to my mother and sister. My mother was then forty-five, and my sister five years old. When the darkness began to fade, I found that there was nothing around me. My house, the next door neighbor's house, and the next had all vanished. I was standing amid the ruins of my house. No one was around. It was quiet, very quiet—an eerie moment. I discovered my mother in a water tank. She had fainted. Crying out, "Mama, Mama," I shook her to bring her back to her senses. After coming to, my mother began to shout madly for my sister: "Eiko! Eiko!"
>
> I wondered how much time had passed when there were cries of searchers. Children were calling their parents' names, and parents were calling the names of their children. We were calling desperately for my sister and listening for her voice and looking to see her. Suddenly, Mother cried "Oh Eiko!" Four or five meters away, my sister's head was sticking out and was calling my mother. . . . Mother and I worked desperately to remove the plaster and pillars and pulled her out with great effort. Her body had turned purple from the bruises, and her arm was so badly wounded that we could have placed two fingers in the wound.

Others were less fortunate in their searches and rescue attempts. In "Unforgettable Fire," a housewife describes a scene she saw:

> A mother, driven half-mad while looking for her child, was calling his name. At last she found him. His head looked like a boiled octopus. His eyes were half-closed, and his mouth was white, pursed, and swollen.

Throughout the city, parents were discovering their wounded or dead children, and children were discovering their wounded or dead parents. Kikuno Segawa recalls seeing a little girl with her dead mother:

> A woman who looked like an expectant mother was dead. At her side, a girl of about three years of age brought some water in an empty can she had found. She was trying to let her mother drink from it.

The sight of people in extremities of suffering was ubiquitous. Kinzo Nishida recalls:

> While taking my severely wounded wife out to the riverbank by the side of the hill of Nakahiro-machi, I was horrified, indeed, at the sight of a stark naked man standing in the rain with his eyeball in his palm. He looked to be in great pain, but there was nothing that I could do for him.

Many people were astonished by the sheer sudden absence of the known world. The writer Yoko Ota later wrote:

> I just could not understand why our surroundings had changed so greatly in one instant. . . . I thought it might have been something which had nothing to do with the war—the collapse of the earth, which it was said would take place at the end of the world, and which I had read about as a child.

And a history professor who looked back at the city after the explosion remarked later, "I saw that Hiroshima had disappeared."

As the fires sprang up in the ruins, many people, having found injured family members and friends, were now forced to abandon them to the flames or to lose their own lives in the firestorm. Those who left children, husbands, wives, friends, and strangers to burn often found these experiences the most awful of the entire ordeal. Mikio Inoue describes how one man, a professor, came to abandon his wife:

> It was when I crossed Miyuki Bridge that I saw Professor Takenaka, standing at the foot of the bridge. He was almost naked, wearing nothing but shorts, and he had a ball of rice in his right hand. Beyond the streetcar line, the northern area was covered by red fire burning against the sky. Far away from the line, Ote machi was also a sea of fire.
>
> That day, Professor Takenaka had not gone to Hiroshima University, and the A-bomb exploded when he was at home. He tried to rescue his wife, who was trapped under a roofbeam, but all his efforts were in vain. The fire was threatening him also. His wife pleaded, "Run away, dear!" He was forced to desert his wife and escape from the fire. He was now at the foot of Miyuki Bridge.
>
> But I wonder how he came to hold that ball of rice in his hand. His naked figure, standing there before the flames with

that ball of rice, looked to me as a symbol of the modest hopes
of human beings.

In "Hiroshima," John Hersey describes the flight of a group
of German priests and their Japanese colleagues through a
burning section of the city:

> The street was cluttered with parts of houses that had slid into
> it, and with fallen telephone poles and wires. From every second
> or third house came the voices of people buried and abandoned,
> who invariably screamed, with formal politeness, "*Tasukete kure!*
> Help, if you please!" The priests recognized several ruins from
> which these cries came as the homes of friends, but because of
> the fire it was too late to help.

And thus it happened that throughout Hiroshima all the ties
of affection and respect that join human beings to one another
were being pulled and rent by the spreading firestorm. Soon
processions of the injured—processions of a kind that had never
been seen before in history—began to file away from the center
of the city toward its outskirts. Most of the people suffered
from burns, which had often blackened their skin or caused it to
sag off them. A grocer who joined one of these processions has
described them in an interview with Robert Jay Lifton which
appears in his book "Death in Life":

> They held their arms bent [forward] . . . and their skin—not
> only on their hands but on their faces and bodies, too—hung
> down. . . . If there had been only one or two such people . . .
> perhaps I would not have had such a strong impression. But
> wherever I walked, I met these people. . . . Many of them died
> along the road. I can still picture them in my mind—like walking
> ghosts. They didn't look like people of this world.

The grocer also recalls that because of people's injuries
"you couldn't tell whether you were looking at them from in
front or in back." People found it impossible to recognize one
another. A woman who at the time was a girl of thirteen, and
suffered disfiguring burns on her face, has recalled, "My face
was so distorted and changed that people couldn't tell who I
was. After a while I could call others' names but they couldn't
recognize me." In addition to being injured, many people were

vomiting—an early symptom of radiation sickness. For many, horrifying and unreal events occurred in a chaotic jumble. In "Unforgettable Fire," Torako Hironaka enumerates some of the things that she remembers:

1. Some burned work-clothes.
2. People crying for help with their heads, shoulders, or the soles of their feet injured by fragments of broken window glass. Glass fragments were scattered everywhere.
3. [A woman] crying, saying "Aigo! Aigo!" (a Korean expression of sorrow).
4. A burning pine tree.
5. A naked woman.
6. Naked girls crying, "Stupid America!"
7. I was crouching in a puddle, for fear of being shot by a machine gun. My breasts were torn.
8. Burned down electric power lines.
9. A telephone pole had burned and fallen down.
10. A field of watermelons.
11. A dead horse.
12. What with dead cats, pigs, and people, it was just a hell on earth.

Physical collapse brought emotional and spiritual collapse with it. The survivors were, on the whole, listless and stupefied. After the escapes, and the failures to escape, from the firestorm, a silence fell over the city and its remaining population. People suffered and died without speaking or otherwise making a sound. The processions of the injured, too, were soundless. Dr. Michihiko Hachiya has written in his book "Hiroshima Diary":

> Those who were able walked silently toward the suburbs in the distant hills, their spirits broken, their initiative gone. When asked whence they had come, they pointed to the city and said, "That way," and when asked where they were going, pointed away from the city and said, "This way." They were so broken and confused that they moved and behaved like automatons.
>
> Their reactions had astonished outsiders, who reported with amazement the spectacle of long files of people holding stolidly to a narrow, rough path when close by was a smooth, easy road going in the same direction. The outsiders could not grasp the fact that they were witnessing the exodus of a people who walked in the realm of dreams.

Those who were still capable of action often acted in an absurd or an insane way. Some of them energetically pursued tasks that had made sense in the intact Hiroshima of a few minutes before but were now utterly inappropriate. Hersey relates that the German priests were bent on bringing to safety a suitcase, containing diocesan accounts and a sum of money, that they had rescued from the fire and were carrying around with them through the burning city. And Dr. Lifton describes a young soldier's punctilious efforts to find and preserve the ashes of a burned military code book while people around him were screaming for help. Other people simply lost their minds. For example, the German priests were escaping from the firestorm, one of them, Father Wilhelm Kleinsorge, carried on his back a Mr. Fukai, who kept saying that he wanted to remain where he was. When Father Kleinsorge finally put Mr. Fukai down, he started running. Hersey writes:

> Father Kleinsorge shouted to a dozen soldiers, who were standing by the bridge, to stop him. As Father Kleinsorge started back to get Mr. Fukai, Father LaSalle called out, "Hurry! Don't waste time!" So Father Kleinsorge just requested the soldiers to take care of Mr. Fukai. They said they would, but the little, broken man got away from them, and the last the priests could see of him, he was running back toward the fire.

In the weeks after the bombing, many survivors began to notice the appearance of petechiae—small spots caused by hemorrhages—on their skin. These usually signalled the onset of the critical stage of radiation sickness. In the first stage, the victims characteristically vomited repeatedly, ran a fever, and developed an abnormal thirst. (The cry "Water! Water!" was one of the few sounds often heard in Hiroshima on the day of the bombing.) Then, after a few hours or days, there was a deceptively hopeful period of remission of symptoms, called the latency period, which lasted from about a week to about four weeks. Radiation attacks the reproductive function of cells, and those that reproduce most frequently are therefore the most vulnerable. Among these are the bone-marrow cells, which are responsible for the production of blood cells. During the latency period, the count of white blood cells, which are instrumental in fighting infections, and the count of platelets, which are instrumental in clotting, drop precipitously, so the body is poorly defended against infection and is liable to hemorrhaging. In the third, and final, stage, which may last for several weeks, the victim's hair may fall out and he may suffer from diarrhea and may bleed from the intestines, the mouth, or other parts of the body, and in the end he will either recover or die. Because the fireball of the Hiroshima bomb did not touch the ground, very little ground material was mixed with the fission products of the bomb, and therefore very little local fallout was generated. (What fallout there was descended in the black rain.) Therefore, the fatalities from radiation sickness were probably all caused by the initial nuclear radiation, and since this affected only people within a radius of a mile and a quarter of ground zero, most of the people who received lethal doses were killed more quickly by the thermal pulse and the blast wave. Thus, Hiroshima did not experience the mass radiation sickness that can be expected if a weapon is ground-burst. Since the Nagasaki bomb was also burst in the air, the effect of widespread lethal fallout on large areas, causing the death by radiation sickness of whole populations in the hours, days, and weeks after the blast, is a form of nuclear horror that the world has not experienced.

In the months and years following the bombing of Hiroshima, after radiation sickness had run its course and most of the injured had either died of their wounds or recovered from them, the inhabitants of the city began to learn that the exposure to radiation they had experienced would bring about a wide variety of illnesses, many of them lethal, throughout the lifetimes of those who had been exposed. An early sign that the harm from radiation was not restricted to radiation sickness came in the months immediately following the bombing, when people found that their reproductive organs had been temporarily harmed, with men experiencing sterility and women experiencing abnormalities in their menstrual cycles. Then, over the years, other illnesses, including cataracts of the eye and leukemia and other forms of cancer, began to appear in larger than normally expected numbers among the exposed population. In all these illnesses, correlations have been found between nearness to the explosion and incidence of the disease. Also, fetuses exposed to the bomb's radiation in utero exhibited abnormalities and developmental retardation. Those exposed within the mile-and-a-quarter radius were seven times as likely as unexposed fetuses to die in utero, and were also seven times as likely to die at birth or in infancy. Surviving children who were exposed in utero tended to be shorter and lighter than other children, and were more often mentally retarded. One of the most serious abnormalities caused by exposure to the bomb's radiation was microcephaly—abnormal smallness of the head, which is often accompanied by mental retardation. In one study, thirty-three cases of microcephaly were found among a hundred and sixty-nine children exposed in utero.

What happened at Hiroshima was less than a millionth part of a holocaust at present levels of world nuclear armament. The more than millionfold difference amounts to more than a difference in magnitude; it is also a difference in kind. The authors of "Hiroshima and Nagasaki" observe that "an atomic bomb's massive destruction and indiscriminate slaughter involves the sweeping breakdown of all order and existence—in a word, the collapse of society itself," and that therefore "the essence of atomic destruction lies in the totality of its impact on man and society." This is true also of a holocaust, of course, except that the totalities in question are now not single cities but nations, ecosystems, and the earth's ecosphere. Yet with the exception of fallout, which was relatively light at Hiroshima and Nagasaki (because both the bombs were air-burst), the immediate devastation caused by today's bombs would be of a sort similar to the devastation in those cities. The immediate effects of a twenty-megaton bomb are not different in kind from those of a twelve-and-a-half-kiloton bomb; they are only more extensive. (The proportions of the effects do change greatly with yield, however. In small bombs, the effects of the initial nuclear radiation are important, because it strikes areas in which people might otherwise have remained alive, but in larger bombs—ones in the megaton range—the consequences of the initial nuclear radiation, whose range does not increase very much with yield, are negligible, because it strikes areas in which everyone will have already been burned or blasted to death.) In bursts of both weapons, for instance, there is a radius within which the thermal pulse can ignite newspapers: for the

twelve-and-a-half-kiloton weapon, it is a little over two miles;
for the twenty-megaton weapon, it is twenty-five miles. (Since
there is no inherent limit on the size of a nuclear weapon,
these figures can be increased indefinitely, subject only to the
limitations imposed by the technical capacities of the bomb
builder—and of the earth's capacity to absorb the blast. The Soviet Union, which has shown a liking for sheer size in so many
of its undertakings, once detonated a sixty-megaton bomb.)
Therefore, while the total effect of a holocaust is qualitatively
different from the total effect of a single bomb, the experience
of individual people in a holocaust would be, in the short term
(and again excepting the presence of lethal fallout wherever
the bombs were ground-burst), very much like the experience
of individual people in Hiroshima. The Hiroshima people's
experience, accordingly, is of much more than historical interest. It is a picture of what our whole world is always poised to
become—a backdrop of scarcely imaginable horror lying just
behind the surface of our normal life, and capable of breaking
through into that normal life at any second. Whether we choose
to think about it or not, it is an omnipresent, inescapable truth
about our lives today that at every single moment each one
of us may suddenly become the deranged mother looking for
her burned child; the professor with the ball of rice in his hand
whose wife has just told him "Run away, dear!" and died in
the fires; Mr. Fukai running back into the firestorm; the naked
man standing on the blasted plain that was his city, holding his
eyeball in his hand; or, more likely, one of millions of corpses.
For whatever our "modest hopes" as human beings may be,
every one of them can be nullified by a nuclear holocaust.

     One way to begin to grasp the destructive power of
present-day nuclear weapons is to describe the consequences
of the detonation of a one-megaton bomb, which possesses
eighty times the explosive power of the Hiroshima bomb, on
a large city, such as New York. Burst some eighty-five hundred
feet above the Empire State Building, a one-megaton bomb
would gut or flatten almost every building between Battery
Park and 125th Street, or within a radius of four and four-tenths
miles, or in an area of sixty-one square miles, and would heavily
damage buildings between the northern tip of Staten Island
and the George Washington Bridge, or within a radius of

about eight miles, or in an area of about two hundred square miles. A conventional explosive delivers a swift shock, like a slap, to whatever it hits, but the blast wave of a sizable nuclear weapon endures for several seconds and "can surround and destroy whole buildings" (Glasstone). People, of course, would be picked up and hurled away from the blast along with the rest of the debris. Within the sixty-one square miles, the walls, roofs, and floors of any buildings that had not been flattened would be collapsed, and the people and furniture inside would be swept down onto the street. (Technically, this zone would be hit by various overpressures of at least five pounds per square inch. Overpressure is defined as the pressure in excess of normal atmospheric pressure.) As far away as ten miles from ground zero, pieces of glass and other sharp objects would be hurled about by the blast wave at lethal velocities. In Hiroshima, where buildings were low and, outside the center of the city, were often constructed of light materials, injuries from falling buildings were often minor. But in New York, where the buildings are tall and are constructed of heavy materials, the physical collapse of the city would certainly kill millions of people. The streets of New York are narrow ravines running between the high walls of the city's buildings. In a nuclear attack, the walls would fall and the ravines would fill up. The people in the buildings would fall to the street with the debris of the buildings, and the people in the street would be crushed by this avalanche of people and buildings. At a distance of two miles or so from ground zero, winds would reach four hundred miles an hour, and another two miles away they would reach a hundred and eighty miles an hour. Meanwhile, the fireball would be growing, until it was more than a mile wide, and rocketing upward, to a height of over six miles. For ten seconds, it would broil the city below. Anyone caught in the open within nine miles of ground zero would receive third-degree burns and would probably be killed; closer to the explosion, people would be charred and killed instantly. From Greenwich Village up to Central Park, the heat would be great enough to melt metal and glass. Readily inflammable materials, such as newspapers and dry leaves, would ignite in all five boroughs (though in only a small part of Staten Island) and west to the Passaic River, in New Jersey, within a radius of about nine and a half miles from ground zero, thereby creating an area of more than two hundred and eighty square miles in which mass fires were likely to break out.

If it were possible (as it would not be) for someone to stand at Fifth Avenue and Seventy-second Street (about two miles from ground zero) without being instantly killed, he would see the following sequence of events. A dazzling white light from the fireball would illumine the scene, continuing for perhaps thirty seconds. Simultaneously, searing heat would ignite everything flammable and start to melt windows, cars, buses, lampposts, and everything else made of metal or glass. People in the street would immediately catch fire, and would shortly be reduced to heavily charred corpses. About five seconds after the light appeared, the blast wave would strike, laden with the debris of a now nonexistent midtown. Some buildings might be crushed, as though a giant fist had squeezed them on all sides, and others might be picked up off their foundations and whirled uptown with the other debris. On the far side of Central Park, the West Side skyline would fall from south to north. The four-hundred-mile-an-hour wind would blow from south to north, die down after a few seconds, and then blow in the reverse direction with diminished intensity. While these things were happening, the fireball would be burning in the sky for the ten seconds of the thermal pulse. Soon huge, thick clouds of dust and smoke would envelop the scene, and as the mushroom cloud rushed overhead (it would have a diameter of about twelve miles) the light from the sun would be blotted out, and day would turn to night. Within minutes, fires, ignited both by the thermal pulse and by broken gas mains, tanks of gas and oil, and the like, would begin to spread in the darkness, and a strong, steady wind would begin to blow in the direction of the blast. As at Hiroshima, a whirlwind might be produced, which would sweep through the ruins, and radioactive rain, generated under the meteorological conditions created by the blast, might fall. Before long, the individual fires would coalesce into a mass fire, which, depending largely on the winds, would become either a conflagration or a firestorm. In a conflagration, prevailing winds spread a wall of fire as far as there is any combustible material to sustain it; in a firestorm, a vertical updraft caused by the fire itself sucks the surrounding air in toward a central point, and the fires therefore converge in a single fire of extreme heat. A mass fire of either kind renders shelters useless by burning up all the oxygen in the air and creating toxic gases, so that anyone inside the shelters is asphyxiated, and also by heating the ground to such high temperatures that the shelters turn, in effect, into ovens, cremating the people inside them. In Dresden, several days after the firestorm raised there by Allied conventional bombing, the interiors of some bomb shelters were still so hot that when they were opened the inrushing air caused the contents to burst into flame. Only those who had fled their shelters when the bombing started had any chance of surviving. (It is difficult to predict in a particular situation which form the fires will take. In actual experience, Hiroshima suffered a firestorm and Nagasaki suffered a conflagration.)

In this vast theatre of physical effects, all the scenes of agony and death that took place at Hiroshima would again take place, but now involving millions of people rather than hundreds of thousands. Like the people of Hiroshima, the people of New York would be burned, battered, crushed, and irradiated in every conceivable way. The city and its people would be mingled in a smoldering heap. And then, as the fires started, the survivors (most of whom would be on the periphery of the explosion) would be driven to abandon to the flames those family members and other people who were unable to flee, or else to die with then. Before long, while the ruins burned, the processions of injured, mute people would begin their slow progress out of the outskirts of the devastated zone. However, this time a much smaller proportion of the population than at Hiroshima would have a chance of escaping. In general, as the size of the area of devastation increases, the possibilities for escape decrease. When the devastated area is relatively small, as it was at Hiroshima, people who are not incapacitated will have a good chance of escaping to safety before the fires coalesce into a mass fire. But when the devastated area is great, as it would be after the detonation of a megaton bomb, and fires are springing up at a distance of nine and a half miles from ground zero, and when what used to be the streets are piled high with burning rubble, and the day (if the attack occurs in the daytime) has grown impenetrably dark, there is little chance that anyone who is not on the very edge of the devastated area will be able to make his way to safety. In New York, most people would die wherever the blast found them, or not very far from there.

If instead of being burst in the air the bomb were burst on or near the ground in the vicinity of the Empire State Building, the overpressure would be very much greater near the center of the blast area but the range hit by a minimum of five pounds per square inch of overpressure would be less. The range of the thermal pulse would be about the same as that of the air burst. The fireball would be almost two miles across, and would engulf midtown Manhattan from Greenwich Village nearly to Central Park. Very little is known about what would happen to a city that was inside a fireball, but one would expect a good deal of what was there to be first pulverized and then melted or vaporized. Any human beings in the area would be reduced to smoke and ashes; they would simply disappear. A crater roughly three blocks in diameter and two hundred feet deep would open up. In addition, heavy radioactive fallout would be created as dust and debris from the city rose with the mushroom cloud and then fell back to the ground. Fallout would begin to drop almost immediately, contaminating the ground beneath the cloud with levels of radiation many times lethal dose, and quickly killing anyone who might have survived the blast wave and the thermal pulse and might now be attempting an escape; it is difficult to believe that there would be appreciable survival of the people of the city after a megaton ground burst. And for the next twenty-four hours or so more fallout would descend downwind from the blast, in a plume whose direction and length would depend on the speed and the direction of the wind that happened to be blowing at the time of the attack. If the wind was blowing at fifteen miles an hour, fallout of lethal intensity would descend in a plume about a hundred and fifty miles long and as much as fifteen miles wide. Fallout that was sublethal but could still cause serious illness would extend another hundred and fifty miles downwind. Exposure to radioactivity in human beings is measured in units called rems—an acronym for "roentgen equivalent in man." The roentgen is a standard measurement of gamma- and X-ray radiation, and the expression "equivalent in man" indicates that an adjustment has been made to take into account the differences in the degree of biological damage that is caused by radiation of different types. Many of the kinds of harm done to human beings by radiation—for example, the incidence of cancer and of genetic damage—depend on the dose accumulated over many years; but radiation sickness, capable of causing death, results from an "acute" dose, received in a period of anything from a few seconds to several days. Because almost ninety per cent of the so-called "infinite-time dose" of radiation from fallout—that is, the dose from a given quantity of fallout that one would receive if one lived for many thousands of years—is emitted in the first week, the one-week accumulated dose is often used as a convenient measure for calculating the immediate harm from fallout. Doses in the thousands of rems, which could be expected throughout the city, would attack the central nervous system and would bring about death within a few hours. Doses of around a thousand rems, which would be delivered some tens of miles downwind from the blast, would kill within two weeks everyone who was exposed to them. Doses of around five hundred rems, which would be delivered as far as a hundred and fifty miles downwind (given a wind speed of fifteen miles per hour), would kill half of all exposed able-bodied young adults. At this level of exposure, radiation sickness proceeds in the three stages observed at Hiroshima. The plume of lethal fallout could descend, depending on the direction of the wind, on other parts of New York State and parts of New Jersey, Pennsylvania, Delaware, Maryland, Connecticut, Massachusetts, Rhode Island, Vermont, and New Hampshire, killing additional millions of people. The circumstances in heavily contaminated areas, in which millions of people were all declining together, over a period of weeks, toward painful deaths, are ones that, like so many of the consequences of nuclear explosions, have never been experienced.

A description of the effects of a one-megaton bomb on New York City gives some notion of the meaning in human terms of a megaton of nuclear explosive power, but a weapon that is more likely to be used against New York is the twenty-megaton bomb, which has one thousand six hundred times the yield of the Hiroshima bomb. The Soviet Union is estimated to have at least a hundred and thirteen twenty-megaton bombs in its nuclear arsenal, carried by Bear intercontinental bombers. In addition, some of the Soviet SS-18 missiles are capable of carrying bombs of this size, although the actual yields are not known. Since the explosive power of the twenty-megaton bombs greatly exceeds the amount necessary to destroy most military targets, it is reasonable to suppose that they are meant for use against large cities. If a twenty-megaton bomb were air-burst over the Empire State Building at an altitude of thirty thousand feet, the zone gutted or flattened by the blast wave would have a radius of twelve miles and an area of more than four hundred and fifty square miles, reaching from the middle of Staten Island to the northern edge of the Bronx, the eastern edge of Queens, and well into New Jersey, and the zone of heavy damage from the blast wave (the zone hit by a minimum of two pounds of overpressure per square inch) would have a radius of twenty-one and a half miles, or an area of one thousand four hundred and fifty square miles, reaching to the southernmost tip of Staten Island, north as far as southern Rockland County, east into Nassau County, and west to Morris County, New Jersey. The fireball would be about four and a half miles in diameter and would radiate the thermal pulse for some twenty seconds. People caught in the open twenty-three miles away from ground zero, in Long Island, New Jersey, and southern New York State, would be burned to death. People hundreds of miles away who looked at the burst would be temporarily blinded and would risk permanent eye injury. (After the test of a fifteen-megaton bomb on Bikini Atoll, in the South Pacific, in March of 1954, small animals were found to have suffered retinal burns at a distance of three hundred and forty-five miles.) The mushroom cloud would be seventy miles in diameter. New York City and its suburbs would be transformed into a lifeless, flat, scorched desert in a few seconds.

If a twenty-megaton bomb were ground-burst on the Empire State Building, the range of severe blast damage would, as with the one-megaton ground blast, be reduced, but the fireball, which would be almost six miles in diameter, would cover Manhattan from Wall Street to northern Central Park and also parts of New Jersey, Brooklyn, and Queens, and everyone within it would be instantly killed, with most of them physically disappearing. Fallout would again be generated, this time covering thousands of square miles with lethal intensities of radiation. A fair portion of New York City and its incinerated population, now radioactive dust, would have risen into the mushroom cloud and would now be descending on the surrounding territory. On one of the few occasions when local fallout was generated by a test explosion in the multi-megaton range, the fifteen-megaton bomb tested on Bikini Atoll, which was exploded seven feet above the surface of a coral reef, "caused substantial contamination over an area of more than seven thousand square miles," according to Glasstone. If, as seems likely, a twenty-megaton bomb ground-burst on New York would produce at least a comparable amount of fallout, and if the wind carried the fallout onto populated areas, then this one bomb would probably doom upward of twenty million people, or almost ten per cent of the population of the United States.

The "strategic" forces of the Soviet Union—those that can deliver nuclear warheads to the United States—are so far capable of carrying seven thousand warheads with an estimated maximum yield of more than seventeen thousand megatons of explosive power, and, barring unexpected developments in arms-control talks, the number of warheads is expected to rise in the coming years. The actual megatonnage of the Soviet strategic forces is not known, and, for a number of reasons, including the fact that smaller warheads can be delivered more accurately, it is very likely that the actual megatonnage is lower than the maximum possible; however, it is reasonable to suppose that the actual megatonnage is as much as two-thirds of the maximum, which would be about eleven and a half thousand megatons. If we assume that in a first strike the Soviets held back about a thousand megatons (itself an immense force), then the attack would amount to about ten thousand megatons, or the equivalent of eight hundred thousand Hiroshima bombs. American strategic forces comprise about nine thousand warheads with a yield of some three thousand five hundred megatons. The total yield of these American forces was made comparatively low for strategic reasons. American planners discovered that smaller warheads can be delivered more accurately than larger ones, and are therefore more useful for attacking strategic forces on the other side. And, in fact, American missiles are substantially more accurate than Soviet ones. However, in the last year or so, in spite of this advantage in numbers of warheads and in accuracy, American leaders have come to believe that the American forces are inadequate, and, again barring unexpected developments in arms-control talks, both the yield of the American arsenal and the number of warheads in it are likely to rise dramatically. (Neither the United States nor the Soviet Union reveals the total explosive yield of its own forces. The public is left to turn to private organizations, which, by making use of hundreds of pieces of information that *have* been released by the two governments, piece together an over-all picture. The figures I have used to estimate the maximum capacities of the two sides are taken for the most part from tables provided in the latest edition of "The Military Balance," a standard yearly reference work on the strength of military forces around the world, which is published by a research institute in London called the International Institute for Strategic Studies.) The territory of the United States, including Alaska and Hawaii, is three million six hundred and fifteen thousand one hundred and twenty-two square miles. It contains approximately two hundred and twenty-five million people, of whom sixty per cent, or about a hundred and thirty-five million, live in various urban centers with a total area of only eighteen thousand square miles. I asked Dr. Kendall, who has done considerable research on the consequences of nuclear attacks, to sketch out in rough terms what the actual distribution of bombs might be in a ten-thousand-megaton Soviet attack in the early nineteen-eighties on all targets in the United States, military and civilian.

"Without serious distortion," he said, "we can begin by imagining that we would be dealing with ten thousand weapons of one megaton each, although in fact the yields would, of course, vary considerably. Let us also make the assumption, based on common knowledge of weapons design, that on average the yield would be one-half fission and one-half fusion. This proportion is important, because it is the fission products—a virtual museum of about three hundred radioactive isotopes, decaying at different rates—that give off radioactivity in fallout. Fusion can add to the total in ground bursts by radioactivation of ground material by neutrons, but the quantity added is comparatively small. Targets can be divided into two categories—hard and soft. Hard targets, of which there are about a thousand in the United States, are mostly missile silos. The majority of them can be destroyed only by huge, blunt overpressures, ranging anywhere from many hundreds to a few thousand pounds per square inch, and we can expect that two weapons might be devoted to each one to assure destruction. That would use up two thousand megatons. Because other strategic military targets—such as Strategic Air Command bases—are near centers of population, an attack on them as well, perhaps using another couple of hundred megatons, could cause a total of more than twenty million casualties, according to studies by the Arms Control and Disarmament Agency. If the nearly eight thousand weapons remaining were then devoted to the cities and towns of the United States in order of population, every community down to the level of fifteen hundred inhabitants would be hit with a megaton bomb—which is, of course, many, many times what would be necessary to annihilate a town that size. For obvious reasons, industry is highly correlated with population density, so an attack on the one necessarily hits the other, especially when an attack of this magnitude is considered. Ten thousand targets would include everything worth hitting in the country and much more; it would simply *be* the United States. The targeters would run out of targets and victims long before they ran out of bombs. If you imagine that the bombs were distributed according to population, then, allowing for the fact that the attack on the military installations would have already killed about twenty million people, you would have about forty megatons to devote to each remaining million people in the country. For the seven and a half million people in New York City, that would come to three hundred megatons. Bearing in mind what one megaton can do, you can see that this would be preposterous overkill. In practice, one might expect the New York metropolitan area to be hit with some dozens of one-megaton weapons."

In the first moments of a ten-thousand-megaton attack on the United States, I learned from Dr. Kendall and from other sources, flashes of white light would suddenly illumine large areas of the country as thousands of suns, each one brighter than the sun itself, blossomed over cities, suburbs, and towns. In those same moments, when the first wave of missiles arrived, the vast majority of the people in the regions first targeted would be irradiated, crushed, or burned to death. The thermal pulses could subject more than six hundred thousand square miles, or one-sixth of the total land mass of the nation, to a minimum level of forty calories per centimetre squared—a level of heat that chars human beings. (At Hiroshima, charred remains in the rough shape of human beings were a common sight.) Tens of millions of people would go up in smoke. As the attack proceeded, as much as three-quarters of the country could be subjected to incendiary levels of heat, and so, wherever there was inflammable material, could be set ablaze. In the ten seconds or so after each bomb hit, as blast waves swept outward from thousands of ground zeros, the physical plant of the United States would be swept away like leaves in a gust of wind. The six hundred thousand square miles already scorched by the forty or more calories of heat per centimetre squared would now be hit by blast waves of a minimum of five pounds per square inch, and virtually all the habitations, places of work, and other man-made things there—substantially the whole human construct in the United States—would be vaporized, blasted, or otherwise pulverized out of existence. Then, as clouds of dust rose from the earth, and mushroom clouds spread overhead, often linking to form vast canopies, day would turn to night. (These clouds could blanket as much as a third of the nation.) Shortly, fires would spring up in the debris of the cities and in every forest dry enough to burn. These fires would simply burn down the United States. When one pictures a full-scale attack on the United States, or on any other country, therefore, the picture of a single city being flattened by a single bomb—an image firmly engraved in the public imagination, probably because of the bombings of Hiroshima and Naga-saki—must give way to a picture of substantial sections of the country being turned by a sort of nuclear carpet-bombing into immense infernal regions, literally tens of thousands of square miles in area, from which escape is impossible. In Hiroshima and Nagasaki, those who had not been killed or injured so severely that they could not move were able to flee to the undevastated world around them, where they found help, but in any city where three or four bombs had been used—not to mention fifty, or a hundred—flight from one blast would only be flight toward another, and no one could escape alive. Within these regions, each of three of the immediate effects of nuclear weapons—initial radiation, thermal pulse, and blast wave—would alone be enough to kill most people: the initial nuclear radiation would subject tens of thousands of square miles to lethal doses; the blast waves, coming from all sides, would nowhere fall below the overpressure necessary to destroy almost all buildings; and the thermal pulses, also coming from all sides, would always be great enough to kill exposed people and, in addition, to set on fire everything that would burn. The ease with which virtually the whole population of the country could be trapped in these zones of universal death is suggested by the fact that the sixty per cent of the population that lives in an area of eighteen thousand square miles could be annihilated with only three hundred one-megaton bombs—the number necessary to cover the area with a minimum of five pounds per square inch of overpressure and forty calories per centimetre squared of heat. That would leave nine thousand seven hundred megatons, or ninety-seven per cent of the megatonnage in the attacking force, available for other targets. (It is hard to imagine what a targeter would do with all his bombs in these circumstances. Above several thousand megatons, it would almost become a matter of trying to hunt down individual people with nuclear warheads.)

The statistics on the initial nuclear radiation, the thermal pulses, and the blast waves in a nuclear holocaust can be presented in any number of ways, but all of them would be only variations on a simple theme—the annihilation of the United States and its people. Yet while the immediate nuclear effects are great enough in a ten-thousand-megaton attack to destroy the country many times over, they are not the most powerfully lethal of the local effects of nuclear weapons. The killing power of the local fallout is far greater. Therefore, if the Soviet Union was bent on producing the maximum overkill—if, that is, its surviving leaders, whether out of calculation, rage, or madness, decided to eliminate the United States not merely as a political and social entity but as a biological one—they would burst their bombs on the ground rather than in the air. Although the scope of severe blast damage would then be reduced, the blast waves, fireballs, and thermal pulses would still be far more than enough to destroy the country, and, in addition, provided only that the bombs were dispersed widely enough, lethal fallout would spread throughout the nation. The amount of radiation delivered by the fallout from a ground burst of a given size is still uncertain—not least because, as Glasstone notes, there has never been a "true land surface burst" of a bomb with a yield of over one kiloton. (The Bikini burst was in part over the ocean.) Many factors make for uncertainty. To mention just a few: the relative amounts of the fallout that rises into the stratosphere and the fallout that descends to the ground near the blast are dependent on, among other things, the yield of the weapon, and, in any case, can be only guessed at; the composition of the fallout will vary with the composition of the material on the ground that is sucked up into the mushroom cloud; prediction of the distribution of fallout by winds of various speeds at various altitudes depends on a choice of several "models" and the calculation of the arrival time of the fallout—an important calculation, since fallout cannot harm living things until it lands near them—is subject to similar speculative doubts. However, calculations on the basis of figures for a one-megaton ground burst which are given in the Office of Technology Assessment's report show that ten thousand megatons would yield one-week doses around the country averaging more than ten thousand rems. In actuality, of course, the bombs would almost certainly not be evenly spaced around the country but, rather, would be concentrated in populated areas and in missile fields; and the likelihood is that in most places where people lived or worked the doses would be many times the average, commonly reaching several tens of thousands of rems for the first week, while in remote areas they would be less, or, conceivably, even nonexistent. (The United States contains large tracts of empty desert, and to target them would be virtually meaningless from any point of view.)

These figures provide a context for judging the question of civil defense. With overwhelming immediate local effects striking the vast majority of the population, and with one-week doses of radiation then rising into the tens of thousands of rems, evacuation and shelters are a vain hope. Needless to say, in these circumstances evacuation before an attack would be an exercise in transporting people from one death to another. In some depictions of a holocaust, various rescue operations are described, with unafflicted survivors bringing food, clothes, and medical care to the afflicted, and the afflicted making their way to thriving, untouched communities, where churches, school auditoriums, and the like would have been set up for their care—as often happens after a bad snowstorm, say. Obviously, none of this could come about. In the first place, in a full-scale attack there would in all likelihood *be* no surviving communities, and, in the second place, everyone who failed to seal himself off from the outside environment for as long as several months would soon die of radiation sickness. Hence, in the months after a holocaust there would be no activity of any sort, as, in a reversal of the normal state of things, the dead would lie on the surface and the living, if there were any, would be buried underground.

To this description of radiation levels around the country, an addition remains to be made. This is the fact that attacks on the seventy-six nuclear power plants in the United States would produce fallout whose radiation had much greater longevity than that of the weapons alone. The physicist Dr. Kosta Tsipis, of M.I.T., and one of his students, Steven Fetter, recently published an article in *Scientific American* called "Catastrophic Releases of Radioactivity," in which they calculate the damage from a one-megaton thermonuclear ground burst on a one-gigawatt nuclear power plant. In such a ground burst, the facility's radioactive contents would be vaporized along with everything nearby, and the remains would be carried up into the mushroom cloud, from which they would descend to the earth with the rest of the fallout. But whereas the fission products of the weapon were newly made, and contained many isotopes that would decay to insignificant levels very swiftly, the fission products in a reactor would be a collection of longer-lived isotopes (and this applies even more strongly to the spent fuel in the reactor's holding pond), since the short-lived ones would, for the most part, have had enough time to reduce themselves to harmless levels. The intense but comparatively short-lived radiation from the weapon would kill people in the first few weeks and months, but the long-lived radiation that was produced both by the weapon and by the power plant could prevent anyone from living on a vast area of land for decades after it fell. For example, after a year an area of some seventeen hundred square miles downwind of a power plant on which a one-megaton bomb had been ground-burst (again assuming a fifteen-mile-an-hour wind) would still be delivering more than fifty rems per year to anyone who tried to live there, and that is two hundred and fifty times the "safe" dose established by the E.P.A. The bomb by itself would produce this effect over an area of only twenty-six square miles. (In addition to offering an enemy a way of redoubling the effectiveness of his attacks in a full-scale holocaust, reactors provide targets of unparalleled danger in possible terrorist nuclear attacks. In an earlier paper, Tsipis and Fetter observe that "the destruction of a reactor with a nuclear weapon, even of relatively small yield, such as a crude terrorist nuclear device, would represent a national catastrophe of lasting consequences." It can be put down as one further alarming oddity of life in a nuclear world that in building nuclear power plants nations have opened themselves to catastrophic devastation and long-term contamination of their territories by enemies who manage to get hold of only a few nuclear weapons.)

If, in a nuclear holocaust, anyone hid himself deep enough under the earth and stayed there long enough to survive, he would emerge into a dying natural environment. The vulnerability of the environment is the last word in the argument against the usefulness of shelters: there is no hole big enough to hide all of nature in. Radioactivity penetrates the environment in many ways. The two most important components of radiation from fallout are gamma rays, which are electromagnetic radiation of the highest intensity, and beta particles, which are electrons fired at high speed from decaying nuclei. Gamma rays subject organisms to penetrating whole-body doses, and are responsible for most of the ill effects of radiation from fallout. Beta particles, which are less penetrating than gamma rays, act at short range, doing harm when they collect on the skin, or on the surface of a leaf. They are harmful to plants on whose foliage the fallout descends—producing "beta burn"—and to grazing animals, which can suffer burns as well as gastrointestinal damage from eating the foliage. Two of the most harmful radioactive isotopes present in fallout are strontium-90 (with a half-life of twenty-eight years) and cesium-137 (with a half-life of thirty years). They are taken up into the food chain through the roots of plants or through direct ingestion by animals, and contaminate the environment from within. Strontium-90 happens to resemble calcium in its chemical composition, and therefore finds its way into the human diet through dairy products and is eventually deposited by the body in the bones, where it is thought to cause bone cancer. (Every person in the world now has in his bones a measurable deposit of strontium-90 traceable to the fallout from atmospheric nuclear testing.)

Over the years, agencies and departments of the government have sponsored numerous research projects in which a large variety of plants and animals were irradiated in order to ascertain the lethal or sterilizing dose for each. These findings permit the prediction of many gross ecological consequences of a nuclear attack. According to "Survival of Food Crops and Livestock in the Event of Nuclear War," the proceedings of the 1970 symposium at Brookhaven National Laboratory, the lethal doses for most mammals lie between a few hundred rads and a thousand rads of gamma radiation; a rad—for "roentgen absorbed dose"—is a roentgen of radiation that has been absorbed by an organism, and is roughly equal to a rem. For example, the lethal doses of gamma radiation for animals in pasture, where fallout would be descending on them directly and they would be eating fallout that had fallen on the grass, and would thus suffer from doses of beta radiation as well, would be one hundred and eighty rads for cattle; two hundred and forty rads for sheep; five hundred and fifty rads for swine; three hundred and fifty rads for horses; and eight hundred rads for poultry. In a ten-thousand-megaton attack, which would create levels of radiation around the country averaging more than ten thousand rads, most of the mammals of the United States would be killed off. The lethal doses for birds are in roughly the same range as those for mammals, and birds, too, would be killed off. Fish are killed at doses of between one thousand one hundred rads and about five thousand six hundred rads, but their fate is less predictable. On the one hand, water is a shield from radiation, and would afford some protection; on the other hand, fallout might concentrate in bodies of water as it ran off from the land. (Because radiation causes no pain, animals, wandering at will through the environment, would not avoid it.) The one class of animals containing a number of species quite likely to survive, at least in the short run, is the insect class, for which in most known cases the lethal doses lie between about two thousand rads and about a hundred thousand rads. Insects, therefore, would be destroyed selectively. Unfortunately for the rest of the environment, many of the phytophagous species—insects that feed directly on vegetation—which "include some of the most ravaging species on earth" (according to Dr. Vernon M. Stern, an entomologist at the University of California at Riverside, writing in "Survival of Food Crops"), have very high tolerances, and so could be expected to survive disproportionately, and then to multiply greatly in the aftermath of an attack. The demise of their natural predators the birds would enhance their success.

Plants in general have a higher tolerance to radioactivity than animals do. Nevertheless, according to Dr. George M. Woodwell, who supervised the irradiation with gamma rays, over several years, of a small forest at Brookhaven Laboratory, a gamma-ray dose of ten thousand rads "would devastate most vegetation" in the United States, and, as in the case of the pastured animals, when one figures in the beta radiation that would also be delivered by fallout the estimates for the lethal doses of gamma rays must be reduced—in this case, cut in half. As a general rule, Dr. Woodwell and his colleagues at Brookhaven discovered, large plants are more vulnerable to radiation than small ones. Trees are among the first to die, grasses among the last. The most sensitive trees are pines and the other conifers, for which lethal doses are in roughly the same range as those for mammals. Any survivors coming out of their shelters a few months after the attack would find that all the pine trees that were still standing were already dead. The lethal doses for most deciduous trees range from about two thousands rads of gamma-ray radiation to about ten thousand rads, with the lethal doses for eighty per cent of deciduous species falling between two thousand and eight thousand rads. Since the addition of the beta-ray burden could lower these lethal doses for gamma rays by as much as fifty per cent, the actual lethal doses in gamma rays for these trees during an attack could be from one thousand to four thousand rads, and in a full-scale attack they would die. Then, after the trees had died, forest fires would break out around the United States. (Because as much as three-quarters of the country could be subjected to incendiary levels of the thermal pulses, the sheer scorching of the land could have killed off a substantial part of the plant life in the country in the first few seconds after the detonations, before radioactive poisoning set in.) Lethal doses for grasses on which tests have been done range between six thousand and thirty-three thousand rads, and a good deal of grass would therefore survive, except where the attacks had been heaviest. Most crops, on the other hand, are killed by doses below five thousand rads, and would be eliminated. (The lethal dose for spring barley seedlings, for example, is one thousand nine hundred and ninety rads, and that for spring wheat seedlings is three thousand and ninety rads.)

When vegetation is killed off, the land on which it grew is degraded. And as the land eroded after an attack life in lakes, rivers, and estuaries, already hard hit by radiation directly, would be further damaged by minerals flowing into the watercourses, causing eutrophication—a process in which an oversupply of nutrients in the water encouraged the growth of algae and microscopic organisms, which, in turn, deplete the oxygen content of the water. When the soil loses its nutrients, it loses its ability to "sustain a mature community" (in Dr. Woodwell's words), and "gross simplification" of the environment occurs, in which "hardy species," such as moss and grass, replace vulnerable ones, such as trees; and "succession"—the process by which ecosystems recover lost diversity—is then "delayed or even arrested." In sum, a full-scale nuclear attack on the United States would devastate the natural environment on a scale unknown since early geological times, when, in response to natural catastrophes whose nature has not been determined, sudden mass extinctions of species and whole ecosystems occurred all over the earth. How far this "gross simplification" of the environment would go once virtually all animal life and the greater part of plant life had been destroyed and what patterns the surviving remnants of life would arrange themselves into over the long run are imponderables; but it appears that at the outset the United States would be a republic of insects and grass.

It has sometimes been claimed that the United States could survive a nuclear attack by the Soviet Union, but the bare figures on the extent of the blast waves, the thermal pulses, and the accumulated local fallout dash this hope irrevocably. They spell the doom of the United States. And if one imagines the reverse attack on the Soviet Union, its doom is spelled out in similar figures. (The greater land mass of the Soviet Union and the lower megatonnage of the American forces might reduce the factor of overkill somewhat.) Likewise, any country subjected to an attack of more than a few hundred megatons would be doomed. Japan, China, and the countries of Europe, where population densities are high, are especially vulnerable to damage, even at "low" levels of attack. There is no country in Europe in which survival of the population would be appreciable after the detonation of several hundred megatons; most European countries would be annihilated by tens of megatons. And these conclusions emerge even before one takes into account the global ecological consequences of a holocaust, which would be superimposed on the local conse-quences. As human life and the structure of human existence are seen in the light of each person's daily life and experience, they look impressively extensive and solid, but when human things are seen in the light of the universal power unleashed onto the earth by nuclear weapons they prove to be limited and fragile, as though they were nothing more than a mold or a lichen that appears in certain crevices of the landscape and can be burned off with relative ease by nuclear fire.

Many discussions of nuclear attacks on the United States devote considerable attention to their effect on the nation's economy, but if the population has been largely killed off and the natural environment is in a state of collapse "the economy" becomes a meaningless concept; for example, it makes no difference what percentage of "the automobile industry" has survived if all the producers and drivers of automobiles have died. Estimates of economic survival after a full-scale holocaust are, in fact, doubly unreal, because, as a number of government reports have shown, the nation's economy is so much more vulnerable to attack than the population that even at most levels of "limited" attack a greater proportion of the economy than of the population would be destroyed. An intact economic plant that goes to waste because there aren't enough people left to run it is one absurdity that a nuclear holocaust does not present us with. At relatively low levels of attack, however, the more or less complete destruction of the economy, accompanied by the survival of as much as twenty or thirty per cent of the population, is conceivable. Since the notion of "limited nuclear war" has recently become attractive to the American leadership, it may not be digressive to discuss what the consequences of smaller attacks would be. Our knowledge of nuclear effects is too imprecise to permit us to know at exactly what level of attack a given percentage of the population would survive, but the fact that sixty per cent of the population lives in eighteen thousand square miles and could be eliminated by the thermal pulses, blast waves, and mass fires produced by about three hundred one-megaton bombs suggests some rough magnitudes. The fallout that would be produced by the bombs if they were ground-burst would very likely kill ten or fifteen per cent of the remaining population (it could lethally contaminate some three hundred thousand square miles), and if several hundred additional megatons were used the percentage of the entire population killed in the short term might rise to something like eighty-five. Or, to put it differently, if the level of attack on civilian targets did not rise above the low hundreds of megatons tens of millions of people might survive in the short term. But that same level of attack would destroy so much of the physical plant of the economy, and, of course, so many of the laborers and managers who make it work, that in effect the economy would be nearly one hundred per cent destroyed. (There is a tendency when one is analyzing nuclear attacks to begin to accustom oneself to such expressions as "a thousand megatons," and therefore to begin to regard lower amounts as inconsequential. Yet even one megaton, which contains the explosive yield of eighty Hiroshimas, would, if it should be dropped in the United States in the form of a number of small bombs, be an unimaginable catastrophe. Ten megatons—eight hundred Hiroshimas—would leave any nation on earth devastated beyond anything in our historical experience. A hundred megatons—eight thousand Hiroshimas—is already outside comprehension.)

As soon as one assumes that many tens of millions of people

might survive the early stages of an attack, what are often called the long-term effects of a holocaust come into view; in fact, it is only when the imagined attack is reduced to this level that it begins to make sense to talk about many of the long-term effects, because only then will there be people left living to suffer them. The most obvious of these is injury. In an attack that killed from fifty to seventy per cent of the population outright, the great majority of the survivors would be injured. In a limited attack, some people might try to make their way to shelters to escape the fallout, which would be less intense than in the larger attack but still lethal in most populated areas. (If we again assume ground bursts, and also assume that two thousand megatons have been used on military targets, then average levels of radiation around the country would be in the low thousands of rems. But in this case averages would have little or no meaning; actual levels would be very high in some places and very low or nonexistent in others, depending on targeting and weather patterns.) People who reached shelters and sealed themselves in in time might have a chance of survival in some areas, but a large number of people would have received lethal doses of radiation without knowing it (since exposure to radiation is painless) and would enter the shelters and die there, making life in the shelters unbearable for the others. With many people seeking to get into the shelters, attempts to decide who was to be allowed to enter and who was to be kept out would begin in bitterness and end in chaos. (In the nineteen-fifties, when Americans gave greater thought to the matter of shelters than they do now, some communities began to prepare to defend their shelters against intruders by arming themselves.) Also, the withdrawal into shelters of the uninjured or lightly injured portion of the population would be more consequential for the survivors as a body, because in a limited attack there might be a considerable number of people on the surface who would have had a chance of surviving if they had not been abandoned. The widespread use of shelters would therefore mean additional deaths; the injured or sick people would die unattended on the surface while the uninjured and healthy people hid underground.

   The injuries from the attack would very likely be compounded by epidemics. Dr. H. Jack Geiger, who teaches community medicine at the School of Biomedical Education of the City College of New York, recently described to me the likely medical conditions after a limited attack. "The landscape would be strewn with millions of corpses of human beings and animals," he pointed out. "This alone is a situation without precedent in history. There would be an immense source of pollution of water and food. If you read the literature concerning natural disasters such as floods and typhoons, you find that there is always an associated danger of cholera or typhoid. The corpses would also feed a fast-growing population of insects, and insects happen to be a prime vector of disease. Naturally, medical measures to fight disease would not be taken, since the blasts would have destroyed virtually all medical facilities. Nor, of course, would there be such elementary sanitary facilities as running water and garbage collection. Finally, the population's resistance to infection would have been weakened, since many would be suffering from sublethal radiation sickness and wounds. It would be impossible to devise circumstances more favorable to the spread of epidemics."

Strategists of nuclear conflict often speak of a period of "recovery" after a limited attack, but a likelier prospect is a long-term radical deterioration in the conditions of life. For a while, some supplies of food and clothing would be found in the rubble, but then these would give out. For a people, the economy—any kind of economy, whether primitive or modern—is the means of survival from day to day. So if you ruin the economy—if you suspend its functioning, even for a few months—you take away the means of survival. Eventually, if enough people do live, the economy will revive in one form or another, but in the meantime people will die: they will starve, because the supply of food has been cut off; they will freeze, because they have no fuel or shelter; they will perish of illness, because they have no medical care. If the economy in question is a modern technological one, the consequences will be particularly severe, for then the obstacles to restoring it will be greatest. Because a modern economy, like an eco-system, is a single, interdependent whole, in which each part requires many other parts to keep functioning, its wholesale breakdown will leave people unable to perform the simplest, most essential tasks. Even agriculture—the immediate means of subsistence—is caught up in the operations of the inter-dependent machine, and breaks down when it breaks down. Modern agriculture depends on fertilizers to make crops grow, on machines to cultivate the crops, on transportation to carry the produce thousands of miles to the consumers, on fuel to run the means of transportation and the agricultural machinery, and on pesticides and drugs to increase production. If fertilizers, machines, transportation, fuel, pesticides, and drugs are taken away, agriculture will come to a halt, and people will starve. Also, because of the interdependence of the system, no sector of the economy can be repaired unless many of the other sectors are in good order.

But in a nuclear attack, of course, all sectors of the economy would be devastated at once. The task facing the survivors, therefore, would be not to restore the old economy but to invent a new one, on a far more primitive level. But the invention of a primitive economy would not be a simple matter. Even economies we think of as primitive depend on considerable knowledge accumulated through long experience, and in modern times this knowledge has been largely lost. The economy of the Middle Ages, for example, was far less productive than our own, but it was exceedingly complex, and it would not be within the capacity of people in our time suddenly to establish a medieval economic system in the ruins of their twentieth-century one. After a limited nuclear attack, the typical predicament of a survivor would be that of, say, a bus driver in a city who was used to shopping at a supermarket and found himself facing the question of how to grow his own food, or of a bookkeeper in a suburb who found that he must make his own clothing, not to mention the cloth for the clothing. Innumerable things that we now take for granted would abruptly be lacking. In addition to food and clothing, they would include: heating, electric lights, running water, telephones, mail, transportation of all kinds, all household appliances powered by electricity or gas, information other than by word of mouth, medical facilities, sanitary facilities, and basic social services, such as fire departments and police. To restore these essentials of life takes time; but there would be no time. Hunger, illness, and possibly cold would press in on the dazed, bewildered, disorganized, injured remnant of the population on the very day of the attack.

They would have to start foraging immediately for their next meal. Sitting among the debris of the Space Age, they would find that the pieces of a shattered modern economy around them—here an automobile, there a washing machine—were mismatched to their elemental needs. Nor would life be made easier for them by the fact that their first need, once they left any shelters they might have found, would be to flee the heavily irradiated, burned-out territories where they used to live, and to start over in less irradiated, unburned territories, which would probably be in the wilderness. Facing these urgent requirements, they would not be worrying about rebuilding the automobile industry or the electronics industry; they would be worrying about how to find nonradioactive berries in the woods, or how to tell which trees had edible bark.

Lastly, over the decades not only would the survivors of a limited attack face a contaminated and degraded environment but they themselves—their flesh, bones, and genetic endowment—would be contaminated: the generations that would be trying to rebuild a human life would be sick and possibly deformed generations. The actual doses received by particular survivors would, of course, depend on their circumstances, but some notion of the extent of the contamination can perhaps be gathered from the fact that if people came out of shelters after three months into an area in which the fallout would in the long run deliver a dose of ten thousand rems they would still receive about three per cent of the total, or three hundred rems, over their lifetimes, with two hundred of those rems being received in the first year. I spoke to Dr. Edward Radford, who is a professor of environmental epidemiology at the University of Pittsburgh, and who was chairman from 1977 to 1980 of the National Academy of Sciences' Committee on the Biological Effects of Ionizing Radiations, about the medical consequences of such exposure. "The present incidence of cancer, exclusive of skin cancer, in the United States population is thirty per cent, and roughly seventeen per cent die of the disease," he told me. "Since the dose of radiation that doubles the cancer rate is about one hundred and fifty rems, we could expect that a dose of three hundred rems would cause just about everybody to get cancer of one kind or another, and perhaps half of them would die from it. In addition, the dose that is estimated to cause a doubling of the spontaneous-mutation rate—which now affects ten per cent of all births—is also one hundred and fifty rems, and therefore we could also expect genetic abnormalities to increase dramatically." Whether a human community could survive bearing this burden of illness and mutation is at best questionable.

In considering the global consequences of a holocaust, the first question to be asked is how widespread the hostilities would be. It is often assumed that a holocaust, even if it were full-scale, would be restricted to the Northern Hemisphere, destroying the United States, the Soviet Union, Europe, China, and Japan, but in fact there is no assurance that hostilities would not spread to other parts of the world. Both Soviet and American leaders believe that the rivalry between their countries has worldwide ideological significance, and in the name of their causes they might well extend their attacks almost anywhere. Furthermore, it takes very little imagination to see that once the superpowers had absorbed several thousand megatons of nuclear explosives each they would no longer *be* superpowers; indeed, they would no longer exist as nations at all. At that point, any sizable nation that had been spared attack—for example, Vietnam, Mexico, Nigeria, Australia, or South Africa—might, in the minds of the leaders of the ex-superpowers, become tempting as a target. It might suddenly occur to them that on a devastated earth mere survival would be the stuff of global might, and either or both of the ex-superpowers might then set about destroying those surviving middle-ranking powers that seemed closest to sharing the ideology of the enemy. Again, it is impossible to know what thoughts would go through the minds of men in caves, or perhaps in airborne command posts, who had just carried out the slaughter of hundreds of millions of people and whose nations had been annihilated in a similar slaughter (and it should always be borne in mind that sheer insanity is one of the possibilities), but it could be that in some confused attempt to shape the political future of the post-holocaust world (if there is one) they would carry their struggle into the would-be-neutral world. It could be that even now the United States has a few dozen megatons reserved in one contingency plan or another for, say, Cuba, Vietnam, and North Korea, while the Soviet Union may have a similar fate in mind for, among others, Israel, South Africa, and Australia. We also have to ask ourselves what the Chinese, the French, and the British, who all possess nuclear arms, and the Israelis, the South Africans, and the Indians, who are all suspected of possessing them, would attempt once the mayhem began. And this list of nuclear-armed and possibly nuclear-armed countries shows every sign of being a growing one.

Although it may seem inappropriate to mention "civilization" in the same breath as the death of hundreds of millions of people, it should at least be pointed out that a full-scale holocaust would, if it extended throughout the Northern Hemisphere, eliminate the civilizations of Europe, China, Japan, Russia, and the United States from the earth.

As I have already mentioned, there are uncertainties inherent in any attempt to predict the consequences of a nuclear holocaust; but when we try to estimate those consequences for the targeted countries it turns out that the readily calculable local primary effects of the bombs are so overwhelming that we never arrive at the uncertainties. Obviously, there can be no tangled interplay of destructive influences in society if there is no society; and the local primary effects are more than enough to remove society from the picture. This is why those observers who speak of "recovery" after a holocaust or of "winning" a nuclear "war" are dreaming. They are living in a past that has been swept away forever by nuclear arms. However, when it comes to inquiring into the global ecological consequences of a holocaust and, with them, the risk of human extinction, the uncertainties, and the political questions they raise, move to the fore. To begin with, this inquiry requires us to concentrate our attention on the earth. The earth is a compound mystery, for it presents us with the mystery of life in its entirety, the mystery of every individual form of life, and the mystery of ourselves, and all our thoughts and works. (Since we are earth-made, investigation of the earth eventually becomes introspection.) The reason for our ignorance is not that our knowledge of the earth is slight—on the contrary, it is extensive, and has grown in this century more than in all other centuries put together—but that the amount to be known is demonstrably so much greater. There is a sense, of course, in which knowledge can increase ignorance. By lead-ing to fresh discoveries, knowledge may open up new wonders to our view but not yet to our understanding. Our century's discoveries in the earth sciences have increased our ignorance in just this sense: they have given us a glimpse of how much there is still to find out. Dr. Lewis Thomas, the noted biologist and essayist, has defined this ignorance in categorical terms, saying, "We are ignorant about how we work, about where we fit in, and most of all about the enormous, imponderable system of life in which we are embedded as working parts. We do not really understand nature, at all." Of all the things to be said in a discussion of the global effects of a nuclear holocaust, this is by far the most important: that because of the extent of what we know that we don't know, we are simply debarred from making confident judgments.

Since an awareness of the boundaries of present knowledge is a necessary part of science's effort to achieve precision and clarity, it is not surprising that the literature on global nuclear effects is littered with reminders of the fallibility and, above all, of the incompleteness of our present understanding. This appropriately modest, tentative spirit has perhaps been best summed up in the opening comments of the Office of Tech-nology Assessment report, which states that the most impor-tant thing to know about a holocaust is not anything that "is known" but "what is not known." A similar acknowledgment of the importance of the unknown is implicit in a remark in a 1977 "interim" report by the National Academy of Sciences on the peril to the stratosphere from man-made disturbances in general. "It is unfortunately true," the report says, "that, accompanying very substantial over-all progress, the recent de-velopment of our understanding of stratospheric chemistry has been dominated by major upheavals caused by the recognition of the importance of processes whose role either had not been properly appreciated . . . or whose rate coefficient had been grossly misjudged. . . . To say how many more major upheavals we should expect in the future is rather like trying to foresee the unforeseeable." The report goes on to note that as knowledge of the chemistry of the stratosphere has improved, it has turned out that "even with the largest computers it is not possible to represent the detailed three-dimensional motions in the

atmosphere while including the detailed chemical reactions."
Before the "upheavals," scientists seemed to "know" a good
deal; afterward, they knew that they knew less.

Our ignorance pertains to the possibility of altogether
unknown major effects of nuclear explosions as well as to the
magnitude of the known ones and their infinite interactions.
Like so much else in science, the discovery of what is known so
far about the effects of nuclear explosions is a story of surprises,
starting with the surprise that the nucleus could be fissioned at
all. Perhaps the second big surprise was the extent of harmful
fallout; this came to light in the fifteen-megaton test at Bikini in
1954, when, to the amazement of the designers of the test, fallout began to descend on Marshall Islanders and on American
servicemen manning weather stations on atolls at supposedly
safe distances from the explosion. It was not until this test that
the world was alerted to the real magnitude—or, at any rate,
to the magnitude as it is understood so far—of the peril from
nuclear fallout. The next surprise was the extent of the effects
of the electromagnetic pulse. Probably the most recent surprise
has been the discovery, in the nineteen-seventies, of the peril to
the ozone layer. Around 1970, a number of scientists became
worried that the use of supersonic transports, which fly in the
stratosphere and emit oxides of nitrogen, would deplete the
ozone layer, and it occurred to two Columbia physicists—Henry
M. Foley and Malvin A. Ruderman—that since nuclear weapons were known to produce nitric oxide in the stratosphere, the
capacity of this compound for depleting the ozone might be
tested by trying to find out whether ozone levels had dropped
as a result of the atmospheric testing of nuclear weapons. The
investigation was inconclusive, but it led the two men to worry
about the fate of the ozone in the event of a nuclear holocaust.
Their concern awakened the concern of other scientists, and
in 1975 the National Academy of Sciences produced its report
"Long-Term Worldwide Effects of Multiple Nuclear-Weapons
Detonations," which attempted, among other things, to measure this peril. The sequence of events leading to our present
awareness of this peril is illuminating, because it shows how a
broad new development in scientific thought—in this case, the
growing awareness in the nineteen-seventies of the vulnerability of the ecosphere to human intervention—brought to light

an immense effect of nuclear weapons which had previously gone unnoticed. It is always difficult to become aware of one's ignorance, but as we try to give due weight to our present ignorance it can help us to recall that little more than a decade ago possibly the gravest global consequence of a holocaust which we now know of was totally unsuspected. Given the incomplete state of our knowledge of the earth, it seems unjustified at this point to assume that further developments in science will not bring forth further surprises.

The embryonic state of the earth sciences is one reason for our uncertainty concerning the outcome of a nuclear holocaust, but there is a moral and political reason that may be even more fundamental. Epistemologically, the earth is a special object. Scientific inquiry into the effects of a holocaust, like every other form of inquiry into this subject, is restricted by our lack of experience with large-scale nuclear destruction. But the lack of experience is not the result of neglect or accident, or even of our reluctance to face the horror of our predicament. In scientific work, experience means experiments, and scientific knowledge is not considered to be knowledge until it has been confirmed by experiment—or, at least, by observation. Until then, no matter how plausible a theory sounds, and no matter how dazzling it may appear intellectually, it is relegated to the limbo of hypothesis. But when it comes to judging the consequences of a nuclear holocaust there can be no experimentation, and thus no empirical verification. We cannot run experiments with the earth, because we have only one earth, on which we depend for our survival; we are not in possession of any spare earths that we might blow up in some universal laboratory in order to discover their tolerance of nuclear holocausts. Hence, our knowledge of the resiliency of the earth in the face of nuclear attack is limited by our fear of bringing about just the event—human extinction—whose likelihood we are chiefly interested in finding out about. The famous uncertainty principle, formulated by the German physicist Werner Heisenberg, has shown that our knowledge of atomic phenomena is limited because the experimental procedures with which we must carry out our observations inevitably interfere with the phenomena that we wish to measure. The question of extinction by nuclear arms—or by any other means, for that matter—presents us with an opposite but related uncertainty principle: our knowledge of extinction is limited because the experiments with which we would carry out our observations interfere with us, the observers, and, in fact, might put an end to us. This uncertainty principle complements the first. Both principles recognize that a limit to our knowledge is fixed by the fact that we are incarnate beings, not disembodied spirits, and that observation, like other human activities, is a physical process and so can interfere both with what is under observation and with the observer. Therefore, it is ultimately extinction itself that fixes the boundary to what we can know about extinction. No human being will ever be able to say with confidence, "*Now* I see how many megatons it takes for us to exterminate ourselves." To the extent that this check stands in the way of investigation, our uncertainty is forced on us not so much by the limitations of our intellectual ability as by the irreducible fact that we have no platform for observation except our mortal frames. In these circumstances, which are rudiments of the human condition, toleration of uncertainty is the path of life, and the demand for certainty is the path toward death.

We have had some experience of moral and political restraints on research in the field of medicine, in which, in all civilized countries, there are restrictions on experimenting with human beings; when the results might be injurious, laboratory animals are used instead. However, in investigating the properties of the earth we lack even any recourse that would be analogous to the use of these animals, for if we have no extra, dispensable earths to experiment with, neither are we in possession of any planets bearing life of some different sort. (As far as we now know, among the planets in the solar system the earth stands alone as a bearer of life.) And while it is true that we can run experiments in various corners of the earth and try to extrapolate the results to the earth as a whole, what is always missing from the results is the totality of the ecosphere, with its endless pathways of cause and effect, linking the biochemistry of the humblest alga and global chemical and dynamic balances into an indivisible whole. This whole is a mechanism in itself; indeed, it may be regarded as a single living being. Dr. Thomas, for one, has likened the earth to a cell. The analogy is compelling, but in one noteworthy respect, at least, there is a difference between the earth and a cell: whereas each cell is one among billions struck from the same genetic mold, the earth, as the mother of all life, has no living parent. If the behavior of cells is often predictable, it is because they exist en masse, and what a billion of them, programmed by their genetic material, have done a billion times the billion and first is likely to do again. But the earth is a member of no class as yet open to our observation which would permit the drawing of such inferences by generalization. When it comes to trying to predict its tolerance to perturbances, we are in the position of someone asked to deduce the whole of medicine by observing one human being. With respect to its individuality, then, the earth is not so much like a cell as like an individual person. Like a person, the earth is unique; like a person, it is sacred; and, like a person, it is unpredictable by the generalizing laws of science.

If we had no knowledge at all of the likely consequences of a holocaust for the earth, there would, of course, be no basis whatever for judgment. However, given the extent of what there is to know about the earth, it is no contradiction to say that while our ignorance is vast and, in a certain sense, irremediable (although, at the same time, the amount that we can and certainly will find out is also probably measureless), our knowledge is also vast, and that what we know is extremely alarming. Since in a global holocaust even the so-called local effects of the explosions may cover the whole land mass of the Northern Hemisphere, they may have secondary consequences that are truly global. The destruction of estuarine life throughout the Northern Hemisphere and the radioactive poisoning of the local waters could cause general harm to life in the oceans. Ecological collapse on the land in large parts of the Northern Hemisphere could have large consequences for the climate of the earth as a whole. Loss of vegetation, for example, increases the surface reflectivity of the earth, and this has a cooling effect on the atmosphere. In heavily irradiated zones, the mutation of plant pathogens might create virulent strains that could, in the words of the 1975 N.A.S. report, "produce disease epidemics that would spread globally." The irradiated northern half of the earth would in general become a huge radioecological laboratory, in which many species would be

driven to extinction, others would flourish and possibly invade
unharmed parts of the earth, and still others would evolve into
new and unpredictable forms.

But more important by far, in all probability, than the
global aftereffects of the local destruction would be the direct
global effects, the most important of which is ozone loss.
The concentration of ozone in the earth's atmosphere is very
small—not more than ten parts by weight per million parts
of air. Yet the ozone layer has a critical importance to life on
earth, because it protects the earth's surface from the harmful
ultraviolet radiation in sunlight, which would otherwise be
"lethal to unprotected organisms as we now know them," to
quote Dr. Martyn M. Caldwell, a leading authority on the
biological effects of ultraviolet radiation, in a recent article of
his in *BioScience* titled "Plant Life and Ultraviolet Radiation:
Some Perspective in the History of the Earth's UV Climate."
I have already mentioned Glasstone's remark that without the
absorption of solar ultraviolet radiation by the ozone "life as
currently known could not exist except possibly in the ocean."
The 1975 N.A.S. report states, "As biologists, geologists, and
other students of evolution recognize, the development of an
oxygen-rich atmosphere, with its *ozone layer, was a precondition
to the development of multicelled plants and animals, and all
life forms on land have evolved under this shield*" (italics in the
original). B. W. Boville, of the Canadian Atmospheric Environment Service, has written that the ozone layer is "a crucial
element to climate and to the existence of all life on earth."
Dr. Fred Iklé, who served as the director of the Arms Control
and Disarmament Agency under Presidents Nixon and Ford,
and now serves as Under Secretary of Defense for Policy under
President Reagan, has stated that severe reduction of the ozone
layer through nuclear explosions could "shatter the ecological
structure that permits man to remain alive on this planet." And
a paper delivered at a United Nations–sponsored scientific conference in March, 1977, states, "The whole biological world,
so dependent on micro-organisms, may, if doses [of ultraviolet
radiation] increase, be in serious trouble."

As the passage from the N.A.S. report states, the beginnings
of multicelled life are associated with the formation of an ozone
layer. In the earliest stages of evolution, when there was little

or no oxygen in the atmosphere, and no ozone layer—ozone (O_3) is formed when sunlight strikes oxygen (O_2) in the upper atmosphere—ultraviolet radiation, which would then have reached the surface of the earth relatively unimpeded, may have been one of the most important sources of the energy that built up the first biological macromolecules, about three and a half billion years ago. But about two billion years ago, when those molecules had formed into single-celled organisms, the organisms freed themselves from dependence on ultraviolet light as a source of energy by coming to rely instead on photosynthesis—a method of extracting energy from sunlight by making use of carbon dioxide and water, which were available everywhere in the environment, as they are today. Photosynthesis was "probably the largest single step on the evolutionary path leading to the growth of higher life forms" (according to Dr. Michael McElroy, a physicist at Harvard's Center for Earth and Planetary Physics, who has done important new work in the study of the earth's atmosphere), and set the stage for terrestrial life as it exists today. For that life to develop, however, the genetic material, DNA, had also to develop, and ultraviolet light, as it happens, is particularly destructive of DNA, causing it to lose "biological activity," as Dr. Caldwell notes. Furthermore, ultraviolet light inhibits photosynthesis, and thus on the earth of two billion years ago it placed another barrier in the way of what turned out to be the next step in evolution. And there was still another barrier to evolution in the fact that oxygen, a by-product of photosynthesis, was poisonous to existing organisms. At first, it is suggested, organisms solved their oxygen problem by fixing oxygen to ferrous iron—a procedure that would explain the existence of banded iron formations found in sedimentary rock that is some two billion years old. But it was life's second solution to its oxygen problem—the development of enzymes capable of returning oxygen harmlessly to the environment—that proved to be the more successful one. It lifted the barriers to evolution just mentioned: by detoxifying oxygen it liberated life from its dependence on iron, leaving life "free to proliferate in the ocean, with rapid growth in oxygen" (McElroy); and by enriching the atmosphere with oxygen it assured the gradual creation of an ozone layer, which blocked out much of the ultraviolet radiation. Once this was done, the way was cleared, in the opinion of some scientists, for the "eruptive proliferation of species" (Caldwell) that geologists find in the fossil record of the Cambrian period, nearly six hundred million years ago. A hundred and eighty million years later, in the Silurian, life made a second leap ahead when, after more than three billion years in the ocean, it made its "dramatic appearance" (Caldwell) on land, and this leap, too, can be associated with the growth of the ozone shield, which, it is thought, around that time reached a density that would permit organisms to survive on land, without the partial protection from ultraviolet radiation which water affords.

If the formation of the ozone layer was one of the necessary preconditions for the "dramatic appearance" of life on land, then the question naturally arises whether heavy depletion of the ozone, by nuclear explosions or any other cause, might not bring about a dramatic disappearance of life, including human life, from the land. (Spray cans, incongruously, are one possible cause of harm to the ozone, because they put chlorocarbons into the atmosphere, and these are broken down by sunlight, releasing chlorine, which depletes ozone.) But that question, having been raised, is one of those which cannot be answered with confidence, given the present state of our knowledge of the workings of the earth. Even the estimates of ozone loss that would be brought about by holocausts of different sizes are highly uncertain (in calculating some of these figures, the National Academy of Sciences found the largest computers insufficient)—as is made clear in the 1975 N.A.S. report, which found that the explosion of ten thousand megatons of nuclear weapons would increase the amount of nitric oxide in the stratosphere to something between five and fifty times the normal amount (a tenfold uncertainty is characteristic of calculations in this field), that it would (as has been mentioned) reduce the ozone layer in the Northern Hemisphere, where the report assumes that the explosions would occur, by anything from thirty to seventy per cent, and that it would reduce it in the Southern Hemisphere by anything from twenty to forty per cent. I recently asked Dr. McElroy what the current estimation of danger to the ozone layer from man-made oxides of nitrogen in general was. "In the years after the N.A.S. report of 1975, the estimates of harm were lowered, but since about 1977 they have

risen again," he told me. He went on to discuss a possible increase in nitrous oxide in the atmosphere brought about by, say,
agricultural fertilizers. "At present, it is estimated that a doubling of the nitrous oxide in the troposphere, which becomes
nitric oxide—one of the compounds that deplete ozone—after
it reaches the stratosphere, would bring about a fifteen-
per cent reduction in the ozone. That is a higher estimate for
the nitrous-oxide effect than the one made in 1975. However,
a nuclear holocaust would inject nitric oxide directly into the
stratosphere, and in amounts much greater than would be produced, indirectly, by the twofold increase in nitrous oxide, and
no one has done any study of the consequences for the ozone
of these larger amounts in the light of the knowledge acquired
since 1975. But my guess is that the figures would not have
changed radically, and that the estimates for ozone reduction
by a nuclear holocaust given in 1975 would not be far off." In
mid-1981, the first measurement of an actual reduction of the
ozone layer was made. The National Aeronautics and Space
Administration reported "preliminary" findings indicating that
ozone in a region of the stratosphere some twenty-five miles
up—in the higher part of the ozone layer—had decreased at
the rate of approximately half a per cent a year over the past
decade. While this chilling discovery does not bear directly on
the consequences of a holocaust for the ozone, it does tend to
confirm the more general hypothesis that the ozone is vulnerable to human intervention.

The extent of the biological damage that would be done by
various increases in ultraviolet radiation is, if anything, even
less well known than what the increases caused by nuclear
detonations might be, but the available information suggests
that the damage to the whole ecosphere would be severe. One
reason is that certain wavelengths of ultraviolet that are known
to be particularly harmful biologically would be disproportionately increased by ozone reduction. Moreover, the cause of
the biological damage—increased ultraviolet radiation—would
be similar everywhere, but the effects would be different for
each of the earth's species and ecosystems. And the effects
of those effects, spreading outward indefinitely through the
interconnected web of life, are not within the realm of the
calculable. However, it is known with certainty that ultraviolet

radiation is harmful or fatal to living things. In fact, precisely because of its abiotic qualities ultraviolet light has long been in use as a sterilizing agent in medical and other scientific work. The most comprehensive study of ultraviolet's effects which has been done so far is the Department of Transportation's Climatic Impact Assessment Program report "Impacts of Climatic Change on the Biosphere." It states that "excessive UV-B radiation"—the part of the ultraviolet spectrum which would be significantly increased by ozone depletion—"is a decidedly detrimental factor for most organisms, including man," and continues, "Even current levels of solar UV-B irradiance can be linked with phenomena such as increased mutation rates, delay of cell division, depression of photosynthesis in phytoplankton, skin cancer in humans, cancer eye in certain cattle, and lethality of many lower organisms, such as aquatic invertebrates and bacteria."

Research concerning the effects of UV-B irradiance on specific organisms—and especially on organisms in their natural habitats—has been slight, and in a recent conversation Dr. Caldwell, who was chairman of the scientific panel that produced the Climatic Impact Assessment Program report, told me that not enough experiments have been done for anyone to generalize with confidence about the ultimate fate of living things subjected to increased ultraviolet radiation. From the experiments that have been done, however, it is known that, among mammals, human beings are especially vulnerable, because of their lack of body hair. Since some ultraviolet light reaches the earth in normal circumstances, human beings (and other creatures) have developed adaptations to deal with it. The main adaptation in man is tanning, which helps to prevent sunburn. The susceptibility of fair-skinned people to these ailments and also to skin cancer is traceable to their relative inability to tan, and one consequence of reduced ozone could be higher rates of skin cancer among human beings. Of much greater seriousness, though, would be the temporary loss of sight through photophthalmia, or snow blindness, which can be contracted by exposure to heightened ultraviolet radiation and may last for several days after each exposure. Photophthalmia is, in the words of the 1975 N.A.S. report, "disabling and painful"; also, "there are no immune groups," and "there is no adaptation." One can avoid photophthalmia by wearing goggles whenever one goes outside, but so far the world has made no provision for each person on earth to have a pair of goggles in case the ozone is depleted. However, if the higher estimates of depletion turn out to be correct, people will not be able to stay outdoors very long anyway. At these levels, "incapacitating" sunburn would occur in several minutes; if the reduction of the ozone reached the seventy per cent maximum that the report assigns to the Northern Hemisphere, the time could be ten minutes. Moreover, the report states that in the months immediately following the attack ozone depletion could be even higher than seventy per cent. "We have no simple way," the report observes, "to estimate the magnitude of short-term depletion." The ten-minute rule is not one that the strategists of "recovery" after a nuclear attack usually figure into their calculations. If high levels of ultraviolet radiation occur, then anyone who crawls out of his shelter after radiation from fallout has declined to tolerable levels will have to crawl back in immediately. In the meantime, though, people would not have been able to go out to produce food, and they would starve. A further possible harmful consequence—in itself a potential human and ecological catastrophe of global proportions—is that increased ultraviolet light would raise the amounts of Vitamin D in the skin of mammals and birds to toxic levels. But the experimentation necessary to determine whether or not this sweeping catastrophe would occur has not been done. The 1975 N.A.S. report observes, alarmingly but inconclusively, "We do not know whether man and other vertebrate animals could tolerate an increased Vitamin D synthesis that might result from a large and rapid increase in [ultraviolet] exposure." The report "urgently" recommends further study of the question.

The skin of many mammals would be protected by fur or other covering, but their eyes would remain exposed. In a recent lecture, Dr. Tsipis said that ozone reduction might bring about the blinding of the world's animals, and that this effect alone would have the makings of a global ecological catastrophe. I discussed the subject with Dr. Frederick Urbach, who teaches medicine at Temple University and is the editor of a volume titled "The Biologic Effects of Ultraviolet Radiation

with Emphasis on the Skin," and who has conducted extensive
research on the effect of ultraviolet radiation on animals. He
confirmed that the peril to the eyes of animals is vast and real.
"If you go much above fifty per cent reduction of the ozone,
the increase in ultraviolet radiation begins to do injury to the
cornea," he told me. "You get a bad sunburn of the eye. People
don't usually get it, because at normal levels the anatomy of the
face gives protection. But when there is snow on the ground
the ultraviolet radiation is reflected back up into the eye. The
problem is easily remedied by wearing glasses, but animals will
hardly be able to do that. There is a story—probably apocry-
phal—that when Hannibal crossed the Alps, where ultraviolet is
more intense, some of his elephants went blind. When animals
can't see, they can't protect themselves. A blind animal does
not survive well in nature. Repeated injury causes scarring of
the cornea, and this would eventually make the animals permanently blind. We see this happening to the mice that we
irradiate with ultraviolet wavelengths in the laboratory; after
a while, they develop opaque corneas. In the event of ozone
depletion, the same thing would happen not only to mammals
but to insects and birds."

Sight and smell permit animals to find their way in the
environment and to fulfill the roles mapped out for them by
nature, and the loss of sight would throw the environment into
disarray as billions of blinded beasts, insects, and birds began
to stumble through the world. The disorientation of insects
would be fateful not only for them but for plant life, much of
which depends on insects for pollination and other processes
essential to survival. Ultraviolet light is, in fact, known to play a
role in many activities of insects, including phototaxis, celestial
navigation, and sex identification, and an increase in ultraviolet light would no doubt impair these capacities. But plant
life would in any case be under direct assault from increased
ultraviolet radiation. While confident generalization about the
fate of plants has to be ruled out, experiments that have been
performed with crops show that while some are quite resistant,
others, including tomatoes, beans, peas, and onions, would be
killed or "severely scalded," according to the N.A.S. report.
Because ultraviolet radiation breaks down DNA, which regulates reproduction, and because it also represses photosynthesis,

which is the chief metabolic process of plants, the direct effect
of increased ultraviolet radiation on plant life is likely to be
widespread and serious. And because many species, the N.A.S.
report states, "survive at an upper limit of tolerance," any
increase in ultraviolet radiation is "a threat to the survival of
certain species and accordingly to entire ecosystems." The
global damage to plants and the global damage to the insects
are synergistic: the damage to the insects damages the plants,
which in turn, damage the insects again, in a chain of effects
whose outcome is unforeseeable. On the question of the harm
to the insects that would be caused by the harm to the rest
of the ecosphere, Ting H. Hsiao, a professor of entomology
at Utah State University, has written in the Climatic Impact
Assessment Program report, "Since insects are important in
the world's ecosystems, any changes in other components of
the ecosystem could have an impact on insect populations.
Ultraviolet radiation is a physical factor that directly influences
all biotic components of the ecosystem. . . . A change in abiotic
factors, such as temperature, rainfall, or wind, associated with
elevated ultraviolet radiation could profoundly affect behavior,
biology, population structure, dispersal, and migration of insects." Dr. Hsiao's observations about insects and the ecosphere
can, in fact, be generalized to include all global effects of a
holocaust, for there are few that do not have potentially large
consequences for the character and severity of all the others.

The web of life in the oceans, perhaps more than any other
part of the environment, is vulnerable to damage from increased ultraviolet radiation. John Calkins, of the Department
of Radiation Medicine of the University of Kentucky, and D.
Stuart Nachtwey, a professor of radiation biology at Oregon
State University, remark in the Climatic Impact Assessment
Program report that the experimentation that has been done
so far, though it is inadequate, suggests that "many aquatic
micro-organisms and invertebrates have little reserve capacity
to cope with surface levels of solar UV-B." The organisms at
greatest risk are the unicellular organisms that lie at the base of
the marine food chain, and thus ultimately sustain the higher
creatures in the oceans. Since the removal of an organism from
the food chain can eliminate all the organisms above it in the
chain, the loss of even part of the chain's base could have huge

consequences. Once again, quantitative judgments are not possible, but such experiments as have been carried out make the danger clear. In the early nineteen-seventies, researchers discovered that even normal levels of UV-B radiation are harmful or fatal to many aquatic organisms if they are not permitted to descend deeper into the water or otherwise shield themselves from exposure. The finding is important, because it means that the question to be asked about increased UV-B radiation is not whether it would be biologically harmful but whether the intensity would be great enough to overpower the mechanisms of defense that organisms have built up over billions of years of evolution to deal with normal levels of ultraviolet radiation. The defense mechanisms include the screening of the DNA molecules with less critical molecules; enzymatic mechanisms by which damage done in the daytime is repaired at night; and delay of cell divisions (when cells can be most sensitive to ultraviolet radiation) until the nighttime. But fleeing, which can save some organisms from the ultraviolet peril, may get them into other kinds of trouble. In general, organisms find the niche in the environment that is best suited to them, and if they are suddenly forced to leave it they may die. Or, if they survive, they may destroy the ecological niche that permits some other species to survive. If a change in the environment occurs slowly, an organism may prove able to adapt, but a holocaust would bring a sudden change, and the usefulness of adaptation would be greatly reduced. A glimpse of a few of the complexities involved in ultraviolet stress is offered by some experiments that were done by Dr. Nachtwey and several colleagues on the unicellular alga called *Chlamydomonas reinhardi.* If the alga is resting near the surface of the ocean on a cloudy day, and the sun suddenly appears, it will dive for safety, and if ultraviolet radiation is at normal levels it will get deep enough fast enough to survive. But if the ozone has been decreased by as little as sixteen per cent, the alga will be killed in mid-dive by the more intense ultraviolet rays. The crucial factor for *C. reinhardi* turns out to be its swimming speed.

Because experimentation has been so slight, and because the complexities are so immense, both the Climatic Impact Assessment Program report and the N.A.S. report hold back from sweeping judgments about the fate of oceanic life as a whole

in the event of severe ozone reduction, but at one point the
N.A.S. report does state that "under extreme circumstances,
certain habitats could become devoid of living organisms," and
at another point, speaking of the global effects in their entirety,
it states, "Large-scale detonations will create conditions sufficient to modify the oceanic environment, on a global basis,
with a resultant modification of the marine biota. In areas of
major perturbations this influence will be in the form of local or
extensive extinctions or reduction in susceptible species, with a
subsequent disruption of the normal food web."

A second global consequence of ozone reduction would be
climatic change. The earth's climate, like the ecosphere as a
whole, the 1975 N.A.S. report reminds us, is "holocoenotic";
in other words, it is a whole in which "any action influencing a
single part of the system can be expected to have an effect on
all other parts of the system." As is hardly surprising, the totality
of those effects is unknown even for a single major climatic
disturbance, and the N.A.S. report notes that "no adequate
climatic models exist that would permit prediction of the
nature and degree of climatic changes that might result from
a large-scale nuclear event." Of the three large components of
the earth's surface—land, sea, and air—the air is probably the
most changeable. The parts of this delicately balanced whole
include, among many others, the chemical composition of both
the troposphere and the stratosphere; the temperature levels of
the atmosphere and the degree of moisture at all altitudes; the
temperature and reflectivity of the earth's surface; the circulatory patterns of the air; the circulatory patterns of the ocean
currents; and the degree of retention of the earth's reflected
warmth by the atmosphere, in the so-called greenhouse effect.
Each of these parts could be disturbed by a holocaust, and the
disturbance of any one could disturb many or all of the others.
According to present thinking, a depletion of the ozone layer
would simultaneously act to warm the surface of the earth, by
permitting more solar radiation to reach it, and act to cool it,
by reducing the layer's capacity to radiate back to earth the heat
reflected from the earth's surface. But, according to the N.A.S.
report, the cooling at the surface of the earth, which might last
for several years, is expected to exceed the warming by, at most,
an amount estimated (very tentatively, considering that "no

adequate climatic models exist") at approximately one degree Fahrenheit. Temperature change at the surface, however, may be less important than temperature change elsewhere in the atmosphere. For example, cooling of the upper troposphere and of the lower stratosphere "is likely to be much larger" than cooling at the surface, and may cause alterations in the cloud cover, which would, in turn, influence the climate. This whole subject, however, is one of the many subjects that remain relatively unexplored. It is estimated that dust and smoke lofted by the explosions would add to the cooling by another degree Fahrenheit. Temperatures on earth can fluctuate tens of degrees in a single day, yet the net reduction of a couple of degrees in the temperature of the entire surface of the earth after a holocaust would be of great consequence. For example, it could cut the biological productivity of deciduous forests by as much as twenty per cent, shift the monsoons in Asia in a way that could be ruinous for both agriculture and ecosystems, and eliminate all wheat-growing in Canada. The N.A.S. report also mentions that climatic change identified as "dramatic" and "major," but not otherwise specified, "cannot be ruled out," and adds that although the change is likely to last only a few years, the possibility exists that it "may not be reversible." Greater reductions would, of course, have larger consequences. Another global consequence of the injection of oxides of nitrogen into the stratosphere by nuclear explosions would be pollution of the environment as these gases fell back into the troposphere. Nitrogen dioxide, for example, is one of the most harmful components of the smog that afflicts many modern cities, such as Los Angeles. It reacts with hydrocarbons present in the air above these cities, actually causing in the process some ozone formation. While ozone in the stratosphere is beneficial to human beings, ozone near ground level is not. It has been found not only to increase respiratory problems among human beings but to be harmful to some plant life. The formation of nitrogen dioxide, accordingly, is still another global effect of a holocaust whose consequences are not calculable. In addition, nitrogen dioxide is responsible in polluted cities for turning the sky brown, and after a holocaust it might happen that the sky of the whole earth would turn from blue to brown for as long as the pollution lasted (perhaps several years).

The known consequences of global contamination by stratospheric fallout (as distinct from the tropospheric fallout on the targeted countries) would seem great in comparison with anything except other nuclear effects, but against this backdrop they seem moderate—although, as usual, the state of knowledge precludes confident prediction. The stratospheric portion of the fallout is much less intense than the tropospheric portion, because it can remain in the atmosphere for several years, and by the time it descends to earth its radioactivity has declined to very low levels. The N.A.S. report estimates that a ten-thousand-megaton holocaust would deliver over the following twenty to thirty years a dose of four rems to every person in the Northern Hemisphere and a third of that to every person in the Southern Hemisphere, and would cause a two-per-cent rise in the death rate from cancer. The same doses would cause serious genetic disease to increase around the world by up to about two per cent, with a noticeable but decreasing number of mutations appearing in the next thirty generations. There would, however, be "hot spots" in some parts of the world, where, because of certain patterns of weather, the doses of radiation would be many times as great. Also, the world would be contaminated with particles of plutonium, which would cause an as yet unestimated rise in the incidence of lung cancer. (All these effects, which were calculated by the N.A.S. in 1975 for a ten-thousand-megaton holocaust, would presumably be greater in a twenty-thousand-megaton holocaust.)

In recent years, scientists in many fields have accumulated enough knowledge to begin to look on the earth as a single, concrete mechanism, and to at least begin to ask how it works. One of their discoveries has been that life and life's inanimate terrestrial surroundings have a strong reciprocal influence on each other. For life, the land, oceans, and air have been the environment, but, equally, for the land, oceans, and air life has been the environment—the conditioning force. The injection of oxygen into the atmosphere by living things, which led to the formation of an ozone layer, which, in turn, shut out lethal ultraviolet rays from the sun and permitted the rise of multicellular organisms, was only one of life's large-scale interventions. The more closely scientists look at life and its evolution, the less they find it possible to draw a sharp distinction between "life," on the one hand, and an inanimate "environment" in which it exists, on the other. Rather, "the environment" of the present day appears to be a house of unimaginable intricacy which life has to a very great extent built and furnished for its own use. It seems that life even regulates and maintains the chemical environment of the earth in a way that turns out to suit its own needs. In a far-reaching speculative article entitled "Chemical Processes in the Solar System: A Kinetic Perspective," Dr. McElroy has described the terrestrial cycles by which the most important elements of the atmosphere—oxygen, carbon, and nitrogen—are kept in proportions that are favorable to life. He finds that in each case life itself—its birth, metabolism, and decay—is chiefly responsible for maintaining the balance. For example, he calculates that if for some reason respiration and decay were suddenly cut off, photosynthesis would devour all the inorganic carbon on the surface of the ocean and in the atmosphere within forty years. Thereafter, carbon welling up from the deep ocean would fuel photosynthesis in the oceans for another thousand years, but then "life as we know it would terminate." Dr. McElroy also observes that the amount of ozone in the stratosphere is influenced by the amount of organic decay, and thus by the amount of life, on earth. Nitrous oxide is a product of organic decay, and because it produces nitric oxide—one of the compounds responsible for ozone depletion—it plays the role of regulator. In the absence of human intervention, living things are largely responsible for introducing nitrous oxide into the atmosphere. When life is exceptionally abundant, it releases more nitrous oxide into the atmosphere, and may thus act to cut back on the ozone, and that cutback lets in more ultraviolet rays. On the other hand, when life is sparse and depleted, nitrous-oxide production is reduced, the ozone layer builds up, and ultraviolet rays are cut back. These speculative glimpses of what might be called the metabolism of the earth give substance to the growing conviction among scientists that the earth, like a single cell or a single organism, is a systemic whole, and in a general way they tend to confirm the fear that any large man-made perturbation of terrestrial nature could lead to a catastrophic systemic breakdown. Nuclear explosions are far from being the

only perturbations in question; a heating of the global atmosphere through an increased greenhouse effect, which could
be caused by the injection of vast amounts of carbon dioxide
into the air (for instance, from the increased burning of coal),
is another notable peril of this kind. But a nuclear holocaust
would be unique in its suddenness, which would permit no observation of slowly building environmental damage before the
full—and, for man, perhaps the final—catastrophe occurred.
The geological record does not sustain the fear that sudden
perturbations can extinguish all life on earth (if it did, we would
not be here to reflect on the subject), but it does suggest that
sudden, drastic ecological collapse is possible. It suggests that
life as a whole, if it is given hundreds of millions of years in
which to recuperate and send out new evolutionary lines, has
an astounding resilience, and an ability to bring forth new and
ever more impressive life forms, but it also suggests that abrupt
interventions can radically disrupt any particular evolutionary
configuration and dispatch hundreds of thousands of species
into extinction.

The view of the earth as a single system, or organism, has
only recently proceeded from poetic metaphor to actual scientific investigation, and on the whole Dr. Thomas's observation
that "we do not really understand nature, at all" still holds. It is
as much on the basis of this ignorance, whose scope we are only
now in a position to grasp, as on the basis of the particular items
of knowledge in our possession that I believe that the following judgment can be made: Bearing in mind that the possible
consequences of the detonations of thousands of megatons
of nuclear explosives include the blinding of insects, birds,
and beasts all over the world; the extinction of many ocean
species, among them some at the base of the food chain; the
temporary or permanent alteration of the climate of the globe,
with the outside chance of "dramatic" and "major" alterations
in the structure of the atmosphere; the pollution of the whole
ecosphere with oxides of nitrogen; the incapacitation in ten
minutes of unprotected people who go out into the sunlight;
the blinding of people who go out into the sunlight; a significant decrease in photosynthesis in plants around the world;
the scalding and killing of many crops; the increase in rates of
cancer and mutation around the world, but especially in the

targeted zones, and the attendant risk of global epidemics; the possible poisoning of all vertebrates by sharply increased levels of Vitamin D in their skin as a result of increased ultraviolet light; and the outright slaughter on all targeted continents of most human beings and other living things by the initial nuclear radiation, the fireballs, the thermal pulses, the blast waves, the mass fires, and the fallout from the explosions; and, considering that these consequences will all interact with one another in unguessable ways and, furthermore, are in all likelihood an incomplete list, which will be added to as our knowledge of the earth increases, one must conclude that a full-scale nuclear holocaust could lead to the extinction of mankind.

To say that human extinction is a certainty would, of course, be a misrepresentation—just as it would be a misrepresentation to say that extinction can be ruled out. To begin with, we know that a holocaust may not occur at all. If one does occur, the adversaries may not use all their weapons. If they do use all their weapons, the global effects, in the ozone and elsewhere, may be moderate. And if the effects are not moderate but extreme, the ecosphere may prove resilient enough to withstand them without breaking down catastrophically. These are all substantial reasons for supposing that mankind will not be extinguished in a nuclear holocaust, or even that extinction in a holocaust is unlikely, and they tend to calm our fear and to reduce our sense of urgency. Yet at the same time we are compelled to admit that there *may* be a holocaust, that the adversaries *may* use all their weapons, that the global effects, including effects of which we are as yet unaware, *may* be severe, that the ecosphere *may* suffer catastrophic breakdown, and that our species *may* be extinguished. We are left with uncertainty, and are forced to make our decisions in a state of uncertainty. If we wish to act to save our species, we have to muster our resolve in spite of our awareness that the life of the species may not now in fact be jeopardized. On the other hand, if we wish to ignore the peril, we have to admit that we do so in the knowledge that the species may be in danger of imminent self-destruction. When the existence of nuclear weapons was made known, thoughtful people everywhere in the world realized that if the great powers entered into a nuclear-arms race the human species would sooner or later face the possibility of extinction. They also realized that in the absence of international agreements preventing it an arms race would probably occur. They knew that the path of nuclear armament was a dead end for mankind. The discovery of the energy in mass—of "the basic power of the universe"—and of a means by which man could release that energy altered the relationship between man and the source of his life, the earth. In the shadow of this power, the earth became small and the life of the human species doubtful. In that sense, the question of human extinction has been on the political agenda of the world ever since the first nuclear weapon was detonated, and there was no need for the world to build up its present tremendous arsenals before starting to worry about it. At just what point the species crossed, or will have crossed, the boundary between merely having the technical knowledge to destroy itself and actually having the arsenals at hand, ready to be used at any second, is not precisely knowable. But it is clear that at present, with some twenty thousand megatons of nuclear explosive power in existence, and with more being added every day, we have entered into the zone of uncertainty, which is to say the zone of risk of extinction. But the mere risk of extinction has a significance that is categorically different from, and immeasurably greater than, that of any other risk, and as we make our decisions we have to take that significance into account. Up to now, every risk has been contained within the frame of life; extinction would shatter the frame. It represents not the defeat of some purpose but an abyss in which all human purposes would be drowned for all time. We have no right to place the possibility of this limitless, eternal defeat on the same footing as risks that we run in the ordinary conduct of our affairs in our particular transient moment of human history. To employ a mathematical analogy, we can say that although the risk of extinction may be fractional, the stake is, humanly speaking, infinite, and a fraction of infinity is still infinity. In other words, once we learn that a holocaust *might* lead to extinction we have no right to gamble, because if we lose, the game will be over, and neither we nor anyone else will ever get another chance. Therefore, although, scientifically speaking, there is all the difference in the world between the mere possibility that a holocaust will bring about extinction and the certainty of it, morally they are the same, and we have no choice but to address the issue of nuclear weapons as though we knew for a certainty that their use would put an end to our species. In weighing the fate of the earth and, with it, our own fate, we stand before a mystery, and in tampering with the earth we tamper with a mystery. We are in deep ignorance. Our ignorance should dispose us to wonder, our wonder should make us humble, our humility should inspire us to reverence and caution, and our reverence and caution should lead us to act without delay to withdraw the threat we now pose to the earth and to ourselves.

In trying to describe possible consequences of a nuclear holocaust, I have mentioned the limitless complexity of its effects on human society and on the ecosphere—a complexity that sometimes seems to be as great as that of life itself. But if these effects should lead to human extinction, then all the complexity will give way to the utmost simplicity—the simplicity of nothingness. We—the human race—shall cease to be.

II. THE SECOND DEATH

IF A COUNCIL were to be empowered by the people of the earth to do whatever was necessary to save humanity from extinction by nuclear arms, it might well decide that a good first step would be to order the destruction of all the nuclear weapons in the world. When the order had been carried out, however, warlike or warring nations might still rebuild their nuclear arsenals—perhaps in a matter of months. A logical second step, accordingly, would be to order the destruction of the factories that make the weapons. But, just as the weapons might be rebuilt, so might the factories, and the world's margin of safety would not have been increased by very much. A third step, then, would be to order the destruction of the factories that make the factories that make the weapons—a measure that might require the destruction of a considerable part of the world's economy. But even then lasting safety would not have been reached, because in some number of years—at most, a few decades—everything could be rebuilt, including the nuclear arsenals, and mankind would again be ready to extinguish itself. A determined council might next decide to try to arrest the world economy in a pre-nuclear state by throwing the blueprints and technical manuals for reconstruction on the bonfires that had by then consumed everything else, but that recourse, too, would ultimately fail, because the blueprints and manuals could easily be redrawn and rewritten. As long as the world remained acquainted with the basic physical laws that underlie the construction of nuclear weapons—and these laws include the better part of physics as physics is understood in our century—mankind would have failed to put many years between itself and its doom. For the fundamental origin of the peril of human extinction by nuclear arms lies not in any particular social or political circumstances of our time but in the attainment by mankind as a whole, after millennia of scientific progress, of a certain level of knowledge of the physical universe. As long as that knowledge is in our possession, the atoms themselves, each one stocked with its prodigious supply of energy, are, in a manner of speaking, in a perilously advanced state of mobilization for nuclear hostilities, and any conflict anywhere in the world can become a nuclear one. To return to safety through technical measures alone, we would have to disarm matter itself, converting it back into its relatively safe, inert, nonexplosive nineteenth-century Newtonian state—something that not even the physics of our time can teach us how to do. (I mention these farfetched, wholly imaginary programs of demolition and suppression in part because the final destruction of all mankind is so much more farfetched, and therefore seems to give us license to at least consider extreme alternatives, but mainly because their obvious inadequacy serves to demonstrate how deeply the nuclear peril is ingrained in our world.)

It is fundamental to the shape and character of the nuclear predicament that its origins lie in scientific knowledge rather than in social circumstances. Revolutions born in the laboratory are to be sharply distinguished from revolutions born in society. Social revolutions are usually born in the minds of millions, and are led up to by what the Declaration of Independence calls "a long train of abuses," visible to all; indeed, they usually cannot occur unless they are widely understood by and supported by the public. By contrast, scientific revolutions usually take shape quietly in the minds of a few men, under cover of the impenetrability to most laymen of scientific theory, and thus catch the world by surprise. In the case of nuclear weapons, of course, the surprise was greatly increased by the governmental secrecy that surrounded the construction of the first bombs. When the world learned of their existence, Mr. Fukai had already run back into the flames of Hiroshima, and tens of thousands of people in that city had already been killed. Even long after scientific discoveries have been made and their applications have transformed our world, most people are likely to remain ignorant of the underlying principles at work, and this has been particularly true of nuclear weapons, which, decades after their invention, are still surrounded by an aura of mystery, as though they had descended from another planet. (To most people, Einstein's famous formula $E=mc^2$, which defines the energy released in nuclear explosions, stands as a kind of symbol of everything that is esoteric and incomprehensible.)

But more important by far than the world's unpreparedness for scientific revolutions are their universality and their permanence once they have occurred. Social revolutions are restricted to a particular time and place; they arise out of particular circumstances, last for a while, and then pass into history. Scientific revolutions, on the other hand, belong to all places and all times. In the words of Alfred North Whitehead, "Modern science was born in Europe, but its home is the whole world." In fact, of all the products of human hands and minds, scientific knowledge has proved to be the most durable. The physical structures of human life—furniture, buildings, paintings, cities, and so on—are subject to inevitable natural decay, and human institutions have likewise proved to be transient. Hegel, whose philosophy of history was framed in large measure in an attempt to redeem the apparent futility of the efforts of men to found something enduring in their midst, once wrote, "When we see the evil, the vice, the ruin that has befallen the most flourishing kingdoms which the mind of man ever created, we can scarce avoid being filled with sorrow at this universal taint of corruption; and, since this decay is not the work of mere Nature, but of Human Will—a moral embitterment—a revolt of the Good Spirit (if it have a place within us) may well be the result of our reflections." Works of thought and many works of art have a better chance of surviving, since new copies of a book or a symphony can be transcribed from old ones, and so can be preserved indefinitely; yet these works, too, can and do go out of existence, for if every copy is lost, then the work is also lost. The subject matter of these works is man, and they seem to be touched with his mortality. The results of scientific work, on the other hand, are largely immune to decay and disappearance. Even when they are lost, they are likely to be rediscovered, as is shown by the fact that several scientists often make the same discovery independently. (There is no record of several poets' having independently written the same poem, or of several composers' having independently written the same symphony.) For both the subject matter and the method of science are available to all capable minds in a way that the subject matter and the method of the arts are not. The human experiences that art deals with are, once over, lost forever, like the people who undergo them, whereas matter, energy, space, and time, alike everywhere and in all ages, are always available for fresh inspection. The subject matter of science is the physical world, and its findings seem to share in the immortality of the physical world. And artistic vision grows out of the unrepeatable individuality of each artist, whereas the reasoning power of the mind—its ability to add two and two and get four—is the same in all competent persons. The rigorous exactitude of scientific methods does not mean that creativity is any less individual, intuitive, or mysterious in great scientists than in great artists, but it does mean that scientific findings, once arrived at, can be tested and confirmed by shared canons of logic and experimentation. The agreement among scientists thus achieved permits science to be a collective enterprise, in which each generation, building on the accepted findings of the generations before, makes amendments and additions, which in their turn become the starting point for the next generation. (Philosophers, by contrast, are constantly tearing down the work of their predecessors, and circling back to re-ask questions that have been asked and answered countless times before. Kant once wrote in despair, "It seems ridiculous that while every science moves forward ceaselessly, this [metaphysics], claiming to be wisdom itself, whose oracular pronouncements everyone consults, is continually revolving in one spot, without advancing one step.") Scientists, as they erect the steadily growing structure of scientific knowledge, resemble nothing so much as a swarm of bees working harmoniously together to construct a single, many-chambered hive, which grows more elaborate and splendid with every year that passes. Looking at what they have made over the centuries, scientists need feel no "sorrow" or "moral embitterment" at any "taint of corruption" that supposedly undoes all human achievements. When God, alarmed that the builders of the Tower of Babel would reach Heaven with their construction, and so become as God, put an end to their undertaking by making them all speak different languages, He apparently overlooked the scientists, for they, speaking what is often called the "universal language" of their disciplines from country to country and generation to generation, went on to build a new tower—the edifice of scientific knowledge. Their phenomenal success, beginning not with Einstein but with Euclid and Archimedes, has provided the unshakable structure that supports the world's nuclear peril. So durable is the scientific edifice that if we did not know that human beings had constructed it we might suppose that the findings on which our whole technological civilization rests were the pillars and crossbeams of an invulnerable, inhuman order obtruding into our changeable and perishable human realm. It is the crowning irony of this lopsided development of human abilities that the only means in sight for getting rid of the knowledge of how to destroy ourselves would be to do just that—in effect, to remove the knowledge by removing the knower.

Although it is unquestionably the scientists who have led us to the edge of the nuclear abyss, we would be mistaken if we either held them chiefly responsible for our plight or looked to them, particularly, for a solution. Here, again, the difference between scientific revolutions and social revolutions shows itself, for the notion that scientists bear primary responsibility springs from a tendency to confuse scientists with political actors. Political actors, who, of course, include ordinary citizens as well as government officials, act with definite social ends in view, such as the preservation of peace, the establishment of a just society, or, if they are corrupt, their own aggrandizement; and they are accordingly held responsible for the consequences of their actions, even when these are unintended ones, as they so often are. Scientists, on the other hand (and here I refer to the so-called pure scientists, who search for the laws of nature for the sake of knowledge itself, and not to the applied scientists, who make use of already discovered natural laws to solve practical problems), do not aim at social ends, and, in fact, usually do not know what the social results of their findings will be; for that matter, they cannot know what the findings themselves will be, because science is a process of discovery, and it is in the nature of discovery that one cannot know beforehand what one will find. This element of the unexpected is present when a researcher sets out to unravel some small, carefully defined mystery—say, the chemistry of a certain enzyme—but it is most conspicuous in the synthesis of the great laws of science and in the development of science as a whole, which, over decades and centuries, moves toward destinations that no one can predict. Thus, only a few decades ago it might have seemed that physics, which had just placed nuclear energy at man's disposal, was the dangerous branch of science, while biology, which underlay improvements in medicine and also helped us to understand our dependence on the natural environment, was the beneficial branch; but now that biologists have begun to fathom the secrets of genetics, and to tamper with the genetic substance of life directly, we cannot be so sure. The most striking illustration of the utter disparity that may occur between the wishes of the scientist as a social being and the social results of his scientific findings is certainly the career of Einstein. By nature, he was, according to accounts, the gentlest of men, and by conviction he was a pacifist, yet he made intellectual discoveries that led the way to the invention of weapons with which the species could exterminate itself. Inspired wholly by a love of knowledge for its own sake, and by an awe at the creation which bordered on the religious, he made possible an instrument of destruction with which the terrestrial creation could be disfigured.

A disturbing corollary of the scientists' inability even to foresee the path of science, to say nothing of determining it, is that while science is without doubt the most powerful revolutionary force in our world, no one directs that force. For science is a process of submission, in which the mind does not dictate to nature but seeks out and then bows to nature's laws, letting its conclusions be guided by that which *is*, independent of our will. From the political point of view, therefore, scientific findings, some lending themselves to evil, some to good, and some to both, simply pour forth from the laboratory in senseless profusion, offering the world now a neutron bomb, now bacteria that devour oil, now a vaccine to prevent polio, now a cloned frog. It is not until the pure scientists, seekers of knowledge for its own sake, turn their findings over to the applied scientists that social intentions begin to guide the results. The applied scientists do indeed set out to make a better vaccine or a bigger bomb, but even they, perhaps, deserve less credit or blame than we are sometimes inclined to give them. For as soon as our intentions enter the picture we are in the realm of politics in the broadest sense, and in politics it is ultimately not technicians but governments and citizens who are in charge. The scientists in the Manhattan Project could not decide to make the first atomic bomb; only President Roosevelt, elected to office by the American people, could do that.

If scientists are unable to predict their discoveries, neither can they cancel them once they have been made. In this respect, they are like the rest of us, who are asked not whether we would like to live in a world in which we can convert matter into energy but only what we want to do about it once we have been told that we do live in such a world. Science is a tide that can only rise. The individual human mind is capable of forgetting things, and mankind has collectively forgotten many things, but we do not know how, as a species, to *deliberately* set out to forget something. A basic scientific finding, therefore, has the character of destiny for the world. Scientific discovery is in this regard like any other form of discovery; once Columbus had discovered America, and had told the world about it, America could not be hidden again.

Scientific progress (which can and certainly will occur) offers little more hope than scientific regression (which probably cannot occur) of giving us relief from the nuclear peril. It does not seem likely that science will bring forth some new invention—some antiballistic missile or laser beam—that will render nuclear weapons harmless (although the unpredictability of science prevents any categorical judgment on this point). In the centuries of the modern scientific revolution, scientific knowledge has steadily increased the destructiveness of warfare, for it is in the very nature of knowledge, apparently, to increase our might rather than to diminish it. One of the most common forms of the hope for deliverance from the nuclear peril by technical advances is the notion that the species will be spared extinction by fleeing in spaceships. The thought seems to be that while the people on earth are destroying themselves communities in space will be able to survive and carry on. This thought does an injustice to our birthplace and habitat, the earth. It assumes that if only we could escape the earth we would find safety—as though it were the earth and its plants and animals that threatened us, rather than the other way around. But the fact is that wherever human beings went there also would go the knowledge of how to build nuclear weapons, and, with it, the peril of extinction. Scientific progress may yet deliver us from many evils, but there are at least two evils that it cannot deliver us from: its own findings and our own destructive and self-destructive bent. This is a combination that we will have to learn to deal with by some other means.

We live, then, in a universe whose fundamental substance contains a supply of energy with which we can extinguish ourselves. We shall never live in any other. We now know that we live in such a universe, and we shall never stop knowing it. Over the millennia, this truth lay in waiting for us, and now we have found it out, irrevocably. If we suppose that it is an integral part of human existence to be curious about the physical world we are born into, then, to speak in the broadest terms, the origin of the nuclear peril lies, on the one hand, in our nature as rational and inquisitive beings and, on the other, in the nature of matter. Because the energy that nuclear weapons release is so great, the whole species is threatened by them, and because the spread of scientific knowledge is unstoppable, the whole species poses the threat: in the last analysis, it is all of mankind that threatens all of mankind. (I do not mean to overlook the fact that at present it is only two nations—the United States and the Soviet Union—that possess nuclear weapons in numbers great enough to possibly destroy the species, and that they thus now bear the chief responsibility for the peril. I only wish to point out that, regarded in its full dimensions, the nuclear peril transcends the rivalry between the present superpowers.)

The fact that the roots of the nuclear peril lie in basic scientific knowledge has broad political implications that cannot be ignored if the world's solution to the predicament is to be built on a solid foundation, and if futile efforts are to be avoided. One such effort would be to rely on secrecy to contain the peril—that is, to "classify" the "secret" of the bomb. The first person to try to suppress knowledge of how nuclear weapons can be made was the physicist Leo Szilard, who in 1939, when he first heard that a nuclear chain reaction was possible, and realized that a nuclear bomb might be possible, called on a number of his colleagues to keep the discovery secret from the Germans. Many of the key scientists refused. His failure foreshadowed a succession of failures, by whole governments, to restrict the knowledge of how the weapons are made. The first, and most notable, such failure was the United States' inability to monopolize nuclear weapons, and prevent the

Soviet Union from building them. And we have subsequently witnessed the failure of the entire world to prevent nuclear weapons from spreading. Given the nature of scientific thought and the very poor record of past attempts to suppress it, these failures should not have surprised anyone. (The Catholic Church succeeded in making Galileo recant his view that the earth revolves around the sun, but we do not now believe that the sun revolves around the earth.) Another, closely related futile effort—the one made by our hypothetical council—would be to try to resolve the nuclear predicament through disarmament alone, without accompanying political measures. Like the hope that the knowledge can be classified, this hope loses sight of the fact that the nuclear predicament consists not in the possession of nuclear weapons at a particular moment by certain nations but in the circumstance that mankind as a whole has now gained possession once and for all of the knowledge of how to make them, and that all nations—and even some groups of people which are not nations, including terrorist groups—can potentially build them. Because the nuclear peril, like the scientific knowledge that gave rise to it, is probably global and everlasting, our solution must at least aim at being global and everlasting. And the only kind of solution that holds out this promise is a global political one. In defining the task so broadly, however, I do not mean to argue against short-term palliatives, such as the Strategic Arms Limitation Talks between the United States and the Soviet Union, or nuclear-nonproliferation agreements, on the ground that they are short-term. If a patient's life is in danger, as mankind's now is, no good cause is served by an argument between the nurse who wants to give him an aspirin to bring down his fever and the doctor who wants to perform the surgery that can save his life; there is need for an argument only if the nurse is claiming that the aspirin is all that is necessary. If, given the world's discouraging record of political achievement, a lasting political solution seems almost beyond human powers, it may give us confidence to remember that what challenges us is simply our extraordinary success in another field of activity—the scientific. We have only to learn to live politically in the world in which we already live scientifically.

Since 1947, the *Bulletin of the Atomic Scientists* has included a "doomsday clock" in each issue. The editors place the hands farther away from or closer to midnight as they judge the world to be farther away from or closer to a nuclear holocaust. A companion clock can be imagined whose hands, instead of metaphorically representing a judgment about the likelihood of a holocaust, would represent an estimate of the amount of time that, given the world's technical and political arrangements, the people of the earth can be sure they have left before they are destroyed in a holocaust. At present, the hands would stand at, or a fraction of a second before, midnight, because none of us can be sure that at any second we will not be killed in a nuclear attack. If, by treaty, all nuclear warheads were removed from their launchers and stored somewhere else, and therefore could no longer descend on us at any moment without warning, the clock would show the amount of time that it would take to put them back on. If all the nuclear weapons in the world were destroyed, the clock would show the time that it would take to manufacture them again. If in addition confidence-inspiring political arrangements to prevent rearmament were put in place, the clock would show some estimate of the time that it might take for the arrangements to break down. And if these arrangements were to last for hundreds or thousands of years (as they must if mankind is to survive this long), then some generation far in the future might feel justified in setting the clock at decades, or even centuries, before midnight. But no generation would ever be justified in retiring the clock from use altogether, because, as far as we can tell, there will never again be a time when self-extinction is beyond the reach of our species. An observation that Plutarch made about politics holds true also for the task of survival, which has now become the principal obligation of politics: "They are wrong who think that politics is like an ocean voyage or a military campaign, something to be done with some end in view, something which levels off as soon as that end is reached. It is not a public chore, to be got over with; it is a way of life."

The scientific principles and techniques that make possible the construction of nuclear weapons are, of course, only one small portion of mankind's huge reservoir of scientific knowledge, and, as I have mentioned, it has always been known that scientific findings can be made use of for evil as well as for good, according to the intentions of the user. What is new to our time is the realization that, acting quite independently of any good or evil intentions of ours, the human enterprise as a whole has begun to strain and erode the natural terrestrial world on which human and other life depends. Taken in its entirety, the increase in mankind's strength has brought about a decisive, many-sided shift in the balance of strength between man and the earth. Nature, once a harsh and feared master, now lies in subjection, and needs protection against man's powers. Yet because man, no matter what intellectual and technical heights he may scale, remains embedded in nature, the balance has shifted against him, too, and the threat that he poses to the earth is a threat to him as well. The peril to nature was difficult to see at first, in part because its symptoms made their appearance as unintended "side effects" of our intended goals, on which we had fixed most of our attention. In economic production, the side effects are the peril of gradual pollution of the natural environment—by, for example, global heating through an increased "greenhouse effect." In the military field, the side effects, or prospective side effects—sometimes referred to by the strategists as the "collateral effects"—include the possible extinction of the species through sudden, severe harm to the ecosphere, caused by global radioactive contamination, ozone depletion, climatic change, and the other known and unknown possible consequences of a nuclear holocaust. Though from the point of view of the human actor there might be a clear difference between the "constructive" economic applications of technology and the "destructive" military ones, nature makes no such distinction: both are beachheads of human mastery in a defenseless natural world. (For example, the ozone doesn't care whether oxides of nitrogen are injected into it by the use of supersonic transports or by nuclear weapons; it simply reacts according to the appropriate chemical laws.) It was not until recently that it became clear that often the side effects of both the destructive and the constructive applications were really the main effects. And now the task ahead of us can be defined as one of giving the "side effects," including, above all, the peril of self-extinction, the weight they deserve in our judgments and decisions. To use a homely metaphor, if a man discovers that improvements he is making to his house threaten to destroy its foundation he is well advised to rethink them.

A nuclear holocaust, because of its unique combination of immensity and suddenness, is a threat without parallel; yet at the same time it is only one of countless threats that the human enterprise, grown mighty through knowledge, poses to the natural world. Our species is caught in the same tightening net of technical success that has already strangled so many other species. (At present, it has been estimated, the earth loses species at the rate of about three per day.) The peril of human extinction, which exists not because every single person in the world would be killed by the immediate explosive and radioactive effects of a holocaust—something that is exceedingly unlikely, even at present levels of armament—but because a holocaust might render the biosphere unfit for human survival, is, in a word, an *ecological* peril. The nuclear peril is usually seen in isolation from the threats to other forms of life and their ecosystems, but in fact it should be seen as the very center of the ecological crisis—as the cloud-covered Everest of which the more immediate, visible kinds of harm to the environment are the mere foothills. Both the effort to preserve the environment and the effort to save the species from extinction by nuclear arms would be enriched and strengthened by this recognition. The nuclear question, which now stands in eerie seclusion from the rest of life, would gain a context, and the ecological movement, which, in its concern for plants and animals, at times assumes an almost misanthropic posture, as though man were an unwanted intruder in an otherwise unblemished natural world, would gain the humanistic intent that should stand at the heart of its concern.

Seen as a planetary event, the rising tide of human mastery over nature has brought about a categorical increase in the power of death on earth. An organism's ability to renew itself during its lifetime and to reproduce itself depends on the integrity of what biologists call "information" stored in its genes. What endures—what lives—in an organism is not any particular group of cells but a configuration of cells which is dictated by the genetic information. What survives in a species, correspondingly, is a larger configuration, which takes in all the individuals in the species. An ecosystem is a still larger

configuration, in which a whole constellation of species forms
a balanced, self-reproducing, slowly changing whole. The ecosphere of the earth—Dr. Lewis Thomas's "cell"—is, finally, the
largest of the living configurations, and is a carefully regulated
and balanced, self-perpetuating system in its own right. At each
of these levels, life is coherence, and the loss of coherence,—the
sudden slide toward disorder—is death. Seen in this light, life is
information, and death is the loss of information, returning the
substance of the creature to randomness. However, the death
of a species or an ecosystem has a role in the natural order that
is very different from that of the death of an organism. Whereas
an individual organism, once born, begins to proceed inevitably
toward death, a species is a source of new life that has no fixed
term. An organism is a configuration whose demise is built into
its plan, and within the life of a species the death of individual
members normally has a fixed, limited, and necessary place, so
that as death moves through the ranks of the living its pace is
roughly matched by the pace of birth, and populations are kept
in a rough balance that enables them to coexist and endure in
their particular ecosystem. A species, on the other hand, can
survive as long as environmental circumstances happen to permit. An ecosystem, likewise, is indefinitely self-renewing. But
when the pace of death is too much increased, either by human
intervention in the environment or by some other event, death
becomes an extinguishing power, and species and ecosystems
are lost. Then not only are individual creatures destroyed but
the sources of all future creatures of those kinds are closed
down, and a portion of the diversity and strength of terrestrial
life in its entirety vanishes forever. And when man gained the
ability to intervene directly in the workings of the global "cell"
as a whole, and thus to extinguish species wholesale, his power
to encroach on life increased by still another order of magnitude, and came to threaten the balance of the entire planetary
system of life.

Hence, there are two competing forces at work in the terrestrial environment—one natural, which acts over periods of
millions of years to strengthen and multiply the forms of life,
and the other man-made and man-operated, which, if it is left
unregulated and unguided, tends in general to deplete life's
array of forms. Indeed, it is a striking fact that both of these

great engines of change on earth depend on stores of information that are passed down from generation to generation. There is, in truth, no closer analogy to scientific progress, in which a steadily growing pool of information makes possible the creation of an ever more impressive array of artifacts, than evolution, in which another steadily growing pool of information makes possible the development of ever more complex and astonishing creatures—culminating in human beings, who now threaten to raze both the human and the natural structures to their inanimate foundations. One is tempted to say that only the organic site of the evolutionary information has changed— from genes to brains. However, because of the extreme rapidity of technological change relative to natural evolution, evolution is unable to refill the vacated niches of the environment with new species, and, as a result, the genetic pool of life as a whole is imperilled. Death, having been augmented by human strength, has lost its appointed place in the natural order and become a counterevolutionary force, capable of destroying in a few years, or even in a few hours, what evolution has built up over billions of years. In doing so, death threatens even itself, since death, after all, is a part of life: stones may be lifeless but they do not die. The question now before the human species, therefore, is whether life or death will prevail on the earth. This is not metaphorical language but a literal description of the present state of affairs.

One might say that after billions of years nature, by creating a species equipped with reason and will, turned its fate, which had previously been decided by the slow, unconscious movements of natural evolution, over to the conscious decisions of just one of its species. When this occurred, human activity, which until then had been confined to the historical realm—which, in turn, had been supported by the broader biological current—spilled out of its old boundaries and came to menace both history and biology. Thought and will became mightier than the earth that had given birth to them. Now human beings became actors in the geological time span, and the laws that had governed the development and the survival of life began to be superseded by processes in the mind of man. Here, however, there were no laws; there was only choice, and the thinking and feeling that guide choice. The reassuring, stable, self-sustaining prehistoric world of nature dropped away, and in its place mankind's own judgments, moods, and decisions loomed up with an unlooked-for, terrifying importance.

Regarded objectively, as an episode in the development of life on earth, a nuclear holocaust that brought about the extinction of mankind and other species by mutilating the exosphere would constitute an evolutionary setback of possibly limited extent—the first to result from a deliberate action taken by the creature extinguished but perhaps no greater than any of several evolutionary setbacks, such as the extinction of the dinosaurs, of which the geological record offers evidence. (It is, of course, impossible to judge what course evolution would take after human extinction, but the past record strongly suggests that the reappearance of man is not one of the possibilities. Evolution has brought forth an amazing variety of creatures, but there is no evidence that any species, once extinguished, has ever evolved again. Whether or not nature, obeying some law of evolutionary progress, would bring forth another creature equipped with reason and will, and capable of building, and perhaps then destroying, a world, is one more unanswerable question, but it is barely conceivable that some gifted new animal will pore over the traces of our self-destruction, trying to figure out what went wrong and to learn from our mistakes. If this should be possible, then it might justify the remark once made by Kafka: "There is infinite hope, but not for us." If, on the other hand, as the record of life so far suggests, terrestrial evolution is able to produce only once the miracle of the qualities that we now associate with human beings, then all hope rides with human beings.) However, regarded subjectively, from within human life, where we are all actually situated, and as something that would happen to us, human extinction assumes awesome, inapprehensible proportions. It is of the essence of the human condition that we are born, live for a while, and then die. Through mishaps of all kinds, we may also suffer untimely death, and in extinction by nuclear arms the number of untimely deaths would reach the limit for any one catastrophe: everyone in the world would die. But although the untimely death of everyone in the world would in itself constitute an unimaginably huge loss, it would bring with it a separate, distinct loss that would be in a sense even huger—the cancellation of all future generations of human beings. According to the Bible, when Adam and Eve ate the fruit of the tree of knowledge God punished them by withdrawing from them the privilege of immortality and dooming them and their kind to die. Now our species has eaten more deeply of the fruit of the tree of knowledge, and has brought itself face to face with a second death—the death of mankind. In doing so, we have caused a basic change in the circumstances in which life was given to us, which is to say that we have altered the human condition. The distinctness of this second death from the deaths of all the people on earth can be illustrated by picturing two different global catastrophes. In the first, let us suppose that most of the people on earth were killed in a nuclear holocaust but that a few million survived and the earth happened to remain habitable by human beings. In this catastrophe, billions of people would perish, but the species would survive, and perhaps one day would even repopulate the earth in its former numbers. But now let us suppose that a substance was released into the environment which had the effect of sterilizing all the people in the world but otherwise leaving them unharmed. Then, as the existing population died off, the world would empty of people, until no one was left. Not one life would have been shortened by a single day, but the species would die. In extinction by nuclear arms, the death of the species and the death of all the people in the world would happen together, but it is important to make a clear distinction between the two losses; otherwise, the mind, overwhelmed by the thought of the deaths of the billions of living people, might stagger back without realizing that behind this already ungraspable loss there lies the separate loss of the future generations.

The possibility that the living can stop the future generations from entering into life compels us to ask basic new questions about our existence, the most sweeping of which is what these unborn ones, most of whom we will never meet even if they are born, mean to us. No one has ever thought to ask this question before our time, because no generation before ours has ever held the life and death of the species in its hands. But if we hardly know how to comprehend the possible deaths in a holocaust of the billions of people who are already in life how are we to comprehend the life or death of the infinite number of possible people who do not yet exist at all? How are we, who are a part of human life, to step back from life and see it whole, in order to assess the meaning of its disappearance? To kill a human being is murder, and there are those who believe that to abort a fetus is also murder, but what crime is it to cancel the numberless multitude of unconceived people? In what court is such a crime to be judged? Against whom is it committed? And what law does it violate? If we find the nuclear peril to be somehow abstract, and tend to consign this whole elemental issue to "defense experts" and other dubiously qualified people, part of the reason, certainly, is that the future generations really are abstract—that is to say, without the tangible existence and the unique particularities that help to make the living real to us. And if we find the subject strangely "impersonal" it may be in part because the unborn, who are the ones directly imperilled by extinction, are not yet persons. What are they, then? They lack the individuality that we often associate with the sacredness of life, and may at first thought seem to have only a shadowy, mass existence. *Where* are they? Are they to be pictured lined up in a sort of fore-life, waiting to get into life? Or should we regard them as nothing more than a pinch of chemicals in our reproductive organs, toward which we need feel no special obligations? What standing should they have among us? How much should their needs count in competition with ours? How far should the living go in trying to secure their advantage, their happiness, their existence?

The individual person, faced with the metaphysical-seeming perplexities involved in pondering the possible cancellation of people who do not yet exist—an apparently extreme effort of the imagination, which seems to require one first to summon before the mind's eye the countless possible people of the future generations and then to consign these incorporeal multitudes to a more profound nothingness—might well wonder why, when he already has his own death to worry about, he should occupy himself with this other death. Since our own individual death promises to inflict a loss that is total and final, we may find the idea of a second death merely redundant. After all, can everything be taken away from us twice? Moreover, a person might reason that even if mankind did perish he wouldn't have to know anything about it, since in that event he himself would perish. There might actually be something consoling in the idea of having so much company in death. In the midst of universal death, it somehow seems out of order to want to go on living oneself. As Randall Jarrell wrote in his poem "Losses," thinking back to his experience in the Second World War, "it was not dying: everybody died."

However, the individual would misconceive the nuclear peril if he tried to understand it primarily in terms of personal danger, or even in terms of danger to the people immediately known to him, for the nuclear peril threatens life, above all, not at the level of individuals, who already live under the sway of death, but at the level of everything that individuals hold in common. Death cuts off life; extinction cuts off birth. Death dispatches into the nothingness after life each person who has been born; extinction in one stroke locks up in the nothingness before life all the people who have not yet been born. For we are finite beings at both ends of our existence—natal as well as mortal—and it is the natality of our kind that extinction threatens. We have always been able to send people to their death, but only now has it become possible to prevent all birth and so doom all future human beings to uncreation. The threat of the loss of birth—a beginning that is over and done with for every living person—cannot be a source of immediate, selfish concern; rather, this threat assails everything that people hold in common, for it is the ability of our species to produce new generations which assures the continuation of the world in which all our common enterprises occur and have their meaning. Each death belongs inalienably to the individual who must suffer it, but birth is our common possession. And the meaning of extinction is therefore to be sought first not in what each person's own life means to him but in what the world and the people in it mean to him.

In its nature, the human world is, in Hannah Arendt's words, a "common world," which she distinguishes from the "private realm" that belongs to each person individually. (Somewhat surprisingly, Arendt, who devoted so much of her attention to the unprecedented evils that have appeared in our century, never addressed the issue of nuclear arms; yet I have discovered her thinking to be an indispensable foundation for reflection on this question.) The private realm, she writes in "The Human Condition," a book published in 1958, is made up of "the passions of the heart, the thoughts of the mind, the delights of the senses," and terminates with each person's death, which is the most solitary of all human experiences. The common world, on the other hand, is made up of all institutions, all cities, nations, and other communities, and all works of fabrication, art, thought, and science, and it survives the death of every individual. It is basic to the common world that it encompasses not only the present but all past and future generations. "The common world is what we enter when we are born and what we leave behind when we die," Arendt writes. "It transcends our life-span into past and future alike; it was there before we came and will outlast our brief sojourn in it. It is what we have in common not only with those who live with us, but also with those who were here before and with those who will come after us." And she adds, "Without this transcendence into a potential earlthy immortality, no politics, strictly speaking, no common world, and no public realm is possible." The creation of a common world is the use that we human beings, and we alone among the earth's creatures, have made of the biological circumstance that while each of us is mortal, our species is biologically immortal. If mankind had not established a common world, the species would still outlast its individual members and be immortal, but this immortality would be unknown to us and would go for nothing, as it does in the animal kingdom, and the generations, unaware of one another's existence, would come and go like waves on the beach, leaving everything just as it was before. In fact, it is only because humanity has built up a common world that we can fear our destruction as a species. It may even be that man, who has been described as the sole creature that knows that it must die, can know this only because he lives in a common world, which permits him to imagine a future beyond his own life. This common world, which is unharmed by individual death but depends on the survival of the species, has now been placed in jeopardy by nuclear arms. Death and extinction are thus complementary, dividing between them the work of undoing, or threatening to undo, everything that human beings are or can ever become, with death terminating the life of each individual and extinction imperilling the common world shared by all. In one sense, extinction is less terrible than death, since extinction can be avoided, while death is inevitable; but in another sense extinction is more terrible—is the more radical nothingness—because extinction ends death just as surely as it ends birth and life. Death is only death; extinction is the death of death.

The world is made a common one by what Arendt calls "publicity," which insures that "everything that appears in public can be seen and heard by everybody." She writes, "A common world can survive the coming and going of the generations only to the extent that it appears in public. It is the publicity of the public realm which can absorb and make shine through the centuries whatever men may want to save from the natural ruin of time." But this publicity does not only shine on human works; it also brings to light the natural foundations of life, enabling us to perceive what our origins are. It thereby permits us not only to endow things of our own making with a degree of immortality but to see and appreciate the preëxisting, biological immortality of our species and of life on the planet, which forms the basis for any earthly immortality whatever. The chief medium of the publicity of the common world is, of course, language, whose possession by man is believed by many to be what separates him from the other animals; but there are also the other "languages" of the arts and sciences. And standing behind language is that of which language is expressive—our reason, our psyche, our will, and our spirit. Through these, we are capable of entering into the lives of others, and of becoming aware that we belong to a community of others that is as wide as our species. The foundation of a common world is an exclusively human achievement, and to live in a common world—to speak and listen to one another, to read, to write, to know about the past and look ahead to the future, to receive the achievements of past generations, and to pass them on, together with achievements of our own, to future generations, and otherwise to participate in human enterprises that outlast any individual life—is part of what it means to be human, and by threatening all this nuclear weapons threaten a part of our humanity. The common world is not something that can be separated from the life we now live; it is intrinsic to our existence—something as close to us as the words we speak and the thoughts we think using those words. Descartes's famous axiom "I think, therefore I am" has perhaps been more extensively rebutted that any other single philosophical proposition. The rebuttal by Lewis Mumford happens to amount to a description of each person's indebtedness to the common world and to the common biological inheritance that the common world has brought to light. "Descartes forgot that before he uttered these words 'I think' . . . he needed the coöperation of countless fellow-beings, extending back to his own knowledge as far as the thousands of years that Biblical history recorded," Mumford writes in "The Pentagon of Power," a book published in 1970. "Beyond that, we know now he needed the aid of an even remoter past that mankind too long remained ignorant of: the millions of years required to transform his dumb animal ancestors into conscious human beings." In our long and arduous ascent out of biological darkness, it seems, we forgot our indebtedness to the natural world of our origins, and now, in consequence, threaten to plunge ourselves into an even deeper darkness. The nuclear predicament is thus in every sense a crisis of life in the common world. Only because there is a common world, in which knowledge of the physical world accumulates over the generations, can there be a threat to the common world and to its natural foundations. Only because there is a common world, which permits us knowledge of other generations and of the terrestrial nature of which human life is a part, can we worry about, or even know of, that threat. And only because there is a common world can we hope, by concerting our actions, to save ourselves and the earth.

The common world has been the work of every generation that has lived in it, back to the remotest ages. Much as poets begin by using language as they find it but, usually as an unself-conscious consequence of their work, leave usage slightly altered behind them, people in general pursue their various ends in the yielding medium of the world and shape its character by their actions. But although the world receives the imprint of the lives of those who pass through it, it has never been given to any single generation to dictate the character of the world. Not even the most thoroughgoing totalitarian regimes have succeeded in wholly shaping the lives of their peoples. One has only to think of Alexander Solzhenitsyn growing up in the Soviet Union but drawing so much of his spiritual sustenance from earlier centuries of Russian life, or to think of China, where so many of the customs and qualities of the people have outlasted what was probably the longest and most concentrated assault in history by a government on the national tradition of its own country, to realize how deeply a people's past is woven into its present.

The links binding the living, the dead, and the unborn were described by Edmund Burke, the great eighteenth-century English conservative, as a "partnership" of the generations. He wrote, "Society is indeed a contract. . . . It is a partnership in all science; a partnership in all art; a partnership in every virtue, and in all perfection. As the ends of such a partnership cannot be obtained except in many generations, it becomes a partnership not only between those who are living, but between those who are living, those who are dead, and those who are to be born." Pericles offered a similar, though not identical, vision of the common life of the generations in his funeral oration, in which he said that all Athens was a "sepulchre" for the remembrance of the soldiers who had died fighting for their city. Thus, whereas Burke spoke of common tasks that needed many generations for their achievement, Pericles spoke of the immortality that the living confer on the dead by remembering their sacrifices. In the Unites States, Abraham Lincoln seemed to combine these two thoughts when he said in his Gettysburg address that the sacrifices of the soldiers who had died at Gettysburg laid an obligation on the living to devote themselves to the cause for which the battle had been fought. And, indeed, every political observer or political actor of vision has recognized that if life is to be fully human it must take cognizance of the dead and the unborn.

But now our responsibilities as citizens in the common world have been immeasurably enlarged. In the pre-nuclear common world, we were partners in the protection of the arts, the institutions, the customs, and all "perfection" of life; now we are also partners in the protection of life itself. Burke described as a common inheritance the achievements that one generation passed along to the next. "By a constitutional policy, working after the pattern of nature, we receive, we hold, we transmit our government and our privileges, in the same manner in which we enjoy and transmit our property and our lives," he wrote. "The institutions of policy, the goods of fortune, the gifts of Providence, are handed down, to us and from us, in the same course and order." These words appear in Burke's "Reflections on the Revolution in France"—the revolution being an event that filled him with horror, for in it he believed he saw a single generation violently destroying in a few years the national legacy of hundreds of years. But, whether or not he was right in thinking that the inheritance of France was being squandered by its recipients, the inheriting generations and their successors were at least biologically intact. In our time, however, among the items in the endangered inheritance the inheritors find themselves. Each generation of mankind still receives, holds, and transmits the inheritance from the past, but, being now a part of that inheritance, each generation *is received, is held, and is transmitted*, so that receiver and received, holder and held, transmitter and transmitted are one. Yet our jeopardy is only a part of the jeopardy of all life, and the largest item in the inheritance that we receive, hold, and must transmit is the entire ecosphere. So deep is the change in the structure of human life brought about by this new peril that in retrospect the Burkean concern about the "perfection" of life, indispensable as this concern is to the quality of our existence, seems like only the barest hint or suggestion of the incomparably more commanding obligation that is laid on us by the nuclear predicament. It strikes modern ears as prophetic that when Burke sought to describe the permanence in human affairs which he so valued he often resorted to metaphors drawn from the natural world—speaking, for example, of a "pattern of nature" that human society should imitate—as though he had had a premonition that an almost habitually revolutionary mankind would one day proceed from tearing society apart to tearing the natural world apart. Speaking of the society into which each of us is born, Burke angrily asked whether it could be right to "hack that aged parent in pieces." His words have acquired a deeper meaning than he could ever have foretold for them now that the parent in question is not merely human society but the earth itself.

Since all human aims, personal or political, presuppose human existence, it might seem that the task of protecting that existence should command all the energy at our disposal. However, the claims that the conduct of life lays upon us, including our desire for individual survival, have not suspended themselves in deference to the peril to life as a whole. As long as we keep from extinguishing ourselves, history continues at full flood, and the needs, desires, fears, interests, and ideals that have always moved people assert themselves with their usual vigor, even though extinction threatens them all with termination forever. For example, although people may want the species to survive, they may also want to be free, to be prosperous, to be treated justly, and so on. We are thus required to weigh the value of these goals of human life against the value of human life in its entirety. But while we are used to weighing the various goals of human life against one another, this new task finds us unprepared. For with what measuring rods should we gauge our worth as a species, and how should we rate ourselves against things whose own worth derives from our existence? These questions are by no means academic. Every government and every citizen in the world—but especially the governments and the citizens of the United States and the Soviet Union—face the decision of how much weight to give to the survival of the world compared with the exigencies of business in the world. Ordinarily, when we look out upon each other and upon the world we measure the worth of what we find by making use of standards. For measuring the products of our labor, we may employ a standard of usefulness; for political activity, a standard of justice; for artistic and intellectual work, standards of beauty and truth; for human behavior in general, a standard of goodness. And when the things we value in life are in conflict we weigh them against one another by the perhaps indefinable but nevertheless comprehensive and useful standard of the common good. But none of these standards, including that of the common good, are suitable for gauging the worth of mankind as a whole, for none of them have any meaning or application unless one first assumes the existence of the very thing whose loss they are supposed to measure; namely, mankind. Anyone who prizes the usefulness of things assumes the existence of human beings to whom things can be useful; anyone who loves justice assumes the existence of a society whose parts can be brought into relationships that are just; anyone who loves beauty and truth assumes the existence of minds to which the beautiful and the true can manifest themselves; anyone who loves goodness assumes the existence of creatures who are capable of exhibiting it and being nourished by it; and anyone who wishes to promote the common good assumes the existence of a community whose divergent aims it can harmonize. These standards of worth, and any others that one might think of, are useful only in relating things that are in life to one another, and are inadequate as measures of life itself. We cannot, for example, say in any simple or unqualified sense that the end of the world is bad and its continuation good, because mankind is not in itself good or evil but is the source of both, providing the theatre in which good and evil actions appear as well as the actors by whom they are all enacted. (No stone, tree, or lion ever did anything either good or evil.) Neither can we say that mankind is useful. For to whom are we of any use? Human life is not needed by someone somewhere; rather, it is the seat of need, and need is one of the modes of our being.

The question of the worth of each individual human life, like the question of the worth of mankind, also poses the question of what life might be "for"—if, indeed, it is right to say that life is "for" anything—but with the crucial difference that while the individual can sacrifice his own life "for" others, mankind cannot do the same, since it includes all possible others within itself. Some philosophers, faced with the perplexing fact that although we can try to judge the worth of everything in creation by asking how well it serves as a means to some end of mankind's, mankind itself does not seem to be a means to anything, and therefore, by this estimation, is, strictly speaking, worthless, have attempted to solve the problem (as Kant, for example, did) by saying that man is "an end in himself" or a "final end," by which they meant that service to human beings was the highest good, and that human life was not to be treated as a means for achieving some other, supposedly higher good. However, this description is open to the criticism that by placing mankind at the final stage of a series of means and ends it seems to suggest that man creates himself—since the process of reaching ends through means is a purely human one—whereas in fact he was created by powers over which he had no influence whatever. It would be more appropriate, perhaps, to say that man is a beginning, for all chains of means and ends, no matter what their ultimate goals may be, start up out of man, whose existence they presuppose, and only then circle back into him, and so are wholly enclosed within human life. In that sense, man does not serve as a "final end" so much as stand prior to all means and ends, shaping and defining them according to his nature and his will. But this "beginning," whose existence is a fait accompli as far as we are concerned, is hard for us to see, because as soon as we start thinking something, intending something, enjoying something, or doing something, we have already taken it—"it" being our very selves and our fellow human beings—for granted. The forms that the life of the species can assume appear in innumerable clearly defined, often visible shapes, but mankind itself—the bare structure of human life, which underlies all these permutations—never appears as such, and remains, in a way, invisible.

One reason that standards fail us in our attempt to grasp the worth of our species is that they are meant to provide a common frame of reference against which the individuals in a given class of things can be measured, whereas mankind is a member of no class that we have as yet discovered. It is theoretically possible, of course, that other creatures endowed with the mental, psychological, and spiritual faculties that now distinguish human beings from all other forms of life will be discovered in outer space, and that we will then be able to rate ourselves in relation to them according to some suitable standard that will suggest itself once the creatures are in view. Even now, we are free to imagine that some extraterrestrial creature or god might take the measure of our loss by regarding it as a gap of a certain character and size in the order of a universal living creation of whose existence we are as yet unaware. But these lofty proceedings, in which we exchange our human perspective for a purely speculative superhuman one, are an evasion, for they lift us clean out of the human predicament that it is our obligation to face. By setting up an intelligence that itself escapes extinction and looks down upon the event, and by endowing that intelligence with suspiciously human characteristics, we in effect deny or evade the reality of extinction, for we have covertly manufactured a survivor. (Could it be that the vogue for science fiction and other types of pure fantasy stems in part from the reassurance we get from believing that there are other forms of life in the universe besides ours? The extra worlds offered by science fiction may provide us with an escape in imagination from the tight trap that our species is caught in in reality.) Seen in religious terms, such an assumption of a godlike perspective would be an attempted usurpation by man of God's omniscience, and, as such, a form of blasphemy. A second reason that standards fail us, then, is that employment of the only ones we actually have in our possession or have any real title to apply—the human ones—is terminated by our extinction, and we are left with the impossibility of a judgment without a judge to pass it.

A closely related, and more serious, perversion of religion is the suggestion, made by some Christian fundamentalists, that the nuclear holocaust we threaten to unleash is the Armageddon threatened by God in the Bible. This identification arrogates to ourselves not only God's knowledge but also His will. However, it is not God, picking and choosing among the things of His creation, who threatens us but we ourselves. And extinction by nuclear arms would not be the Day of Judgment, in which God destroys the world but raises the dead and then metes out perfect justice to everyone who has ever lived; it would be the utterly meaningless and completely unjust destruction of mankind by men. To imagine that God is guiding our hand in this action would quite literally be the ultimate evasion of our responsibility as human beings—a responsibility that is ours because (to stay with religious interpretation for a moment) we possess a free will that was implanted in us by God.

Human beings have a worth—a worth that is sacred. But it is *for* human beings that they have that sacred worth, and for them that the other things in the creation have their worth (although it is a reminder of our indissoluble connection with the rest of life that many of our needs and desires are also felt by animals). Hence, while our standards of worth have reference to the various possible worthy things in life, they all also point back to the life of the needy, or suffering, or rejoicing, or despairing, or admiring, or spiritually thirsting person in whose existence the things are found to be worthy or lacking in worth. To borrow elementary philosophical language, as objects the members of the species are among many things in existence that have worth in human eyes, but as the sum of all possible human subjects the species comprises all those "eyes," and in that sense is the sole originator of all worth as it is given to us to be aware of it. The death of an individual person is a loss of one subject, and of all its needs, longings, sufferings, and enthusiasms—of its being. But the extinction of the species goes farther, and removes from the known universe the human *kind* of being, which is different from any other kind that we as yet know of. It is, above all, the death of mankind as this immortal source of all human subjects, not the death of mankind as an object, that makes extinction radically unique and "unthinkable." In extinction, a darkness falls over the world not because the lights have gone out but because the eyes that behold the light have been closed. To assert this, however, is not to assert that only that which the human eye beholds is real. There is nothing in a holocaust that calls into doubt the existence of the physical world, which we can be confident will go on existing whether we destroy ourselves or not. We are even free to suppose that in a certain sense the worth of things will still reside in them in our absence, waiting for creatures who can appreciate it to reappear. But, without entering into the debate over whether beauty is in the eye of the beholder or in "the thing itself," we can at least say that without the beholder the beauty goes to waste. The universe would still exist, but the universe as it is imprinted on the human soul would be gone. Of many of the qualities of worth in things, we can say that they give us a private audience, and that insofar as they act upon the physical world they do so only by virtue of the response that they stir in us. For example, any works of art that survived our extinction would stare off into a void without finding a responding eye, and thus become shut up in a kind of isolation. (The physical qualities of things, on the other hand, will go on interacting among themselves without us.) Or, to put it differently, the qualifies of worth find in us their sole home in an otherwise neutral and inhospitable universe. I believe that Rilke was saying something of this kind when, in the "Duino Elegies," he wrote the lines:

Earth, isn't this what you want: an invisible
re-arising in us? Is it not your dream
to be one day invisible? Earth! invisible!
What is your urgent command, if not transformation?
Earth, you darling, I will! Oh, believe me, you need
your Springs no longer to win me: a single one,
just one, is already more than my blood can endure.

Because we are the ones who hold everything that is of
worth to be so, the attempt to assign a worth to our species
leads us in an intellectual circle. We find ourselves trying to
gauge the usefulness of usefulness, the goodness of goodness,
the worth of worth, and these are questions that have no
resolution. Mankind is to be thought of not as something that
possesses a certain worth (although in the eyes of one another
we have that, too)—as something with a certain measurable
degree of usefulness, beauty, or goodness (for just as often as
we are useful, beautiful, or good we are destructive, ugly, or
evil)—but as the inexhaustible source of all the possible forms
of worth, which has no existence or meaning without human
life. Mankind is not, in the ancient phrase, the measure of all
things; he is the measurer, and is himself measureless.

For the generations that now have to decide whether or not
to risk the future of the species, the implication of our species'
unique place in the order of things is that while things in the
life of mankind have worth, we must never raise that worth
above the life of mankind and above our respect for that life's
existence. To do this would be to make of our highest ideals so
many swords with which to destroy ourselves. To sum up the
worth of our species by reference to some particular standard,
goal, or ideology, no matter how elevated or noble it might be,
would be to prepare the way for extinction by closing down
in thought and feeling the open-ended possibilities for human
development which extinction would close down in fact.
There is only one circumstance in which it might be possible
to sum up the life and achievement of the species, and that
circumstance would be that it had already died; but then, of
course, there would be no one left to do the summing up.
Only a generation that believed itself to be in possession of
final, absolute truth could ever conclude that it had reason to

put an end to human life, and only generations that recognized the limits to their own wisdom and virtue would be likely to subordinate their interests and dreams to the as yet unformed interests and undreamed dreams of the future generations, and let human life go on.

From the foregoing, it follows that there can be no justification for extinguishing mankind, and therefore no justification of any nation ever to push the world into nuclear hostilities, which, once inaugurated, may lead uncontrollably to a full-scale holocaust and to extinction. But from this conclusion it does not follow that any action is permitted as long as it serves the end of preventing extinction. The grounds for these two propositions become clearer if we consider the nature of ethical obligation. It seems especially important to consider the ethical side of the question, because the other common justification for military action—self-interest—obviously can never justify extinction, inasmuch as extinction would constitute suicide for the perpetrator; and suicide, whatever else it may be, is scarcely in the interest of the one who commits it.

I shall let the behavior of Socrates at his trial in Athens, in the fourth century B.C., on charges of corrupting youth and denigrating the gods, stand as a model of ethical behavior. His example has a special, direct relevance to the nuclear question, because every attempt to justify the use of nuclear weapons has been based on some variation of the conviction, first given full expression by him, in words that still sound with their full force, that the highest good is not life itself—mere survival—but the moral life. The possible application of the Socratic principle to the question of extinction is obvious: if under certain circumstances it is the duty of the individual to sacrifice his life for something higher than his life, might it not be the obligation of mankind under certain circumstances to do the same? The philosopher Karl Jaspers, for one, thought so, and was one of the few who have had the courage to state such a belief outright. In his book "The Future of Mankind," published in 1958, he writes, concerning the nuclear question, "Man is born to be free, and the free life that he tries to save by all possible means is more than mere life. Hence, life in the sense of existence—individual life as well as all life—can be

staked and sacrificed for the sake of the life that is worth living."
He asks, "And if no such way [to the life worth living] is found,
does the substance of humanity then lie where failure is no
longer an objection—where indeed man's ultimately real, truly
serious purpose is his doom?" To which he answers, "It could
be necessary only as a sacrifice made for the sake of eternity."
I have suggested, though, that doom can never be a human
purpose at all, truly serious or otherwise, but, rather, is the end
of all human purposes, none of which can be fulfilled outside
of human life.

Jaspers's opposite conclusion, I believe, depends on an
application to the species as a whole of a canon of morality
that properly applies only to each individual person. Ethical
commandments have often been regarded as "absolute" for
the individual (and thus as justifying any sacrifice made in their
name), and, in a certain sense, Socrates regarded them in that
light, too. He even claimed that a "voice," or "God," sometimes
commanded him not to do certain things. The commands were
absolute in two ways. First, once the voice, which we may take
to be the voice of conscience, had spoken, he could not be
released from it by appeal to any outside authority, such as the
majority voice of the community. Second, the commands were
absolutely binding on him, and had to be followed even unto
death. Therefore, when the city of Athens put him on trial he
was not at liberty to abandon the dictates of his conscience
and to save his life. Instead, he chided the jury for "trying to
put an innocent man to death," and added, for good measure,
that since to commit such an injustice would be in his opinion
a worse fate than to suffer it, then "so far from pleading on
my own behalf, as might be supposed, I am really pleading on
yours." In these bold words and actions, which cost him his life,
Socrates asserted the absolute sovereignty of his conscience over
his actions. But, having asserted that sovereignty, he did not go
on to suppose that he had thereby won the right to exercise a
similar sovereignty over others. On the contrary, it was of the
essence of his conduct at the trial and at the execution that he
placed himself wholly at the service of his community, and that
his belief in the worth of his actions in fact consisted in this. His
radical assertion of the independence of his conscience was thus
inseparable from a no less radical subordination of his interests

to the good of his city. This subordination was evident in his decision to stand trial, in his decision after the trial to stay in Athens and suffer the death penalty rather than flee (as friends advised him to do), and in the words that he spoke throughout the proceedings. He persisted in dedicating himself to the service of his community even though the community might kill him for his pains. In this devotion, he resembled Christ, of course, who appeared on earth to be "a servant of all," and gave up His life for the sake of the people who put Him to death.

In the present context, the point is that if Socrates is taken as the example, there are no ethics apart from service to the human community, and therefore no ethical commandments that can justify the extinction of humanity. Ethical obligation begins with the assumption that we are naturally inclined to look out for our own interests, and asks that we pay regard to the interests of others—that we do unto them as we would have them do unto us. But since extinction annihilates the community of others it can never be an ethical act, and to say that it could be is like saying that to kill the children in a school would be an educational experience for them, or to starve a country to death would be a beneficial economic measure for it. And even if all the people in the world somehow managed to persuade themselves that their death was justified (thus overlooking the question of for what or for whom it was justified), this suicidal action would still be wrong, because it would also cancel the unconsulted and completely innocent future generations. (Can anybody be more innocent than they are?) In actuality, of course, no one is proposing the voluntary suicide of everyone on earth; on the contrary, what is being claimed is that one or two countries have the right to jeopardize all countries and their descendants in the name of certain beliefs. Hence, those who, to defend risking extinction, start with the moral obligation of "individual life" to sacrifice itself and generalize from that to an obligation of "all life" to sacrifice itself (in Jaspers's phrases) in fact pass from a principle of individual self-sacrifice to a principle of aggression by a few against all—"all" in this case including the unborn generations.

The question remains whether there might be some super-ethical, ultramundane principle, perhaps of religious inspiration, that could justify the destruction of the world. Is it possible, for example, that one day it might be our obligation to set both human interests and human morality aside and destroy the species for the sake of God? There is a long history of wars waged in the name of one god or another, but in the possible justifications for a nuclear holocaust theological principles could play a role of special importance, because they might seem to offer something to "fight" for that would not itself be destroyed in a holocaust. For example, the extinction of an "evil" mankind might be regarded as acceptable or pleasing to a wrathful God—or, at least, as representing the fulfillment of some plan of His (as in the identification by some Christian fundamentalists of a holocaust with Armageddon). When armies take up the banner of God, the "absolute" sovereignty of each person's individual conscience over his own actions is transmuted into a claim of absolute sovereignty over other people; and the absolute submission owed by each person to the voice of conscience is transmuted into a claim of submission owed by other people to those who, as representatives of religious orthodoxy, have taken it on themselves to speak for God. Then the Christian commandment to sacrifice oneself for one's neighbor at God's command is transformed into permission to sacrifice one's neighbor for God's sake. In the pre-nuclear world, the assumption of these claims led to considerable slaughter; in the nuclear world, it could lead to the end of the species. But all this is infinitely remote from the teaching of Christ, at least, who taught people not to kill their enemies but to love them, and who died rather than lift His hand in violence against His tormentors. It speaks powerfully against any Christian justification for destroying the world that when the Christian God appeared on earth in human form not only did He not sacrifice a single human being for His sake but He suffered a lonely, anguishing, degrading human death so that the world might be saved.

In no saying of His did Christ ever suggest that the two great commandments—to love God and to love one's neighbor—could in any way be separated, or that the former could be used as a justification for violating the latter. In fact, He explicitly stated that religious faith that is divorced from love of human beings is empty and dangerous. For example, He said,

"If thou bring thy gift to the altar, and there rememberest that thy brother hath aught against thee; Leave there thy gift before the altar, and go thy way; first be reconciled to thy brother, and then come and offer thy gift." We who have planned out the deaths of hundreds of millions of our brothers plainly have a great deal of work to do before we return to the altar. Clearly, the corpse of mankind would be the least acceptable of all conceivable offerings on the altar of this God.

If there is nothing in the teachings of either Socrates or Christ that could justify the extinction of mankind—nothing, in fact, that could teach us to do anything in regard to this act but hold back from performing it—neither is there anything that would justify the commission of crimes in order to prevent extinction. In the teachings of both men, a person's obligation is to answer even the utmost evil not with more evil but with good. This refusal to be goaded by evil into evil may be the closest thing to an "absolute" that there is in their teachings. (I wonder whether it might not have been this absolute refusal to participate in evil which was in the back of Jaspers's mind when he said that in order to avoid certain evils it was permissible to perpetrate extinction.) Rather, the altogether un-Socratic and un-Christian teaching that the end justifies the means is the basis on which governments, in all times, have licensed themselves to commit crimes of every sort; the *raison d'état* of governments, in fact, enshrines the opposite of the Socratic principle, for it holds that states may do virtually anything whatever in the name of survival. Extinction nullifies the ends-means justification by destroying every end that might justify the means (the *raison d'état* is not well served if the nation is biologically exterminated), but the goal of *preventing* extinction, if it ever became operative as an end, could lend to this expedient line of thinking an immensely enlarged scope, since if the end justifies the means, and the end is human survival, then any means short of human extinction can be countenanced. Herein lies another peril of the nuclear predicament—albeit a lesser one by far than extinction itself, since any political system, no matter how entrenched, is subject to change and decline, whereas extinction is eternal. In most countries, "national security" is found to be justification enough for abusing every human right, and we can only imagine what governments might feel entitled to do once they had begun to claim that they were defending not just national but human survival.

It has not been the mistake of governments of our time to lay too much emphasis on the imperative of human survival, yet in the period of détente between the United States and the Soviet Union the world was given a glimpse of policies in which the aim of avoiding extinction was offered as a justification for repression. Both superpowers, while hardly abandoning the defense of their national interests, made a disturbingly smooth transition between using national interests to rationalize repression and using human survival to rationalize it. In the Soviet Union, a totalitarian country, it was not long before the authorities were supplementing their usual list of charges against critics of the regime by calling them "wreckers of détente," and the like. And in the United States, a democracy, but one that was presided over at the time by an Administration with a criminal and authoritarian bent, President Nixon was quick to invite the public to accept his usurpations and violations of the Constitution as a small price for the country to pay for the grandiose "structure of peace" that he believed he was building together with the Soviets. This incipient alliance of the champions of peace in repression went a step further when the Soviet leaders emerged as vocal defenders of Nixon's constitutional abuses in the Watergate crisis. It is noteworthy also that the Nixon Administration was conspicuously silent about abuses of human rights in the Soviet Union. Regrettably, it may be that the cause of peace can be used no less readily than war as a justification for repression. There is even a superficial resemblance between peace and repression—both tend to be quiet—which should put us on our guard. In the period of détente, the first, tentative steps were taken toward nuclear-arms control (only to stall subsequently), but the totalitarian murk around the world thickened noticeably.

Having said that each generation has an obligation to survive, so that the future generations may be born, I would like to guard against a possible misinterpretation. It has become fashionable recently to suggest that in circumstances of extreme evil—including, especially, imprisonment in concentration camps—personal survival becomes a moral principle, and one that, indeed, takes precedence over the obligation to treat others decently. If this notion were accepted, then the Socratic message that mere survival is empty, and only an honorable life is worth living, would be overruled, and each person would be invited to treat other people however he liked as long as he survived. It might be thought that the obligation of the species to survive adds weight to this point of view. However, each generation's obligation to survive does not in fact lead to a similar obligation on the part of the individual, any more than the individual's obligation to sacrifice himself implies an obligation of self-sacrifice on the part of the species. On the contrary, the species' obligation to survive lays on each individual a new obligation to set aside his personal interest in favor of the general interest. (After all, his personal survival, which cannot last beyond the natural span of his life in any case, in no way aids the survival of the species, since the world's peril does not stem from any shortage of people.) For whereas there is no principle, whether practical, ethical, or divine, that overarches mankind and would offer a justification for its self-destruction, mankind still overarches each person, as it always has done, and summons him, at times, to act in favor of something larger than he is.

Implicit in everything that I have said so far about the nuclear predicament there has been a perplexity that I would now like to take up explicitly, for it leads, I believe, into the very heart of our response—or, rather, our lack of response—to the predicament. I have pointed out that our species is the most important of all the things that, as inhabitants of a common world, we inherit from the past generations, but it does not go far enough to point out this superior importance, as though in making our decision about extinction we were being asked to choose between, say, liberty, on the one hand, and the survival of the species, on the other. For the species not only overarches but contains all the benefits of life in the common world, and to speak of sacrificing the species for the sake of one of these benefits involves one in the absurdity of wanting to destroy something in order to preserve one of its parts, as if one were to burn down a house in an attempt to redecorate the living room, or to kill someone to improve his character. But even to point out this absurdity fails to take the full measure of the peril of extinction, for mankind is not some invaluable object that lies outside us and that we must protect so that we can go on benefitting from it; rather, it is we ourselves, without whom everything there is loses its value. To say this is another way of saying that extinction is unique not because it destroys mankind as an object but because it destroys mankind as the source of all possible human subjects, and this, in turn, is another way of saying that extinction is a second death, for one's own individual death is the end not of any object in life but of the subject that experiences all objects. Death, however, places the mind in a quandary. One of the confounding characteristics of death—"tomorrow's zero," in Dostoevski's phrase—is that, precisely because it removes the person himself rather than something in his life, it seems to offer the mind nothing to take hold of. One even feels it inappropriate, in a way, to try to speak "about" death at all, as though death were a thing situated somewhere outside us and available for objective inspection, when the fact is that it is within us—is, indeed, an essential part of what we are. It would be more appropriate, perhaps, to say that death, as a fundamental element of our being, "thinks" in us and through us about whatever we think about, coloring our thoughts and moods with its presence throughout our lives.

Extinction is another such intangible, incomprehensible, yet all-important presence, surrounding and pervading life without ever showing its face directly. Extinction is, in truth, even less tangibly present than death, because while death continually strikes down those around us, thereby at least reminding us of what death is, and reminding us that we, too, must die, extinction can, by definition, strike only once, and is, therefore, entirely hidden from our direct view; no one has ever seen extinction and no one ever will. Extinction is thus *a human future that can never become a human present.* For who will suffer this loss, which we somehow regard as supreme? We, the living, will not suffer it; we will be dead. Nor will the unborn shed any tears over their lost chance to exist; to do so they would have to exist already. The perplexity underlying the whole question of extinction, then, is that although extinction might appear to be the largest misfortune that mankind could ever suffer, it doesn't seem to happen *to* anybody, and one is left wondering where its impact is to be registered, and by whom.

Lucretius wrote, "Do you not know that when death comes, there will be no other you to mourn your memory, and stand above you prostrate?" And Freud wrote, "It is indeed impossible to imagine our own death: and whenever we attempt to do so, we can perceive that we are in fact still present as spectators." Thought and feeling try to peer ahead and catch a glimpse of death, but they encounter their own demise along the way, for their death is what death is. In the same way, when we try to picture extinction we come up against the fact that the human faculties with which someone might see, hear, feel, or understand this event are obliterated in it, and we are left facing a blankness, or emptiness. But even the words "blankness" and "emptiness" are too expressive—too laden with human response—because, inevitably, they connote the *experience* of blankness and emptiness, whereas extinction is the end of human experience. It thus seems to be in the nature of extinction to repel emotion and starve thought, and if the mind, brought face to face with extinction, descends into a kind of exhaustion and dejection it is surely in large part because we know that mankind cannot be a "spectator" at its own funeral any more than any individual person can.

It might be well to consider for a moment the novel shape of the mental and emotional predicament that the nuclear peril places us in—a predicament that exists not because of a psychological failing or the inadequacy of the human mind but because of the actual nature of the thing that we are trying to think about. Strange as it may seem, we may have to teach ourselves to think about extinction in a meaningful way. (This seems less strange when we recall that whereas people may have a natural aversion to death no similar instinct moves them to ward off extinction—although most people's spontaneous reaction to the idea is hardly favorable, either. Like the peril of extinction itself, recognition of the peril and understanding of it can come only as a product of our life together in the common world—as a product, that is, not of instinct but of civilization. Other species not only do not resist extinction but are completely unaware that it is happening; the last passenger pigeon had no way of knowing that it *was* the last passenger pigeon, much less of doing anything about it.) On first looking into the consequences of nuclear holocaust, one is struck by the odd fact that, beyond a certain point, the larger the imagined attack is, the less there is to say about it. At "low" levels of attack—the tens or hundreds of megatons—there is the complexity of the countless varieties of suffering and social and ecological breakdown to reflect on. But at higher levels—the thousands of megatons—the complexity steadily gives way to the simplicity and nothingness of death. Step by step, the "spectators" at the "funeral"—the sufferers of the calamity, in whose eyes it retains a human reality, and in whose lives it remains a human experience—dwindle away, until at last, when extinction is reached, all the "spectators" have themselves gone to the grave, and only the stones and stars, and whatever algae and mosses may have made it through, are present to witness the end.

Yet no matter how poor and thin a thing for imagination to grasp extinction may be, it seems to be in imagination alone that it can be grasped at all. Lacking the possibility of experience, all we have left is thought, since for us extinction is locked away forever in a future that can never arrive. Like the thought "I do not exist," the thought "Humanity is now extinct" is an impossible one for a rational person, because as soon as *it* is, *we* are not. In imagining any other event, we look ahead to a moment that is still within the stream of human time, which is to say within a time in which other human beings will exist, and will be responding to whatever they see, looking back to our present time and looking forward to future times that will themselves be within the sequence of human time. But in imagining extinction we gaze past everything human to a dead time that falls outside the human tenses of past, present, and future. By adopting a coldly scientific frame of mind, we can imagine that inert scene, but the exercise is oddly fruitless, and seems to hold no clue to the meaning of extinction. Instead, we find that almost everything that might engage our attention or stir our interest—even if only to repel us—has passed away. Struggling in this way to grasp the meaning of extinction, we may be led to wonder whether it can be grasped at all, and begin to suspect that nature provided an instinctual drive for the perpetuation of the species because it knew that our consciousness and will were so poorly equipped to deal with this task.

Given the special role of our mental faculties in any attempt to come to terms with extinction, it is not very surprising that a great deal of the writing that has been done about nuclear strategy is characterized by a highly abstract tone. The atmosphere in which this work goes forward is perfectly suggested by the nickname for the sort of institution in which much of it takes place: "the think tank." This term, evoking a hermetic world of thought, exactly reflects the intellectual circumstances of those thinkers whose job it is to deduce from pure theory, without the lessons of experience, what might happen if nuclear hostilities broke out. But, as Herman Kahn, the director of one of these think tanks (the Hudson Institute), and the author of "Thinking About the Unthinkable," among other works on nuclear strategy, has rightly said, "it will do no good to inveigh against theorists; in this field, everyone is a theorist." Hence, while in one sense Kahn is right to call a nuclear holocaust "unthinkable," it is also true, as his remark suggests, that when it comes to grasping the nature of this peril thinking about it is all that we *can* do.

The intellectual and affective difficulties involved in trying to understand the nuclear predicament have no precedent (unless one is to count individual death as a precedent), but they were foreshadowed in at least some respects by certain barriers that have impeded understanding of other sudden revolutionary developments of the modern age. In "Democracy in America," Tocqueville, speaking of the democratic revolution of his times, wrote, "Although the revolution that is taking place in the social condition, the laws, the opinions, and the feelings of men is still very far from being terminated, yet its results already admit of no comparison with anything that the world has ever before witnessed. I go back from age to age up to the remotest antiquity, but I find no parallel to what is occurring before my eyes; as the past has ceased to cast its light upon the future, the mind of man wanders in obscurity." But if in Tocqueville's day the past had ceased to cast its light upon the future, the present—what was occurring before his eyes—could still do so. Although the democratic revolution had not "terminated," it was nevertheless in full swing, and democratic America provided Tocqueville with enough factual material to fill the two thick volumes of his book. Drawing on this material, he was able to cast so much light on the future that we still see by it today.

The radical novelty of events became an even more troubling impediment to the understanding of totalitarian revolutions of our century. Arendt, who, more than anyone else, performed the offices of a Tocqueville in casting light on totalitarianism, wrote, "The gap between past and future ceased to be a condition peculiar only to the activity of thought and restricted as an experience to those few who made thinking their primary business. It became a tangible reality and perplexity for all; that is, it became a fact of political relevance." The totalitarian regimes, of course, made active attempts to revise or erase the factual record of both the past and the present. Yet these attempts have not been successful, and, in spite of the sense of unreality we feel when we confront the acts of the totalitarian regimes, totalitarianism is for us today something that has left its bloody marks on history, and these events, when we are told of them by credible witnesses, fill us with active revulsion. In Hitler's Germany and Stalin's Russia, horrifying events of dreamlike incredibility occurred, and pure, everyday common sense might reject their very possibility if the historical record were not there. In Arendt's "Eichmann in Jerusalem," we read the following description of the gassing to death by the Nazis of Jews in Poland:

> This is what Eichmann saw: The Jews were in a large room; they were told to strip; then a truck arrived, stopping directly before the entrance to the room, and the naked Jews were told to enter it. The doors were closed and the truck started off. "I cannot tell [how many Jews entered, Eichmann said later], I hardly looked. I could not; I could not; I had had enough. The shrieking, and . . . I was much too upset, and so on, as I later told Müller when I reported to him; he did not get much profit out of my report. I then drove along after the van, and then I saw the most horrible sight I had thus far seen in my life. The truck was making for an open ditch, the doors were opened, and the corpses were thrown out, as though they were still alive, so smooth were their limbs. They were hurled into the ditch, and I can still see a civilian extracting the teeth with tooth plyers."

We don't want to believe this: we find it all but impossible to believe this. But our wishful disbelief is stopped cold by the brute historical fact that it *happened*: we are therefore forced to believe. But extinction *has not happened*, and hides behind the veil of a future time when human eyes can never pierce. It is true that the testimony of those who survived the bombings of Hiroshima and Nagasaki offers us a vivid record of devastation by nuclear arms, but this record, which already seems to exhaust our powers of emotional response, illumines only a tiny corner of a nuclear holocaust, and, in any case, does not reach the question of extinction, which, instead of presenting us with scenes of horror, puts an end to them, just as it puts an end to all other scenes that are enacted by human beings. After several centuries of bringing a variety of nightmarish futures into existence, we have now invented one so unbelievable and overwhelming that it cannot come to pass at all. ("Come to pass" is a perfect phrase to describe what extinction cannot do. It can "come," but not "to pass," for with its arrival the creature that divides time into past, present, and future—the creature before whose eyes it would "pass"—is annihilated.) Deprived of both past and present experience to guide us as we try to face the nuclear predicament, we are left in the unpromising position of asking the future to shed light on itself.

As we look ahead to the possibility of extinction, our secret thought, which is well founded in the facts of the case, may be that since everyone will then be dead no one will have to worry about it, so why should we worry about it now? Following this unacknowledged but logical line of thinking, we may be led to the shrug of indifference that seems to have characterized most people's conscious reaction to the nuclear peril for the last thirty-six years. If extinction is nothing, we may unconsciously ask ourselves, may not no reaction be the right one? By contrast, our thoughts and feelings experience no such defeat when we consider a privation of future generations which falls short of denying them their existence—when we imagine, for example, that their supply of oil will run out, or that their supply of food will grow short, or that their civilization will go into decline. Then, through the widest possible extension of our respect for individual life, we can picture their plight, sympathize with their suffering, and perhaps take some action to forestall the evil. In effect, we are still following the ethical precept of doing unto others as we would have them do unto us, now expanding our understanding of who the others are to include the unborn, as Burke did. This comes naturally to us, as Burke pointed out, because a moment's reflection reveals to us the debt of gratitude that we owe past generations. However, in extending our sympathetic concern in this way, of course, we make the tacit assumption that there will *be* future generations, taking it for granted that nature, acting in and through us, will bring them forth, as it always has done. And in the pre-nuclear world, before it was in our power to extinguish the species, this confidence was warranted. But now the creation of new human beings is just the thing that is in question; and, in our attempt to grasp not the suffering and death of future generations but their failure to come into existence in the first place, a sympathetic response is inappropriate, for sympathy can extend only to living beings, and extinction is the foreclosure of life. The shuddering anticipation that we may feel on behalf of others when we realize that they are threatened with harm is out of place, because the lack of any others is the defining feature of extinction.

In removing the sufferer and his suffering with one blow, extinction again shows its resemblance to death. Montaigne writes, "Death can put an end, and deny access, to all our other woes," and adds, "What stupidity to torment ourselves about passing into exemption from all torment!" Extinction likewise brings not suffering but the end of suffering. Among feelings, suffering and joy are opposites, but both, like all feelings, are manifestations of life, and, as such, are together opposites of either death or extinction. Never having faced the end of human life before, we are led by mental habit to try to respond to it as though it were a disaster of one kind or another, in which people were going to be harmed or bereaved. But in doing so we strain for a reaction that, to our puzzlement, perhaps, does not come, for the excellent reason that in extinction there is no disaster: no falling buildings, no killed or injured people, no shattered lives, no mourning survivors. All of that is dissolved in extinction, along with everything else that goes on in life. We are left only with the ghostlike cancelled future generations, who, metaphorically speaking, have been waiting through all past time to enter into life but have now been turned back by us.

The distinction between harm to people in the world and the end of the world—or even the end of *a* world, such as occurred to European Jewry under Hitler—may give us some clue to the nature of what Arendt, borrowing a phrase of Kant's in order to describe the unparalleled crimes of Hitler's Germany and Stalin's Soviet Union, has called "radical evil." The "true hallmark" of radical evil, "about whose nature so little is known," she says, is that we do not know either how to punish these offenses or how to forgive them, and they therefore "transcend the realm of human affairs and the potentialities of human power, both of which they radically destroy wherever they make their appearance." By crimes that "transcend the realm of human affairs and the potentialities of human power," she means, I believe, crimes so great that they overwhelm the capacity of every existing system of jurisprudence, or other organized human response, to deal with them adequately. She goes on to say, "Here, where the deed itself dispossesses us of all power, we can indeed only repeat with Jesus: 'It were better for him that a millstone were hanged about his neck, and he cast into the sea.'" I would like to suggest that evil becomes radical whenever it goes beyond destroying individual victims (in whatever numbers) and, in addition, mutilates or destroys the *world* that can in some way respond to—and thus in some measure redeem—the deaths suffered. This capacity of evil was demonstrated on a large scale in modern times by the totalitarian regimes, which, in a manner of speaking, attempted to tear gaping, unmendable holes in the fabric of the world—holes into which entire peoples or classes would sink without a trace—but now it has fully emerged in the capacity of the species for self-extinction, which, by ending the world altogether, would "dispossess us of all power" forever. When crimes are of a certain magnitude and character, they nullify our power to respond to them adequately because they smash the human context in which human losses normally acquire their meaning for us. When an entire community or an entire people is destroyed, most of those who would mourn the victims, or bring the perpetrators to justice, or forgive them, or simply remember what occurred, are themselves destroyed. When that community is all mankind, the loss of the human context is total, and no one is left to respond. In facing this deed, we will either respond to it before it is done, and thus avoid doing it, or lose any chance to respond, and pass into oblivion.

If this interpretation is correct, every episode of radical evil is already a small extinction, and should be seen in that light. Between individual death and biological extinction, then, there are other possible levels of obliteration, which have some of the characteristics of extinction. The "end of civilization"—the total disorganization and disruption of human life, breaking the links between mankind's past and its future—is one. Genocide—the destruction of a people—which can be seen as an extinction *within* mankind, since it eliminates an element in the interior diversity of the species, is another; in fact, genocide, including, above all, Hitler's attempt to extinguish the Jewish people, is the closest thing to a precursor of the extinction of the species that history contains. What the end of civilization, genocide, and extinction all have in common is that they are attacks not merely on existing people and things but on either the biological or the cultural heritage that human beings transmit from one generation to the next; that is, they are crimes against the future. The connection between genocide and extinction is further suggested by the fact that what the superpowers *intend* to do if a holocaust breaks out (leaving aside the unintended "collateral effects" for the moment) is to commit genocide against one another—to erase the other side as a culture and as a people from the face of the earth. In its nature, human extinction is and always will be without precedent, but the episodes of radical evil that the world has already witnessed are warnings to us that gigantic, insane crimes are not prevented from occurring merely because they are "unthinkable." On the contrary, they may be all the more likely to occur for that reason. Heinrich Himmler, a leading figure in the carrying out of the destruction of the Jews, assured his subordinates from time to time that their efforts were especially noble because by assuming the painful burden of making Europe "Jew-free" they were fighting "battles which future generations will not have to fight again." His remark applies equally well to a nuclear holocaust, which might render the earth "human-free." This is another "battle" (and the word is as inappropriate for a nuclear holocaust as it was for the murder of millions of Jews) that "future generations will not have to fight again."

If our usual responses to disasters and misfortunes are mis-matched to the peril of extinction, then we have to look in some other quarter of our being to find its significance. Individual death once more offers a point of departure. We draw closer to death throughout our lives, but we never arrive there, for just as we are about to arrive we are gone. Yet although death thus always stands outside life, it nevertheless powerfully conditions life. Montaigne writes, "You are in death while you are in life; for you are after death when you are no longer in life. Or, if you prefer it this way, you are dead after life; but during life you are dying; and death affects the dying much more roughly than the dead, and more keenly and essentially." We are similarly "in extinction" while we are in life, and are after extinction when we are extinct. Extinction, too, thus affects the living "more roughly" and "more keenly and essentially" than it does the nonliving, who in its case are not the dead but the unborn. Like death, extinction is felt not when it has arrived but beforehand, as a deep shadow cast back across the whole of life. The answer to the question of who experiences extinction and when, therefore, is that we the living experience it, now and in all the moments of our lives. Hence, while it is in one sense true that extinction lies outside human life and never happens to anybody, in another sense extinction saturates our existence and never stops happening. If we want to find the meaning of extinction, accordingly, we should start by looking with new eyes at ourselves and the world we live in, and at the lives we live. The question to be asked then is no longer what the features and characteristics of extinction are but what it says about us and what it does to us that we are preparing our own extermination.

Because the peril is rooted in basic scientific knowledge, which is likely to last as long as mankind does, it is apparently a permanent one. But in the presence of that peril opposite poles of response, both in feeling and, above all, in action, are possible, and the quality of the lives we live together is conditioned in opposite ways according to which response we choose. The choice is really between two entire ways of life. One response is to decline to face the peril, and thus to go on piling up the instruments of doom year after year until, by accident or design, they go off. The other response is to recognize the peril, dismantle the weapons, and arrange the political affairs of the earth so that the weapons will not be built again. I remarked that we do not have two earths at our disposal—one for experimental holocausts and the other to live on. Neither do any of us have two souls—one for responding to the nuclear predicament and the other for living the rest of our lives. In the long run, if we are dull and cold toward life in its entirety we will become dull and cold toward life in its particulars—toward the events of our own daily lives—but if we are alert and passionate about life in its entirety we will also be alert and passionate about it in its dailiness.

It is a matter of record that in our thirty-six years of life in a nuclear-armed world we have been largely dead to the nuclear peril, and I would like to consider more closely what this failure of response seems to have been doing to our world. Pascal, taking note of the cerebral character of the condition of mortality, once observed that "it is easier to endure death without thinking about it than to endure the thought of death without dying." His observation perfectly describes our response so far to the peril of extinction: we have found it much easier to dig our own grave than to think about the fact that we are doing so. Almost everyone has acknowledged on some level that the peril exists, but the knowledge has been without consequences in our feelings and our actions, and the superpowers have proceeded with their nuclear buildups, in the recent words of George Kennan, "like the victims of some sort of hypnotism, like men in a dream, like lemmings heading for the sea."

For a very short while before and after the first bomb was produced, a few men at and near the top of the American government seemed prepared to deal with the nuclear predicament at its proper depth. One of them was Secretary of War Henry Stimson, who knew of the Manhattan Project and, in March of 1945—four months before the Trinity test, at Alamogordo—confided to his diary an account of a discussion he had had about the new weapon with Harvey Bundy, his closest personal assistant. "Our thoughts," he wrote, "went right down to the bottom facts of human nature, morals, and governments, and it is by far the most searching and important thing that I have had to do since I have been here in the Office of the Secretary of War because it touches matters which are deeper even than the principles of present government." Yet those deep thoughts somehow did not take root firmly enough in the hearts of the American leaders or of the world at large, and the old ways of thinking returned, in the teeth of the new facts. The true dimensions of the nuclear peril, and of its significance for mankind, had been glimpsed, but then the awareness faded and the usual exigencies of international political life—including, shortly, the Cold War between the United States and the Soviet Union—laid claim to people's passions and energies. The nuclear buildup that has continued to this day began, and the nuclear question, having emerged abruptly from the twofold obscurity of scientific theory and governmental secrecy, was almost immediately thrust into the new obscurity of the arcane, abstract, denatured world of the theorists in the think tanks, who were, in effect, deputized to think the "unthinkable" thoughts that the rest of us lacked the will to think.

Thus began the strange double life of the world which has continued up to the present. On the one hand, we returned to business as usual, as though everything remained as it always had been. On the other hand, we began to assemble the stockpiles that could blow this supposedly unaltered existence sky-high at any second. When the scientists working on the Manhattan Project wanted to send word to President Truman, who was at the Potsdam Conference, that the detonation near Alamogordo had been successful, they chose the horrible but apt code phrase "Babies satisfactorily born." Since then, these "babies"—which are indeed like the offspring of a new species, except that it is a species not of life but of anti-life, threatening to end life—have "proliferated" steadily under our faithful care, bringing forth "generation" after "generation" of weapons, each more numerous and more robust than the last, until they now threaten to do away with their creators altogether. Yet while we did all this we somehow kept the left hand from knowing—or from dwelling on—what the right hand was doing; and the separation of our lives from awareness of the doom that was being prepared under us and around us was largely preserved.

It is probably crucial psychologically in maintaining this divorce that, once Hiroshima and Nagasaki had been pushed out of mind, the nuclear peril grew in such a way that while it relentlessly came to threaten the existence of everything, it physically touched nothing, and thus left people free not to think about it if they so chose. Like a kindhearted executioner, the bomb permitted its prospective victims to go on living seemingly ordinary lives up to the day that the execution should suddenly and without warning be carried out. (If one nuclear bomb had gone off each year in one of the world's cities, we can well imagine that public attitudes toward the nuclear peril would now be quite different.) The continuity, however illusory, between the pre-nuclear world and the nuclear world which was made possible by these years of not using nuclear weapons was important in preserving the world's denial of the peril because it permitted a spurious normality to be maintained—although "normality" was at times embraced with a fervor that betrayed an edge of hysterical insecurity. The spectacle of life going on as usual carried with it a strong presumption that nothing much was wrong. When we observed that no one seemed to be worried, that no one was showing any signs of alarm or doing anything to save himself, it was hard to resist the conclusion that everything was all right. After all, if we were reasonable people and we were doing nothing how could there be anything the matter? The totality of the peril, in particular, helped to disguise it, for, with everyone and everything in the world similarly imperilled, there was no flight from imperilled things to safe things—no flow of capital from country to country, or migration of people from one place to another. Thoughts of the nuclear peril were largely banned from waking life, and relegated to dreams or to certain fringes of society, and open, active concern about it was restricted to certain "far-out" people, whose ideas were on the whole not so much rejected by the supposedly sober, "realistic" people in the mainstream as simply ignored. In this atmosphere, discussion of the nuclear peril even took on a faintly embarrassing aura, as though dwelling on it were somehow melodramatic, or were a sophomoric excess that serious people outgrew with maturity.

It was not unless one lifted one's gaze from all the allegedly normal events occurring before one's eyes and looked at the executioner's sword hanging over everyone's head that the normality was revealed as a sort of mass insanity. This was an insanity that consisted not in screaming and making a commotion but precisely in *not* doing these things in the face of overwhelming danger, as though everyone had been sedated.

Passengers on a ship who are eating, sunning themselves, playing shuffleboard, and engaging in all the usual shipboard activities appear perfectly normal as long as their ship is sailing safely in quiet seas, but these same passengers doing these same things appear deranged if in full view of them all their ship is caught in a vortex that may shortly drag it and them to destruction. Then their placidity has the appearance of an unnatural loss of normal human responses—of a pathetic and sickening acquiescence in their own slaughter. T. S. Eliot's well-known lines "This is the way the world ends/Not with a bang but a whimper" may not be literally correct—there will decidedly be a very big bang—but in a deeper sense it is certainly right; if we do end the world, the sequence is likely to be not a burst of strong-willed activity leading to a final explosion but enervation, dulled senses, enfeebled will, stupor, and paralysis. Then death.

Since we have not made a positive decision to exterminate ourselves but instead have chosen to live on the edge of extinction, periodically lunging toward the abyss only to draw back at the last second, our situation is one of uncertainty and nervous insecurity rather than of absolute hopelessness. We know that we may fall into the abyss at any moment, but we also know that we may not. So life proceeds—what else should it do?—but with a faltering and hesitant step, like one who gropes in darkness at the top of a tall precipice. Intellectually, we recognize that we have prepared ourselves for self-extermination and are improving the preparations every day, but emotionally and politically we have failed to respond. Accordingly, we have begun to live *as if* life were safe, but living *as if* is very different from just living. A split opens up between what we know and what we feel. We place our daily doings in one compartment of our lives and the threat to all life in another compartment. However, this split concerns too fundamental a matter to remain restricted to that matter alone, and it begins to influence the rest of life. Before long, denial of reality becomes a habit—a dominant mode in the life of society—and unresponsiveness becomes a way of life. The society that has accepted the threat of its utter destruction soon finds it hard to react to lesser ills, for a society cannot be at the same time asleep and awake, insane and sane, against life and for life.

To say that we and all future generations are threatened with extinction by the nuclear peril, however, is to describe only half of our situation. The other half is that we are the authors of that extinction. (For the populations of the superpowers, this is true in a positive sense, since we pay for extinction and support the governments that pose the threat of it, while for the peoples of the non-nuclear-armed world it is true only in the negative sense that they fail to try to do anything about the danger.) Like all those who are inclined to suicide, we approach the action in two capacities: the capacity of the one who would kill and that of the one who would be killed. As when we dream, we are both the authors and the sufferers of our fate. Therefore, when we hide from ourselves the immense preparations that we have made for our self-extermination we do so for two compelling reasons. First, we don't want to recognize that at any moment our lives may be taken away from us and our world blasted to dust, and, second, we don't want to face the fact that we are potential mass killers. The moral cost of nuclear armament is that it makes of all of us underwriters of the slaughter of hundreds of millions of people and of the cancellation of the future generations—an action whose utter indefensibility is not altered in the slightest degree by the fact that each side contemplates performing it only in "retaliation." In fact, as we shall see, this retaliation is one of the least justified actions ever contemplated, being wholly pointless. It is another nonsensical feature of the nuclear predicament that while each side regards the population of the other side as the innocent victims of unjust government, each proposes to punish the other government by annihilating that already suffering and oppressed population. Nor is there any exoneration from complicity in this slaughter in the theoretical justification that we possess nuclear arms not in order to use them but in order to prevent their use, for the fact is that even in theory prevention works only to the degree that it is backed up by the plausible threat of use in certain circumstances. Strategy thus commits us all to actions that we cannot justify by any moral standard. It introduces into our lives a vast, morally incomprehensible—or simply immoral—realm, in which every scruple or standard that we otherwise claim to observe or uphold is suspended. To be targeted from the cradle to the grave as a victim of indiscriminate mass murder is degrading in one way, but to target others for similar mass murder is degrading in another and, in a sense, a worse way. We endeavor to hold life sacred, but in accepting our roles as the victims and the perpetrators of nuclear mass slaughter we convey the steady message—and it is engraved more and more deeply on our souls as the years roll by—that life not only is not sacred but is worthless; that, somehow, according to a "strategic" logic that we cannot understand, it has been judged acceptable for everybody to be killed.

As it happens, our two roles in the nuclear predicament have been given visual representation in the photographs of the earth that we have taken with the aid of another technical device of our time, the spaceship. These pictures illustrate, on the one hand, our mastery over nature, which has enabled us to take up a position in the heavens and look back on the earth as though it were just one more celestial body, and, on the other, our weakness and frailty in the face of that mastery, which we cannot help feeling when we see the smallness, solitude, and delicate beauty of our planetary home. Looking at the earth as it is caught in the lens of the camera, reduced to the size of a golf ball, we gain a new sense of scale, and are made aware of a new relation between ourselves and the earth: we can almost imagine that we might hold this earth between the giant thumb and forefinger of one hand. Similarly, as the possessors of nuclear arms we stand outside nature, holding instruments of cosmic power with which we can blot life out, while at the same time we remain embedded in nature and depend on it for our survival.

Yet although the view from space is invaluable, in the last analysis the view that counts is the one from earth, from within life—the view, let us say, from a bedroom window in some city, in the evening, overlooking a river, perhaps, and with the whole colored by some regret or some hope or some other human sentiment. Whatever particular scene might come to mind, and whatever view and mood might be immediately present, from this earthly vantage point another view—one even longer than the one from space—opens up. It is the view of our children and grandchildren, and of all the future generations of mankind, stretching ahead of us in time—a view not just of one earth but of innumerable earths in succession, standing out brightly against the endless darkness of space, of oblivion. The thought of cutting off life's flow, of amputating this future, is so shocking, so alien to nature, and so contradictory to life's impulse that we can scarcely entertain it before turning away in revulsion and disbelief. The very incredibility of the action protects it from our gaze; our very love of life seems to rush forward to deny that we could do this. But although we block out the awareness of this self-posed threat as best we can, engrossing ourselves in life's richness to blind ourselves to the jeopardy to life, ultimately there is no way that we can remain unaffected by it. For finally we know and deeply feel that the ever-shifting, ever-dissolving moments of our mortal lives are sustained and given meaning by the broad stream of life, which bears us along like a force at our backs. Being human, we have, through the establishment of a common world, taken up residence in the enlarged space of past, present, and future, and if we threaten to destroy the future generations we harm ourselves, for the threat we pose to them is carried back to us through the channels of the common world that we all inhabit together. Indeed, "they" are we ourselves, and if their existence is in doubt our present becomes a sadly incomplete affair, like only one word of a poem, or one note of a song. Ultimately, it is subhuman.

Because the weight of extinction, like the weight of mortality, bears down on life through the mind and spirit but otherwise, until the event occurs, leaves us physically undisturbed, no one can prove that it alters the way we live. We can only say that it hardly stands to reason that the largest peril that history has ever produced—a peril in which, indeed, history would swallow itself up—should leave the activities of life, every one of which is threatened with dissolution, unaffected; and that we actually do seem to find life changing in ways that might be expected. Since the future generations are specifically what is at stake, all human activities that assume the future are undermined directly. To begin with, desire, love, childbirth, and everything else that has to do with the biological renewal of the species have been administered a powerful shock by the nuclear peril. The timeless, largely unspoken confidence of the species that although each person had to die, life itself would go on—the faith that on earth life was somehow favored, which found one of its most beautiful expressions in Christ's admonition "Consider the lilies of the field, how they grow; they toil not, neither do they spin: And yet I say unto you, That even Solomon in all his glory was not arrayed like one of these"—has been shaken, and with it the also largely unspoken confidence that people had in their own instinctual natures has been upset. It seems significant that Freud, who pioneered our century's self-consciousness in sexual matters, should have been one of the first observers to warn that humanity was headed down a path of self-destruction. In the last paragraph of "Civilization and Its Discontents," published in 1930, he wrote:

> The fateful question for the human species seems to me to be whether and to what extent their cultural development will succeed in mastering the disturbance of their communal life by the human instinct of aggression and self-destruction. It may be that in this respect precisely the present time deserves a special interest. Men have gained control over the forces of nature to such an extent that with their help they would have no difficulty in exterminating one another to the last man. They know this, and hence comes a large part of their current unrest, their unhappiness and their mood of anxiety. And now it is to be expected that the other of the two "Heavenly Powers," eternal Eros, will make an effort to assert himself in the struggle with his equally immortal adversary [death]. But who can foresee with what success and with what result?

It is as though Freud perceived that the balance between man's "lower," animal, and instinctual nature, which had historically been so much feared and despised by religious men and philosophers as a disruptive force in man's spiritual development, and his "higher," rational nature had tipped in favor of the latter—so that now the greater danger to man came not from rampant, uncontrolled instinct breaking down the restraining bonds of reason and self-control but from rampant reason oppressing and destroying instinct and nature. And rampant reason, man found, was, if anything, more to be feared than rampant instinct. Bestiality had been the cause of many horrors, but it had never threatened the species with extinction; some instinct for self-preservation was still at work. Only "selfless" reason could ever entertain the thought of self-extinction. Freud's merciful, solicitous attitude toward the animal in our nature foreshadowed the solicitude that we now need to show toward the animals and plants in our earthly environment. Now reason must sit at the knee of instinct and learn reverence for the miraculous instinctual capacity for creation.

It may be a symptom of our disordered instinctual life that, increasingly, sexuality has lost its hiding place in the privacy of the bedroom and been drawn into the spotlight of public attention, where it becomes the subject of debate, advice, and technical instruction, just like any other fully public matter. In Freud's day, open discussion of sexual questions helped to free people from a harshly restrictive Victorian morality, but in our day it appears that sex, which no longer suffers from that traditional suppression, is drawn into the open because something has gone wrong with it and people want to repair it. By making it a public issue, they seem to acknowledge indirectly that our instincts have run up against an obstacle, as indeed they have, and are in need of public assistance, as indeed they are. Odd as it may seem, the disorder of our private, or once private, lives may require a political solution, for it may not be until the human future has been restored to us that desire can again find a natural place in human life.

The biological continuity of the species is made into a fully human, worldly continuity by, above all, the institution of marriage. Marriage lends permanence and a public shape to love. Marriage vows are made by a man and a woman to one another, but they are also made before the world, which is formally present at the ceremony in the role of witness. Marriage *solemnizes* love, giving this most inward of feelings an outward form that is acknowledged by everyone and commands everyone's respect. In swearing their love in public, the lovers also let it be known that their union will be a fit one for bringing children into the world—for receiving what the Bible calls "the grace of life." And the world, by insisting on a ceremony, and by attending in the role of witness, announces its stake in its own continuity. Thus, while in one sense marriage is the most personal of actions, in another sense it belongs to everybody. In a world that is perpetually being overturned and plowed under by birth and death, marriage—which for this reason is rightly called an "institution"—lays the foundation for the stability of a human world that is built to house all the generations. In this sense as well as in the strictly biological sense and the emotional sense, love creates the world.

The peril of extinction surrounds such love with doubt. A trembling world, poised on the edge of self-destruction, offers poor soil for enduring love to grow in. Everything that this love would build up, extinction would tear down. "Eros, builder of cities" (in Auden's phrase, in his poem eulogizing Freud on the occasion of his death) is thwarted. Or, to put it brutally but truthfully, every generation that holds the earth hostage to nuclear destruction holds a gun to the head of its own children. In laying this trap for the species, we show our children no regard, and treat them with indifference and neglect. As for love itself, love lives in the moment, but the moment is dying, as we are, and love also reaches beyond its moment to dwell in a kind of permanence. For

> Love's not Time's fool, though rosy lips and cheeks
> Within his bending sickle's compass come;
> Love alters not with his brief hours and weeks,
> But bears it out even to the edge of doom.

But if doom's edge draws close, love's vast scope is narrowed and its resolve may be shaken. The approach of extinction drives love back into its perishable moment, and, in doing so, tends to break up love's longer attachments, which now, on top of all the usual vicissitudes, have the weight of the whole world's jeopardy to bear.

There is, in fact, an odd resemblance between the plight of love and the plight of war in the nuclear world. Military hostilities, having been stopped by dread of extinction from occurring on the field of battle, are relegated to a mental plan—to the world of strategic theory and war games, where the generals of our day sit at their computer terminals waging shadow wars with the ostensible aim of making sure that no real hostilities ever happen. Love, too, although it has not been prevented altogether, has in a way lost its full field of action—the world that included the future generations—and so has tended to withdraw to a mental plane peculiarly its own, where it becomes an ever more solitary affair: impersonal, detached, pornographic. It means something that we call both pornography and nuclear destruction "obscene." In the first, we find desire stripped of any further human sentiment or attachment—of any "redeeming social value," in the legal phrase. In the second, we find violence detached from any human goals, all of which would be engulfed in a holocaust—detached, that is, from all redeeming social value.

The Japanese used to call the pleasure quarters of their cities "floating worlds." Now our entire world, cut adrift from its future and its past, has become a floating world. The cohesion of the social realm—the dense and elaborate fabric of life that is portrayed for us in the novels of the nineteenth century, among other places, inspiring "nostalgic" longing in us—is disintegrating, and people seem to be drifting apart and into a weird isolation. The compensation that is offered is the license to enjoy life in the moment with fewer restrictions; but the present moment and its pleasures provide only a poor refuge from the emptiness and loneliness of our shaky, dreamlike, twilit world. The moment itself, unable to withstand the abnormal pressure of expectation, becomes distorted and corrupted. People turn to it for rewards that it cannot offer—certainly not when it is ordered to do so. Plucked out of life's stream, the moment—whether a moment of love or of spiritual peace, or even of simple pleasure in a meal—is no longer permitted to quietly unfold and be itself but is strenuously tracked down, manipulated, harried by instruction and advice, bought and sold, and, in general, so roughly manhandled that the freshness and joy that it can yield up when it is left alone are corrupted or destroyed.

It is fully understandable that in the face of the distortion and disintegration of human relationships in a doom-ridden world a "conservative" longing for a richer, more stable, and more satisfying social existence should spring up. Unfortunately, however, this longing, instead of inspiring us to take political measures that would remove the world from jeopardy, and thus put life on a solid footing again, all too often takes the form of a simple *wish* that the world would stop being the way it is now and return to its former state, with what are often called "the old values" intact. Rather than take cognizance of the radical causes of the world's decline, with a view to doing something about them, these would-be upholders of the past tend to deny the existence of our new situation. It is only one more part of this denial—the most dangerous part—to imagine that war, too, still exists in its traditional form, in which one's enemies can be defeated on the field of battle without bringing an end to everything. Conservatism in personal and social questions has often gone together with militarism in the past, but now the combination is far more perilous than ever before. It represents a denial of what the world has now become which could lead to the end of the world. If a nation indulges itself in the illusion that, even with nuclear arms, war is possible, and that "victory" can be won with them, it risks bringing about its own and the world's extinction by mistake. Alert and realistic conservatives, by contrast, would see that everything that anyone might wish to conserve is threatened by nuclear weapons, and would recognize in them a threat not only to "the old values" but to any values whatever. And instead of dreaming of the vanished wars of past times they would place themselves in the forefront of a movement for disarmament.

Politics, as it now exists, is even more thoroughly compromised than personal and social life by the peril of extinction. Marriage lays down its map of hereditary lines across the unmarked territory of generational succession, shaping the rudiments of a common world out of biological reproduction, which without marriage would continue anyway, as it did before civilization was born, and does still among animals. Marriage is thus half submerged in the unconscious, instinctual, biological life of the species, and only half emergent into the "daylight" (in Hegel's term) of history and the common world. Politics, on the other hand, is wholly the creature of the common world, and could have no existence without it. (If people did not have reason and language, they could still reproduce but they could not set up a government among themselves.) There is no political "moment," as there is a sensual moment, to fall back on in an attempted retreat from the futility of a jeopardized common world. Politics, accordingly, is fully stuck with the glaring absurdity that with one hand it builds for a future that with the other hand it prepares to destroy. Each time a politician raises his voice to speak of making a better world for our children and grandchildren (and this is an intrinsic part of what politics is about, whether or not it happens to be explicitly stated), the peril of extinction is there to gainsay him with the crushing rebuttal: But there may *be* no children or grandchildren. And when, far more ridiculously, politicians let us know of their desire for a "place in history," it is not only their swollen vanity that invites anger but their presumption in trying to reserve a place in a history whose continued existence their own actions place in doubt.

Since Aristotle, it has often been said that the two basic aims of political association are, first, to assure the survival of members of society (that is, to protect life) and, second, to give them a chance to fulfill themselves as social beings (that is, to enable them to lead a noble or a good life). The threat of self-extermination annuls both of these objectives, and leaves the politics of our day in the ludicrous position of failing even to aim at the basic goals that have traditionally justified its existence. If our economy were to produce a wonderful abundance of silverware, glasses, and table napkins but no food, people would quickly rebel and insist on a different system. The world's political arrangements, which now aim at providing some accoutrements of life but fail to lift a finger to save life itself, are in no less drastic need of replacement. People cannot for long place confidence in institutions that fail even to recognize the most urgent requirement of the whole species, and it is therefore not surprising that, more and more, people do actually look on politicians with contempt, though perhaps without having quite figured out why.

As long as politics fails to take up the nuclear issue in a determined way, it lives closer than any other activity to the lie that we have all come to live—the pretense that life lived on top of a nuclear stockpile can last. Meanwhile, we are encouraged not to tackle our predicament but to inure ourselves to it: to develop a special, enfeebled vision, which is capable of overlooking the hugely obvious; a special, sluggish nervous system, which is conditioned not to react even to the most extreme and urgent peril; and a special, constricted mode of political thinking, which is permitted to creep around the edges of the mortal crisis in the life of our species but never to meet it head on. In this timid, crippled thinking, "realism" is the title given to beliefs whose most notable characteristic is their failure to recognize the chief reality of the age, the pit into which our species threatens to jump; "utopian" is the term of scorn for any plan that shows serious promise of enabling the species to keep from killing itself (if it is "utopian" to want to survive, then it must be "realistic" to be dead); and the political arrangements that keep us on the edge of annihilation are deemed "moderate," and are found to be "respectable," whereas new arrangements, which might enable us to draw a few steps back from the brink, are called "extreme" or "radical." With such fear-filled, thought-stopping epithets as these, the upholders of the status quo defend the anachronistic structure of their thinking, and seek to block the revolution in thought and in action which is necessary if mankind is to go on living.

Works of art, history, and thought, which provide what Arendt calls the "publicity" that makes an intergenerational common world possible, are undermined at their foundations by the threat of self-extermination. Each such work is a vessel that bears the distillation of some thought, feeling, or experience from one generation to another. In his 1970 Nobel Prize acceptance speech, Solzhenitsyn said, "Woe to that nation whose literature is disturbed by the intervention of power. Because that is not just a violation against 'freedom of print,' it is the closing down of the heart of the nation, a slashing to pieces of its memory." In reminding us that totalitarian governments seek to break the connections between generations, which are so inconvenient to all monomaniacal campaigns, Solzhenitsyn might well have been demonstrating that totalitarianism is indeed one of the precursors of the peril of extinction, which puts an end to all the generations. (The difference is that whereas totalitarianism destroys the memories, extinction destroys all the rememberers.) A work of art will often celebrate the most evanescent thing—a glance, a vague longing, the look of a certain shadow—but as soon as the artist picks up his brush or his pen he takes up residence in the immortal common world inhabited by all generations together. As the poets have always told us, art rescues love and other mortal things from time's destruction. And it is not only the artists who reach beyond their own lifetimes with art; it is also the readers, listeners, and viewers, who while they are in the presence of a work of art are made contemporary with it and, in a way, with all other readers, listeners, and viewers, in all ages. Through art, we "are able to break bread with the dead, and without communion with the dead a fully human life is impossible" (Auden). The timeless appeal of the greatest works of art, in fact, testifies to our common humanity as few other things do, and is one of the strongest grounds we have for supposing that a political community that would embrace the whole earth and all generations is also possible.

The other side of art's communion with the dead (which is the basis for Camus's lovely remark "As an artist . . . I began by admiring others, which in a way is heaven on earth") is its communion with the unborn. In nothing that we do are the unborn more strongly present than in artistic creation. It is the very business of artists to speak to future audiences, and therefore it is perhaps not surprising that they—probably more than any other observers, at least in the modern age—have been gifted with prophetic powers. (In our century, the name of Kafka, who seemed to foresee in so many particulars the history of our time, inevitably comes to mind.) Indeed, great works of art are often so closely attuned to the future that it takes the world a few decades to understand them. There is no doubt that art, which breaks into the crusted and hardened patterns of thought and feeling in the present as though it were the very prow of the future, is in radically altered circumstances if the future is placed in doubt. The ground on which the artist stands when he turns to his work has grown unsteady beneath his feet. In the pre-nuclear world, an artist who hoped to enable future generations to commune with his time might be worried that his work would be found wanting by posterity and so would pass into oblivion, but in the nuclear world the artist, whose work is still subject to this danger, must also fear that even if he produces nothing but timeless masterpieces they will fall into oblivion anyway, because there will be no posterity. The masterpieces cannot be timeless if time itself stops. The new uncertainty is not that one's work will be buried and forgotten in the tumult of history but that history, which alone offers the hope of saving anything from time's destruction, will itself be buried in the indifference of the nonhuman universe, dragging all human achievements down with it. The two fates, which now constitute a double jeopardy for artistic creation, are utterly different. In the first, it is life—the "onslaught of the generations," in Arendt's phrase—that undoes the work while itself surviving. In the second, it is death that swallows up both life and the work. The first peril makes us feel our individual mortality more keenly, but, for that very reason, makes us feel the common life of the species more strongly, and both feelings may inspire us to increase our efforts to accomplish whatever it is that we hope to offer the world before we die. The second peril threatens not each individual work but the world to which all works are offered, and makes us feel that even if we did accomplish our individual aims it would be pointless, thus undercutting our will to accomplish anything at all.

It would be futile to try to prescribe to art what it "can" and "cannot" do, as though we in the present had a visionary capacity to foresee art's future forms and, like an omniscient critic, accept some while ruling out others; but it is possible to reflect on what has already occurred, and to wonder what role political and other events in the world may have played in this or that development. Bearing in mind the irreducible mysteriousness of artistic creativity, we may note that some of the developments in art in recent decades have the look of logical, if unconscious, adjustments to the newly imperilled condition of the species. The art critic and social and political observer Harold Rosenberg has spoken of a "de-definition" of art, by which he meant a blurring of the boundary lines that have traditionally separated artistic creation from other human activities. Among the distinctions that have been lost—or deliberately breached—are the ones between the artist and his work of art and between the work of art and its audience. Rosenberg found the first breach in Action painting, in which the meaning of the work came to reside in the action of painting rather than in the finished canvas, and he found the second in all those artistic events that are called "happenings," in which the audience is more or less dispensed with and the "aesthetic effects are given by the event itself, without intervention on the part of the spectator-participant." In trying to do away with the enduring, independently existing art product and its audience, and concentrating on the act of creation, these artists, who "left art behind," seemed to be working toward an art that would fulfill itself—like the sexual act that is isolated from the past and the future—in the moment, thus giving up on communion with the dead and with the unborn: doing away, in fact, with art's whole dependence on the common world, which assumes the existence of the human future. If art could manage this, of course, it would escape the futility of trying to communicate with generations that now may never arrive. Politics is simply powerless to cut itself off from the future and compress itself into a highly charged present (although some of the radical students of the nineteen-sixties seemed at times to be making the attempt), but art may have more leeway for experimentation, perhaps because, as the traditional rescuer of fleeting things from oblivion, it starts off being closer to life in the moment. Whether these experiments can produce much that is worthwhile is another question. Rosenberg spoke of "all those ruses of scrutinizing itself and defiantly denying its own existence" by which art has survived in recent decades, but he held out little hope that these devices could sustain art much longer. Looked at in terms of the predicament of the species as a whole, art appears to be in a quandary. Art attempts both to reflect the period in which it was produced and to be timeless. But today, if it wishes to truthfully reflect the reality of its period, whose leading feature is the jeopardy of the human future, art will have to go out of existence, while if it insists on trying to be timeless it has to ignore this reality—which is nothing other than the jeopardy of human time—and so, in a sense, tell a lie. Art by itself is powerless to solve its predicament, and artists, like lovers, are in need of assistance from statesmen and ordinary citizens.

By threatening to cancel the future generations, the nuclear peril not only throws all our activities that count on their existence into disorder but also disturbs our relationship with the past generations. We need the assurance that there will be a future if we are to take on the burden of mastering the past—a past that really does become the proverbial "dead past," an unbearable weight of millennia of corpses and dust, if there is no promise of a future. Without confidence that we will be followed by future generations, to whom we can hand on what we have received from the past, it becomes intolerably depressing to enter the tombs of the dead to gather what they have left behind; yet without that treasure our life is impoverished. The present is a fulcrum on which the future and the past lie balanced, and if the future is lost to us, then the past must fall away, too.

Death lies at the core of each person's private existence, but part of death's meaning is to be found in the fact that it occurs in a biological and social world that survives. No one can be a spectator at his own funeral, but others can be there, and the anticipation of their presence, which betokens the continuity of life and all that that means for a mortal creature, is consolation to each person as he faces his death. Death suffered in the shadow of doom lacks this consolation. It is a gap that threatens soon to be lost in a larger gap—a death within a greater death. When human life itself is overhung with death, we cannot go peacefully to our individual deaths. The deaths of others, too, become more terrible: with the air so full of death, every death becomes harder to face. When a person dies, we often turn our thoughts to the good he did while he was alive—to that which he gave to the world, and which therefore outlasts him in the world's affection. (When someone who did great harm to the world dies, we feel that death has had a more thorough victory, since there is so little of his that the world wishes to preserve. Rather, it may wish to bury him even more thoroughly than any grave can.) But when the whole world, in which the dead in a sense live on, is imperilled, this effort at remembrance and preservation seems to lose its point, and all lives and deaths are threatened with a common meaninglessness.

There have been many deaths in our century that in certain respects resembled those that would be suffered in a nuclear holocaust: the deaths of the millions of people who died in the concentration camps of the totalitarian regimes, which sought not only to kill their victims but to extirpate their memory from the historical record. Because the camps threatened people not only with death but with oblivion, remembrance has become for some survivors a passion and a sacred obligation. When Solzhenitsyn accepted the Nobel Prize, he was at pains to remind the world that he spoke on behalf of millions who had not survived, and his whole historical reconstruction of the Soviet camp system is pitted against totalitarian forgetfulness. Likewise, the command "Never forget," so often heard in connection with the Nazis' genocidal attack on the Jews, is important not only because it may help the world to prevent any repetition but because remembering is in itself an act that helps to defeat the Nazis' attempt to send a whole people into oblivion. Just because genocide, by trying to prevent

the future generations of people from being born, commits
a crime against the future, it lays a special obligation on the
people of the future to deal with the crime, even long after its
perpetrators are themselves dead. The need to bear witness and
then to remember was felt first by the inmates of the camps and
only later by the world at large. The French journalist David
Rousset, a survivor of several camps, including Buchenwald,
has written of his experiences in those camps:

> How many people here still believe that a protest has even his-
> toric importance? This skepticism is the real masterpiece of the
> S.S. Their great accomplishment. They have corrupted all human
> solidarity. Here the night has fallen on the future. When no wit-
> nesses are left, there can be no testimony. To demonstrate when
> death can no longer be postponed is an attempt to give death a
> meaning, to act beyond one's own death. In order to be success-
> ful, a gesture must have social meaning. There are hundreds of
> thousands of us here, all living in absolute solitude.

Thanks to a few heroic witnesses, and to the existence outside the totalitarian world of a nontotalitarian world, which
could find out about what happened and then remember it,
the connections between the camp victims and the rest of humanity were never altogether severed. There *was* testimony, the
"historic importance" of the events in the camps *was* preserved,
"human solidarity" *was* partly maintained, however tragically
late, and the "masterpiece" of the S.S. was spoiled. Indeed, if
we read the testimony of those in the camps deeply enough
it may help us in our effort to avoid our extinction. Arendt,
writing in her classic study "The Origins of Totalitarianism,"
made the connection:

> Here [in the camps], there are neither political nor historical
> nor simply moral standards but, at the most, the realization that
> something seems to be involved in modern politics that actually
> should never be involved in politics as we used to understand it,
> namely all or nothing—all, and that is an undetermined infinity
> of forms of human living-together, or nothing, for a victory of
> the concentration-camp system would mean the same inexorable
> doom for human beings as the use of the hydrogen bomb would
> mean the doom of the human race.

Yet we must insist, I think, that in fact extinction by nuclear arms would be the more profound oblivion, since then the very possibility of remembrance or renewal—of the existence of a Solzhenitsyn or Rousset to bear witness, or of an Arendt to reflect on their testimony, or of readers to ponder what happened and take it to heart—would be gone. In extinction, and only in extinction, the connections between the victims and the rest of humanity would really be severed forever, and the "masterpiece" of the mass murderers would be perfected, for the night would have "fallen on the future" once and for all. Of all the crimes against the future, extinction is the greatest. It is the murder of the future. And because this murder cancels all those who might recollect it even as it destroys its immediate victims the obligation to "never forget" is displaced back onto us, the living. It is we—the ones who will either commit this crime or prevent it—who must bear witness, must remember, and must arrive at the judgment.

A nuclear holocaust would destroy the living and cancel the unborn in the same blow, but it is possible, as I mentioned earlier, at least to imagine that, through sterilization of the species, the future generations could be cancelled while the living were left unharmed. Although the condition of being extinct is by definition beyond experience this remnant—the living cells of the dead body of mankind—would, like a prisoner who knows that he is condemned to die on a certain day, be forced to look extinction in the face in a way that we, who can always tell ourselves that we may yet escape extinction, are not. To them, the futility of all the activities of the common world—of marriage, of politics, of the arts, of learning, and, for that matter, of war—would be driven home inexorably. They would experience in their own lives the breakdown of the ties that bind individual human beings together into a community and a species, and they would feel the current of our common life grow cold within them. And as their number was steadily reduced by death they would witness the final victory of death over life. One wonders whether in these circumstances people would want to go on living at all—or whether they might not choose to end their own lives. By killing off the living quickly, extinction by nuclear arms would spare us those barren, bitter decades of watching and feeling the end close in. As things are, we will never experience the approach of extinction in that pure form, and are left in an irremediable uncertainty. Nevertheless, the spectre of extinction hovers over our world and shapes our lives with its invisible but terrible pressure. It now accompanies us through life, from birth to death. Wherever we go, it goes, too; in whatever we do, it is present. It gets up with us in the morning, it stays at our side throughout the day, and it gets into bed with us at night. It is with us in the delivery room, at the marriage ceremony, and on our deathbeds. It is the truth about the way we now live. But such a life cannot go on for long.

Because the unborn generations will never experience their cancellation by us, we have to look for the consequences of extinction before it occurs, in our own lives, where it takes the form of a spiritual sickness that corrupts life at the invisible, innermost starting points of our thoughts, moods, and actions. This emphasis on us, however, does not mean that our only reason for restraining ourselves from elimination of the future generations is to preserve them as auxiliaries to *our* needs—as the audience for our works of art, as the outstretched hands to receive our benefactions (and so to bring our otherwise frustrated charitable impulses to fulfillment), as the minds that will provide us with immortality by remembering our words and deeds, and as the successors who will justify us by carrying on with the tasks that we have started or advanced. To adopt such an expedient view of the future generations would be to repeat on a monumental scale the error of the philanthropist who looks on the needy only as a convenient prop with which he can develop and demonstrate his moral superiority, or the more familiar and more dangerous figure of the politician who looks on the public only as a ladder on which he can climb to power. It would also put us in the company of those who, in pursuit, very often, of visionary social goals, make the opposite but closely related error of regarding the *present* generations only as auxiliaries—as the expendable bricks and mortar to be used in the construction of a glorious palace in which the future generations will take up residence. (We have merely to remember how many people have been murdered so that "history" might "go forward" to be reminded how great the costs of this mistake have been.) Whether we were subordinating the living or the unborn generations, this reduction of human beings to a supporting role in the completion of cross-generational tasks would suggest that we had come to place a higher value on the achievements of life than we did on life itself, as though we were so dazzled by the house man lives in that we had forgotten who lives there. But no human being, living or unborn, should be regarded as an auxiliary. Although human beings have their obligations to fulfill, they are not to be seen as beasts of burden whose purpose in existing is to carry on with enterprises that are supposedly grander and more splendid than they are. For in the last analysis these enterprises, which together make up the common world, are meant to serve life, not to be served by it. Life does not exist for the sake of the governments, the buildings, the books, and the paintings; all these exist for the sake of life. The works of man are great, but man himself is greater.

The reason that so much emphasis must be laid on the living generations is not that they are more important than the unborn but only that at any given moment they, by virtue of happening to be the ones who exist, are the ones who pose the peril, who can feel the consequences of the peril in their lives, and who can respond to the peril on behalf of all other generations. To cherish life—whether one's own or someone else's, a present life or an unborn life—one must already be in life, and only the living have this privilege. The question that the peril of extinction puts before the living, however, is: Who would miss human life if they extinguished it? To which the only honest answer is: Nobody. That being so, we have to admit that extinction is no loss, since there cannot be loss when there is no loser: and we are thus driven to seek the meaning of extinction in the mere anticipation of it by the living, whose lives this anticipation corrupts and degrades. However, there is another side to the entire question. For while it is true that extinction cannot be felt by those whose fate it is—the unborn, who would stay unborn—the same cannot be said, of course, for extinction's alternative, survival. If we shut the unborn out of life, they will never have a chance to lament their fate, but if we let them into life they will have abundant opportunity to be glad that they were born instead of having been prenatally severed from existence by us. The idea of escaping extinction before one was born is a strange one for us, since it is so new, but to generations that live deep in nuclear time, and who know that their existence has depended on the wisdom and restraint of a long succession of generations before them, we can be sure that the idea will be familiar.

Of every other bequest that the present makes to the future it can be said that that which would be gratefully received if it was given would also be sorely missed if it was withheld. Of life alone is it the case that while its receipt can be welcomed, its denial cannot be mourned. The peril of extinction, by bringing us up against this reality, concentrates our attention in a new way on the simple and basic fact that before there can be good or evil, service or harm, lamenting or rejoicing there *must be life*. (Even those who wish to exploit and harm other human beings must first want human beings to exist.) In coming to terms with the peril of extinction, therefore, what we must desire first of all is that people be born, for their own sakes, and not for any other reason. Everything else—our wish to serve the future generations by preparing a decent world for them to live in, and our wish to lead a decent life ourselves in a common world made secure by the safety of the future generations—flows from this commitment. Life comes first. The rest is secondary.

To recapitulate: In a nuclear holocaust great enough to extinguish the species, every person on earth would die; but in addition to that, and distinct from it, is the fact that the unborn generations would be prevented from ever existing. However, precisely because the unborn are not born, they cannot experience their plight, and its meaning has to be sought among the living, who share a common world with the unborn as well as with the dead, and who find that if they turn their backs on the unborn, and deny them life, then their own lives become progressively more twisted, empty, and despairing. On the other hand, if instead of asking what the act of extinction means we ask what the act of survival means—and in the nuclear world survival has, for the first time, become an act—we find that the relationship between the generations is reconstituted, and we can once again ask what the meaning of our actions will be for the people directly affected by them, who now, because they are presumed to exist, can be presumed to have a response.

By acting to save the species, and repopulating the future, we break out of the cramped, claustrophobic isolation of a doomed present, and open a path to the greater space—the only space fit for human habitation—of past, present, and future. Suddenly, we can think and feel again. Even by merely imagining for a moment that the nuclear peril has been lifted and human life has a sure foothold on the earth again, we can feel the beginnings of a boundless relief and calm—a boundless peace. But we can open this path only if it is our desire that the unborn exist for their own sake. We trace the effects of extinction in our own world because that is the only place where they can ever appear, yet those sad effects, important as they are, are only the side effects of our shameful failure to fulfill our main obligation of valuing the future human beings themselves. And if at first we find these future people to be somewhat abstract we have only to remind ourselves that we, too, were once "the future generation," and that every unborn person will be as vivid and important to himself as each of us is to himself. We gain the right perspective on extinction not by trying to peer into the inhuman emptiness of a post-human universe but by putting ourselves in the shoes of someone in the future, who, precisely because he has been allowed to be born, can rejoice in the fact of being alive.

With the generation that has never known a world unmenaced by nuclear weapons, a new order of the generations begins. In it, each person alive is called on to assume his share of the responsibility for guaranteeing the existence of all future generations. And out of the new sense of responsibility must come a worldwide program of action for preserving the species. This program would be the guarantee of existence for the unborn and the measure of the honor and the humanity of the living. Its inauguration would mark the foundation of a new common world, which would greatly transcend the old, pre-nuclear common world in importance and in the strength of its ties. Without such a program in place, nothing else that we undertake together can make any practical or moral sense. Thus, the nuclear peril, while for the first time in history placing the whole common world in jeopardy, at the same time draws into that common world much that was formerly left out, including, above all, the terrestrial biological inheritance. Through the jeopardy of our biological substance, even the things that belong to what Arendt called the "private realm" are affected, so that ultimately it is not only the institutions, arts, and sciences—the enduring, heavy structure of the world—whose meaning is changed but also the fleeting things: sensation, desire, "the summer lightning of individual happiness" (Alexander Herzen). Against the background of the new double mortality of life, the fleeting things seem even more flickering, and more to be protected and cherished.

By threatening life in its totality, the nuclear peril creates new connections between the elements of human existence—a new mingling of the public and the private, the political and the emotional, the spiritual and the biological. In a strikingly pertinent remark, Arendt, speaking of the individual's capacity for action, writes, "With word and deed we insert ourselves into the human world, and this insertion is like a second birth, in which we confirm and take upon ourselves the naked fact of our original physical appearance." Now the whole species is called on literally to take on itself the naked fact of its original physical appearance—to protect our being through an act of our will. Formerly, the future was simply given to us; now it must be achieved. We must become the agriculturalists of time. If we do not plant and cultivate the future years of human life, we will never reap them. This effort would constitute a counterpart in our conscious life of reason and will of our instinctual urge to procreate. And in so doing it would round out and complete the half-finished common world of pre-nuclear times, which, by the time nuclear weapons were invented, had enabled mankind to learn and to suffer but not to act as one.

In asking us to cherish the lives of the unborn, the peril of extinction takes us back to the ancient principle of the sacredness of human life, but it conducts us there by a new path. Instead of being asked not to kill our neighbors, we are asked to let them be born. If it is possible to speak of a benefit of the nuclear peril, it would be that it invites us to become more deeply aware of the miracle of birth, and of the world's renewal. "For unto us a child is born." This is indeed "good news." Yet when we turn from extinction, which silences us with its nothingness, to the abundance of life, we find ourselves tongue-tied again, this time by the fullness of what lies before our eyes. If death is one mystery, life is another, greater one. We find ourselves confronted with the essential openness, unfathomability, and indefinability of our species. (Auden has observed that human nature is indefinable because definition is a historical act that can upset the human reality it seeks to define.) We can only feel awe before a mystery that both is what we are and surpasses our understanding.

Without violating that mystery, we can perhaps best comprehend the obligation to save the species simply as a new relationship among human beings. Because the will to save the species would be a will to let other people into existence rather than a will to save oneself, it is a form of respect for others, or, one might say, a form of love. (By contrast, the will to avoid the holocaust, which would kill off every living person, involves self-interest, and would grow, in part, out of fear. Thus, as we face the nuclear predicament in its entirety, both love and fear are present, but they are inspired by threats to different things.) This love, I believe, would bear a resemblance to the generative love of parents, who in wanting to bring children into the world have some experience of what it is to hope for the renewal of life. They know that when a child is born the whole world is reborn with it, as in a sunrise, since it is only in the mind, heart, and spirit of each human being that the human world has existence. If the ideal for the relationship among living people is brotherhood, then the ideal for the relationship of the living to the unborn is parenthood. Universal brotherhood, which seeks to safeguard lives that are already in existence, embodies the solicitude and protectiveness of love, and its highest command, therefore, is "Thou shalt not kill." Universal parenthood, which would seek to bring life into existence out of nothing, would embody the creativity and abundant generosity of love, and its highest commandment, therefore, would be "Be fruitful and multiply." But this commandment is not the strictly biological one. The nuclear peril makes all of us, whether we happen to have children of our own or not, the parents of all future generations. Parental love, which begins even before any child exists, is unconditional. It does not attach to any quality of the beloved; it only wants him to be. But then all love, when it is deep, has something in it of this character, and is ready to forgive every particular failing in the beloved. Shakespeare says that "love is not love which alters when it alteration finds," and we know from the Bible that "love keeps no accounts."

The common world itself can be seen as a product of the superabundance of life's fruitfulness. It is like a surplus, beyond what each generation can use for itself, that is passed on in a steadily growing accumulation, enabling all the generations to participate in a *life* of mankind which transcends individual life and is not undone by individual death. Extinction is a second death, and this second life is the life that it destroys.

Since the future generations will surely do and suffer wrong, it is part of the work of this love to come to terms with evil. Love is given Job's task: to accept and affirm the creation even in the full knowledge of the unspeakable injustice and suffering that it contains. Thus, while our capacity for sympathizing with the suffering of others is of no help in understanding extinction, because there is no suffering (or any other human experience) in it, it would not be right to say that the question of suffering does not come up, for *in saving* the future generations we will bring them every kind of suffering that life holds (together with every other human experience). The fact that it is not extinction but life that brings suffering, and even death, is the clearest proof that extinction is misconceived as a disaster in any ordinary sense. On the contrary, survival means disaster— endlessly, as long as life is beset by accident and folly. In the pre-nuclear common world, our aim was to spare all generations every particular evil that it was in our power to resist, but now our determination must be first to give the future generations all the evils, which are as much a part of life as breathing, and only then to set about mitigating them. Fortunately or unfor- tunately, we cannot pick and choose which experiences of life to give the future generations. Either we keep them out of life completely or we get them in for all of it.

To favor life on these terms is difficult, but it is not inhuman. We find this affirmation in one form in parental love and we find it in another form in religious faith, as the example of Job attests. Augustine wrote that after his introduction to Christianity "no more did I long for better things, because I thought of all things, and with a sounder judgment I held that the higher things are indeed better than the lower, but that all things together are better than the higher things alone." And he wrote, "All things, by the very fact that they *are*, are good." A Japanese Buddhist monk seems to have been saying the same thing even more simply when he said, "Every day is a good day." A similar affirmation runs through the ceremonial words of Christian sacramental occasions. Marriage vows, in which the couple swear to love one another in sickness and in health and "for better for worse," seem to signify an affirmation not only of the married condition but of the whole human condition. And in the words sometimes spoken in burial services the affirmation is made outright: "Ashes to ashes, dust to dust. The Lord gave, and the Lord hath taken away; blessed be the name of the Lord."

The first principles of life in the new common world would be respect for human beings, born and unborn, based on our common love of life and our common jeopardy in the face of our own destructive powers and inclinations. This respect would grow out of each generation's gratitude to past generations for having permitted it to exist. Each generation would look on itself as though it were a delegation that had been chosen by an assembly of all the dead and all the unborn to represent them in life. The living would thus look on the gift of life the way any political representative should look on election to office—as a temporary trust to be used for the common good. For if the surface of the globe is the breadth of the world, time, which politics is now called on to guarantee, is its depth, and we cannot expect the world to cohere horizontally if it is not joined together vertically as well. In this new world, the people of the present generations, if they acquit their responsibility, would be the oldest of the grandfathers, and their role would be that of founders.

A second principle of life in the nuclear common world would be respect for the earth. This is nothing but a full realization of the ecological principle, according to which the earth's environment is seen not merely as a surrounding element in which it is more or less pleasant to live but as the foundation of human as of other life. The oneness of the earth as a system of support for life is already visible around us. Today, no matter how strenuously statesmen may assert the "sovereign" power of their nations, the fact is that they are all caught in an increasingly fine mesh of global life, in which the survival of each nation depends on the survival of all. There is no "sovereign" right to destroy the earthly creation on which everyone depends for survival (although such a right is exactly what each superpower now claims for itself). More and more, the earth is coming to resemble a single body, or, to use Dr. Thomas's metaphor, a single cell, which is inhabited by billions of separate intelligences and wills. In these circumstances, the use of violence is like the left hand attacking the right, or like both hands attacking the throat. We want to maintain the independence of each person's mind and will—for our liberty consists in this—but in doing so we must not kill the one terrestrial body in which we are all incarnated together.

A third principle would be respect for God or nature, or whatever one chooses to call the universal dust that made, or became, us. We need to remember that neither as individuals nor as a species have we created ourselves. And we need to remember that our swollen power is not a power to create but only a power to destroy. We can kill all human beings and close down the source of all future human beings, but we cannot create even one human being, much less create those terrestrial conditions which now permit us and other forms of life to live. Even our power of destruction is hardly our own. As a fundamental property of matter, nuclear energy was nature's creation, and was only discovered by us. (What is truly our own is the knowledge that has enabled us to exploit this energy.) With respect to creation, things still stand as they have always stood, with extra-human powers performing the miracle, and human beings receiving the fruits. Our modest role is not to create but only to preserve ourselves. The alternative is to surrender ourselves to absolute and eternal darkness: a darkness in which no nation, no society, no ideology, no civilization will remain; in which never again will a child be born; in which never again will human beings appear on the earth, and there will be no one to remember that they ever did.

III. THE CHOICE

Four and a half billion years ago, the earth was formed. Perhaps a half billion years after that, life arose on the planet. For the next four billion years, life became steadily more complex, more varied, and more ingenious, until, around a million years ago, it produced mankind—the most complex and ingenious species of them all. Only six or seven thousand years ago—a period that is to the history of the earth as less than a minute is to a year—civilization emerged, enabling us to build up a human world, and to add to the marvels of evolution marvels of our own: marvels of art, of science, of social organization, of spiritual attainment. But, as we built higher and higher, the evolutionary foundation beneath our feet became more and more shaky, and now, in spite of all we have learned and achieved—or, rather, because of it—we hold this entire terrestrial creation hostage to nuclear destruction, threatening to hurl it back into the inanimate darkness from which it came. And this threat of self-destruction and planetary destruction is not something that we will pose one day in the future, if we fail to take certain precautions; it is here now, hanging over the heads of all of us at every moment. The machinery of destruction is complete, poised on a hair trigger, waiting for the "button" to be "pushed" by some misguided or deranged human being or for some faulty computer chip to send out the instruction to fire. That so much should be balanced on so fine a point—that the fruit of four and a half billion years can be undone in a careless moment—is a fact against which belief rebels. And there is another, even vaster measure of the loss, for stretching ahead from our present are more billions of years of life on earth, all of which can be filled not only with human life but with human civilization. The procession of generations that extends onward from our present leads far, far beyond the line of our sight, and, compared with these stretches of human time, which exceed the whole history of the earth up to now, our brief civilized moment is almost infinitesimal. And yet we threaten, in the name of our transient aims and fallible convictions, to foreclose it all. If our species does destroy itself, it will be a death in the cradle—a case of infant mortality. The disparity between the cause and the effect of our peril is so great that our minds seem all but powerless to encompass it. In addition, we are so fully enveloped by that which is menaced, and so deeply and passionately immersed in its events, which are the events of our lives, that we hardly know how to get far enough away from it to see it in its entirety. It is as though life itself were one huge distraction, diverting our attention from the peril to life. In its apparent durability, a world menaced with imminent doom is in a way deceptive. It is almost an illusion. Now we are sitting at the breakfast table drinking our coffee and reading the newspaper, but in a moment we may be inside a fireball whose temperature is tens of thousands of degrees. Now we are on our way to work, walking through the city streets, but in a moment we may be standing on an empty plain under a darkened sky looking for the charred remnants of our children. Now we are alive, but in a moment we may be dead. Now there is human life on earth, but in a moment it may be gone.

Once, there was time to reflect in a more leisurely way on our predicament. In August, 1945, when the invention of the bomb was made known through its first use on a human population, the people of Hiroshima, there lay ahead an interval of decades which might have been used to fashion a world that would be safe from extinction by nuclear arms, and some voices were in fact heard counselling deep reflection on the looming peril and calling for action to head it off. On November 28, 1945, less than four months after the bombing of Hiroshima, the English philosopher Bertrand Russell rose in the House of Lords and said:

> We do not want to look at this thing simply from the point of view of the next few years; we want to look at it from the point of view of the future of mankind. The question is a simple one: Is it possible for a scientific society to continue to exist, or must such a society inevitably bring itself to destruction? It is a simple question but a very vital one. I do not think it is possible to exaggerate the gravity of the possibilities of evil that lie in the utilization of atomic energy. As I go about the streets and see St. Paul's, the British Museum, the Houses of Parliament, and the other monuments of our civilization, in my mind's eye I see a nightmare vision of those buildings as heaps of rubble with corpses all round

them. That is a thing we have got to face, not only in our own country and cities, but throughout the civilized world.

Russell and others, including Albert Einstein, urged full, global disarmament, but the advice was disregarded. Instead, the world set about building the arsenals that we possess today. The period of grace we had in which to ward off the nuclear peril before it became a reality—the time between the moment of the invention of the weapons and the construction of the full-scale machinery for extinction—was squandered, and now the peril that Russell foresaw is upon us. Indeed, if we are honest with ourselves we have to admit that unless we rid ourselves of our nuclear arsenals a holocaust not only *might* occur but *will* occur—if not today, then tomorrow; if not this year, then the next. We have come to live on borrowed time: every year of continued human life on earth is a borrowed year, every day a borrowed day.

In the face of this unprecedented global emergency, we have so far had no better idea than to heap up more and more warheads, apparently in the hope of so thoroughly paralyzing ourselves with terror that we will hold back from taking the final, absurd step. Considering the wealth of our achievement as a species, this response is unworthy of us. Only by a process of gradual debasement of our self-esteem can we have lowered our expectations to this point. For, of all the "modest hopes of human beings," the hope that mankind will survive is the most modest, since it only brings us to the threshold of all the other hopes. In entertaining it, we do not yet ask for justice, or for freedom, or for happiness, or for any of the other things that we may want in life. We do not even necessarily ask for our personal survival; we ask only that we *be survived*. We ask for assurance that when we die as individuals, as we know we must, mankind will live on. Yet once the peril of extinction is present, as it is for us now, the hope for human survival becomes the most tremendous hope, just because it is the foundation for all the other hopes, and in its absence every other hope will gradually wither and die. Life without the hope for human survival is a life of despair.

The death of our species resembles the death of an individual in its boundlessness, its blankness, its removal beyond experience, and its tendency to baffle human thought and feeling, yet as soon as one mentions the hope of survival the similarities are clearly at an end. For while individual death is inevitable, extinction can be avoided; while every person must die, mankind can be saved. Therefore, while reflection on death may lead to resignation and acceptance, reflection on extinction must lead to exactly the opposite response: to arousal, rejection, indignation, and action. Extinction is not something to contemplate, it is something to rebel against. To point this out might seem like stating the obvious if it were not that on the whole the world's reaction to the peril of extinction has been one of numbness and inertia, much as though extinction were as inescapable as death is. Even today, the official response to the sickening reality before us is conditioned by a grim fatalism, in which the hope of ridding the world of nuclear weapons, and thus of surviving as a species, is all but ruled out of consideration as "utopian" or "extreme"—as though it were "radical" merely to want to go on living and to want one's descendants to be born. And yet if one gives up these aspirations one has given up on everything. As a species, we have as yet done nothing to save ourselves. The slate of action is blank. We have organizations for the preservation of almost everything in life that we want but no organization for the preservation of mankind. People seem to have decided that our collective will is too weak or flawed to rise to this occasion. They see the violence that has saturated human history, and conclude that to practice violence is innate in our species. They find the perennial hope that peace can be brought to the earth once and for all a delusion of the well-meaning who have refused to face the "harsh realities" of international life—the realities of self-interest, fear, hatred, and aggression. They have concluded that these realities are eternal ones, and this conclusion defeats at the outset any hope of taking the actions necessary for survival. Looking at the historical record, they ask what has changed to give anyone confidence that humanity can break with its violent past and act with greater restraint. The answer, of course, is that everything has changed. To the old "harsh realities" of international life has been added the immeasurably harsher new reality of the peril of extinction. To the old truth that all men are brothers has been added the inescapable new truth that not only on the moral but also on the physical plane the nation that practices aggression will itself die. This is the law of the doctrine of nuclear deterrence—the doctrine of "mutual assured destruction"—which "assures" the destruction of the society of the attacker. And it is also the law of the natural world, which, in its own version of deterrence, supplements the oneness of mankind with a oneness of nature, and guarantees that when the attack rises above a certain level the attacker will be engulfed in the general ruin of the global ecosphere. To the obligation to honor life is now added the sanction that if we fail in our obligation life will actually be taken away from us, individually and collectively. Each of us will die, and as we die we will see the world around us dying. Such imponderables as the sum of human life, the integrity of the terrestrial creation, and the meaning of time, of history, and of the development of life on earth, which were once left to contemplation and spiritual understanding, are now at stake in the political realm and demand a political response from every person. As political actors, we must, like the contemplatives before us, delve to the bottom of the world, and, Atlas-like, we must take the world on our shoulders.

The self-extinction of our species is not an act that anyone describes as sane or sensible; nevertheless, it is an act that, without quite admitting it to ourselves, we plan in certain circumstances to commit. Being impossible as a fully intentional act, unless the perpetrator has lost his mind, it can come about only through a kind of inadvertence—as a "side effect" of some action that we do intend, such as the defense of our nation, or the defense of liberty, or the defense of socialism, or the defense of whatever else we happen to believe in. To that extent, our failure to acknowledge the magnitude and significance of the peril is a necessary condition for doing the deed. We can do it only if we don't quite know what we're doing. If we did acknowledge the full dimensions of the peril, admitting clearly and without reservation that any use of nuclear arms is likely to touch off a holocaust in which the continuance of all human life would be put at risk, extinction would at that moment become not only "unthinkable" but also undoable. What is needed to make extinction possible, therefore, is some way of thinking about it that at least partly deflects our attention from what it is.

And this way of thinking is supplied to us, unfortunately, by our political and military traditions, which, with the weight of almost all historical experience behind them, teach us that it is the way of the world for the earth to be divided up into independent, sovereign states, and for these states to employ war as the final arbiter for settling the disputes that arise among them. This arrangement of the political affairs of the world was not intentional. No one wrote a book proposing it; no parliament sat down to debate its merits and then voted it into existence. It was simply there, at the beginning of recorded history; and until the invention of nuclear weapons it remained there, with virtually no fundamental changes. Unplanned though this arrangement was, it had many remarkably durable features, and certain describable advantages and disadvantages; therefore, I shall refer to it as a "system"—the system of sovereignty. Perhaps the leading feature of this system, and certainly the most important one in the context of the nuclear predicament, was the apparently indissoluble connection between sovereignty and war. For without sovereignty, it appeared, peoples were not able to organize and launch wars against other peoples, and without war they were unable to preserve their sovereignty from destruction by armed enemies. (By "war" I here mean only international war, not revolutionary war, which I shall not discuss.) Indeed, the connection between sovereignty and war is almost a definitional one—a sovereign state being a state that enjoys the right and the power to go to war in defense or pursuit of its interests.

It was into the sovereignty system that nuclear bombs were born, as "weapons" for "war." As the years have passed, it has seemed less and less plausible that they have anything to do with war; they seem to break through its bounds. Nevertheless, they have gone on being fitted into military categories of thinking. One might say that they appeared in the world in a military disguise, for it has been traditional military thinking, itself an inseparable part of the traditional political thinking that belonged to the system of sovereignty, that has provided those intentional goals—namely, national interests—in the pursuit of which extinction may now be brought about unintentionally, or semi-intentionally, as a "side effect." The system of sovereignty is now to the earth and mankind what a polluting factory is to its local environment. The machine produces certain things that its users want—in this case, national sovereignty—and as an unhappy side effect extinguishes the species.

The ambivalence resulting from the attempt to force nuclear weapons into the preëxisting military and political system has led to a situation in which, in the words of Einstein—who was farseeing in his political as well as in his scientific thought—"the unleashed power of the atom has changed everything save our modes of thinking, and we thus drift toward unparalleled catastrophes." As Einstein's observation suggests, the nuclear revolution has gone quite far but has not been completed. The question we have to answer is whether the completion will be extinction or a global political revolution—whether the "babies" that the scientists at Alamogordo brought forth will put an end to us or we will put an end to them. For it is not only our thoughts but also our actions and our institutions—our global political arrangements in their entirety—that we have failed to change. We live with one foot in each of two worlds. As scientists and technicians, we live in the nuclear world, in which whether we choose to acknowledge the fact or not, we possess instruments of violence that make it possible for us to extinguish ourselves as a species. But as citizens and statesmen we go on living in the pre-nuclear world, as though extinction were not possible and sovereign nations could still employ the instruments of violence as instruments of policy—as "a continuation of politics by other means," in the famous phrase of Karl von Clausewitz, the great philosopher of war. In effect, we try to make do with a Newtonian politics in an Einsteinian world. The combination is the source of our immediate peril. For governments, still acting within a system of independent nation-states, and formally representing no one but the people of their separate, sovereign nations, are driven to try to defend merely national interests with means of destruction that threaten not only international but intergenerational and planetary doom. In our present-day world, in the councils where the decisions are made there is no one to speak for man and for the earth, although both are threatened with annihilation.

The peril that the scientists have brought into our lives stems from hitherto unknown properties of the physical universe, but it is not an external, self-propelled peril—as though they had discovered that forces in the interior of the earth were one day going to blow it up, or that a huge asteroid was one day going to collide with it. Rather, the peril comes from our own actions—from within us—and if we had never sought to harm one another the energy latent in matter would have remained locked up there, without posing any threat to anybody. Thus, the peril of extinction by nuclear arms is doubly ours: first, because we have it in our power to prevent the catastrophe, and, second, because the catastrophe cannot occur unless, by pursuing our political aims through violence, we bring it about. Since military action is the one activity through which we deliberately threaten to employ our new mastery over nature to destroy ourselves, nothing could be more crucial to an understanding of the practical dimensions of the nuclear predicament than a precise understanding of what nuclear weapons have done to war, and, through war, to the system of sovereignty of which war has traditionally been an indispensable part. All war is violent, but not all violence is war. War is a violent means employed by a nation to achieve an end, and, like all mere means, is subject to Aristotle's rule "The means to the end are not unlimited, for the end itself sets the limit in each case." The possible ends of war are as varied as the desires and hopes of men, having ranged from the recovery of a single beautiful woman from captivity to world conquest, but every one of them would be annihilated in a nuclear holocaust. War is destructive, but it is also a human phenomenon—complex, carefully wrought, and, in its way, fragile and delicate, like its maker—but nuclear weapons, if they were ever used in large numbers, would simply blow war up, just as they would blow up everything else that is human.

One of the respects in which war is unique among the uses to which mankind's steadily increasing technical skills have been put is that in war no benefit is obtained and no aim achieved unless the powers involved exert themselves to the limit, or near-limit, of their strength. In the words of Clausewitz: "War is an act of violence pushed to its utmost bounds; as one side dictates to the other, there arises a sort of reciprocal action which logically must lead to an extreme." For only at the extremes are victory and defeat—the results of war—brought

about. Even when victory and defeat are not absolute, the
terms of the disengagement are determined by the nearness
of one side to defeat. In this case, the antagonists, like chess
players near the end of the game, see the inevitable outcome
and spare themselves the trouble of actually going through the
final moves. As Clausewitz writes, "everything is subject to a
supreme law: which is the *decision by arms.*" Therefore, "all
action . . . takes place on the supposition that if the solution by
force of arms which lies at its foundation should be realized,
it will be a favorable one." For "the decision by arms is, for
all operations, great and small, what cash payment is in bill
transactions," and "however remote from each other these
relations, however seldom the realization may take place, still
it can never entirely fail to occur." Nuclear arms ruin war by
making the decision by arms impossible. The decision by arms
can occur only when the strength of one side or the other is
exhausted, or when its exhaustion is approached. But in nuclear "war" no one's strength fails until *both* sides have been
annihilated. There cannot be a victor without a vanquished,
the collapse of whose military efforts signals the end of the
hostilities, permitting the victor to collect his spoils. But when
both adversaries have nuclear arms that moment of collapse
never comes, and the military forces—the missiles—of both
countries go on "fighting" after the countries themselves have
disappeared. From the point of view of a power contemplating
war in the pre-nuclear world, war appeared to depend on the
possession of great strength, since the side that possessed the
greater strength had the better chance of being victorious. But
when war is seen from the point of view of the nuclear world
it becomes clear that as an institution—as the mechanism with
which sovereign states settled their disputes—war depended,
above all, on weakness: the weakness of the defeated party,
whose collapse made the decision by arms (the whole purpose
of war) possible. And this weakness, in turn, depended on the
presence of certain technical limitations on the ability of mankind in general to avail itself of natural forces for destructive
purposes. When science made the energy in mass available to
man, the crucial limits were removed, for everybody, forever,
and the exhaustion of the defeated party—and so the triumph
of the victor—was rendered impossible. War itself has thus

proved to be a casualty of the tremendous means that were put at its disposal by science. We are now in a position to see that helplessness has always been the specific product of war, and weakness its essential ingredient. War has never been anything but unilateral disarmament—the disarmament of one side by the other. But now, before the exhaustion of either party can be reached, everyone will be dead, and all human aims—the aims pursued in the "war" and all others—will have been nullified. In a nuclear conflict between the United States and the Soviet Union—the holocaust—not only the adversaries but also the world's bystanders will vanish. In this "war," instead of one side winning and the other losing, it is as though all human beings lost and all the weapons won. Clausewitz writes, "War can never be separated from political intercourse, and if, in the consideration of the matter, this is done in any way, all the threads of the different relations are, to a certain extent, broken, and we have before us a senseless thing without an object." War can, for example, decline into mere looting or banditry or some other form of aimless violence. But, of all the "senseless things" that can ever occur when war's violence (its means) is severed from its political purposes (its ends), a nuclear holocaust is the most senseless. To call this senseless thing "war" is, in fact, simply a misnomer, and to go on speaking of "nuclear war," and the like, can only mislead and confuse us. Thus, while the Soviet Union and the United States are perfectly free to fire their thousands of nuclear weapons at one another, the result would not be war, for no end could be served by it. It would be comprehensive destruction—a "senseless thing." With the invention of nuclear weapons, it became impossible for violence to be fashioned into war, or to achieve what war used to achieve. Violence can no longer break down the opposition of the adversary; it can no longer produce victory and defeat; it can no longer attain its ends. It can no longer be war.

It must be emphasized that what nuclear weapons have ruined is not only "nuclear war" but all war (that is, all war between nuclear powers). "Conventional war," which in fact encompasses everything that deserves to be called war, is ruined because as long as nuclear weapons are held in reserve by the combatants, in accordance with the supposedly agreed-upon rules of some "limited war," the hostilities have not run to that extreme of violence at which the essential helplessness of one side or the other has been produced. If a decision were to be reached while the "defeated" party held potentially decisive means of violence in its possession, then that decision would be not "by arms" but by something else. We have to imagine that this power would accept its defeat while knowing that the use of its bombs would reverse it. A current example illustrates how little willingness there is among nuclear powers to accept such an outcome. For some time, it has been widely believed that the Soviet Union enjoys a preponderance in conventional forces over the NATO powers in Europe, and the United States has reserved for itself the right to resort to nuclear weapons in Europe rather than accept a conventional defeat there. Thus, the United States has already publicly discarded the notion of abiding by any rules of "limited war" if those rules should prove to mean a defeat for the United States. And there is certainly very little reason to suppose that the Soviet Union is any more willing to volunteer for defeat than the United States. That being the likely state of things, there seems little chance that a conventional war between nuclear powers could stay limited. And this means that a conventional war between nuclear powers must not even be begun, since it threatens the same holocaust that the limited use of nuclear weapons threatens. As a practical matter, this rule has up to now been followed by the statesmen of the nuclear world. Disregarding theoretical treatises on the possibility of "limited war" between nuclear powers, including "limited nuclear war," they have held back from any war; thus, in our thirty-six years of experience with nuclear weapons no two nuclear powers have ever entered into even conventional hostilities. The same cannot be said, of course, of hostilities between nuclear powers and non-nuclear powers, such as the Vietnam War or the Soviet-Afghanistan war. These remain possible—although, for reasons that I shall not go into here, they are not, it would seem, profitable.

It is often said that nuclear arms have made war obsolete, but this is a misunderstanding. Obsolescence occurs when a means to some end is superseded by a new and presumably better means—as when it was discovered that vehicles powered by internal-combustion engines were more efficient than vehicles pulled by horses at transporting people and goods from one place to another. But war has not been superseded by some better means to its end, which is to serve as the final arbiter of disputes among sovereign states. On the contrary, war has gone out of existence without leaving behind any means at all—whether superior or inferior—to that end. The more than three decades of jittery peace between the nuclear superpowers which the world has experienced since the invention of nuclear weapons is almost certainly the result of this lack. There is thus no need to "abolish war" among the nuclear powers; it is already gone. The choices don't include war any longer. They consist now of peace, on the one hand, and annihilation, on the other. And annihilation—or "assured destruction"—is as far from being war as peace is, and the sooner we recognize this the sooner we will be able to save our species from self-extermination.

When nuclear weapons were invented, it was as though a battlefield on which two armies had been fighting for as long as anyone could remember had suddenly been bisected in an earthquake by a huge chasm, so that if the armies tried to rush at one another in order to engage in battle they would plunge into this chasm instead, pulling their nations in with them. And it was as though, further, the generals of these armies, having spent their lifetimes fighting this war and hearing about their forebears' exploits in it, periodically forgot about the existence of the chasm, and therefore from time to time sent their armies into the field—only to discover that the chasm was still there.

The disabling of war is in itself something to be welcomed (although not if the price is extinction, or even the perpetual threat of extinction), but the system of sovereignty was bereft by it. The ultimate purpose of military forces in the system of sovereignty—the defense of one's nation by combating and defeating the attacking forces of the enemy—was nullified in a stroke, for there could be no defense against nuclear weapons. The "final arbiter" had been taken away, and nations, now living in terror of their annihilation but also terrified of being taken over by their enemies, were left to figure out some new means of securing their survival and of pursuing their aims in the world. In effect, the system of sovereignty faced a breakdown. The world now had to decide whether to reject sovereignty and "war" (which, suddenly, no longer was war) and institute global political arrangements that would arbitrate international disputes or to try to shore up sovereignty with the use or deployment of nuclear weapons. Lord Russell and a few other people favored the first course, but a larger number favored the second. Still others favored the first course in the abstract but turned out to be unwilling in practical terms to make the radical political changes that were called for. It was easy to say, as many did, that in a nuclear world mankind had to live in peace or perish; it was a far different matter to make actual political sacrifices that would permit the nuclear peril to be lifted. The present-day United Nations is the empty husk of those irresolute good intentions. But, whatever people said, or ineffectually hoped for, the world in fact chose the course of attempting to refashion the system of sovereignty to accommodate nuclear weapons.

The doctrine that resulted was the doctrine of nuclear deterrence: the forbidding political and intellectual product of our attempt to live simultaneously in the two worlds—the nuclear, scientific world and the pre-nuclear military and political one. Since the doctrine is the means by which the world now endeavors to escape its doom from moment to moment, it deserves our most searching examination. In its intellectual, emotional, and moral tone as well as in its content, the doctrine was something new. Not surprisingly, the people in charge of framing this doctrine and putting it into practice seem at times to suffer from double vision, as though at some moments they recognized that we live in a nuclear world, in which the life of the species is at stake, but at other times forgot this, and believed that wars could still be fought without the risk of self-extermination. It is a symptom of the schism between what Einstein called our "thinking" and the reality around us that when our strategists set out to think their "unthinkable" thoughts they feel obliged to quite deliberately leave the rest of their human equipment—their feelings, their moral sense, their humanity—behind. For the requirements of strategy in its present form force them to plan actions that from any recognizable moral point of view are indefensible. One strategic thinker, in a striking inversion of the usual understanding of ethical obligation, has said that an "iron will" is required if one is to recommend the slaughter of hundreds of millions of people in a nuclear attack—a point of view that is uncomfortably close to that of Heinrich Himmler, who told the commanders of the SS that in order to carry out the extermination of the Jews they had to be "superhumanly inhuman." In both statements, it is not obedience to our moral feelings but resistance to those feelings that is presented as our obligation, as though moral feeling were a siren call that it would be weak to give in to and that it is our duty to resist. Once the "strategic necessity" of planning the deaths of hundreds of millions of people is accepted, we begin to live in a world in which morality and action inhabit two separate, closed realms. All strategic sense becomes moral nonsense, and vice versa, and we are left with the choice of seeming to be either strategic or moral idiots. The feeling of unreality that present strategic thinking arouses is compounded by the fact, itself a unique feature of life in the nuclear world, that the strategist must incessantly plan for future attacks and counterattacks whose prevention is supposedly the planning's whole purpose. Strategic thinking thus refers to a reality that is supposed never to come into existence. Therefore, not only is morality deliberately divorced from "thinking" but planning is divorced from action. The result of all these novel mental operations is a fantastic intellectual construct—the body of strategic theory built up over more than thirty years—in which ratiocination, unrestrained either by moral feelings or by facts, has been permitted to run wild in a riot of pure theory. On this "thinking" almost no bounds are set, and the slaughter of whole populations and the extinction of man become all too "thinkable." But the divorce of thought from feeling, of strategy from morality, and of planning from action are all only manifestations of the more fundamental divorce between the pre-nuclear basis of our whole approach to political life and the reality of our nuclear world. The reason we cannot bear emotionally and morally to face the actions that we "think" about and plan and the reason the aim of all our strategic planning must be to prevent the actions we are planning to take are the same: the actions we have in mind, which risk the termination of our species, are irredeemably senseless. And as long as we continue to accept the underlying assumptions of this strategy we will be condemned to go on sketching "scenarios" for futures that must never be, while neglecting all planning for futures that *can* be, and that would permit us to be.

The central proposition of the deterrence doctrine—the piece of logic on which the world theoretically depends to see the sun rise tomorrow—is that a nuclear holocaust can best be prevented if each nuclear power, or bloc of powers, holds in readiness a nuclear force with which it "credibly" threatens to destroy the entire society of any attacker, even after suffering the worst possible "first strike" that the attacker can launch. Robert McNamara, who served as Secretary of Defense for seven years under Presidents Kennedy and Johnson, defined the policy, in his book "The Essence of Security," published in 1968, in the following terms: "Assured destruction is the very essence of the whole deterrence concept. We must possess an actual assured-destruction capability, and that capability also must be credible. The point is that a potential aggressor must believe that our assured-destruction capability is in fact actual, and that our will to use it in retaliation to an attack is in fact unwavering." Thus, deterrence "means the certainty of suicide to the aggressor, not merely to his military forces, but to his society as a whole." Let us picture what is going on here. There are two possible eventualities: success of the strategy or its failure. If it succeeds, both sides are frozen into inaction by fear of retaliation by the other side. If it fails, one side annihilates the other, and then the leaders of the second side annihilate the "society as a whole" of the attacker, and the earth as a whole suffers the consequences of a full-scale holocaust, which might include the extinction of man. In point of fact, neither the United States nor the Soviet Union has ever adopted the "mutual-assured-destruction" doctrine in pure form; other aims, such as attempting to reduce the damage of the adversary's nuclear attack and increasing the capacity for destroying the nuclear forces of the adversary, have been mixed in. Nevertheless, underlying these deviations the concept of deterring a first strike by preserving the capacity for a devastating second strike has remained constant. The strategists of deterrence have addressed the chief issue in any sane policy in a nuclear-armed world—the issue of survival—and have come up with this answer: Salvation from extinction by nuclear weapons is to be found in the nuclear weapons themselves. The possession of nuclear weapons by the great powers, it is believed, will prevent the use of nuclear weapons by those same powers. Or, to put it more accurately, the threat of their use by those powers will prevent their use. Or, in the words of Bernard Brodie, a pioneer in nuclear strategy, in "The Absolute Weapon: Atomic Power and World Order," a book published in 1946: "Thus far, the chief purpose of our military establishment has been to win wars. From now on its chief purpose must be to avert them. It can have almost no other useful purpose." Or, in the classic, broad formulation of Winston Churchill, in a speech to the House of Commons in 1955: "Safety will be the sturdy child of terror, and survival the twin brother of annihilation."

This doctrine, in its detailed as well as its more general formulations, is diagrammatic of the world's failure to come to terms with the nuclear predicament. In it, two irreconcilable purposes clash. The first purpose is to permit the survival of the species, and this is expressed in the doctrine's aim of frightening everybody into holding back from using nuclear weapons at all; the second purpose is to serve national ends, and this is expressed in the doctrine's permitting the defense of one's nation and its interests by threatening to use nuclear weapons. The strategists are pleased to call this clash of two opposing purposes in one doctrine a paradox, but in actuality it is a contradiction. We cannot both threaten ourselves with something and hope to avoid that same thing by making the threat—both intend to do something and intend not to do it. The head-on contradiction between these aims has set up a crosscurrent of tension within the policies of each superpower. The "safety" that Churchill mentions may be emphasized at one moment, and at the next moment it is the "terror" that comes to the fore. And since the deterrence doctrine pairs the safety and the terror, and makes the former depend on the latter, the world is never quite sure from day to day which one is in the ascendant—if, indeed, the distinction can be maintained in the first place. All that the world can know for certain is that at any moment the fireballs may arrive. I have said that we do not have two earths, one to blow up experimentally and the other to live on; nor do we have two souls, one for reacting to daily life and the other for reacting to the peril to all life. But neither do we have two wills, one with which we can intend to destroy our species and the other with which we can intend to save ourselves. Ultimately, we must all live together with one soul and one will on our one earth.

For all that, the adoption of the deterrence doctrine represented a partial recognition that the traditional military doctrine had become an anachronism—a doctrine that was suited well enough to the pre-nuclear world but lost all application and relevance when the first nuclear bomb flashed over the New Mexico desert. In assessing the advance made by deterrence, we must acknowledge how radically it departed from traditional military doctrine. Traditional military doctrine and nuclear doctrine are based on wholly different factual circumstances, each set of which corresponds to the technical realities of its period. Traditional military doctrine began, as I have suggested, with the premise that the amounts of force available to the belligerents were small enough to permit one side or the other to exhaust itself before both sides were annihilated. Nuclear doctrine, on the other hand, begins with the premise that the amounts of force are so great that both sides, and perhaps all mankind, will be annihilated before either side exhausts its forces. Like postulates in geometry, these two premises determine the entire systems of thought that follow, and no discussion of military strategy can make any sense unless one clearly specifies which premise one is starting from. But, as I pointed out at some length at the outset of these observations, there is no longer room for doubt that in our time the second premise is the correct one.

The chief virtue of the doctrine of nuclear deterrence is that it begins by accepting this basic fact of life in the nuclear world, and does so not only on the rhetorical plane but on the practical plane of strategic planning. Hence, it acknowledges that victory can no longer be obtained in a contest between two well-armed nuclear powers, such as the United States and the Soviet Union. Senator Barry Goldwater wrote a book, published in 1962, whose title was "Why Not Victory?" To this question the strategists of deterrence have a decisive answer: Because in the present-day, nuclear world "victory" is oblivion. From this recognition flows the conclusion, arrived at by Brodie in 1946, that the sole purpose of possessing nuclear strategic arms is not to win war but to prevent it. The adoption of the aim of preventing rather than winning war requires the adoption of other policies that fly in the face of military tradition. One is abandonment of the military defense of one's nation—of what used to be at the center of all military planning and was the most hallowed justification of the military calling. The policy of deterrence does not contemplate doing anything in defense of the homeland; it only promises that if the homeland is annihilated the aggressor's homeland will be annihilated, too. In fact, the policy goes further than this: it positively requires that each side leave its population open to attack, and make no serious effort to protect it. The requirement follows from the basic logic of deterrence, which is that safety is "the sturdy child of terror." According to this logic, the safety can be only as great as the terror is, and the terror therefore has to be kept relentless. If it were to be diminished—by, for example, building bomb shelters that protected some significant part of the population—then safety would be diminished, too, because the protected side might be tempted to launch a holocaust, in the belief that it could "win" the hostilities. That is why in nuclear strategy "destruction" must, perversely, be "assured," as though our aim were to destroy, and not to save, mankind.

In strategic terms, the requirement that the terror be perfected, and never allowed to deteriorate toward safety, translates into the requirement that the retaliatory force of both sides be guaranteed—first, by making sure that the retaliatory weapons cannot be destroyed in a first strike, and, second, by making sure that the society of the attacking power *can* be destroyed in the second strike. And since in this upside-down scheme of things the two sides will suffer equally no matter which one opens the hostilities, each side actually has an interest in maintaining its adversary's retaliatory forces as well as its own. For the most dangerous of all the configurations of forces is that in which one side appears to have the ability to destroy the nuclear forces of the other in a first strike. Then not only is the stronger side theoretically tempted to launch hostilities but—what is probably far more dangerous—the other side, fearful of completely losing its forces, might, in a crisis, feel compelled to launch the first strike itself. If on either side the population becomes relatively safe from attack or the retaliatory strike becomes vulnerable to attack, a temptation to launch a first strike is created, and "stability"—the leading virtue of any nuclear balance of power—is lost. As Thomas Schelling, the economist and noted nuclear theorist, has put it, in "The Strategy of Conflict," a book published in 1960, once instability is introduced on either side, both sides may reason as follows: "He, thinking I was about to kill him in self-defense, was about to kill me in self-defense, so I had to kill him in self-defense." Under deterrence, military "superiority" is therefore as dangerous to the side that possesses it as it is to the side that is supposedly threatened by it. (According to this logic, the United States should have heaved a sigh of relief when the Soviet Union reached nuclear parity with it, for then stability was achieved.) All these conclusions follow from the deterrence doctrine, yet they run so consistently counter to the far simpler, more familiar, and emotionally more comprehensible logic of traditional military thinking—not to mention instinct and plain common sense, which rebel against any such notion as "assuring" our own annihilation—that we should not be surprised when we find that the deterrence doctrine is constantly under challenge from traditional doctrine, no matter how glaringly at odds with the facts traditional doctrine may be. The hard-won gains of deterrence, such as they are, are repeatedly threatened by a recrudescence of the old desire for victory, for national defense in the old sense, and for military superiority, even though every one of these goals not only would add nothing to our security but, if it should be pursued far enough, would undermine the precarious safety that the deterrence doctrine tries to provide.

If the virtue of the deterrence policy lies in its acceptance of the basic fact of life in the nuclear world—that a holocaust will bring annihilation to both sides, and possibly the extinction of man as well—its defect lies in the strategic construct that it erects on the foundation of that fact. For if we try to guarantee our safety by threatening ourselves with doom, then we have to mean the threat; but if we mean it, then we are actually planning to do, in some circumstance or other, that which we categorically must never do and are supposedly trying to prevent—namely, extinguish ourselves. This is the circularity at the core of the nuclear-deterrence doctrine; we seek to avoid our self-extinction by threatening to perform the act. According to this logic, it is almost as though if we stopped threatening ourselves with extinction, then extinction would occur. Brodie's formula can be reversed: if the aim of having nuclear forces is to avert annihilation (misnamed "war" by him), then we must cling for our lives to those same forces. Churchill's dictum can be reversed, too: If safety is the sturdy child of terror, then terror is equally the sturdy child of safety. But who is to guarantee which of the children will be born? And if survival is the twin brother of annihilation, then we must cultivate annihilation. But then we may *get* annihilation. By growing to actually rely on terror, we do more than tolerate its presence in our world: we place our trust in it. And while this is not quite to "love the bomb," as the saying goes, it decidedly is to place our faith in it, and to give it an all-important position in the very heart of our affairs. Under this doctrine, instead of getting rid of the bomb we build it ever more deeply into our lives.

The logical fault line in the doctrine runs straight through the center of its main strategic tenet—the proposition that safety is achieved by assuring that any nuclear aggressor will be annihilated in a retaliatory strike. For while the doctrine relies for its success on a nuclear-armed victim's resolve to launch the annihilating second strike, it can offer no sensible or sane justification for launching it in the event. In pre-nuclear military strategy, the deterrent effect of force was a useful by-product of the ability and willingness to wage and win wars. Deterrence was the shadow cast by force, or, in Clausewitz's metaphor, the credit that flowed from the ability to make the cash payment of the favorable decision by arms. The logic of pre-nuclear deterrence escaped circularity by each side's being frankly ready to wage war and try for victory if deterrence failed. Nuclear deterrence, however, supposedly aims solely at forestalling any use of force by either side, and has given up at the outset on a favorable decision by arms. The question, then, is: Of what object is nuclear deterrence the shadow? Of what cash payment is it the credit? The theoretical answer, of course, is: The retaliatory strike. Yet since in nuclear-deterrence theory the whole purpose of having a retaliatory capacity is to deter a first strike, one must ask what reason would remain to launch the retaliation once the first strike had actually arrived. Nuclear deterrence requires one to prepare for armed conflict not in order to "win" it if it breaks out but in order to prevent it from breaking out in the first place. But if armed conflict breaks out anyway, what does one do with one's forces then? In pre-nuclear times, the answer would have required no second thought: it would have been to strive for the decision by arms—for victory. Yet nuclear deterrence begins by assuming, correctly, that victory is impossible. Thus, the logic of the deterrence strategy is dissolved by the very event—the first strike—that it is meant to prevent. Once the action begins, the whole doctrine is self-cancelling. In sum, the doctrine is based on a monumental logical mistake: one cannot credibly deter a first strike with a second strike whose *raison d'être* dissolves the moment the first strike arrives. It follows that, as far as deterrence theory is concerned, there is no reason for either side not to launch a first strike.

What seems to be needed to repair the doctrine is a motive for retaliation—one that is not supplied by the doctrine itself and that lies outside its premises—but the only candidates are those belonging to traditional military doctrine; namely, some variation of victory. The adherents of nuclear victory—whatever that would be—have on occasion noted the logical fallacy on which deterrence is based, and stepped forward to propose their solution: a "nuclear-war-fighting" capacity. Thus, the answer they give to the question of what to do after the first strike arrives is: Fight and "win" a "nuclear war." But victory does not suddenly become possible simply because it offers a solution to the logical contradiction on which the mutual-assured-destruction doctrine rests. The facts remain obdurately what they are: an attack of several thousand megatons will annihilate any country on earth many times over, no matter what line of argument the strategists pursue; and a "nuclear exchange" will, if it is on a large scale, threaten the life of man. Indeed, if victory were really possible there would have been no need for a deterrence strategy to begin with, and traditional military strategy would have needed no revision. This "solution" is therefore worse than the error it sets out to remedy. It resolves the contradiction in the deterrence doctrine by denying the tremendous new reality that the doctrine was framed to deal with, and that all of us now have to deal with on virtually every level of our existence. Consequently, this "solution" could lead us to commit the ultimate folly of exterminating ourselves without even knowing what we were doing. Aiming at "victory," we would wind up extinct.

In the last analysis, there can be no credible threat without credible use—no shadow without an object, no credit without cash payment. But since use is the thing above all else that we don't want, because it means the end of all of us, we are naturally at a loss to find any rationale for it. To grasp the reality of the contradiction, we have only to picture the circumstances of leaders whose country has just been annihilated in a first strike. Now their country is on its way to becoming a radioactive desert, but the retaliatory nuclear force survives in its silos, bombers, and submarines. These leaders of nobody, living in underground shelters or in "doomsday" planes that could not land, would possess the means of national defense but no nation to defend. What rational purpose could they have in launching the retaliatory strike? Since there was no longer a nation, "national security" could not be the purpose. Nor could defense of other peoples be the purpose, since the retaliatory strike might be the action that would finally break the back of the ecosphere and extinguish the species. In these circumstances, it seems to me, it is really an open question whether the leaders would decide to retaliate or not.

This conclusion is not one that is likely to be breathed aloud by anyone in or near power in either the Soviet Union or the United States. Since deterrence depends fully as much on one's adversary's perception of one's "unwavering" will to retaliate as on one's technical ability to do it, an acknowledgment that retaliation is senseless would in a way amount to unilateral disarmament by verbal means. The doctrine of nuclear deterrence thus deters debate about itself, and this incidental "deterrence" may have been no small factor in the sharp limits placed on the definition of "respectable," so-called "realistic" thinking about nuclear strategy. Nevertheless, the contradiction at the heart of the doctrine has occasioned considerable indirect intellectual twisting and turning among the nuclear theorists, and the resulting recommendations lead one into byways of the maze of strategic theory which stand out as bizarre and frightening even for the catalogues of nuclear strategic "options." The commonest solution to the problem of the missing motive for retaliation is to suggest that the policymakers try to cultivate an appearance of unreason, for if one is insane one doesn't need to supply any motive for retaliating—one might do it simply out of madness. The nuclear theorist Herman Kahn, for example, suggests that "it might best deter the attack" by an "*appearance* of irrationally inexorable commitment." Kahn first wonders whether it might not be enough merely to "pretend" to be irrationally committed, but he concludes that a pretense of unreason is not reliable, and that one must "*really intend to do it.*" The prescription, then, which he calls the policy of "the rationality of irrationality," is to coolly resolve to be crazy. How statesmen are to go about this, Kahn does not say. Another solution, quite closely related, is to try to create either the appearance or the reality of being out of control. Uncontrol, like insanity, removes the need for a rational motive in retaliating, this time by arranging for the retaliation to occur "by accident." Thomas Schelling, addressing the general question "How can one commit himself in advance to an act that he would in fact prefer not to carry out in the event?," suggests the tactic either of pretending that the crucial decisions will be in part up to "chance" or of actually arranging things so that this is true, thus adding to Kahn's concept of reasoned insanity the planned accident. With this strategy in effect, he writes, "the brink is not . . . the sharp edge of a cliff, where one can stand firmly, look down, and decide whether or not to plunge." Rather, "the brink is a curved slope that one can stand on with some risk of slipping." Therefore, "brinkmanship involves getting onto the slope where one may fall in spite of his own best efforts to save himself, dragging his adversary with him." That these astonishing remedies are no less consequential in the real world than the doctrinal illogicality they try to remedy is testified to by, among other things, a statement in the memoirs of President Richard Nixon's chief of staff H. R. Haldeman that Nixon believed in the "Madman Theory" of the Presidency, according to which the nation's foes would bow to the President's will if they believed that he had taken leave of his senses and was ready to risk a holocaust in order to secure some limited national gain. Whether or not Nixon had read the writings of Kahn and Schelling, he was following their counsel to the letter.

The recommendation of these tactics naturally raises the questions of whether, with the life of our species at stake, we want our nuclear decision-makers to be cultivating irrationality and uncontrol, and whether a slippery slope over the nuclear abyss is where we all want to be. But these questions, which I think must be answered with a resounding "no," come up only as a consequence of our reliance on "terror" to provide "safety," and on the threat of "annihilation" to provide "survival." For it is in an effort to strengthen and shore up the terror and make annihilation more certain that the strategists and statesmen are forced into these appalling postures. Their problem is to find a way of appearing "inexorably" resolved to do things that can never make any sense or ever be justified by any moral code, and irrationality and uncontrol fulfill the requirements for the very reason that they represent the abandonment of morality and sense. Adopted as policy, they lend credibility to actions that are—conveniently for strategic purposes, if not for the safety of mankind—immoral and insane.

It must be added that there is another extreme solution, which would entirely remove the defect in the doctrine of nuclear deterrence. This solution, described (but not recommended) by Kahn, would be to construct a literal doomsday machine, which would blow up the whole world as soon as an adversary engaged in some activity that had previously been defined as "unacceptable" by the machine's possessor. Kahn, who estimated in 1960 that a doomsday machine might be built for as little as ten billion dollars, points out that the machine would eliminate any doubt concerning the retaliatory strike by making it fully automatic. The retaliatory strike would still be senseless, but this senselessness would no longer cloud its "credibility," since the action would have been predetermined: the foundation would have been provided for a fully consistent policy of nuclear deterrence, under which nations would be deterred from launching nuclear attacks by the prearranged certainty that their own countries would perish in the ensuing global annihilation. But Kahn is also quick to point out a disadvantage of the doomsday machine which makes its construction immediately repugnant and intolerable to anyone who thinks about it: once it is in place, "there is no chance of human intervention, control, and final decision." And behind this objection, we may add, is an even simpler and more basic one: the chief reason we don't want a doomsday machine is that we don't want doom—not in any circumstances. Doom doesn't become any more acceptable because it comes about as someone's "final decision." And, of course, even though no enemy attack has been launched, in a moment of computer confusion the doomsday machine might make its own "final decision" to go off.

Because deterrence, on which we all now rely for whatever safety we have, is a psychological strategy, which aims at terrorizing the adversary into holding back from attacking us, it might seem that the discovery in one or the other command center of the logical absurdity of the policy would lead to the breakdown of the system—or, at least, to the abandonment of the doctrine. That this has not occurred is an indication that, even in the abstruse realm of nuclear doctrine, theory and practice, thought and reality are still different. In the real world, there are several stand-ins for the missing motive for the crucial retaliatory strike. The first stand-in is revenge, which, even though retaliation is not a rational action, might cause it to be carried out anyway. According to the emotional logic of revenge, the living act to right the wrong inflicted on the unjustly slain, who, being dead, cannot themselves realign the unbalanced scales of justice. Revenge is neither sensible nor constructive—especially not in a nuclear holocaust—but it is human, and the possibility that it would well up in the breasts of the leaders of a country that has just been effaced from the earth can by no means be ruled out by an aggressor; he has to consider that, even without any irrationality of the planned sort, a "rational" response to a nuclear attack can hardly be counted on. The second, and perhaps more important, stand-in for the missing motive is the irreducible unpredictability of events once the nuclear threshold is crossed. At this verge, with the survival of the species at stake, the human mind falters. The leaders of the nuclear powers have no choice, as they stare into McNamara's "vast unknown," but to assume that the stakes are total. Certainly there is no need for anyone to strain to appear irrational, as Kahn suggests, or out of control, as Schelling suggests: a world that has embarked on a holocaust is in its nature irrational and out of control.

Our experience of nuclear crises leads us to believe that when the leaders of nuclear powers are forced to contemplate the reality of a holocaust at close quarters they have looked on it in this light. That is, they have assumed that if limited nuclear war, or even conventional war between the superpowers, breaks out, a holocaust is the likely result. Michael Mandelbaum, in his history of nuclear strategy and experience, "The Nuclear Question," published in 1979, observes that when the Soviet and American leaders confronted one another in the Cuban missile crisis they discovered that the fearful nature of a holocaust, which during the days of the crisis partly emerged from abstraction and unreality to become almost palpable in people's emotions, strongly deterred them from inaugurating hostilities at no matter how minor a level. Brought face to face with the beast, both sides realized that "there was no way to fight a nuclear war." Thus, "in striving to avoid having to fight a nuclear war they took great care not to start a war of any kind, which they feared would become nuclear." This lesson of experience offered some complementary lessons. One was that although no one had decided to establish a doomsday machine, people had to act as though one were in place. They had to assume that one misstep could be the misstep that ended the world. The notion that there was a middle ground of "tactical" nuclear hostilities of a limited kind, or even of conventional hostilities, disappeared under the awful pressure of the crisis. The doorway to the "vast unknown" seemed always right at hand, and all the scenarios of "limited war" and the like tended to crumble.

A final "deterrent," which, although fallible, is both rational and human, but which goes unmentioned in deterrence theory, is the humanity of the leaders of the nuclear powers. History is crowded with ruthless, berserk actions, yet there are none that have attained the horror and insanity of a nuclear holocaust, and very few that have gone as far as the worst crime of which we do have experience—genocide. I believe that without indulging in wishful thinking we can grant that the present leaders of both the Soviet Union and the United States are considerably deterred from launching a nuclear holocaust by sheer aversion to the unspeakable act itself.

The inconsistencies that bedevil the doctrine of nuclear deterrence—the reliance upon a second strike that has no explicable purpose, the need to cultivate irrationality and uncontrol to remedy this and other defects, the reliance upon the logic of the doomsday machine combined with the failure to carry the logic through to its conclusion, and many others that might be mentioned—are all consequences of the larger, inherent inconsistency of reliance upon preparations for annihilation to prevent annihilation. The result of relying on this contradictory system for our survival is our present half-numb, half-terror-stricken world, in which growing mountains of nuclear weapons are supposed to improve the world's safety, and in which we do not know from one moment to the next whether we will survive or be exploded back into our original atoms. Reflecting on the frightful effects of this arrangement—effects that, even without a holocaust, corrupt our lives—we are led to wonder why it should be necessary to seek safety in terror, survival in annihilation, existence in nothingness, and to wonder why we shouldn't resort to the more straightforward measure of disarmament: of seeking survival by banning the instruments of death.

Even to put this question, however, is to reveal that in Churchill's and Brodie's formulations, which have been echoed with great regularity, in many versions, by the statesmen who have been in charge of the world's nuclear arsenals (President Kennedy, for example, said in his Inaugural Address, "Only when our arms are certain beyond doubt can we be certain beyond doubt that they will never be used"), an essential part of the truth is being left out. The missing element is the political aim of strategy. For the fact is that the nuclear powers do *not*, as the statesmen so often proclaim, possess nuclear weapons with the sole aim of preventing their use and so keeping the peace; they possess them also to defend national interests and aspirations—indeed, to perpetuate the whole system of sovereign states. But now, instead of relying on war for this enforcement, as nations did in pre-nuclear times, they rely on the threat of extinction. The proposition based on the aim of survival is that one prepares for extinction only in order to secure survival; however, the aim of holding on to the system of sovereignty introduces a much less reassuring, much less frequently voiced, and much less defensible proposition, which is that one prepares for extinction in order to protect national interests. This threat not only makes no sense in its own terms, since actual execution of the threat would eradicate any national interest in whose pursuit the hostilities were launched, but also undercuts the policy of deterrence, by continually propelling nations to threaten to bring about the holocaust whose avoidance is supposedly the policy's main justification. For while the aim of survival causes statesmen to declare regularly that no purpose could ever be served by a holocaust, and that the aim of nuclear policy can only be to prevent such insanity, the pursuit of national objectives forces them to declare in the next breath that they are unwaveringly resolved to perpetrate exactly this unjustifiable and insane action if some nation threatens a "vital interest" of theirs.

Thus, the peril of extinction is the price that the world pays not for "safety" or "survival" but for its insistence on continuing to divide itself up into sovereign nations. Without this insistence, there would be no need to threaten annihilation in order to escape annihilation, and the world could escape annihilation by disarming, as Russell, Einstein, and others recommended as early as the mid-nineteen-forties. Churchill's aphorism thus needs revision to read, "National sovereignty will be the sturdy child of terror and the twin brother of annihilation." This is less pithy and less palatable than the original, but it is the truth about our present nuclear arrangements. Or, to be exact, and to give those arrangements their due, the statement should read, "Safety will be the sturdy child of terror, and survival the twin brother of annihilation, *provided that nations respect one another's vital interests; otherwise, we end the world.*" But, no matter how one phrases it, the fact, which is rarely, if ever, mentioned either in the cold, abstract language of the theorists or in the ringing tones of the statesmen, is that the nuclear powers put a higher value on national sovereignty than they do on human survival, and that, while they would naturally prefer to have both, they are ultimately prepared to bring an end to mankind in their attempt to protect their own countries.

That we have let extinction replace war as the final protector of national interests is concealed to a certain extent by the fact that so far nuclear threats have been used, broadly speaking, for defensive purposes, to preserve rather than upset the status quo. For example, no one has attempted simply to conquer other countries through the threat or the use of nuclear weapons. Our reliance on extinction to thus freeze the world more or less in its present state is, in a sense, flushed out of hiding in times of crisis, when the status quo is challenged. At these moments—the Berlin crisis, the Cuban missile crisis, the American mining of Haiphong Harbor in 1972, the Soviet invasion of Afghanistan in 1979, among others—the world suddenly glimpses how far the superpowers are ready to go in pursuit of their interests. When calm returns, however, we are permitted to forget this ugly fact about the nuclear world, and to indulge ourselves again in the illusion that we possess nuclear arms solely in order to prevent their use.

As I have noted earlier, the crisis brought about by the Soviet invasion of Afghanistan serves to illustrate the contradictory pressures that operate on statesmen in any nuclear crisis. When the Soviet Union began the airlift of thousands of troops into Afghanistan, early in December of 1979, and, a few weeks later, oversaw the murder of the country's leader, President Hafizullah Amin (an extreme leftist who had fallen out of favor with Moscow), and installed its own man, Babrak Karmal, in his place, the American reaction was immediate and strong, but it involved neither the use nor the threat of force. President Carter sharply curtailed the sale of grain and certain other items to the Soviet Union, asked the United States Olympic Committee not to participate in the Olympics in Moscow in the summer of 1980 (the request was honored), and announced that he was asking the Senate to delay consideration of the SALT II treaty, which he and Brezhnev had already signed. The lack of military action, or even a threat of such action, against the Soviets in Afghanistan signalled that, while the American government was greatly disturbed by the invasion, it did not regard it as menacing the "vital interests" of the United States. The same could not be said, however, of a possible invasion of Afghanistan's neighbor Iran, which supplied oil in large quantities to the West, or of nearby Saudi Arabia, which has the largest oil reserves of any country in the world. The independence of these nations was indeed considered to be a vital interest of the United States, because the nations of the Western alliance and Japan had come to depend on Middle Eastern oil for the functioning of their economies; and it was a growing fear that the Soviet Union might next threaten these countries that gave the crisis a nuclear dimension. The fact was that the United States was worried not so much about Afghanistan and its people as about Western oil supplies. And to counter that perceived peril the United States did resort to a military threat, which took the form of Carter's statement, in his State of the Union address, in January, that "an attempt by any outside force to gain control of the Persian Gulf region will be regarded as an assault on the vital interests of the United States of America," and that "such an assault will be repelled by any means necessary, including military force." And shortly afterward any ambiguity about the meaning of the threat was dispelled by the story in the *Times* concerning a Defense Department "study" (apparently leaked by the Administration) that found that in the event of a Soviet invasion of northern Iran the United States should consider the use of nuclear weapons. However, just as everyone knew that the Soviet Union had conventional superiority in the Persian Gulf, everyone also knew that the Soviet Union possessed nuclear weapons and would be perfectly capable of using them in retaliation if the United States used them first. No one could suppose that the Soviet Union would advance into Iran only to give up and go home once the United States had used nuclear weapons against its troops. Rather, it was thought, the Soviet Union would either hold off from such an invasion in the first place or have some plan in mind for responding to an American nuclear attack. Furthermore, it was clear to all observers that neither side could expect to "win" a nuclear "war" in the Middle East. Only after all the missiles were fired—not only at targets in the Middle East but at targets throughout the world—would any outcome be reached, but that outcome, of course, would be mutual annihilation. Since these elementary facts were well known to both sides, and had certainly been rehearsed countless times in "war games" and the like, both sides were well aware that President Carter in threatening to use "any means necessary" to defend the Persian Gulf was in effect invoking the ultimate sanction: the threat of pushing the world into a nuclear holocaust. I shall not deal here with the question of whether or not Carter was correct in his judgment that the Soviet Union was considering the conquest of the Persian Gulf countries, and thus needed to be deterred from doing so. I only wish to observe that in the present global political system a leader of a nuclear power who comes to believe that his nation's vital interests are being threatened by another nuclear power faces a pair of alternatives that never confronted any statesman of pre-nuclear times: he can acquiesce in the aggression—a policy that, if it were to be followed consistently, could leave his nation at the adversary's mercy—or he can threaten, as Carter did, to unleash a holocaust in which the life of mankind might be lost, his hope being, of course, that the threat alone will deter the enemy from its aggressive action.

We are left to wonder what Carter would have done if the Soviets had ignored his threat and invaded Iran or Saudi Arabia, just as we are left to wonder what any Soviet or American leaders would do if an "unacceptable" move against the "vital interests" of their countries ever actually materialized—if, for example, the Soviet Union invaded West Germany, or the NATO forces invaded East Germany. This is what the world had to ask itself during the Cuban missile crisis, and what it has to ask itself whenever the interests of the superpowers clash in any part of the world. (And the question also comes up now in Sino-Soviet disputes—as it did when the Chinese recently engaged in a border war against the Soviet-backed Vietnamese. The divide that defines "the brink" now runs between the Soviet Union and China as well as between the Soviet Union and the United States.) As in the case of the retaliatory strike in deterrence theory, we encounter the disparity between the supposed rationality of *threatening* the use of nuclear weapons and the irrationality of actually *using* them if the threat should fail. For while it arguably makes sense to *deter* the foe from some action with the threat of a holocaust, it can never make sense to *launch* the holocaust if the foe is not deterred, since there is no human purpose that can justify extinction. And yet the success of the deterrence doctrine depends on the credibility of the threat of this unjustifiable use. Would Carter—a dedicated Christian—have risked extinction in the attempt to hold on to Middle Eastern oil? When he made his threat, did he consider his obligation to all of mankind and to the numberless future generations of human beings? Would he have plunged the world into the "vast unknown"? And did Brezhnev consider those obligations when he jarred the peace of the world by sending his armies across Soviet borders to subjugate one of the earth's sovereign peoples? Would Brezhnev, who has stated that to launch a nuclear holocaust would be "suicide," commit that suicide if he believed that the West was about to gain control of Eastern Europe? Would Deng Xiaoping take that risk to keep hold of a piece of Inner Mongolia? Did Khrushchev weigh the importance of the earth and the human species when he sent into Cuba missiles capable of carrying nuclear warheads? And did Kennedy weigh the importance of those things when he blockaded Cuba and then, according to his brother, waited to find out whether events over which "he no longer had control" would lead the world into a holocaust? These are the questions that hang in the air over our nuclear world, leaving us perpetually uncertain whether the next moment may not be the world's last.

When one great power adopts a strategic theory, it becomes a doctrine; when two rival great powers adopt it, it becomes a system; and when those rivals more or less abide by the rules of the system, and even hold negotiations aimed at strengthening it (I am thinking of SALT), and are prepared to see new nations enter it as they develop the necessary technical equipment, the system can be described as entrenched. This is the point at which the system of deterrence has arrived today. In essence, it is, as we have seen, a system of sovereign nation-states presided over by a hedged, or qualified, doomsday machine, with which we hope to reap the deterrent benefits of the threat of doom without clearly committing ourselves to doom if deterrence should fail—as we know that it well may, especially with the number of nuclear powers in the world growing. The basic dictate of the system is that if in the opinion of any nuclear power any other nuclear power seriously breaks the rules, then all powers are to be annihilated. Since in a holocaust the consequences may be the same for the aggressor, its punisher, and bystanders, the distinction between friendly and hostile nuclear forces has lost most of its meaning, and the nuclear arsenals of the world are effectively combined by policy into one great arsenal, which is looked to by all powers equally for their "safety." By the same token, even conventionally armed nations have the potential of blowing the world up, for they may draw the superpowers into one of their wars. We can picture this system in simple form if we imagine it as a doomsday machine possessed jointly by all nuclear powers. It is as though a number of people, each one possessing certain valuables that the others want and, furthermore, think they have a right to, are grouped in a room around a single bomb that is large enough to kill them all if it goes off. Each person holds in his hands a switch with which he can detonate the bomb. Every once in a while, a new person enters, also holding a switch. These people constantly reassure one another that the purpose of the whole system is to frighten everyone into inaction and let everyone enjoy in peace the valuables he has, and that for anyone to pull the switch would be suicidal and insane. Yet whenever a dispute breaks out over which valuables rightfully belong to whom, those same people hotly declare that enjoyment of their valuables is more important to them than everyone's life, their own included, and declare their "unwavering" and "inexorable" determination to set off the bomb if they cannot have their way. To this description we must add that some of the people in the room are not quite sure that the system works the way they have been told it does, and suspect that if they are the ones to set off the bomb they may be spared and only the others killed.

Examined in theoretical terms, the deterrence system emerges as a monstrous hybrid, stuck halfway between what the political philosophers call a "state of nature," in which individuals live together without founding any central authority among them, and the so-called "civil state," in which such an authority has been founded. In the passage from the state of nature to the civil state, each individual surrenders his capacity for violence to the central authority, which then employs the gathered resources, according to a system of laws, in the service of the common good. In the deterrence system, the individuals have combined their forces into a single force—the machine that will punish everyone with annihilation if anyone breaks the rules—but have failed to establish any central authority to preside over it. Thus, they have centralized the means of violence while leaving the decision-making decentralized—in effect, delegating to each member of the community a veto power over the continued survival of the species. It is no overstatement to say that if any society organized its affairs in this way, giving to each citizen the power to kill all the others, it would be regarded as deranged.

(The system is even worse than anarchy, in which the evil that each person can do is at least limited by the limits of his own strength.) But, for some reason, when it comes to organizing the whole world, and providing for its survival, we regard such a system as a masterpiece of prudent statesmanship.

The dilemma of the nation that in order to protect its national sovereignty finds that it must put the survival of mankind at risk is a trap from which there is no escape as long as nations possess arsenals of nuclear weapons. The deterrence doctrine seeks to rationalize this state of affairs, but it fails, because at the crucial moment it requires nations to sacrifice mankind for their own interests—an absurdity as well as a crime beyond reckoning. Indeed, the deterrence doctrine actually almost *compels* the world to live perpetually on the brink of doom, for any nation that took a step or two back would put its interests, and ultimately, its independence at the mercy of the military forces of its adversaries. And although, for any number of reasons, an adversary might not press its advantage (as, for example, the United States did not right after the Second World War, when it possessed a monopoly on nuclear weapons), no nation has yet volunteered to put itself at this competitive disadvantage. It appears that the only way to escape from the trap is to change the system, and take away from nuclear weapons the responsibility for defending nations. But unless one supposes that, in a global spread of quietism, nations and people in general are going to give up the pursuit of their interests and their ideals and become wholly inactive, this separation can be achieved only if a new way—a nonviolent way—of making and guaranteeing these decisions is found.

In the decades since nuclear arms first appeared in the world, the doctrine of nuclear deterrence has commanded the sincere respect and adherence of many people of good will—especially when they found themselves arguing, as they so often did, with the adherents of traditional military doctrine, who even today, in the face of extinction itself, go on arguing for "military superiority," and the like. And if one once accepts the existence of the doomsday machine, then deterrence theory, however flawed, does offer the hope of certain benefits, the main one being a degree of "stability." Therefore, the perpetual struggle of its adherents against the sheer lunacy of "fighting a nuclear war" is a creditable one. But the fundamental truth about the doctrine and about its role in the wider political—and, it must be added, biological—scheme of things also has to be recognized. For the doctrine's central claim—that it deploys nuclear weapons only in order to prevent their use—is simply not true. Actually, it deploys them to protect national sovereignty, and if this aim were not present they could be quickly dismantled. The doctrine, then, has been the intellectual screen behind which the doomsday machine was built. And its deceptive claim that only by building nuclear weapons can we save ourselves from nuclear weapons lent the doomsday machine a veneer of reason and of respectability—almost of benevolence—that it should never have been given. For to build this machine at all was a mistake of the hugest proportions ever known—without question the greatest ever made by our species. The only conceivable worse mistake would be to put the machine to use. Now deterrence, having rationalized the construction of the machine, weds us to it, and, at best, offers us, if we are lucky, a slightly extended term of residence on earth before the inevitable human or mechanical mistake occurs and we are annihilated.

Yet the deterrence policy in itself is clearly not the deepest source of our difficulty. Rather, as we have seen, it is only a piece of repair work on the immeasurably more deeply entrenched system of national sovereignty. People do not want deterrence for its own sake; indeed, they hardly know what it is, and tend to shun the whole subject. They want the national sovereignty that deterrence promises to preserve. National sovereignty lies at the very core of the political issues that the peril of extinction forces upon us. Sovereignty is the "reality" that the "realists" counsel us to accept as inevitable, referring to any alternative as "unrealistic" or "utopian." If the argument about nuclear weapons is to be conducted in good faith, then just as those who favor the deterrence policy (not to speak of traditional military doctrine) must in all honesty admit that their scheme contemplates the extinction of man in the name of protecting national sovereignty, so must those who favor complete nuclear and conventional disarmament as I do, admit that their recommendation is inconsistent with national sovereignty; to pretend otherwise would be to evade the political question that is central to the nuclear predicament. The terms of the deal that the world has now struck with itself must be made clear. On the one side stand human life and the terrestrial creation. On the other side stands a particular organization of human life—the system of independent, sovereign nation-states. Our choice so far has been to preserve that political organization of human life at the cost of risking all human life. We are told that "realism" compels us to preserve the system of sovereignty. But that political realism is not biological realism; it is biological nihilism—and for that reason is, of course, political nihilism, too. Indeed, it is nihilism in every conceivable sense of that word. We are told that it is human fate—perhaps even "a law of human nature"—that, in obedience, perhaps, to some "territorial imperative," or to some dark and ineluctable truth in the bottom of our souls, we must preserve sovereignty and always settle our differences with violence. If this is our fate, then it is our fate to die. But must we embrace nihilism? Must we die? Is self-extermination a law of our nature? Is there nothing we can do? I do not believe so. Indeed, if we admit the reality of the basic terms of the nuclear predicament—that present levels of global armament are great enough to possibly extinguish the species if a holocaust should occur; that in extinction every human purpose would be lost; that because once the species has been extinguished there will be no second chance, and the game will be over for all time; that therefore this possibility must be dealt with morally and politically as though it were a certainty; and that either by accident or by design a holocaust can occur at any second—then, whatever political views we may hold on other matters, we are driven almost inescapably to take action to rid the world of nuclear arms. Just as we have chosen to make nuclear weapons, we can choose to unmake them. Just as we have chosen to live in the system of sovereign states, we can choose to live in some other system. To do so would, of course, be unprecedented, and in many ways frightening, even truly perilous, but it is by no means impossible. Our present system and the institutions that make it up are the debris of history. They constitute a noose around the neck of mankind, threatening to choke off the human future, but we can cut the noose and break free. To suppose otherwise would be to set up a false, fictitious fate, molded out of our own weaknesses and our own alterable decisions. We are indeed fated by our acquisition of the basic knowledge of physics to live for the rest of the time with the knowledge of how to destroy ourselves. But we are not for that reason fated to destroy ourselves. We can choose to live.

In this book, I have not sought to define a political solution to the nuclear predicament—either to embark on the full-scale reëxamination of the foundations of political thought which must be undertaken if the world's political institutions are to be made consonant with the global reality in which they operate or to work out the practical steps by which mankind, acting for the first time in history as a single entity, can reorganize its political life. I have left to others those awesome, urgent tasks, which, imposed on us by history, constitute the political work of our age. Rather, I have attempted to examine the physical extent, the human significance, and the practical dimensions of the nuclear predicament in which the whole world now finds itself. This predicament is a sort of cage that has quietly grown up around the earth, imprisoning every person on it, and the demanding terms of the predicament—its durability, its global political sweep, its human totality—constitute the bars of that cage. However, if a description of the predicament, which is the greatest that mankind has ever faced, cannot in itself reveal to us how we can escape, it can, I believe, acquaint us with the magnitude and shape of the task that we have to address ourselves to. And it can summon us to action.

To begin a summary with the matter of war: By effectively removing the limits on human access to the forces of nature, the invention of nuclear weapons ruined war, which depended for its results, and therefore for its usefulness, on the exhaustion of the forces of one of the adversaries. War depended, above all, on the weakness of human powers, and when human powers came to exceed human and other earthly endurance—when man as master of nature grew mightier than man as a vulnerable, mortal part of nature—war was ruined. Since war was the means by which violence was fashioned into an instrument that was useful in political affairs, the ruin of war by nuclear weapons has brought about a divorce between violence and politics. I submit that this divorce, being based on irreversible progress in scientific knowledge, not only is final but must ultimately extend across the full range of political affairs, and that the task facing the species is to shape a world politics that does not rely on violence. This task falls into two parts—two aims. The first is to save the world from extinction by eliminating nuclear weapons from the earth. Just recently, on the occasion of his retirement, Admiral Hyman Rickover, who devoted a good part of his life to overseeing the development and construction of nuclear-powered, nuclear-missile-bearing submarines for the United States Navy, told a congressional committee that in his belief mankind was going to destroy itself with nuclear arms. He also said of his part in the nuclear buildup that he was "not proud" of it, and added that he would like to "sink" the ships that he had poured so much of his life into. And, indeed, what everyone is now called on to do is to sink all the ships, and also ground all the planes, and fill in all the missile silos, and dismantle all the warheads. The second aim, which alone can provide a sure foundation for the first, is to create a political means by which the world can arrive at the decisions that sovereign states previously arrived at through war. These two aims, which correspond to the aims mentioned earlier of preserving the existence of life and pursuing the various ends of life, are intimately connected. If, on the one hand, disarmament is not accompanied by a political solution, then every clash of will between nations will tempt them to pick up the instruments of violence again, and so lead the world back toward extinction. If, on the other hand, a political solution is not accompanied by complete disarmament, then the political decisions that are made will not be binding, for they will be subject to challenge by force. And if, as in our present world, there is neither a political solution nor disarmament, then the world will be held perpetually at the edge of doom, and every clash between nuclear powers will threaten to push it over the edge.

The significance of the first aim—disarmament—which, without being paradoxical, we can describe as a "strategic" aim, can be clarified if we extend to its logical conclusion the reasoning that underlies the doctrine of deterrence. At present, the world relies on nuclear weapons both to prevent the use of nuclear weapons and to regulate the behavior of nations; but let us go a step—a very large step—further, and suppose, for a moment, that the world had established a political means of making international decisions and thus had no further need for nuclear or any other weapons. In order for such a thing to happen, we may ask, would the doctrine of deterrence and the fears on which it is based have to evaporate in the warmth of global good will? They would not. On the contrary, fear of extinction would have to increase, and permeate life at a deeper level: until it was great enough to inspire the complete rearrangement of world politics. Indeed, only when the world has given up violence does Churchill's dictum that safety is the sturdy child of terror actually become true. (At present, as we have seen, it is not safety but sovereignty that is the sturdy child of terror.) Under the current deterrence doctrine, one might say, safety is only the frail, anemic child of terror, and the reason is precisely that the terror is not yet robust enough to produce a sturdy offspring. For we still deny it, look away from it, and fail to let it reach deep enough into our lives and determine our actions. If we felt the peril for what it is—an urgent threat to our whole human substance—we would let it become the organizing principle of our global collective existence: the foundation on which the world was built. Fear would no longer dictate particular decisions, such as whether or not the Soviet Union might place missiles in Cuba; rather, it would be a moving force behind the establishment of a new system by which every decision was made. And, having dictated the foundation of the system, it would stand guard over it forever after, guaranteeing that the species did not slide back toward anarchy and doom.

This development would be the logical final goal of the doctrine of nuclear deterrence. In the pre-nuclear world, the threat of war, backed up by the frequent practice of war, served as a deterrent to aggression. Today, the threat of extinction, unsupported, for obvious reasons, by practice but backed up by the existence of nuclear arms and the threat to use them, serves as the ultimate deterrent. Thus, in today's system the actual weapons have already retired halfway from their traditional military role. They are "psychological" weapons, whose purpose is not to be employed but to maintain a permanent state of mind—terror—in the adversary. Their target is someone's mind, and their end, if the system works, is to rust into powder in their silos. And our generals are already psychological soldiers—masters of the war game and of the computer terminal but not, fortunately, of the battlefield. In this cerebral world, strategy confronts strategy and scenario battles scenario, the better to keep any of them from ever actually unfolding. But we need to carry this trend further. We need to make the weapons *wholly* cerebral—not things that sit in a silo ready to be fired but merely a thought in our minds. We need to destroy them. Only then will the logical fallacy now at the heart of the deterrence doctrine be removed, for only then will the fear of extinction by nuclear arms be used for the sole purpose of preventing extinction, and not also for the pursuit of national political aims. In a perfected nuclear deterrence, the knowledge in a disarmed world that rearmament potentially means extinction would become the deterrent. Now, however, it would be not that each nuclear-armed country would deter its nuclear-armed adversary but that awareness of the peril of extinction would deter all mankind from reëmbarking on nuclear armament. All human beings would join in a defensive alliance, with nuclear weapons as their common enemy. But since that enemy could spring only from our own midst, deterrer and deterred would be one. We thus arrive at the basic strategic principle of life in a world in which the nuclear predicament has been resolved: *Knowledge is the deterrent.* The nuclear peril was born out of knowledge, and it must abide in knowledge. The knowledge in question would be, in the first place, the unlosable scientific knowledge that enables us to build the weapons and condemns us to live forever in a nuclear world. This knowledge is the inexpungible minimum presence that the nuclear peril will always have in the life of the world, no matter what measures we adopt. In the second place, the knowledge would be the full emotional, intellectual, spiritual, and visceral understanding of the meaning of extinction—above all, the meaning of the unborn generations to the living. Because extinction is the end of mankind, it can never be anything more than "knowledge" for us; we can never "experience" extinction. It is *this* knowledge— this horror at a murderous action taken against generations yet unborn, which exerts pressure at the center of our existence, and which is the whole reality of extinction insofar as it is given to us to experience it—that must become the deterrent.

In a disarmed world, we would not have eliminated the

peril of human extinction from the human scene—it is not in our power to do so—but we would at least have pitted our whole strength against it. The inconsistency of threatening to perpetrate extinction in order to escape extinction would be removed. The nuclei of atoms would still contain vast energy, and we would still know how to extinguish ourselves by releasing that energy in chain reactions, but we would not be lifting a finger to do it. There would be no complicity in mass murder, no billions of dollars spent on the machinery of annihilation, no preparations to snuff out the future generations, no hair-raising lunges toward the abyss.

The "realistic" school of political thinking, on which the present system of deterrence is based, teaches that men, on the whole, pursue their own interests and act according to a law of fear. The "idealistic" school looks on the human ability to show regard for others as fundamental, and is based on what Gandhi called the law of love. (Whereas the difference between traditional military thinking and nuclear strategic thinking lies in the different factual premises that they start from, the difference between the "realistic" and the "idealistic" schools of political philosophy lies in different judgments regarding human nature.) Historically, a belief in the necessity of violence has been the hallmark of the credo of the "realist"; however, if one consistently and thoroughly applies the law of fear in nuclear times one is driven not to rely on violence but to banish it altogether. This comes about as the result not of any idealistic assumption but of a rigorous application to our times of the strictly "military" logic of traditional war. For today the only way to achieve genuine national defense for any nation is for all nations to give up violence together. However, if we had begun with Gandhi's law of love we would have arrived at exactly the same arrangement. For to one who believed in nonviolence in a pre-nuclear setting the peril of extinction obviously adds one more reason—and a tremendous one, transcending all others—for giving up violence. Moreover, in at least one respect the law of love proves to fit the facts of this peril better than the law of fear. The law of fear relies on the love of self. Through deterrence—in which anyone's pursuit of self-interest at the expense of others will touch off general ruin that will destroy him, too—this self-love is made use of to protect everyone. However, self-love—a narrow, though intense, love—cannot, as we have seen, extend its protection to the future generations, or even get them in view. They still do not have any selves whose fear of death could be pooled in the common fund of fear, and yet their lives are at stake in extinction. The deterrence doctrine is a transaction that is limited to living people—it leaves out of account the helpless, speechless unborn (while we can launch a first strike against them, they have no forces with which to retaliate)—and yet the fate of the future generations is at the heart of extinction, for their cancellation is what extinction is. Their lives are at stake, but their vote is not counted. Love, however, can reach them—can enable them to be. Love, a spiritual energy that the human heart can pit against the physical energy released from the heart of matter, can create, cherish, and safeguard what extinction would destroy and shut up in nothingness. But in fact there is no need, at least on the practical level, to choose between the law of fear and the law of love, because ultimately they lead to the same destination. It is no more realistic than it is idealistic to destroy the world.

In supposing for a moment that the world had found a political means of making international decisions, I made a very large supposition indeed—one that encompasses something close to the whole work of resolving the nuclear predicament, for, once a political solution has been found, disarmament becomes a merely technical matter, which should present no special difficulties. And yet simply to recognize that the task is at bottom political, and that only a political solution can prepare the way for full disarmament and real safety for the species, is in itself important. The recognition calls attention to the fact that disarmament in isolation from political change cannot proceed very far. It alerts us to the fact that when someone proposes, as President Carter did in his Inaugural Address, to aim at ridding the world of nuclear weapons, there is an immense obstacle that has to be faced and surmounted. For the world, in freeing itself of one burden, the peril of extinction, must inevitably shoulder another: it must assume full responsibility for settling human differences peacefully. Moreover, this recognition forces us to acknowledge that nuclear disarmament cannot occur if conventional arms are left in place, since as long as nations defend themselves with arms of any kind they will be fully sovereign, and as long as they are fully sovereign they will be at liberty to build nuclear weapons if they so choose. And if we assume that wars do break out and some nations find themselves facing defeat in the conventional arena, then the reappearance of nuclear arms, which would prevent such defeat, becomes a strong likelihood. What nation, once having entrusted its fortunes to the force of arms, would permit itself to be conquered by an enemy when the means of driving him back, perhaps with a mere threat, was on hand? And how safe can the world be while nations threaten one another's existence with violence and retain for themselves the sovereign right to build whatever weapons they choose to build? This vision of an international life that in the military sphere is restricted to the pre-nuclear world while in the scientific realm it is in the nuclear world is, in fact, thoroughly implausible. If we are serious about nuclear disarmament—the minimum technical requirement for real safety from extinction—then we must accept conventional disarmament as well, and this means disarmament not just of nuclear powers but of all powers, for the present nuclear powers are hardly likely to throw away their conventional arms while non-nuclear powers hold on to theirs. But if we accept both nuclear and conventional disarmament, then we are speaking of revolutionizing the politics of the earth. The goals of the political revolution are defined by those of the nuclear revolution. We must lay down our arms, relinquish sovereignty, and found a political system for the peaceful settlement of international disputes.

The task we face is to find a means of political action that will permit human beings to pursue any end for the rest of time. We are asked to replace the mechanism by which political decisions, whatever they may be, are reached. In sum, the task is nothing less than to reinvent politics: to reinvent the world. However, extinction will not wait for us to reinvent the world. Evolution was slow to produce us, but our extinction will be swift; it will literally be over before we know it. We have to match swiftness with swiftness. Because everything we do and everything we are is in jeopardy, and because the peril is immediate and unremitting, every person is the right person to act and every moment is the right moment to begin, starting with the present moment. For nothing underscores our common humanity as strongly as the peril of extinction does; in fact, on a practical and political plane it establishes that common humanity. The purpose of action, though, is not to replace life with politics. The point is not to turn life into a scene of protest; life is the point.

Whatever the eventual shape of a world that has been re-invented for the sake of survival, the first, urgent, immediate step, which requires no deep thought or long reflection, is for each person to make known, visibly and unmistakably, his desire that the species survive. Extinction, being in its nature outside human experience, is invisible, but we, by rebelling against it, can indirectly make it visible. No one will ever witness extinction, so we must bear witness to it before the fact. And the place for the rebellion to start is in our daily lives. We can each perform a turnabout right where we are—let our daily business drop from our hands for a while, so that we can turn our attention to securing the foundation of all life, out of which our daily business grows and in which it finds its justification. This disruption of our lives will be a preventive disruption, for we will be hoping through the temporary suspension of our daily life to ward off the eternal suspension of it in extinction. And this turnabout in the first instance can be as simple as a phone call to a friend, a meeting in the community.

However, even as the first steps are taken, the broad ultimate requirements of survival must be recognized and stated clearly. If they are not, we might sink into self-deception, imagining that inadequate measures would suffice to save us. I would suggest that the ultimate requirements are in essence the two that I have mentioned: global disarmament, both nuclear and conventional, and the invention of political means by which the world can peacefully settle the issues that throughout history it has settled by war. Thus, the first steps and the ultimate requirements are clear. If a busload of people is speeding down a mountainside toward a cliff, the passengers do not convene a seminar to investigate the nature of their predicament; they see to it that the driver applies the brakes. Therefore, at a min-imum, a freeze on the further deployment of nuclear weapons, participated in both by countries that now have them and by countries that do not yet have them, is called for. Even better would be a reduction in nuclear arms—for example, by cutting the arsenals of the superpowers in half, as George Kennan suggested recently. Simultaneously with disarmament, political steps of many kinds could be taken. For example, talks could be started among the nuclear powers with the aim of making sure that the world did not simply blunder into extinction by mistake; technical and political arrangements could be drawn up to reduce the likelihood of mechanical mistakes and misjudgments of the other side's intentions or actions in a time of crisis, and these would somewhat increase the world's security while the predicament was being tackled at a more fundamental level. For both superpowers—and, indeed, for all other powers—avoiding extinction is a common interest than which none can be greater. And since the existence of a common interest is the best foundation for negotiation, negotiations should have some chance of success. However, the existence of negotiations to reduce the nuclear peril would provide no reason for abandoning the pursuit of other things that one believed in, even those which might be at variance with the beliefs of one's negotiating partner. Thus, to give one contemporary example, there is no need, or excuse, for the United States not to take strong measures to oppose Soviet-sponsored repression in Poland just because it is engaged in disarmament talks with the Soviet Union. The world will not end if we suspend shipments of wheat to the Soviet Union. On the other hand, to break off those talks in an effort to help the Poles, who will be as extinct as anyone else if a holocaust comes about, would be self-defeating. To seek to "punish" the other side by breaking off those negotiations would be in reality self-punishment. All the limited aims of negotiation can be pursued in the short term without danger if only the ultimate goal is kept unswervingly in mind. But ordinary citizens must insist that all these things be done, or they will not be.

If action should be concerted, as it eventually must be, in a common political endeavor, reaching across national boundaries, then, just as the aim of the endeavor would be to hold the gates of life open to the future generations, so its method would be to hold its own gates open to every living person. But it should be borne in mind that even if every person in the world were to enlist, the endeavor would include only an infinitesimal fraction of the people of the dead and the unborn generations, and so it would need to act with the circumspection and modesty of a small minority. From its mission to preserve all generations, it would not seek to derive any rights to dictate to the generations on hand. It would not bend or break the rules of conduct essential to a decent political life, for it would recognize that once one started breaking rules in the name of survival no rule would go unbroken. Intellectually and philosophically, it would carry the principle of tolerance to the utmost extreme. It would attempt to be as open to new thoughts and feelings as it would be to the new generations that would think those thoughts and feel those feelings. Its underlying supposition about creeds and ideologies would be that whereas without mankind none can exist, with mankind all can exist. For while the events that might trigger a holocaust would probably be political, the consequences would be deeper than any politics or political aims, bringing ruin to the hopes and plans of capitalists and socialists, rightists and leftists, conservatives and liberals alike. Having as the source of its strength only the spontaneously offered support of the people of the earth, it would, in turn, respect each person's will, which is to say his liberty. Eventually, the popular will that it marshalled might be deployed as a check on the power of whatever political institutions were invented to replace war.

Since the goal would be a nonviolent world, the actions of this endeavor would be nonviolent. What Gandhi once said of the spirit of nonviolent action in general would be especially important to the spirit of these particular actions: "In the dictionary of nonviolent action, there is no such thing as an 'external enemy.'" With the world itself at stake, all differences would by definition be "internal" differences, to be resolved on the basis of respect for those with whom one disagreed. If our aim is to save humanity, we must respect the humanity of every person. For who would be the enemy? Certainly not the world's political leaders, who, though they now menace the earth with nuclear weapons, do so only with our permission, and even at our bidding. At least, this is true for the democracies. We do not know what the peoples of the totalitarian states, including the people of the Soviet Union, may want. They are locked in silence by their government. In these circumstances, public opinion in the free countries would have to represent public opinion in all countries, and would have to bring its pressure to bear, as best it could, on all governments.

At present, most of us do nothing. We look away. We remain calm. We are silent. We take refuge in the hope that the holocaust won't happen, and turn back to our individual concerns. We deny the truth that is all around us. Indifferent to the future of our kind, we grow indifferent to one another. We drift apart. We grow cold. We drowse our way toward the end of the world. But if once we shook off our lethargy and fatigue and began to act, the climate would change. Just as inertia produces despair—a despair often so deep that it does not even know itself as despair—arousal and action would give us access to hope, and life would start to mend: not just life in its entirety but daily life, every individual life. At that point, we would begin to withdraw from our role as both the victims and the perpetrators of mass murder. We would no longer be the destroyers of mankind but, rather, the gateway through which the future generations would enter the world. Then the passion and will that we need to save ourselves would flood into our lives. Then the walls of indifference, inertia, and coldness that now isolate each of us from others, and all of us from the past and future generations, would melt, like snow in spring. E. M. Forster told us, "Only connect!" Let us connect. Auden told us, "We must love one another or die." Let us love one another—in the present and across the divides of death and birth. Christ said, "I come not to judge the world but to save the world." Let us, also, not judge the world but save the world. By restoring our severed links with life, we will restore our own lives. Instead of stopping the course of time and cutting off the human future, we would make it possible for the future generations to be born. Their inestimable gift to us, passed back from the future into the present, would be the wholeness and meaning of life.

Two paths lie before us. One leads to death, the other to life. If we choose the first path—if we numbly refuse to acknowledge the nearness of extinction, all the while increasing our preparations to bring it about—then we in effect become the allies of death, and in everything we do our attachment to life will weaken: our vision, blinded to the abyss that has opened at our feet, will dim and grow confused; our will, discouraged by the thought of trying to build on such a precarious foundation anything that is meant to last, will slacken; and we will sink into stupefaction, as though we were gradually weaning ourselves from life in preparation for the end. On the other hand, if we reject our doom, and bend our efforts toward survival—if we arouse ourselves to the peril and act to forestall it, making ourselves the allies of life—then the anesthetic fog will lift: our vision, no longer straining not to see the obvious, will sharpen; our will, finding secure ground to build on, will be restored; and we will take full and clear possession of life again. One day—and it is hard to believe that it will not be soon—we will make our choice. Either we will sink into the final coma and end it all or, as I trust and believe, we will awaken to the truth of our peril, a truth as great as life itself, and, like a person who has swallowed a lethal poison but shakes off his stupor at the last moment and vomits the poison up, we will break through the layers of our denials, put aside our fainthearted excuses, and rise up to cleanse the earth of nuclear weapons.

THE ABOLITION

I dedicate this book
with love to William Shawn.

Contents

I. DEFINING THE GREAT
PREDICAMENT

I<small>N A SPEECH</small> given in Hiroshima in February of 1981, Pope John Paul II said, "In the past, it was possible to destroy a village, a town, a region, even a country. Now it is the whole planet that has come under threat. This fact should fully compel everyone to face a basic moral consideration: from now on, it is only through a conscious choice and then deliberate policy that humanity can survive." The Pope's deceptively simple statement contains an invaluable anatomy of the challenge that the invention of nuclear weapons has placed before mankind. In distinguishing between "a conscious choice" and "deliberate policy," he defines two stages—one individual and spiritual, the other public and political—that we must pass through if we are to resolve the nuclear predicament. Because by building large nuclear arsenals we threaten to extinguish ourselves as a species, each of us is called on to do something that no member of any generation before ours has had to do: to assume responsibility for the continuation of our kind—to *choose* human survival. There is nothing perfunctory or easy about making this choice. For example, it is wholly inadequate for us to remind ourselves that "nuclear war is horrible," and to assure ourselves that we are not "for" extinguishing mankind. The potential extermination of the human species by nuclear arms presents, like every monumental crime—Hitler's genocidal attack on the Jewish people being the most monstrous in memory—a challenge to the human spirit, and not one that we can be at all sure in advance that we are up to meeting. But even among monumental crimes the extermination of the species is unique. For the risk of extinction is not just one more item on the agenda of issues that faces us. Embracing, as it does, the life and death of every human being on earth and every future human being, it embraces and transcends all other issues. It is the ground in which they and every issue that might arise in the future have their significance and their being. But even to say that it is a life-and-death matter does not go far enough, because while the individual person may choose to give his life for causes that he considers to be greater and more important than his own life, including the cause of saving the lives of others, the extinction of mankind would destroy not only every person's life but also every larger cause, including the lives of all others, for which a person might be willing to give up his life. Extinction therefore threatens not so much each person's life (which is threatened at the same time by many other things, and will one day end anyway) as the *meaning* of our lives. It threatens life with meaninglessness as individual death never can. In doing so, it not only encompasses all human life but reaches deep into each life, requiring each of us to make this business his own. Sometimes it is suggested that it is ignoble to give the highest priority to our effort to save mankind from destruction, because in doing so we supposedly place our animal wish to stay alive above our higher, more specifically human obligation to live a morally decent life. But just the opposite is the case. It is precisely all those things *for which* people have throughout history been willing to sacrifice their lives that we have, indecently, now placed, in their entirety, at risk. And it is our desire to save those things— not merely the desire to save our own necks—which moves us to choose to save our species. It is also sometimes suggested that fear will inspire us to combat the nuclear peril, but that reasonable-sounding idea seems to me equally mistaken. Fear, a more or less reflexive response that we share with other species, drives each of us, as an individual, to save himself in the face of danger. Fear cannot distinguish between a fire in one's own house and a nuclear holocaust—between one's own death and the end of the world—and is therefore useless even to begin to suggest to us the meaning of the nuclear peril. Its meaning can be grasped only to the extent that we feel the precise opposite of fear, which is a sense of responsibility, or devotion, or love, for other people, including those who have not yet been born. In Germany, the peace movement has inverted the traditional Biblical admonition "Fear not" to say "You must fear." But the original version was the right one, for nuclear matters as for others. Fear isolates. Love connects. Only insofar as the latter is strong in us are we likely to find the resolve to prevent our extinction.

The conscious choice to take responsibility for the continuation of human life is further complicated and confused by the fact, which also is peculiar to the nuclear peril, that we are able to respond to it only before it happens. Since after extinction no one will be present to take responsibility, we have to take full responsibility now. It follows that we incur the full burden of guilt for extinguishing our species merely by preparing to do the deed, even without actually pushing the button. Sometimes it is suggested that while it would be a crime to extinguish mankind we are blameless if we intend—and threaten—to do so, provided that some laudable goal is being served by the threat. But if we absolve ourselves of responsibility for the intent, then we in effect evade responsibility altogether, since we can hardly assume responsibility after we are all dead. Therefore, insofar as we are going to take any responsibility whatever, we must in fact take it for the intent alone. To combine strategic with Christian terminology, we must adopt a policy of preemptive repentance. We must repent the crime before we commit it, and in that repentance find the will not to commit it. This displacement of repentance from the aftermath of the crime to the time preceding it would be, to paraphrase William James, the moral equivalent of deterrence. The only difference between it and the strategic sort is that whereas in strategic deterrence we are deterred by what the enemy may do to us, in moral deterrence we are deterred by what we may do to him—and to countless innocents, including all potential future generations of human beings. Or, to put it simply, we are not only fearful at the thought of suffering a nuclear holocaust but repelled by the thought of perpetrating one. Still, it would be misleading, perhaps, to try to distinguish too sharply between our fearful, selfish impulses and our altruistic, selfless ones. The holocaust itself will make no such distinctions. The fallout will fall on the just and the unjust alike. After the Cuban missile crisis, Premier Nikita Khrushchev remarked that the smell of burning flesh was in the air. But, in truth, that smell is never far from our nostrils now. The world's nuclear arsenals threaten to annihilate everyone in response to a transgression or mistake by any one party. That is how the doctrine of deterrence is designed. In consenting to live under it, we bear responsibility not only for the lives of the people whom "we" may kill but also for the lives of those whom "they" would kill; namely, our families, our friends, and our other fellow-citizens. Through the balance of terror, we all come to hold a dagger to the hearts of those nearest and dearest to us as well as to threaten those far away, down to the uttermost generations of human beings. The parent threatens the child, the lover the lover, the friend the friend, the citizen the citizen. Our acceptance of nuclear weapons is in that sense a default of parenthood, of love, of friendship, of citizenship, in which we all, like hijackers of airplanes, take one another hostage and threaten to kill one another. In acquiescing in the balance of terror, we become irresponsible parents, coldhearted lovers, faithless friends, and apathetic citizens. And in making a "conscious choice" to lift the nuclear peril we resolve to escape this pervasive corruption of our lives. We resolve to clear the air of the smell of burning flesh.

In making the choice, however, one decides nothing about the *means* of attaining the goal. That task is left to the second stage: framing the "deliberate policy." In fact, one has not even determined whether the goal of bringing the species to safety is attainable. If it is not, then our situation is tragic in the full sense of the word. Then our species, while willing to live, would be fated to die. And, indeed, there are many distinguished observers today who, while they do not write off the human species, believe that its safety cannot be very much improved. In particular, they rule out the abolition of nuclear weapons as impossible. For example a *New York Times* editorial critical of the recent pastoral letter of the National Conference of Catholic Bishops on war and peace, in which the bishops advocated the eventual abolition of nuclear weapons, stated, "Fundamentally, the American bishops' approach falters on the assumption that the nuclear dilemma can eventually be resolved by eliminating rather than controlling nuclear weapons. But there is no known way to get rid of The Bomb, no way to guard against all possible production or concealments of warheads." And in *Living with Nuclear Weapons*, a book written at the request of Derek Bok, the president of Harvard, by five professors and a graduate student associated with Harvard—Albert Carnesale, Paul Doty, Stanley Hoffmann, Samuel P. Huntington, Joseph S. Nye, Jr., and Scott D. Sagan, and published in 1982—it is stated that a world without nuclear weapons is "a fictional utopia," and "humanity has no alternative but to hold this threat at bay and to learn to live with politics, to live in the world we know: a world of nuclear weapons, international rivalries, recurring conflicts, and at least some risk of nuclear crisis." In the closing paragraph of the Harvard book, there is a memorable sentence, which the authors apparently thought important enough to make use of for their title. It reads, "Living with nuclear weapons is our only hope." This sentence could be engraved on our currency, alongside "In God we trust," or perhaps replacing it, for it reflects accurately the faith of our time. We truly not only "live with" nuclear weapons but place our hope for the future in them. And now some of us have apparently arrived at a point at which we profess to have lost all hope without them. Yet if a nuclear-free world is really "a fictional utopia," and if there is really "no known way to get rid of The Bomb"—not even "eventually"—then one must wonder what hope there is for mankind. Given the incurable fallibility of men and machines, doesn't it follow that sooner or later the bomb will get rid of us?

In the last few years, much of the public, having very largely ignored the nuclear peril for almost four decades, has been discovering a different faith. To express it in the Pope's terms, these people have been making their conscious choice: they have been choosing human survival. This long-delayed but deep and powerful public response is, like the predicament it addresses, a unique phenomenon, and familiar terms have to be stretched or altered to describe it, or even to name it. For example, it is both more and less than a "peace movement"—the usual, and probably inescapable, term for it. It is more because the word "movement" suggests something of a political character, whereas this response was born and has gathered strength outside politics. It has begun as a pre-political stocktaking, in which people have been reexamining life itself, and every activity in life, in the light of the present peril to all life. This psychological and spiritual process, which is the very substance of the conscious choice, might be described as an awakening rather than a movement. The response is less than a traditional movement for much the same reason: though it stands poised at the edge of the political arena, and has already intervened, or tried to intervene, in certain decisions (the deployment of the new American missiles in Europe, for example), it has yet to find full political expression. That is, it has decided that it wants man to survive, but it has not (as its critics are quick to point out) settled on a "deliberate policy" for reaching its goal. Thus, it might be described as an awakening seeking to become a movement. This awakening is new, and its extent and its consequences are still uncertain, but it promises to be one of those great changes of heart in mankind—such as the awakening to the evil of slavery in the nineteenth century—that alter the psychological and spiritual map of the world, and, first acting outside politics, sweep into it with decisive effect. If politics is the art of the possible, then deep changes in opinion of this kind extend the boundaries of what the possible includes. (The political process in a democracy is broader than is sometimes supposed. When politicians speak of what is "possible" or "impossible," they are often referring to nothing more than what is or is not acceptable to current public opinion. What they often really mean when they say that something is "impossible" is that they cannot win the next election if they advocate it. But if public opinion changes, then their opinion changes, too, and all of a sudden yesterday's impossible thing is possible.)

Just what may have triggered the new movement is a matter for speculation, but several circumstances and events are usually mentioned. They include the large buildup of nuclear arms by the Soviet Union in the last two decades, which has brought it up to the level of nuclear parity with the United States; the breakdown of the Strategic Arms Limitation Talks and the stalemate of the Strategic Arms Reduction Talks that succeeded them; the collapse of a mood of "détente" between the United States and the Soviet Union; the growing deployment by both the Soviet Union and the United States of missiles with the power to achieve a first strike against at least some missiles of the other side; the decision by the North Atlantic Treaty Organization to deploy intermediate-range nuclear missiles in Europe; and many provocative or ignorant-seeming statements regarding nuclear arms by officials of the Reagan Administration—statements such as one by T. K. Jones, the Deputy Under-Secretary of Defense for Research and Engineering, Strategic and Theatre Nuclear Forces, that "if there are enough shovels to go around, everybody's going to make it" through a nuclear holocaust, and, most important, the statement, in a top-secret Department of Defense planning document obtained by the *Times*, that the United States not only is planning for "prolonged" nuclear war but has as its aim to "prevail" in it—in plain language, to win it. But standing in the background of all these circumstances and events, I believe, is a development so simple and elementary that it is often overlooked. It is the fact that the doomsday machine—that immense collaborative undertaking of the United States and the Soviet Union, with minor assistance from other countries—has, over the last thirty-nine years, been assembled, with the finishing touches perhaps having been put on by the Soviet buildup. What was once merely a phrase in books is now actuality. And the real doomsday machine, lowering over the world, looks, feels, and is different in innumerable ways from the theoretical article. Of course, the doomsday machine didn't spring into existence all at once. The superpowers held no unveiling ceremony to announce to mankind that the preparations for the annihilation of the human species were now complete. Yet when people turned their attention to the nuclear peril they tended to see it all at once, with astonishment and horror, as though they had suddenly turned around and found themselves looking at a ferocious beast in the room with them. But looking at the nuclear peril was unlike any other looking. Because people were looking at things that they already in a sense knew about (the existence of nuclear arms had never been a secret), and not at some facts that had just been brought to light by reporters, it was a kind of looking within—a kind of introspection. And because these things that everyone already knew about were sickening and almost unbelievable, and because each person doing the looking was himself both implicated in and condemned by the evil, this looking within was anguishing. It seems not to be given to human beings to hold great horrors unremittingly before their mind's eye, and particularly not when the beholder is himself the potential perpetrator of the horror. We falter. We need respite. We forget. Then perhaps we look again. Alertness and stupor alternate. And we seem to lack any way of picturing extinction. The recent television film *The Day After* performed a public service by portraying Kansas after a nuclear attack. But no film can ever show the full consequences of a holocaust. It would have to display nothingness on the screen, and last forever. Even to try to understand the notion of extinction requires both intellectual and emotional effort. The boundlessness, the invisibility, and the emptiness of extinction are confounding. Extinction lacks the intricacy and detail that would permit our intellects to take hold of it—to analyze, to draw distinctions, to judge. Yet it is important to try to achieve an intellectual understanding of it, if only because by holding that in our mind we can sustain our effort and maintain our resolve without being dependent on the uncertainties of emotion. And, of course, as we strive, daily life in all its profusion goes on making its claims, introducing an at times comical disproportion in our lives between the immensity of our thoughts about the life and death of man and the smallness of our preoccupations with a particular personal quarrel, or meal, or financial worry, that may be absorbing us at a given moment. Weighing these incommensurables—deciding, for example, how much effort to expend to save the human species for all time as against how much to expend on, say, buying a sofa—is itself a considerable feat of balance and judgment.

Looking within themselves at the nuclear peril prepared people for action, and also was in itself a kind of action, albeit action taken within the privacy of each person's soul. Because this preparatory action—this coming to grips as a human being with the altered human situation—was not yet a political action, and prescribed no political course, it seemed to some as if it were nothing. That may be one reason the public awakening caught so many politicians and so much of the press by surprise: it had come about in domains of existence—the moral and spiritual—in which they ordinarily take little professional interest. That may also be the reason that, insofar as the movement has had leaders (a peculiar characteristic of it, apparently related to its grass-roots origin, has been its lack of conspicuous political leadership), they have tended to be doctors, including psychiatrists, and clergymen—people ordinarily concerned not with politics but with disturbances in the body, the psyche, and the soul. The new disturbances were, in fact, seismic. Suddenly, people were awash in fathomless questions of human existence. How did it happen, people started to ask themselves, that we have become the underwriters of the slaughter of billions of innocent people? Can such slaughter ever be justified? How? What is the meaning of human life on earth? What would its extermination mean? What does it mean about us that we have built the equipment with which to carry out that extermination, and are apparently prepared to perform the act? What does it mean that we—one link in the chain of the generations—are prepared to cut the chain, and set adrift in darkness all the future generations of human beings? What is our responsibility to these unborn people, and how can we fulfill it?

These questions are no newer than the technical invention that propelled them into the thick of history: they were raised in 1945, in the stunned aftermath of the Hiroshima bombing. Yet before long they receded from people's thoughts, as though they were too shocking for people to take to heart on such short notice. We who are alive today, however, thirty-nine years into the nuclear world, stand on different historical ground. Some of us have moved through the years of our lives in the shadow of the peril—have grown up, come of age, married, had children, worked, and approached death in the knowledge that before long all mankind may die. In one sense, our experience of the peril is oblique (no nuclear blast has been directed against human beings since Nagasaki), but in another sense it is fundamental, since if mankind destroys itself with nuclear weapons no one will experience our disappearance after the fact, and our experience of that fate now, before it happens, is all the experience of it that anyone will ever get. It *is* the experience of extinction. What we feel, therefore, is not so much fear of a future event, such as we feel when we realize that one day something terrible may happen to us, as it is disgust at the debasement of life right now because it is threatened by and threatens the extinction of man.

To make the choice is essential, for without it we are simply becalmed—as we were until very recently. If the inner landscape of our souls does not change, the outer landscape of the world will not change, either. And once the choice has been made it must, like every profound moral and spiritual decision, be continually refreshed and renewed. Since the beginning of history, human beings have stood in wonder at the blessing of life within them and around them. But now, for the first time, that wonder implies a political obligation. Every beautiful morning, every note of song, every infant's smile must propel us into action. Making and sustaining the conscious choice is a labor that has an integrity of its own, independent of what we may propose to do about the nuclear predicament. Just as in medicine the diagnosis precedes the prescription, and lays the basis for it, the conscious choice must precede the deliberate policy. But then we must frame the deliberate policy. If we fail, the cost to us—even if it happens that we do not stumble into oblivion—is that our wonder at life and our joy in it will be progressively diminished and corrupted. The choice must be made so that the policy can follow; but if the policy does not follow—if, instead, we sink back into stupefaction and complacency—the choice itself will be undone. Worse, it will, in effect, be reversed: by default, we will have chosen annihilation. In these pages, I propose to address the question of deliberate policy—specifically, the question of how we might abolish nuclear arms—but first, as a way of framing the policy question, I would like, by sketching out the chief features of our predicament (including, briefly, the facts that underlie the peril itself, some of which have come to light only recently), and by discussing some of the responses to the predicament over the years, to describe the elements of what appears to be a historic impasse, in which the world has now been stuck for almost four decades.

As citizens, we would like to know what the consequences of a nuclear holocaust at various levels of nuclear armament would be. We would like to know how many weapons of what size would kill how many people; how many weapons would be necessary to annihilate a particular country (our own, for example); and how many would be necessary to destroy our whole species. In search of answers to these questions, we naturally turn to scientists. But when we do we find that they can offer us only a portion of the information that either they or we need in order to make a firm judgment. That this should be so is not the fault of today's scientists, who have made impressive strides in understanding the natural world. Rather, it is due to humanity's still having only a rudimentary over-all comprehension of the living systems whose destruction or mutilation is in question; namely, human societies, ecosystems, and, ultimately, the earth itself—which is to say life itself, insofar as it has been given to human beings to know life. What is known about the earth is awesome—as readers of the September, 1983, issue of *Scientific American*, for example, which takes the workings of the earth as its subject, can appreciate. Yet what remains unknown is more awesome still. What is known seems towering until one looks at how much there remains to find out, and then it seems minuscule.

The crucial role of uncertainty in assessing the consequences of a nuclear holocaust needs some emphasis, because it is often overlooked or misunderstood by people who, for understandable reasons, would like simple and clear factual answers. The scientists can speak with great confidence about the properties of the weapons, which they invented and have observed in tests. But as soon as they begin to speak about the effects of those weapons on the surrounding world uncertainty sets in. For instance, it is known that land-surface nuclear explosions would create large amounts of radioactive fallout. Yet there has never been a true land-surface explosion of a bomb with a yield of more than one kiloton. The farther we get from the simple, immediate effects of the weapons—the initial nuclear radiation, the electromagnetic pulse, the thermal pulse, the blast wave, the local fallout—the more speculative our knowledge becomes. Maximum uncertainty is reached when we get to the question of extinction. Nuclear weapons threaten our species with extinction not because every last person on earth would be blown up or irradiated in a nuclear holocaust (something that could conceivably come close to happening in the targeted nations, though not in all the nations of the earth) but because a holocaust might so drastically alter the ecosphere that the earth would become uninhabitable by human beings.

The story of the advances that have been made in our understanding of the effects of a holocaust implies the unfinished state of our present knowledge of the total effects. That story has been one of continual surprises. The first surprise was the atomic bomb itself, which not ten years before its invention had been declared by many eminent scientists to be an unlikelihood bordering on an impossibility. Even Albert Einstein is reported to have remarked in 1935 that to split the atom would be akin to shooting birds in the dark in a country where there were few birds. Perhaps the next surprise, which came as a result of atmospheric testing, was the huge amount and range of radioactive fallout; its extent was unsuspected until it began falling on Pacific islanders and American servicemen after the American test on Bikini Atoll, in 1954. A further surprise that came during testing was the electromagnetic pulse—a gigantic surge of electricity that is generated by gamma radiation acting on air. The electromagnetic pulse of just one big nuclear bomb, if it is detonated high above the United States, may, it is now believed, damage solid-state electrical circuits throughout the continental United States and in parts of Canada and Mexico. A more recent surprise was the discovery, made in the early 1970s, of a danger to the ozone layer—one that in terms of global damage could be the most serious of the dangers that had been discovered up to that time. A report by the National Academy of Sciences in 1975 on *Long-Term Worldwide Effects of Multiple Nuclear-Weapons Detonations* found that after a holocaust in which ten thousand megatons were detonated ozone reduction might be as high as seventy per cent in the Northern Hemisphere (where all the detonations were assumed to have occurred) and forty per cent in the Southern Hemisphere. The formation of an ozone layer is believed to have been a precondition for the emergence of multicellular life, and of life on land, because ozone blocks out wavelengths of ultraviolet light that are harmful to many forms of life, and while reductions in the ozone of the magnitudes mentioned in the report would not eliminate all organisms with more than one cell or drive life back into the sea they could pervasively harm both plant and animal life, and their ultimate consequences for the earth's varied ecosystems are unforeseeable. Weighing these effects of a nuclear holocaust, scientists gave us warning that extinction was a possibility. For example, in March of 1982, in support of a proposal for joint hearings by the House Foreign Affairs Committee and the Senate Foreign Relations Committee on the effects of a holocaust, a number of scientists made statements on the subject. Marvin Goldberger, the president of the California Institute of Technology, said, "Full-scale war would eliminate humanity to all intents and purposes. Survival itself would be questionable." Paul Marks, the president of the Memorial Sloan-Kettering Cancer Center, said, "Nuclear war would wipe out the [human] race where the war was fought, and it could exterminate the entire race. It would make half

THE GREAT PREDICAMENT 233

the world uninhabitable. I'm not sure of the effect on the other half. It would probably make it uninhabitable, too." Other scientists who were quoted in favor of the proposal placed greater stress on the chances for survival. For example, Lewis Thomas, president emeritus of Sloan-Kettering, said, "Nuclear war would almost surely destroy human society. We would lose all of what we call culture. U.S.–U.S.S.R. conflict would eliminate the Northern Hemisphere for all practical purposes. The Southern Hemisphere might survive. I doubt that all humans would be exterminated." But whether they were pessimistic or optimistic about the chances for human survival the scientists surrounded their opinions with appropriate expressions of doubt, saying that extinction was "possible," or that the Southern Hemisphere "might" survive. Their common ground was uncertainty.

The wisdom of these scientists' reluctance to make final judgments became abundantly clear late last year, when, at a conference in Washington called "The World After Nuclear War," another group of eminent scientists revealed the latest surprise in the unfolding and obviously unfinished story of the effects of a nuclear holocaust. They had concluded that in a holocaust soil and dust from the explosions and smoke from fires set by the explosions would create a dark cloud over the earth which would largely block out sunlight, turning day into twilight or night, and drastically lowering the temperature, to create a "nuclear winter." The way in which this discovery was made is instructive of the unexpected ways in which science moves forward. One important new element in the discovery was space travel. In 1971, Mariner 9—the first spacecraft to go into orbit around another planet—began to circle Mars. Aboard was an infrared interferometric spectrometer—an instrument that could measure temperatures on the surface of Mars and at various heights in the atmosphere above it. As it happened, Mars was enveloped in a global dust storm when Mariner 9 arrived. The spectrometer showed that the atmosphere of Mars was considerably warmer than it usually was, and the surface considerably cooler: the dust in the atmosphere was absorbing sunlight, thus warming the atmosphere, and was blocking it from reaching the surface, thus cooling the surface. A group of scientists concerned with parallels between the earth and

other planets—Richard Turco, an atmospheric physicist in
Marina del Rey, California; Owen Toon, Thomas Ackerman,
and James Pollack, all from the National Aeronautics and Space
Administration's Ames Research Center; and Carl Sagan, the
director of the Laboratory for Planetary Studies at Cornell—set
about applying these findings to terrestrial questions. Their
interest was spurred by a recently advanced hypothesis that
the extinction of the dinosaurs at the end of the Cretaceous
period, sixty-five million years ago, might have resulted from a
drop in light and temperature brought about when an asteroid
crashed into the earth, lofting a cover of dust into the terrestrial
atmosphere.

Meanwhile, two other scientists—Paul Crutzen, of the Max
Planck Institute for Chemistry, in Mainz, Germany, and John
Birks, of the University of Colorado—had calculated that
smoke generated by the fires that would be started by nuclear
explosions would greatly decrease the sunlight reaching the
earth. (In fact, the smoke would be more important than the
dust in blocking sunlight.) The earth—its cities and its forests
in particular—is like a well-laid fire. If you light it with enough
nuclear matches, it will burn, and as it burns it will fill the
atmosphere with smoke and plunge much of the world into a
frigid darkness for several months. These findings, which were
published in 1982, and the findings from Mars led Turco and
his colleagues to conduct a study that they eventually called
Nuclear Winter: Global Consequences of Multiple Nuclear Explo-
sions. They concluded that within two weeks after a holocaust
in which five thousand megatons were used had occurred in
the Northern Hemisphere the cloud of smoke would circle
the hemisphere. A deep gloom would have gathered, and land
temperatures would be falling. Also, a toxic smog, loaded with
hydrogen cyanide and other debris of the burned cities, could
cover the hemisphere. A few weeks later, the cloud would
penetrate the Southern Hemisphere, and land temperatures
there would also begin to fall. After a holocaust in which ten
thousand megatons were used (the study estimated this to be
about three-quarters of what is available in present strategic
arsenals, whose exact megatonnage is unknown), temperatures
at the center of continents in the Northern Hemisphere could
sink as low as twenty-three degrees below zero Fahrenheit,

even in summer. Near coastlines, the temperatures would be more moderate, because of the warming influence of the sea, but violent, monsoon-like storms caused by the difference between inland and ocean temperatures could be expected. After a period lasting from several months to a year, the cloud would have largely dissipated, and sunlight, now unfortunately including the biologically harmful ultraviolet light let in by the ozone loss, would reach the surface again. In the Southern Hemisphere, the drops in temperature and the other effects would be less severe. One of the most surprising findings of the study was that as little as a hundred megatons—less than one per cent of the world's arsenals—could, if it were to be targeted on urban centers, trigger a less severe but still catastrophic nuclear winter, in which temperatures could drop more than fifty degrees Fahrenheit. Thus, there appears to be a threshold—determined by the number of explosions it would take to set a significant number of cities on fire—above which the major features of this climatic catastrophe would occur.

The human and biological consequences of the nuclear winter literally defy representation. Some are gross and obvious. People would freeze. They would find it difficult to see what they were doing. Crops wouldn't grow, so they would starve. Other animals would freeze and starve. If the holocaust occurred during the growing season, then "virtually all land plants in the Northern Hemisphere would be damaged or killed," in the words of Paul Ehrlich, professor of biological sciences at Stanford University, who presented a report to the conference on the biological consequences of the nuclear winter. "In the oceans, the darkness would inhibit photosynthesis in the tiny green plants (algae) that form the base of all significant marine food chains," Ehrlich said. "Tropical forests could largely disappear." The combined consequences of the nuclear winter, coming on top of the other effects, which in themselves could kill or wound billions of people and would shatter the elementary equipment of civilization by which modern man survives, lie far beyond our power of prediction, but they could, in words of Ehrlich's that, in the light of the new discoveries, add urgency to the words of warning we had already had from other scientists, "entrain the extinction of humanity."

The question of whether nuclear weapons might extinguish

mankind first came up in the 1940s, in a context slightly different from the present one. As the team of scientists at Los Alamos was preparing for the detonation of the first bomb, it occurred to someone that the heat of the explosion might be so great that it would ignite the earth's atmosphere and burn it up, ending not only human life but all life on earth. Robert Oppenheimer, the director of the project, took the danger seriously enough to ask a group of scientists on the team to figure out whether or not this would happen. The group found not only that the temperature of the bomb would be insufficient to set the atmosphere on fire but that the temperature needed to do that was so high that it could never be reached by any nuclear explosion. Armed with this assurance, the Los Alamos team went ahead and set off the bomb. (In social, if not in scientific, terms, the group's calculation may be described as the most important ever made by scientists.) One wonders whether the team would have done so if the group had come back with a less reassuring answer—if, for example, it had said that there was a one-in-a-hundred chance that the bomb would set the atmosphere on fire. Whatever the team might have done then, now that more than fifty thousand nuclear weapons stand ready to be detonated in the world's arsenals no such assurance regarding the survival of our species in the event of a holocaust is, or can be, forthcoming from responsible scientists. The physicist Theodore Taylor has said, "The consequences of nuclear war are unpredictable. The extinction of the species forever cannot be ruled out by any process of scientific investigation." We will gain more knowledge. (Already, a Russian scientist at the "World After Nuclear War" conference has suggested that the warming of the upper atmosphere by the smoke and soot from a holocaust will melt glaciers and snows in high mountain ranges, creating floods "of continental magnitude.") But our knowledge will never be complete. To accept uncertainty is essential in facing the nuclear peril honestly, and to learn to make judgments, and to act on them, in the midst of uncertainty is the beginning of wisdom in dealing with the nuclear predicament. It is especially important to avoid all false assurances and pseudo certainty. These, unfortunately, are rife, and include not only baseless, dogmatic judgments about the ultimate effects of a holocaust but also a large array of doubtful "strategic" predictions concerning precisely what moves and countermoves might be made in a holocaust.

Once the citizen has gone to the scientists and received the information that they have available, he must, without further professional help, take counsel with himself. The scientists can tell what they know; they can tell what they suspect; and they can guess with the rest of us about how much there may still be to find out. In putting his questions to the scientists, the citizen has already in a way asked them to venture beyond the proper limits of their disciplines, for he has asked them not for the proved results of experimentation but for speculation that is unprovable, unless we blow up the earth in search of answers. Because of the importance of the issue, the scientists oblige us with their best answers while candidly confessing the uncertainty and incompleteness of their findings. It would obviously be a mistake for the citizen to do what the scientists have warned against, and treat educated speculation as hard, scientific fact. The most valuable thing that the citizen carries away from the scientists' report, I suggest, is not any particular estimate—the percentage of ozone reduction, for example, or the level of temperature drop in the nuclear winter—for most of these estimates have been revised many times in the past and may be revised again in the future, and are, in any case, almost certainly an incomplete catalogue of effects. It is, rather, a broad sense of the power of a nuclear holocaust to throw the ecosphere as a whole into catastrophic disorder.

As the citizen takes stock of the perils, at least two considerations that lie outside the range of scientific evidence must come into play. The first is that effects of a nuclear holocaust will not fail to occur merely because they haven't been predicted. It may be that, say, only fifty per cent of them have been discovered, but a hundred per cent of them will occur. Unless—like the advocates of Newtonian physics at the end of the nineteenth century, who thought that with the scientific achievements of their time the edifice of physics had essentially been completed—we have the arrogance to believe that our present knowledge of the earth is perfect, we have no choice but to assume that the list of surprises is not complete. It should help us to preserve modesty in making judgments about the effects of a nuclear holocaust to recall that if we had sought in, say, 1950 to make a final judgment about those effects we would have seriously underestimated or left entirely out of account what are perhaps the three most important global effects that have been discovered so far: the extent of fallout; ozone loss; and the nuclear winter. The second consideration is that from a human point of view our extinction is an unlimited consequence. It would not only put an end to the living generations but foreclose all future generations, down to the end of time. It would mark the defeat of all human strivings, all human hopes, all human ideals, past and future. For now human beings, engaged, as always, in the ambitions and disputes of their particular place and time, can end the human story in all places for all time. The eternal has been placed at stake in the temporal realm, and the infinite has been delivered into the care of finite human beings. It is because of this special nature of the peril, I believe, that the very existence of uncertainty about whether or not a holocaust would extinguish our species should lead us to treat the issue morally and politically *as though* it were a certainty. That is, when we turn to the nuclear predicament we should muster all the commitment that loyalty to our species can inspire. In my book *The Fate of the Earth* (1982), I wrote a passage that emphasizes the importance of uncertainty, and I repeat it here to clarify the reason for treating the uncertainty *as though* it were certainty:

> We know that a holocaust may not occur at all. If one does occur, the adversaries may not use all their weapons. If they do use all their weapons, the global effects, in the ozone and elsewhere, may be moderate. And if the effects are not moderate but extreme, the ecosphere may prove resilient enough to withstand them without breaking down catastrophically. These are all substantial reasons for supposing that mankind will not be extinguished in a nuclear holocaust, or even that extinction in a holocaust is unlikely, and they tend to calm our fear and to reduce our sense of urgency. Yet at the same time we are compelled to admit that there *may* be a holocaust, that the adversaries *may* use all their weapons, that the global effects, including effects of which we are as yet unaware, *may* be severe, that the ecosphere *may* suffer catastrophic breakdown, and that our species *may* be extinguished. We are left with uncertainty.

I concluded, "Once we learn that a holocaust *might* lead to extinction we have no right to gamble, because if we lose, the game will be over, and neither we nor anyone else will ever get another chance. Therefore, although, scientifically speaking, there is all the difference in the world between the mere possibility that a holocaust will bring about extinction and the certainty of it, morally they are the same, and we have no choice but to address the issue of nuclear weapons as though we knew for a certainty that their use would put an end to our species." It is in this spirit that I continue here to speak of nuclear weapons as an issue of life or death for mankind.

The totality of the peril (in the sense just defined) is, of course, the most important feature of the nuclear predicament. It must inevitably shape and color all our thinking on the subject, including our thinking on what we should do about the predicament. A second, less often mentioned feature, which is of importance to the policy question, is the abruptness with which the peril arrived. Great changes had occurred in the conditions of life before, but they had arrived gradually. The industrial revolution, for example, transformed the way people lived, but it was made up of innumerable technical innovations that were released into the world over centuries, so that people had time to make their adjustments. The industrial revolution would offer a closer analogy if all the inventions made between, say, 1700 and 1945 had somehow arrived at once, in 1700. The nuclear predicament—the result of the invention of a *single* device—sprang into the world full-fledged, offering little time for reflection or adjustment. (There did remain the time required to build up the arsenals—a sort of grace period—but it was very short, and, in any case, has been squandered.) Slavery offers another analogy. It was there at the beginning of history, and it took mankind millennia to finally confront the practice and abolish it. But when nuclear weapons were invented a brand-new evil was suddenly created, as though slavery had been lowered into our midst in an instant. And we did not have the luxury of millennia in which to react. The peril was immediate, and called on us to act right away.

A third feature of the predicament, which is also of importance to the policy question, is the peril's apparent everlastingness. While nuclear weapons can, I believe, one day be eliminated, the knowledge of how to make them, which is rooted in our century's fundamental discoveries in physics, appears likely to be with us forever, and since that is so the possibility that nuclear arsenals will be rebuilt and used cannot be ruled out. We are not condemned to live always in a world armed with nuclear weapons, but we shall always live in a nuclear world. In that respect, nuclear energy is like a new sun that has risen over the earth—a sun that will beam its bleak light on human affairs as long as the sun in the sky will. We speak of "the nuclear age," but since, strictly speaking, that "age," like the period "after Christ," has no end in view, it would be more appropriate to speak, in the Latin phrase, of "a new order of the ages." But perhaps if we optimistically suppose that nuclear weapons (though not the knowledge of how to make them) will one day be abolished we can call the period up to then "the nuclear age"—and pray that it will be short.

As if it were not enough that the threat posed by the nuclear peril was unlimited in its scope, instantaneous in its appearance, and everlasting in its staying power, a fourth key feature of the predicament is that nuclear weapons immediately lodged themselves at the very heart of international decision-making, and so carried revolutionary global political implications. Given all the rest, it might seem that the revolutionary political implications would hardly need mention, but the fact is that one can imagine perils on an equal scale physically whose political solution would be relatively simple. For example, it was discovered some years ago that certain types of spray cans release gases which, like the products of nuclear explosions, can rise into the stratosphere, where they decompose, and that their components erode the ozone layer. Let us suppose that scientists had discovered (as in fact they have not) that at present levels of spray-can use the erosion of the ozone layer would go far enough to doom all land animals in ten years. We can have little doubt that the nations of the earth would quickly sign a treaty abolishing spray cans. Or let us suppose that scientists had discovered (as, again, they have not) that, beyond a certain threshold, the burning of fossil fuels would trigger a runaway "greenhouse effect" in the atmosphere, in which the temperature of the earth would rise to lethal levels. (Scientists suspect that a runaway greenhouse effect may be responsible for the seven-hundred-degree surface temperature of Venus. They also suspect that a greenhouse effect produced by the burning of fossil fuels will warm the earth by several degrees in the next hundred years.) Once again, it is hard to doubt that, despite the importance of fossil fuels, the nations of the earth would quickly sign a treaty bringing their use under control. For it would surely very soon become clear to people everywhere that they valued humanity more than they valued fossil fuels. Or if we imagine that one day we were attacked by creatures from space whose aim was to destroy mankind and take over the planet, it is again hard to doubt that the nations of the earth would unite to defend their planet. (The Soviet Union and the United States even managed to unite to defeat the earthly peril of Nazi Germany.) Yet when it comes to saving the earth from the peril of a nuclear holocaust the necessary agreements are not arrived at so easily—as the history of the last thirty-nine years attests. And for this failure there is a substantial cause that would not be a factor in any of the foregoing, imagined situations. The solution of each of those threats would require us to give something up—spray cans, fossil fuels, the immediate pursuit of earthly rivalries. But if we ask what it is that we would have to give up in order to resolve the nuclear predicament we find that it is nothing less than the whole present structure of international affairs. For the very first effect of the invention of nuclear weapons—which occurred even without their going off—was to fatally undermine the institution of war.

It may seem odd to speak of war, the nemesis of human institutions, as an institution itself, liable to change and decline like any other, yet we are now in a position to see that it has been just that: a particular kind of organization of human affairs, with a particular character, a particular technical foundation, and particular uses. Its preeminent use has been to serve as what has been called since Roman times "the final arbiter" of disputes among nations—as the world's means of last resort for getting things settled. But when nuclear weapons entered the arsenals of nations war could no longer arbitrate anything, because the levels of force available would destroy every prize that a nation might want either to seize or to defend. Nations bent on achieving some aim by the use of force, whether the aim was their own survival or another country's subjugation, could not hope to succeed in a nuclear-armed world. To be sure, nuclear-armed nations could still attack one another (if they were foolish enough), but at the end of the road only their "mutual assured destruction" now awaited them. This would not be war—once defined as "the continuation of politics by other means"—but only suicide, which is the continuation of nothing.

It's worth noting that the point in the nuclear buildup at which mutual assured destruction became possible (and victory in war impossible) is different from the point at which extinction became possible. Perhaps because both results are absurd, the two are sometimes lumped together. The difference becomes obvious if we imagine that two small countries, each of which can be annihilated with just a few dozen nuclear weapons, are faced off against one another. Each would destroy the other long before the two together could extinguish the species. When the countries are large, however, the gap between mutual assured destruction and extinction is narrower, and the new conclusion that even "limited nuclear war" might trigger the nuclear winter narrows this gap still further. In a general holocaust, the mutual destruction of the belligerents would be only a minor absurdity within the major, unlimited absurdity of the end of humanity. Nevertheless, the potential for mutual assured destruction needs to be underscored, because it is precisely *this* minor absurd outcome—which does not depend on the presence of a peril of extinction—that spoils war as a rational instrument of national policy, and forces nations to look for a substitute. (The possibility of extinction, above and beyond mutual assured destruction, gives their search a transcendent importance.)

To avoid misunderstanding: When I say that war has been spoiled as a means of settling international disputes, I mean that it has been spoiled in those theatres of potential conflict in which the rivals are abundantly armed with nuclear weapons, as the United States and the Soviet Union are. In other theatres, in which one or both powers lack nuclear weapons, nations can and do go on fighting wars. To avoid further misunderstanding: What has been ruined is, precisely, war—no more and no less. Violence between nuclear-armed states is still possible on any scale, from terrorist acts right up to the end of the world, but none of this would, properly speaking, be war. For war is not just violence; it is violence shaped to achieve state ends. But all these ends would be unattainable by "war" as it exists today, for by the time anyone had "won" the "war" both sides would have been annihilated.

In sum, the underlying *human* question that the invention of nuclear weapons confronts us with is whether we will live or die as a species, but the underlying *political* question, which must be tackled before the human question can be favorably resolved, is how disputes among nations are to be handled in a world in which war has been spoiled as an instrument of state policy. Nuclear weapons are radical biologically and spiritually because they threaten our species with extinction, but they are radical politically because they have spoiled war. For traditionally the political character of our world has been determined in large part by the outcome of wars—by whether the Romans or the Carthaginians, Napoleon or Wellington, the Axis or the Allies, were victorious. At stake, therefore, *in addition* to the life or death of mankind, is everything that nations are and everything that they stand for, since it is through war that nations in the past have sought ultimately to protect their existence. How, we are now forced to ask, are we to defend the things that we believe in—or, on a more prosaic level, that we merely want? (For the United States, and for the Western alliance, the chief question of this sort is, perhaps, how we can protect our liberties and, by a reasonable extension, liberty in the world as a whole.) How are nations to respond to aggression? Or should there any longer even *be* nations, which, continuing their historical reliance on the resort to force in pursuit of their parochial interests, now menace the survival of all mankind? At issue is *who* is going to decide international disputes and *how*—and these are, of course, the fundamental issues of politics. Should nations decide through violence, as in the past? Should an international authority decide? Is there another way of deciding? No proposal that fails to give an answer to this underlying question can inspire confidence, and only a proposal that deals with it to the world's satisfaction seems likely to stand a chance of finally resolving the nuclear predicament.

There is a strong temptation to underestimate either the biological or the political dimension of the peril, because then the job of finding a solution is much simplified. For example, if we choose to disregard the radical nature of the political issue, then responding without impediment to the totality and immediacy of the peril, we are free to imagine that we can "ban" nuclear weapons without further ado—without, that is, having to account for how, politically, a nuclear-free world would work, what would be likely to happen in it, and whether or not it would be likely to stay nuclear-free. On the other hand, if, duly impressed by the intractability of the political challenge, we choose instead to play down the physical immediacy and totality of the peril, we may complacently and unconscionably leave our species at risk of annihilation. Such, I believe, is our present condition.

The difficulty of taking all the features of the nuclear predicament into account was made clear in the first attempts to discover solutions. Sheer thought, of course, was able to see its way to a solution quite easily. The steps in the reasoning were simple ones. If war now meant nuclear war—and no one could doubt that it did—and nuclear war meant, at best, the mutual assured destruction of the belligerents and, at worst, human extinction, then war no longer made any sense and would have to be given up. But if war was given up, then some other means would have to be found to resolve the disputes that war had always resolved. A means was not hard to find—at least, on the purely intellectual plane. It was government—world government. The rule of law would supplant the rule of force, and what had once been decided by violence would now be decided by courts, parliaments, and all the other institutions of civil society. In the early days of the nuclear age, many people, including, notably, many scientists, were swayed by this compelling logic, and soon set to work to bring a world government into existence. Preeminent among them, perhaps, was Albert Einstein, who, at the beginning of the century, had first revealed that energy and matter are the same. As early as September 29, 1945—less than two months after the bomb was dropped on Hiroshima, on August 6—he wrote:

> The pathetic attempts made by governments to achieve what they consider to be international security have not the slightest effect on the present political structure of the world, nor is it rec-ognized that the real cause of international conflicts is due to the

existence of competing sovereign nations. Neither governments nor people seem to have learned anything from the experiences of the past and appear to be unable or unwilling to think the problem through. The conditions existing in the world today force the individual states, out of fear for their own security, to commit acts which inevitably produce war.

At the present high level of industrialization and economic interdependence, it is unthinkable that we can achieve peace without a genuine supranational organization to govern international relations.

At about the same time, Einstein was one of the signatories of a letter, published in the *New York Times*, that said, in part:

We have learned, and paid an awful price to learn, that living and working together can be done in one way only—under law. There is no truer and simpler idea in the world today. Unless it prevails, and unless by common struggle we are capable of new ways of thinking, mankind is doomed.

And in June of 1946 he told an interviewer:

Our defense is not in armaments, nor in science, nor in going underground. Our defense is in law and order.

Einstein knew very well that the political climate of his time was hostile to his proposal, and he knew that many people regarded it as, in his words, "illusory, even absurd." Nevertheless, in a reply to critics, he asked:

Is it really a sign of unpardonable naiveté to suggest that those in power decide among themselves that future conflicts must be settled by constitutional means rather than by the senseless sacrifice of great numbers of human lives? Once such a firm decision has been reached, nothing will be "impossible." . . .

A "sophisticated" person might well comment: We have been working toward the same goal by means of small, patient steps, which, in view of human psychology, is the only possible method. But I, the so-called "idealist," regard this attitude as a fatal illusion. There is no *gradual* way to secure peace. As long as nations have no real security against aggression, they will, inevitably, continue to prepare for war. And, as history has proven conclusively, preparation for war always leads to actual war. When the North American Colonies united and created a central government in Washington, it came about not through a slow process but through a resolute and creative act.

In interviews, articles, letters, and public statements, Einstein, continuing to state his case with his customary clarity, modesty, simplicity, and passion, advocated this position until the end of his life, in April, 1955.

Einstein's view that the nuclear predicament could be resolved and mankind saved only if the world renounced force and adopted peaceful political means for the settlement of its disputes possessed a straightforward logic that no one ever refuted and that was apparently irrefutable. (His view that the only such means possible was world government was more debatable.) But what logic called for and what the world was prepared to accept were two different things. Einstein set out to change minds. He knew, as few other men did, what the measure of the peril was, and he worked tirelessly to impart that knowledge to others. As a scientist, he was used to thinking a problem through to its end, and he thought the political implications of the nuclear predicament through to their end, too. He placed his faith in reason—in people's ability to learn, and to act on what they have learned. He had changed the world through scientific thought, and now he wanted to change it further through political thought. In that sense, world government was a scientists' *sort* of idea. Using reason, scientists analyzed the problem, came up with a formula that would solve it, and then invited the world to apply that formula. Einstein wrote, "Just as we have changed our thinking in the world of pure science to embrace newer and more useful concepts, so we must now change our thinking in the world of politics and law. It is too late to make mistakes." And, even more simply, "Past thinking and methods did not succeed in preventing world wars. Future thinking *must* prevent wars." But politics was different from science, and thinking turned out not to have the effectiveness in world affairs that it had had in the laboratory. In politics, the process was different and the tempo was different. Political ideas moved at a slower pace than scientific ones from one mind to the minds of many, and from the minds of many into action.

Certainly one cause of the world's apparent indifference to the nuclear peril, and of the short shrift it gave the idea of world government, was the peril's all-or-nothing character, which removed it from people's direct experience. Most evils arrive in the world a little bit at a time, so that in pushing people into action the bite of painful experience is added to the voice of pure reason. If a factory is polluting the water supply, for example, deadly poison doesn't suddenly start running from the tap; the pollution appears gradually, and people are driven to do something before a catastrophe occurs. But after Hiroshima and Nagasaki the nuclear peril turned out to leave the world physically untouched, and the field was left to "thinking" alone. There can be little doubt that if in the last thirty-nine years one Hiroshima-sized nuclear weapon had gone off each day in a city somewhere in the world (thus releasing, in all, only about one per cent of the explosive power of today's arsenals) Einstein's proposal, or something of an equally radical nature, would have found acceptance by now. As it was, the nuclear weapons fortunately stayed unexploded (while unfortunately multiplying in the world's arsenals), and people were not impelled to think or do very much about them.

The stronger reasons for the rejection of the sweeping changes that Einstein wanted, however, were unquestionably political. Arrayed against his argument was not so much counterargument as brute fact—everything that comes under the heading of political "reality," which in the short run, at least, has a weight and an inertia that are independent of argument and the light of reason. On the immediate level, reality was two great powers—the United States and the Soviet Union—whose systems of government were wholly antithetical. While it was quite conceivable that these two powers could live together without war—that is, "coexist"—there seemed little or no possibility that they could fuse into a single government. Reality was, in addition, the countless unresolved struggles that went on, and go on, among the less powerful nations of the world, dividing Arab from Jew, Irishman from Englishman, Turk from Greek, and so on. On the deepest level, however, reality was the entire political organization of the world. Standing in the way of Einstein's "thinking," that is, was nothing less than the world's political institutions as they had existed throughout history—the entire system of independent states, whose defense now threatened extinction. The invention of nuclear

weapons brought basic physical and biological reality, now radically transformed by the revolution in scientific thought, into
head-on collision with basic political reality, where no similar
revolution appeared likely soon. And the collision was not just
a clash of styles, or a failure of scientists and politicians to speak
one another's language; it was objective and real. Science had
moved with the speed of thought to alter physical reality and
to give technical man the ability to place the whole world in
peril of annihilation, but the political thinkers were powerless
to perform a comparable miracle in political affairs. Political
affairs, weighted with tradition and habit—in this case, a way
of doing things which had lasted throughout history—moved
with a ponderous gait of their own, and were not to be hurried.
The nuclear predicament had emerged in an instant from the
laboratory, but the resolution of the predicament could not
emerge from any laboratory. It would have to be born in its
own time, in the hearts of the billions of the earth's people.

The disparity between the swiftness of science in presenting
the peril (a swiftness much accentuated, from the world's point
of view, by the governmental secrecy out of which the bomb
sprang) and the seemingly built-in slowness of the world's
thinking and the world's institutions to adjust to it presented
the world, in effect, with a monumental problem of timing.
While the predicament might not be inherently beyond resolution, the mismatch between the immediacy of the peril and
the magnitude of the psychological, spiritual, and political work
required for mankind to make an adequate response—which
might conceivably take generations—could in itself prove fatal.
The proposal for world government therefore engendered as
much discouragement as hope. Many people believed that a
solution might lie there, but they could not see how to arrive
at it soon enough to respond to the pressing emergency in
which the species found itself. Nor did sovereignty show any
signs of expiring on its own. If anything, it was tightening its
hold—especially in the Third World, where patriotic feeling was
showing itself to be an almost irresistible force, against which
the great colonial empires of the West were proving powerless.

In those circumstances, it was anything but surprising that a
second school of thought about how to handle the nuclear

predicament soon emerged—a school that was ready to accept the unwillingness of nations to surrender their sovereignty and enter into a world government. In 1946, in a book called *The Absolute Weapon*, by a group of academics at the Yale Institute of International Studies, there appeared two chapters written by the political scientist Bernard Brodie, which have come to be considered a founding document of American nuclear strategy, and which we may take as representative of the second school of thought. Brodie begins by accepting as given the continuation of the sovereign state—the very thing whose abolition Einstein saw as the only hope for survival in the nuclear world. As befits someone stating a premise, Brodie does not so much argue the point as simply assert it, saying, with light irony, that "the wholesale conversion of mankind away from those parochial attitudes bound up in nationalism is a consummation devoutly to be wished" but "the mere existence of the bomb does not promise to accomplish it at an early enough time to be of any use." If the existence of the nation-state is a given, then the possibility of the use of force becomes another given, because it is through the use of force that nations have ultimately sought to assure their survival. And if the possibility of the use of force is a given, then the existence of nuclear weapons becomes still another given, because nuclear weapons are the most powerful instruments of force available. Thus, while it may be true that, as Einstein said, if you want to rid the world of nuclear weapons you will have to establish a world government, neither of these things, in Brodie's view, can be accomplished, and the truly important and interesting question, therefore, is what policy to adopt in a world in which both sovereign states and nuclear weapons are present. Significantly, Brodie does not see this task as an end in itself; rather, he sees it as a way of buying time while more radical solutions, of the Einsteinian variety, are worked on. He wants merely to "transmute what appears to be an immediate crisis into a long-term problem," so as to give society the opportunity it needs to adjust its politics to its physics. His answer to the problem of mismatched timing is to work within the realm of the politically "possible" for the present, and postpone more ambitious efforts. It is noteworthy, though, that while he and the other authors of *The Absolute Weapon* acknowledge the need to find radical solutions sometime in the future they have no suggestions to offer about how to proceed with this work. The "short term" occupies them completely.

It is in framing policy for a world in which nuclear weapons are a given that Brodie shows his prescience and his originality. He begins with an unsparing description of the destructive power of the atomic bomb—a description that Einstein, for one, would surely have approved of. He points out that to destroy any city in the world, from one to ten atomic, or fission, bombs will suffice (the hydrogen, or fusion, bomb, which can be thousands of times as powerful as the fission bomb, and so can do the job much more efficiently, had, of course, not yet been invented); that no defense against the bomb is possible; and that therefore "it is now physically possible for air forces no greater than those existing in the recent war to wipe out all the cities of a great nation in a single day." He then notes that some "scientists and laymen" who have a "passionate" preoccupation with "proposals for 'world government'" have concluded from these admittedly terrifying facts that "the safeguards to security formerly provided by military might are no longer of any use," and that the bomb must therefore be regarded as "the apotheosis of aggressive instruments." And he quotes J. Robert Oppenheimer as saying that the bomb "is a weapon for aggressors, and the elements of surprise and of terror are as intrinsic to it as are the fissionable nuclei." Brodie disagrees. In a key paragraph, he says, "The truth of Professor Oppenheimer's statement depends on one vital but unexpressed assumption: that the nation which proposes to launch the attack will not need to fear retaliation. If it must fear retaliation, the fact that it destroys its opponent's cities some hours or even days before its own are destroyed may avail it little." The would-be aggressor, who knew that he faced retaliation, Brodie thinks, would very likely give up its aggression. "Multilateral possession of the bomb," therefore, will discourage, not encourage, aggression, provided that it is "as nearly certain as possible that the aggressor who uses the bomb will have it used against him."

Here, in a nutshell, and without the jargon and intellectual adornment of the "strategic theory" that unfolded luxuriantly in later years, is the doctrine of nuclear deterrence—although Brodie did not use that word. From Brodie's observations flowed the basic tenets of the doctrine of deterrence: that nuclear weapons offer nations effectively unlimited force; that winning a nuclear war is impossible; that it is imperative, therefore, to stop such a war from ever beginning; that the weapons themselves play the crucial role in that effort; that an invulnerable retaliatory force is of particular importance; that there is a special danger inherent in any capacity, on either side, for destroying the nuclear forces of the other side in a first strike; and that "perceptions" and "psychology" play an essential role in convincing the adversary that any aggression by him will lead only to his annihilation, and so in maintaining the "stability" of the whole arrangement. Summing up in a way that must have been jarring to military sensibilities at that time, Brodie wrote, "The writer . . . is not for the moment concerned about who will *win* the next war in which atomic bombs are used. Thus far the chief purpose of our military establishment has been to win wars. From now on its chief purpose must be to avert them. It can have almost no other useful purpose." The policy of deterrence did not, of course, remove the peril of nuclear annihilation. On the contrary, it deliberately and firmly increased it (by sanctioning a buildup of nuclear arms), in the hope that the immediacy of the threat, felt by each side in the face of the other side's nuclear arsenals, would produce a stalemate in which the world would live on the very edge of the abyss but for precisely that reason would take special care not to lose its balance. The great advantage of deterrence was not the high degree of safety that it offered—for under it a single miscalculation could tip the world into the abyss—but its immediate practicability. For while it was doubtful in the extreme that that world would soon put together a world government, there was little doubt that in the absence of such a step the world's great powers could and would build large nuclear arsenals and threaten one another with them. To be sure, once the Soviet Union had acquired nuclear weapons, and the nuclear stalemate had been established, no one in either Washington or Moscow needed any political scientists to tell him that a nuclear attack might be met with retaliation in kind, and was, for that reason, among others, a bad idea. But it was the distinction of Brodie and his fellow-strategists to foresee this in 1946, when only one power possessed the bomb. His discovery was that a balance of nuclear forces might make possible a world more stable than any before it in our century. While he agreed with the advocates of world government that the bomb could not be defended against, he saw, as many of them did not, that the threat of retaliation could play the role that defenses had played in the past, and that in this threat there might lie a measure of safety for a nuclear-armed world.

The argument between the Einsteinian school and the Brodiean school reflected not just a split in opinion but a split in the world itself. For the arrival of nuclear weapons in the world had at a stroke opened a fissure down the center of human life, placing whole realms of human existence at odds with one another. The traditional demands of man's international political existence, rooted in sovereignty and pursued through the use of force, were suddenly at variance with the demands of man's existence pure and simple, which was now mortally endangered. Political man held a knife to the throat of biological man, but since politics, like every other human activity, is possible only where there are human beings, political man also held a knife to his own throat. At the same time, the demands of man's moral existence, which were meaningless if they did not call on us to hold back at all costs from slaughtering billions of people and perhaps putting our species to death, were at variance with those of man's political existence, which seemed to require that we threaten to do just that, on pain of military defeat by our enemies if we did not. Einstein and Brodie, in a manner of speaking, took up positions on opposite sides of the gap, with Einstein standing alongside trembling, imperilled biological man and asking political man to yield, and Brodie standing alongside dug-in, unbudgeable political man and asking biological man to endure the peril. And each, of course, had a compelling reason for standing where he did, since no one could deny, on the one hand, that the peril was great—indeed, unlimited—and its urgency extreme or, on the other, that the immediate top-to-bottom transformation of international political life was, at the very least, doubtful. A bystander looking for guidance was left to contemplate two conclusions, each of which had apparently been established incontrovertibly by experts: (1) that the nature of physical reality as it had now been revealed by physics made a swift revolution in global politics necessary if human survival was to be assured, and (2) that the nature of political reality as it had revealed itself throughout history made such a revolution impossible.

People of Einstein's persuasion came to be called "idealists," as he had noted, while those of Bridie's persuasion came to be called "realists," but in fact both camps were characterized by a spirit of realism. This was not a debate in which there was reality on one side and a mistaken idea on the other. Rather, there were two opposed realities: the reality of the peril of extinction by nuclear arms, and the reality of the existing political institutions of the world. The two schools of thought therefore did not so much clash irreconcilably as fail even to join the argument; it was as though each were addressing a different "nuclear predicament"—and, in a way, each was. Einstein took as his point of departure his knowledge of the laws of physics and of the peril they defined; he went on to ask what had to be done to remove the peril, and concluded that the whole political realm had to be revolutionized. Since not only politics but everything human was in danger of "being disintegrated someday into atoms and swept up into the atmosphere," as he put it, revolution in just one department of life seemed to him a small price to pay. Brodie, by contrast, took as his point of departure his knowledge of the laws of politics and of the existing political world, and concluded that for the immediate future the peril would have to be lived with. Rarely in a great debate had each side had so many seemingly incontestable points to make. Could anyone seriously doubt that, as a supporter of Einstein's views said, quoting Alexander Hamilton, "to look for a continuation of harmony between a number of independent, unconnected sovereignties situated in the same neighborhood would be to disregard the uniform course of human events, and to set at defiance the accumulated experience of ages"? On the other hand, could anyone argue with William T. R. Fox, one of the authors of *The Absolute Weapon*, when, in the final chapter of that book, he observed, "It would be very dangerous to create a machine of central force before one created a machinery of central justice. For a machinery of central justice to work satisfactorily, its judgments would have to be based upon a worldwide community of values. That community of values does not exist today"? Wasn't it a fact that, as Einstein said, "today the atomic bomb has altered profoundly the nature of the world as we know it, and the human race consequently finds itself in a new habitat to which it must adapt its thinking"? But wasn't it also a fact that, as Fox noted, a Soviet commentator had just called the idea of world government a smoke screen for "renunciation of the basis of the struggle against fascist aggression"; and that the United States was also "unwilling to surrender a degree of control over its own destinies sufficient to permit a world authority to enforce its declared policy against any challenger"?

Einstein and Brodie, each rooted firmly in the reality he knew best, were unable to find common ground. Einstein, the proponent of what was necessary for survival, could not persuade the world that it was politically possible. Brodie, the definer of what was politically possible, could not enlarge his conception of it to encompass what was necessary for survival. The world was offered two problematic proposals: one that would solve the problem but could not be brought into being, and one that could be brought into being but did not solve the problem. The gap between them—between imperilled biological man and entrenched political man; between the irresistible force of nuclear weapons and the immovable object of the world's political institutions (immovable, that is, except by nuclear weapons, which could move them right out of existence in an instant); between a resolution of the broad human crisis of the peril of extinction and a resolution of the political crisis of how the world was to be organized without war; between the laws of science and the laws of history; between the dictates of conscience and the dictates of policy; between "idealism" and "realism"; between the "long term" and the "short term"; between the necessary and the possible; between the slowness of political change and the swiftness of the approach of doom— remained unbridged. And it has remained so to the present day.

Whoever may have had the better of the debate between the two schools, it was, of course, the deterrence doctrine that eventually became official policy. People couldn't, or wouldn't, or just did not, establish world government, and they turned to the only prominent alternative. Before that happened, however, the United States launched an initiative at the United Nations to prevent a nuclear-arms race and abolish nuclear weapons. The initiative failed, but in failing it threw a spotlight on the mountainous political obstacles to a solution of the nuclear problem. The initiative originated, in January of 1946, with the appointment by Secretary of State James Byrnes of a committee headed by Under-Secretary of State Dean Acheson whose work would be to frame a proposal for nuclear disarmament which the United States would make at a forthcoming meeting of the Atomic Energy Commission of the United Nations. Acheson proceeded to appoint a board of consultants, under the chairmanship of David E. Lilienthal, who was then the director of the Tennessee Valley Authority, and including Robert Oppenheimer. On March 17, after intense labors, the committee and the board of consultants concluded their deliberations and embodied them in a document commonly known as the Acheson-Lilienthal report, which was transmitted to Byrnes the following day. At the heart of the committee's recommendations was a proposal that nuclear activities be placed under international control. The report had arrived at an ingenious solution (which may yet prove useful to the world one day) to the thorny problem arising from the need for inspection under any agreement by nations to forgo the production and possession of nuclear arms. Impressed by the political difficulties that would face teams charged with inspecting a large number of independent, national nuclear facilities, the report recommended that all "dangerous" nuclear activities—from uranium mining to the construction of nuclear reactors—be placed under the direct ownership of an international authority associated with the United Nations. (Individual nations would be licensed by the authority to carry out certain "safe" nuclear activities.) This authority, they reasoned, could readily inspect that which it was doing itself.

On March 18, President Truman announced the appointment of Bernard Baruch, a financier who served as an adviser to several Presidents, to represent the United States at the disarmament talks at the United Nations, and Baruch was given the Acheson-Lilienthal report. Much to the dismay of the report's authors, Baruch turned out to have many reservations about it, including its assumption that major violations of the proposed system of international controls would ultimately come before

the United Nations Security Council, whose decisions could be
nullified by a veto by any one of five nations: the United States,
the Soviet Union, England, France, and China. It was the Soviet veto that worried Baruch. He recommended that the veto
power in the Security Council be abolished for decisions having
to do with atomic energy. And, in a second major departure
from the report, he recommended that penalties be established
for violations of the agreement concerning atomic energy. (The
report had not proposed any penalties.) Without these, he said,
the proposal as a whole would amount to nothing more than a
warning system, which would put the world on notice if nuclear
arming began but would be unable to do anything about it.
In short, he had noted the lack in the report of any means for
dealing with the underlying political question of how disputes
among nations—in this case, disputes concerning the life-and-
death matter of atomic energy—were to be decided, and his
recommendations were designed to repair the omission: the
Security Council would decide. What he recommended was not
world government, but it contained something like the essence
of world government: an authority with the power to make
and enforce decisions concerning the most critical element
of military power. President Truman agreed with Baruch and
adopted his recommendations.

In June, Baruch presented the proposal to the United Nations, and it was immediately turned down by Andrei Gromyko,
the Soviet representative at the arms negotiations. The Soviet
Union had substantial reasons for turning it down. The United
Nations, which did not yet include most of the hundred-odd
nations that make up what we now call the Third World, could
be counted on in those days to vote in favor of Western proposals, and the Soviet Union's veto in the Security Council was its
only means of undoing the results. To accept an international
authority that controlled mining rights in the Soviet Union and
held a monopoly on nuclear energy could thus mean accepting
not only a large measure of American control over Soviet nuclear
energy but also American intervention in Soviet life—an idea as
repugnant to the Soviet Union as the converse would have been
to the United States if the Soviet Union had enjoyed majority
support at the United Nations. Besides, the Soviet Union was

at the time well on its way to getting the bomb. (It succeeded in 1949.) However, the Soviet Union went far beyond rejecting the repeal of the veto. It also denounced inspection, as a breach of national sovereignty. Gromyko stated, "When the Charter of the United Nations was prepared by the conference at San Francisco, the question of sovereignty was one of the most important questions considered. This principle of sovereignty is one of the cornerstones on which the United Nations structure is built; if this were touched the whole existence and future of the United Nations would be threatened." But Gromyko did not go on to suggest ways in which the Baruch plan could be made acceptable. Instead, he made a proposal that seemed almost designed to be unacceptable to the United States—as we may suspect that it was, given the Soviet Union's strong interest in developing the bomb for itself, and its imminent ability to do so. Gromyko called for an international convention to ban the production of nuclear weapons, which was to be followed some time later by the establishment of two committees at the United Nations—one for an exchange of scientific information, and the other to fashion safeguards for the abolition agreement. In short, the United States was *first* to give up its atomic monopoly, and *then* the Soviet Union would consent to *discuss* inspection and international control. The predictable United States rejection came quickly.

The amendment of the Acheson-Lilienthal report by Baruch, and then the rejection of the Baruch proposal by the Soviet Union—accompanied by a wholly unacceptable proposal of its own—illustrated the likely fate of any plan, however brilliant, that did not take into account the political questions at the outset. Once again—this time in action rather than in theory—the world had reached the impasse that seemed to block any radical or full solution of the nuclear predicament. The Acheson-Lilienthal committee had repaired to the relatively uncontroversial ground of technology, and offered a technical solution to the problem. But the problem could not in fact be divorced from the political issue, which meant at bottom how the world was going to be making its decisions in the international arena from then on, and the two governments, whose very business was politics, had no choice but to put politics back into the negotiations. When they did that, however, the proposal foundered, because there was no willingness on either side to make the radical political concessions that alone could have put the two sides on negotiable ground. It was as though in the course of the negotiations they had recognized the validity of Einstein's conviction that the predicament could be resolved only if a global authority with real power was established. But the plain truth, as William T. R. Fox had noted in *The Absolute Weapon*, was that neither side wanted a real international authority—not presiding over nuclear matters, and not presiding over any other matters, either—whose actions it could neither control nor derail. (When the United States lost its majority support at the United Nations, it quickly lost its enthusiasm for the idea that any binding decisions should be made by that body.) Both sides preferred a nuclear-arms race, with the United States hoping to use its technical superiority to increase its lead, and the Soviet Union hoping to catch up. (As was virtually inevitable, the latter is what eventually happened.)

The arms race began. Other proposals for full nuclear disarmament were made, but they never occupied the center of the political stage. Much of what Brodie and other advocates of deterrence had foreseen for a nuclear-armed world came to pass. In the succeeding decades, no war, conventional or nuclear—much less a third world war—broke out between the great nuclear powers. Whether war was avoided because of the balance of terror or for some other reason we cannot know (a negative is impossible to prove), but it is only common sense to suppose that the fear of nuclear destruction, while it was not the only factor involved, contributed heavily to the resolve of the great powers to remain at peace. However, another of Brodie's hopes went unfulfilled—his hope that deterrence would serve as a stopgap to buy time in which the world could find its way to the long-term political solution he saw as ultimately necessary. For many years, deterrence continued to be explained as a time-buying measure. As late as 1960, for example, Herman Kahn, a prominent theorist of nuclear strategy, was arguing for a policy of deterrence by saying, "We must take seriously the problem of reaching 1975." The possibility of a long-term solution still seemed real to him, and in 1962 he wrote:

We probably must accept the notion that the world as we know it is passing from the stage of history, and that attempts to preserve this five-hundred-year-old nation-state system would probably be as futile as the earlier attempts of some of the small German or Italian states to stave off the unification of their countries. If we wish to influence these coming changes, we simply must learn much more about existing and potential international orders— and learn fast.

But none of the sweeping changes occurred, or even began to occur—not after 1946, not after 1960, and not after the world had made it to 1975. The short term had a way of stretching on indefinitely and the long term a way of receding into the future. Deterrence had been presented as a sort of trailer that mankind would live in while the permanent home of a full political resolution of the nuclear predicament was being constructed. But what happened as the years passed was that the trailer was built up and elaborated, while the home went unstarted.

The failure of the long term ever to arrive was no small defect in the justification for the doctrine of deterrence, inasmuch as it had been in considerable measure by presenting deterrence as a short-term, time-buying device that its advocates had answered objections to the doctrine's glaring shortcomings: that it held mankind perpetually dangling over the nuclear abyss, suspended on the slender thread of whatever wisdom the statesmen, all of them fallible, and many of them extremely so, might happen to possess at a given instant; that by defining safety in terms of possessing nuclear arsenals it not only permitted but actually encouraged their proliferation; that it kept us all in the intolerable position of standing ready to slaughter billions of our fellow human beings; and, in general, that it required us all to rely for our safety on the criminal and absurd "threat" to blow our species off the face of the earth forever. What the world actually experienced was not the hoped-for slow progress toward a full solution but steady retrogression, in the form of the arms race and the proliferation of nuclear weapons, which were developed by more and more countries. Sometimes our performance in the postwar period is called a great success, on the ground that we have so far avoided a nuclear holocaust, and much of the credit for the success is given to the policy of deterrence. What this reckoning overlooks is that in that same period the world has built up arsenals of more than fifty thousand nuclear warheads—in short, that behind the screen of our deterrence policy we have built the means of our annihilation. Seen in the best possible light, this self-endangerment of our species was a tragic necessity. Seen less forgivingly—and, I believe, more justly—it was the greatest collective failure of responsibility by any generation in history. But, whichever of these it was, self-congratulation is certainly out of order. If someone climbs out on the ledge of a high building and threatens to jump off, we do not stand around congratulating him on his wisdom and restraint in not having jumped yet, and expounding on how safe a place the ledge of a building must be; we seek to pull him in at the earliest possible opportunity.

Part of the nuclear buildup was sanctioned—in fact, required—by the doctrine of deterrence, which founded the world's safety not on Einstein's "law and order" but on terror. To that extent, deterrence must share in the blame for our suicidal preparations. But the nuclear buildup—apparently fueled by a tremendous internal momentum—went far, far beyond what was required under that doctrine. Strictly speaking, the deterrence doctrine should have set a limit on the number of bombs required by a nation. It would have been the number needed to guarantee the destruction of the adversary's society in a retaliatory strike. Brodie wrote in 1946, "It appears that for any conflict a specific number of bombs will be useful to the side using it, and anything beyond that will be a luxury. . . . We can say that if two thousand bombs in the hands of either party is enough to destroy entirely the economy of the other, the fact that one side has six thousand and the other two thousand will be of relatively small significance." This is another idea of Brodie's that went unnoticed. Instead of stopping the arms race when several thousand Hiroshima-sized weapons had been stockpiled on each side, the superpowers invented the hydrogen bomb and went on to build tens of thousands of those, giving each side the preposterously redundant capacity for raining down hundreds of thousands of Hiroshimas on the adversary. Deterrence theory, it seemed, was competent to start an arms race but not to stop one.

There was a retrogression in thinking as well. While the nuclear arsenals grew to tower up to the sky around us, people seemed to forget that anyone had ever hoped for any other kind of world. People got accustomed to life in the trailer and forgot about the permanent home they were supposed to have had. Intellectual horizons narrowed and hopes dimmed. The vision of a world without nuclear weapons all but died. People's eyes became adjusted to the nuclear darkness, in a sort of moral equivalent of the nuclear winter. The time that Brodie had hoped to win was won, but it had not been used to achieve the ends he had had in mind. Instead, the champions of deterrence lost their former modesty and began to advance their makeshift as a permanent solution. The journalist Thomas Powers has spoken in the past few years to many of the military men who are responsible for carrying out the nuclear policies of the United States, and he has made a special point of asking them how they view the future. In his recent book *Thinking About the Next War*, he reports that he found two convictions to be nearly universal: first, that even with the arsenals in place—in fact, *because* the arsenals are in place—nuclear weapons will *never* be used and, second, that the military men "*know* we shall never get rid of nuclear weapons": that their abolition not only is "not on the horizon" but is not even "*over* the horizon." That is also the view of the Harvard authors of *Living with Nuclear Weapons*, who ask, "Why not abolish nuclear weapons? Why not cleanse this small planet of these deadly poisons?" They answer categorically, "Because we cannot," and go on to explain that the discovery of nuclear weapons "lies behind us" and "cannot be undone." In this prognosis, the hope of abolishing nuclear weapons has been extinguished, and the short-term stopgap of deterrence has completely usurped the place of full nuclear disarmament, which is frankly ruled out.

The doctrine of deterrence reigned supreme in official circles in the United States for the better part of the postwar period, during which the public, for its part, showed only sporadic interest in nuclear matters—being only too willing, it seemed, to hand the whole sickening business over to the specialists. Then, toward the end of the 1970s, this wide consensus—consisting, on the one hand, of widespread doctrinal agreement among government officials and, on the other, of public acceptance of their stewardship—was unexpectedly shattered by two upheavals: one in public opinion, in the form of the new peace movement, and the other in government policy, in the form of a subtle but profound and many-sided crisis in the doctrine of deterrence itself, which is now in a state of confusion amounting almost to disintegration. And this confusion, in turn, forced the world to face once again the elemental questions that Brodie and Einstein, among many others, had confronted, but not resolved, in the first days of the nuclear age. Even as the doctrine's theorists were elevating it to the position of dogmatic truth, support for it was beginning to erode. As so often seems to happen in the history of both men and ideas, the moment of apotheosis was the signal for decline. The crisis in the doctrine emerged into full public view under the Reagan Administration, but cracks had been appearing in it for at least half a decade before that. As the balance prescribed by deterrence was attained (with lots of overkill thrown in for good measure), contradictions that had always underlain the doctrine but had gone largely unremarked on before began to emerge into prominence. These contradictions all had to do, in one way or another, with the central, unresolvable contradiction of "defending" one's country by threatening to use weapons whose actual use would bring on the annihilation of one's country and possibly of the world as well. And the emergence of the contradictions was in turn propelled, I believe, by a recognition—this time on the part of nuclear strategists rather than citizens at large—of what a doomsday machine really is, and what it means to intend, in certain circumstances, to use one. This gigantic new reality, which has quietly grown up behind our backs in the decades since the weapons were invented, is, I suggest, the underlying cause of both the crisis in public confidence and the crisis in policy, and so in that sense they are part of a single, deeper crisis. Both, in their different ways, are responses to the fantastic, horrifying, brutal, and absurd fact that we human beings have actually gone ahead and wired our planet for its and our destruction. Whereas for the public, which was not much interested in the subtleties of doctrine, the crisis appeared in the stark form of the over-all senselessness and horror of the species' highly advanced preparations to commit suicide, for the strategists it took the form of a thousand inconsistencies, anomalies, and logical faults that kept cropping up irrepressibly in the details of nuclear policies and in their justifications. Yet when these various internal faults are looked at closely they turn out to be symptoms of the larger absurdity that is upsetting the public.

According to strict deterrence theory, the attainment of parity over the years should have had a stabilizing effect, for only then did the deterrence system become fully operational. The world should have breathed easier. Superiority on either side, theory decreed, lessens the security of both, because it creates an incentive on the stronger side to strike first, which, in turn, creates an incentive on the weaker side to avoid that first strike by itself striking first, and so on. When the strategists actually found themselves looking at parity, however, they discovered that it made them nervous. For one thing, parity put in question several American policies of long standing, perhaps the most important being the policy for the defense of Europe, where, in the opinion of many experts, the Soviet Union enjoyed superiority in conventional forces. In the event of a Soviet conventional attack in Europe, the American plan was—and still is—to make up for NATO's possible conventional inferiority by resorting to nuclear weapons early in the hostilities. (The American reliance on nuclear weapons to defend Europe goes back to the first years of the postwar period, when the United States had a monopoly on nuclear weapons and, in response to strong public demand, had partly demobilized the conventional forces that had been fighting in the Second World War.) As long as the United States possessed clear nuclear superiority, it could be argued that this plan had a certain plausibility—or "credibility," to use the favored term—because it was at least possible to imagine that if the Soviet Union was faced with a nuclear attack in Europe it would refrain from responding in kind, for fear of coming off worse in a general holocaust. But when the Soviet Union reached nuclear parity with the United States this thinking no longer obtained. Then there remained no basis (in deterrence theory, at any rate) for believing that the Soviet Union would hold back from nuclear retaliation if the United States had used nuclear weapons first. And if after that Soviet retaliation the United States attacked again, at a higher level of force, there was no reason to suppose that the Soviet Union would not retaliate in kind again, and so on up the line, until both sides' arsenals were depleted and both sides were annihilated. While one supposed virtue of nuclear superiority was that with it you could get an advantage in a war, it also had another theoretical virtue, which was that it might supply a stopping point in any hostilities that got going—the point at which the weaker side, foreseeing the unfavorable consequences to itself of continuing, gave up. But when the forces became equal that point would never be arrived at and the escalation would climb smoothly to oblivion. In the succinct (if ungrammatical) words of Henry Kissinger in an address in Brussels in 1979, which were quoted recently by former Secretary of Defense Robert McNamara in an article on NATO's nuclear policy, and on the role of nuclear weapons in general, in *Foreign Affairs*, "the European allies should not keep asking us to multiply strategic assurances that we cannot possibly mean, or if we do mean, we should not want to execute because if we execute, we risk the destruction of civilization." And, in Mr. McNamara's own words in the article, "if deterrence fails and conflict develops, the present NATO strategy carries with it a high risk that Western civilization, as we know it, will be destroyed"—to which one can add that *Homo sapiens* in its entirety may be destroyed into the bargain.

At the outset of a crisis, it is true, the President may not have to make the final, drastic choice. The policy of "flexible response"—of responding to each level of attack with a comparable level of retaliation—offers him less drastic steps to take. And certainly we should hope that even after the madness has begun it can somehow be stopped. (One excellent proposal that has been made recently is for a joint Soviet-American control center, where in the event of a crisis information could be exchanged, so that the two powers wouldn't miscalculate one another's intentions.) However, flexible response, even if it works, can only postpone, not evade, that final decision. If the foe is determined—and we have to assume that he is if he has launched a nuclear war against a nuclear-armed adversary—then the moment will still come, after the "limited" salvos have been fired, when a choice must be made between defeat and annihilation. But that moment may come well before some of the scenarists of nuclear war imagine that it will come, for there is good reason to doubt whether the limited attacks supposedly made available by flexible response will stay limited. The hope that nuclear hostilities, once they are started, can be limited depends on at least four very doubtful assumptions: that the leaders on both sides will retain control over their forces and that their orders will be obeyed (if, that is, the leaders survive); that the adversary will grasp one's "limited" intent even as he sees nuclear bombs tearing up his armies and his country; that if he does grasp this he will, in the interests of restraint all around, forgo the real or imagined advantages of a full-scale preemptive strike; and, finally, that the two sides, showing a wisdom in the midst of a nuclear holocaust which they failed to show in the days and hours leading up to it, while the world was intact, will come to their senses, establish diplomatic contact, and agree to halt the descent into the abyss in mid-course. No one knows how diplomacy would fare halfway to the end of the world, but it seems unwise to rely on it very heavily. In any case, the conclusion that the nuclear winter may descend after only a fraction of the world's present arsenals have been detonated may have made the distinction between "limited" and "total" nuclear war academic. "Limited war" itself has turned out to have potentially unlimited consequences.

In an effort to remedy the flaws in the American plan for the defense of Europe, the NATO governments hit on a plan that turned out only to exacerbate the underlying tensions. If the American threat to defend Europe with nuclear weapons was losing credibility, the NATO planners feared, then the Soviet leaders might start to believe that they could conquer or intimidate Europe without encountering an American response. This fear was increased when the Soviet Union began to withdraw its one-warhead SS-4 intermediate-range missiles that it had targeted on Europe and replace them with more modern, three-warhead SS-20 missiles. What was needed, the NATO planners decided—both to "reassure" the Europeans and to frighten the Russians—was a way of binding the defense of Europe more tightly to the defense of the United States. The upshot was the Euromissiles—intermediate-range ballistic and cruise missiles that would be based in Europe and would be capable of striking the Soviet Union. Their deployment, it was believed, would convince the Soviet Union once and for all that the Americans were serious about the defense of

Europe. The problem was that a mere change in the place of deployment—from the United States to Europe—of American missiles capable of reaching Soviet territory did little to cure the incredibility of the threat of their use. In Mr. McNamara's words, "for the same reason that led Henry Kissinger to recognize that a U.S. President is unlikely to initiate the use of U.S.-based strategic nuclear weapons against the U.S.S.R., so a President would be unlikely to launch missiles from European soil against Soviet territory." Meanwhile, a large segment of the European citizenry was anything but reassured by the plan. On the contrary, it was frightened. People in Europe felt that they were becoming all too dependent on the United States, and they feared that the United States might drag them against their will into a holocaust of its own making. They believed that they were becoming (in the recent words of Rudolf Augstein, the publisher of *Der Spiegel*) a "computer component" in a broader superpower game, over which they had no control. Furthermore, unconvinced that the Euromissiles, which were to be under the sole control of the United States, would bind the fortunes of Europe and the United States closer together, they feared that the missiles might be used to try to fight a "limited" nuclear war in Europe alone, sparing the United States. (These fears were fanned when President Reagan opined at a briefing for news editors in October of 1981 that a limited nuclear war might indeed be possible.) Before long, a very large number of these people began to make their apprehensions known in demonstrations throughout Europe.

Meanwhile, in the United States four Americans with long experience in government—George Kennan; McGeorge Bundy; Gerard Smith, head of the delegation that negotiated the SALT I agreement; and Robert McNamara—had a quite different solution to suggest to the problem of the defense of Europe. They recommended that the United States consider adopting a policy of no first use of nuclear weapons in Europe while building NATO conventional forces to whatever level was necessary to achieve a balance with Warsaw Pact conventional forces. As they saw it, a policy of no first use would improve on the existing policy in a number of ways: it would add to the credibility of an American response to Soviet conventional attack (since at least the initial American response would no longer have to be suicidal); it would remove from the United States the responsibility and the onus of actually planning to be the first to use nuclear weapons (the Soviets have already declared a no-first-use policy); it would, by giving the United States something better to do in the event of aggression in Europe than start a nuclear holocaust, somewhat reduce the chances of a holocaust. These benefits, all of which appear to be real and substantial, are perhaps reason enough to adopt the policy of no first use, yet that policy would nevertheless fall short of fully resolving the contradiction that underlies the American plan for the defense of Europe. In conventional war, there is no guarantee of success in any engagement—and certainly not when the opposing forces are, by design, evenly balanced. Hence, in the event that a conventional war broke out in Europe it is quite possible that, even if there should be a conventional balance in place, the NATO forces would begin to lose, and so would be forced to decide anyway between defeat and a first use of nuclear weapons—or, if the Warsaw Pact started to lose, it would face the decision. In either case, there seems to be a fair chance that nuclear weapons would be used. Conventional defeat is the Achilles' heel of no first use. A policy of no first use thus can never really live up to its name. There is always an invisible asterisk attached, referring us to a footnote that reads, "Unless we start to lose." Without this qualification, a policy of no first use would really be a form of unilateral nuclear disarmament by verbal means, in which the foe was invited to take what he could, provided only that he did it with conventional forces. (If he used nuclear forces, nuclear deterrence would come into play.)

This limitation of no first use, of which the authors of the proposal were well aware, is worth mentioning not because it discredits the recommendation (it does not) but because it points to the contradiction at the heart of deterrence itself. The underlying problem, which both citizens and policymakers are now wrestling with, is that, given the difficulty of limiting nuclear war, and given the extreme consequences even if the war *is* limited, *any* actual use of nuclear weapons is likely to be self-defeating and senseless. For whether or not there is a policy of no first use, and whether or not the hostilities begin with the use of conventional weapons, there is, ultimately, no way to spare the President (if it is he who faces the decision) from having to make the final, terrible choice between defeat and annihilation. This is the moment at which the President has to decide whether or not actually to carry out the notorious "threat of suicide"—also known as the "threat to end the world"—with which the two great nuclear powers ultimately hope to deter one another from aggression. (Deployment of the Euromissiles commits him to making it earlier rather than later.) The crux of the matter is that while there may be a benefit in making the threat it can never make sense to carry it out, no matter what the circumstances. For how can it make sense to "save" one's country by blowing it to pieces? And what logic is there in staving off a limited defeat by bringing on unlimited, eternal defeat? Nuclear deterrence is like a gun with two barrels, on which one points ahead and the other points back at the gun's holder. If a burglar should enter your house, it might make sense to threaten him with this gun, but it could never make sense to fire it.

The dilemma is even more sharply defined if one turns from Europe, where the West has conventional forces in place with which to at least try to repel possible Soviet aggression, to the Middle East, where it has almost none and, furthermore, has no chance of dispatching enough in time to make a military difference. The fault line in the doctrine here is wider. In the Middle East, the military policy is either one of nuclear first use or nothing. The United States is making provision for a rapid-deployment force that could be sent to the Middle East in a crisis, but in the face of a full-scale Soviet conventional attack it could do no more than be a trip wire for the American launching of nuclear weapons. Yet the Soviet Union can retaliate with nuclear weapons in the Middle East just as easily as it can in Europe, and the ladder of escalation climbs up just as smoothly from the Persian Gulf as it does from the plains of Germany. The President appears to have no way to "protect" Middle Eastern oil militarily other than by launching nuclear weapons. But for whose use will the oil have been protected if everyone winds up dead in the process of protecting it?

If the threat of nuclear war is irrational, one might ask, why do nations go on making it, and why do they bother even to build nuclear weapons instead of, say, building more conventional weapons, which, according to some theorists, they might sensibly use? Why doesn't the absurdity of "defending" one's country by threatening suicide lead to the collapse or abandonment of the policy? The answer, of course, is that the minute a nation gives up nuclear weapons it puts itself militarily at the mercy of its nuclear-armed foes, for no one has yet devised a successful defense against nuclear attack. Rather than be put in this position, nations prefer to make irrational threats—and hope never to be forced to decide whether or not to carry them out. As for the problem of credibility, in the real world—as opposed to the world of logic and theory—the irrationality of the threat to commit suicide probably doesn't do a great deal to reduce its effectiveness. There has been enough insanity in history to lend credibility to even the maddest threats, and for governments to threaten to do something irrational is quite enough to get everybody to believe they will do it. (It is one of the humiliating aspects of our nuclear policy that if rationality ever prevailed in the world our policy would become untenable.) Another point in favor of the deterrence doctrine is its probable descriptive honesty. It discards all dubious assumptions regarding the likelihood of limiting a nuclear holocaust; or, at the very least, it acknowledges and no sensible statesman can *count on* these assumptions, and therefore invites statesmen to look on the use of nuclear weapons as the beginning of the end. The morality of the doctrine of mutual assured destruction has been assailed on the ground that it calls for the mass slaughter of innocents, as indeed it does. But this immorality is inherent in the very possession of tens of thousands of nuclear weapons, whatever the doctrine. There is no conceivable way that these can be used without mass slaughter on an incalculable scale, and no theoretical sophistry can eliminate this basic fact. The doctrine of mutual assured destruction is in that sense not so much a policy as an acknowledgment of reality. It brings us—statesman and citizen alike—face to face with the way things really are in a nuclear-armed world.

In an article in *The New York Review of Books*, in June of 1983, McGeorge Bundy proposed a policy of what he called "existential deterrence," in which we would make political use of some of the inherent qualities of nuclear arsenals. One of these qualities is uncertainty. He observes that "the existing systems on both sides are now so powerful and varied that no political leader can have or hope to have any clear idea of what would in fact happen 'if deterrence failed'—that is, if nuclear war began." And he goes on to remark that "scenarios" that pretend to predict what would happen "reflect nothing more than the state of mind of their authors." Our knowledge of the immense destructive power of nuclear weapons and our incurable ignorance of the exact course that that destruction would take are, he suggests, irreducible, "existential" properties of our nuclear arsenals, and he suggests that we can count on these properties to deter a foe, even without spelling out our murderous retaliatory intentions in detail. The reason for this uncertainty is, of course, the same as the reason for our uncertainty concerning our survival as a species "if deterrence failed": we have never had any experience with nuclear holocausts. The new finding that limited war could cause nuclear winter adds extremely important support to "existential" deterrence. This finding shows that an attacker might even destroy himself with his own first strike. Now, therefore, our own missiles are not only figuratively but literally pointed at ourselves. But there is, of course, no cause for rejoicing in this, because while it is true that the new finding may make statesmen more reluctant than before to launch nuclear hostilities this gain is won at the cost of an increase in the danger of an accidental or inadvertent extinction of mankind.

Because of the "existential" properties of large nuclear arsenals, deterrence overcomes its cracked logical foundations and "works"; that is, it inspires a well-justified terror in the minds of our adversaries, just as their arsenals inspire a reciprocal terror in us. The illogic of deterrence does not lead to a direct weakening of the fear that it inspires. No statesman in his right mind is so foolish as to stake his country's existence on the surmise that if he launches a nuclear attack against his foe the foe, guided by pure reasonableness and logic, will sit back and endure the attack without responding. The consequences of the doctrine's illogic are to be found somewhere else: in another audience, in ourselves. This audience very much includes the people who make up the new peace movement—people who are increasingly repelled by the idea of putting mankind to the sword because some crisis in Europe or Lebanon or the Falkland Islands, or wherever, has got out of hand. But before the peace movement arose another group, closer to power and more influential, had begun to ponder the dilemma. Its members were, and are, the strategists of "counterforce" and "nuclear-war-fighting," some of whom now guide the policies of the Reagan Administration. Having in many cases spent their lives studying nuclear strategy, they were well aware of the contradiction between the benefits of threatening to start a nuclear war and the senselessness of actually doing so. These people took theory seriously, and they took the contradiction seriously. They were not reassured by the uncertainty in nuclear affairs which restored the credibility that logic undermined, or by any of the other "existential" properties of nuclear arsenals. But what worried them chiefly was not, as with the peace movement, that a small crisis could bring on the end of the world; it was that the Soviet Union—counting on the reluctance of the United States to commit suicide by launching a nuclear attack—might go ahead with some act of aggression, including even a limited nuclear attack, hoping that there would be no response. But, having identified in deterrence the same inconsistency that the peace movement had identified, they struck off in an entirely different direction, embarking on a critique of mutual assured destruction from a new angle. The new strategists wanted to repair American credibility, and in order to do it they set out to find some rational goal for the United States to pursue "if deterrence failed." How would the adversary be deterred, they asked, if there was no sensible or reasonable threat to deter him with? Their solution—which marked a radical shift in strategic thought—was the idea of actually fighting and winning a nuclear war, just as though it were a conventional war. If the United States could fight and win a nuclear war, then the *threat* to use nuclear weapons would no longer be a suicide threat, and would become credible again. Once the new thinking had found wide acceptance in the Reagan Administration, the Administration, without rejecting the doctrine of deterrence outright, began to make statements and take actions that could be interpreted only as part of a war-fighting, or war-winning, strategy. Navy Secretary John Lehman said, "You have to have a war-winning capability if you are to succeed." Secretary of

Defense Caspar Weinberger said, "You show me a Secretary of Defense who's planning not to prevail [in a war], and I'll show you a Secretary of Defense who ought to be impeached." And, as I have mentioned, a top-secret plan stated that the United States should prepare to fight "a prolonged" nuclear war and to be able to "prevail" in it and "force the Soviet Union to seek earliest termination of hostilities on terms favorable to the United States."

A decision to "prevail" in the event of nuclear war necessarily wreaked havoc on the traditional tenets of deterrence. Deterrence called for equality of forces, but prevailing required superiority; deterrence was upset by the power of either side to destroy the forces of the other side in a first strike, but prevailing required such a power; deterrence acknowledged the impossibility of an effective defense against a nuclear attack, but prevailing required such a defense; deterrence sought stability and was consistent with arms-control agreements based on equality, but prevailing, since it required superiority, was inconsistent with such agreements. And the Reagan Administration set out to achieve the objectives required for prevailing. The President called for the development and deployment of first-strike weapons. His Administration proposed ambitious programs both for civil defense and for space-based defense against Soviet ballistic missiles. All the while, it kept up a barrage of rhetoric against the Soviet Union more bellicose than anything heard from any other Administration in the postwar period.

As it happened, technical developments had for some time abetted the development by the United States of first-strike, nuclear-war-fighting weapons. One of these developments was the invention, in the mid-1960s, of the Multiple Independently Targeted Reentry Vehicle (MIRV), which permitted one missile to be equipped with many warheads, each of them guided to a different target. If the targets were the silos of enemy missiles, then just one missile fired offensively could menace many missiles sitting defensively in their silos. Another destabilizing technical development was a revolution in accuracy, which improved the chances that the warheads, multiplied or not, would actually reach the silos they were aimed at. The doctrine of deterrence had always rested on the twin foundations of the vulnerability of civilian populations to nuclear attack and the invulnerability of nuclear forces to nuclear attack. But now offensive capacity was improving to a point at which nuclear forces were beginning to become vulnerable. Although bombers in the air and submarines at sea still remained safe from a first strike, the safety of land-based missiles was dwindling. Meanwhile, the Soviet Union, too, although its public statements were more restrained than those of the United States had become, was developing weapons with a first-strike capacity. The United States had been the first to deploy MIRVs but the Soviet Union was the first to place them on giant land-based missiles capable of carrying ten warheads apiece. (The MX, which will carry as many as ten warheads, is an attempt to match this dangerous achievement.) The move on both sides to build first-strike weapons shows the vulnerability of the nuclear balance in general to technical advances. The arms race is always, in effect, afloat on a stream of technical discovery, which can upset its most carefully laid plans. It is always as much a race against the scientific unknown as against the adversary per se. This aspect of the race—the qualitative, rather than the quantitative—has nothing to do with any malign influence of scientists. Rather, it is inherent in an arms race in a world in which experience has shown that the greatest advantages are to be gained not so much by mounting gigantic industrial efforts as by fishing new devices out of the unknown. At bottom, it stems from each side's well-justified fear that the other side will arrive at an advantageous discovery first. (An example would be a device that could detect the positions of submarines from a great distance.)

The debate between the mutual-assured-destruction school and the new nuclear-war-fighting school happens to have been encapsulated in an exchange of letters between the writer Theodore Draper and Secretary of Defense Weinberger in *The New York Review of Books*. (In entering into correspondence with Draper, Weinberger, as Draper acknowledged, showed a respect for the views of a private citizen—and, by implication, a sense of accountability to the public—that is all too often lacking in public officials.) It gives us a portrait in miniature of the stresses that are now tearing deterrence apart. The occasion for the exchange was an open letter written by Weinberger which appeared in *The New York Review* in November of 1982. In an "open reply," Draper takes note of the top-secret document parts of which were obtained by the *New York Times*—"Fiscal Year 1984–1988 Defense Guidance," which was approved by Weinberger and provides general strategic direction over a five-year period for America's armed services—which states that American nuclear forces "must prevail and be able to force the Soviet Union to seek earliest termination of hostilities on terms favorable to the United States," and he goes on to accuse the Administration of planning to try to "win" a nuclear war. In a letter to Draper, Weinberger denies the charge, saying, "We believe neither side could win," and he also denies that the Administration hopes to "prevail" in a protracted nuclear war. But, going on to broach the question that has occasioned the rise of the nuclear-war-fighting school—namely, what the United States should actually do with its nuclear weapons "if deterrence fails"—he says, "U.S. contingency planning, to serve deterrence, must also envision the possible employment of nuclear weapons." The answer of the mutual-assured-destruction school to the question of what to do if deterrence fails is that one goes ahead with mutual assured destruction. This answer Weinberger rejects, explaining that "it would be militarily, politically and morally unsound to confine the President to resorting either to capitulation or massive retaliation." Then, giving his own formulation of what to do, he says, "Our policy requires that, if necessary, we prevail in denying victory to the Soviets and in protecting the sovereignty and continued viability of the United States and of the Western democracies as free societies." But this goal—with its "viability of the United States," its preserved "sovereignty," its intact "free societies," and its "denying victory" to the Soviet Union—has about it a suspicious look of prevailing, not to say winning.

Weinberger's tortured and evasive formulation gives Draper his opening to respond. In a second letter, he accuses Weinberger of rejecting the goal of prevailing at the beginning of his letter "only to reinstate it in a peculiarly negative form"—in which the phrase "terms favorable to the United States" mentioned in the "Defense Guidance" plan has been replaced by the less provocative "denying victory to the Soviet Union." Draper then accuses Weinberger of both "denying the aim to 'prevail' and affirming the plan to prevail." Weinberger, in a final letter, seems to have little to say in rebuttal of this point. He writes that American military policy as a whole is "defensive," as though Draper had accused the Administration of planning aggression (he had not), and then, once more addressing the crucial question of what the American plan should be if deterrence fails, merely comes up with a slightly milder and even more euphemistic version of his previous answer. This time, he says that the United States should seek to "terminate the conflict quickly at the lowest level of destruction possible, to restore deterrence, and to protect the sovereignty and continued viability of the United States and of the Western democracies as free societies with fundamental institutions and values intact." But then he shifts from defense of Administration policies to criticism of the policy supported by Draper, who believes that the United States should possess enough nuclear forces to annihilate the Soviet Union in a retaliatory strike and then stop. "Although . . . you believe massive response against the Soviet population is the response necessary to provide for deterrence, for political, military, and yes, moral reasons, we do not target civilian populations as such," Weinberger writes. "If we are forced to retaliate and can only respond by destroying population centers, we invite the destruction of our own population. Such a deterrent strategy could lack conviction, particularly as a deterrent to nuclear—let alone conventional—attack on an ally." In other words, he articulates the nuclear-war-fighters' complaint against mutual assured destruction: that suicide is not a very plausible threat.

Now it is Draper's turn to lack an answer. In fact, in his next letter he fails to take up the question of what he proposes that the United States should do if deterrence breaks down; instead he concentrates more fire on Weinberger's unconvincing answers to the same question. Weinberger's charge that to unleash mutual assured destruction is senseless as an action and implausible as a threat is permitted to stand. In short, in responding (or, in Draper's case, failing to respond) to the question of what to do "if deterrence fails," each man succeeds in demonstrating the senselessness of the other man's plan and does not succeed in defending his own plan. It's a case of mutual assured destruction. And both are right. Draper succeeds in showing that Weinberger really wants to win a nuclear war, and that this hope is utterly illusory, but he cannot find any justification for actually carrying out the mutual assured destruction that he supports. He is reduced to saying, in effect, that deterrence *won't* fail. Thus, in his second letter he says that the only "effective use" of nuclear weapons is to "prevent their use" in the first place. But that answer begs the question under discussion, which is what to do with them *if prevention fails* and nuclear bombs are landing on one's soil. In other words, there is no deterrence without a threat. The question is: Threat of what? As Weinberger points out, the answer given to *this* question by policymakers *now*, before any attack has been made, theoretically bears on whether prevention itself will work, since under the deterrence doctrine it is fear of retaliation that keeps the first strike from being launched. Weinberger, for his part, succeeds in showing that mutual assured destruction is a senseless action and therefore an unconvincing threat, but he cannot demonstrate that in the nuclear war he apparently has in mind we can actually preserve our "institutions and values intact" or "force" the Soviet Union to accept "terms favorable to the United States," or achieve any of the other things he promises in his long string of euphemisms for victory.

The truth that neither man wants to face up to is that there is nothing that it would make sense to do "if deterrence fails"— nothing, that is, but to get on the hot line and try to stop the whole debacle as soon as possible. But that intention cannot be spelled out in advance by government officials as their "response" to nuclear attack, because deterrence requires that they threaten devastating retaliation of one kind or another, be it attempted nuclear-war-fighting or straight mutual assured destruction. When the President is asked what the United States will do if it is subjected to nuclear attack by the Soviet Union, he cannot answer, "I will immediately call up the Soviet Premier and ask him to please stop." He cannot tell the world that if we suffer nuclear attack our retaliation will be a phone call. For the instant he gave that answer deterrence would dissolve. Once again, we arrive at the very core of what is wrong with deterrence, which can be stated very simply: it commits us in certain circumstances to do what we must never do in any circumstances—plunge into a nuclear holocaust, in which our species could be destroyed and the human story ended forever. Deterrence theory is indeed a marvel of circularity and contradiction. To obtain the benefit of the policy, we must threaten to perform an insane action. But the benefit we seek is precisely *not* to perform that action. We thus seek to avoid performing an act by threatening to perform it. As long as the policy succeeds, of course, everyone is happy. But the moment it fails we would like to scrap the whole thing, because then we find ourselves committed to performing an insane action—to doing the very thing whose avoidance was the purpose of the policy. But if, looking ahead to this terrible moment, we admit now that once the breakdown occurs (and Soviet troops are flooding into Western Europe, for example) we don't want to perform the insane act of shoving the world into the abyss of doom we lose the pre-breakdown benefits that we now enjoy. So we don't admit it—perhaps not even to ourselves—and continue to stand ready to perform the act.

Draper and Weinberger have their separate ways of evading this terrible truth of our time. Draper simply declines to acknowledge the illogic of making a threat whose execution would be senseless. Weinberger, in an apparent step forward, acknowledges the illogic, but then, in his attempt to repair it, takes two steps backward, by taking leave of the reality that gave rise to the whole problem in the first place—the reality of the overwhelming destructive force of the weapons, which are more than a match for any institutions we have, not to speak of "values." (It's when *we* annihilate *them* that our "values" are destroyed.) In effect, he and the Administration he speaks for have escaped from illogic into fantasy. Of the two defects, the illogic, as I have noted, is preferable, in part because it is compensated for by the "existential" qualities of the arsenals, including the impenetrable uncertainty that, in the real world, must reside in the minds of all sensible people regarding what would happen once a nuclear holocaust actually started. If there must be nuclear weapons, then this uncertainty, and not the iron resolve to annihilate the adversary and suffer annihilation oneself, in mutual assured destruction, or the supposed ability to defeat him in a "nuclear war," is the strongest buttress of such stability as our jeopardized world now enjoys. The necessity of relying on uncertainty, however—on our *in*ability to control or predict our actions—is only one more demonstration that there is no truly rational or humanly justifiable way either to use or to threaten to use nuclear weapons, and that only their abolition can return our lives to sanity and normality.

In 1946, Bernard Brodie and a number of other strategic thinkers devised the doctrine of deterrence as a means of gaining time for the world while it worked on a true solution to the nuclear problem. But the world, instead of using the time won in this way, chose to forget the underlying issues and to elevate the temporary expedient into a dogma. And improvisation became orthodoxy. Meanwhile, the world, lulled into a false sense of reassurance, in effect went to sleep. In the decades following the invention of the bomb, the doctrine of deterrence achieved a seemingly unchallengeable dominance. Its triumphant progress perhaps reached its apogee in the early 1970s, when the first nuclear-arms-control agreements between the United States and the Soviet Union were signed. So widely accepted in our country had the doctrine become that some likened it to a religious faith, and referred to its experts as a "priesthood"—a priesthood that might argue back and forth in specialized journals over the fine points of theology but was united on the basic articles of the faith. It even had its paradoxes and mysteries (such as what to do if deterrence failed)—an essential ingredient in any theology worth the name. And when the arms-control agreements were signed it seemed that the faith had spread from Washington to Moscow. If all this was "elitist," it was also reassuring. A doctrine was in place that promised "stability" in the world. The two great nuclear adversaries seemed to subscribe to it. (The sheer fact of agreement on *something* was important.) What was better, under its guidance they had reached agreements that promised to be only the first in a long series—a series in which the weapons would be, if not abolished, at least "managed." The direction the two powers were moving in seemed to be the right one. And yet within a few years this solid-seeming edifice had disintegrated. The doctrine of deterrence on which it was based had come apart, the priesthood was scattered, the arms-control "process" was at a standstill, the two great nuclear powers were exchanging insulting and menacing remarks, and the arms race, unguided now by any coherent philosophy on either side—much less by one shared by the two sides—was spiraling out of control.

Deterrence had not been assailed from without. No enemy had challenged it. No consistent new doctrine had taken its place in men's minds. ("Nuclear-war-fighting" remained an uncertain and ambivalent mishmash of atavistic military impulses and abstruse theorizing presented in the teeth of the most elementary facts of the nuclear age.) Rather, deterrence was unraveling from within; it was a victim of its own contradictions, which were seized upon in large measure by its own practitioners. Yet when the contradictions were looked at unblinkingly it turned out that they were inherent in the existence of the doomsday machine itself. For the truth was that there was nothing wrong with the doctrine of deterrence which was not wrong simply with the possession of vast nuclear arsenals—with or without the doctrine of deterrence. The reason that no repair of the doctrine was possible was that the problem did not lie in doctrine. It lay in the world's possession of nuclear arsenals—in their "existential" features, if you like. For, whatever government spokesmen might say about possessing nuclear weapons only to prevent their use, the inescapable truth was that possession inevitably implied use, and use was irredeemably senseless, since it threatened to bring about the destruction of whatever one might think one was trying to defend: if you tried to reject deterrence while holding on to the weapons, you only wound up with nuclear-war-fighting. Thus, at bottom, the crisis in doctrine stemmed from the reliance on nuclear arms. Indeed, deterrence was probably the least obnoxious and most sensible doctrine consistent with the absurd situation of possessing the arsenals. Most important, it was based on an acknowledgment of the true extent of the peril. Furthermore, it renounced the aggressive use of the weapons, and sought stability rather than military advantage from them. It endeavored to increase the element of *threat* to the maximum while reducing the risk of *use* to the minimum. If this effort was self-contradictory—since the threat was credible only insofar as use was a real possibility—and was in that sense like trying to make use of the shadow of an

object without having the object itself, it was certainly better
than imagining that after a nuclear holocaust we would wind
up with our societies and "values" intact.

It was against this background of official confusion and international discord that the new peace movement arose. But while
the movement may have been triggered in part by the crisis
in the deterrence doctrine it has not taken the restoration of
deterrence as its goal. To be sure, some members of the old nuclear priesthood have come to the defense of their beleaguered
doctrine, but only to find real priests challenging it, in the bishops' pastoral letter. It turned out that while the nuclear-war-
fighters were looking at the contradictions of deterrence and
worrying about a loss of credibility people on the outside were
looking at those same contradictions and worrying about the
loss of mankind itself. Having made their conscious choice in
favor of human survival, they could hardly be content with a
policy that left mankind perched on the edge of doom and
prescribed that in certain not altogether unlikely circumstances
we jump. And when the proponents of deterrence began to
present the arrangement as permanent, and to rule out full
nuclear disarmament even in the long run, the doctrine came
to seem an abomination. It began to look like a death sentence
for the human race. Yet while extreme dissatisfaction with
deterrence was implicit in making the "conscious choice" to
try to preserve the human species a critique of deterrence was
not yet a deliberate policy of the peace movement.

The world was awakening, but what it was awakening *to* was
not a ready solution to the nuclear predicament but, rather,
the impasse that the world had reached in the first years of the
nuclear age. When the world woke up, it was therefore only to
find itself manacled to the bed on which it was lying, for the
"impossibility" of any real relief from the nuclear peril—and
the impossibility, in particular, of the abolition of nuclear
weapons—had been affirmed by decades of strategic thinking.
It was perhaps not surprising, then, that many people wanted
to go back to sleep—in effect, saying, "Wake us up again when
you have some answers." For trailing after the elemental human
questions raised by the peace movement was a whole new set
of questions, concerning what should be done. Can the goal

of a nuclear-free world actually be reached, or is it in fact impossible—a "fictional utopia," as *Living with Nuclear Weapons* tells us? If the Harvard book is right, what then is the outlook? If it is wrong, and the path is open, what then is the path? Is it unilateral disarmament? If so, what would happen to our independence and our liberties? Or is bilateralism best? If it is, how can we in the West, including both governments and the peace movement, bring our influence to bear on the Soviet Union, where no independent peace movement is permitted? Must political détente precede disarmament? If the superpowers are to get rid of half of their weapons, must they first get rid of half of their political differences? Or can disarmament go ahead with the political differences intact? If so, how far can it go? *Can* they get rid of half of the weapons? Three-quarters? All? Does world government then become necessary? Or will something else do? In addressing these questions, the peace movement finds itself up against the issues that divided Einstein and Brodie; and the old debate on these issues, which has been in abeyance for some time, has been resumed.

Much of it is the same as in 1945. Once again, supposed "realists" tilt against supposed "idealists"; once again, moralists call strategists immoral, and strategists call moralists naïve; once again, the necessary is called impossible, and the impossible is called necessary. In short, rhetorical warfare has broken out afresh along the whole front of the still unbridged divide that the invention of nuclear weapons opened between the world's historical political organization of human life and human life itself. Yet there are some changes in the debate. Perhaps the most significant change is that the political program of the peace movement, in contrast to that of Einstein and his school, has so far been modest and tentative. There is little appetite for sweeping proposals that might resolve the predicament all at once if they were acted upon but that probably would not be acted upon, because they would be unlikely to meet with official or public acceptance. In particular, there are virtually no new calls for world government—a pair of words so thoroughly out of fashion that merely uttering them seems guaranteed to sink in political oblivion any plan connected with them. For Einstein, the boundlessness of the peril of extinction and the sweeping, radical solution of world government were so tightly connected as to be almost two parts of one thought, with the latter simply implicit in the former. For the peace movement of the 1980s, however, the question has been broken into many thoughts, and there has been a sense of a great distance to be crossed, intellectually as well as politically, between an analysis of the problem and an analysis of its resolution. This dissection of the issue—this opening up of its moral and political dimensions, revealing a richer complexity than had previously been recognized—is probably one more result of the world's years of experience of living with the doomsday machine. In 1945, the peril was on the horizon and was approaching quickly, yet it remained distant and abstract. The bombings of Hiroshima and Nagasaki were soon seen as part of a war that was over, not as harbingers of everybody's future. In 1984, the peril, while still in a sense invisible and abstract, nevertheless surrounds and pervades our lives. It is the sky overhead and the ground underfoot. We are immersed in it and permeated by it. In sum, we now live in a *nuclear world*, and our reactions, our thoughts and feelings, conscious and unconscious, have reference to that world. They have a flavor of experience, which the reactions of people in 1945 could not have.

The American bishops' pastoral letter exemplifies both the spirit and the substance of the new movement. It subjects the nuclear policies of the great powers to searching moral and intellectual scrutiny. The question that the bishops start by asking is not so much "What shall we do?" as the more uncomfortable, prior question "What are we doing?" Though their goal is not novelty—they hold established policies up to the light of time-honored standards and principles—their investigation breaks new ground, for hitherto as a society we have permitted our nuclear policies to escape such examination. By insisting that our political and military practices be judged according to traditional ethical standards, the bishops are taking the first step toward making our sundered world whole. This is a fitting effort for the Catholic Church, which over the centuries has made an effort to find and apply moral standards that are appropriate to all domains of life, public and private. Invoking the just-war theory of Catholic teaching, which says that it is at times permissible to kill in defense of one's country, the bishops sanction the existence of a breach of some size between the moral standards for private conduct and the moral standards for governmental conduct. But they draw limits. First, they declare that nuclear weapons must *never* be used against cities. Quoting the Second Vatican Council, they state, "Any act of war aimed indiscriminately at the destruction of entire cities or of extensive areas along with their population is a crime against God and man himself. It merits unequivocal and unhesitating condemnation." Second, they condemn the initiation of nuclear war, finding it "not justified by rational political objectives." Third, they reject the notion of "limited" nuclear war, stating that to cross the nuclear threshold is "to enter a world where we have no experience of control, much testimony against [limited war's] possibility, and therefore no moral justification for submitting the human community to this risk."

Having made these firm and far-reaching moral judgments, the bishops do not go on to make equally firm and far-reaching recommendations for action on the basis of them. Rather, they subscribe to such moderate and partial proposals as the nuclear freeze and no first use. Like the peace movement as a whole, the bishops are diagnostic radicals but prescriptive moderates. They reserve judgment on the deeper political questions, perhaps because they believe (as I do) that it is only on the prior foundation of a solid moral and intellectual understanding of the predicament that a sound political solution can be built. According to this line of thinking, the present system of deterrence, while possessing virtues that should not be overlooked, is a perfect example of a solution built on shaky foundations, and its recent disarray, which is due more to internal disintegration than to assault from without, is a symptom of its basic infirmity. Seen in this light, the political hesitancy of the bishops and of the movement as a whole must be judged a strength, not a weakness. It bespeaks a wise open-mindedness, not a fatal impracticality or a neglect of the realities of political life. It means only that the bishops are addressing the issue in the two stages recommended by the Pope: first the "conscious choice," then the "deliberate policy." Before the nuclear question could be re-answered, it had to be reopened, and they have reopened it. However, if those who have raised the question withhold judgment on the policy question for a prolonged period the strength will become a fatal weakness. Beyond a certain point, a failure to follow up the choice with a policy will breed discouragement. The peace movement, like the world as a whole, is in need of proposals for action which are commensurate with the hopes that it has raised, and are answerable to the moral standards it uses to measure present policies. If no such proposals are forthcoming, the peace movement seems sure to dissipate, just as peace movements in the past have dissipated. In that event, a yet more profound atmosphere of fatalism than people have felt so far seems likely to descend over the world, because people will be convinced that even popular action—previously their one untried hope—is helpless in the face of the nuclear peril, which will then truly take on the final aspect of a doomsday machine: something that has been made by human beings but has slipped beyond human control.

For the time being, the movement has given its backing to proposals that are somewhat more ambitious than those normally considered feasible by the arms-control experts but are still moderate enough to win widespread approval. In the United States, the outstanding proposal of this kind is, of course, the freeze, which from the moment it became widely known enjoyed broad public support. (In Europe, the comparable effort, which has now failed, was to block deployment of the Euromissiles.) In fact, the freeze proposal was adopted by the movement perhaps as much for its political "salability" as for its merits, which I believe are nevertheless great. The freeze answers the urgent need to head off the next advance in the arms race, which promises to be a particularly perilous one. The first-strike weapons already deployed by the Soviet Union and the United States have undermined stability, and the weapons planned for the near future—weapons such as the MX and the Trident D-5 missile—would undermine it further. Another peril to stability is the plan to put arms in space, by developing both anti-satellite weapons and space-based anti-missile weapons. Anti-satellite weapons are destabilizing because they threaten to blind the warning systems and the intelligence-gathering systems of one or both sides in a crisis, and leave the statesmen acting in the dark as nuclear hostilities begin. Space-based anti-missile weapons are destabilizing because they could menace the retaliatory capacity of the other side—a threat that would certainly be met either by a further buildup of missiles or by the development of still other weapons, designed to attack the space-based anti-missile ones, or by both. Still another technical development that threatens stability is the cruise missile, which promises to greatly complicate future arms-control talks. Unlike most ballistic missiles, which are large and relatively easy to spot by satellite, cruise missiles are small—as little as eighteen feet long and twenty-one inches in diameter—and therefore easy to conceal. Moreover, cruise missiles, whose eventual deployment may be in the tens of thousands, can be equipped with either nuclear or conventional warheads, and a rival power cannot always know from the outside which is which. Both this difficulty in determining which of them are nuclear-armed and the ease with which they can be hidden would make the verification of arms-control agreements incomparably more complicated than it is today.

While the freeze is fully defensible as a measure in its own right, virtually none of the advocates of the freeze (or of any of the other moderate measures that have been put forward by the peace movement) present it (or any of the others) as the final goal of their efforts. They are well aware that, as an answer to the question of what mankind should do about the threat of human extinction by nuclear arms, the proposal that one should freeze the doomsday machine in place would, if it were to be offered without promise of a further proposal, be a non sequitur. They all, therefore, regard it as only "a first step." A step, however, implies a direction, and a direction implies a goal. Neither the direction nor the goal has yet been defined. If one asks what "the next step" should be, the answer is very likely to be "reductions," or "deep reductions." But when one asks how far the reductions should go, and what sort of world they would lead to, haziness and ambiguity set in. The goal of complete nuclear disarmament is sometimes mentioned, but in a perfunctory, almost casual way. Few details are offered, and no convincing picture of a nuclear-free world has yet been presented.

These lacks are only part of another lack—the lack of any doctrine that could guide the steps toward the goal of complete nuclear disarmament. A doctrine is a comprehensive policy—or, if you like, a "deliberate policy"—for dealing with an entire issue. It offers both a broad picture of the world and long-term goals to strive toward, so that the short-term measures are not a groping in a void, and do not contradict one another. When the issue is nuclear disarmament, the basic question that a doctrine must address is the underlying political one of how, in a world in which war has become mutual annihilation, the bitterest and most intractable disputes among nations are to be settled. In other words, the issue is nothing less than how the world is to be organized politically. Deterrence deserves to be called a doctrine because it offers an answer—however unsatisfactory one may find it—to the political question. It holds that the disputes among nations which in the past have been resolved through war must now be averted by the maintenance of a balance of terror with huge nuclear arsenals. It invites us to tolerate a degree of risk of extinction as the price for national defense and international stability. The proposal for world government, too, deserves to be called a doctrine, because it also answers the basic question—holding that these disputes must be resolved by civil procedures under a global authority. This solution invites us to revolutionize the politics of the earth as the cost of lifting the peril of extinction. Whatever one thinks of the bargain struck by either of these resolutions of the nuclear predicament, both deserve to be recognized as politically "serious," in the sense that both face the basic political issue without evasion. There have, by contrast, been any number of suggestions that have lacked seriousness in this sense. They may, for example, call for nuclear disarmament, or for total disarmament, but without acknowledging the need for the vast political changes that would enable nations to resolve their disputes bindingly by peaceful means, and without specifying any such means. Sometimes the intent behind such incomplete proposals may be purely rhetorical, as when a politician wishes to end his speech with an uplifting thought, and sometimes genuine political naïveté may be responsible. Inasmuch as the settlement of the disputes that arise among men is of the very essence of politics, these proposals are truly—to use a much-abused term—politically "unrealistic." They simply evade the political dimension of the issue altogether.

So far, the current peace movement has not given any significant backing to proposals that ignore the political dimension of the predicament. Rather, to the extent that it has recommended actions it has largely insisted on political workability throughout, and has chosen the course of backing modest but useful plans of action, such as the freeze, within the framework of existing broad policy, and of leaving the deeper political question open for the time being. Uneasy with deterrence but uninterested in world government, the peace movement seeks to chart a new course, but it has not yet found a way to do it. Lacking any doctrine to call its own, the movement has been driven reluctantly to rely for now on the basic framework of deterrence to justify its moderate proposals. Thus, it defends the freeze in part on the ground that it will stabilize deterrence, and protect the nuclear balance from the technical developments that threaten to destabilize it in the near future. And, in fact, the broad acceptability of the freeze is probably attributable in no small measure to its compatibility with deterrence. (A recent poll showed that seventy per cent of the American public favored a freeze.) Accordingly, in putting forward the freeze the peace movement offers the world a new step to take but borrows an old doctrine to justify it. This borrowing is in itself unexceptionable (since it is a clear benefit to everybody for the present system to be made safer and for future deterioration of its stability to be headed off), but it has a high price attached if it continues for very long. For the premise of the doctrine of deterrence—that safety can be maintained only by the maintenance of large nuclear arsenals—is at odds with the deepest premise of the new movement, which is that we must somehow stop threatening ourselves with annihilation. The bishops' pastoral letter can again serve as an illustration.

The bishops begin by unequivocally condemning the mass slaughter of innocents with nuclear weapons. Yet deterrence requires such slaughter—or, at the very least, cannot promise to avoid it—simply because any large-scale nuclear attack, even if it is aimed at military targets, will involve the mass slaughter of innocents. There is, of course, a policy that would succeed in translating the pastoral letter's ban on nuclear mass slaughter into actual policy. It is unilateral disarmament—and not some unilateral "gesture" or other but the real thing: an immediate declaration by the President that he was dismantling the nation's nuclear arsenal in the shortest possible time, and that meanwhile he renounced the use of nuclear weapons. Yet if there are two words that in the present political climate doom a proposal to political oblivion even more swiftly than "world government" they are "unilateral disarmament," and the bishops explicitly reject this course. Nevertheless, they seem at times to steer in its direction. At one point in the letter, they observe that "the political paradox of deterrence has also strained our moral conception." Then they pose a series of questions: "May a nation threaten what it may never do? May it possess what it may never use? Who is involved in the threat each superpower makes: Government officials? Or military personnel? Or the citizenry in whose defense the threat is made?" This series of questions has the look of an exploratory probe of dangerous territory—a probe in which the bishops reconnoitre the perilous ground of unilateral disarmament only to veer away again. For if these questions are answered in a certain way they make the moral argument for unilateral nuclear disarmament: "A nation may never threaten what it may never do. It must never possess what it may never use. Not only government officials and military personnel but also the citizenry in whose defense the threat is made are involved in the threat." Judged by traditional ethical standards, including, specifically, the Catholic teaching on war, this position is not an extreme one. It does not rule out all killing, for example. It does not even rule out killing on quite a large scale. It merely spells out the measures necessary if the injunction against the mass slaughter of innocents is to be more than exhortation and become policy. The bishops boldly ask us whether we are willing, under any conceivable circumstances, to kill countless millions of innocent people, and to this their and our immediate impulse is to cry out "No!" And, indeed, at one point the bishops state that we must say a clear "no" to nuclear weapons. If I may use myself as an example, I know that if the nuclear button were on my desk and a nuclear attack were launched against the United States I would be unable to retaliate in kind. I would utterly lack the "resolve" to do this. In fact, my whole resolve would be that it not be done. This "retaliation" would seem to me to be a separate, new, unspeakable crime in its own right, which was in no way an appropriate response to the unspeakable crime that had just been committed against my country. As I see it, it would, in fact, not even *be* retaliation, since most of the people it would kill—innocent citizens, including children—would have had nothing to do with their government's criminally insane decision. Yet I know that this unwillingness of mine would, if it were generalized into a policy, be so far outside the pale politically as to have virtually no acceptance. In that sense, to truly say "no" to nuclear weapons forces one into a position that is politically irrelevant—at least, as far as present policy is concerned. Although I can't speak for others, I suspect that there are many people who want to say a real "no" to nuclear weapons but find that majority opinion is overwhelmingly against them. So, in desperation, they, like the bishops, seek partial and gradual measures that, if they are pursued long enough, may enable us one day not only to say but to practice our "no."

The fissure that nuclear weapons have created between our political selves and our moral selves is precisely delineated by the fact that as long as there are nuclear weapons in the world we are compelled to choose between a position that is politically sound but immoral and one that is morally sound but politically irrelevant. The bishops, who have had the rare courage to articulate the dilemma, oscillate between these two positions and conclude with a compromise. Having begun by condemning the slaughter of innocents with nuclear arms, they appear to catch a glimpse of the political implication of that stand (unilateral disarmament) and reject it, and finally fall back on deterrence, to which they give a "strictly conditioned" acceptance—the condition being that deterrence be recognized as a provisional remedy while full-scale nuclear disarmament is being worked out. (On this point, I find myself in disagreement with the bishops. My unwillingness to support the use or the threat to use nuclear weapons is unconditional. There are simply some means that I think are wrong, no matter what the end pursued, and this is one of them. And if it is wrong in that sense, then it is wrong in all times and places and circumstances, including now, right here, and in our present circumstances. If we are attacked with nuclear weapons, I *want* the retaliation to be a phone call. Thus, unlike the bishops, I cannot support deterrence conditionally, because I think that it is as wrong conditionally as it is eternally. If, while awaiting a full solution to the nuclear problem, we, in obedience to the dictates of deterrence policy, take action that leads to the death of billions of people, they will not be conditionally dead. And if we extinguish mankind it will not be conditionally extinguished. It will be extinguished forever. At the same time, however, precisely because extinction is forever, I believe that moderate steps that fall short of a full solution to the nuclear peril should receive everyone's wholehearted support. We can and must morally boycott evil in this world, but we cannot boycott the world. The purity of an individual person's conduct has immeasurable importance for *the world*. But if in seeking to preserve our purity we let *the world* perish, of what use will our purity be then?) The bishops state that we must say a clear "no" to nuclear weapons. Ultimately, however, their "no" is qualified, and nuclear weapons are accepted, if only temporarily. The bishops articulate the soul's demand that we desist at all costs from carrying out mass murder and the extinction of our species, but they do not find a home for that demand in our present world. Yet the choked-back "no" continues to sound beneath the argumentation and compromise. It becomes the banked moral fire that is needed to keep the idea of disarmament active in our thoughts and efforts.

The bishops' U-turn, in which they criticize but then embrace deterrence, although only provisionally and with barely contained revulsion, reflects the whole peace movement's rejection of the premises of deterrence and its simultaneous reliance on deterrence to justify the moderate and politically popular proposals that it has put forward. Moral and intellectual torment, of which the pastoral letter is a paradigm, is one of the results of that reliance. Another, which has greater practical consequences, is that of leaving the movement without any road map to full nuclear disarmament to offer the world—and, worse, we are all left to rely on a road map that specifically precludes full nuclear disarmament. For while the people of the peace movement have not examined in detail the possibility of nuclear disarmament in the framework of deterrence, the theorists of deterrence have, and they have all but unanimously ruled it out as unattainable—as "a fictional utopia."

The popular notion of a whole series of "steps," which evokes the image of a stairway, encourages the simple but hopeful idea that if enough steps are taken the top of the stairway will be reached and complete nuclear disarmament will be attained. And certainly the usefulness of distinguishing between short-term steps and long-term goals seems obvious and undeniable. It needs to be said—once and for all, one would hope—that there is no need whatever to choose between short-term, moderate "steps" that are within our immediate grasp and long-term, radical goals whose achievement would bring us real safety. Nothing is more arid and fruitless than the abuse-laden exchanges between the champions of these two approaches, with one side saying that the moderate steps are useless because they don't go far enough, and the other side saying that long-term goals should be barred from the discussion because they will distract us from moderate measures that we can really achieve. These arguments are like the wasted breath of two people standing at the bottom of a stairway arguing about whether it is more important to take the first step or the last step to get to the top. Isn't it self-evident that both are needed? The two camps would do well to call a cease-fire and become allies, with the short-term people gaining hope and a sense of direction from a new understanding that long-term goals are both essential and achievable, and the long-term people taking heart from the actual accomplishments of the short-term people. And then, of course, they could pit their combined efforts against the steady retrogression that has been our real record over the last thirty-nine years.

However, an agreement on the obvious point that all the steps—first, middle, and last—must be traversed if one is to get to the top of the stairs would hardly solve the substantive question of just *which* stairway leads to safety (if such a thing is attainable at all in the nuclear world). Close examination of the doctrine of deterrence dashes the hope that *this* doctrine is such a stairway. The problem is inherent in the very nature of deterrence as it is currently practiced. Under deterrence, "safety" lies in the weapons themselves, and in the terror they inspire. More particularly, it lies in the power of each side to destroy the society of the other side after suffering a first strike. If that power is lost, then the balance of terror is lost, and deterrence

dissolves. Deterrence thus establishes a level beneath which "reductions" may not go, and the level is the number of weapons
necessary to destroy the society of the adversary in a retaliatory
strike. This situation is often called "minimum deterrence," and
it marks the lower limits of arms reductions under the doctrine
of deterrence in its present form. Under deterrence, arms control can theoretically eliminate redundancy, but it must never
touch the essential capacity for "assuring" the annihilation of
the other side. In other words, it can get rid of the overkill
but not the kill—an advance, but not one that offers much
relief to people in the targeted countries. Indeed, in the light
of the conclusion that even a fraction of the present arsenals
could trigger a nuclear winter, it turns out that there might not
even be any relief for untargeted nations, whose interests might
otherwise be served by a policy of minimum deterrence. From
the point of view of a mortal human being, the first time you
lose your life is the time that counts, and whether or not your
ghost is being stalked through the rubble by further nuclear
explosions is a point of small interest. Another problem with
minimum deterrence, which was seized on by Weinberger in his
argument with Draper (who, however, favors not "minimum"
but what he calls "sufficient" deterrence), is that it leaves the
statesmen with an all-or-nothing choice as soon as the brink is
reached, and deprives them of all flexibility.

   Reduction to zero is, of course, ruled out. For, according to
the terms of the doctrine, if nations had no nuclear weapons to
threaten one another with, deterrence would evaporate. In fact,
there is a sense in which even reductions are antithetical to the
logic of deterrence: if under this doctrine safety relies on terror,
then it may be dangerous—destabilizing—to undermine, or
even to "minimize," that terror, because one might at the
same time minimize the safety. The only reason to minimize
the number of weapons would be to minimize the damage "if
deterrence fails," but such minimizing runs directly counter
to the essence of the logic of deterrence, which is that everyone will be dissuaded from launching an attack only because
everyone knows that the damage to his own society will be
the maximum possible. It can even be argued that overkill is
useful in producing a deterrent effect. It may eliminate every
last shred of doubt on either side that to make war in a nuclear

world is to commit suicide. (And the recent statements by our own government officials show how durable the illusion is that one might survive—or even come out on top—in a nuclear war.)

A goal for arms control which does make sense under the doctrine of deterrence is stability, but stability is not necessarily served by reductions; rather, increases to assure "the survivability of the retaliatory force," for example, or to heighten that force's destructive power might in some circumstances be judged necessary. In fact, a minor argument has broken out in the arms-control world between the advocates of reductions and the advocates of stabilization. The former aim at reducing the numbers of nuclear weapons, apparently in the hope that the momentum achieved might lead the world to safety. The latter argue that, given the existence of nuclear arsenals, the numbers are unimportant, and the thing to do is to remove the technical imbalances and the political tensions that could lead to use of the arsenals—whatever their size. (The ultimate stabilization, of course, would be for the Soviet Union and the United States to come to an understanding regarding their international differences.) However, both schools accept the underlying framework of deterrence. Deterrence is a system—a way of organizing the nuclear world. As such, it has an underlying logic (though a flawed one), definite rules and provisions, and definite military and technical requirements. If in order to achieve the abolition, or even the severe reduction, of nuclear weapons this logic is to be abandoned, its rules broken, and its provisions violated, then some other system—some other way of organizing the world—has to be offered in its stead.

The theorists of deterrence do not altogether rule out the abolition of nuclear weapons; they rule it out only as a measure that is possible in a world of sovereign states. If we are to achieve the abolition of nuclear weapons—not to mention complete disarmament—then, they say, we must establish world government. World government, they admit, could at least theoretically replace deterrence. But they reject world government, and, with it, abolition. According to this view, we must choose between a nuclear-armed world of sovereign states and a nuclear-free world ruled by world government. The one thing they see as truly impossible, in the long run as well as the short run, is a world of still sovereign states from which nuclear weapons have been abolished. This is because they see no way that the political question—how disputes among nations are to be resolved—can be answered in such a world. They foresee that if in such a world a dispute arises and diplomatic efforts are unavailing, then one or both countries will shortly rearm, and war will break out. What is worse, in anticipation of such a conflict some nations may secretly stockpile or actually produce nuclear weapons, in undetectable violation of the abolition agreement, so as to have an immediate and overwhelming advantage over their potential adversaries—or, at any rate, to avoid being left at a hopeless disadvantage if it turns out that the adversary has cheated. And the deterrence theorists note, as a clinching argument, that even if it should happen that no one was violating the agreement the knowledge of how to make the weapons would remain in the world, and nations could rebuild nuclear weapons openly as soon as some unresolvable political dispute broke out. Since in this view political disputes are sooner or later inevitable, it would not be long before the whole world had embarked again on a chaotic, pell-mell nuclear-arms race—the worst of all possible results. This line of thinking, though it is no secret, is not widely known among the public, yet among strategic analysts it is broadly accepted. And since it is to the analysts, by and large, that the politicians turn when they wish to translate hopeful rhetoric into action this view stands as a serious obstacle to any plan for full nuclear disarmament—and should so stand unless the points made can be answered. The following are but a few examples of this reasoning. Herman Kahn wrote in 1960:

> It has probably always been impractical to imagine a com-
> pletely disarmed world, and the introduction of the thermo-
> nuclear bomb has added a special dimension to this impracti-
> cality. Given the large nuclear stockpiles in the Soviet Union,
> the United States, and the British Isles, it would be child's play
> for one of these nations to hide completely hundreds of these
> bombs. . . . The violator would then have an incredible advantage
> if the agreement ever broke down and the arms race started again.
> This surely means that even if all nations should one day agree to
> total nuclear disarmament, we must presume that there would be

the hiding of some nuclear weapons or components as a hedge against the other side doing so. An international arrangement for banishing war through disarmament will not call for total disarmament but will almost undoubtedly include provisions for enforcement that cannot be successfully overturned by a small, hidden force. Otherwise it would be hopelessly unstable. . . .

While total disarmament can be ruled out as an immediate possibility, one can conceive of some sort of international authority which might have a monopoly of war-making capability. . . . However, it is most doubtful in the absence of a crisis or war that a world government can be set up in the next decade.

Living with Nuclear Weapons makes some of these same points:

> Complete disarmament would require some form of world government to deter actions of one nation against another. In a disarmed world, without such a government armed with sufficient force to prevent conflict between or among nations, differences in beliefs and interests might easily lead to a renewal of war. But any world government capable of preventing world conflict could also become a world dictatorship. And given the differences in ideology, wealth, and nationalism that now exist in the world, most states are not likely to accept a centralized government unless they feel sure of controlling it or minimizing its intrusiveness.

And the M.I.T. political scientist and arms-control expert George Rathjens, in an essay published in 1977 in which he advocates large reductions in the nuclear arsenals of both sides, writes:

> We reject the possibility of complete nuclear disarmament as being unrealistic for the foreseeable future. This becomes clear as soon as one faces up to the changes in the political environment that would be required. . . .
>
> (a) All states would have to be parties to disarmament agreement. . . .
>
> (b) All would have to accept such intrusive inspection as to preclude weapons manufacture. . . .
>
> (c) To be sure of timely access to any suspected installation where nuclear weapons might be stored or produced, the forces available to the international authority would have to be sufficiently strong to overcome resistance rapidly. . . .

We are, then, for all practical purposes, dealing with the question of the establishment of a world government (or something very close to it), and one with rather extraordinary powers of search and seizure at that.

As it happens, agreement on this point extends even to the advocates of world government. Both see an unbreakable linkage between full nuclear (or total) disarmament and world government. In *World Peace Through World Law*, published in 1958, which is one of the most carefully thought through of the proposals for world government, Grenville Clark and Louis B. Sohn spell out the minimum that they think would be necessary:

> Apart from an effective inspection system to supervise the disarmament process from the outset, it will be indispensable simultaneously to establish an adequate world police force in order that, after complete disarmament has been accomplished, the means will exist to deter or apprehend violators of the world law forbidding any national armaments and prohibiting violence or the threat of it between nations. It will then become equally clear that along with the prohibition of violence of the threat of it as the means of dealing with international disputes, it will be essential to establish alternative peaceful means to deal with all disputes between nations in the shape of a world judicial and conciliation system. It will doubtless also be found advisable, in the interest of a solid and durable peace, to include a World Development Authority, adequately and reliably financed, in order to mitigate the vast disparities between the "have" and the "have not" nations.
>
> The necessity will also be seen for a world legislature with carefully limited yet adequate powers. . . . In addition, it will be necessary to constitute an effective world executive, free from any crippling veto, in order to direct and control the world inspection service and the world police force and to exercise other essential executive functions. Finally, it will follow as surely as day follows night that an effective world revenue system must be adopted.

And, in 1955, Bertrand Russell wrote:

> It would be wholly futile to get an agreement prohibiting the H-Bomb. Such an agreement would not be considered binding after war has broken out, and each side on the outbreak of war would set to work to manufacture as many bombs as possible.

I might add that in *The Fate of the Earth* (in which I sought to define the political task posed by nuclear weapons but did not propose any course of action) I wrote:

> This task [of resolving the nuclear predicament] falls into two parts—two aims. The first is to save the world from extinction by eliminating nuclear weapons from the earth. . . . The second aim, which alone can provide a sure foundation for the first, is to create a political means by which the world can arrive at the decisions that sovereign states previously arrived at through war. These two aims . . . are intimately connected. If, on the one hand, disarmament is not accompanied by a political solution, then every clash of will between nations will tempt them to pick up the instruments of violence again, and so lead the world back toward extinction. If, on the other hand, a political solution is not accompanied by complete disarmament, then the political decisions that are made will not be binding, for they will be subject to challenge by force.

(I take the liberty of quoting myself again only because I wish to acknowledge my former adherence to a point of view with which I now propose to argue.)

These statements, and countless others that might be quoted, form a remarkable consensus. One school favors world government and the other opposes it, yet they agree that if full nuclear disarmament (or total disarmament) is to be achieved world government is necessary. They make different choices, but they agree on what the choices are, and they agree that between the two there is no middle ground. The changeover is from one fundamental organization of the world to another. And each organization has its own logic and fundamental structure, radically different from the other's. Deterrence, as we have seen, cannot countenance any reductions below what is necessary for "minimum deterrence," and even these reductions, it is sometimes argued, may be destabilizing. But world government, as the passage by Clark and Sohn makes clear, has an even more comprehensive and indivisible logic—one that moves from an inspection force to a police force, and from a police force to a court, so that by the time you reach the end of the paragraph you have a "World Development Authority," set up to hand over the money of the "have" nations to the "have not" nations. The real problem with world government, as this passage suggests, is not that it is "impossible," or "utopian"—for if enough people want it they can surely have it—but that if we choose it we get more than we want. The heart sinks at the thought of world government not because it is "unrealistic" but because it is all too real. To use a homely metaphor, it is like one of those mail-order clubs in which to receive an attractive introductory offer of, say, a book or a plant one must accept for the rest of the year a monthly book or plant that one may not want. We want relief from the nuclear peril, but if we sign up for world government as the means of getting it we find that global institution after global institution is inexorably delivered on our doorstep thereafter, each one equipped to meddle in some new area of our lives. We are caught up, seemingly for purely technical reasons, in a whirlwind of political change that, in and of itself, we do not want. (The reason for what seems the illimitably sweeping character of world government is easier to understand when one recalls that it is being instituted as a replacement for war, which was previously the "final arbiter" of *all* international disputes, no matter what their character or origin might be.) We would like world government to make just one decision—to "ban" (as it's often put) nuclear weapons—but we find that in order to do that it must apparently have the power to make almost any decision we can think of. And from this unlimited delegation of power we shrink back. (Most proposals for world government, and particularly those made by Americans or Englishmen, are hedged about with all kinds of restraints, but, while the restraints might indeed work and be useful, experience tells us that they can always break down, and it is hard to place much trust in them.)

In sum, I am suggesting that the reason we have failed to achieve nuclear disarmament in the last thirty-nine years is not merely that we have lacked the fortitude or the will or the moral sensitivity (although we can hardly exonerate ourselves on those counts) but also that even on the purely intellectual level we have been missing a piece of the puzzle: a way of abolishing nuclear weapons that does not require us to found a world government, which the world shows virtually no interest in founding. The requirement for world government as the inevitable price for nuclear disarmament is at the heart of the impasse that the world has been unable to break through in almost four decades of the nuclear age. It stops citizens and government officials alike from clearly advocating the natural and obvious goal of their anti-nuclear efforts: the abolition of nuclear arms. The linkage is in itself paralyzing. Until it is re-moved—until we find some way of ridding ourselves of nuclear weapons without having to establish world government, or something like it—major relief from the nuclear peril seems unlikely.

Once the early hopes for a nuclear-free world raised by the advocates of world government had, in the late 1940s, been effectively buried, the tone and content of the continuing discussion of the nuclear question in official circles came to be conditioned by a key piece of reasoning. The reasoning ran: If nuclear weapons are to be abolished, there must be world government; world government is impossible; therefore, we must arm ourselves with nuclear weapons. Once this piece of reasoning was accepted, the greatest of the human and moral questions that were raised by nuclear weapons—questions such as whether it was acceptable to annihilate whole nations, or whether it made sense to build the machinery for the self-extermination of mankind—were, in effect, ruled out of order. For if there was only one path—world government—that led to complete nuclear disarmament, and that path was blocked, a nuclear buildup became inevitable. There is moral responsibility only where there is choice, but here no choice was seen, and therefore no responsibility was seen, either. While the necessity for threatening to use, and perhaps one day actually using, nuclear weapons was certainly regrettable, it was suggested that there was no sense in losing sleep over it until someone showed a plausible way of abolishing them. The remaining questions were details: how many millions you had to threaten to kill to make deterrence take effect, how many bombs you needed to do it, how to keep your retaliatory force safe, etc. The underlying logic constituted a license, which has been honored until the present, to "think the unthinkable" without any qualms. And if anyone protested the amoral cold-ness of this thinking, the burden of proof was on him. Did he propose world government? Did he suppose that it could be established and established in time to prevent a nuclear holocaust? Could he point to some other way of abolishing nuclear weapons? If not, it was said, he should hold his tongue.

In 1961, James Newman, an editor on the staff of *Scientific American*, reviewing Herman Kahn's book *On Thermonuclear War* in that periodical, described it as "a moral tract on mass murder: how to plan it, how to commit it, how to get away with it, how to justify it." Kahn's book was exactly that, but so was every book on nuclear strategy—unless it advocated unilateral disarmament—and if Newman could not show the way to avoid this mass murder, then the question was whether he really had the standing to complain. He could be seen to be just as deeply implicated as Kahn was, the only difference being that Kahn was ready to think about the mass murder and talk about it, while Newman was not. (So firmly rooted was the underlying justification for nuclear strategizing that the theorists of the unthinkable at times assumed an air of martyred dignity, as though they were being held in disrepute for volunteering to take up a necessary but painful burden that the rest of society was too weak or squeamish to shoulder. And the theorists were absolutely right—as long as everyone agreed that a nuclear-armed world was the only realistic one.)

The new peace movement now finds itself in the same position as James Newman. Its members have exhumed the elemental human and moral questions that are posed by nuclear weapons. They have discovered their revulsion against the idea of enjoying a precarious "safety" at the price of holding hostage the life of every human being on earth and every future, unborn human being. They have awakened with shock and horror to the realization that, like a demented person who has filled the basement of his house with TNT and threatens to set it off, the human family has crammed its planetary home, unmenaced by any outside power, with nuclear weapons. They have rebelled against the belief that mankind's "no" to nuclear slaughter and self-annihilation is untranslatable into action, and must always be blocked by an impenetrable shield of political impossibility. And all this has been essential work, without which mankind would never be able to escape from its self-constructed trap. But now they are asked—and rightly—what plan they have to offer to show the way out of the impasse. If they have none, it is said, they are airing their anguish and indignation before the public for nothing—behavior comparable to running up to someone on death row and shouting "You must die! You must die!" Their challenge, and everyone's challenge, is to unmake the chain of reasoning that locks us in inaction, to break through the shield of political impossibility, and to chart the path that leads back to survival.

II. A DELIBERATE POLICY

THE CONSENSUS, among so many of those who have thought deeply about the nuclear predicament, that nuclear weapons cannot be abolished unless world government is established seems to find support in traditional political theory: in the distinction between the so-called state of nature, in which men live in anarchy and resolve their disputes among themselves, with war serving as the final arbiter, and the so-called civil state, in which men live under a government and submit their disputes to its final arbitration. In reflecting on the formation of states out of warring tribes or principalities, political thinkers have often observed that the transition from the state of nature to the civil state is usually radical and abrupt, frequently involving some act of conquest or other form of violence, and admits of no partial or halfway solutions, in which, say, a central authority is given the legislative power to "decide" the outcome of disputes but not the executive power to enforce its decisions. We seem to be faced with the same radical, either-or choice in the world as a whole, in which nations, although each constitutes a civil state within its own borders, have, according to the traditional view, always lived in an anarchic state of nature in their relations with each other. The United Nations, which has been helpful in moderating hostilities in our tense and warlike world but has not been empowered to resolve basic disputes among nations, appears to exemplify what halfway measures toward entry into the civil state lead to in the global arena.

The reason that halfway measures toward the civil state never seem to amount to very much is straightforward and basic. Human beings, existing on earth in large numbers and possessed of separate and independent wills, inevitably get into disputes, and government and war are the two immemorial means by which the disputes have been bindingly resolved. Nations do not dare to give up war and disarm until world government, or some equivalent, is in place, because if they did they would be left without any final arbiter for settling disputes. This situation would be inherently unstable, because as soon as a serious dispute arose—concerning, for example, who was to control a certain piece of territory—nations would reach for the instruments of war, and the impotent, halfway civil measures would be ignored or swept aside (as happened, for example, to the League of Nations in the 1930s). That is why the political thinkers of our time have, with rare unanimity, declared that either total disarmament or full nuclear disarmament is impossible without the simultaneous establishment of world government—and we are left with the unfortunate choice between living with a full balance of nuclear terror, which we would like to get away from, and instituting a full global state, which we would like to avoid. (Mere nuclear disarmament is seen as impossible without world government because among the instruments of war nuclear arms overrule all the others. They have the final word.)

The key event in the transition from the state of nature to the civil state is the centralization of power, in which the individual nations (or people) renounce their right to resort to force at their own discretion, yielding it to the central authority, which is then empowered to make and enforce final decisions. Unfortunately, the centralization of power does not necessarily require a shift from "lawlessness" to "law," as advocates of world government sometimes seem to suggest. The central authority can be, in a moral sense, as "lawless" as any individual. When the central authority in question is a world government, this possibility assumes terrifying proportions, which have no precedent in the annals of politics. Moreover, the establishment of a central authority does not necessarily entail a reduction in the levels of violence, as the record of the totalitarian regimes in the first half of our century makes clear (and as the record of the Pol Pot government in Kampuchea has made clear more recently). Governments, we are forced to acknowledge, are fully as capable of slaughtering huge numbers of people as war is. And if a lawless government were to assume control of the world and such slaughter were to be carried out in the global darkness of the oppression of all mankind the horror of the situation would be beyond all imagining.

What the world's entry into the civil state would accomplish, however, is, as everyone acknowledges, an end to war—or, in our time, an end to the possibility of "mutual assured destruction" and human extinction. In war, the level of force used is bid up to the maximum, because victory (if any) goes to the side that keeps on fighting longer. War is, in Clausewitz's words, a form of "reciprocal action" that "must lead to an extreme" in order to reach a conclusion. And for that reason nuclear weapons spoil war as a final arbiter of international disputes: the extreme they run to is total annihilation. Central governments, on the other hand, don't need to run to any extremes of force to carry out even the most extensive slaughter. One bullet for each "subversive," fired into the back of the head, will suffice. In fact, strictly speaking, no active violence at all is necessary. Vast populations can be killed off by simple deprivation. If you place a multitude of people in a camp, force them to work hard, and cut back their rations, you can kill as many of them as you want to. Certainly no nuclear bombs will be necessary to kill them. In that limited, tragic sense, world government, even at its worst, would be a way out of the nuclear predicament. (Of course, if world government were to break down, and civil war were to arise, the nuclear peril might re-arise with it; but just at the moment the peril of a nuclear holocaust resulting from a breakdown of world government is, I should say, the least of our worries.) Even if one regards these worst-case nightmares of world government run amok as unlikely, the prospect of a supreme political power ruling over the whole earth remains chilling. Anarchy is not liberty, yet it could be that in anarchy, with all its violence, the human spirit has greater latitude to live and grow than it would have in the uniform shadow of a global state.

To be sure, for a number of people it is not the attractions of world government that lead them to favor that particular resolution of the nuclear predicament. It is their dismay at what they see as the alternative: an indeterminate period of life on the edge of the abyss, terminated by extinction. The real choice, they say, is not between world government and anarchy but between world government and nothing—"one world or none," as people used to put it. Nevertheless, most people are agreed that the immediate political choice before us is between an anarchic state of nature, in which nations possess nuclear weapons, and the civil state, or world government, in which they would not. (Some people, it is true, have suggested that the world government itself might have to possess nuclear weapons—a prospect that can only increase one's misgivings about this institution.) This definition of the actions open to us is at the heart of an impasse in which the world has been stuck throughout the nuclear age.

In *The Nuclear Revolution: International Politics Before and After Hiroshima*, of 1981, the political scientist Michael Mandelbaum, reflecting the opinion of the consensus—which includes both the advocates of world government and the advocates of our present-day policy of nuclear deterrence—writes, "Relations among sovereign states are still governed by the principles of anarchy. War is still possible." And he goes on:

> A logical way to do away with war among nation-states is to abolish national armaments altogether. This, in turn, requires abolishing the incentives for states to have armaments. They have them because of the insecurity that arises from the anarchical structure of the international system. So the requirement for disarmament is the disappearance of anarchy, in favor of an international system organized along the lines of the state in domestic politics. States must give up sovereignty. This is the political revolution that some anticipated in 1945 but that has not come to pass.

In this view, evidently, our world of nuclear-armed deterrence remains in the traditional anarchic state of nature. I should like to argue, however, that inasmuch as nuclear weapons have spoiled war—the final arbiter in the state of nature—we are mistaken about this, having been misled by the habits of pre-nuclear political thought, which so often lead us astray in the new and strange nuclear world. A deterred world, I believe, is no longer in anarchy—in the traditional state of nature. Nor, of course, is it in the civil state. It is not even quite in between the two but, rather, is in a new state altogether—the deterred state—which has been brought into being by the all-pervasive, deeply rooted, man-made reality of a nuclear-capable world. It was, I believe, an unacknowledged change of this kind that Einstein was referring to when he made his famous remark, "The unleashed power of the atom has changed everything save our modes of thinking, and thus we drift toward unparalleled catastrophe." But if our world, because of the invention of nuclear weapons, has already departed from the traditional state of nature, then the possibility seems to open up that our choices may not be restricted to the either-or one between nuclear-armed anarchy and world government. New and more promising alternatives may be available. I believe that they are. In particular, I believe that within the framework of deterrence itself it may be possible to abolish nuclear weapons. But to understand how this might be so we need to examine deterrence more deeply—its mechanisms, its scientific and technical foundations, and its political goals.

A simple analogy may help to clarify the full novelty of the deterred state. Let us suppose that one day my neighbor comes into my house and starts to carry off my furniture. If he and I live in the civil state, I will call the police, and some organ of government will eventually decide what is to be done. If he and I live in a state of nature, there are no police or organs of government, and it is for me alone to try to stop him—by persuasion, if possible, or, if that fails, by force. Force is my last resort, the final arbiter of my dispute with my neighbor, and what then ultimately decides our dispute is whether it is he or I who lies dead on the ground. It's worth noting, though, that there is nothing inherently violent in the fact of a dispute. My neighbor may have quietly carried off my furniture while I was out. It is as a solution to the dispute that violence—or some alternative—enters the picture. In the civil state, my dispute with my neighbor is arbitrated by government, and in the state of nature it is arbitrated by the fight between him and me (if it comes to that). But when one turns to deterrence one finds that neither of these things is happening. Deterrence arbitrates nothing. Underlying the traditional belief that my neighbor and I must resolve our dispute either by violence or by government was the unstated assumption that the disputes must *be* resolved. Deterrence, however, discovers another possibility—that disputes can be suspended, can be kept in abeyance, without any resolution. It uses terror to prevent disputes from ever coming into being. Under deterrence, I neither call the police nor shoot my neighbor—or even lay hands on him—because he doesn't enter my house to begin with. For under deterrence I have, in anticipation of my neighbor's depredations, filled my house with explosives, wired them to go off the moment any unauthorized person crosses my threshold, and (an essential step) informed my neighbor of what I have done—hoping, of course, that he will then have the good sense to give up any plans he might have for stealing my furniture. Deterrence intervenes at a point in the action quite different from that at which either force or an organ of government intervenes. Force or an organ of government steps in after the dispute has arisen and has reached an impasse, to settle it, whereas deterrence steps in before anyone has made a move, to keep the dispute from taking place.

The mechanism of deterrence is as different from the mechanism of war as its end result is from the end result of war. Deterrence is essentially psychological in its action. It uses terror to produce a mental result—the decision not to act. In the international sphere, its aim is to make government leaders *reflect* before they engage in aggression. When its action is effective, no one lies dead on the ground (although if it fails all do). It relies for its success not on the corpse of the fallen soldier but on the prudence of the live, thinking statesman. War, by contrast, while it has its psychological elements, including an element of deterrence, is in essence physical in its action: it blasts the opponent out of the way, as though he were a thing rather than a person, and his soon to be darkened psyche is of purely secondary interest.

In making deterrence possible, nuclear weapons have thus offered a new answer to the question (which lies at the heart of the nuclear predicament) of how disputes among nations are to be handled—an answer in which the disputes, instead of being arbitrated either by government or by war (or by anything else, for that matter), are kept out of "court" altogether. Because both government and war were ways of settling disputes, the civil state and the state of nature were both states of change. The deterred state, by contrast, is a stalemate. In the sphere of international politics, all is held stationary, in a sort of global-political version of "the freeze"—a version in which it is not arms that are frozen in place but national boundaries—and change is relegated to other spheres, such as the economic, the cultural, and the spiritual, and to domestic turmoil, including revolution. (Revolutionary war escapes incapacitation by nuclear weapons because the enemies—often belonging to the same families—are too closely intertwined to be able to kill one another by such indiscriminate means. Furthermore, while people have shown themselves willing to consider precipitating the annihilation of their own countries by antagonizing another nuclear power, they have yet to show themselves willing to threaten their own countries with nuclear weapons.)

Whatever may be the advantages or disadvantages of the state of deterrence, its foundations are solid. They are deeply lodged in the nature of things. They lie, in the last analysis, in the structure of matter, which we are powerless to return to its former, Newtonian state—a feat that would require us to forget twentieth-century physics. We are used to thinking of deterrence as a policy, but before it is a policy it is a simple fact of life for nuclear-armed nations. Hand two nations the wherewithal to dip their buckets into the bottomless pools of energy that lie in the heart of matter and a state of deterrence springs up between them, whatever their policies may be. For their leaders, if they are rational, will grasp without the help of theory that if they drop nuclear bombs on their nuclear-armed foe, the foe may drop nuclear bombs on them in return. In the last analysis, victory is ruled out in the nuclear world because the adversaries are matched not against reserves of power that belong in any basic way to either of them individually but against the unlimited, universal power of nuclear energy, which is now more or less available to all. And what human power can hope to defeat the universe? The role of deterrence *policy* is to acknowledge, codify, and shore up this situation, and then seek certain advantages from it.

It would be a mistake, however, to suggest that the deterred state has been added to the two traditional ones, as though we were now free to choose among three states. Rather, the foundations of the traditional state of nature have themselves been altered, so that now we must distinguish between two states of nature—the pre-nuclear one and the nuclear one. The idea of an alteration in nature comes as something of a shock to us, as the very word "nature" suggests that it might. The word suggests the *given*—all that exists, has always existed, and always will exist, independent of human power to alter it. It was not in this realm that we expected alteration. We looked for alteration, on the whole, in the civil state, where our efforts and our will were supposed to make a difference. Whatever else might change, "anarchy" appeared to be a constant—stable, if you will. But we failed to reckon with modern physics (one of the "natural" sciences), which proved capable of transforming nature. Anarchy rested on a shaky base. When the atom was cracked open and its vast energy was spilled into our human world, anarchy's underpinnings were washed away. Thanks to physics, the supposedly changeless physical world was unexpectedly changed, and nations were simply obliged to adjust as best they could. (One of the ironies of our situation is that the natural world has proved to be more changeable than the supposedly flexible political world.)

Of course, the phrase "altering nature" is not literally accurate. In literal fact, nature remains just as it was before we pried into its secrets (as far as we know, neither the detonation of a few tens of thousands of nuclear weapons on our planet nor our disappearance as a species would have the slightest effect on any of the hundred billion or so galaxies in the universe), and what we really mean by the expression is that the physical world in which human beings live and conduct their affairs has been altered. We are not the inventors but only the discoverers of the energy in matter. The universe has always been built this way, and human beings, belonging to a rational and inquiring species, were bound to discover the fact. And then we were bound to try to figure out—as we are now doing—how to survive in such a universe. Nothing now seems more "unnatural" to us than the nuclear peril, and yet in reality nothing is more "natural," inasmuch as the peril is rooted in the basic structure of nature itself.

Whether or not one subscribes to the policy of nuclear deterrence—the threat to strike back with nuclear weapons if one's country is attacked with them or if it starts to lose a conventional war—one has to recognize as an objective fact that the equations of war and peace have had to be rewritten in our nuclear world, and that in those rewritten equations war comes out a suicidal proposition. Not only has war been taken away from us by physics—been "spoiled"—but we can't get it back. Some have tried. Among them are the devotees of "nuclear-war-fighting," who believe that it is possible to fight and survive, and even prevail in, a nuclear war, and who are now in the ascendancy in Washington. But their efforts inevitably founder in the boundless destruction of the more than a million Hiroshimas that are waiting to happen in the world's fifty-thousand-odd nuclear weapons. What these strategists can never explain is how anyone can "prevail" in a "war" after which no one would be left. Their "victories," or restorations of the peace "on terms favorable to the United States," are apparently of an extra-human sort—"victories" in which after all the people have been killed, our bombs triumph over the other side's bombs. And the strategists' sometimes intricate and ingenious scenarios of nuclear-war-fighting are testimony only to the ability of the human mind, transported by pure abstract theory, to take leave of reality altogether.

In short, under deterrence the passage to a world in which the use of force is given up as the means of settling international differences *has already begun.* In a way, it has been accomplished. In the first days of the nuclear age, it seemed to some "idealists" that the task facing mankind was to abolish war, but "realists" replied that this was impossible—at least, in the short run— because it required the establishment of world government; instead, they proposed the policy of deterrence. However, when one looks at deterrence closely it turns out that war has not been preserved by it. Isn't this what the political scientist Bernard Brodie was getting at when he said, in 1946, in *The Absolute Weapon,* that in the nuclear world the only purpose of military preparations was to avert wars, not to win them? And isn't this what countless statesmen of our time have been telling us in saying that the purpose of their nuclear policies is only to prevent the use of nuclear and other weapons? The statement "War has been spoiled," which stands in such sharp contrast to Mandelbaum's "War is still possible," thus refers not to an idealistic aspiration but to a fait accompli. We cannot abolish war, because nuclear weapons have already done the job for us. What we can and must abolish is mutual assured destruction and the possibility of human extinction, the threat of which we now trade on to keep the peace. Our ambivalence toward this threat, which we try simultaneously to renounce and to exploit for our political ends, defines our new predicament. Just by thinking a little harder, and by looking a little bit more closely at both theory and practice in our nuclear world, we seemingly have already accomplished this "impossible" thing of abolishing war (among nuclear powers, anyway). This is not a mere phrase but a bedrock reality of our time, on which we may rely as we seek elements with which to build the edifice of our future safety. All the debates, carried over from the pre-nuclear age, about whether or not war is moral, and whether or not world government might be preferable, are no doubt extremely interesting, but they are anachronistic, for the world to which they have reference has gone out of existence.

Nuclear weapons, we see, have knocked the sword of war from our hands. Now it is up to us to decide what we will pick up in its place. The question before us shifts from how to abolish war to how to get along in a world from which war has been abolished. And we can start by seeing the first alternative that we have hit on—deterrence—in a new light: not as a continuation of international "anarchy," in which "war is still possible," but as *one* possible system for getting along in a world without war. Without quite recognizing it, we have taken the first steps toward global agreement. It is true that force, while it is no longer the final arbiter, or any sort of arbiter, still plays the central role, as it did in the pre-nuclear state of nature, for a by-product of force, terror, is what holds everybody immobile. Yet it is also true that, as in the civil state, each individual's force, in a kind of tacit agreement, is supposed never to be used. And, as in the civil state, the whole system depends on the recognition by each individual actor of a common interest—survival—that must take precedence over individual interests. Since everybody knows and acknowledges that the use of force by any party may push everybody toward a common doom, all make efforts together to ensure that the "first use" never occurs—although at the same time each side, paradoxically, must constantly bristle with resolve to use force to repel any aggression, should it somehow occur. Moreover, right at the heart of deterrence there is an element of cooperation and consent—a crucial ingredient of every civil state, no matter how oppressive. This is the "psychological" element in deterrence, on which all else depends. For while it is true that sheer terror is the operative force in deterrence it is also true that the statesman on whom it operates must give his consent if it is to work. To be sure, his freedom of action is no greater than that of someone who is being told to do something at gunpoint; nevertheless, he remains a free agent in extremely important ways. His state of mind—his self-interest, his sanity, his prudence, his self-control, his clear-sightedness—is the real foundation of his country's and everyone else's survival. In short, he must *decide* that the world he lives in is not one in which aggression pays off. In all these respects, a deterred world is not a state of anarchy awaiting the imposition of a world order but, rather, already a sort of world order, albeit one that is in many ways contradictory and absurd.

In a deep sense, unless the species does destroy itself our world will remain a deterred world. By this I do not mean that we shall forever maintain nuclear weapons and threaten one another with mutual assured destruction. I mean that whether we possess nuclear weapons or abolish them the terror they inspire will dominate our affairs and dictate the character of our political decisions. Even if mankind were now to enter formally into the civil state, and found a world government to replace war, deterrence would, in a way, still be in effect. In the pre-nuclear world, entry into the civil state would have been a free act, arising out of an abundant faith in humanity and confidence in its betterment. For us, however, who live surrounded by doom, like people in a town at the foot of a rumbling volcano (it is our peculiar distinction not to have built our town next to Vesuvius but to have built Vesuvius next to our town), entry into the civil state would be a compelled act: a measure taken not so much to better life as only to hold on to it—not to bring heaven to earth but only to preserve the earth. Being inspired by terror, entry into the civil state would be a variant of the balance of terror under deterrence—a variant in which nations, instead of deterring each other from starting a nuclear holocaust, would all join together to deter the species as a whole from extinguishing itself. While the shift from multiplicity to unity would require a global political revolution—it would be some equivalent of what Einstein called for—even that revolution would not suspend the underlying transformation of human existence which was brought about by the development of nuclear weapons. We can never recover war. We will always be at risk, somewhere down the road, of extinguishing ourselves. We will always live in a state of deterrence. These changes mark a transformation of our world. And it is this transformed world, not the vanished, pre-nuclear one, that is our true starting point as we face the nuclear peril.

The great aim—the supreme good—that we seek through deterrence is "stability." However, this aim, to which we often refer as though it were single and indivisible, actually comprises two separate and conflicting aims. The first is to preserve the political stalemate—to freeze the status quo. The status quo in question is the one that was more or less fixed in place (at least in the central theatres of superpower rivalry, where the influence of nuclear weapons made itself felt most keenly) in the years immediately following the Second World War. What recommended this status quo as the one in which to freeze the world was not the virtue of its particular arrangements—in fact, terrible injustices, including Soviet domination of Eastern Europe, were institutionalized by it—but only the fact that it *was* the status quo when the nuclear age began, and was thus the logical starting place for a system whose essence was going to be that no changes through military action were permitted. In a broader sense, however, the status quo was the system of independent states, which had existed throughout history but whose continued existence was called into question by the nuclear peril. The second aim is to avert a nuclear holocaust, which the great powers hope to head off by the paradoxical, ju-jitsulike means of threatening one another (if only in retaliation) with that same holocaust. In other words, the policy seeks to give satisfactory resolutions of the two great issues that were raised by the development of nuclear weapons—*how* man should live (in nation-states or in some other way; under capitalism, Communism, or something else; and so on) and *whether* he would live.

The principle that binds these two aims of deterrent policy together, and whose observance would make them obtainable simultaneously, is the principle of nonaggression. This principle embodies no millennial dreams, yet its realization has been much sought (through the League of Nations and the United Nations, among other organizations) and rarely achieved. Nuclear weapons lend tremendous support to the principle of nonaggression. Traditionally, victory—the light at the end of the tunnel of war—has been the great incentive for aggression; but nuclear weapons have killed this hope in the breasts of all realistic government leaders and have thus robbed aggression of its point. Confusingly—and regrettably—they have robbed defense of *its* point, too, since in a nuclear "war" the defender is as thoroughly annihilated as the aggressor. For both parties, the tunnel of war now leads only to eternal darkness. The development of nuclear weapons has therefore, at least in theory, laid the foundation for a world at peace. And, in fact, ever since the balance of terror was established the great powers have enjoyed the stability promised by deterrence. They have never used military force against one another, although the air has been filled with threats (which are of the essence of deterrence), and although they have felt free to use their forces against non-nuclear powers. No one has liked this stalemate very much, yet people have made do with it. It is "acceptable": we have accepted it.

No one knows what any of the statesmen of our day would really do if, in the moment of truth, they were forced to choose between the two goals of deterrence policy, and either suffer military defeat or launch a nuclear holocaust. But there can be no doubt about which course the doctrine of deterrence specifies: it specifies the holocaust. If it doesn't specify the holocaust, then it isn't deterrence but something else. In that sense, deterrence gives a clear priority to national defense over human survival (although government leaders, of course, hope never to have to make the choice). If this weren't so, the resolution of the nuclear predicament would be easy. We could simply "ban the bomb," and let political matters sort themselves out however they might. If human survival had been the world's overriding goal from the time the nuclear threat first presented itself, and *not* to use nuclear weapons had really been the dominant consideration in nuclear policy—that is, if people had been ready to risk or sacrifice their particular ways of life for the sake of life itself (not their individual lives but the survival of the species)—then they would have at least seriously considered either disarming unilaterally or establishing world government, or doing both. Sometimes it is suggested that unilateral disarmament might itself lead to the use of nuclear weapons, because by creating a military imbalance it would invite the very aggression that the disarmers were hoping to head off. This argument, however, holds true only for halfhearted, faltering unilateral disarmament, which would be reversed as soon as an enemy attack materialized. Thoroughgoing, resolute disarmament would not lead to any use of nuclear arms, because the enemy could get what it wanted from the now militarily undefended country simply by walking into it. What unilateral disarmament might really lead to is not a nuclear holocaust but military defeat and foreign occupation. If by "stability" we meant only the absence of war, then unilateral disarmament would be a matchless way of achieving it. Defeat could be entirely "stable."

In the present context, however, the point is not to advocate or oppose either unilateral disarmament or world government but only to make it clear that the rejection of both by just about everybody in favor of a policy of deterrence shows that the principal goal of deterrence is to preserve national sovereignty and everything that goes with sovereignty. At the very heart of the riddle of deterrence sits sovereignty, whose preservation the policy achieves by subjecting mankind to the risk of extinction. Whatever final judgment one might make on this bargain—and it is extreme dissatisfaction with it that has fueled the new peace movement—the arguments in its favor are substantial enough not to require obfuscation by the misleading claim that we possess nuclear arms chiefly in order to avoid using them. National sovereignty *in itself*—the full political control by local people of their own territories—is, most people would agree, highly desirable. Certainly most people treasure the independence of their own countries. And probably very few even of those whose countries are not defended by nuclear arsenals would like to see either the establishment of a world government or the collapse of the balance of terror through unilateral disarmament. Furthermore, liberty in the world at large may depend on the political survival of a certain number of countries, including, above all, the democracies of the West. The strongest and most honest argument in favor of the possession of nuclear weapons, then—for those who believe in liberty—is that upholding liberty is worth the risk of extinction. (For the Soviet government, of course, the justification would be that socialism is upheld.) The argument is strengthened if one maintains—as the Catholic bishops, in their pastoral letter, and Brodie do but *Living with Nuclear Weapons* does not—that deterrence is a temporary, emergency arrangement, soon to be replaced by some better system, in which we no longer secure our safety by threatening our doom.

Nevertheless, it remains true that, within the limits imposed by the fundamental decision to defend national sovereignty with nuclear arsenals, the mutual-assured-destruction strategists do, as an additional goal, seek to deploy the weapons in such a way as to reduce to a minimum the chance of a holocaust. They do their best to see to it that the threat of annihilation by which sovereignty is preserved also prevents the execution of the threat. Above all, they seek to adopt strategic policies that add to stability—by, for example, building retaliatory rather than first-strike weapons, forgoing attempts at civil defense, establishing hot lines and the like with the adversary, and, of course, entering into arms-control agreements. (It is regarding these measures, which assume the existence of nuclear arsenals, that the sometimes arcane disputes between the advocates of mutual assured destruction and the advocates of nuclear-war-fighting take place, with the mutual-assured-destruction school, on the whole, favoring measures that will stop the holocaust from even occurring in the first place and the nuclear-war-fighting school favoring measures that would supposedly enable the United States to get some advantage over the Soviet Union if a holocaust did occur.)

Such are the means and ends of the doctrine of deterrence, on which we rely today for the safety of the nuclear world. They present us with a striking disparity. The over-all end—the military stalemate—is modest and conservative. The means, however—two nations' threats to annihilate one another and, perhaps, all mankind—are extreme in a way that gives new meaning to that word. The problem with deterrence is not that it doesn't "work"—it is, I am sure, a very effective (though far from infallible) way of restraining the superpowers from attacking one another, should they be inclined to do so—but that we must pay an inconceivable price if it fails. Regarded as a sort of world order, deterrence is a regime in which every

crime is punished by the severest possible penalty, as though
the ruler of a state had decreed that if just one of the citizens
commits a burglary all the citizens must be put to death. This
radical disproportion between ends and means invites us to
inquire whether we might not be able to achieve our modest
ends by less extreme means—a means by which we did not
threaten ourselves with doom. This definition of our task is, of
course, quite different from the one in which we were invited
to found world government in the midst of "anarchy" or else
accept a life lived perpetually on the edge of extinction. Now
we would be working within deterrence defined in its broadest
sense—as the new "state of nature," brought into being by
the very peril that we wish to alleviate. This could come about
because deterrence offers us elements to work with that were
not available in the pre-nuclear age. Two stand out. The first
is the stalemate itself, which was made possible only because
of the fearsome destructive power of the military invention
that backs it up. The second is the unlosable nature of the
knowledge that underlies the invention, and prevents us from
ever wholly expunging the possibility of nuclear destruction
from our affairs.

Our first step would be to accept the political verdict that
has been delivered by deterrence, and formalize the stalemate.
The achievement of the stalemate was, in the broadest sense,
accidental: conceived as a makeshift for coping in the short term
with a sudden peril that the world lacked either the imagination
or the will (or both) to tackle head-on, it gradually took shape,
over a period of decades, through trial and error. Its creation
was the principal work of a generation. The question for that
generation (once world government and full nuclear disarmament were jointly ruled out) was whether, given the presence
of nuclear weapons in the world, stability could be achieved.
It could be. It was. But now, with the answer to that question
in hand, we can start with the stability—the stalemate—and
invert the question, asking whether, within the new context of
our transformed world, there might not be a better means of
preserving that same stability: a means with less extreme risk
attached. What for the people of the earlier generation was the
end point of their efforts can for us be the starting point. For
even as we see that deterrence is possible we know, and have

felt in our hearts, that the bargain now struck by it is unworthy of human life, because it turns us into potential mass slayers of our species. This lesson, too, is a fruit of our experience in the nuclear age, and it drives us to seek to dismantle the doomsday machine at the earliest possible moment. A deepening awareness of the full meaning of that bargain—frequently and rightly described as "Faustian"—for strategy, for the state of our civilization, and for the state of our souls is what now inspires the world's gathering protest against nuclear arms.

Our method can be to convert into a settlement in principle the settlement of political differences which we have achieved in fact under the pressure of the nuclear threat. We can, in a manner of speaking, adopt our present world, with all its injustices and other imperfections, as our ideal, and then seek the most sensible and moderate means of preserving it. This effort is consistent with the spiritual task that nuclear weapons have put before us, which is at bottom to awaken ourselves to a new appreciation and gratitude for the world that is given to each of us at birth. For the time being, instead of asking ourselves how, in the light of the peril to all life, we must transform all life, we ask what the best way is to keep everything just the same. Not improvement but mere continuation is our dream. This, of course, is a deeply conservative aim, but then the nuclear peril seems to call on us to be conservative, inasmuch as *conserving* ourselves and our world is the challenge that we now face. To many peoples, the idea of freezing the status quo might seem discouraging, especially if for them the status quo includes intervention in their affairs by a great power. The peoples of Eastern Europe are a case in point. They cannot wish to formalize Soviet domination of their countries. The formalization of the status quo envisioned here, however, would not do that. It would permit those peoples every means to liberate themselves that they now have at their disposal, and would remove only means that they now already lack—Western military intervention in their struggles.

The next question is whether, after formalizing the status quo, we can reduce our reliance on the extreme means by which we now uphold it, and how far a reduction can go. The invaluable lesson of deterrence theory is that in the nuclear age the use of force is self-cancelling. This is the profound truth that the statesmen of our day are struggling to articulate when—expressing, no doubt, their fervent desire, though it is not the actual case—they tell us that they possess nuclear weapons only in order *not* to use them. At first, the simple and almost irresistible implication of that truth for policy seems to be that we can take the whole hateful machinery of force—conventional and nuclear—and clear it out of our lives. The moment we did that, all the paradoxes, contradictions, absurdities, and abominations that we live with under deterrence would evaporate. If the whole doomsday machine is intended only to paralyze itself—to do nothing—why do we need it? Can't we accomplish nothing without threatening suicide? But the very question reveals that after all—semi-covertly and somewhat shamefacedly—we actually rely on the doomsday machine to serve another end: the preservation of our sovereignty. We still exploit the peril of extinction for our political ends. And we don't know how to wean ourselves from that reliance without taking radical steps, such as unilateral disarmament or world government. But while some of us may be ready for radical steps the world as a whole, it is clear, is not, and demands that we preserve the sovereignty of states, even though it requires a risk to our survival. Given this political reality—which shows no sign of changing soon—it appears that, in one form or another, our reliance on the nuclear threat cannot be broken. Nevertheless, even under these terms we have far more flexibility than we have thought. It is a flexibility that, I believe, extends all the way to the abolition of nuclear arms.

On the face of it, there appears to be a contradiction between the two goals we have set for ourselves. It appears that we want to keep the stalemate but to abolish the weapons that make it possible. Yet this contradiction exists in present policy—taking the form of our threatening to use the weapons in order *not* to use them. Either way, paradox is our lot. We seek to preserve a stalemated, purely defensive world but must apparently make use of—or at least make provision for—purely offensive weapons to do it. Indeed, one way of looking at the nuclear predicament is to see it as the final outcome of a competition between offense and defense which has been going on throughout the history of war, in a sort of war within war. The invention of nuclear weapons gave the victory once and for all, it appears, to the offensive side. Although the unpredictability of science prevents a truly definitive judgment, the chances that the defense will ever catch up look vanishingly dim. The entire history of warfare supports this conclusion: although the balance between offense and defense has swung back and forth, the general trend has been unvaryingly toward the increasing destructiveness of offensive war. It is this rising general destructiveness, and not the recent success of one particular offensive weapon in eluding destruction by a defensive counterpart, that has now culminated in the whole planet's being placed in mortal peril. The ultimate vulnerability of human beings is the result of the frailty of nature itself, on which we depend utterly for life; as is now clearer to us than ever before, nature cannot stand up to much nuclear destruction. Given this flood tide of destructive power, which was rising steadily even before nuclear weapons were developed, and has continued since their development (in the fields of chemical and biological warfare, for example), the hopes for defense are not so much slight as beside the point. Most of these hopes rest on weapons that counter not the effects of nuclear weapons but, rather, the nuclear weapons' delivery vehicles. Yet a delivery vehicle is simply anything that gets from point A to point B on the face of the earth. A horse and cart is a delivery vehicle. An army battling its way into enemy territory is a delivery vehicle. A man with a suitcase is a delivery vehicle. There seems little chance that all existing vehicles—not to mention all the vehicles that science will dream up in the future—can be decisively countered. And it is even more unlikely that the devices designed to attack all the delivery vehicles would remain invulnerable to devices that scientists would soon be inventing to attack *them*. The superiority of the offense in a world of uninhibited production of nuclear weapons and their delivery vehicles therefore appears to be something that will last for the indefinite future.

The contradiction between the end we seek and the means of attaining it becomes even clearer when we try to imagine the situation we would have if in 1945 the scientists, instead of handing us the ultimate offensive weapon, had emerged from their laboratory with an ultimate defensive weapon—perhaps one of those impenetrable bubbles with which science-fiction writers like to surround cities. Then a thoroughgoing, consistent defensive world would be possible. Aggressively inclined nations might hurl their most lethal weapons at their neighbors, but the weapons would all bounce off harmlessly, and no one would be hurt. Peoples would then live safely within their own borders, suffering only the torments that they managed to invent for themselves. Under our present circumstances, by contrast, we have not perfect defense but perfect vulnerability.

It was in addressing this contradiction that the strategists came up with the doctrine of deterrence in the first place. Their chief discovery was that the threat of retaliation could substitute for the missing defenses. But while defense and deterrence have the same ends the way they work is nearly opposite. In a defensive system, you rely on your military forces actually to throw the enemy forces back: the swung sword falls on the raised shield without inflicting damage; the advancing foot soldier falls into the moat; the warhead is pulverized by the laser beam. But in a system of deterrence you have given up all hope of throwing the enemy back, and are hoping instead, by threatening a retaliatory attack that *he* cannot throw back, to dissuade him from attacking at all. Deterrence thus rests on the fear of a double offense, in which everyone would destroy everyone else and no one would be defended. The crucial element in deterrence is the foreknowledge by the potential aggressor that if he starts anything this is how it will end. Offensive means are made to serve defensive ends. But in the process the continuation of our species is put in jeopardy.

Inasmuch as the goal we have chosen is to shore up a stalemated, defensive world, one way of defining our task would be to ask whether, having agreed to live with the status quo, we might by further agreement accomplish what we are unable to accomplish through technical efforts; namely, to snatch the victory away from offensive arms and hand it, at least provisionally, back to defensive ones. The question is whether as political and diplomatic actors we could rush into the fray on the side of the defense and turn the tables. I think that, within certain all-important limits, we can. The key is to enter into an agreement abolishing nuclear arms. Nations would first agree, in effect, to drop their swords from their hands and lift their shields toward one another instead. They would agree to have not world government, in which all nations are fused into one nation, but its exact opposite—a multiplicity of inviolate nations pledged to leave each other alone. For nations that now possess nuclear weapons, the agreement would be a true abolition agreement. For those that do not now possess them, it would be a strengthened nonproliferation agreement. (A hundred and nineteen nations have already signed the non-proliferation treaty of 1968.) Obviously, an agreement among the superpowers on both the nature of the status quo and the precise terms of abolition would be the most difficult part of the negotiation. The agreement would be enforced not by any world police force or other organ of a global state but by each nation's knowledge that a breakdown of the agreement would be to no one's advantage, and would only push all nations back down the path to doom. In the widest sense, the agreement would represent the institutionalization of this knowledge. But if nuclear weapons are to be abolished by agreement, one might ask, why not go all the way? Why not abolish conventional weapons and defensive weapons as well? The answer, of course, is that even in the face of the threat of annihilation nations have as yet shown no willingness to surrender their sovereignty, and conventional arms would be one support for its preservation. While the abolition of nuclear arms would increase the margin of mankind's safety against nuclear destruction and the peril of extinction, the retention of conventional arms would permit the world to hold on to the system of nation-states. Therefore, a second provision of the agreement would stipulate that the size of conventional forces be limited and balanced. In keeping with the defensive aim of the agreement as a whole, these forces would, to whatever extent this was technically possible, be deployed and armed in a defensive mode.

There is also another reason for retaining defenses. One of the most commonly cited and most substantial reasons for rejecting the abolition of nuclear arms, even if the nuclear powers should develop the will to abolish them, is that the verification of a nuclear-abolition agreement could never be adequate. And, as far as I know, it is true that no one has ever devised a system of verification that could, even theoretically, preclude significant cheating. Like defense, it seems, inspection is almost inherently imperfect. When arsenals are large, the argument runs, a certain amount of cheating on arms-control agreements is unimportant, because the number of concealed weapons is likely to be small in relation to the size of the arsenals as a whole. But as the size of the arsenals shrinks, it is said, the importance of cheating grows, and finally the point is reached at which the hidden arsenals tip the strategic balance in favor of the cheater. According to this argument, the point of maximum—indeed, total—imbalance is reached when, after an abolition agreement has been signed, one side cheats while the other does not. Then the cheater, it is said, has an insuperable advantage, and holds its innocent and trusting cosigner at its mercy. But if anti-nuclear defenses are retained the advantage in cheating is sharply reduced, or actually eliminated. Arrayed against today's gigantic nuclear forces, defenses are helpless. Worse, one side's defenses serve as a goad to further offensive production by the other side, which doesn't want the offensive capacity it has decided on to be weakened. But if defenses were arrayed against the kind of force that could be put together in violation of an abolition agreement they could be crucial. On the one side would be a sharply restricted, untested, and clandestinely produced and maintained offensive force, while on the other side would be a large, fully tested, openly deployed, and technically advanced defensive force. Such a force might not completely nullify the danger of cheating (there is always the man with a suitcase), but no one can doubt that it would drastically reduce it. At the very least, it would throw the plans of an aggressor into a condition of total uncertainty. Moreover, as the years passed after the signing of the agreement the superiority of the defense would be likely to increase, because defensive weapons would continue to be openly developed, tested, and deployed, while offensive weapons could not be. Therefore—probably as a separate, third provision of the agreement—anti-nuclear defensive forces would be permitted.

President Reagan recently offered a vision of a world protected from nuclear destruction by defensive weapons, many of which would be based in space. The United States, he said, should develop these weapons and then share them with the Soviet Union. With both countries protected from nuclear attack, he went on, both would be able to scrap their now useless nuclear arsenals and achieve full nuclear disarmament. Only the order of events in his proposal was wrong. If we seek first to defend ourselves, and not to abolish nuclear weapons until after we have made that effort, we will never abolish them, because of the underlying, technically irreversible superiority of the offensive in the nuclear world. But if we abolish nuclear weapons first and then build the defenses, as a hedge against cheating, we can succeed. Abolition prepares the way for defense.

However, none of these defensive arrangements would offer much protection if the agreement failed to accompany them with one more provision. The worst case—which must be taken into account if nations are to have confidence in the military preparations for thwarting aggressors—is not mere cheating but blatant, open violation of the agreement by a powerful and ruthless nation that is determined to intimidate or subjugate other nations, or the whole world, by suddenly and swiftly building up, and perhaps actually using, an overwhelming nuclear arsenal. This possibility creates the all-important limits mentioned earlier. As soon as it happened, the underlying military superiority of the offensive in the nuclear world would again hold sway, and the conventional and anti-nuclear defenses permitted under the abolition agreement would become useless. (Just how soon in this buildup the offensive weapons would eclipse the defensive ones would depend on the effectiveness of the defenses that had been built up.) The only significant military response to this threat would be a response in kind: a similar nuclear buildup by the threatened nations, returning the world to something like the balance of terror as we know it today. But in order to achieve that buildup the threatened nations would probably have to have already in existence considerable preparations for the manufacture of nuclear arms. Therefore, a fourth provision of the abolition agreement would permit nations to hold themselves in a particular, defined state of readiness for nuclear rearmament. This provision would, in fact, be the very core of the military side of the agreement. It would be the definition, in technical terms, of what "abolition" was to be. And it would be the final guarantor of the safety of nations against attack. However, this guarantor would not defend. It would deter. The most important element in this readiness would simply be the knowledge of how to make the weapons—knowledge that nations are powerless to get rid of even if they want to. This unlosable knowledge is, as we have seen, the root fact of life in the nuclear world, from which the entire predicament proceeds. But, just as the potential for nuclear aggression flows from the knowledge, menacing the stability of the agreement, so does the potential for retaliation, restoring the stability of the agreement. Its persistence is the reason that deterrence doesn'tt dissolve when the weapons are abolished. In other words, in the nuclear world the threat to use force is as self-cancelling at zero nuclear weapons as it is at fifty thousand nuclear weapons. Thus, both in its political ends—preservation of a stalemate—and in its means—using the threat of nuclear destruction itself to prevent the use of nuclear weapons—the abolition agreement would represent an extension of the doctrine of deterrence: an extension in which the most terrifying features of the doctrine would be greatly mitigated, although not finally removed.

The agreed-upon preparations would be based on the knowledge. In all likelihood, they would consist both of inspectable controls on nuclear reactors and on other facilities producing weapons-grade materials and of rules regarding the construction of delivery vehicles. One question that the policymakers would put to the scientists would be what precise level of technical arrangements would permit some particular, defined level of armament to be achieved in a fixed lead time to nuclear rearmament—say, six weeks. Possible lead times would be defined in such terms as the following: an eight-week lead time to the production of two hundred warheads mounted on cruise missiles, or a six-week lead time to a hundred warheads mounted in military aircraft. The lead time would have to be short enough so that the would-be aggressor, seeking to make use of the interval as a head start, would not be able to establish a decisive lead. "Decisive" in this, or any, nuclear context refers to the ability to destroy the victim's retaliatory capacity in a pre-emptive first strike. Preemption is the spectre that haunts the deterrence strategists, for if one side can destroy the retaliatory capacity of the other side in a preemptive strike, then deterrence dissolves. This is the point at which victory looms up again as a possibility, and force stops being self-cancelling. (At least, it does in the short run. It's much more difficult to see how a nuclear aggressor could escape retaliation over a longer run.)

So it is today, and so it would be in a world of zero nuclear weapons.

The task for strategy in a nuclear-weapon-free world would be to design a capacity for nuclear rearmament which could not be destroyed in a first strike by a nation that took the lead in rearmament by abrogating the abolition agreement, secretly or openly. Retaliatory capacity would have to be able to keep pace with aggressive capacity—to the extent that a disarming first strike would be excluded. If that requirement was satisfied, possession in a nuclear-weapon-free world of the capacity for rebuilding nuclear weapons would deter nations from rebuilding them and then using them, just as in our present, nuclear-armed world possession of the weapons themselves deters nations from using them. Today, missile deters missile, bomber deters bomber, submarine deters submarine. Under what we might call weaponless deterrence, factory would deter factory, blueprint would deter blueprint, equation would deter equation. In today's world, when the strategists assess one another's arsenals they see that every possible escalation in attack can be matched by an escalation on the other side, until the arsenals of both sides are depleted and both nations are annihilated. So the two sides are deterred from attacking one another. With weaponless deterrence in effect, the strategists would see that any possible escalation in rearmament by one side could be matched by an escalation on the other side, until both were again fully armed and ready to embark on mutual assured destruction. So they would be deterred from rearming.

It has often been said that the impossibility of uninventing nuclear weapons makes their abolition impossible. But under the agreement described here the opposite would be the case. The knowledge of how to rebuild the weapons is just the thing that would make abolition *possible*, because it would keep deterrence in force. Indeed, the everlastingness of the knowledge is the key to the abolition of nuclear arms within the framework of deterrence. Once we accept the fact that the acquisition of the knowledge was the essential preparation for nuclear armament, and that it can never be reversed, we can see that every state of disarmament is also a state of armament. And, being a state of armament, it has deterrent value. In pointing out the deterrent value of preparations for nuclear rearmament, and even of the mere knowledge of how to rebuild the weapons, we make the reply to the present opponents of abolition which Bernard Brodie made to Robert Oppenheimer. Oppenheimer, rightly observing that nuclear weapons could not be defended against, called them inherently "aggressive" weapons and predicted that they would inevitably be used in lightning-swift aggressive war. In such a world, of course, there would have been no stability whatever. But to this Brodie responded that the would-be aggressor would not be the only one possessing nuclear weapons, and that when the aggressor saw that its foe possessed them—and was ready to retaliate with them—its aggressive fever would be cooled down. Now we are told that aggressors will take advantage of the abolition of nuclear weapons to rebuild and use nuclear weapons, and to this the answer again is that the intended victims will have the same capacities, and these will act as a deterrent, saving the world's stability.

The notion that abolition is impossible because uninvention is impossible appears to stem from a failure to distinguish clearly between these two things. The confusion is exemplified in *Living with Nuclear Weapons*, in which, in support of their conclusion that a world without nuclear weapons is "a fictional utopia," the Harvard authors write, "The discovery of nuclear weapons, like the discovery of fire itself, lies behind us on the trajectory of history: it cannot be undone. Even if all nuclear arsenals were destroyed, the knowledge of how to reinvent them would remain and could be put to use in any of a dozen or more nations. The atomic fire cannot be extinguished." The authors fear that "the knowledge of how to reinvent" the weapons will upset any abolition agreement. But if one has "the knowledge," there is no need to "reinvent" anything, because one can go ahead and rebuild the weapons right away by using that knowledge. If, on the other hand, reinvention is really required, then one must have somehow lost the knowledge, but this is impossible. Of course, if one speaks of the knowledge of how to rebuild the weapons rather than "the knowledge of how to reinvent" them, the inconsistency disappears; but then one is speaking of rearming after abolition rather than after uninvention. By inadvertently blurring the distinction between the two, the Harvard authors, like many other proponents of deterrence, make abolition appear to be, like uninvention,

impossible, and confer upon the world's nuclear arsenals a durability and irremovability that in fact only the knowledge of how
to make them possesses. Though uninvention is impossible,
abolition is not. Or if it were true that both were impossible it
would have to be for completely different reasons—in the case
of uninvention because we don't know how to rid the world of
basic scientific knowledge, and in the case of abolition because
we lack the necessary political will. If the distinction is kept
clear, then the hope opens up that the impossibility of uninvention, which is the fundamental fact of life in the nuclear world,
makes abolition, which is just one of the conceivable ways of
organizing that world, possible. For it was the invention, not
the buildup, of nuclear arms that irreversibly placed mankind
within reach of its own self-slaughtering hand, ruined war as
the final arbiter in global affairs, and set mankind adrift in a new
and unfamiliar political world.

The stages of nuclear escalation are often pictured as a ladder
reaching from a peaceful but nuclear-armed world up through
various levels of nuclear attack and retaliation to the end of the
world. Deterrence calls for the ability of each potential adversary to match the others at each rung of the ladder. The levels
of nuclear armament, from zero up to a full-scale doomsday
machine, can be pictured as lower rungs on that same ladder,
and the levels of technical and industrial preparation for the
production of nuclear arms as still lower rungs. On this extended ladder, the bottom rung is not zero nuclear weapons
but the bare knowledge of how to make them, unaccompanied
by any preparations to rebuild them. In actuality, however, this
lowest rung can never be reached, because every general level
of technical proficiency, whether geared to weapons production
or not, is a state of readiness for nuclear armament at one level
or another. That is why there can be no such thing as a return
to the pre-nuclear world but only increases in the lead time to
nuclear armament and from there to a holocaust. At present,
the lead time is virtually the shortest possible: we might say
that it is seven minutes—approximately the time that it would
take for forward-based strategic missiles on each side to reach
targets in the opposing country. If world government, or
some equivalent political solution, were in place, the lead time
might arguably be centuries, but there would still *be* a lead

time, because the knowledge of how to build nuclear weapons would remain in the world. Under the abolition agreement described here, our modest but invaluable achievement would be in increasing this lead time from its present seven minutes to weeks or months.

The technical choice available to us, then, is not whether to possess or to eradicate nuclear weapons but what should be the state of readiness—or, if you want to look at it that way, of unreadiness—for nuclear hostilities in which, by international agreement, we would hold the world. The either-or character of the choice between deterrence with full-scale nuclear arsenals and world government without them no longer has to paralyze the world, for we find that within deterrence itself there are endless gradations, leading all the way down to zero and beyond, as the state of readiness is reduced and diplomatic and political arrangements are improved. Deterrence has more extensive possibilities than we have yet acknowledged. It is our curse—a kind of second fall from grace—that the knowledge of how to extinguish ourselves as a species will never leave us. And it is perhaps only modest compensation that that same knowledge, by ruining war—a lesser but more ancient curse under which our species has labored—has laid the foundations for a world at peace. Nevertheless, to throw this advantage away would be a monumental mistake, since it is one of the few elements that work in our favor as we seek to avoid extinction. The durability of the invention and the collapse of war which has come with it provide a strong foundation on which to begin to build our safety. But on this strong foundation we have so far built only a rickety, improvised shelter. We suffer the danger that flows from the fact that the fateful knowledge is inexpungible from our world, but we have so far turned down the advantages that flow from that fact. We arrange to terrorize one another with annihilation, but we have so far failed to achieve the full measure of safety obtainable from the terror. It is a paradox fully worthy of this elaborate doctrine that if we were to permit ourselves to recognize clearly the breadth and depth of the peril—to assure ourselves once and for all of its boundlessness and durability—we might thereby clear a path to our salvation.

Deterrence depends on foreknowledge. Without that, we have no barrier between ourselves and our doom. It is a system in which government leaders who might be inclined toward aggression look at the end of the story they would be setting in motion, see their own and everyone else's doom written there, and therefore decide not to take even the first step. Deterrence under an abolition agreement would work in precisely the same way, except that the story at the end of which doom was written would be somewhat longer and the foreknowledge a little farther-sighted. It would now take in all the rungs on the ladder, from the construction of the first nuclear weapon up to the end of the world. The changeover from today's system would be less drastic than it might at first appear. Even under the present doctrine, the weapons are only "psychological" arsenals, meant to create terrifying "appearances." Their targets are not people's bodies but their minds, and, theoretically, the weapons' physical destiny is to rust into powder in the silos, or to pass into honored retirement, as a new and still more fearsome "generation" is groomed to take their place. Indeed, because they are wholly devoted to creating the right menacing appearances and inducing the right states of mind, no one has ever been able to suggest any sensible or sane mission for them "if deterrence fails" and the moment for their supposed actual use arrives. The manifest failure of the nuclear-war-fighters to fill the gap only underscores the point. Furthermore, the weapons have been pulled back to a purely responsive—if not exactly a "defensive"—role. Everyone says that he will use them only if he is attacked. So, theoretically, if everyone behaves well, and no one attacks, no one will use them. (Unfortunately, though, if someone does attack we are committed to using them.) In military history (if we can call such unalloyed posturing "military"), these arsenals are unique in that they can fail simply by being employed in action. They have become semi-real, shadow things, designed to play a merely supporting role in a public-relations game. This role could be filled just as well by a sham, papier-mâché arsenal, if only we could be sure that the fraud would not be discovered. Abolition would carry the present quasi-retirement of the weapons one more step. Instead of literal-mindedly requiring that we keep the actual physical things under our noses to frighten ourselves with, we would make do with the capacity for rebuilding them, which should be frightening enough.

In chess, when skilled players reach a certain point in the play they are able to see that, no matter what further moves are made, the outcome is determined, and they end the game without going through the motions. This is also our situation in the nuclear world—with the difference that the predetermined outcome is not the victory of one side or the other but the destruction of both. The difference between our present world and a nuclear-weapon-free world would be only that people had all learned to see a few steps farther ahead than they do now—as though the chess players, having gained in experience, were to call off their game four moves before checkmate rather than two. Every statesman would see, just as he does today, that aggression leads inevitably to annihilation, and would feel no need to test the proposition in action. This does not seem too much for people to have learned after thirty-nine years of staring oblivion in the face.

The great advantage of our present situation is that by actually having built a doomsday machine we have played all the moves in this game except the last, and so know from experience, as people in the first years of the nuclear age could not, where the moves lead. We've played the game this far, and the result of the final moves is before our eyes—not the victory of one side over the other but doom. If mankind were ever to lift the nuclear peril, one saying that people might employ to keep themselves from backsliding would be "Remember 1984." (But if we use 1984 to turn the nuclear-arms race around we might give this year, prospectively slated for infamy by George Orwell, a place of honor.) It seems likely that, to an extent that we today can hardly begin to imagine, future generations, if there are any, will look back on our recent history with unutterable horror. They will recall incredulously a generation that, bowing down abjectly to a technical device of its own invention, set up the machinery for the destruction of humanity. They are likely to look back with particular incredulity, it seems to me, on us in the West. The world must count on us in the West to take the lead in resolving the nuclear predicament, because we enjoy freedom here, including the freedom to examine the nuclear predicament in a creative and unfettered way. But of what avail will our freedom have been to us and to the world if by making use of it we arrive only at fatalism? Perhaps it will be concluded in defense of our generation as a whole that it was *necessary* to build the doomsday machine, so that, like a child that makes a mask to frighten itself with, we could make the nuclear peril real to ourselves—real enough so that we would finally do something about it. If that is so, we could regard the nuclear-arms race of the last several decades as a gigantic educational device—a sort of classroom aid designed to teach us all about nuclear weapons and the doom they portend. (Such a role would be consistent with the "psychological" role which we now assign to the weapons in strategic doctrine.) The result offered by this perilous exercise, at any rate, is the advantage that we have over people who faced the question in 1945. But if we fail to avail ourselves of the advantage—if we fail to learn the lesson that our indirect experience offers—then there will be little to be said in our favor, and perhaps no one to say it.

Before we examine in greater detail how an abolition agreement might work, a cautionary word seems in order concerning hypothetical constructions of future events—or "scenarios," as they are called—and, in particular, scenarios involving deterrence. We want to arrive at a judgment about the general workability of an abolition agreement under which an ability to rebuild nuclear weapons would serve as a deterrent. The key word is "judgment." It is emphatically not "prediction." Judgment never claims certainty; it never pretends to *know* what the future holds. It is not a science, and in a world dominated by the relative certainties of science and the pseudocertainties of pseudoscience its admittedly fallible claims often fail to command respect. Judgment does not rely on reason alone; it also summons into play intuition, emotion, experience, temperament—in a sense, our whole being. But in the nuclear field judgment has a competitor—strategic "theory," which tries, like science, to proceed by reasoning. Strategic theory, however, lacks an element that is crucial to science: empirical verification. There is always the danger with theory that it will come to supplant reality in the minds of the theorists; and in nuclear-strategic theorizing the danger is especially acute, because, fortunately, mankind has had no direct experience of "nuclear war"—of two-sided nuclear combat—against which to measure its hypotheses. Strategic theory is in that respect like a physics without the benefit of experimentation, or a social science without the benefit of a society to observe. Never, perhaps, has pure deduction, uncorrected by empirical knowledge, been given freer rein or assigned a more important role in the regulation of human affairs.

When experience is replaced by theory, the possibility always exists that the theory's assumptions will be generally accepted as conclusions. One particularly harmful assumption of this kind in the theory of deterrence is that only the balance of terror counts in the decision-making of statesmen, so that if your adversary gets the slightest opening to do his worst to you he will do it. The effect of making this assumption is to introduce into policy an extreme reductionism, in which moral and psychological, and even diplomatic and political, influences on governmental conduct are ruled out of consideration. And since deterrence is not merely a theory but a policy there is a further danger that this reductionist assumption can take on the quality of a self-fulfilling prophecy. Two nations, starting by assuming unmitigated enmity between them, and proceeding on both sides to build their military forces accordingly, can soon find that the unmitigated enmity has become real. It has become a fact that each side menaces the other with annihilation, and this fact has emotional and psychological consequences of its own, independent of any prior, underlying enmity. At this point, the assumption, which may at the beginning have masked a more complex and subtly shaded reality, has become "true." The British historian E. P. Thompson has pointed out, in his recent book *Beyond the Cold War*, "By conditioning military and political élites, on both sides, to act in accord with the first premises of adversary posture—to seek ceaselessly for advantage and to expect annihilating attack upon the first sign of weakness—[strategic doctrine] could tempt one side (if a manifest advantage should arise) to behave as theory prescribes, and to seize the opportunity for a preemptive strike. And what would the war, then, have been *about*? It would have been about fulfilling a theorem in deterrence theory." It's a striking historical fact, and one that should make us reflect, that the severest crisis of the nuclear age, the Cuban missile crisis, was *about* the weapons themselves.

In truth, there is much evidence that contradicts the pessimistic chief assumption of deterrence. Three historical episodes, among many that could be mentioned, can serve as illustration. The first is the behavior of the United States between 1945 and 1949, when it possessed a monopoly of nuclear weapons. The United States not only did not immediately annihilate the Soviet Union but did not even seek any drastic change in Soviet policy—by, for example, using nuclear blackmail to force the Soviet Union out of Eastern Europe. The second episode is the behavior of the Soviet Union between roughly the mid-1950s and the present, during which time it has had complete nuclear superiority over China and has also been in a state of hostility toward China at least as intense as its hostility toward the United States. According to purely theoretical considerations, the Soviet Union has had every reason to launch a preemptive strike against China, for in all likelihood it could destroy China's nuclear forces entirely. Yet it has not launched a preemptive strike. This restraint is all the more telling because it involves a totalitarian country, which is relatively immune to public opinion. The third episode is the behavior of Britain in its recent successful war to regain the Falkland Islands from Argentina. Argentina, which is not a nuclear power (although it is now able to become one), seized territory that was claimed by a nuclear-armed Britain. According to present theory, Britain should at that point have used its absolute nuclear superiority to force Argentine withdrawal. Britain could, for example, have begun with threats; then backed these up by stationing a nuclear-armed submarine with range of Argentina; then set off a demonstration nuclear explosion, perhaps over the sea, or over an unpopulated part of Argentina; then destroyed an Argentine military base with a "small" (Hiroshima-sized) bomb; then destroyed a small city or two; and, finally, blown Argentina off the map (a feat well within the capacity of Britain's nuclear forces, comparatively small though they are). But, as far as I'm aware, the British government did not breathe the merest suggestion that any of these things were remotely possible. What it did do was launch and win a conventional war, at a high cost in lives and in money. It is interesting to speculate on what Britain might have done if it had faced conventional defeat, but the complete lack of any mention of nuclear arms by government spokesmen, during the war or afterward, allows us to suppose that it would have suffered the defeat rather than resort to nuclear weapons. What was equally striking was the failure of outside observers of the war—columnists, diplomats of other countries, and the like—to mention Britain's nuclear arsenal. Somehow, its complete irrelevance to the situation was intuitively assumed by everybody.

These lessons of experience are of great value to the world—especially since they are hopeful. They prove to us, as we try to shape a safer future, that we have more—much, much more—to work with than terror. In our world, there is also courage, trust, prudence, imagination, decency. There is even love. Can it be "realistic" to exclude these proved good qualities of our species from our calculations? To do so would be to libel mankind and cripple our efforts. Indeed, the whole abolition agreement suggested here can be seen as a mere holding operation, giving us time in which these good qualities can be brought to bear on the vast political work that alone can lead to a true and fully satisfactory resolution of the nuclear predicament.

The theorists correctly justify their resort to pure theory on the ground that no experience of a nuclear holocaust is available; but this justification has been stretched too far, for while post-Nagasaki history does not show what starts nuclear hostilities it shows many examples of what does *not* start them. We should become careful students of negative history, inasmuch as the chief aim of our political efforts in the nuclear age must be to see to it that something does *not* happen—that we do *not* blow ourselves up. High-school students are required to study the "three causes," or the "four causes," of the First World War, or the Second World War, or whatever. We must study the causes of the lack of war—the causes of peace. Leaving the study of "nuclear war" to the theorists, we as historians can study its prevention. One of the first things our study shows us is that, while in theory even slight imbalances in nuclear forces lead to instability and war, in actuality they have not done so. Another thing it shows is that with a war in progress a power possessing a monopoly of nuclear weapons may choose not to use them, or even to remind the world that it possesses them.

The statesmen of the nuclear age seem to act with a sobriety not credited to them by our theorists. Some of the assumptions of deterrence theory can never be tested in action (not if we hope to survive), but others can be and have been. Among them is the assumption that nuclear powers will seek out and exploit any nuclear imbalance to obtain political or military advantage. This assumption has now been put to the test of experience many times, and has proved each time to be false. Why did the United States not preemptively attack the Soviet Union in the 1940s? Why has the Soviet Union not preemptively attacked China? Why did Britain choose to expend the lives of its soldiers in the Falkland Islands rather than even rattle its nuclear sword at Argentina? We can only guess at answers. Perhaps in the back of the minds of the leaders of these nations was some notion that what you do to others will one day be done to you. Perhaps they felt that even to threaten a nuclear attack would shame them before the world and history. Perhaps they feared that a nuclear attack of any sort would engulf the world in a chaos in which their own nations would suffer. Or perhaps their consciences stayed their hands.

It would be self-defeating folly to deny the common sense of the central axiom of deterrence—that the fear of nuclear retaliation provides nations with an overwhelming incentive not to launch nuclear attacks—but it would also be folly if, granting that, we concluded that the fear of retaliation was the only sentiment at work in holding the world back from nuclear destruction. So it is not meaningless, after showing that no country could expect to profit by violating an abolition agreement, to point out that even if some statesmen mistakenly concluded that his country could profit from aggression he might be restrained for any number of reasons, including the sense of shame and repugnance that almost every human being feels at the thought of murdering millions, and possibly billions, of innocent people in cold blood.

It is in the spirit of seeking to reach a broad judgment, not of trying to produce a whole new crop of scenarios, that I want to address the question of whether or not an abolition agreement would be workable. In the years ahead, a profusion of plans and ideas defining not just steps but whole stairways to nuclear disarmament will, in all likelihood, be put forward as people seek instruments for their newfound will to save the species. At the same time, people will be seeking to understand more profoundly what it means to live in a world in which we have the power to exterminate ourselves. And out of a deepening understanding will come still further thoughts about what we should be doing. For no single plan can guide us. And no single person can possess the wisdom to chart our course. It is in the very nature of things that the effort will be collective. The world is not to be approached, blueprint in hand, as if it were so much raw material waiting to be fashioned to someone's design. We—the people of the earth, each of us possessing an independent will—are that material, and it will be only out of the combined resolve of all of us that, probably at unexpected times and in unexpected ways, our will, the will of the world, will make itself known and felt. If the remarks in these pages are not predictions, neither are they would-be blueprints for the future. Rather, they, and the whole proposal for abolition described here, are an attempt to make a contribution to the broader discussion out of which, we must hope, will come the actual steps that lead us away from the abyss.

As the examples of nuclear restraint I have cited demonstrate, there are more motives acting in favor of military restraint in the nuclear age than a simple fear of nuclear retaliation. Strict deterrence theory recognizes only this fear, and disregards all other factors, and it is in that respect like an insurance policy—it deals with the worst case. It offers assurance that even if an aggressor were to disregard all other constraints and try his worst he could not hope for victory. It does not tell us that our adversary *will* try to burn our house down, or even that he necessarily wants to, but only that if this thought ever crosses his mind, and he is rational, he will have cause to dismiss it. Therefore, to whatever extent we fear that the adversary will do his worst, including his nuclear worst, and to whatever extent we are willing in return to do our worst, including our nuclear worst, the assurances offered by credible deterrence are important. To some people, they are all-important. But to someone who, like me, feels that he cannot find a justification for even threatening to use, to say nothing of using, nuclear weapons, in support of either armed or weaponless deterrence, any proposal that relies on a threat to use them, including the proposal for weaponless deterrence, raises an ethical question. I oppose any use of nuclear weapons, whether in a first strike or in a second strike or in any strike at all. But, as I have said, I believe that in dealing with the nuclear predicament we must support interim measures—measures such as the establishment of a Soviet-American control center for the exchange of information in a crisis; SALT or START agreements; a policy of no first use of nuclear weapons; the freeze; reductions in the nuclear arsenals; or the abolition of nuclear arms coupled with weaponless deterrence—that will help steer mankind away from its extinction, even though in the meantime we go on depending on morally obnoxious means. Today, mankind is like a person who lies bleeding to death on the street after an accident. Eventually, this person will require major surgery. But right now he needs to be rushed to the hospital in an ambulance, and given first aid on the way. It is pointless to say at this moment, "This person doesn't need an ambulance, he needs major surgery." The passage from our nuclear-armed world to a nuclear-weaponless world would be that ambulance ride. Once the life of mankind is out of immediate danger, we will have the time—we will have won it for ourselves—to address the radical and sweeping measures of global political renovation which alone can fully deliver us from the evil.

As we consider whether deterrence could remain in force under an abolition agreement, the work of present-day theorists of deterrence is helpful, because under the agreement the requirements of deterrence would be exactly what they are today. Deterrence would require stability, which would mean that under the system every statesman in his right mind would see that the almost certain result if he launched aggression would be the pointless destruction of all concerned, including, most definitely, his own country; that is, it would require that the hope of military victory vanish from his mind. It would require credibility, which would mean that the ability to visit devastation on an aggressor would have to be secure. It would therefore require a retaliatory nuclear capacity that would survive any first strike the adversary could mount. In connection with these requirements, the most important question to ask about a nuclear-weapon-free world is whether it could be arranged in such a way that no nation, by sudden or surreptitious rearmament, or by military action, could defeat an adversary or blackmail it into submission. (Obviously, the ability to defeat and the ability to blackmail are linked, since no country is going to allow itself to be blackmailed unless the prospect of defeat is virtually certain.) This question is far more complicated than is commonly acknowledged. Usually, it is disposed of in a few sentences that are prefatory to the author's getting down to his real interest, which, typically, is either to discuss the mechanics of armed deterrence or to set forth the provisions for world government. (The near-total lack of interest of each of these schools in the details of the other's thinking is remarkable.)

If the abolition of nuclear weapons were the same as their uninvention, a sudden violation of the agreement (by a nation that had somehow invented them again) would really constitute an insuperable advantage. The violator would then be in the position that the United States was in vis-à-vis Japan in July of 1945. But since abolition is not uninvention, and the intended victim of nuclear blackmail would be able to retaliate in several weeks' time, the imbalance between the violator and his victim would be much less than it at first appears to be. In 1946, as I have mentioned, Brodie pointed out that if the aggressor "must fear retaliation," then "the fact that it destroys its opponent's cities some hours or even days before its own are destroyed may avail it little." A delay of a month or so would make equally little difference. The unimportance of delays is one more of the differences between deterrence and defense. In defense, the shield has to be raised at the moment the sword falls, not a few days later. But the avenging sword of nuclear retaliation is not dulled by a wait. There is, indeed, something awful—something "deterring"—about the prospect of delayed retaliation. It's interesting to ponder whether the United States would have used the atomic bomb against Japan if Japan had been known to be a few weeks away from having one itself (as in fact it was not). Would the United States have been ready to risk New York and Chicago for Hiroshima and Nagasaki? I doubt it. The point in the present context is that the imbalance between a country that has invented the bomb and one that

hasn't is categorically greater than the imbalance that exists
between two nations that have both developed the bomb but
one of which has dismantled its arsenal.

As deterrence theory teaches us, to have a really decisive
advantage in a first strike the violator would have to possess
forces sufficient to erase the victim's capacity of retaliation. To
be really worth anything, therefore, a first strike delivered out of
secrecy under an abolition agreement would have to be utterly
devastating to the victim's nuclear capacity and be followed up
by the immediate and total occupation of the victim's country
with conventional forces, in order to prevent its nuclear rearmament. It is perhaps imaginable that if the defenses of the capacity
for retaliation were left to chance a determined aggressor could,
with the use of concealed arsenals only, so thoroughly devastate
and then so swiftly occupy its victim that the victim could not
retaliate. However, the defenses of the retaliatory capacity would
not be left to chance. Rather, under the abolition agreement
not only would the readiness to rebuild nuclear weapons be in
place but so would the anti-nuclear defenses and the defensively
arrayed conventional forces. The violator's aggression would
fail, because the abolition agreement would have been *designed*
for it to fail. Under this agreement, whatever is necessary to
defeat such aggression would be built in, probably redundantly,
for the sake of everyone's peace of mind.

The question of the state of readiness for nuclear rearmament
is complex. It would have to meet two basic requirements. First,
it would have to permit a lead time long enough to be of real
benefit to the world. (Yet any increase would be beneficial. For
example, if the nuclear powers today did nothing more than
remove the nuclear warheads from their missiles and store them
nearby, so that it would take, say, six hours to put them in again,
the gain would be great. It would increase the lead time by
several thousand per cent.) Second, it would have to provide a
smooth and assured path back to nuclear armament, in order to
fulfill the need, as it is defined by deterrence theory, for the retaliatory force to be invulnerable. In all likelihood, the best way
of providing such a path while at the same time lengthening the
lead time would be to establish controls on fissionable materials. A more radical measure would be to ban nuclear reactors in
general (probably with certain narrowly defined exceptions), or

else to place them—as the Baruch Plan, proposed by the United States to the United Nations in 1946, did—under the control of an international body. Banning reactors would carry a higher economic cost, but it would provide a longer lead time, and it might be more easily verifiable, since nuclear reactors and the industry that builds and maintains them are a great deal more difficult to hide than bombs or delivery vehicles. Another set of provisions could cover delivery vehicles. Since any vehicle, whether it is a missile or the suitcase carried by a pedestrian, can be a delivery vehicle for nuclear weapons, removing delivery vehicles for nuclear weapons from the world forever is impossible, just as removing forever the ability to build the weapons themselves is impossible. The important, attainable goal would be to restrict national capacities for deploying delivery vehicles, much as nuclear-arms-control agreements attempt to do today.

Clearly, the complexity of the nuclear balance at the level of zero weapons would be great—though not, perhaps, as great as the complexity is today, with thousands of weapons and their varied delivery systems in existence. The decisions to be made would have to deal not only with the state of readiness to rearm but also with the extent of the technical means permitted, its deployment, and so on. For example, it would be an advantage to the agreement as a whole if the technical means were decentralized to begin with and, in addition, were further dispersible in the event of the agreement's breakdown. (In the agreement, a nation's right to rearm if an adversary had done so would, of course, be recognized.) Dispersibility, in particular, would be invaluable. It could suffice in itself to defeat nuclear blackmail by a violator of the agreement. Blackmail requires that a threat be openly made and that time be allowed for compliance with its demands. But that time could be used to disperse the technical means from their known and inspected places to secret places. Once dispersal had occurred, it would be impossible for the small, secretly assembled nuclear force of the violator to threaten the retaliatory capacity of the victim. The question of what to do if the abolition agreement should be violated would be analogous to the question today of what to do "if deterrence fails." But whereas today we cannot think of one single thing that it would make sense to do if deterrence fails, there would be many sensible things to do if the abolition agreement broke down, including beginning to rearm. To be sure, if the violations continued to grow, and the world began to return to full armament, the actions in response would start to make less and less sense. Yet, even as they continued, the world would have time—as it would not today "if deterrence fails"—to see where it was heading, to reflect, and to pull back.

The principal mission of the anti-nuclear defensive forces set forth in the agreement would be not to protect their nations—a task that in the long run they could perform no better than they can today—but to protect the retaliatory capacity as it was being mobilized for action. They would thus have the limited role of a hedge against cheating. For the defensive superiority that was arranged for in the abolition agreement would last only as long as that agreement did—or, rather, as long afterward as the defensive retained the upper hand. And this would not be indefinitely. It would be only long enough for the attacked nation to assemble its retaliatory force, at which point the balance of terror as we know it today would be restored. But, of course, just as today we keep our retaliatory force at the ready in the hope that its very existence will prevent the attack that would cause us to use it, so in a world of zero nuclear weapons we would preserve our well-defended readiness to rearm in the hope that it would prevent the rearmament that would lead us to rearm. Thus, although we would be relying provisionally on defense we would still be living in a deterred world. Defense would provide protection while the deterrent forces were assembled, but then deterrence would take over. The underlying facts of life in a nuclear-weapon-free world would be just what they are today—that defense is impossible and deterrence inescapable. And under deterrence, armed or unarmed, our hope is that deterrence itself would gradually become obsolete while the conditions for a real, full peace were being established. Our chief protection, then, which would operate before either defenses or deterrence was called into play, would be whatever political will we had mustered to institute, and then to uphold, the abolition agreement.

None of this is to say that defense of the population should be ruled out. The question of whether or not to deploy civil defense, as a further hedge against cheating, is debatable. It could be argued (as it is today by the advocates of deterrence) that civil defense, if it could be made to work (as it can't today, in the face of our giant nuclear arsenals), would be destabilizing, because it would erode the "effectiveness" of the foe's retaliatory capacity. With an abolition agreement in force, however, the world would not be *counting* on cheating; it would be trying to discourage it, and in that effort protection of the population would be helpful, because it would reduce the effectiveness of blackmail. In general, defensive measures would constitute a sort of obstacle that would-be aggressors would know that they had to overcome before their aggression began to pay off. But since they would also know that before that moment came their intended victims would have armed themselves with nuclear weapons, in preparation for retaliation, the moment would actually never come, and they would abandon their aggressive plans.

A provision for a balance in conventional forces would be essential to the agreement as a whole, because it would prevent the nuclear-arms race from being replaced by a conventional-arms race. "Conventional" arms today are in fact anything but that. Though they are overshadowed by nuclear weapons, they have increased in destructive power to a point at which the doctrine of mutual assured destruction might be maintained by them alone—especially when biological and chemical weapons are taken into account. The principal strategic mission of these limited and balanced conventional forces would be to do their part in deterring a disarming first strike by a violator of the agreement. Since to be successful in preventing nuclear rearmament and retaliation such a strike would require full occupation of the attacked country, the conventional forces would be deployed to prevent invasion. But this would be so in two senses: they would be armed in such a way that they *could* repel an invasion by another country, yet they would be armed in such a way that they *could not* themselves invade another country. These armies would, for example, be loaded down with anti-tank weapons but low on tanks; well equipped with anti-aircraft weapons but ill equipped with aircraft. The present Swiss Army, which bristles with weapons to repel invaders but itself never invades anybody, might serve as a model. Equipping those armies would admittedly be a novel military task but not

an impossible one, especially when we remember that all the
military planners would be on the same side: the side of defense.
Their aim would be to equip every army with steel shields and
rubber swords. It is only a little bit facetious to suggest that
the two sides might establish a joint "defense department"
(properly named, for once), devoted to the development of
defensive weaponry. A new "arms race" would begin, between
offensive and defensive arms, but, fortunately, all the nations of
the world would be working together to support the defense.

The preservation on both sides of an ability to rebuild
nuclear weapons, arrangements for inspection on whatever
level was necessary to provide a safeguard against cheating,
and the presence of limited and balanced conventional forces
defensively arrayed would, it seems to me, be more than adequate to provide for the requirements of deterrence in a world
without nuclear weapons. Each of these elements would exist
in a balance with the others. For example, an estimate would
be needed of how much cheating might be possible under a
particular level of inspection. When the estimate was given, the
deployment of the capacity for rearming would be adjusted
to meet, or more than meet, that potential threat. As more
inspection was made possible, the less ready the capacity for
rearming would have to be, and the less extensive the defenses
would have to be (although it seems that there would be little
to be lost in making defenses redundant). Every advance in
inspection, then, would permit a lengthening of the world's nuclear fuse, and an increase in the world's safety. For example—to
pick arbitrary figures—if the estimated amount of conceivable
cheating associated with a particular level of inspection was a
hundred bombs on a hundred commercial airliners, then the
level of readiness could be quite low and the needed defenses
quite thin. If, however, the estimated amount of conceivable
cheating was two hundred bombs on two hundred cruise
missiles, then the readiness would have to be higher and the
defenses stronger. Conversely, the better the defenses were, the
less strict the inspection would have to be. And, of course, the
precise technical form of the agreed-upon readiness to rearm
would have a bearing on how effective the defense of it could
be. The important point in the present context is that the levels
of inspection, of readiness, and of defense are interdependent

and adjustable, with considerable room for margins of safety to be built in when the abolition agreement is designed.

The difficulties facing a violator of an abolition agreement only multiply when one turns from purely technical considerations to strategic ones. Let us suppose that a violator of the agreement has assembled a clandestine nuclear arsenal. But an arsenal is not in itself a policy. How to gain a military or political advantage from it remains to be figured out. To begin with, the cheater has to take into account the possibility that its intended victim has cheated as well. The possibility of cheating cuts two ways: it permits violation of the agreement, but it also sows suspicion in the mind of the would-be cheater that the other side may have cheated, too. Those who cheat know from their own action that cheating is possible, and are likely to suppose that others have done it also. If that has happened, the cheater, when he pulls back the curtain of secrecy, reveals the hidden arsenal, and starts making demands, will find himself facing an opposing arsenal right away, and the exercise will be fruitless. In short, uncertainty about cheating can have a deterrent as well as a destabilizing effect. (Uncertainty, it seems, is in all circumstances the most steadfast ally of deterrence.)

A cheater might have either of two possible aims: to hedge against suspected cheating on the other side or to engage in aggression. If the aim was to secure a hedge, then the cheating, while dangerous and undesirable, would remain clandestine and without disastrous consequences. (This would be so even if it had occurred on both sides, because then, although nobody would know it, a nuclear balance would have been created, at very low levels of armament.) There is reason to believe, however, that nations would not find it in their interest to cheat even as a hedge. The protective benefit of the hedge would be offset by the extremely serious cost of being caught in a violation. When one considers that in order to act as a hedge a violation would have to continue indefinitely, and therefore discovery would be likely sooner or later, it is hard to imagine that a nation would find it worthwhile—especially if it knew that in the event of a violation by another nation its legitimate capacity to rearm was secure. If, on the other hand, the aim was aggression, then the violator would face all the defensive and retaliatory penalties that are built into the agreement to deter aggression. And yet, even without considering these, the government leader weighing the costs of cheating would have to reflect that his victim, or one of his victim's allies, might have cheated, and that in that case his plans would be aborted right there. In other words, the violator, after revealing himself to the world as an international outlaw of the most hateful and terrifying kind, might be thwarted immediately, without having a chance even to attempt some mischief in a brief moment of nuclear superiority.

In the event that a government overlooked all these obstacles and decided that it was ready to violate the agreement anyway, it would still need a strategy. It would have to have both an attainable political goal in mind and a plan for reaching it. Neither is easy to conceive of. Just as is true in our present world, the strategy for a first strike, whether only threatened or actually carried out, would have to be, in the jargon terms, either "counterforce" or "countervalue"; that is, the bombs would have to menace or destroy either the foe's military forces, in the hope of achieving a crippling first strike, or the foe's cities and population, in the hope of terrorizing him into submission. A successful counterforce strike would be impossible for all the reasons just mentioned; the entire abolition agreement would have been framed to preclude it. The idea, for example, that the Soviet Union, using a clandestine nuclear force, could destroy the ability of the United States to make nuclear weapons and then, in the space of a few weeks, conquer Europe, cross the Atlantic, and occupy the United States to prevent nuclear rearmament is patent fantasy. And if one adds that the first strike with the clandestine arsenal would be opposed by large-scale defenses, including swift dispersal of the nuclear-weapon-making capacity, and that the conventional forces of the Soviet Union had, under the agreement, been reduced from their present size and deprived of many of their offensive arms, then the idea of such an attack positively enters the realm of the surreal. That would leave the possibility of blackmail against cities or actual attacks on them—a possibility that is often pointed to as the decisive advantage of violating an abolition agreement. Such a threat or attack, however, would be even easier than the counterforce one to reply to. In the first place, the elaborate and technically advanced defenses of the victim might be adequate to actually defend in considerable measure against a threat made with the small, probably technically backward offensive forces of the aggressor. But even if the defenses were inadequate the victim's ability to retaliate with nuclear arms in a few weeks' time would erase the aggressor's advantage. The response of the threatened country would be exactly what it is today: it would threaten nuclear attack in return. Deterrence would be fully in force.

It is not, however, until one turns from the methods of a violator to his possible political goals that the ground for believing in the stability of a nuclear-weapon-free world stands fully revealed. The traditional nightmare of global politics is that some single nation or bloc will grow so strong that it will upset the balance of power and then move to dominate all other nations. The Romans once did it. In more recent times, Napoleon and Hitler came close. This larger possibility, standing in the background of smaller crises, can give even minor aggression, when it is launched by a great power, a momentous importance. It also provides the temptation that lures a statesman with grandiose longings onto the path of conquest. When nations are faced with such aggression, the question that their leaders always have to ask themselves is where it will be stopped if not in the instance at hand. This is the famed "lesson of Munich," learned from the experience of France and England in 1938, when, at a meeting with Hitler in Munich, they agreed, essentially, that, rather than go to war with him, they would let him take over Czechoslovakia—only to find that they had to go to war with him anyway a short while later. It is the lesson, too, that is embodied in the so-called domino theory, of more recent times, which holds that aggression must be prevented at the earliest possible moment or it will run out of control and engulf everything. The wedding of this lesson to the doctrine of deterrence is what has led to the disproportion of means and ends in our current military strategy—forcing us to defend, say, the Persian Gulf by, in effect, risking the end of the world. The reason our statesmen are willing to risk the end of the world to protect the Persian Gulf is not that the Persian Gulf is so important (its oil *is* very important, of course, but not worth the extinction of mankind); it is that they are persuaded that if aggression is permitted there—or almost anywhere—it cannot be stopped later. The leader we fear—the one we build nuclear arsenals to deter—is not the one who wants to grab a disputed piece of territory from his neighbor but the one whose dreams are filled with triumphal visits to subjugated foreign capitals. (Hitler's early-morning visit to Paris in 1940, captured on film by his propagandists, comes to mind.) Our nation's leaders believe that Soviet leaders are determined to dominate the world and will actually do it if they are not stopped in an early stage. The Soviet leaders have reciprocal fears. It may be that in fact neither nation has these unlimited ambitions, but since each believes that the other has them both base their foreign policies on this conviction.

A precise way of posing the question of the stability of a nuclear-weapon-free world is to ask how such a would-be world conqueror might fare in it. I have argued that even the very first step, in which the aspiring Caesar of our time, having nursed his dream of world conquest behind a veil of feigned peacefulness, whipped back the curtain of secrecy, displayed his arsenal to the world, and demanded some political prize, on pain of nuclear devastation if it was denied, would meet with failure—and not for just one reason but for many, redundant reasons—and that, furthermore, he would know this before he started, and would not start. But what is even surer is that if this first act of aggression somehow occurred and was successful it could have no sequel. For before it had been completed it would have set in motion all over the world the countermeasures that would prevent any repetition: not only the victimized nation but every other nuclear-capable nation in the world could rearm with nuclear weapons to confront the violator. And our budding Caesar would know all this, too: if he couldn't figure it out for himself, people would tell him. To an extent perhaps not yet fully appreciated, the development of nuclear arms has provided a surefire antidote to the world's ancient nightmare of military conquest by a single power. Such grandiose ambitions cannot be realized in our world, nor could they be in the world of an abolition agreement. The reason is not that nations are less ambitious or less ruthless than they were in the past; it is that the world has changed. And in this changed world it is not the physical existence of nuclear arsenals but the knowledge of how to build them that is fundamental.

It could be said that this knowledge, which is destined to spread over the whole globe, is like a quicksand in which the feet of the armies of the great powers are sunk. And the reason is deterrence, in the broadest sense of the word: no one wants to embark on an obviously self-defeating enterprise. In our strategic thinking, we seem to have become mesmerized by numbers, speaking easily of a thousand, ten thousand, fifty thousand nuclear weapons. But in reality just ten of them—which can carry the explosive force of *ten thousand* Hiroshimas—provide a level of destructive power outside all historical experience. What government leader in his right mind, knowing that these weapons are available to his enemies, can dream of the military conquest of the world? At best, the great powers can fight desultory, drawn-out, small wars—often unsuccessful—against non-nuclear-armed local peoples (the North Vietnamese, the Afghans). Never again can they sweep victoriously from nation to nation, as the armies of the great conquerors of the past did. They know what likely fate awaits them if they try: some justly infuriated enemy will let off the E in the m of a few kilograms of plutonium, multiplied by c^2, and their armies will go up in a puff of vapor. You can't conquer the world with vapor armies. Regrettably, none of this means that nuclear weapons will not be used; it means only that they are unlikely to be used in the service of premeditated schemes of conquest or aggression. Their use, if it occurs, is likely to come by accident, or in the confusion and misunderstanding of a crisis, in which neither side is ready to back down. In a way, it is the very existence of the arsenals, rather than any intention to use them, that makes their use possible. As long as they exist, they can be used. And the moment we abolished them the chances of their use, although still present, would become comfortingly small.

Paradoxically, the anachronism of campaigns of world conquest in the nuclear age might emerge into view more clearly in a nuclear-weapon-free world than it does in our nuclear-armed world. Precisely because our present arsenals are so immense and no government leader can be assured that if he sets off one nuclear bomb they will not all go off, a shadow of doubt hangs over the threat of their use as a means of preventing aggression, and it seems conceivable (though very far from likely, once we think about it) that some power might get away with a serious act of aggression. In a nuclear-weapon-free world, however, with no preposterously overstocked arsenals ready to go off the moment a single bomb was used, the threatened nuclear retaliation for aggression would be less irrational and more "credible." To put it in terms of present strategy, "flexible response" would come into its own, for the self-paralysis that results from our natural reluctance to "defend" ourselves by taking steps that might start an unstoppable slide to the end of the world would no longer occur. Because in a nuclear-weapon-free world the path of aggression and rearmament would be broken into steps, we could see with greater clarity than we can today that every escalation of aggression—every crossing of a new national border—could be met with fully commensurate retaliation.

A further bar to world conquest deserves mention, though it is not nuclear in origin. Through our century, local people, inspired by an aroused national consciousness and by patriotic feeling, have put up increasingly strong, and increasingly successful, resistance to foreign domination. Whatever other political principles people may subscribe to, they appear to be mightily determined to take charge of their countries. In our world, the "dominoes" have taken on a life of their own and are in rebellion against the players. The classical empires of the West have been effectively dissolved by this force, and so has the somewhat later Soviet aim of a Communist world revolution under Soviet leadership—today it is virtually a dead letter. Whatever atrocities people may suffer, it seems, they want to suffer at the hands of their own monsters and madmen. More and more, we live in a world in which local people rule in their own places. The single great exception to this local takeover from great powers is in Eastern Europe, where the continued Soviet domination is ultimately maintained by occupying armies. But even there local resistance—especially in Poland—though it is not yet intense enough to expel the Soviets, makes one wonder how long this anachronistic form of political control can last. Today, even the greatest powers must think many times before embarking on a Vietnam or an Afghanistan. For this reason alone, quite apart from the influence of nuclear weapons, world domination by a single power has now become unthinkable. Thus, the ambitions of the great powers are doubly checked: while their nuclear forces are immobilized in the balance of nuclear terror, their conventional armies sink in the swamps of local resistance.

The abolition agreement might be accompanied by collective-security agreements, designed to make the fate of aggressors still clearer to any statesmen who were having trouble perceiving the realities of the world they lived in. Weaponless deterrence would not require collective-security agreements in order to work, but it would lend itself naturally to them and would be strengthened by them. The abolition of nuclear arms would be a militarily equalizing measure. With a number of the technically competent nations standing at the same starting line (the agreed-upon readiness) in any race to rearm, their power would be more nearly equal—at least, in the short run—than it is today. This relative equality would give added importance to alliances. There would be safety in numbers, for even if the potential violator should think that he could escape retaliation by his immediate victim he would know that he could not escape it from a dozen or so nations to which the victim was allied in a collective-security agreement. In our nuclear-armed world, proliferation—of capacity, not of weapons—could be stabilizing. It would multiply the reasons for holding back from aggression. (It's interesting that at least one nation that is now nuclear-capable—India—has forgone actual construction of a nuclear arsenal. Its leaders may count it sufficient that their adversaries know that they *can* build the weapons if they want to.) Of all the developments occurring today, proliferation of nuclear weapons may well be the most dangerous. It raises the possibility that sooner or later a madman may have everyone's fate in his hands. An abolition agreement would not fully insure against this terrifying prospect, but it would give us incomparably more security against it than we have now.

Everyone agrees that nations want to survive, and we can be sure that, given the opportunity, they will take steps to assure their survival. Today, however, there are few steps that any but the two most powerful nations can take to protect themselves from the worst fate of all—annihilation in a general holocaust.

All the others must simply wait and watch as their life or death is decided by a few men in Washington and Moscow. In a nuclear-weapon-free world, a field of action would open to them. In peacetime, they could work diplomatically and politically to strengthen the abolition agreement. A good way to begin would be with collective-security agreements. But even if nuclear aggression or nuclear blackmail should be attempted there would still be time to act. There would be an interval of some weeks between the original act of aggression and any nuclear response, and in that period pressures of all kinds— including the pressure of the threat of nuclear retaliation by any number of nations—could be exerted to resolve the crisis. These courses of action could be spelled out in advance, so that any would-be aggressor would be able to see clearly what was in store for him.

In judging a system of deterrence, one needs to concentrate on the train of thought that one believes would run through the mind of any national leader inclined toward aggression. In a nuclear-weapon-free world of the kind I have described, a would-be world conqueror contemplating the technical, strategic, and political consequences of aggression would see, I suggest, nothing but a vast field of insurmountable obstacles and, at the end of it—or even quite early—the same mutual assured destruction that we see today when we contemplate "nuclear war." The nuclear world is unconquerable. The peoples of the world refuse to be subjugated, and they have the means, including—in a world in which twentieth-century physics is an open book to all comers—the nuclear means, to prevent their subjugation. Where once a smooth plain stretched before the conqueror's eye, a would-be conqueror today looks out over a terrain that, like one of those glaciers high in the mountains which claim the lives of climbers, is crisscrossed with slippery crevasses, any one of which can prove fatal. Every step courts suicide. The tiny split atom yawns to swallow him up. One might just as well try to cross the desert in a sailing ship or cross the ocean in a tank as try to conquer the nuclear world with military force. And the abolition of nuclear arms would not change this outlook in any basic way. In the foreground of the nuclear-weapon-free world would be the victim's capacity for rearming, itself protected by powerful defensive forces. Beyond that would be the nuclear capacity of the victim's allies, and, beyond that, the nuclear and other retaliatory capacities of the whole world, enraged that it had been pushed back toward its doom by the violator, and possessing both the will and the means to resist further aggression. And, finally, there would be the ferocious local resistance of the peoples of the earth to subjugation: fifty, a hundred, two hundred Vietnams. The potential violator would see that even his first step was extremely unlikely to succeed, the second step impossible, the third pure fantasy. And, seeing all that, he would not take the first step. He would be deterred.

We fear cheating under an abolition agreement because we fear aggression; we fear aggression primarily because we fear that it will upset the balance of power; and we fear an upset of the balance of power because we fear that some single nation or bloc will gain irresistible military superiority and, with it, domination of the world. But in the nuclear world, whether armed or unarmed, these things cannot happen—not because cheating is impossible but because the entire military and political organization of the world in which cheating might have been the first step toward world domination has passed away. No balance of power can be upset, because there is no balance of power—only a balance of terror, which is something different. In a balance of power, each side faces the *power* of the other—power to achieve victory in war, to conquer and occupy other countries or the world—but in the balance of terror all *power* has evaporated, and the two sides are impotent in the face of the same oblivion: not anyone's victory or domination but unlimited and universal defeat; not a foe having its way with the world but the end of the world. All human powers are overmatched by the universal power that was unleashed in the world when the atom was split, and that universal power is what, in the final analysis, checks the would-be world conqueror at every step, including the step in which his maniacal dream might crystallize in his brain. When it turned out that E equals mc^2, his sort was doomed. The dreams of world conquest are dead dreams. They belong to a world that has vanished. Its ways and practices—the marching and retreating armies, the contests for "control of the seas" or "control of the air," the long strings of victories and defeats, spanning the continents, and all the rest of the moves and countermoves, the noise and the fire, of those great global pitched battles by which in the pre-nuclear world the political fortunes of mankind were settled—have, like the lances, armor, and escutcheons of feudalism, sunk under the waves of time forever. We cannot get that world back. Yet its loss can be our gain, for we can profit from it as we turn to face the real peril that has been put before us: the featureless, timeless nothingness of our doom.

In political affairs, it's a great advantage to be able to start with what is in place and improve on it, rather than to have to start over. An agreement freezing the world's boundaries in place and abolishing nuclear arms while keeping deterrence in force by retaining the ability to rebuild them offers this advantage. It would be a logical, evolutionary outgrowth of present-day deterrence. Deterrence is built on the foundation of the world's horror at the idea of either suffering a nuclear holocaust or, for that matter, perpetrating one. The abolition agreement would build a stronger and more effective policy on that same foundation. It would be a more reliable, more rational, and (within regrettably defined limits) more humane way of profiting from our horror. Under it, the rationale that the only sensible role for nuclear weapons is to guarantee that those same weapons are never used would not, it is true, be fully carried through to its logical conclusion, but it would be buttressed and strengthened. The latent agreement among adversaries on which deterrence depends would be made explicit and *acted upon*. Their de facto acceptance of the status quo would be institutionalized. Nations would still, in the last analysis, rely on their own nuclear capacities to preserve their independence. But the grotesque disproportion between the causes and the results of "war"—the threat to end the world so as to prevent every threat to the status quo—would be greatly reduced (although not yet removed).

The precise steps by which abolition might be reached would be the product of negotiations, but the most important stage in the great powers' negotiations would consist of an initial formal affirmation and definition, in technical, military, and political terms, of the goal. Agreement on the goal would have to come first because it is impossible to decide on precise steps until one knows where one is heading. At present, strangely, our procedure is the reverse. We concentrate all our energy on the steps (SALT, START, the freeze, and so on), and simply leave unanswered the question of where all this is going. (At the moment, it seems to be going nowhere.) Is our aim the stability of existing arsenals? Is it President Reagan's defensive world, protected from nuclear attack by weapons in space and elsewhere? Is it "reductions"? "Deep reductions"? If so, how deep? Down to "minimum deterrence"? What then? Or do we—as a number of Presidents, including President Carter and President Reagan, have hinted—seek abolition? If we do, what is the world going to look like then, and what are we going to do if trouble starts? Up to now, these questions have somehow been seen as unfit for government to answer. In this matter—the most important matter of all—government has been content to grope along a path that lacks a clearly defined destination. Even the peace movement has been shy about advocating full nuclear disarmament—showing a reluctance as crippling to its cause as hesitation to advocate the abolition of slavery would have been to that of the anti-slavery movement. The answer one gives to the question of the goal determines the character of the steps one takes. And the lack of an answer—of a destination for arms control—means that the steps falter, grow uncertain, cross back over each other, and finally stop. With no consensus in place on where we are going, policy shifts from Administration to Administration; and even within each Administration there is a lack of clarity about what would be desirable. The general public, for its part, is left in total confusion, unable to bring its will to bear, or even to form its will, on questions of specific policy. One Administration concentrates on delivery systems, another on throw-weight and numbers of warheads. Two Presidents say that they seek abolition, and Harvard and the *New York Times* say that abolition is impossible. One President sees anti-nuclear defenses as injurious to stability, and the next sees them as the key to stability. One school of expert thought says that the stabilization of forces, even at something like present levels, should be the goal of arms control, and another school thinks that reductions should be the goal. The point here is not so much to argue that any of these views is right or wrong per se as to suggest that without agreement on a single, clear goal for arms control we have no standard by which to measure anyone's views.

A clear goal, once adopted, would serve as an organizing principle for both our steps and our ideas. If after study our government adopted abolition as its goal—not as a rhetorical flourish for the peroration of presidential speeches but as a practical, thought-out destination—many points currently under discussion would be clarified. The issue of anti-nuclear defenses is a case in point. As we have seen, such defenses are destabilizing *before* an abolition agreement (because they only spur increased offensive measures on the other side) but become stabilizing *after* an abolition agreement (as a hedge against cheating). Thus, until the great powers were well on their way to abolition we would rein in defenses, but once they were on their way we would encourage defenses. The issue of reductions would also be clarified. Reductions become unambiguously necessary. Because they would be the path leading to zero, they would lose the air of pointlessness that they necessarily have as long as it is believed that mutual assured destruction must be preserved, if only "minimally." (Reductions short of abolition, it should be said, might serve one invaluable purpose: they might—though when we consider the nuclear winter we can't be sure—bring the arsenals down to a level still adequate for mutual assured destruction but not sufficient to cause extinction.) The goal of stability, too, would gain a new context.

Once the goal had been studied, defined, and accepted, the steps, it seems to me, would not be hard to find. Without trying to go into detail, I shall mention a few principles by which they might be established. A basic principle governing the whole process would be that deterrence would remain in effect at every stage, including, of course, the final one—abolition itself. Most important, at every step, all the way down to zero, each side would retain a secure retaliatory capacity. The deterrence theory in use, however, would be "existential deterrence," rather than any of the more theoretically elaborate kinds. Instead of being guided by detailed scenarios of possible nuclear wars, we would rely on common sense and the lessons of history, which show that nations are even more reluctant to use nuclear weapons than deterrence theory suggests. Guided by this rough-and-ready version of deterrence, which, though

it is less intellectually dazzling than some of the others, corresponds better to our actual, fallible human predictive powers,
the negotiating partners would seek a balance at all stages of
the reductions but would not get unduly alarmed if imbalances
appeared in one area or another now and then.

As reductions continued, the capacity for retaliation would
consist less and less of the possession of weapons and more and
more of the capacity for rebuilding them, until, at the level of
zero, that capacity would be all. Indeed, the more closely we
look at the zero point the less of a watershed it seems to be. Examined in detail, it reveals a wide range of alternatives, in which
the key issue is no longer the number of weapons in existence
but the extent of the capacity and the level of readiness for
building more. (At even quite high levels of warheads—say, the
hundreds—the importance of capacity might eclipse the importance of stockpiles.) But there would also be the issue of control
of delivery vehicles—an issue that at the zero level might well
be even more important than the abolition of warheads. Since
the man with a suitcase is a delivery vehicle, attaining "zero
delivery systems" is in principle impossible. Instead, the task
would be to set specifications for those which were allowed
and those which were not. Defining the permissible states of
readiness for building the bombs and for building delivery
vehicles of various sorts would be the first task of negotiations.

One further strategic notion that would gain in depth and
meaning in the context of negotiations to establish weaponless
deterrence would be the principle of no first use. The value
of this concept lies not only in the contribution it makes
toward present stability but in its establishment of an almost
purely deterrent role for nuclear weapons. (I say "almost"
because of the unspoken reservation attached to no first use
which specifies that it ceases to apply as soon as one side faces
conventional defeat.) If two sides have declared a policy of no
first use, then each side possesses its nuclear arsenals only to
retaliate in the event that the other side uses them, and since
neither side intends ever to strike first neither has any reason
to keep its arsenals, and they can be abolished. All that remains
is for each side to convince the other that it really *is* abolishing
the weapons. When people are persuaded—as so many analysts have been since 1945—that a nuclear-weapon-free world

is, in the absence of world government, inherently the least stable of worlds, the opportunity opened up by the two sides' willingness to forswear aggression is lost. But if, as I have argued here, a nuclear-weapon-free world can be stable, with deterrence remaining in effect, then the opportunity can be seized. The no-first-use principle coupled with the principle of achieving weaponless deterrence could provide the foundation for complete nuclear disarmament.

When a person or a society or, as in this case, a whole planet is embarked on a self-destructive and ultimately suicidal course, the first order of business is a decision to *reverse course*. To reverse course is not in itself to arrive at the safe shore, which may still be far in the distance, but it is at least to glimpse that shore and to turn one's craft in its direction. A discussion of what the ultimate aims of the United States' disarmament policy should be, culminating in the actual adoption of a goal, could be the means by which the needed course reversal would take place. The arena in which the debate over the ultimate goals of disarmament takes place should be government, but not government alone. Ideally, it should encompass all of society, but since it is in fact only in the West that free discussion can occur, the debate should begin here. One step in the direction of such a deliberation might be, for example, the appointment of a presidential commission to restudy the whole issue, from the ground up. Another might be for Congress to hold joint hearings on the question—hearings that would be televised in full before the nation. The press, the universities, and the other independent voices in the society could join in. But it may not be necessary for anyone to take any self-conscious steps to start this discussion. When the time is right, it will be unstoppable. Indeed, it may have already begun.

Just as the steps in arms control need to be placed in the context of the abolition of nuclear arms, so abolition needs to be placed in the context of a full resolution of the nuclear predicament. Abolition would not give us a world from which nuclear weapons had been eradicated forever, which is to say that it would not return us to the pre-nuclear world. Nothing can do that. Even in the realm of the possible, however, abolition would be only a halfway house—an interim solution. We sometimes say that we live on the brink of nuclear destruction. But, with no more than a mechanical or human mistake or two between us and the end of the world, it would be more accurate to say that we are hanging by one arm from a branch that sticks out over the brink. Abolition would get us up onto the brink. It would get us onto solid ground, where we would have the time and the peace of mind to look at the lay of the land and plan our next steps. Or, to change the metaphor, it would be like reaching a base camp, from which we could reconnoitre to plan the ascent of the mountain itself. To us now, who are unable to restrain ourselves from heaping up more and more nuclear weapons until we hardly know where to deploy them, abolition looks like the peak of Mount Everest. But when we got there we would find that we had climbed only a foothill, and that the real Everest—the political challenge of finding peaceful means for handling all disputes in the international sphere—still rose up before us.

It is tempting to suppose that a nuclear-weapon-free world of stalemated sovereign states could be long-lasting, or even permanent. To resort to one more metaphor, nations in the state of deterrence are like trains on the tracks of a roundhouse, all of which converge upon a central point, like the spokes of a wheel. Let us imagine that reaching the central point would give the engineer of any one train, if he rushed forward with his train and seized it, the means to control all the other trains ("world domination"). To prevent this, the engineers resolve that if they see any engineer rushing his train toward the center they will all do the same, destroying the first train and themselves in a single huge collision. But now let us suppose that these tracks extend outward indefinitely, that the trains have all retreated miles into the countryside, and that, furthermore, the engineers have voluntarily entered into a solemn agreement not to come within a defined distance of the center. This, it seems to me, is a fair representation of weaponless deterrence. In recognition of the futility of the resort to force in the nuclear age, nations would have pulled far back from the abyss. The agreement would be their first line of defense against threats both to their national sovereignty and to human survival. They would bend their efforts to preserve it. Yet ultimately they would still rely on the nuclear threat. The engineers are deep in the quiet of the countryside, but if, against all expectation and all reason, one of their number starts rushing toward the central point they are able and ready to do likewise. If we suppose, however, that they manage to stay in their pulled-back state long enough—say, centuries—then we can entertain the hope that something like permanence has been achieved. Theoretically, the trains are ready to rush suicidally to the central point, but actually they have, more and more, been conducting relations along branch lines that they have been building up. The whole business of crashing into each other at the central point has gradually become fantastic and unreal—a nightmare from a barbaric and insane past. The converging tracks fall into disuse and become overgrown. Then one day, perhaps, this paraphernalia of mass destruction can be carted off to village greens, to take its place alongside the naval cannons of the past, and to be played on by small children.

But life is movement and change. No stalemate can be eternal. Differences must arise. They will have to be resolved, and a means of resolving them will have to be found—a means other than violence. And then we are faced again with the revolution in our political affairs which some called for in the mid-1940s but which never happened. At issue in this revolution would be not just the outcome of one dispute or another—not even the outcome of the East-West struggle in its entirety—but how all nations were to conduct their political relations with one another from then on. Some observers have suggested that, given the limits of what we can hope to accomplish in the near future, it is meaningless to define the predicament in such broad terms. But it seems to me that even while we recognize these limits it is an essential element of honesty for us to measure our accomplishments not against what we have decided it is possible for us to do at a particular moment but against the objective magnitude of the task that, without our willing it or wanting it, has actually been imposed on us by nuclear weapons. This is the first requirement of realism in the nuclear age, and, I believe, it is in a spirit of realism that we should acknowledge that the abolition of nuclear weapons would be only a preliminary to getting down to the more substantial political work that lies ahead. The size of the predicament is not ours to choose; only the resolution is.

The resolution of the nuclear predicament as a whole, then, would fall into two broad stages. In the first (discussed here), the world would, by agreement, institutionalize the broad global stalemate that we are already in, and abolish nuclear weapons. Political changes would still occur, but no longer by military means. In this stage, the differences between nations would not be taken up and resolved but suppressed and postponed. The nuclear peril would still exist in our affairs, but passively. Nuclear weapons would not, by virtue of this arrangement, have become anachronistic, but to whatever extent we took advantage of the respite by finding diplomatic and political means for conducting the world's business peacefully we would *make* them anachronistic. And that process of invention and construction would constitute the second stage (not discussed here) of the resolution of the nuclear predicament. In it, the frozen world of deterrence would begin to melt and move—peacefully—as new, nonviolent means for decision-making were discovered and instituted. With the critical issue of national security provisionally taken care of, it would no longer be necessary for this political work to take the form of a desperate and unwanted plunge into world government. Instead, the world could deal with its international business step by step—not out of panic that the world was about to end but out of a specific and positive desire to take care of the business at hand. Already the agenda of business calling for such attention is long. It comprises all those matters which come under the heading of "interdependence," including global ecological issues and global economic issues. In these and other areas of international life, "sovereignty" has already dissolved. There is no sovereign power over migratory birds, or over migratory capital, either. The current global debt crisis is a case in point. The world needs to institute a peaceful, orderly means of resolving it and other economic crises of its kind, in which the individual interests of nations can be served only to the extent that the common interest of all is attended to first. The resolution of the current debt crisis will not save the world from nuclear weapons. But if those weapons had been abolished, then the resolution of that crisis would be one of the limited steps along the path of global political changes ultimately necessary if we are to put nuclear weapons behind us once and for all.

Abolition backed up by weaponless deterrence would thus crack the link between nuclear disarmament and world government in not just one way but two: first, it would enable abolition to occur without our having to solve the underlying political problems; and, second, it would provide a foundation on which those political problems could be addressed piecemeal and gradually rather than all at once. In a word, it would resolve not the nuclear predicament—something that does require that we pursue the solution of the political question all the way to its revolutionary conclusion—but the problem of timing that was presented when, one July morning in 1945, our quick-thinking scientists handed our slow-moving politicians a device that simultaneously put our species in peril of self-extermination and made nonsense of the system of international relations with which, for better or worse, we had lived since the beginning of history. Abolition in this form would enable us to move swiftly to rescue our species from its desperate, moment-to-moment peril of self-destruction while allowing the political solution to proceed at the much slower pace that such vast work seems almost in the nature of things to require. When we first snap awake to the nearly unbelievable fact that our species is teetering on the edge of its doom, we are moved, like someone who sees a child wandering near the edge of a cliff, to spring forward immediately and save it. Yet as long as everyone—radicals and moderates alike—believed that we could not do this without first establishing world government our impulse was checked. If that requirement is waived, however, then, although the path ahead of us may still be difficult, we are free to obey our impulse and spring forward. In clearing away this obstacle, we would, for the first time since nuclear weapons were developed, stretch a frail bridge across the gap that opened at the onset of the nuclear age between the demands of the present global political system and the demands of survival. This would be the first major step toward bringing our policies back into some semblance of alignment with our scruples, and making our mortally imperilled, broken life well and safe and whole.

It might be objected that arranging to keep the world immobilized in national units unchallengeable from without would be a step away from, not toward, a world community—a step backward, in which such units, instead of passing from the world scene, would become more firmly entrenched than ever. And it is certainly true that this world of weaponless deterrence is the direct opposite of the "world without boundaries" of which so many have dreamed. In fact, in a world of weaponless deterrence boundaries, far from disappearing, would become virtually sacrosanct. The world would, in effect, be crystallized into units unchangeable from without—units in which peoples were sequestered, unable to conquer others but also safe from conquest by others. Yet, seen in another light, this organization of our global affairs, instead of impeding the eventual peaceful arbitration of international disputes, could set the stage for it nicely. If international institutions are ever to acquire real power—power to solve a world debt crisis, power to legislate a law of the sea, power to decide whom the Falkland Islands should belong to—then we want that power to be balanced and checked by local power. The great and growing patriotic feeling in the world today could be the source of that power. A world of intense patriotism would be the hardest sort of world in which to carry out either aggression or repression. It is sometimes said that patriotism is an obstacle to peace, and insofar as it has been used to feed and justify hatred of other peoples it has certainly been that. Yet patriotism, before it curdles into hatred, can be a generous, large-spirited sentiment, which lifts one out of one's private concerns and reinforces one's attachment and devotion to the community in which one lives. It might serve well as a staging ground for building the broader loyalties that we must develop if we are to survive.

A nuclear-weapon-free but conventionally armed and nuclear-capable world of sovereign and independent states linked together under an abolition agreement would remain an uneasy, dangerous world. Events in it could veer off in unexpected and unwanted directions. It would be subject to breakdowns of many kinds. One has many questions and doubts. Would some local crisis (and we can be sure there will continue to be many crises) draw the great powers into its vortex, and tempt one or more of them back down the path of rearmament, plunging the world into a mad scramble to get back to mutual assured destruction, or something worse? Would it all unravel—precipitately and catastrophically? Would some stern and resolute power, harboring an aggressive will behind smiles of friendship, suddenly burst forth and attack a peaceful and unsuspecting world? Would the West, breathing a vast sigh of relief at having abolished nuclear weapons, also push them out of mind, and grow complacent and soft, while the Soviet Union, still kept under a harsh discipline by totalitarian rule, remained militant and tough? Would the deterrent effect of mere preparations for nuclear armament be impressive enough to influence the actions of governments—to deter them? Would some power see nuclear disarmament as its opportunity to grab some advantage by launching conventional war? No one can say that these or any number of other disasters are impossible. And even if the system worked exactly as we wanted it to it would remain inherently flawed, because we would still be relying on nuclear weapons for our national defense. We would still be implicated in the intention—somewhere, someday, perhaps—of slaughtering millions of people. Instead of rejecting nuclear destruction categorically, we would still be relying on it. Our "no" to nuclear weapons would still be qualified. That this would be so is one more measure of how small a part of the distance to a full resolution of the nuclear predicament we would have travelled.

Our point of comparison, however, is not a world in which the disputes among nations have melted away or are being settled peacefully. It is today's world, in which in order to preserve a precarious "safety" we think we are obliged to threaten ourselves with doom. If we were to compare the world of an abolition agreement with the Garden of Eden, we would find it very unsatisfactory—very unstable. (But then the Garden of Eden turned out to be rather "unstable" itself.) But if we compare the world of weaponless deterrence with our present world, we find it to be immeasurably better: the impasse would be broken, and our long and difficult journey to a full resolution could begin. Nuclear weapons *would* be abolished. At first glance, a mere increase in the lead time to nuclear hostilities may seem a disappointingly modest gain to be won from the abolition of nuclear weapons. (It seems more impressive when one remembers that, given the everlastingness of the knowledge of how to build the weapons, an increase in the lead time of one length or another is technically the best we can do.) But in fact that modest increase in lead time—from about seven minutes to a month or six weeks—would mark a revolution in stability. The two most shocking features of our present system for organizing the world are the extreme precariousness of our balance on the nuclear tightrope—a precariousness defined by the short lead time—and the extreme price to be paid "if deterrence fails." In a world of weaponless deterrence, both these features would be removed. Strategic analysts largely agree that the two likeliest causes of a nuclear holocaust are, first, a preemptive strike launched out of fear that the other side would launch one and, second, miscalculation, confusion, panic, or accident (human or technological) in the midst of a crisis. Both perils arise from the presence of the arsenals themselves, and both would vanish with the abolition of the arsenals. Nuclear hostilities could begin only as the result of long premeditation and long preparation leading to cold-blooded aggression out of the blue—a course of action that present analysts regard as the unlikeliest of all causes of nuclear hostilities.

We are concerned with the stability of the nuclear world. The absence of the peril of a preemptive strike and the peril of the accidental or semi-accidental strike in a crisis would lend to a nuclear-weapon-free world a stability that we cannot even dream of in our present world of huge nuclear arsenals. For the same reason, the extremity of the penalty would have been reduced, too. Since there would be no huge arsenals, there would, of course, be no peril that the world would be blown up in an instant. Instead, in the event of a breakdown the number of nuclear weapons used—if any—would be small at first. In our present, abundantly armed world, the gruesome lessons of nuclear experience—of nuclear bombs killing people—could not be brought to bear to save us from the final abyss; once we went over the brink, there would be no hope that, horrified by what we had wrought, we would be able to turn back. But in a nuclear-weapon-free world, the lessons of experience would reinforce deterrence. It would be not only foreknowledge of the horror of nuclear destruction that would stop us from exterminating ourselves but, in the event of a breakdown, the actual spectacle of it. In short, diplomatic and political processes would not be suspended at the brink of nuclear hostilities, as they are likely to be today, but could be continued even after nuclear hostilities had begun. And while there is little hope that these processes could halt a holocaust involving tens of thousands of weapons and lasting a few hours, there is great hope that they could halt one involving hundreds of weapons and lasting weeks or months.

In a recent speech, George Kennan asked, "Can we not at long last cast off our preoccupation with sheer destruction, a preoccupation that is costing us our prosperity and preempting the resources that should go to the solving of our great social problems?" He continued, "For this entire preoccupation with nuclear war is a form of illness. It is morbid in the extreme. There is no hope in it—only horror." Nuclear weapons are truly an evil obsession: they can somehow drag us down even as we try to fight them. They degrade us. They soil us. It is unfortunately true that in a world of unarmed deterrence we would still be relying for our defense on terror—relying for our safety on the threat of terrible crimes. Yet we would have succeeded in pushing the terror and the crimes into the background of our affairs. We would have withdrawn them from the center of the stage, thereby clearing a space into which the peaceful, constructive energies of humanity could flood. But even this retirement of the weapons would not be the most important thing that we had accomplished. It would be that we had made a decision as a species in favor of our survival and then had acted on it. We would have adopted a "deliberate policy"—an unfinished and imperfect one, but a deliberate policy nevertheless. It would not resolve the nuclear predicament, yet the day that the last nuclear weapon on earth was destroyed would be a great day. It would be a day for celebrations. We would have given substance to our choice to create the human future. We would have dispelled once and for all the fatalism and lack of faith in man which, like some dark shadow of extinction itself, have crept over us. And when the celebrations ended, we could turn with new hope and new strength to the unfinished business that lay before us.

THE
UNCONQUERABLE WORLD:
POWER, NONVIOLENCE, AND
THE WILL OF THE PEOPLE

*I dedicate this book
to the memory of my mother,
fighter for peace.*

Liberty, when men act in bodies, is power.
—EDMUND BURKE
Reflections on the Revolution in France

Contents

The Towers and the Wall

December 17, 2002, New York City

"Of Arms, and the man I sing." So wrote Virgil, celebrator of the imperial Rome of his patron Caesar Augustus, in the opening lines of *The Aeneid*, as rendered in the seventeenth century by Dryden and memorized by generations of English schoolboys, who were soon sent out to rule an empire even more far-flung than Rome's. "The man": a patriot, bound to fight, and perhaps to die, for his country and all that it possessed and stood for. "Arms": the means whereby the man could vindicate his honor and defend his country or aggrandize its power and interests. The fighting man took life but also was ready to lay down his own, thereby bowing, in the mayhem of war, to a kind of rudimentary justice. Four centuries before Virgil, the Athenian statesman Pericles, much admired in both imperial Rome and imperial England, eulogized him in his funeral oration for the soldiers of Athens who had died at Marathon. "As for success or failure," Pericles said, "they left that in the doubtful hands of Hope, and when the reality of battle was before their faces, they put their trust in their own selves . . . and, in a small moment of time, the climax of their lives, a culmination of glory, not of fear, would be swept away from us." And so they would be accorded "praises that never grow old, the most splendid of sepulchres—not the sepulchre in which their bodies are laid, but where their glory remains eternal in men's minds, always there on the right occasion to stir others to speech or to action." On these foundations was reared a system—a system, at its best, of standing up for principle with force, right with might; at its worst, of plunder, exploitation, and massacre—that was to last from Pericles' time down to ours.

Yet alongside the martial tradition another, contrary one was born. At almost the very moment that Virgil was writing his lines, Jesus, the New Testament says, was speaking the even better-known words, "Put up thy sword. For they that live by the sword shall die by the sword." Following in the tradition of some of the Old Testament prophets, he sang of the man without arms. The sword in question was no symbolic weapon. It was the disciple Simon Peter's sword, and he had just cut off the ear of one Malchus, a servant of the high priest, who had been in the act of arresting Jesus in Jerusalem. It was in the heat and fury of this bloody altercation, not in the quiet of a philosopher's study, that Jesus gave his advice. And these words, too, took root somehow in people's hearts, and lasted down the centuries.

Since then, the two conflicting traditions—one worldly, sanctioning violence, the other spiritual, forbidding it—have coexisted. Each has seemed to express an ineradicable truth. Each has retained its power to inspire in spite of the other. Neither has been discarded in the name of the other. Western civilization has lived according to the rules laid down by Virgil's patron Augustus but has dated its calendar from the birth of Jesus. On the intellectual plane, many attempts to reconcile the two traditions have been made. The most notable was to declare, with St. Augustine—the great conjoiner of Roman and Christian thought of the early fifth century—that each principle applied to a distinct realm of existence. One was the City of God, a spiritual and personal realm, in which Jesus' law of nonviolence and love should be followed, the other the fallen City of Man—the public, political realm, in which Caesar's law of force must, however regrettably, hold sway. Echoes of this distinction also sounded down the centuries: in Catholic just-war theory, in Machiavelli's distinction between what is good for one's soul and what is good for the republic, in Montesquieu's distinction between the virtue of the political man and the virtue of the Christian man. There is even a shadow of it in the modern separation of church and state. Certainly, Jesus' counsel was rejected for political affairs, except among a few people, regarded by almost everyone as dreamers or fools, blind to the iron laws that govern the political world.

And who with the slightest acquaintance with history, whether in the Western world or elsewhere, can deny the primal connection between politics and violence? Indeed, what may be the earliest historical document discovered so far, the so-called Scorpion Tableau, carved in stone some 5,250 years ago in Egypt and unearthed by archaeologists in 1995, seems to depict a scene of victory in battle. It shows a man with an upraised mace standing over a bound captive. The captor, the discoverers of the document believe, is one King Scorpion, the first unifier of ancient Egypt, and the captive is a king he has defeated and is leading to public execution.

Yet history has not left the character of violence unchanged. The bloody record of the twentieth century, which seemed to confirm as never before the strength of the tie between politics and violence, also showed that violence did not stay everlastingly the same. It was capable of fantastic mutation and expansion. If an evil god had turned human society into an infernal laboratory to explore the utmost extremes of violence, short only of human extinction, he could scarcely have improved upon the history of the twentieth century. Totalitarian rule and total war each in its own way carried violence to its limits—reaching what we can call total violence, as distinct from the technically restricted violence of earlier times. Violence was old, but total violence—violence that, as in nuclear conflict, can kill without limit, reaching no decision, no point of return—was new. Rule, when it resorted to total violence, turned out no longer to be rule, for rule is domination over living human beings, and the totalitarian regimes, in their most ferocious epochs, became factories of corpses. And war, when it laid hold of its ever more powerful instruments of destruction, was no longer war but annihilation, and annihilation was as unlike war as it was unlike peace. The means of annihilation paradoxically put their possessors in a predicament that was better described by the precepts of Jesus than by those of Augustus. Through the creation of the nuclear arsenals of the Cold War and their doctrinal accoutrement the strategy of nuclear deterrence, it became literally true that the users of the sword would die by the sword. (Nuclear rivals have been likened to scorpions in a bottle, creating the possibility that history's last document as well as its first will refer to the doings of scorpions.) The increase in available force, rooted in, among other things, fundamental scientific discoveries of the twentieth century, is not a change in attitude or beliefs but an irrevocable change in the world, at least as durable as any state or empire. It has called into question the age-old reliance of politics on violent means. The iron laws of the world have become different laws, and those who wish to live and act in the world as it really is must think and act differently.

The people of the twentieth century were, of course, dismayed by the unprecedented violence visited upon them and tried to find ways to escape it. Twice in the first half of the century the world went to war. Twice in the aftermath the victors attempted to uproot the system of war and replace it with a system of law—with the League of Nations in 1919 and the United Nations in 1945. And twice they failed. In the latter half of the century, a third global struggle was waged—not a hot war this time but the cold one—and on November 9, 1989, the day the Berlin Wall was breached by joyful East Berliners, it ended. In many respects, the opportunity to found an enduring peace appeared more favorable than ever before. No defeated power awaited the hour of vengeance, as defeated Germany had after its humiliation by the onerous terms of the Versailles treaty at the end of the First World War. No ideological division threatened to divide the camp of the victors, as the antagonism between Soviet communism and liberal democracy had at the end of the Second World War. This time, however, no great effort was made to secure the peace. The victorious powers turned their minds to economic and other matters. A conviction seemed to settle in that the horrors of the twentieth century had ended of their own accord. Mere opportunity was mistaken for accomplishment, and nothing was done.

It is difficult to assign a cause to neglect, and perhaps it would be a mistake to spend much effort trying. Why, at the beginning of the twentieth century, did Europe blind itself to the approach of the First World War? Why, after that war, did the United States withdraw into isolation, condemning itself to fight again in the Second World War? The insouciance of the 1990s is equally hard to explain. Perhaps the victors of the Cold War wanted a vacation from its chronic apocalyptic anxieties, and so turned their attention to more agreeable matters— above all, to the getting and spending of the era of economic globalization. Perhaps they believed that the welcome reduction of the threat of nuclear war that the end of the Cold War brought had removed all nuclear peril. Or perhaps the United States, where a sort of complacent triumphalism developed, was simply too pleased with the status quo to imagine that it could be upset.

Whatever the reason, the spell was broken, of course, on September 11, 2001. The slumbering dragon of total violence had only twitched its tail; and yet with that one stroke the United States was brutally startled out of its sleep. This crime, in which, out of a clear blue sky one sparkling fall morning, the most imposing buildings in New York and Washington were attacked and struck down, leaving thousands dead, drove home a truth that the world should never have forgotten but did: that in our age of weapons of mass destruction all buildings, all cities, all nations, all people can likewise be reduced to ash in an instant.

And yet the awakening was selective. Even as the underlying dangers of the time were brought to shocking life, the equally remarkable and equally neglected opportunities to create a lasting peace that had appeared with the end of the Cold War were pushed into still deeper obscurity. The United States, facing the threat of further attack from a global, stateless terrorist network, launched its war on terrorism. Then it embarked on a full-scale revolution in its foreign policy that, while taking September 11 as its touchstone, adopted goals and means that extended far beyond the war on terror. The policy's foundation was an assertion of absolute, enduring American military supremacy over all other countries in the world, and its announced methods were the overthrow of governments ("regime change") in preemptive, or preventive attacks. Almost immediately, other nations, as if taking their cue from the United States, also went to war or the brink of war. Palestinians stepped up their campaign of suicide bombings against Israel, and Israel responded with military incursions against the Palestinian Authority in the West Bank and Gaza. Russia intensified its war against "terrorism" in Chechnya. Nuclear-armed India embarked on its confrontation with nuclear-armed Pakistan after the parliament in New Delhi was attacked by terrorists whom India linked to Pakistan, and the danger of nuclear war became a permanent feature of life in South Asia. The optimism and hope of the immediate post–Cold War years gave way to war fever and war. The burning towers of 2001 eclipsed the broken wall of 1989.

What never occurred, as complacency gave way to sudden

alarm, was a considered stocktaking of both the perils and the opportunities of the new era. In these pages, I will try to look past history's feints and tricks of timing and, in a view that encompasses both the wall and the towers, pose afresh the issue of war and peace, of annihilation and survival. The terrible violence of the twentieth century, I will argue, holds a lesson for the twenty-first. It is that in a steadily and irreversibly widening sphere, violence, always a mark of human failure and a bringer of sorrow, has now also become dysfunctional as a political instrument. Increasingly, it destroys the ends for which it is employed, killing the user as well as his victim. It has become the path to hell on earth and the end of the earth. This is the lesson of the Somme and Verdun, of Auschwitz and Bergen-Belsen, of Vorkuta and Kolyma; and it is the lesson, beyond a shadow of a doubt, of Hiroshima and Nagasaki.

As the British scholar and political thinker Isaiah Berlin has rightly observed, no revolution in the twentieth century had a formative influence comparable to that of the French revolution on the nineteenth. It was not in fact a revolution but a war—the First World War—that played this decisive role, setting in motion a spiral of violence whose effects are still felt today. The century's first decade, like its last, was a period of economic growth, globalization, spreading liberalism, and peace. At a stroke, the First World War reversed all four tendencies, ushering in an era of depression, contraction of global trade, dictatorship, and war. In August 1914 there were two hundred divisions prepared to go to battle in Europe. When war broke out, "The submerged warrior society . . . sprung armed through the surface of the peaceful landscape," as the historian of war John Keegan has put it. In a sense, that warrior society never returned to its barracks. In defeated Germany and Russia, the suffering, humiliation, and incalculable social disorganization caused by the war created conditions that made possible the rise to power of mass totalitarian parties in the two countries. The seventy-five-year Bolshevik terror—which Solzhenitsyn called the Red Wheel—rolled out of the trenches of the First World War, as did its jagged counterpart the Nazi swastika, and the aggression and antagonism of these regimes led straight to the Second World War. For the next three decades, every effort to restore peace and sanity seemed doomed to failure in advance. In the words of the twentieth-century political thinker Hannah Arendt, "Nothing which was being done, no matter how stupid, no matter how many people knew and foretold the consequences, could be undone or prevented. Every event had the finality of a last judgment, a judgment that was passed neither by God nor by the devil, but looked rather like the expression of some unredeemably stupid fatality."

As the new century begins, no question is more important than whether the world has now embarked on a similar cycle of violence, condemning the twenty-first century to repeat, or even outdo, the bloodshed of the twentieth. The elements of the danger are obvious. They are not, as before, the massed conventional armies and systematized hatreds of rival great powers. They are the persistence and steady spread of nuclear weapons and other weapons of mass destruction, the unappeased demons of national, ethnic, religious, and class fury, and, I believe, the danger that the world's greatest power, the United States, responding disproportionately and unwisely to these realities, will pursue the Augustan path of force and empire. These elements could, at some unforeseeable point of intersection, bring an explosion, some nuclear 1914 or anthrax 1914, that would send history off the rails as irremediably as the guns of August did almost a hundred years ago. The use of just a few dozen of the world's thirty thousand or so nuclear weapons, let us recall, could kill more people in a single unthinkable afternoon than the two world wars put together. These dark prospects require that we step back from the emergencies of the moment and ask whether there is another path to follow.

I contend that, notwithstanding the shock of September 11 and the need to take forceful measures to meet the threat of global terrorism, such a path has opened up, and remains open. For in twentieth-century history another, complementary lesson, less conspicuous than the first but just as important, has been emerging. It is that forms of nonviolent action can serve effectively in the place of violence at every level of political affairs. This is the promise of Mohandas K. Gandhi's resistance to the British Empire in India, of Martin Luther King, Jr.'s civil-rights movement in the United States, of the nonviolent movements in Eastern Europe and in Russia that brought down the Soviet Union, and of the global success of democracy in its long contest with the totalitarian challenge. It is even one of the unexpected lessons of the nuclear strategies of the Cold War. The century of total violence was, however discreetly, also a century of nonviolent action. Its success often surprised those who used it and always surprised those against whom it was used. Some of its forms, such as Gandhi's satyagraha and the social movements that pushed the Soviet Union into its grave, were radically new; others, such as the revival of liberal democracy in the century's last decades, were a fulfillment of developments whose roots went back hundreds, even thousands, of years.

The appearance of these forms did not herald the Second Coming. They did not float down from the City of God but were born in strife on the streets of the City of Man. They sprang up in revolution, in civil life, and even in the midst of war. They were as real and as consequential in history as the new forms of violence to which they were a response. They were mainly a product of action, as often stumbled upon as consciously invented, although political imagination of the highest order was also at work. In the mountainous slag heaps of twentieth-century history, they are the flecks of gold that the twenty-first century must sift out and put to use.

As I wrote these pages, I often paused to ask myself whether I had become a pacifist. Although my debt to pacifist thinkers and activists was large, I had to answer that I had not. As soon as I pictured myself a pacifist, my mind would teem with situations, both historical and imaginary, in which it was clear that I would support the use of force or myself use it. The difficulty with the creed for me was not the root of the word, *pax*, but its suffix, *ist*—suggesting that one rule was applicable to all imaginable situations. The emphasis of the word was at any rate wrong for this book. For it was not so much the horrors of twentieth-century violence, immense as they were, that I was seeking to describe as the birth, fostered by historical events, of an alternative—of what William James called "the moral equivalent of war." The path of relying on violence as the answer to violence lies open, and the world has seemed, in a wrong turn of epic proportions, to start down it, as it did in August of 1914. But there is another way.

Then shall the world, at long last, say its farewell to arms?

That unrealized vision, I know, is as old as arms themselves. Is it necessary to add that today, too, the obstacles are mountainous; that the temptations of violence, including the longing for revenge, power, or loot—or, for that matter, visions of heaven on earth or of mere safety—still grip the imagination; that the quandaries facing the peacemakers confound the best minds; that as old forms of violence exit the historical scene new ones enter; that in many parts of the world growing scarcity and ecological ruin add new desperation to the ancient war of all against all; that one day's progress unravels the next day; that while in some places nonviolence advances, in others barbarism, including genocide, is unleashed with new vigor and ferocity; that both terror and counterterror are escalating; that the callousness of the rich incites the fury of the poor; that the dream of dominion has fresh allure in the counsels of the powerful; and that hardly a single step toward peace takes place without almost superhuman tenacity and sacrifice, including the supreme sacrifice, made by such heroes as Gandhi, King, Jan Palach, Anwar Sadat, and Yitzhak Rabin, to mention just a few? In downtown Grozny, the Congo jungles, Sierra Leone, Kashmir, Jenin, or Jerusalem, it is difficult to make out, even in the distance, the outlines of a world at peace. I shall contend, nevertheless, that quiet but deep changes, both in the world's grand architecture and in its molecular processes, have expanded the boundaries of the possible. Arms and man have both changed in ways that, even as they imperil the world as never before, have created a chance for peace that is greater than ever before. To describe those changes is the business of this book.

PART ONE

VIOLENCE

1

The Rise and Fall of the War System

Some of the most important changes for the future of war have come from within war itself. Those who have planned, equipped, and fought wars have done more to alter the character of war than those who have opposed it. In the modern age, war has in fact undergone a metamorphosis so thorough that its existence has been called into question. This metamorphosis has proceeded in two distinct arenas: the traditional one of conventional war and the new one of people's war. The transformation of conventional war, propelled above all by the scientific revolution of modern times, led finally to the invention of nuclear weapons and the gruesome riddles of nuclear deterrence, whereby great-power war was immobilized, and the immense arsenals were deployed, according to the strategists, mostly to prevent their own use. At the same time, the advent of people's war was paradoxically foreshadowing the forms of peaceful resistance that proved so successful against dictatorial regimes of both the right and the left in the final decades of the twentieth century. At no stage in either journey did the warriors involved in either transformation cultivate principles of nonviolence; on the contrary, they often were bent on using violence to the hilt. Nevertheless, nonviolence of a sort was the destination at which each journey wound up.

CLAUSEWITZ ON WAR

In trying to understand the changes that have overtaken war in modern times, it's useful to begin with the eighteenth-century Prussian general and philosopher of war Carl von Clausewitz, who was born in 1780 and died in 1831. He lived and fought and wrote during one of the most important turning points in the history of war. For most of the eighteenth century, war had been largely the business of kings and aristocrats and whatever commoners they could hire or force into their service. Battles usually involved tens of thousands, not hundreds of thousands, of men on each side. The ends of war were often modest, and military strategy often consisted as much of maneuvers as of combat.

With the success of the French Revolution and the rise a decade later of Napoleon Bonaparte, a new force—the energy of an entire population fired with patriotic zeal—was poured onto the battlefield. As an officer in the Prussian service, Clausewitz experienced the effects of the change at first hand, and never more painfully than at the battle of Jena, in 1806, when Napoleon led his forces to a decisive victory over the numerically superior but antiquated and ill-led Prussian force. The French completed the conquest of Prussia in six weeks, and forced her to accept a 50 percent reduction of her territory in the Treaty of Tilsit, in 1807.

Clausewitz's experience turned him into one of the leaders of Prussian military reform. It also propelled him into a lifetime of reflection on the nature of war in general and the reasons for Napoleon's victories in particular. His magnum opus, *On War*, which many have called the greatest formal analysis of war ever made, was neither published nor even completed in his lifetime. His description of war does not fit war as we know it today. But precisely because he defined the war of his time and of times past more carefully and exactly than anyone had done before or has since, he provided us with a benchmark against which we can measure the revolutionary changes that it is the business of this inquiry to understand. It is exactly the dated aspects of his analysis that make it most interesting.

Three basic concepts define the structure of war as Clausewitz understood it. The first is his concept of "ideal war." By "ideal," Clausewitz did not mean ideally good, as when we speak of the ideal society; he meant what is perfect of its kind, as when we speak of an ideal specimen. He believed that war possesses a singular nature and, once the decision to draw the sword has been taken, develops according to a "logic" peculiar to itself. When this development is allowed to proceed unfettered, ideal war—war without constraint, fought to the death—is the result. If two armies are supplied with all their needs (munitions, logistics, manpower, a clear field of operation) but otherwise battle in a vacuum, like gladiators in a stadium, they will fight an ideal war.

Clausewitz recognized, however, that in actuality war is rarely supplied with all the materials it ideally needs and is never fought in a vacuum. Constraints are always present. For one thing, the plans and operations of armies are impeded by innumerable practical obstacles, all of which Clausewitz subsumes under the heading of "friction." Owing to friction, Clausewitz added to ideal war a second concept, that of "real war." Real war differs from ideal war in the way that a real vase, because it is chipped or slightly misshapen, differs from an ideal vase. A greater constraint than friction on ideal war is politics. Politics, in Clausewitz's view, is not something that unfortunately gets in the way of war; it is, or should be, in command of the entire operation. For war, Clausewitz believes, should be completely subordinate to the goals of the state that wages it. The supremacy of political goals over military goals is the third of his basic concepts. "War"—to give one variant of his most famous saying—"is a true political instrument, a continuation of political intercourse, carried on with other means." Clausewitz's writings sometimes seem to reflect a disappointment that ideal war is spoiled by friction, but he does not regret that war is held in check by politics. On the contrary, he regarded war that has broken free of political guidance as "something pointless and devoid of sense."

THE LOGIC OF WAR

The formulations that Clausewitz gave for the operations of ideal war may at first seem obvious, but when he has placed them in the wider context of politics, any appearance of self-evidence vanishes. On the first page of *On War*, Clausewitz wrote, "Countless duels go to make up war, but a picture of it as a whole can be formed by imagining a pair of wrestlers. Each tries through physical force to compel the other to do his will; his *immediate* aim is to *throw* his opponent in order to make him incapable of further resistance."

From this definition, a basic rule followed: Both sides must exert themselves to the utmost: "War is an act of force, and there is no logical limit to the application of that force. Each side, therefore, compels its opponent to follow suit; a reciprocal action is started which must lead, in theory, to extremes."

There is nothing abstract or metaphysical about this logic. It is the logic of any contest of strength in which the last one standing is the winner: "The fact that slaughter is a horrifying spectacle must make us take war more seriously, but not provide an excuse for gradually blunting our swords in the name of humanity. Sooner or later someone will come along with a sharp sword and hack off our arms." Attempts in principle to avoid the extremes "always lead to logical absurdity."

The reciprocal action pressing the two sides to the extremes of available force is the logic that drives war to assume its ideal nature, which Clausewitz also calls "absolute war." Ideal war and absolute war are the same. So are real war and limited war—except in those few cases in which the demands of politics and the absence of crippling friction permit war to run to its extremes. Then the real approaches the ideal and the absolute.

It's important to understand, however, that even though each side is driven to employ its strength to the limit, weakness is an indispensable element of war *as a system*. The importance of weakness for war is usually overlooked. Yet without it war could never decide anything, for no one could ever be rendered powerless. "All war," Clausewitz wrote, "presupposes human weakness and seeks to exploit it." Defeat—in which the strength of one side buckles and gives way—is the pivot of war. The victor only goes on doing what he had wanted to do and planned to do in the first place. It's on the losing side that the crisis, the reversal of fortune, the shattering of expectations, and the collapse of all plans, takes place. That is why "the loser's scale falls much further below the original line of equilibrium than the winner's side rises above it."

WHAT IS DEFEAT?

The weakness, or "powerlessness," that precipitated defeat was not a simple thing. How could the victor know when defeat had occurred? Was it when the foe's armed forces fled the field of battle? When their capital was occupied? Clausewitz's definitions of war contain an ambiguity. In the metaphor of the wrestling match, the victor renders his opponent "incapable of further resistance." If we picture this—let's call it physical defeat—we see the opponent lying flat on the ground, incapacitated or dead. But Clausewitz calls this merely the immediate aim of war. The victor's larger—and crucially different—goal is to make the enemy "do his will." The distinction between the two becomes clearer in another passage: "The battle . . . is not merely reciprocal slaughter, and its effect is more a killing of the enemy's courage than of the enemy's soldiers," for "loss of moral force is the chief cause of the decision." Following Clausewitz's cue, let us call this moral defeat.

In physical defeat, scenes of which are familiar from heroic paintings, we see slain soldiers carpeting the battlefield, perhaps with the victorious general and a few of his aides surveying them on horseback. But in the second (less often painted) picture of moral defeat, we see the former enemies up and about, busily doing what the victor has commanded—for example, paying tribute, handing over a portion of the harvest, paying a tax, or even worshiping the victor's god. In this scene, the battle is long over. The victor or his proconsul has taken up residency in the capital of the defeated nation. He issues an order. Do the defeated people obey? Do they "do his will"? Perhaps he thought he had won the victory when the enemy forces dissolved; but now it turns out, according to Clausewitz, that the decision made by civilians far from the field of battle will determine whether he really was victorious after all. For the war "cannot be considered to have ended so long as the enemy's *will* has not been broken: in other words, so long as the enemy government and its allies have not been driven to ask for peace, or the population made to submit."

Even the early nineteenth century offered examples of generals who believed a foe had been defeated only to find that he went on fighting, and sometimes prevailed. Clausewitz cites Napoleon's invasion of Russia in 1812. Napoleon won every battle on his march to Moscow. The Russian forces retreated steadily, until he finally occupied the city, which then burned in a great fire. (It has never been determined whether it was started deliberately by the population or was accidental.) Weren't the Russians beaten? In fact, as all readers of Tolstoy's *War and Peace* know, the will of Russia was intact. It was Napoleon who was on his way to ruin.

THE GREAT DEMOCRATIC REVOLUTION

The reciprocal action of the duel pushes it toward the extremes, toward absolute war. *Friction* clogs the gears, slows things down, perhaps brings them to a halt. Fear is a potent form of friction, as are exhaustion, faulty intelligence, and chance events so various that no category can easily encompass them. Weather is a good example of friction in war: "Rain can prevent a battalion from arriving, make another late by keeping it not three but eight hours on the march, ruin a cavalry charge by bogging horses down in the mud."

These are mundane matters, seemingly unsuitable for philosophical reflection, yet friction—this "resisting medium," in which war takes place—does have a grander aspect. Clausewitz is acutely conscious that different historical periods impose extremely different degrees of friction on war. He firmly believes that his picture of ideal war describes a potentiality that is timeless, but he is aware that it can be realized only in certain periods. In some periods, conditions are like molasses, in which war can scarcely get started and, if it does, remains a sorry, sluggish business.

When Clausewitz surveyed the history of war, he found his own period all but unique. Rarely, if ever, he believed, had war come so close to realizing its ideal form. The underlying reason was the French Revolution, which began in 1789, when Clausewitz was a boy. In 1793, when France sent immense conscripted armies into the field, he wrote, "a force appeared that beggared all imagination. Suddenly, war again became the business of the people—a people of thirty million, all of whom considered themselves to be citizens. . . . Nothing now impeded the vigor with which war could be waged." Not since the days of ancient Rome, he believed, had the ideal face of war shown itself more clearly. In the intervening centuries, war had for the most part been a crippled, faltering affair, dragging itself along "slowly, like a faint and starving man." In the preceding century, monarchical governments, cut off from popular support, had fought war in a formal, gentlemanly style. "Their means of waging war came to consist of the money in their coffers and of such idle vagabonds as they could lay their hands on." War thereby had been deprived of its "most dangerous" innate characteristic, the "tendency toward the extreme" dictated by its inner logic.

The larger force that swept aside these cobwebs of restraint was what the French political writer Alexis de Tocqueville, in 1835, called "the great democratic revolution" that "is going on amongst us." Because this democratic revolution touches the story of both war and nonviolence at every point, it requires discussion here. The revolution embraced not only the political upheavals that, beginning in the late eighteenth century, brought democratic governments to power, first in the United States and France and later in other parts of the world, but also the much deeper and broader democratization of the public world associated with a steady increase in the participation by masses of people in every phase of public life. This was the revolution that the early-nineteenth-century French novelist and political thinker Benjamin Constant envisioned as "mankind, emerging from an impenetrable cloud that obscures its birth, advancing toward equality over the debris of all sorts of institutions"; that the English historian Thomas Carlyle around the same time called "the new omnipotent Unknown of Democracy"; that in 1932 the Spanish philosopher Ortega y Gasset balefully assessed in *The Revolt of the Masses*, asserting that "one fact [of] the utmost importance in the public life in Europe" is "the accession of the masses to complete social power."

Those masses arrived by innumerable paths and in innumerable roles—as climbers in all the old hierarchies of privilege, as crowds on the barricades, as soldiers in conscripted armies, as guerrillas in jungles and deserts, as citizens in town meetings, as trade unionists on strike, as patriotic cheering sections for imperial conquests, as outraged native populations protesting those same conquests, as the ghostly bearers of "public opinion" in opinion polls, and, most recently, as women leaving the confines of the home, to take their places in the worlds of work and politics, or as homosexual men and women asserting their human dignity and demanding equality with heterosexuals. Everywhere these masses came, they brought a new, popular energy, a new power, destined to transform politics, war, and the relationship between the two.

What were the causes of this democratic revolution? Almost anything you cared to mention, according to its most profound expositor, Tocqueville. "The various occurrences of national existence have everywhere turned to the advantage of democracy," he wrote; "all men have aided it by their exertions: those who have intentionally labored in its cause and those who have served it unwittingly; those who have fought for it and those who have declared themselves its opponents, have all been driven along in the same track, have all labored to one end, some ignorantly and some unwillingly; all have been blind instruments in the hands of God." Even the achievements of democracy's enemies helped it, by "throwing into relief that natural greatness of man," which was perhaps the true source of the new energy. So deep-seated was the democratic principle of equality, Tocqueville thought, that its gradual development should be regarded as "a providential fact."

The French Revolution was the channel through which the stream of the democratic revolution first flowed onto the battlefields of Europe. In the words of the nineteenth-century French historian Adolphe Thiers, "The revolution, by setting the public mind in motion, prepared the epoch of great military achievements." In 1793, when the French Revolutionary Convention ordered the mass recruitment of citizens known to history as the *levée en masse*, its decree was the definitive announcement of society's unprecedented militarization. "From this moment on, until the enemies have been chased from the territory of the Republic," the convention ordained, "all Frenchmen are in permanent requisition for the service of the armies. The young men will go to combat; married men will forge weapons and transport food; women will make tents and uniforms and will serve in the hospitals; children will make bandages from old linen; old men will present themselves at public places to excite the courage of the warriors, to preach hatred of kings and the unity of the Republic." But it was Napoleon, the Corsican corporal who had himself been crowned emperor of France, who first made full use of the modern democratic army. It was under him that war, as Clausewitz put it, "took on an entirely different character, or rather closely approached its true character, its absolute perfection." Finally, "War, untrammeled by any conventional restraints, had broken loose in all its elemental fury."

WAR AS THE FINAL ARBITER

Friction, in Clausewitz's scheme, was an impediment to the logic of absolute war only *in fact*. The supremacy of politics over war was an impediment *in principle*. The first was an obstacle to war, like another foe in the field, the second a guiding rule that, in his view, must shape strategy from start to finish. Clausewitz has often been scolded as the intellectual founding father of absolute war, and has even been held responsible for the militarism in Germany that did so much to bring on the two world wars of the twentieth century. Nothing, as Clausewitz's biographer Peter Paret has pointed out, could be further from the truth. Having set forth his concept of ideal war, Clausewitz went on to argue with rigor and passion that the operations of war must be thoroughly subordinated to political ends. What is more, he fully understood that his two prescriptions for action—that, on the one hand, the logic of war required that it must be fought to the limit of one's strength and that, on the other, political considerations must limit and constrain war—were in conflict across the board. A lesser thinker might have expounded just one of these rules, but Clausewitz embraces both, and his attempt to reconcile them, though perhaps unavailing, forms one of the richest and most invaluable parts of his work. The following passage gives the context of his renowned saying, already quoted, concerning politics and war:

> It is, of course, well-known that the only source of war is politics—the intercourse of government and peoples; but it is apt to be assumed that war suspends that intercourse and replaces it by a wholly different condition, ruled by no law but its own.
>
> We maintain, on the contrary, that war is simply a continuation of political intercourse, with the addition of other means. . . . How could it be otherwise? Do political relations between peoples and between their governments stop when diplomatic notes are no longer exchanged?

In holding that war must be subordinate to politics, Clausewitz placed himself in the mainstream of the Western political tradition. Since Pericles praised the Athenian soldiers for their defense of their city and its way of life, war has been considered the ultima ratio—the final arbiter—in international affairs. In this tradition, war was seen not as an end in itself but as a servant of the polis—necessary for both its defense and its aggressive purposes. Whatever the costs of war or the wisdom or unwisdom of its goals, it was a political instrument of unquestionable worth. With war, empires were created, enlarged to the edges of the known world, or broken up; countries founded or extinguished; trade protected or cut off; plunder seized; tribute exacted; enemies punished; religions propagated or suppressed; balances of power preserved or upset. We shall never understand war until, even as we face its horror, we acknowledge, with Clausewitz and so many others, how great its usefulness and appeal as an arbiter has been. If we ask, "Arbiter of what?" the response is: Of those political disputes that could not be resolved peacefully. If we ask "Why final?" the tradition answers: Force should be introduced only after peaceful means have been exhausted. Arbitration by force is final, in the last analysis, because death is final, because the dead on the battlefield cannot pick themselves up to fight.

If the saying that war is the continuation of politics by other means assigned to war the last word in disputes, it also fixed limits on war by subordinating it to political goals. "Is war not just another expression of [a government's] thoughts?" Clausewitz asked. "Its grammar, indeed, may be its own, but not its logic." Yet this assertion apparently contradicted his claim that war did have a logic of its own—the logic that drove it to become absolute war. War thus appeared to be in the grip of two contending logics: one proceeding from war itself, the other from politics. If the politicians fixed upon "absolute" political ends (for example, the full conquest of an enemy's territory), then military and political policy might move smoothly in tandem. Clausewitz had lived through such a time—Napoleon's rise and fall. But in most periods, he knew, the logic of politics had worked against the absolutizing logic of war. Usually, the war aims fixed on by statesmen were not large enough to justify the extraordinary efforts and sacrifices required by absolute war. If in those circumstances the politicians let the logic of war take over, then "all proportion between action and political demands would be lost: means would cease to be commensurate with ends, and in most cases a policy of maximum exertion would fail because of domestic problems it would raise"—or, worse, the military tail would begin to wag the political dog. "Were [war] a complete, untrammeled, absolute manifestation of violence . . . war would of its own independent will usurp the place of policy the moment policy had brought it into being; it would then drive policy out of office and rule by the laws of its own nature." Clausewitz has been called a militarist, but rarely has a clearer warning against militarism been sounded by a military man.

The necessary remedy was to make certain that the restraining hand of policy overruled the logic of war, even though this might convert "the terrible battle-sword that a man needs both hands and his entire strength to wield, and with which he strikes home once and no more, into a light, handy rapier—sometimes just a foil for the exchange of thrusts, feints and parries." If we can hear a note of regret at this diminution of war, that only underscores the strength of Clausewitz's resolve to place politics in command.

Clausewitz was the first analyst to clearly identify the two logics that contended for the direction of war. The logic born out of war itself was not some Platonic form, floating above events; it was a dynamic principle, a compulsion, located in the activity of war itself. War was like the biblical mustard seed. You might choose not to plant that seed, but if you did, and nourished it properly, you should expect a mustard plant, not a lily. War had a life of its own, which, if not checked or limited (and the democratic revolution, by firing entire peoples with martial enthusiasm, removed limits previously in place), would dominate events. But since political logic, more often than not, defined aims that were less than absolute, it usually worked against the logic of war, reducing it to the level of modest, restrained real war—the thing encountered in most of history.

Clausewitz's account, however, contained an inconsistency. If politicians, unable to get the results they wanted by peaceful means, turned to soldiers to get them by force of arms, but then restrained those soldiers from running to the extremes at which decisions by arms occurred, how was war to be of any use to politics? Let us suppose, for example, that the politicians had in mind a limited military campaign to seize an island of only modest importance, and the enemy stalemated the attack with equal force. No extreme would have been reached, no one would have been rendered "powerless," no decision would have been rendered. What to do next? Give up? But then why make the attempt in the first place? Escalate? But then the vital "proportion" between the political goal and the military means that were used to attain it would be lost.

Napoleonic war, which extended the extremes at which the decision by arms was reached, only made this conflict more acute. Clausewitz saw the problem plainly. The growing mismatch between political logic and military logic, he wrote, "poses an obvious problem for any theory of war that aims at being thoroughly scientific." By asserting the primacy of politics, he believed, the restraint needed to fight for small objectives could still be achieved. "The natural solution soon emerges," he explained: mastered by political calculation, "the art of war will shrivel into prudence, and its main concern will be to make sure the delicate balance is not suddenly upset in the enemy's favor, and the halfhearted war does not become a real war after all." Once this process is understood, "no conflict need arise any longer between political and military interests."

With the advantage of almost two centuries of hindsight, we can see that Clausewitz was mistaken. The gap between the two logics was in fact about to widen steadily. Indeed, what some historians are calling the "long nineteenth century" in Europe—lasting from Napoleon's defeat in 1815 to the outbreak of the First World War in 1914—can be seen as a protracted, ultimately unsuccessful effort to reconcile the two logics. With the outbreak of the First World War, the logic of war triumphed over the logic of politics, engulfing the world in a series of violent catastrophes that were to dominate the rest of the twentieth century.

Clausewitz's main misjudgment was to regard Napoleonic war as absolute war. The term "absolute," borrowed from philosophy and theology, clearly suggested a culmination, with no further developments to be expected. But we know now that Napoleonic war was in fact only an early stage of a lengthy development that would steadily expand the extremes of which war was capable. War should be a mere "instrument," Clausewitz had said. But the instrument was about to come alive in the hands of its user, and embark on a process of non-stop development that in the next century and a half would produce a revolution not only in war but in the relationship of war to its would-be employer and master, politics. It was not, indeed, until the invention of nuclear weapons that any true absolute—the unquestionable power of each side to annihilate the other—was reached. At that point, strange to say, war ceased, strictly speaking, to exist among the greatest powers. True absolute war, it turned out, was not war at all but some new thing, for which no one really had a good name.

THE WAR SYSTEM

The transformation of war that lay ahead took place in the context of the European conquest of most of the globe. When, as in Clausewitz's Europe, a number of armed states contend in a single geographical arena, sometimes making war, sometimes peace, sometimes making alliances, sometimes breaking or switching them, we can speak not merely of war but of a war system—or, when the arena is the whole world, of a global war system. In a war system, the logic of war is extended to the entire system, now pushing far-flung alliances toward the extremes at which decisions by arms are rendered. Military necessity then becomes such a powerful force that the formation of alliances may override all ideological or political considerations.

As in a game, the action in a war system may be complex, but the underlying strategies available to the players are simple and well known. All were discovered by the ancient Greek city-states. The most aggressive is the strategy of universal empire, and in the West ancient Rome was the first and last to succeed in it. The most common strategy historically has been the defensive one of seeking to maintain a balance of power, whereby one or more nations or an alliance of nations tries to hold any hegemonist at bay, as England did in Europe in the face of the rising power of France in the seventeenth, eighteenth, and nineteenth centuries. An alternative to both is collective security—rarely, if ever, successful—in which a league of nations agrees to keep peace among themselves by pooling their collective force to constrain any aggressor.

It would be wrong, however, if, by referring to a war system, we seemed to suggest that it was designed by somebody. It was not. Lack of a designer, however, does not mean lack of design. There are unintended systems as well as intended ones. The street grid of New York City and the constitutional system of the United States are intentional systems. Evolution and the market economy are unintended ones—systems that had no designer (though the market system soon had many powerful champions). In both, certain patterns and rules developed of their own accord, out of conditions that were provided largely or completely without planning.

The war system is such a system. When the curtain of recorded history goes up, a plurality of states are simply there, bristling with arms and ready to fight. To suggest that the war system was an intentional system would be to falsify and simplify the dilemma of war by seeming to suggest that it was the product of some "masters of war" to whom humanity could appeal to unmake their work.

Systems may also be either static—governed by rules that do not change—or dynamic, thus subject to development. The solar system is a static system. The planets will wheel around the sun without change until the system expires. Evolution and the market economy, by contrast, are dynamic systems. More specifically, they are dynamic systems of the adapt-or-die variety. An adapt-or-die system is one in which competitors can, by adapting themselves with particular skill to a changing environment, put themselves in a position to drive their rivals out of existence. The war system is a system of this kind. Adapt-or-die systems must be supplied with some reliable source of innovation—of new, advantageous possibilities *to which* the actors can strive to be the first to adapt. In the evolutionary system one source of innovation is the random mutation of genes. In the market system, the chief source of change is technical innovation, which provides a ceaseless supply of new inventions that producers can exploit to make better or cheaper products.

For most of the history of war, few innovations were available. Combat was chiefly hand to hand, and the instruments of war—the sword, the spear, the bow and arrow, the chariot, the horse, the battering ram, the trireme, the fortification— were widely available and slow to evolve. Nations could rarely achieve a sudden, decisive advantage through an improvement in weapons or technique. (Briefly, the longbow conferred such an advantage.) In the modern period, however, the pace of innovation picked up abruptly, and the adapt-or-die character of the war system became all-important.

THE VORTEX OF POWER

It was an adaptive innovation—the mobilization of citizens by democratic revolutions—that prompted Clausewitz to announce prematurely that the era of absolute war had arrived. In the modern age, however, the democratic revolution was only one of four distinct great forces that poured newly created energy into the war system. The other three were the scientific revolution; the industrial revolution, whose mass-produced goods began to be incorporated into military armories in the mid-nineteenth century; and imperialism, which dragged the rest of the globe into the European war system. "The Great Powers were, as their name implies, organizations for power, that is, in the last resort for war," the historian A. J. P. Taylor has written. "They might have other objects—the welfare of their inhabitants or the grandeur of their rulers. But the basic tenet for them as Great Powers was their ability to wage war." Defining power this way was hardly new. What was new was the availability of the new forces of the modern age for military purposes. It was the dependence of military power on all four of its new sources of strength that turned the war system into a fast-paced, world-spanning, inescapable, adapt-or-die system, from whose ever-increasing pressure virtually no social enterprise—and certainly no nation—was exempt.

These forces did a great deal more than transform war. They were the constitutive elements in the rise of what some have called the modern world system and others have called the Western world system, as it led to Western domination of the globe. In the late nineteenth and early twentieth centuries, this system, implacable and merciless, compelled all "backward" nations to reform on pain of death—in short, to adapt to the modern Western system or die as independent countries. And which country was not, at some historical moment or other, "backward" and forced to play catch-up with some feared "advanced" nation? In the early modern age, only England—the first nation to avail itself of the modern financial, industrial, and scientific resources for war—escaped this role, with its burden of humiliation, *ressentiment*, and well-justified fear of subjugation. (Joseph Stalin, who explained many of his most ruthless measures as attempts to catch up with the capitalist West, said, "She [Russia] was beaten [in the First World War] because of her backwardness, because of her military, cultural, political, industrial, and agricultural backwardness. . . . Do you want our socialist fatherland to be beaten and to lose its independence? If you do not want that, then you must in the shortest possible time abolish its backwardness and develop a really Bolshevik pace in the establishment of its socialist economy.") Bolshevization, in the minds of its practitioners, was emergency modernization.

Military power, indeed, can be seen as a sort of clearinghouse in which the new forces of the modern age were assembled, brought into relation, and thrown into the contests in which the life or death of nations and empires was determined. We might say that in relation to this modern military exchange-market, each force brought forth both a benefit proper to it, analogous to what the economists call a "use-value," and a secondary, military benefit, analogous to what the economists call an "exchange-value." Use-value is the value a thing has directly for life. (The use-value of a glass of water is to slake a person's thirst, the use-value of a diamond is to be displayed.) Exchange-value is the price the thing will get when it is sold or bartered. So also in the modern world system, the fruits of democracy, science, industry, and imperialism had both a kind of direct use-value and a kind of exchange-value in the burgeoning market of military power. The democratic revolution brought the Rights of Man *and* millions of willing recruits for war; the scientific revolution offered pure knowledge *and* better artillery and explosives; the industrial revolutions created consumer goods *and* provided more matériel for larger and longer wars; imperial possession won trade and spoils *and* strategic global position.

Many writers have pointed out that through the process of "commodification" the free market possesses a remarkable capacity to draw ever-widening spheres of life into its orbit. The exchange market of modern military power had an even greater capacity to subordinate other realms of endeavor to its purposes, for, in that market, not just commodities but the democratic loyalty of citizens, the knowledge of scientists, the material wealth of industry, and the territories of empire were traded in for the common coin of military power—power that, in turn, could be used to gain more fervent loyalty, more material wealth, more territory, and so forth.

PURSUIT OF KNOWLEDGE, PURSUIT OF POWER

The scientific revolution, as many observers have said, has changed the conditions of human life more radically than any other single, sustained force in history. The first round of the technical transformation of war of modern times—the gunpowder revolution—had already occurred by Clausewitz's time. Its effects had been felt in the entire organization of the modern state, having been no small factor in the rise of the absolute monarchs of continental Europe. In the succinct formulation of the sociologist Charles Tilly, "War made the state and the state made war." A technical and economic rivalry among states was triggered, dictating, in an early demonstration of the modern adapt-or-die process, that the smaller states, like small firms in a cutthroat market, "must increase in size or go bankrupt." The cannon-bearing sailing ship, in its turn, laid the basis for the armed seafaring expeditions of the sixteenth and seventeenth centuries.

Fundamental characteristics of modern science—its grant of power, its irrevocability, its mobility, and its unpredictability—have been of immense importance for the development of war. In 1608, Francis Bacon, the first great philosopher of modern science, made the essential point regarding irrevocability. "The benefits of [scientific] discoveries may extend to the whole race of men, civil benefits only to a few particular places; the latter last not beyond a few ages, the former through all time." When analysts of the nuclear question rightly point out that nuclear weapons cannot be disinvented, they are describing a characteristic of all scientific invention. Scientific findings are mobile for the same reason that they are unrepealable—once made, they sooner or later can be repeated by any competent person in the world. Knowledge is by its nature ambulatory. And because science is a process of discovery, its findings—no less than its social applications—are unpredictable. A scientist's investigations are directed by hypotheses, which are in turn directed by theories, both of which enable scientists to make reasonable guesses regarding what they may find in any particular investigation. But they are in the dark when it comes to guessing what other scientists years in the future, guided by still undreamed-of hypotheses and theories, will discover. They are as unable to predict what science will bring to light fifty years ahead as Columbus was to predict what he would discover when he sailed west across the Atlantic.

These characteristics of science—each a positive feature in the context of science's own remarkable progress—are responsible in no small measure for the tyrannous, lethal pressure that the modern war system has placed on nations. They have left society quadruply helpless. Because science was power, nations felt unable to forgo the most destructive inventions; because science was irrevocable, they were unable to rid themselves of any invention once acquired; because science was unpredictable, they were helpless to know what inventions they would be handed next by scientists, and so to foresee the direction in which science was dragging them. On the bridge of the great ship of basic science, where, as Bacon put it, pure scientists were enjoying "contemplation of things as they are, without superstition or imposture, error or confusion," all was peaceful, calm, and orderly, but in the ship's mighty wake every other vessel, especially every military vessel, was buffeted by the currents or sucked under the waves.

The resemblances between the scientific and the democratic revolutions are striking. If ours has been an age of fantastic growth of human powers, then science and democracy have been the two deepest wellsprings of it. Both have been sleepless dynamos of historical change, spilling fresh energy decade after decade into the modern world. Both revolutions seemed to most observers in the eighteenth and nineteenth centuries to be agencies of continuous, cumulative human betterment. Both have been global and have tended to produce uniformity—eroding not only tradition but all local particularity. Both have proved, to use Tocqueville's word, "irresistible" and (so far, at least) irreversible. Both have transformed and continue to transform the world, including war, in ways unanticipated by the actors involved. Both have proffered gifts of previously undreamed-of human power yet have left nations unable to reject these gifts (new destructive inventions, new recruits for armies) if they so wished. Hasn't this powerlessness of humankind *not* to accept windfalls of unimagined power been a defining feature of the modern period?

FROM THE RIGHTS OF MAN TO THE *LEVÉE EN MASSE*

In the nineteenth century, a pattern emerged in which the benefits proper to each of the new forces of the modern age yielded to exigencies of military need. The promise of both the American and the French revolutions was democracy itself—liberty, fraternity, equality, the Rights of Man. But the American revolutionaries found themselves instantly at war, and the French Revolution, as Clausewitz noted, was immediately militarized. No sooner had the Frenchman become a citizen than he rushed off to the front. The revolutionary zeal for war was memorably articulated by the leader of the dominant Gironde faction in the French Assembly, Jacques-Pierre Brissot, who proclaimed, "We cannot rest till Europe, and all Europe, is ablaze."

In one respect, as it turned out, the Girondins fatally miscalculated, for the emergency of war created ideal conditions for the rise of the Jacobin terror, in which many of them perished. But in another respect, the Girondins had prophesied truly, for after initial reverses the French revolutionary armies embarked on a series of smashing triumphs over neighboring monarchies that was not reversed until Waterloo, in 1815. "Here begins modern war," the nineteenth-century French historian Jules Michelet wrote. "Tacticians could never have invented such tactics. No calculation was involved."

Whereas the French had started with democracy and only then discovered the power of mass armies, the Prussians began with mass armies—French ones, invading their country—and only then discovered the need for popular reforms. Democracy always and everywhere involves the participation of the people; but whereas in France democracy initially meant the elevation of the French people over aristocrats and kings, in Germany it meant, from the start, recruitment of the people to fight other

404 THE UNCONQUERABLE WORLD

peoples, including, above all, the detested French conquerors (who were indeed defeated by the Germans in 1871). These effects of the democratic revolution deepened and were systematized throughout the nineteenth century, as states, in the wake of the French revolutionaries' *levée en masse*, mastered the techniques of conscription and mass propaganda. During the nineteenth century, Europe as a whole witnessed a slow evolution from "liberal nationalism," which pitted the common people ("the nation") of each country against its own monarchs and privileged classes, toward an increasingly militaristic, right-wing nationalism, which pitted all classes of the nation, plebeian and privileged alike, against other nations. Nationalism (a word that doesn't come into wide use until the end of the nineteenth century) was the militarization of democracy.

FROM LAISSEZ-FAIRE TO THE MILITARY REVOLUTION

A parallel process of militarization occurred in the evolution of the industrial revolution. In Clausewitz's day, the effects of industrialization had yet to make themselves fully felt in war. The early champions of the free market, most of them British, had in fact looked to industry mainly to create the wealth of nations, as the title of Adam Smith's classic book had it, not the *power* of nations, which had been the preoccupation of their mercantilist predecessors. The advocates of laissez-faire declared the independence of economics from state power. (The eventual coining of the word "economics," identifying a distinct realm of human activity subject to its own laws, was one sign of their faith in that independence.) The market worked best, the worldly philosophers of the late eighteenth century believed, when the government kept its hands off it. Classical economics, in fact, "had no place for the nation, or any collectivity larger than the firm."

Smith's successors proceeded even further in this line of thinking. In the early nineteenth century, the most prominent champions of the market, including the British champions of laissez-faire Richard Cobden and John Bright, contended that free trade, by breaking down or ignoring national boundaries, naturally tended to foster world peace. The market, they ardently believed, was a solvent of national units and a pacifier of national conflicts. "I see in the Free Trade principle," Richard Cobden said in a speech in 1846, "that which shall act on the moral world as the principle of gravitation in the universe, drawing men together, thrusting aside the antagonism of race, and creed, and language, and uniting us in the bonds of eternal peace." In the United States, Ralph Waldo Emerson declared that "trade was the principle of Liberty; that trade planted America and destroyed Feudalism; that it makes peace and keeps peace; and it will abolish slavery." An unbroken thread of faith in free trade as an abettor of peace runs through the entire tradition of liberal internationalism, surviving many disappointments and continuing, if in attenuated form, to this day.

Yet soon a different relationship of markets to war emerged. Just as the nations of Europe could scarcely help noticing, in the wake of the French Revolution, that the mobilization of masses of people had hugely strengthened armies, so as the nineteenth century progressed they observed that the industrial revolution was doing the same. The military advantages of industrialism were put on convincing display in the American Civil War. Railroads and the mass manufacture of weapons played an important part in both its immense destructiveness and the ultimate victory of the North. In 1871, the Prussian victory over France drove the lesson home in Europe. If in the Napoleonic wars France had taught Prussia the value of patriotic masses, now Prussia's taught France—and all Europe—the value of industrialization and organizational skill. The Prussian victory was due in part to what came to be called the Prussian military revolution, in which the resources of industry, technology, and even education were exploited as never before for military purposes. This superiority of machine over man in war was sealed in the slaughter of the First World War, in which artillery and the machine gun—the emblems par excellence of the mechanization of war—laid waste to so many millions of young men. For the rest of the history of war, the strength of industrial economies and military power would be closely linked.

Imperialism's gift to the modern war system was access to nearly every inch of the earth for the military operations of the imperial powers. In the late nineteenth century, economic motives for empire steadily yielded to geopolitical ones. The importance of territory for war had always been recognized. It was not, however, until the forced opening of China and Japan in the mid-nineteenth century and the ensuing "scramble" for Africa and other imperial possessions that the whole earth became an indivisible military theater whose center was Europe. Between 1870 and 1900, European nations seized control of some ten million square miles of territory, on which a hundred and fifty million people lived. Only then was it possible to regard military initiatives in Siam, Natal, or Peking as moves on the chessboard of a truly global war system. The nineteenth-century English historian Frederic Seebohm famously commented that the British Empire was "acquired in a fit of absence of mind," but by the 1880s, absence of mind was at an end, replaced by jingoistic pride and ceaseless global military strategizing. In *Africa and the Victorians*, the scholars Ronald Robinson and John Gallagher have chronicled the change. The early Victorians, faithful to their laissez-faire principles, were content to let private interests take the lead in empire-building. The British government abjured direct rule, believing that the spread of commerce would itself lead "civilization with one hand, and peace with the other, to render mankind happier, wiser, better," in the words of Britain's foreign secretary, Lord Palmerston, in 1842. Even his gunboat diplomacy was aimed only at "opening" countries to trade, not ruling them. As late as 1890, the prime minister, Lord Salisbury, opposing direct British rule of Egypt, said, somewhat facetiously, "The only form of control we have is what is called moral influence, which in practice is a combination of nonsense, objurgation, and worry." He added, "In this, we are supreme."

However, events did not proceed as the liberal dabblers in empire expected—neither in Asia nor in Africa nor in the Ottoman Empire. The economic arrangements forced upon those lands did not strengthen and liberalize their governments but undermined them and drove them, one after another, toward collapse. The Egyptian government, for example, accepted loans from Europe, spent the funds on large but unproductive public projects, and, when these failed, sought to keep up payments on the loans by raising taxes on the poor, who grew discontented and rebellious. The imperial powers then were faced with what seemed a drastic choice: between withdrawing entirely and imposing direct rule. They chose direct rule.

By the turn of the century, most of the territories of the globe had been incorporated by imperialism into the European vortex. Any move anywhere—in the heart of Africa, in the Bay of Bengal, in the Strait of Tsushima—by any of the great powers now seemed to the others likely to upset a global balance of power and to require a countermove. The conservative British politician Lord Curzon spoke for his whole generation of statesmen when, after a long journey to the Middle East in 1890, he wrote, "Turkestan, Afghanistan, Transcaspia, Persia—to many these names breathe only a sense of utter remoteness or a memory of strange vicissitudes and of moribund romance. To me, I confess, they are the pieces on a chessboard upon which is being played out a game for the dominion of the world." Lord Haldane, describing his participation in the unsuccessful Anglo-German negotiations on naval reductions of 1912, said, "I thought, from my study of the German General Staff, that once the German war party had got into the saddle, it would be war not merely for the overthrow of France or Russia but for the domination of the world." From that time on, fear that one power or another would take control of the planet became the nightmare of statesmen and peoples. It was a dread inherent in the logic of war once the war system had drawn all nations into its sphere.

THE TRIUMPH OF THE LOGIC OF WAR

As the nineteenth century came to a close, the European war system, nourished by science, democracy, industry, and imperial conquest, was swollen with powers hardly dreamed of at the century's beginning. If, elaborating on Clausewitz, we liken war to a race that must be run to its finish before the prizes of victory and defeat can be handed out, then we might say that what had been a hundred-yard dash in Napoleon's time had become a potential marathon. Then, states might have had to sacrifice tens of thousands of men before the race was won; now the price would be the blood of millions. Then, Europe was chiefly involved; now the struggle would involve every continent. Then, soldiers marched to battle with muskets on their shoulders; now they would arrive by train with machine guns. The gap between the often modest political objectives of international diplomacy and the military means necessary to secure or defend them had widened into an abyss. And yet, because the war system was now global, tiny events in out-of-the-way places, in themselves without significance to the great powers, were vested with apocalyptic importance. Europe was at peace, but the logic of war had eclipsed the logic of politics.

Two diplomatic-military events—one in the colonial world, another in the heart of Europe—can illustrate the depth of the abyss with particular clarity. One is the Fashoda crisis of 1898, which brought France and England to the brink of war over minuscule claims in what is now southern Sudan. England, in full control of Egypt, did not yet rule its neighbor Sudan, which a few years earlier had been taken over by a radical Islamic movement, whose leader was called the Khalifah. The French, embittered by their exclusion from Egypt when England had occupied it in 1882, concocted a far-fetched scheme to turn the tables against England. An expedition of a hundred and fifty Senegalese and eleven Frenchmen under the leadership of Captain Jean-Baptiste Marchand was dispatched on a thousand-mile overland expedition from West Africa to seize a small Sudanese town called Fashoda—a godforsaken place of "blazing heat, solvent humidity, elephant grass, and enveloping mud (when the rain began in May) and horizon-to-horizon mosquitoes."

Meanwhile, England dispatched an army of thirty thousand men under Lord Kitchener to destroy the Islamic forces in Sudan. For two years, he marched his army south along the Nile, accompanied by gunboats on the river, until, on August 31, 1898, he encountered the Khalifah and his forces at Omdurman and annihilated them. On September 19, he reached Fashoda. Marchand had arrived two months earlier with his small band of fellow explorers and claimed the town for France.

The two men met and had a cordial conversation. Yet for the next few weeks Britain and France stood at the edge of war over a fetid swampland, which neither country valued. The verdict of political logic regarding Fashoda was clear: it was worthless. But the logic of the military chessboard led to an opposite evaluation. Because Fashoda, like Egypt, supposedly sat astride England's "road to India," and since India was the heart of the British Empire, Fashoda must be defended at all costs. The disparity between the puniness of the prize and the immensity of the war being risked in Europe disturbed even the most pugnacious imperialists. Queen Victoria, ordinarily a hard-liner in imperial matters, remarked to Prime Minister Salisbury that "a war for so miserable and small an object is what I could hardly consent to." Yet at the height of the crisis war orders were sent to the English fleet in the Mediterranean. France, lacking comparable naval forces in the region, and holding a position at Fashoda that was, in Kitchener's words by telegraph to London, "as impossible as it is absurd," backed down. The crisis, which bore a close resemblance to others of the period—in Morocco, in Siam, in China—was one of many clear but unheeded warnings that confrontations in out-of-the-way places could push the world toward a pointless, global catastrophe.

The event in Europe that illustrated the same widening abyss between military and political logic was the negotiation, four years earlier, of the Franco-Russian alliance, forged to counter the growing power of Germany, which was allied with Austria and Italy. The treaty's aims, as the American diplomat and scholar George Kennan observes in his book *The Fateful Alliance*, were solely to win a war with Germany, and the treaty made no mention of any political object of the fighting. Instead, its provisions simply stated that if either power were attacked, no matter what the reason, the other would come to its aid by launching all-out war.

The framers of the treaty seem to have learned everything that Clausewitz had to say about the requirements of absolute war but nothing of what he said about the need to subordinate war to the goals of policy. In a state paper that laid the foundation for the treaty, Russian adjutant general Nikolai Obruchev observed, "Once we have been drawn into a war, we cannot conduct that war otherwise than with all our forces, and against all our neighbors. In the face of the readiness of entire peoples to go to war, no other sort of war can be envisaged than the most decisive sort." Not only must the war be total but it must be instantaneous. "The term 'mobilization' must now signify the inauguration of military operations themselves," Obruchev wrote. Therefore, once war had begun, "further diplomatic hesitation is impermissible." Would the diplomats and the statesmen at least have an opportunity to decide on political goals for the war *before* embarking on it? Not according to Obruchev. War against "all neighbors" meant that even partial mobilization by any member of the opposing alliance would have to be met with an immediate, full-scale attack on the entire alliance, for "it is hard to conceive that any war beginning on the continent could be limited to an isolated struggle between any two states."

The politicians undertaking the agreement apparently did not see a need to specify any war aims. The Russian foreign minister, Nikolai Giers, asked Czar Alexander III what the purpose of victory over Germany would be, and the Czar answered, "What we would gain would be that Germany, as such, would disappear." And when General Raoul Mouton de Boisdeffre, the principal architect of the treaty on the French side, was asked what France's intentions regarding Germany would be after a victory, he replied, "Let us begin by beating them; after that it will be easy." Regarding the war's aim, Kennan concluded, "There is no evidence, in fact, that it ever had been discussed between the two governments."

In the Fashoda crisis and the Franco-Russian treaty, we catch two glimpses of a world in which, though peace still reigned, military victory had become an end in itself. The logic of politics had not been merely challenged by the logic of war, it had been shut out completely. The war that now threatened had become the senseless thing that Clausewitz had once feared: "a complete, untrammeled, absolute manifestation of violence" that would "drive policy out of office and rule by the laws of its own nature."

The causes of war now arose not so much from political differences as from the structure of the war system itself—from each country's fear that, if war broke out, some small advantage won by a speedier or better-prepared rival would tip the scales of victory and defeat. When war did come in 1914, it fit this description exactly. It exhibited the grotesque disproportion foreshadowed by the Fashoda crisis and the Franco-Russian treaty. The immediate cause of war—the political fortunes of the small state of Serbia in southeastern Europe—was of negligible intrinsic importance to the great powers, but once the full machinery of the global system was mobilized for battle, the slaughter proved unstoppable until a true Clausewitzian victory had been won by the Allied forces. Nations that had no direct stake in the fortunes of Serbia—England, for example— suffered millions of casualties. As the war historian John Keegan has observed, "The war's political objects—difficult enough to define in the first place—were forgotten. . . . Politics played no part in the conduct of the First World War worth mentioning."

The statesmen of 1914 were notoriously unaware how bloody and protracted total war would be. Most believed that the fighting would last only a few months. One reason was that they saw at least three of the four great modern forces that had fed the war machine—science, democracy, and industry—chiefly as motors of human progress. They identified these forces with the advance of civilization, not its downfall. Even imperialism, in such bad repute later, was touted then as an advance guard of the "three Cs": civilization, Christianity, and commerce.

Among military men, however, the idea that war in Europe could only be total was widespread. In France, Marshal Foch, soon to command the French forces, was saying, "You must henceforth go to the limits to find the aim of war. Since the vanquished party now never yields before it has been deprived of all means of reply, what you have to aim at is the destruction of those very means of reply." From a Clausewitzian point of view, such a statement, which left political goals out of military calculations, was folly. But was it in fact baseless? The advocates of total war, who were ready to unleash war over a Fashoda and did so over Serbia, have often been blamed. Several generations of historians have accused them of losing a sense of proportion—"of forgetting that force should be used in amounts commensurate to the purpose at hand, no more, no less," in Kennan's words. Given the pressures of the adapt-or-die war system, however, was it realistic to expect nations to exercise restraint?

Attempts to reach disarmament agreements, such as the Anglo-German naval discussions of 1912, almost invariably failed; and unilateral restraints were as unthinkable for patriotic publics as they were for governments. Which country, in the name of preserving a peace that might shortly break down, dared to be the one to stop its armies short of a Fashoda or a Sarajevo and let the enemy plant his flag there first, or rest content with a smaller naval gun, or fix a slower timetable for mobilization, or reject an alliance with another power in the face of mortal peril from a third and fourth? And when war did come, was it possible *then*, in the midst of unprecedented slaughter, to *reintroduce* political calculations, and bring the fighting under control? Once the tremendous twentieth-century war machines had been assembled and hurled at one another, was it likely, or even conceivable, that they could be used in a refined, controlled manner—like Clausewitz's hand rapier—to adjudicate such modest, or even trifling, issues as the future of this or that African swamp or Balkan backwater? History famously discloses no alternatives, but the military history of the entire twentieth century strongly suggests that, whatever theorists might have recommended, the modern war machines, once built, had to be used to the full or left unused. Since 1870, no great powers have fought "limited" wars directly against one another (although many have fought small powers). They have fought total war or they have not fought at all.

THE COLLAPSE OF WEAKNESS

The First World War was a watershed not only for war but for the civilization that produced it. Europe, without quite knowing what it was doing, had for more than a century been pouring the awesome energies of modernity into the war system, and the result was the catastrophe of 1914. Now the influence between war and society started to run in the opposite direction, shaping the domestic life of nations, above all in ravaged Russia and Germany, which, in the wake of defeat and anarchy, soon gave birth to the Bolshevik and Nazi regimes. Meanwhile, the technology of war kept improving. By 1918, the democratic revolution—which had galvanized people, fueled the conscription of millions of young men into the armies, and propelled them to the front to die—had contributed all it had to offer to the war system. Mutinies in the French and Russian armies in the last years of the war had even suggested a limit to popular endurance for patriotic gore. The art of harnessing industry to war had been mastered. Imperialism likewise had reached its high tide. Science and industry, however, had much yet to give. The decades ahead would witness the development of tanks, more powerful explosives, and air forces, including long-range bombers, rockets, radar, and aircraft carriers, to name just a few of technology's new contributions to war. After the First World War, the biologist J. B. S. Haldane recollected his wartime experience with artillery and poison gas this way:

> Through a blur of dust and fumes there appear, quite suddenly, great black and yellow masses of smoke which seem to be tearing up the surface of the earth and disintegrating the works of man with an almost visible hatred. These form the chief parts of the picture, but somewhere in the middle distance one can see a few irrelevant-looking human figures, and soon there are fewer. It is hard to believe that these are the protagonists in the battle. One would rather choose those huge substantive oily black masses which are much more conspicuous, and suppose that the men are in reality their servants, and playing an inglorious, subordinate and fatal part in the combat. It is possible, after all, that this view is correct.

In *Weapons and Hope*, the physicist Freeman Dyson comments that observations such as this, which he absorbed as a child, led him and many of his friends in the interwar years to regard technology as "a malevolent monster broken loose from human control." Technology, however, had no will of its own, and to think that it did people had to hide from themselves the human wills that were in fact propelling it. We know who they were—the scientists who developed the technology and the statesmen and generals who ordered its use. And yet in a sense Haldane and Dyson were right, because these people lacked the discretion, except at terrible risk to their nations, to forgo the new inventions of war. They were as thoroughly trapped on the treadmill of the modern adapt-or-die war system as the soldiers in the trenches.

All the new inventions were used to the full in the Second World War, in which an estimated seventy million human beings were killed. But it was the last time. Even as the war was being fought, an instrument that would make such wars forever impossible was being prepared in the desert of New Mexico. Never has a single technical invention had a more sudden or profound effect on an entrenched human institution than nuclear weapons have had on war. For war was a paradoxical freak of evolution: a creature that depended for its survival on that unsung virtue of arms, their weakness—without which war's critical event, its gift to politics, defeat, could not occur. But human weakness, in the twentieth century, proved a dwindling asset. Like clean air, rain forests, stratospheric ozone, and passenger pigeons, it was being steadily depleted by technical progress. In July of 1945, it ran out. The logic of total war had carried its practitioners to the brink of a destination, the far side of human existence, to which the logic of politics could never follow. For politics was a human activity, and in the post-nuclear landscape there might be no human beings. The bomb revealed that total war was not an everlasting but a historical phenomenon. It had gone the way of the tyrannosaurus rex and the saber-toothed tiger, a casualty not of natural but scientific evolution, whose new powers, as always, the war system could not refuse. Its day was done.

2

"Nuclear War"

The atomic bomb that destroyed Hiroshima reverberated in every domain of human existence. It placed the human species at risk of extinction by its own hand. It signaled a reversal in the balance of power between humankind and nature, placing nature in jeopardy from human depredation. It threw into doubt the moral faith on which all civilization must be based—that the collective efforts of human beings will make life better than it otherwise would have been. But in our present context its most important consequence was that it rendered the global war system unworkable beyond any hope of repair. The new state of affairs was recognized by a succession of leaders of the nuclear powers. As early as 1952, President Harry Truman said, in his farewell broadcast to the nation, "Starting an atomic war is totally unthinkable for rational men." At the height of the Cuban missile crisis, the chairman of the Communist Party of the Soviet Union, Nikita S. Khrushchev, acknowledged in a letter to President John F. Kennedy that only "lunatics or suicides, who themselves want to perish and to destroy the whole world before they die," would start a nuclear war. The clearinghouse of the adapt-or-die war system, where the powers of the modern age were cashed in for the universal currency of military power, was abruptly closed for business at the global level. The vast set-piece battles that had long been history's favorite grand decision-making device sank into the past. (Where they did occur—between Iran and Iraq in the 1980s, or between Ethiopia and Eritrea in the nineties—they seemed anachronistic, as "backward" as the countries that were waging them.) Industrialists might still offer their products, scientists their inventions, and citizens their patriotic zeal, but now their contributions could only increase overkill—"strengthen our deterrent," or some such. The critical link between military power and political power, which Clausewitz had struggled to preserve, was severed at the highest level of international operations.

The most obvious solution to the new predicament was

to abolish nuclear weapons, or even to liquidate the entire disabled war system. And in fact abolition was proposed by President Truman's representative to the United Nations, Bernard Baruch, in June of 1946. He asked the world to join with the United States in placing all nuclear facilities under international inspection and control and restricting their use to peaceful purposes. The Soviet Union rejected the proposal, and put forward one of its own, which the United States in turn rejected. Liquidation of the whole war system was attempted with the foundation of the United Nations. The U.N.'s central mechanism for peacekeeping was to be a system of collective security enforced by the powers that had just won the Second World War, all of whom were given permanent memberships on the Security Council and a right to veto its decisions. The operations of the council were soon spoiled for these purposes by the onset of the Cold War, which rendered collective decision making in the council impossible. In 1949, the Soviet Union detonated its first atomic bomb.

The great powers of the Cold War now had to decide how to conduct their business in a world that was *not* going to replace the rule of force with the rule of law but instead *was* going to equip itself with nuclear arsenals. Their dilemma was that they could neither use the most powerful instruments of force now at their disposal nor get rid of them. The bomb had ruined war by transforming it into mutual annihilation. Now the most important question was whether humankind would live or die; but the military paralysis of the great powers also raised the separate question of how, in war's absence, international conflicts would be resolved. What would be the final arbiter now?

Never had war "arbitrated" the destines of nations more sweepingly than in the first half of the twentieth century. The First World War had undone the three imperial dynasties of continental Europe, swept a multitude of national governments from power, and sharpened the appetite for self-determination in colonies around the world. The Second World War had given Hitler the mastery of Europe, then taken it back; subjected the peoples of Asia to Japanese rule and then released them; drawn the Soviet Union deep into Europe; drained the power of England even in victory, giving the coup de grâce to its global empire; and raised up the United States to global preeminence. And now the question had become how, if global war could no longer be fought, conflict in the global order would proceed. People who wanted to make things happen would have to search for other means; but what were they to be? Through what riverbeds would the streams of historical change flow, now that this ancient one was blocked? What were to be the instruments of power?

For human strife had not dried up in deference to the energy released from the atom. On the contrary, a classic global confrontation between two blocs inspired by hostile ideologies was taking shape. At the same time, anticolonial movements were in full flood around the world, and often intersected with the Cold War struggle. Sometimes, regional antagonists dragged the superpowers into their conflicts, and sometimes the superpowers, thwarted by nuclear terror from pursuing their military ambitions directly, deflected them into proxy regional struggles, which, now vested with apocalyptic significance, often escalated back up the military ladder to "the brink," threatening nuclear war. Hanging over the scene was the old fear that one of two great powers, if left unchecked, would dominate the world.

Nuclear strategy had little if anything to offer to the resolution of the burning political issues of the time. At best, the leaders of the day increasingly realized, nuclear arsenals could freeze a global stalemate in place. Even this goal, however, was hard to achieve. Preserving the status quo, after all, is not a modest goal for statesmanship. For almost half a century, for example, it was the primary mission of the Concert of Europe, established following the Congress of Vienna in the wake of Napoleon's defeat, and it has generally been the broad goal of balance-of-power policies wherever these have been practiced. Under the dominant strategic doctrine of the new age, nuclear deterrence, force thus still did in a sense "arbitrate," and on a global scale. That arbitration, however, could deliver only one monotonous verdict: no one can move a muscle, everything must remain as it is.

The question that remained was how nuclear weapons could achieve even this limited goal when they could not be used. A solution was attempted by turning the war system into a system of pure nuclear terror, to which the name "balance of terror" was soon attached. Terror had been employed for political ends from the time of King Scorpion on, and never more lavishly than during the first half of the twentieth century—a period that witnessed the rise of totalitarianism, which used terror as a mainstay of rule, and also the rise of "strategic bombing," whose explicit aim was not to destroy military targets but to break civilian morale. The destruction of Hiroshima was in fact the culmination of a series of destructions of cities by firebombing, in both Germany and Japan.

The nuclear terror of the Cold War nevertheless was categorically different from all previous terror. As a tactic in war, terror is the use of force against some people to intimidate others. A classic example was the Nazi practice in occupied countries of announcing their intention to execute ten or more political prisoners in their jails for every German soldier killed by resistance fighters. Nuclear terror, by contrast, is the paradoxical attempt to produce terror on a mass scale without actually using force—an idea embodied in nuclear deterrence. Under this strategy, military force was handed a role—to prevent its own use—that it had never previously played in the same way before.

The doctrine, which took shape in the 1950s, became the declared policy of the United States in the 1960s, then won a partial, grudging acceptance by the Soviet Union, and went on to become the basis for the first nuclear-arms-control negotiations. According to its central tenet, each side would be stopped from attacking the other by the knowledge that it would be annihilated in return. Historically, military forces had been employed as often to deter war as to fight it. Military leaders had long been fond of the old Roman saying "If you seek peace, prepare for war." But that proposition had in fact been a mere corollary of another, which was too obvious for aphoristic expression: If you seek to fight and win wars, prepare for war. It was this second proposition that the bomb nullified. Seeking war made no sense when war to the finish meant annihilation for all involved. A new proposition, appropriate to the nuclear age, was articulated as early as 1946 by, among others, the American military analyst Bernard Brodie. He wrote, "Thus far the chief purpose of a military establishment has been to win wars. From now on its chief purpose must be to avert them. It can have no other useful purpose." The same argument was put forward by Winston Churchill, when he made his famed remark "It may be that we shall by a process of sublime irony have reached a stage in this story where safety will be the sturdy

child of terror, and survival the twin brother of annihilation."
Even though the system of nuclear terror was no longer a war
system, it was still, let us stress, a system based on force; that is,
force had not been exchanged for obedience to law, or for any
form of willing cooperation. It was the way in which force was
to be exploited that had changed.

If in the new system the *unleashed* force was no longer the
final arbiter, we need to ask, then what, exactly, was? The answer
was that there occurred a sweeping displacement of military
conflicts from theaters of actual combat to a theater of appearances. The battles that *could not* be fought physically were to be
fought out instead on psychological terrain. To borrow Clausewitz's concepts again, it was as if the policy makers wanted to
achieve their opponents' moral defeat without passing through
the stage of physical defeat. Clausewitz had written that "the
destruction of the enemy's force underlies all military actions;
all plans are ultimately based on it, resting on it like an arch on
its abutment." He added, "The decision by arms is for all major
and minor operations in war what cash payment is in commerce.
Regardless how complex the relationship between the parties,
regardless how rarely settlements actually occur, they can never
be entirely absent." But trying to preserve credit—or, in that
much-used term of the nuclear age, "credibility"—without ever
having to make the cash payment (engaging in nuclear war) was
exactly the feat that the superpowers were attempting.

Nuclear credibility—the appearance of a readiness to use
nuclear weapons when the chips were down—was a compound
of several elements. One was obviously possession of a nuclear
arsenal. A second was the readiness to use it. But these were
entirely useless without an essential, if strangely intangible,
third element, the *appearance* of having the first two. Creating
this appearance was therefore *the* essential requirement of
nuclear policy. Even with an arsenal in hand, however, creating
the desired appearance was no simple matter, considering the
suicidal consequences of performing the terrible deed; and a
central—almost an obsessive—preoccupation of the Cold War
leaders was with making people believe that they possessed the
doubtful will to carry out their nuclear threats.

Such demonstrations were necessarily racked with contradictions, all of which were variations on a theme: under no
circumstances could the act that gave the deterrent threat

its effectiveness—namely, the actual launching of a nuclear attack—make any sense. The operational puzzle was what to do "if deterrence failed." It was a question without a reasonable answer, for it can never be in the interest of a country to perform an act (fighting a nuclear war) whose prevention is itself the goal of its policy. All of which is only a complicated way of saying that it could never make sense for the two rivals to blow themselves off the face of the earth.

In practice, the problem was solved by knowledge on all sides that, whether retaliation was rational or not, it was likely to happen. "The essence of the problem is the difficulty of attaching any rationality whatsoever to the initiation of a chain of events that could well end in the utter devastation of one's own society (even assuming indifference to the fate of the enemy society)," the historian of nuclear energy Lawrence Freedman has written. "The resulting sense of an enormous bluff is, however, more likely to worry those relying on these threats . . . than those against whom they are directed." He concludes, "The Emperor Deterrence may have no clothes, but he is still Emperor." The mighty sword, curiously, had turned into a mere picture of a mighty sword. Freedman suggested that the Emperor Deterrence had no clothes, but considering the primacy of appearances in nuclear policy, it would perhaps be more appropriate to say that the clothes had no emperor. What this meant in practice can be illustrated by the most perilous episode of the Cold War—the Cuban missile crisis.

A CRISIS OF APPEARANCES

By the time of the crisis, the peculiar new rules of the nuclear game were in full force, and the progress of the crisis reveals them in operation. On Sunday, October 13, 1962, American U-2 spy aircraft discovered Soviet nuclear-missile sites under construction in Cuba. On Monday, October 22, after a week of secret deliberations, President Kennedy made the fact known in a television address to the American people, and announced that he had imposed a naval quarantine on military goods being sent to Cuba, and was demanding the removal of the missiles. He made clear that the stakes in the crisis were total when he warned that any launch of nuclear weapons from Cuba would be met with "a full retaliatory response upon the Soviet Union," and, in a sentence that summed up the dilemma at the heart of policy in the nuclear age, stated, "We will not prematurely or unnecessarily risk the costs of worldwide nuclear war in which even the fruits of victory would be ashes in our mouth—but neither will we shrink from that risk at any time it must be faced."

Khrushchev's reasons for the deployment were unclear to Kennedy and his advisers. Secretary of Defense Robert McNamara flatly stated to the president that the missiles in Cuba would not materially alter the balance of strategic nuclear power. Most of Kennedy's other advisers agreed. What were Khrushchev's motives, then? Something like a consensus on this matter has subsequently emerged among historians. In the first place, Khrushchev saw the deployment as a means to protect Cuba against a repeat of the kind of attack that the United States had mounted at the Bay of Pigs to overthrow the socialist government of Fidel Castro in 1961, shortly after Kennedy had arrived in office. In the second place, he sought to redress a nuclear imbalance that favored the United States. In the late 1950s and early 1960s, the United States outmatched the Soviet Union in nuclear striking power. In 1960, for example, the United States possessed six thousand nuclear warheads, the Soviet Union three hundred. Of these, only a fraction were mounted on the Soviet Union's mere thirty-five missiles capable of reaching the United States. Khrushchev of course knew this, although during the presidential campaign of 1960 Senator Kennedy had erroneously claimed that it was the United States that suffered from a "missile gap" with the Soviet Union. For a while the error suited the needs of Khrushchev, who was not only aware of his country's nuclear inferiority but afraid that the Americans would use it to advantage. He adopted a policy of bluster and bluff. In August of 1961, the head of the K.G.B., Aleksandr Shelepin, had proposed to an enthusiastic Khrushchev that the U.S.S.R. launch a campaign of disinformation to persuade the United States that its nuclear forces were more powerful than in fact they were. Khrushchev also threatened intermittently to shut off Western access to Berlin and, if the United States should oppose him, to annihilate its European allies. On one occasion, for example, he noted that six hydrogen bombs would be "quite enough" to destroy the British Isles, and nine would be enough for France. "Why should two hundred million people die for two million Berliners?" he asked.

Once in office, the Kennedy administration discovered, or feigned to discover, that there was no missile gap—or, rather, that there was one and it overwhelmingly favored the United States. In a speech delivered by Undersecretary of Defense Roswell Gilpatric in October of 1961, the administration set forth the facts. "The destructive power which the United States could bring to bear even after a Soviet surprise attack upon our forces," he stated, "would be as great as, perhaps greater than, the total undamaged force which the enemy can threaten to launch against the United States in a first strike." Now Khrushchev's bluff had been publicly called. One of his responses was to detonate the largest hydrogen bomb ever exploded on earth to date or since—a monster that unleashed fifty megatons of explosive power, equivalent to almost four thousand Hiroshima bombs. Another response may have been the decision to place nuclear-armed missiles in Cuba.

Kennedy's national security adviser, McGeorge Bundy, later noted that the administration he served did not believe that its immense nuclear superiority was a source of great political advantage. At the time of the missile crisis, American officials were more impressed, Bundy believed, by the tens of millions of casualties that the Soviet Union *could* cause than by the imbalance in the two countries' nuclear arsenals. Hence they were blind to the danger that Khrushchev, thinking the U.S.S.R. weak, might take reckless action to redress the inequality.

This persuasive account of the origins of the Cuban missile crisis illustrates the novel rules of the game in a nuclear-armed world. Only in the nuclear age could it be considered reckless for a great power to publicly expose the weakness of its adversary. For only in an age in which appearances in military matters take precedence over actualities would an inequality of forces *in fact* appear far more tolerable to the weaker side than an inequality of forces *in appearance*.

The resolution of the crisis teaches the same lesson. Khrushchev, perhaps without quite knowing it, had breached the rules of the game in a nuclear-armed world. He had taken a step that, in his adversary's eyes, threatened fatal damage to its own credibility. And yet reversal of that step would threaten *Soviet* credibility. The logic of credibility, once this situation had arisen, pointed toward war; but war in the nuclear age, as Kennedy and Khrushchev were aware, was senseless.

At the height of the crisis, Khrushchev wrote in his memoirs, he privately asked his generals if they could assure him "that holding fast would not result in the death of five hundred million human beings." He went on to report, "They looked at me as though I was out of my mind or, what was worse, a traitor. The biggest tragedy, as they saw it, was not that our country might be devastated and everything lost, but that the Chinese or the Albanians would accuse us of appeasement or weakness." He was led to wonder, "What good would it have done me in the last hour of my life to know that, though our great nation and the United States were in complete ruin, the national honor of the Soviet Union was intact?" Khrushchev's recollection of his fit of sanity in insane circumstances goes to the heart of the contradiction inherent in the nuclear policies of the Cold War era. On the one side of the nuclear ledger was the need to uphold "national honor," or credibility. This required shows of resolve, even military action. On the other side was the threat to the lives of hundreds of millions of human beings. This required restraint. The main aims that nuclear arsenals were meant to serve—preventing war and pursuing national interests—were now in collision, and one, it seemed, had to be given up.

In a parallel episode, Kennedy at a certain moment took his aide Pierre Salinger outside the room in which the Executive Committee dealing with the crisis was meeting, and asked him whether he thought the people inside realized that if he made a mistake there might be two hundred million dead. It's striking that both leaders felt so alone in their terrible knowledge that they were able to communicate it only in side conversations, or later in their memoirs. Perhaps Kennedy at that moment remembered some advice given him a few months earlier by former secretary of state Dean Acheson regarding the use of nuclear weapons in the Berlin crisis of 1961. Acheson counseled that "the president should himself give that question [whether to use nuclear weapons in a crisis in Europe] the most careful and private consideration, well before the time when the choice might present itself, that he should reach his own clear conclusion in advance as to what he would do, and that he should tell no one at all what that conclusion was." Bundy, who was present, drew the obvious conclusion: that Acheson, "the most ardent and eloquent advocate of energetic action to make nuclear risk credible to Khrushchev, a true believer in fighting hard with strong conventional forces for the freedom of West Berlin, nevertheless believed that at the moment of final choice, the course of 'wisdom and restraint' might be to accept local defeat without the use of nuclear weapons." What is notable about the story is that at the hour of truth the decision not to use nuclear weapons—certainly the most important that any president would ever make—had to be such a deep secret that even the man giving the recommendation to him in a private meeting dared not utter it in plain English. All *public* counsel, all statements of theory and policy, including, most especially, those made by the president, had to support the use of nuclear weapons. To do otherwise would be unilateral disarmament by verbal means. Only the president's private resolve, never to be spoken aloud—frail refuge of sanity, of safety for all humankind!—could counsel restraint. National leaders have often spoken of the loneliness of the decisions they must make. Surely, no decision could ever be lonelier than this.

Later, Kennedy formulated the quandary in which the Cuban missile crisis had placed him no less succinctly than Khrushchev had, and in almost identical terms. He and his advisers were well aware that the Cuban missiles did not change the strategic balance of power significantly. But, Kennedy explained, "it would have politically changed the balance of power. It would have appeared to, and appearances contribute to reality."

How, then, did Kennedy and Khrushchev escape war? The answer, in a word, was *secrecy*. If appearances—of soiled honor, of "weakness," of lost credibility, of lack of resolve, of humiliation in the eyes of Albanians, and so forth—were the problem, then what better solution than to hide the facts that might create those appearances? Khrushchev was the first to resort to this method. He sent two messages to Kennedy—one public, the other private. In the private message—a long, secret, personal letter expressing in vivid terms his horror of nuclear war and his determination to avoid it—he offered a deal in which the Soviet missiles in Cuba would be removed in exchange for a promise by the United States not to invade the island. This was highly acceptable to the United States. However, in his public stance, made known the next day, Khruschev added a crucial condition—he demanded the removal of American missiles stationed near the Soviet Union in Turkey. While in private Khrushchev could afford to seem "weak," in public he had to appear "tough."

The administration had planned to remove the Turkish missiles soon in any case. Couldn't it simply go ahead with the plan as part of the settlement? The problem was credibility. The actual strategic position of the United States would not be harmed by the removal of the Turkish missiles. However, any public decision for removal under pressure of the Soviet deployment in Cuba would harm U.S. credibility, especially with its NATO allies.

Now it was the United States' turn to take refuge in secret assurances. The president resorted to the ploy of ignoring Khrushchev's tough, public stand while seeking to agree to the more moderate, private one. That was Kennedy's public position—a tough-seeming one, since it yielded no ground on the Turkish missiles. However, like Khrushchev, he also put forward a "weak" private position: he gave in on the Turkish missiles. But he did so only on condition that the concession remain forever secret. Keeping the missiles in Turkey, however useless militarily, had been declared American policy. Invading Cuba had not. Therefore, giving the no-invasion pledge would leave American credibility intact, while removing the missiles would undermine it.

This consideration illuminates an extraordinary action now taken by President Kennedy and a few officials of his administration. Without telling the whole Executive Committee what they were doing, they traded away the Turkish missiles in a back-channel deal. Then they took a vow of silence regarding the secret agreement, demanding and receiving assurances that the Soviets would do the same. We may suspect that the reason was domestic politics, especially when we recall that at a meeting of the Executive Committee McNamara said, "I'll be quite frank: I don't think there *is* a military problem here. . . . This is a domestic political problem." And unquestionably politics was on the minds of the president and his advisers, who feared Republican charges that they were "soft on Communism." But the dictates of high strategy seconded the requirements of domestic politics. In his speech to the nation on October 22, the president had confirmed the crucial geopolitical role of credibility in his thinking when he referred to the placement of the missiles in Cuba as an "unjustified change in the status quo which cannot be accepted by this country if our courage and our commitment are ever to be trusted again by either friend or foe." In a world in which appearances were not an afterthought of policy but its substance, the president and his advisers felt compelled to make their decisions on the basis not of the actual strategic balance but of what it looked like to the world at large.

From beginning to end of the crisis, the president and his advisers never deviated from this iron rule. When the Soviet ambassador, Anatoly Dobrynin, later gave Robert Kennedy a letter expressing his government's agreement to the Turkish missile deal in writing, Kennedy angrily handed it back, saying (according to Kennedy's notes of talking points for the conversation), "Take your letter—Reconsider it & if you feel it is necessary to write letters then we will also write one which you cannot enjoy. Also if you should publish any document indicating a deal then it is off & also if done afterward will further affect the relationship." The Soviets withdrew the letter, and the vow of secrecy was kept on both sides for years afterward.

The ingenuity, if not the propriety, of this bigovernmental conspiracy of silence against the rest of the world is remarkable. At first glance, it might appear that by agreeing to the American demand for secrecy Khrushchev was permitting the United States to preserve its credibility at the expense of his own—no small concession, given the central role that credibility played at all moments in the crisis on both sides. Certainly, Khrushchev was widely perceived by the general public as having backed down without having received much in return. In assessing this question, however, it is important to remember that credibility is an impression made by one party on another. Its value depends on the audience you wish to impress. In the case of the United States that audience included America's allies as well as congressional and public opinion. The record shows that the Kennedy men were particularly worried about the response of

NATO to a deal to surrender the Turkish missiles. Secrecy regarding the deal preserved American credibility with its crucial
audiences. Khrushchev, who presided over a closed society, on
the other hand, needed to maintain his credibility with a much
smaller audience: high party members, generals, and the leaders
of a few independent-minded communist parties. No congress
or public would review his decisions. And no allied government other than the Chinese and Albanian communist parties
was in a position to second-guess him. Only his immediate
colleagues (who did in fact remove him from power in 1964)
were a danger. Khrushchev sent his first, "weak" letter privately
but drafted his second, "tough" one in front of the Politburo.
With this all-important audience, who knew that Kennedy
had yielded on the Turkish missiles, therefore, Khrushchev's
credibility might well be preserved. As for the world at large,
Khrushchev would have to make do with an American pledge
not to invade Cuba.

Two years later, Robert McNamara was asked at a congressional committee hearing, "Are you aware of any agreement,
any assurance, by yourself or anyone else in high government
office, to Khrushchev that if he would withdraw at the time
under the conditions that you showed us, the United States
would thereby commit itself to any particular course of action?" McNamara answered, "I am not only unaware of any
agreement, it is inconceivable to me that our President would
enter in a discussion of any such agreement. Moreover, there
were absolutely no undisclosed agreements associated with the
withdrawal of the Soviet missiles from Cuba." In calling the
decision that the president had actually taken "inconceivable,"
McNamara kept the administration's vow of secrecy, and gave
powerful evidence of the primacy of appearances in the strategies of the nuclear age.

Even if we are critical of this conspiracy of silence, *which included the Soviet government while excluding the American people,*
we can still admire the dexterity with which both Khrushchev
and Kennedy extricated themselves from a logic that pushed
both of them toward annihilation. Precisely because the most
important moves had been made in secret, however, that logic
remained unimpaired and in full force throughout the years of
the Cold War, though without producing any further crises as

severe as the Cuban missile crisis. It's a sobering commentary on the nuclear policy to which the two men were committed that their most statesmanlike decisions were those they had to hide most assiduously from the world.

The shift from the primacy of force to the primacy of appearances was momentous in the history of war. It signified a real, if equivocal, official recognition that the age-old war system had become an anachronism. The true targets of the missiles of the nuclear age have, in the more than half century since Nagasaki, been the minds, not the bodies, of opponents. The true instruments of this warfare have been not actual warheads flying across oceans but the images of those warheads conveyed in public statements and in the media. And the goal of policy, however shot through with contradiction and apocalyptic danger, was to head off war, not to fight it.

The gap between the political ends of foreign policy and the military logic of strategy that had been growing steadily since Clausewitz's time had widened to the point of no return. And if, possibly, the benefits of nuclear deterrence were real, in that a peace that otherwise might have broken down was preserved, so was its unremitting, intolerable cost: that, day by day, it risked the extinction of the human species and involved all the nuclear powers and their peoples in the complicity of actively planning for this supreme crime. But was there some other final arbiter—some method whereby freedom of action would be restored? To answer this question, we need to examine a military development that ran parallel to the nuclear revolution—the rise of people's war.

3

People's War

The ascending spiral of violence in which Clausewitzian war, driven by its own "logical" need to run to extremes, drew the newborn Promethean energies of the modern age, one after another, into its mighty orbit—leading, in a paradoxical culmination, to the terrorized calm of the nuclear stalemate—was one of the two major developments in the metamorphosis of war in the modern age. The second, concurrent development led in an opposite direction: away from the blackboards and computer screens in the superpowers' think tanks, scientific laboratories, and missile ranges, where they pursued ever-more-costly, technically elaborate methods of war, and down into poor, "underdeveloped" peasant villages and remote swamps and jungles, where scientifically unsophisticated people were incubating methods of warfare that, in their own way, were scarcely less "absolute" than the total war of the great powers and, in the long run, were to prove the more successful invention. These were the methods of people's war. If, to anticipate, nuclear weapons, by spoiling the old final arbiter, conventional war, posed the question of how disputes in the international sphere were *now* to be settled, then people's war, though not itself yet the answer the world needed, pointed the way to an answer. For while nuclear weapons were producing stalemate people's war was changing the political map of the earth.

THE WORLD REVOLT

Like the invention of nuclear weapons, the rise of people's war has a wider context—the centuries-long movement of the peoples of the earth to achieve self-determination. Some rebellions were of colonies in revolt against a mother country, some were of nations with long histories of battling conquerors, and some were of indigenous populations oppressed by imperial overlords. The guiding principle of all of them, however, was to drive out a hated occupier and establish rule by local people—the "self" of the word "self-determination." The freedom to which a movement for self-determination aspired was *sometimes* freedom of the individual; it was *always* freedom of the national, collective self from foreign rule. The period in question is roughly the same as that of the democratic revolution, of which the self-determination movement has been a part.

As its beginning we can plausibly name July 4, 1776, when the American Continental Congress declared to the world that the American people meant to "assume among the powers of the earth the separate and equal station to which the laws of nature and nature's God entitled them." It was also in the American Revolution that a form of people's war, the use of militias, made its first appearance in an anti-imperial cause of modern times. Some years later, one of the signers of the declaration, John Adams, looking toward what would prove a distant future, asked, "When will France, Spain, England and Holland renounce their selfish, contracted, exclusive systems of religion, government, and commerce?" And he answered with a prophecy: "They may depend upon it, their present systems of colonization cannot endure. Colonies universally, ardently breathe for independence. No man who has a soul will ever live in a colony under the present establishments one moment longer than necessity compels him."

Substantial fulfillment of Adams's prophecy came in August of 1991, when the president of Russia, Boris Yeltsin, and the presidents of two other republics of the Soviet Union declared the foundation of the Commonwealth of Independent States and the dissolution of the Soviet Union, the last of the European empires. Between 1776 and that date, all the empires that had existed, whether dynastic, colonial, or both, and all the territorial empires that subsequently arose, including those built on revolutionary foundations, were destroyed. In the former category were the Russian empire of the czars; the Austro-Hungarian Empire of the Hapsburgs; the German empire of the Hohenzollerns; the Ottoman Empire; and the colonial empires of Holland, England, France, Belgium, Spain, and Italy. In the latter category were the Napoleonic empire in the early nineteenth century, the Japanese "Co-Prosperity Sphere" in Asia in the 1930s and forties, Hitler's "thousand-year

Reich," and the Soviet empire. (I leave until later the special case of the mainly nonterritorial empire of the United States that arose in the second half of the twentieth century.)

Broadly speaking, the peoples of the earth assumed their "rightful stations" in three waves. The first, which followed soon after the American War of Independence, commenced when the victims of Napoleon's imperial ambitions, including Clausewitz's Prussia, threw off the French yoke, giving birth, in the process, to a full-fledged conservative nationalism that would be replicated in various versions down to our time. It continued until the First World War, when the last of the great European monarchies fell. The example of the nation-states of Europe, in which peoples created states, or else the states created peoples, and in which both were wedded to a precisely defined, jealously defended national territory, became the model for the subsequent waves. Concurrently, the Spanish empire, an early victim of the anticolonial rebellion, was overthrown by the Latin American peoples.

In the second wave, which lasted roughly from 1905, when Japan defeated Russia, until the mid-1970s, when Portugal gave up its empire in Africa, the rest of the peoples of the European colonies and dependencies rose up, in what Leonard Woolf called a "world revolt," to liberate themselves from their Western (and Japanese) masters. Combining imitation with resistance, they adopted whatever they needed of European ideas and techniques to drive the Europeans out. In the nineteenth century, even as the nations of Europe were learning democracy at home, they had been practicing its opposite in the world at large. Their philosophy in the colonies was, on the whole, that of Lord Milner, the English proconsul in Egypt in the 1880s, who wrote in his *England in Egypt* that although, "As a true born Briton, I of course take off my hat to everything that calls itself Franchise, Parliament, Representation of the People, the Voice of the Majority, and all the rest of it," nevertheless, "as an observer of the actual condition of Egyptian society, I cannot shut my eyes to the fact that popular government, as we understand it, is for a longer time than anyone can foresee at present out of the question." Or, as Kipling, describing his vision of imperial rule, wrote approvingly of the English:

> They terribly carpet the earth with dead,
>   and before their cannons cool,
> They walk unarmed by twos and threes,
>   to call the living to school.

As this picture of massacre as a prelude to educational uplift suggests, the imperial policies of the European democracies were founded on a thoroughgoing contradiction. Claiming democracy and national independence, they denied it to the colonial peoples, who unsurprisingly resolved the contradiction in favor of independence.

In the third wave of self-determination, which occurred suddenly, as if the accumulated experience of the anti-imperial movements were now being applied in a hurry, the peoples of Eastern Europe and of the Soviet Union rose up against the Soviet empire, which, like a dynasty of old, departed the stage of history entirely.

The self-determination movement cut across all political dividing lines. No political system, feudal or modern, proved capable of resisting it. Neither monarchies (the Romanovs, the Hapsburgs, the Hohenzollerns, the Ottomans, Spain) nor liberal democracies (England, Holland, the United States) nor military dictatorships (France under Napoleon, Portugal under Salazar and Caetano) nor communist regimes (the Soviet Union; Vietnam, in its Cambodian venture) were able, in the long run, to perpetuate colonial rule. On the other hand, almost every political creed was adequate for winning independence. Liberal democracy (the United States in 1776, Eastern Europe in the 1980s and nineties), communism (China, Vietnam, Cambodia), racism (the Boers of South Africa), militarism (many South American states), theocracy (Iran and Afghanistan in the 1980s), and even monarchy (Germany in the first half of the nineteenth century), have all proved adequate foundations on which to base self-determination.

The methods of the movements were as diverse as their contents. Some resorted to military force (the United States, China, Vietnam, Algeria, to name only four); some were nonviolent (India, the nations of Eastern Europe, with the exceptions of Yugoslavia and Romania). Some arose from "below," after the pattern of the American and French revolutions, and some were led from "above," after the pattern of the foundation, under Bismarck, of modern Germany. Some won success overnight (the republics of the former Soviet Union), others so slowly that the process was almost imperceptible (Canada).

The independence of the countries of the world was not, on the whole, granted willingly but compelled. Even when independence was achieved by mutual agreement—as in India after the Second World War—it was the result of decades of national struggle. The rulers of empires searched their tool kits of power in vain for the instruments that would bring rebellious colonial populations to heel—a lesson driven home once and for all by the failures of the United States in Vietnam and the Soviet Union in Afghanistan. The movement of resistance and reform in Eastern Europe and the Soviet Union, in the third wave, placed the power of popular resistance on even clearer display. Their victories posed in the sharpest possible form the question that the entire two-century-long movement for self-determination has put before the world: What power has enabled poorly armed or unarmed or entirely nonviolent popular movements to defeat the military forces of the most powerful empires of the past two centuries?

A TRANSFORMATION OF POLITICS

Although people's war was above all a phenomenon of the twentieth century, it first appeared in Europe during the peninsular war of 1807–14, in which the Spanish people mounted fierce resistance to Napoleonic conquest. (This is the war whose savagery is recorded in the work of Francisco Goya.) As it happens, Clausewitz devoted only one brief section of *On War* to people's war, but in those few pages he recognized the novelty and importance of the new kind of conflict. Guerrilla war per se (the Spanish rebellion gave the world this Spanish word) was not a new phenomenon. In the eighteenth century, it had been called *la petite guerre*, and before that, among other things, Parthian war, after the Parthians of antiquity, who were given to hit-and-run attacks on horseback. The unprecedented element in the early years of the nineteenth century was not guerrilla war but the sustained support given the guerrillas by the civilian population of the nation. Guerrilla bands took control of large areas of the Spanish countryside; waylaid French couriers, forcing them to travel with large armed guards; worked to deny the French supplies; harassed and attacked French troops; and spied on the French for the English. Just as important, they crippled the administration of Joseph Bonaparte by an organized refusal to pay taxes to his regime or otherwise cooperate with it. Soon, Joseph's administrators were going unpaid, his commands unfollowed. The French responded with draconian measures that would become all too familiar over the next two centuries: looting, rape, torture, burning of villages, wholesale executions and reprisals. The rebellion blazed most intensely in the city of Saragossa, where the population fought to "the last wall in the last house." "No supreme command had ordered the city to hold out; there was no supreme command. There was only the instinctive knowledge that a nation cannot keep its identity unless it is prepared to fight for it against all hope." Such was the new form of warfare that flared up in Spain—spontaneous, uncalculating, desperate, savage, unquenchable.

Clausewitz placed the new phenomenon in the wider context of the transformation of war that he was witnessing and analyzing. As examples of the "enormous contribution the heart and temper of a nation can make to the sum total of its politics, war potential, and fighting strength," he listed "the stubborn resistance of the Spaniards" which showed "what can be accomplished by arming a people"; the Russian campaign of 1812, which, by defeating Napoleon, showed that "eventual success does not always decrease in proportion to lost battles, captured capitals, and occupied provinces"; and the Prussian military recovery of 1813, which showed that a "militia can fight as well in foreign countries as at home." The recruitment of Napoleon's revolutionary armies had been Act I in the drama of the democratic revolution's influence on warfare, but now, with the Spanish guerrilla resistance to those armies, there was a second act. Clausewitz observed, "Clearly, the tremendous effects of the French Revolution abroad were caused not so much by new military methods and concepts as by radical changes in policies and administration, by the new character of government, altered conditions of the French people, and the like." He further explains:

> The military art on which the politicians relied was part of a world they thought was real—a branch of current statecraft, a familiar tool that had been in use for many years. But *that* form of war naturally shared in the errors of policy, and therefore could provide no corrective. It is true that war itself has undergone significant changes in character and methods, changes that had brought it closer to its absolute form. But these changes did not come about because the French government freed itself, so to speak, from the harness of policy; they were caused by the new political conditions which the French Revolution created.

In a word, "It follows that the transformation of the art of war resulted from the *transformation of politics*."

There is no doubt that Clausewitz was right in seeing the French Revolution and the Spanish popular revolt as expressions of a single underlying phenomenon, the democratic revolution of his time. However, with the benefit of our century and a half of hindsight, it's clear that each was also the starting point for one of two long, diverging evolutionary transformations of war that led in different directions. The Prussian mobilization and reform, for example, aimed at raising vast armies of patriotic citizens in imitation of France, and so was a stage in the expansion of the conventional war system that led eventually to the nuclear stalemate of the Cold War. The commanders of conventional war had always wanted more men to fight with; now the "nation in arms" supplied men in unparalleled abundance. The commanders had always sought zealous, brave soldiers; now the recruits, fired by revolutionary and national enthusiasm, brought their inspiration with them.

The relationship of people's war, as practiced in Spain, to conventional war, on the other hand, was entirely different. Whereas the *levée en masse* of the patriotic citizens, like its later Prussian and other derivatives, nourished conventional war, people's war subverted it. In Spain, as in people's war of later times, the side with more men, more and better weapons, more logistical support was regularly bested by a militarily weaker opponent. Such results were completely contrary to the rules that were supposed to govern conventional war. The renowned military writer Henri Jomini, who fought in the French army in Spain, was one of the first to note the change. "No army, however disciplined," he wrote, "can contend successfully against such a system [people's war] applied by a great nation unless it be strong enough to hold all the essential points of the country, cover its communications and at the same time furnish an active force sufficient to defeat the enemy wherever he may present himself." The experience left Jomini with a feeling of awestruck horror: "The spectacle of a spontaneous uprising of a nation is rarely seen; and, though there be in it something grand and noble which commands our admiration the consequences are so terrible that, for the sake of humanity, we ought to hope never to see it." In later years, it would become a commonplace to say that to defeat guerrilla forces a conventional army needed a numerical advantage of ten to one, or even, some said, twenty to one. But how could that be? If superior force, supposedly the final arbiter, was no longer decisive, then what was? Was there, in people's war, an arbiter *beyond* the conventional final arbiter?

In an even more confusing departure from the rules governing conventional war, victory in battles over guerrilla forces did not advance victory in the war as a whole. Clausewitz had firmly stated the seemingly inarguable proposition (and several generations of German and other military leaders were to learn his advice by heart) that "All action is undertaken in the belief that if the ultimate test of arms should actually occur, the outcome would be *favorable*." Yet a French captain who accompanied Napoleon in Russia, where his army, in addition to facing the Russian winter, was harassed by guerrilla bands, said, "Every victory is a loss to us"—a saying that the historian of guerrilla war Robert B. Asprey has called "a book of wisdom in a single sentence."

Inasmuch as neither possessing superior forces nor winning battles appeared to be the key to victory in people's war, the race to Clausewitz's "extremes"—to the massing and concentration of ever greater resources of violence characteristic of conventional war—did not take place. The Spanish guerrilla leader Mina, anticipating Mao Zedong by more than a century, said, "When the French pressure gets too hard, I retreat. . . . The French pursue me, and get tired, they leave people behind, and on these I jump." And a Prussian officer serving with the

French later penned a lamentation of a kind that was on the lips of many a subsequent soldier sent to fight a guerrilla opponent. "Wherever we arrived, they disappeared," he complained, "whenever we left, they arrived—they were everywhere and nowhere, they had no tangible center which could be attacked." The pitched battle, which was the centerpiece of conventional war, was simply sidestepped in people's war. Rather than seeking to win battles, the people in arms sought mainly to endure. The superior importance in guerrilla campaigns of endurance was summed up by an American who had been in Vietnam, the foreign-service officer Norman B. Hannah, who said, "We ran out of time. This is the tragedy of Vietnam—we were fighting for time rather than space. And time ran out."

THE WEAPONS OF CIVILIZATION

The expansion of conventional war in the modern age was continuous and smooth. Once mass conscription, light artillery, or tanks were invented by one country, they were available for adoption by every country possessing the necessary technical abilities. The evolution of people's war, by contrast, was fitful. The experience and achievement of one generation often was unknown to the next. Books on people's war written in the nineteenth century went unread in the twentieth. Each imperial power, it seemed, tackled guerrilla resistance to its rule with refreshed ignorance.

During the balance of the nineteenth century, conventional war and the conventional thinking that went with it remained dominant. The center of Europe proved to be stony soil for people's war (although the French fought a rearguard partisan campaign after their defeat by Germany in 1871). By the turn of the century, the big army divisions appeared firmly in charge, and "the days of guerrilla wars seemed to be over," in the words of the historian Walter Laqueur. However, appearances misled. The twentieth century was to witness the fullest flowering of people's war. Colonial resistance to imperialism was its breeding ground.

The confrontation between the modern imperial West and the world's traditional societies presents one of the most extreme disparities in the power of civilizations that has ever existed—a disparity wider by far, for instance, than that between ancient Rome and the peoples she subjugated. When, in 1519, the Spaniard Cortés arrived in Mexico, dreaming of gold; when, in 1620, the first Puritan pilgrims landed in Massachusetts to practice their faith; when, in 1743, the Englishman Robert Clive arrived in India to make his fortune; when, in the early 1840s, English gunboats steamed up the rivers of China to enforce her acceptance of the opium trade; when, in 1853, Commodore Matthew Perry sailed an American fleet into Japanese waters to compel Japan to enter into trade and other relations with the rest of the world; when, throughout the nineteenth century, a swelling stream of merchants, adventurers, missionaries, outcasts, con men, criminals, philanthropists, soldiers, and explorers—in short, the whole gamut of imperial intruders—arrived in the villages of Africa, each of these Westerners was backed by instruments of modern power that most of the native populations were helpless to resist, or even to comprehend. (Incomprehension, at least, was mutual.)

The traditional civilizations of Asia, Africa, the Near East, and South America were compelled, at gunpoint, to inaugurate full-scale revolutions not just in their politics but also, in most cases, in their economies, their cultures, and their social structures. In Leonard Woolf's words, "in no other period of the world's history has there been such a vast revolution as this conquest of Asia and Africa by Europe in less than 100 years." All felt compelled to Westernize, or modernize (two processes that were all but impossible to distinguish), almost every aspect of their collective lives. A generation of Chinese political reformers and intellectuals, for example, were forced to ask themselves what the sources of Western power were, and what China would have to do to create them. How much of traditional Chinese society and culture could be saved, how much should be thrown out? Could Western technical achievements be grafted onto Eastern social structures? Or were the roots of China's weakness, and of her humiliation at the hands of other powers, deeper still?

Such was the form that the implacable pressure of the adapt-or-die war system took in the colonial world. The pressure on the colonial peoples was of a piece with that felt not so long before by Prussia and Napoleon's other European victims. The difference was that whereas the latter, sharing the achievements of European civilization, were capable of catching up quite rapidly, the former, possessing civilizations largely unrelated to the European, needed more than a century to make their adjustments—if they have yet adjusted. Although the increasing power of the modern West had many roots, its cutting edge, in the East as elsewhere, was military force. Nowhere did A. J. P. Taylor's observation that for the great powers of the nineteenth century power meant the power to make war hold true more obviously than in the imperial theater, where the Great Game was played. And nowhere, in the adapt-or-die system that fastened its grip on the world at this time, was more of the dying going on than in the imperial colonies, in which nations by the dozen, and even whole peoples (for example, the native tribes in the Americas), were being propelled toward the evolutionary scrap heap designated for them in the social Darwinist theory fashionable at the time.

Although imperialism began as often as not with economic exploitation, almost all the confrontations between a traditional society and the West were resolved by a decisive test of arms, in which the power relations of the two sides were brutally clarified. For India, for example, it was the battle of Plassey of 1757; for China, the Opium Wars; for Japan, the mission of Commodore Perry. The sword of the West, honed and tempered in the fires of the modern scientific and social revolutions, sliced with terrifying ease through the Chinese "melon" (as it was called at the turn of the century), through the limbs of the Ottoman "sick man of Europe," through the grass houses of the defenseless villages of Kipling's "lower breeds without the law" in Africa and elsewhere. The story of colonial battles forms a monotonous record of one-sided slaughter, relieved only occasionally by the exceptions (the defeat of an English army by the Afghans in the early 1840s and of Italy by Ethiopia at Adowa in 1896).

The battle of Omdurman waged against the Sudanese forces of the Khalifah in 1898 by Lord Kitchener, on his way to his rendezvous with Marchand at Fashoda, can stand as a representative of all of these battles—the better for having been described firsthand by the talented young war correspondent Winston Churchill.

As Lord Kitchener's army moved up the Nile there stretched behind it those two prime symbols of power in the late nineteenth century, a new-built railroad and a telegraph wire. On the Nile, alongside Kitchener's line of march, proceeded two gunboats, transported, by way of the river, hundreds of miles into the desert. On the day of the battle, young Churchill took up a position on a hill overlooking the scene, and had lunch ("like a meal before the races"). Below him, the British forces had formed a square. Inside the square were Maxim guns; to one side a light-artillery regiment. The two gunboats on the Nile moved within range. The Khalifah's men massed behind a ridge. In midmorning, they appeared on its crest, looking, from where Churchill stood, like bushes. He describes what happened next:

> Suddenly the whole black line . . . began to move. It was made of men, not bushes. Behind it other immense masses and lines of men appeared over the crest; and while we watched, amazed by the wonder of the sight, the whole face of the slope became black with swarming savages. Four miles from end to end, and as it seemed in five great divisions, the mighty army advanced swiftly. The whole side of the hill seemed to move. Between the masses horsemen galloped continually; before them many patrols dotted the plain; above them waved hundreds of banners, and the sun, glinting on many thousand hostile spear-points, spread a sparkling cloud.

Churchill confesses to a moment of anxiety. However, he had confidence in "the weapons of science," which he also called "the weapons of civilization." He knew what was waiting for the onrushing Sudanese army: "The ranges were known. It was a matter of machinery." The weapons of civilization opened fire, and

> about twenty shells struck them in the first minute. Some burst high in the air, others exactly in their faces. Others, again, plunged into the sand and, exploding, dashed clouds of red dust, splinters, and bullets amid their ranks. The white banners toppled over in all directions.

For a moment, it seemed that the charging cavalry might reach the English camel corps, but just in time one of the gunboats began to fire its Maxim guns:

> The range was short; the effect tremendous. The terrible machine, floating gracefully on the waters—a beautiful white devil—wreathed itself in smoke. The river slopes of the Kerreri Hills, crowded with the advancing thousands, sprang up into clouds of dust and splinters of rock.

And the English? Churchill describes a scene more like assembly-line production than war.

> They fired steadily and stolidly, without hurry or excitement, for the enemy were far away and the officers careful. Besides, the soldiers were interested in the work and took great pains. But presently the mere physical act became tedious. The tiny figures seen over the slide of the back-sight seemed a little larger, but also fewer at each successive volley. The rifles grew hot—so hot that they had to be changed for those of the reserve companies. . . . Their empty cartridge-cases, tinkling to the ground, formed small but growing heaps beside each man. And all the time out on the plain on the other side bullets were shearing through flesh, smashing and splintering bone; blood spouted from terrible wounds; valiant men were struggling on through a hell of whistling metal, exploding shells, and spurting dust—suffering, despairing, dying.

When it was over, the tally of the dead was thirteen thousand Sudanese and forty-eight Englishmen. The youthful Churchill turned reflective. The Khalifah's military plan had been excellent, he thought. Its only flaw had been the "extraordinary miscalculation of the power of modern weapons." He rejected the thought that the Khalifah's forces were guilty of "mad fanaticism." He had been stirred by the courage of the Sudanese in the face of modern war. "For I hope," he wrote, "that if evil days should come upon our own country, and the last army which a collapsing Empire could interpose between London and the invader were dissolving in rout and ruin, that there would be some—even in these modern days—who would not care to accustom themselves to a new order of things and tamely survive the disaster." Thus did England's future prime minister, as he watched the Khalifah's army fall in the desert of Omdurman, anticipate the battle of Britain—a battle with a better result for the defenders. As he watched the British airmen in their silver planes hold the Nazis across the channel at bay, we may wonder, did he remember the sparkling cloud of the Khalifah's charge almost a half century before?

The lopsided casualty figures were typical of colonial battles. Cortés overthrew the civilization of the Aztecs with five hundred men, ten bronze cannons, and twelve muskets. In the battle of Blood River, in 1838, Boer forces slew three thousand Zulus while losing only three themselves. At the battle of Plassey, Clive, with a force of eight hundred Europeans and two thousand Indians, defeated an army of fifty thousand, with a loss of only twenty-two men. In 1865, in Tashkent, in just one of a series of such battles, a Tatar army of thirty thousand was defeated by a Russian army of two thousand. In 1897, "a Royal Niger Co. force composed of 32 Europeans and 507 African soldiers armed with cannons, Maxim guns, and Snider rifles defeated the 31,000-man army of the Nupe Emirate of Sokoto." In a "battle" that the English invader Younghusband waged against the Tibetans in 1903, six hundred Tibetans were killed without British losses, and then "The remnant simply turned and walked away with bowed heads."

People's war was a means to redress the shocking imbalance revealed by these battles, though not, it is true, the only means. In Japan, the solution was hell-bent imitation of the Western conventional model, including the highly self-conscious importation of the political and social organizations of the West. The Japanese race to adopt Western ways, which the writer Natsumei Soseki likened to an Olympics run by the insane, resulted in Japan's victory over Russia in 1905. Japan had accepted the military system whose rules had been fixed by the West, met a Western country on its own ground, and won. In India, the solution was Gandhi's satyagraha—the nonviolent path to independence from imperial rule, of which we will have more to say later. In China, in Vietnam, and in Algeria, among other places, the solution was people's war.

POLITICS IN COMMAND

Its first practitioners were the people of China. The Chinese revolutionary war of the 1920s through the 1940s was a war for independence (against the Japanese invaders) grafted onto a civil war (between the Communist Party and the Kuomintang government) associated with a worldwide revolutionary movement (the communist movement, presided over by the Soviet-run Comintern) fought within the overall context of a world war (the Second World War). Within this larger framework, however, the specific engine that propelled China toward communist rule was people's war. China was not as weak in relation to Japan as Sudan had been in relation to Lord Kitchener, yet battle after battle demonstrated China's inability to face Japan in conventional war. Mao Zedong, only recently confirmed as the undisputed leader of the Communist Party of China, acknowledged this humiliating fact with complete candor in June of 1938. He stated, "We are still a weak country, and, in striking contrast to the enemy, are inferior in military, economic and political-organizational power." Japan, by contrast, was "a powerful imperialist country which ranks first in military, economic and political-organizational power in the East and counts as one of the five or six outstanding imperialist countries in the world." Unable to compete on the conventional, Clausewitzian field of battle, China would, in a manner of speaking, open up a new field of battle—one on which, Mao believed, China's people themselves could appear in strength.

But how, exactly, could people's war enable a weak and backward people to defeat a modern nation-state equipped with the most technically advanced arms? What advantage did it possess? In a single chorus, the leaders of the Chinese revolution broadcast their answer to the world. It was the very word that Clausewitz had used to explain the surprising power of the Spanish guerrillas in their fight against Napoleon: "politics." Everything—tactics, strategy, recruitment, logistics, intelligence—must be subordinated to politics. Mao never tired of making the point:

> What is the relationship of guerrilla warfare to the people? Without a political goal, guerrilla warfare must fail, as it must if its

political objectives do not coincide with the aspirations of the people and their sympathy, co-operation, and assistance cannot be gained.

And the most famous:

Many people think it impossible for guerrillas to exist for long in the enemy's rear. Such a belief reveals lack of comprehension of the relationship that should exist between the people and the troops. The former may be likened to water and the latter to the fish who inhabit it. How may it be said that these two cannot exist together? It is only undisciplined troops who make the people their enemies and who, like the fish out of its native element, cannot live.

The politics in question were revolutionary politics, which meant winning the support of the population at large. Backed by the people, the communist forces could preserve the high morale of their forces, conceal themselves among the people when necessary, provision themselves in the countryside without incurring resentment, and enjoy an almost bottomless supply of fresh recruits. In the war years, China experienced a double political vacuum. In the first place, the ostensible government, the Kuomintang, had never fully succeeded in unifying the country after the fall of the Qing dynasty, in 1912. The power of the provincial warlords who had moved in to fill the political vacuum left by the dynasty's fall had never been completely broken. In the second place, by 1940 the Japanese invaders in the north of China and in selected areas in the south had pulled down such structures of central authority as existed and replaced them either with military rule or with a variety of puppet administrations. It was into this double vacuum that the Communists, who now enjoyed a secure base area among the peasants in the impoverished northwestern province of Yan'an, moved. In wide areas, and especially behind Japanese lines, "politics" therefore meant the creation from the ground up of civil administration.

In this, the Communist Party excelled. As early as the late 1920s, the Communists had governed "liberated" rural areas of China, and by the late 1930s had fully developed their techniques for educating and indoctrinating entire villages and enlisting them in a web of overlapping groups, associations, and governing units, all of which were finally answerable to the Party. The most enduring and important goal of these organizations was land reform, meaning the redistribution of land from the rich to the poor. In traditional rural China, where the gentry class had been supported largely by rents from its landholdings, the redistribution of farming land meant the destruction of one social class by another.

The Communists' guerrilla campaign against the Japanese, starting in 1937, was both an expression of the Party's political strength and a further source of it. It's no justification of Japanese atrocities, which were on a scale with those of the Nazis in Ukraine and Russia, to point out that when a whole population is enlisted in people's war, then the whole population is exposed to retaliation. The Japanese were the first—but unfortunately not the last—antiguerrilla force to whom it occurred that if the guerrillas were the fish and the people were the water, then one way to fight guerrillas was to drain the water. They engaged in a campaign of annihilation using the "Three-All Method"—"Burn all, kill all, destroy all"—in which the destruction of villages and crops and the massacre of all villagers and even animals was common procedure. It is estimated that in the region of greatest Communist strength, in north China, the population dropped in those years from an estimated forty-four million to twenty-five million. China scholars have debated whether the Communist Party's popular support was due more to their program of land reform or more to their resistance to the Japanese—whether more to revolution or more to nationalism. Whatever the answer, the salient point for the evolution of modern warfare is that in both revolution and national resistance "politics" was an essential source of military power.

The thoroughgoing politicization of war, which lent the Communists the strength that so surprised their Chinese and Japanese foes, was accompanied, however, by an equally thoroughgoing militarization of politics. For while it was true that "the better the political reform, the more enduring the War of Resistance," as Mao said, so also was it true that "the more enduring the War of Resistance, the better the political reform." While military "simpletons" had to be taught to place politics first, politicians had to learn to place war first, for "the whole party must pay attention to war, learn military science and be ready to fight." (In Mao's hands, militarized politics would soon come to mean totalitarian politics, whereby enemies were crushed, critics "reeducated," and citizens required to follow a political line determined by the government.)

It is illuminating to compare the formulas of Mao with those of Clausewitz, whose works Mao had studied. On one occasion, for example, Mao, quoting Clausewitz, said, "War is the continuation of politics; in this sense, war is politics and war itself is a political action, and there has not been a single war since ancient times that does not bear a political character." But even as he approves Clausewitz's dictum, he goes on to reverse it: "It can therefore be said that politics are bloodless war while war is the politics of bloodshed." In Clausewitz, the philosopher of conventional war, war seems to take over where politics leaves off. In Mao, the originator of full-scale people's war, war and politics are intermixed. This *fusion* of war and politics, so disturbing to the liberal conscience—torn between admiration for the political restraints placed on the communist soldiers, whose proper treatment of civilians and prisoners was legendary, and horror at the revolutionary brutalization of politics, including the lavish coercion and violence of the totalitarian regime to which people's war often gave birth—is the distinctive contribution that the Communist Party of China made to modern war.

CLAUSEWITZ AND MAO

In the Western military tradition, it would have been considered absurd to introduce *political* activities onto the field of battle: whatever decisions they led to would instantly be overruled by arms. Wherever guns were doing the arguing, the last word was conceded to them. In the words of the Roman general, "Don't speak to me of laws; here the sword rules." Only when the fighting was over could the diplomats reach agreements, which, within certain limits of maneuver, would be ratifications of the new, military "facts on the ground."

In the world of Maoist thought and practice, however, it's obvious that no such priority can be given to force. For Mao,

politics meant, above all, the activities and the interests, as
he conceived them, of common people—and above all, as it
turned out, the interests of the peasants. If anything, politics
is the final arbiter, with force playing only an assisting role.
All the special strengths of a people's army—its invisibility to
the foe, its knowledge of enemy plans, its spirit, its indigenous
sources of supply and recruitment—are likewise bound up
with the local people and the local territory. It was political
struggle that would enable "weak" China eventually to defeat
"strong" Japan. Faced with superior political strength, superior
military strength would over the long run (in "protracted war")
slowly yield. Mao derided those who, as he said, proclaimed
that "China's weapons are inferior and she will certainly be
defeated in war." Rather, "Our view is opposite; we see not only
weapons but also the power of man." In Mao's vision, political
action without a military arm attached was at least thinkable,
if unwise in the extreme, but military action without a political
foundation was an absurdity.

However, the Chinese Communists' belief that political
power was greater than military power was not unqualified. For
all their hammering away at the folly of military action without
political preparation, they still held on to the idea that the last
stage of victory could be accomplished in a conventional battle.
In the same essay in which Mao asserted the primacy of man
over weapons he set forth a three-stage program for war: "mobile war," then "guerrilla war," and finally "positional"—that is,
conventional—war. Mao rejected the idea that "the concept of
guerrilla war is an end in itself and that guerrilla activities can
be divorced from those of the regular forces."

And so it happened. Beginning in late 1948, the Communists, having mobilized more than two million peasants into
their armies, embarked on a series of conventional campaigns
against the Kuomintang (now backed by American money and
arms), which carried them to victory, in 1949. Even in these
final, conventional battles of the Chinese civil war, however,
the dividends of political activity poured in, in the form of
abundant support from the countryside and vast desertions
by disillusioned Kuomintang soldiers. By the last months, it
was hard to say which was occurring faster, the collapse of the
government or the advance of the rebels.

THE FOREST OF POLITICAL DEFEAT

The new relationship between political power and military power that had emerged in people's war was displayed to even more startling effect in the war in Vietnam. The world was slow to absorb the military lessons of people's war in China—just as, in the nineteenth century, it had been slow to absorb the lessons of people's war in Spain. The Second World War had been the greatest conventional war of all time, and guerrilla fighting—whether in China, Yugoslavia, Russia, or elsewhere—had been of secondary importance. When the Japanese occupation of China was cut short by the atomic bomb—an unparalleled display of brute firepower—it seemed clearer than ever that Churchill's "weapons of science," not Mao's irregular peasant armies, were to dominate military affairs.

There was in any case little inclination to reflect on the phenomenon of people's war. The defeated Japanese, living under American occupation, were scarcely in a position to launch a "Who lost China?" debate, which might have illuminated the nature of the Communist victory. That privilege was reserved for the United States, which had supported the Kuomintang until its defeat in 1949. But even then American officialdom, instead of studying the reasons for the Communist success, responded by hounding out of the foreign service as Communist sympathizers the few American firsthand observers who had made such a study. It was an act of willful blindness that, as many historians have noted, prepared the way for the American debacle in Vietnam. In retrospect, we can see, this self-inflicted wound, which occurred in the early 1950s, was part of a deeper policy mistake. Just at the moment when people's war was about to become the principal instrument of political change in the Third World, the United States turned its attention toward the sterile, changeless field of nuclear strategy, where the policy of "massive retaliation" became the order of the day.

It was in Vietnam—the hottest as well as the longest of the Cold War's limited wars—that the West's post–Second World War education in people's war got under way in earnest. After the Japanese were forced out of Vietnam, the French proceeded, with American help, to restore control over their former colony. The United States, which regarded the anticolonial struggle of the Vietnamese as the leading edge of "world communism," soon began to provide the French with supplies. Among all the Western powers, the French had had the most experience with people's war. Although Napoleon's experience in Spain was mostly forgotten, France had faced sporadic anticolonial opposition not only in Vietnam before the war but in its northern African colonies of Tunisia, Morocco, and, above all, Algeria.

The Vietnamese leaders, too, were veterans of people's war, having been steeped in Chinese revolutionary politics for two decades. Ho Chi Minh had lived in China in the twenties and thirties, and had even spent time in prison there. Many of the strategies the Vietnamese were to use against the French had already been battle-tested in China. They included concentration on the rural village as the essential unit of political organization; the foundation of multiple associations (the Peasant Association, the Women's Association, the Youth Association, and so forth) that drew everyone in the village into a tight network of participation and control; the fusion of communist revolution and nationalism; the targeted use of terror against the functionaries of the government; the appeal to popular sentiment together with the suppression of individual thought and opinion; a determined application of land reform; and, most important, an insistence, from start to finish, on the subordination of military action to political goals. The following quotations are a few among a superabundance that express this subordination. (In the first, the ritual bow to Clausewitz is worth noting.)

> Politics forms the actual strength of the revolution: politics is the root and war is the continuation of politics.—*Resolution of the Central Committee of the National Liberation Front.*

> Our political struggle is the manifestation of our absolute political superiority and of the enemy's basic weakness.—*Captured N.L.F. document, 1963.*

Douglas Pike, who served as an official of the U.S. Information Agency in Vietnam, agreed that the key to the N.L.F.'s strength was its political organization. In his book *Viet Cong*, which was written while the war was still in progress, he wrote:

The purpose of this vast organizational effort was not simply population control but to restructure the social order of the village and train the villagers to control themselves. This was the N.L.F.'s one undeviating thrust from the start. Not the killing of A.R.V.N.'s [Army of the Republic of Vietnam's] soldiers, not the occupation of real estate, not the preparation for some great pitched battle at an Armageddon or a Dien Bien Phu but organization in depth of the rural population through the instrument of self-control—victory by means of the organizational weapon. The Communists in Vietnam developed a sociopolitical technique and carried it to heights beyond anything yet demonstrated by the West working with developing nations. The National Liberation Front was a Sputnik in the political sphere of the Cold War.

But it was French observers—among them the writers Jean Lacouture and Bernard Fall—who, among Westerners, were the first to come fully to terms with the nature and significance of people's war as it was being waged by the Vietnamese. Fall—an eyewitness to both the French and the American phases of the war—was in a position to compare the two. In *The Two Vietnams*, published in 1967, he stated boldly that North Vietnam's victory over the French lay "in the effective control of much of the countryside—*despite its occupation by a large Western army*—through the establishment of small but efficient administration units that duplicated the existing Franco-Vietnamese administration." This, of course, was precisely what the Chinese Communists had done behind Japanese lines in the 1940s. Fall called these Vietnamese administrative units "*hiérarchies parallèles*," and said that it was they rather than "the existence of guerrilla battalions" that were "the source of France's defeat." So important was the point that Fall, a political writer immune to pseudoscience, went as far as to distill the essence of what he had learned into a formula. It was

$$RW = G + P$$

where *RW* is revolutionary war, *G* is guerrilla warfare, and *P* is political action. This formula called for violence, he noted, yet "the 'kill' aspect, the military aspect, definitely always remained the minor aspect: the political, administrative, ideological aspect is the primary aspect."

Of particular interest are Fall's applications of the lessons he learned in Vietnam to France's war in Algeria, where the Front de Libération Nationale had launched a guerrilla campaign to free its country from French colonial domination. The war had begun to heat up just as the French war in Vietnam was ending, in 1954. In the next several years, Fall noted, the French generals, by now steeped in the tactics of Mao Zedong that they had ignored in Vietnam, actually succeeded, to all intents and purposes, in militarily defeating the Algerian F.L.N., which, by 1958, had been reduced to a fraction of its former strength. Nevertheless, when Charles de Gaulle, the former leader of the Free French Force in the Second World War, returned to power as the president of the Republic, he understood that the native population of Algeria remained united in opposition to the French, and that as long as this remained the case French rule would be untenable. Fall comments pithily, "This is where the word 'grandeur' applies to President de Gaulle. He was capable of seeing through the trees of military victory to a forest of political defeat, and he chose to settle the Algerian insurgency by other means." Fall did not say so, but the Algerian story suggested a revision of his formula, for if revolutionary war could triumph even after the defeat of guerrilla operations, then political action alone might sometimes be enough for victory, and we would obtain

$$RW = P$$

in which force was missing altogether from the equation of revolution.

Notwithstanding the importance of revolutionary politics, the fall of the French in Vietnam, like the fall of the Kuomintang in China, came in a conventional engagement, the battle of Dien Bien Phu, in 1954, in which superior Vietnamese forces surrounded and decisively defeated the French. Once again, the underlying realities, though not themselves military in character, were given final expression in a set-piece battle, in accord with Mao's three-stage program. At the Geneva conference in 1954, the northern half of Vietnam was ceded to the revolutionary Viet Minh, and South Vietnam, destined soon to become a dependency of the United States, embarked on its brief, doomed existence.

A comment made by de Gaulle after he agreed to give Algeria

its independence sheds further light on the contradictions explored by his countryman Fall. De Gaulle remarked that France could have prevailed in Algeria if she had been "a mastodon," and added that "only Russia, with its communist methods," could have won such a struggle. In fact, just two years earlier, in 1956, the Soviet Union had suppressed an uprising against it in Hungary. France, it seemed at the time, had suffered a failure while the Soviet Union had enjoyed a success. However, de Gaulle's use of the word "mastodon," an extinct animal, proved accurate. He appears to have understood that the Soviet Union's reliance on terror as the method of rule, although a seeming strength, might be a fatal weakness in the end.

His comment is one of the few on record in that era hinting that the Soviet empire might collapse. But before that could happen, the United States intervened in Vietnam.

THE WILLS OF TWO PEOPLES

Much of the American experience on the ground in Vietnam consisted of bloodily learning the lessons that the French had already bloodily learned. Above all, the United States had to discover that the crucial war in Vietnam was not military but political. The immense American military buildup—a half million men at its peak, backed by a naval armada and the most powerful air force ever assembled for a single campaign—could not remedy the political failure but only mask it. In the words of Marine General Victor (Brute) Krulak, the big-unit battles with the National Liberation Front and the North Vietnamese "could move to another planet today, and we would still not have won the war," because "the Vietnamese people are the prize."

But if on the Vietnamese side the war remained the struggle for independence it had always been, the American war was quite different from the French. The United States saw it as just one of many theaters in its global struggle against communism—in the war that had to remain cold because hot war might mean the end of the world. As such, the Vietnam War for the first time brought face-to-face the two new kinds of power that stood at the end of the long, double transformation of war we have described. On the one side was the military power of the nuclear-armed—and nuclear-paralyzed—"superpower," seeking to create and maintain the elusive appearance of deliverable might summed up in the word "credibility." On the other side was the political power of a small nation waging a people's war.

In the broader picture of American strategic policy, the conceptual slot that Vietnam occupied was limited war, as distinct from "general war," which meant unfightable nuclear war. Limited war—as long as it did not get out of control, sending the antagonists back to the brink of nuclear war—*could* be fought, and in Vietnam it was. Limited war was thus the product of two, opposing strategic pressures. The first was the need to confine fighting to the nonnuclear level—meaning, probably, the "periphery." (On several occasions during the Vietnam War, military advisers to the president considered and recommended the use of nuclear weapons or the adoption of policies, such as attacking North Vietnam, that might have drawn Chinese troops into the war, and so precipitate nuclear war; but repeatedly the presidents, fearful of general war, refused.) The second, contrary pressure was the will to actively resist the communist foe—more particularly, to answer the challenge thrown down by Nikita Khrushchev when, in a speech in 1961, seeking to offset his nuclear weakness, he had vowed to support "wars of national liberation." In affirming this policy, which conformed to the long-standing Soviet opposition to Western colonialism, Khrushchev was aligning himself with one of the most durable and powerful movements of the twentieth century—the self-determination movement.

It was the misfortune of the United States that by misnaming the national movements for independence in Vietnam and elsewhere as the advance guard of "world communism," it placed itself on the losing side of these struggles, and so, in Vietnam as elsewhere, found itself on the defensive. On the campaign trail in 1960, Kennedy had already identified Third World revolutions as Soviet emanations. "Their missile power," he had said of the Soviets, "will be the shield from behind which they will slowly but surely advance—through Sputnik diplomacy, limited brush-fire wars, indirect non-overt aggression, intimidation and subversion, internal revolution, increased prestige or influence, and the vicious blackmail of our allies. The periphery of the Free

World will slowly be nibbled away. . . . Each such Soviet move will weaken the West; but none will seem sufficiently significant by itself to justify our initiating a nuclear war which might destroy us." On other occasions, invoking the two-century-old fear of global domination by a single power, he called this unconventional conflict a "twilight struggle"—blazing, high-noon war being inadvisable. (In an age when total war was ruled out, fear of indirect techniques, such as "subversion" and spying, became obsessive on both sides.)

The pressures that collided in America's Vietnam policy were more complex still. Although limited war had been conceived as an escape from the paralysis of nuclear deterrence, the Vietnam War in fact became tangled in it. In Vietnam, it turned out that limited war, just because it was supposed to be a surrogate for the unfightable all-out nuclear war at the center, became charged with an apocalyptic importance that it otherwise would have lacked. For if "indirect" fighting on the periphery was the only kind possible, then the country that mastered it might gradually win the Cold War, as the domino theory predicted. And if that were so, Vietnam was not a refuge from the Third World War, it *was* the Third World War.

Thus did Vietnam, a real war, acquire a symbolic importance in the war of appearances that now dominated nuclear strategy. In this thinking, collapse in Vietnam could lead to nuclear war, or to the collapse of the United States, or both—for all of this supposedly stood at the end point of a long row of collapsing dominos that would leave the United States at bay in a hostile, communized world. It would lead to "our ruin and almost certainly to a catastrophic war," in the words of Secretary of State Dean Rusk in June of 1965.

The consequence was that although the superpowers had gone to the periphery of their global struggle in order to liberate themselves from the futility of nuclear paralysis, they ended up importing that futility into the peripheral situations, to the high cost and sorrow of the resident peoples. In retrospect, it's easy to see that the two blocs were superimposing their struggle onto anticolonial struggles. The outcomes were sharp comeuppances for all concerned. The United States was not only defeated in Vietnam but suffered grievous domestic political harm. Yet it was the Soviets who were to experience the most bitterly ironic consequences. No doubt genuinely believing that they were supporting "international communism" in Vietnam (an illusion both superpowers shared), they were in fact supporting the final stages of a revolt against colonial rule. It apparently never occurred to the Soviet leaders that, in a world of triumphant national liberation, their own empire and union, which held half a dozen Eastern European nations in forcible subjection, and was itself composed of more than a dozen distinct major nationalities, might be a target for insurrection. They apparently thought they were to be the exception to the verdict history had rendered on all other empires of the modern age. They were wrong.

The differences between the geopolitical roles and strategies of France, a fading colonial power, and the United States, a global superpower, were reflected in the way each country fought its war in Vietnam. The most obvious difference was the incomparably greater firepower at the disposal of the United States. Vietnam was a limited war only in the sense that certain expansions of the war (for example, a ground invasion of North Vietnam) were ruled out. Within South Vietnam, the American military effort was unconstrained. By the end of 1966, the United States was pouring more explosive power day by day into that small territory than all the allies together had been using against Germany and Japan at the height of the Second World War. The B-52, an intercontinental bomber designed for a nuclear war with the Soviet Union, was retooled to drop a mile-long path of conventional bombs. Herbicides defoliated thousands of square miles of the country. Other large, populated areas were designated "free-fire zones," in which anything that moved was considered a target.

The immensity of the American military machine confronted the Vietnamese revolutionaries with a strategic problem that the French had never posed. In 1954, the French were defeated at Dien Bien Phu in a classic conventional siege and battle, but there was no hope of defeating American forces by these means. How—to give just one example—were the Vietnamese, who had no planes in the air in South Vietnam, even to touch the B-52s whose flights originated thousands of miles away, on the Pacific island of Guam, and loosed their payloads from an altitude of thirty thousand feet? No amount of political organizing in the Mekong Delta could have the slightest effect on these raids. In reserving the final act of people's war for a conventional victory on the battlefield, Mao, for all his insistence on the supremacy of political over military struggle, had kept one foot in the Clausewitzian world of conventional war, and Vo Nguyen Giap had done the same in his war against the French. Now Mao's blueprint for a three-stage war, culminating in a conventional victory, had to be thrown out. For the first time, the Vietnamese faced the question of how to eject a foreign power without a conventional finale.

The United States, on the other hand, was still unable even to begin to win the political victory without which all its battlefield successes were valueless. By about 1967, the war had reached a perfectly asymmetrical stalemate, from which no Dien Bien Phu could release the antagonists. Each side was supreme in its own sphere of activity—the Vietnamese communists in the sphere of politics, the United States in the sphere of force. Once the United States had committed ground troops in the hundreds of thousands, there was no chance that the Vietnamese could beat the Americans militarily. On the other hand, there was equally little possibility that the Americans and their client Vietnamese, who had all but destroyed the country they were supposedly saving, could win the political allegiance of the Vietnamese people. The two sides, each victorious in a different struggle, lacked, it appeared, any common playing field on which the match could be decided. Political victories won by the N.L.F. and the North Vietnamese in villages, which then were wiped off the face of the earth by American bombing, were as worthless as American military successes won without political support from Vietnamese villagers. In the meantime, everyone involved—the American soldiers, the South Vietnamese soldiers, the N.L.F., the North Vietnamese Army, and, above all, the civilian population of Vietnam—was being killed in growing numbers.

The force that broke the stalemate came from without. It was a change of heart by yet another player in the game, the American public. The event that precipitated the change was the Tet offensive, in February of 1968. The Vietnamese revolutionaries, faced with unbeatable American military superiority, modified Mao's three-stage plan, with its conventional finale, and came up with a new idea—the general uprising. At Tet they sought to put it into practice. The concept was bold and original. The immediate target would be not United States forces but the South Vietnamese government. Military attacks at all points of the country would sweep aside this weak reed. Simultaneously, a general uprising among the urban population would demand the establishment of a new government. The Americans, though still undefeated militarily, would be left in a sea of visibly hostile Vietnamese, and would be forced to withdraw.

Measured by its own goals, the offensive failed disastrously. The military attacks did not spark a general uprising among the urban population, which remained, for the most part, passive. For once, the N.L.F. had made a huge political miscalculation. The South Vietnamese government did not fall, nor did its members defect to the N.L.F. Finally, in the absence of the uprising, the military attacks, although well coordinated and daring, were driven back by American forces, with high losses for the N.L.F. (In the process, the imperial capital of Hue was almost leveled, and parts of Saigon were bombed.) The attacks did not even pay political dividends in the Vietnamese countryside. A number of writers have shown that the N.L.F., badly weakened, lost organizational ground there.

And yet the offensive did bring the long American withdrawal, leading to the eventual victory of the Vietnamese. How, we need to ask, did this unequivocal battlefield defeat win a war? In the old Clausewitzian dispensation, in which force was the final arbiter, defeats in battles were the path to losing a war. But those rules were no longer in effect. In the new world of politically committed and active peoples, it was not force per se but the collective wills of those peoples that were decisive. And, in such a context, even a battlefield defeat could be a decisive victory for the losing side. So it was at Tet. When Richard Nixon was preparing to take office as president in 1968, he asked Rusk, "Where was the war lost?" Rusk answered, "In the editorial rooms of this country."

In March of 1968, President Johnson ducked defeat in the Democratic primaries by resigning his candidacy, stopping the bombing of North Vietnam, and opening peace talks. The Tet offensive had knocked an American president out of office.

The war was to continue under Presidents Nixon and Ford for another seven years, yet the decision had been made. After Tet, in the regretful words of Henry Kissinger, Nixon's national security adviser and then secretary of state, "no matter how effective our actions, the prevalent strategy could no longer achieve its objectives within a period or with force levels politically acceptable to the American people." In 1958, President de Gaulle had seen through the trees of military victory to the forest of political defeat in Algeria, and had granted the country its independence. In the United States in 1968, it was not the head of state but the public at large that came to the same conclusion with regard to Vietnam.

However accidentally, the Vietnamese communists had added a new chapter to the annals of people's war: a war that is won not because the enemy is defeated in a conventional showdown but because the people on the other side, made to understand at last that the cause is ill-conceived and hopeless, *decides* to abandon the effort. Though relying on arms, such an outcome cannot be called a decision by arms. Mao had an inkling that political opinion in the country of the invading army might be decisive in people's war, and in 1938 predicted that revolution in Japan would eventually put an end to its invasion of China—a hope that, of course, was unrealized. It wasn't until the invader was a constitutional democracy that dissension on the home front could prove decisive. The United States lacked a de Gaulle, possessed of sufficient "grandeur" (a word impossible to apply to Richard Nixon), to write a quick finish to the tragedy, and the war staggered on to its humiliating conclusion; but the shift in opinion against the war was never reversed. Military force had played an important role on both sides, but in the last analysis it was the political will of the two peoples involved that was the *final* arbiter of the Vietnam War.

BEYOND THE FINAL ARBITER

In many respects, nuclear deterrence and people's war, each appearing at the end of the twofold metamorphosis of war that we have been tracing, were at opposite poles. One was a fruit of the scientific revolution, and depended on new technical instruments of unlimited destructive power; the other was mainly a fruit of the democratic revolution, and depended on the aroused will of peoples. One was a strategy of the powerful, the other a strategy of the wretched of the earth. One was geopolitical in scope, the other local. Yet in some respects the two strategies were interestingly akin. In both, a certain dematerialization of power occurred. In deterrence, it was the decline of actual war-fighting in favor of creating fearful appearances—credibility—that became the coin of military might in the nuclear age. In people's war, it was the eclipse of the power that flowed "from the barrel of a gun" by the political power that flowed from the hearts and minds of the people. In both shifts, violence became not so much an instrument for producing physical effects as a kind of bloody system of communication, through which the antagonists delivered messages to one another about will. In both, the intangible effect upon hearts and minds was paramount, and the tangible effect upon the opposing military forces was secondary. In both, we seem to see the human will detaching itself from physical fighting, as if getting ready to make a break and turn to other means, though without doing so. In both, the capacity of force to decide political issues is thrown into doubt. In both, in short, the old final arbiter has lost its finality, and some new arbiter seems to be acting in the background. It is because of these developments, somehow occurring simultaneously at the apex and the base of the world's system of military power in the middle decades of the twentieth century, that it is more than a paradoxical phrase to speak of a kind of nonviolence, or at least a turn away from violence, that was occurring *within* war in this period.

The similarities between deterrence and people's war should not, however, unduly surprise us. Both were responses to the same broad, underlying historical development—the steady increase throughout the modern age of the violence at the disposal of military forces. Through people's war, non-Western peoples found a way to defend themselves against the awesome technical superiority of the superpowers. Through the strategy of nuclear deterrence, those superpowers themselves, finding that their weapons had become too destructive to be used against one another, tried as best they could to accomplish the old purposes with mere threats. The twentieth century had produced the most extreme violence that the human species had ever visited upon itself. It was natural—indeed, it was a necessity—that, in different ways, people would react against it, would seek ways to overcome it, to escape it, to go around it, to replace it. In earlier times, violence had been seen as the last resort when all else had failed. "Hallowed are those arms where no hope exists but in them," Livy had written. But in the twentieth century, a new problem forced itself on the human mind: What was the resort when that "last resort" had bankrupted itself? Nuclear deterrence and people's war were two groping, improvised, incomplete attempts to find answers to this question.

It is also true—to state what is perhaps more obvious—that nuclear deterrence and people's war marked two extremes of physical violence, two apogees of total war. Deterrence promised peace only at the price of threatening the world with annihilation. People's war sought to assert the people's interests, but only by turning every section of the population, including women and children, into fighters and victims. Both strategies simultaneously evoke admiration and horror. Even as we are pleased with the peace that deterrence takes as its goal, we are revolted by the unlimited slaughter it menaces. Even as we are awed by the epic of human courage that people's war presents and the nobility of its goal of serving the interests of the least fortunate, we are disgusted by its frequent use of terror and by the totalitarian governments, with their various gulags and "reeducation camps," to which it has often given birth. Deterrence is only a stay of execution, not a reprieve. People's war immerses the people in the violence from which it seeks to deliver them. And yet, I suggest, in reaching each of these ambiguous extremes, we can, for the first time, catch a glimpse of a true rejection of the twentieth century's terrible legacy of violence, as when climbers, upon reaching a mountaintop, and able to climb no higher, first see the new land beyond, and turn their steps down the other side.

PART TWO

NONVIOLENCE

4

Satyagraha

For most of history, military victory has been the royal road to political rule over a rival country, a sequence crystallized in the single word "conquest." The reason was no mystery. If, as Clausewitz said, an enemy was defeated only when he was ready to "do our will," then obviously military victory made rule possible by turning bold, angry enemies into frightened, obedient subjects. It was the genius of the inventors of people's war to challenge this deceptively self-evident proposition by discovering, in the very midst of battle, the power of politics. What if, the inventors of people's war asked, the people on the losing side declined to do the will of the conqueror and, taking a further step, organized itself politically to conduct its own business? In people's war, political organization did not stand on its own; it was interwoven with the military struggle into Mao's seamless fabric. Yet Mao and others placed politics first in the order of importance and military action only second, and this ranking at least suggested the question of whether, if the fabric were unraveled, political action alone might thwart an occupying power. Did revolutions have to be violent? Could nonviolent revolution—that is, *purely* nonviolent revolution—succeed?

The main schools of Western political theory in the modern age answered the question, with one voice, in the negative. Most thinkers, whether left, right, or center, agreed that revolution was in its nature violent. They believed, with Max Weber, that "politics operates with very special means, namely power backed up by *violence.*" For many, the resort to violence was the defining feature of the revolutionary act. Liberals no less than conservatives took it for granted that, as John Locke said, when the government uses "force without right upon a man's person," and "the remedy is denied by a manifest perverting of justice and a barefaced wresting of the laws to protect or indemnify the violence of injuries of some men," then people "are left to the only remedy in such cases—the appeal to heaven"—that is, to arms. For "in all states and conditions, the true remedy of force without authority is to oppose force to it." The upholders of absolutist monarchy had denied a right to revolt even in that case, but they certainly agreed that revolution was in its nature a bloody affair. Revolution, in the words of the eighteenth-century conservative parliamentarian and writer Edmund Burke, "becomes a case of war, and not of constitution. Laws are commanded to hold their tongues amongst arms; and tribunals fall to the ground with the peace they are no longer able to uphold."

The left-wing revolutionaries of the nineteenth and twentieth centuries more than agreed with the liberal contractarian thinkers who preceded them. "*Aux armes, citoyens!*" was the cry of the left from the time of the French Revolution down to the day of Mao and Ho. At the beginning of the nineteenth century, Napoleon, in exile on St. Helena, laid down the law in the following dictum: "General rule: No social revolution without terror. Every revolution is, by its nature, a revolt which success and the passage of time legitimize but in which terror is one of the inevitable phases." Karl Marx's famous formulation was "Violence is the midwife of every old society pregnant with a new one." (We must add that he didn't regard violence as the essence of revolution, which in his view was prepared above all by economic developments.) The leader of the Russian revolution of 1917, Vladimir Ilyich Lenin, asserted that "Not a single question pertaining to the class struggle has ever been settled except by violence." In a still broader generalization, he said, "Great problems in the life of nations are decided only by force."

Voices disagreeing with this wide consensus—the voices of a smattering of anarchists, some moderate Marxists and other socialists, and a few writers, including, above all, the Russian novelist and pacifist Leo Tolstoy—were rarely taken seriously by those who were in power, or even thinking about power. Lenin sneered at Tolstoy's "imbecile preaching about not resisting evil with force." And Max Weber, having declared that "the decisive means for politics is violence," added that "anyone who fails to see this is a political infant." It's hardly necessary to add to this list such right-wing enthusiasts of violence as Joseph de Maistre, who proclaimed, "All greatness, all power, all subordination rest on the executioner. He is the terror and the bond of human association." And when the right, turning revolutionary, produced fascism, it not only justified violence but reveled in it.

This consensus survived all but unshaken until recently, and undoubtedly played a role in the nearly universal failure to predict the downfall of the Soviet Union. The Soviet regime's monopoly on all the instruments of force seemed to render it invulnerable. If revolution had to be violent in order to succeed, then it seemed to have no chance against such a regime, which would thus have been well justified in its expectation (shared by so many of its awed detractors) that it would last, in effect, forever. The conviction that force was always the final arbiter was not in truth so much an intellectual conclusion as a tacit assumption on all sides—the product not of a question asked and answered but of one unasked. Only in the aftermath of the Soviet collapse have people been ready, perhaps, to open their minds to the idea that some power other than force can prevail in revolution and war. That was the utterly unexpected accomplishment of activists in Eastern Europe and the Soviet Union; but the man who first put the question fully to the historical test was Mohandas Karamchand Gandhi.

A QUESTION OF LIFE AND DEATH

The inventors of people's war rewrote the rules governing the connection of politics to war. Gandhi, whose campaign to end British rule in India was contemporaneous with Mao's revolution, was an even more radical tamperer with the relationships among basic human activities. He was a tireless workman in the shop in which new forms of human action and living are forged. He entered public life as the defender of a small, immigrant minority in a dusty corner of a global empire, but before he was done he had led a movement that, more than any other force, dissolved that empire, and in the process had proposed a way of life in which the constituent activities of existence—the personal, the economic, the social, the political, the spiritual—were brought into a new relationship.

Most important in our context was his fusion of politics and religion. Gandhi believed that to drive the gun out of politics he had to invite God in. It was an operation that, in his day of mostly secular politics, raised an array of new questions and problems even as it offered new solutions to old ones. But in order to better understand Gandhi's vision, in all its originality, strangeness, and greatness, we must first place it in its historical context.

As a youth, Gandhi, who was born in 1869 in the Indian city of Porbandar, on the Indian Ocean, exhibited no extraordinary talents of the testable kind. He takes his place on the long list of remarkable people who performed indifferently at school. His biographer Judith M. Brown titles her chapter on his young manhood "An Indian Nonentity." Sent by his family from India to London to study the law, he continued not to shine. He couldn't learn to dance; he couldn't master the violin; he failed his bar examinations on the first try, succeeding only on the second. Back in India, he couldn't get a law practice going. When he was finally given a case, in Bombay, he was struck dumb with shyness in the cross-examination and felt obliged to refund his client's fee. Proper employment did not come until 1893, when he accepted an invitation to handle a legal case for an Indian merchant in South Africa. In the new land, however, the mediocre student and failed barrister promptly demonstrated that he possessed at least one human quality to a superlative degree, and that was the capacity and the will to translate his beliefs into action.

Everyone forms opinions and beliefs, but most act on them only up to a certain point, beyond which fears, desires, doubts, prudence, laziness, and distractions of all kinds take over. Gandhi, as it turned out in South Africa, belonged to the small class of people, many of them religious or political zealots, who are able to act according to their beliefs almost without condition or reservation. On several occasions, he would read some advice in a book, or arrive at some new idea on his own, and put it into practice the next day. On a train from Durban to Pretoria, a white man had him thrown out of the first-class compartment for which he had paid, and when he protested the conductor dumped him onto the station platform. "I should try if possible," as he later wrote, "to root out the disease [of color prejudice in South Africa] and suffer hardships in the process." It was a decision, as things turned out, that would guide his actions for the next twenty-one years.

In 1894, having completed the legal business for which he had come, he had decided to leave South Africa, and a farewell dinner was held in his honor. That day, he had noticed an article in the *Natal Mercury* reporting that the British colony of Natal was about to pass a bill to disenfranchise Indians. His colleagues at dinner implored him to stay to fight the ordinance, and on the spur of the moment he decided he would. A decade later, he read John Ruskin's *Unto This Last* during a twenty-four-hour train ride from Johannesburg to Durban. The book recommended a life of austerity, material simplicity, and self-control. "I arose with the dawn," he wrote later, "ready to reduce these principles to practice." The result was Phoenix Farm, the first of several experimental communities he was to found.

The political and racial issues in South Africa that Gandhi had committed himself to solving were many-layered. South African society was arranged in a four-tier, multinational, multiracial hierarchy. At the bottom was the completely unenfranchised and virtually rightless native black majority, outnumbering everyone else put together by about four to one. Next in the scale were Indians, who, by the turn of the century, were slightly more numerous than whites. Next were the local dominant whites, divided among Boers, who were the descendants of Dutch settlers, an English population, and a scattering of others. (In 1897 in Natal there were about four hundred thousand blacks, forty thousand Indians, and forty thousand whites.) At the top were the British imperial masters, trying to exercise ultimate control from London. In this hierarchy, the British, who would wage the Boer War at the turn of the century to prevent the Boers from seceding from the empire, were logical allies for the Indians, who suffered oppression at the hands of the local whites. South Africa was one of those complicated imperial situations in which a passion for self-rule by one group (the Boers, who by and large were more thoroughly racist than the British) meant even more severe repression for other groups.

Conflict arose when the Indians, imported to South Africa in the late nineteenth century under a system of indenture solely to serve as easily managed labor, began to acquire the aspirations of a normal human community: they began to buy and sell goods, to acquire land and farm it, to trade, to practice their religions, even to enter onto the fringes of political life. The local whites, Boer and English, were resentful and afraid of this new competition. Indian farming, they thought, would bring down the prices of agricultural goods by adding to the supply of food; Indian traders would take business from whites; Indian entry into politics would threaten white supremacy (though the modest Indians were far from having any such ambition).

Seized by a terror, which had no basis in fact, that millions of Indians would inundate South Africa, destroying the foundations of white rule, the whites took steps to suppress all the new signs of vigor and life in the Indian community. They passed bills that disenfranchised the free Indians who could vote; imposed exorbitant taxes on free Indians, to force them to re-indenture themselves; hampered and destroyed Indian traders by entangling them in a rigmarole of licensing and other restrictions; limited the areas in which freed Indians could live; restricted their travel; forbade them to use public facilities, including sidewalks; and even passed legislation to make non-Christian marriages illegal. In the background was the implicit threat that the Indian community would be driven out of South Africa altogether. "I clearly saw that this was a question of life and death for them," Gandhi wrote of his fellow Indians.

LOVER OF THE BRITISH EMPIRE

In theory, the ideals of the British Empire were liberal. In 1858, Queen Victoria had issued a proclamation declaring her wish that "our subjects, of whatever race or creed, be freely and impartially admitted to offices in our service." It was therefore not only to the local government but to London that the Indians of South Africa sent their numerous petitions and delegations for redress. A nascent black movement followed a similar strategy.

In 1903, we find the following characteristic peal of praise from Gandhi for the British Empire:

The Empire has been built up as it is on a foundation of justice and equity. It has earned a worldwide reputation for its anxiety and ability to protect the weak against the strong. It is the acts of peace and mercy, rather than those of war, that have made it what it is.

In 1905, on Empire Day, he is still eulogizing Queen Victoria:

By her large heart and wide sympathy; by her abilities and queenly virtues; above all, by her personal goodness as a woman, she has forever enshrined herself in the hearts of every nation under the British flag.

At times, he seems a more eager imperialist than the British. On the eve of the Boer War, which aroused broad protest among liberals in England and was not popular with all South African Indians, either, Gandhi wrote to an English friend, "We are all fired with one spirit, viz., the imperial." Gandhi had made a decision to support the empire on the ground that although "justice is on the side of the Boers," the Indians, as citizens seeking to enjoy the rights promised by the empire, should "accord their support to acts of state." His enthusiasm was more for what he hoped the empire might become than for what he currently found it to be. His strategy was to shame the imperialists into living up to their professed ideals. He backed up his words by organizing an ambulance corps of Indians to support the British army in the war. In 1906, when war broke out with the Zulus, he repeated the performance.

Somehow coexisting with this enthusiasm for the British Empire, however, was a growing dislike for modern, technological civilization, of which England was obviously the chief global representative and disseminator. He called the "wonderful discoveries and the marvelous inventions of science, good as they undoubtedly are in themselves," an "empty boast," as they did nothing to advance the spiritual life. He denounced "the invention of the most terrible weapons of destruction, the awful growth of anarchism," and the "frightful disputes between capital and labor." His enthusiasm for the British Empire and his mounting dislike of the modern civilization that it embodied were obviously headed for a collision, and it was not long in coming.

Like many other Asian reformers of the late nineteenth and early twentieth centuries, Gandhi had begun by distinguishing between a strong, materialist West and a weak but spiritual East. He recognized that England's power did not depend on technology alone. It depended also, he firmly believed, on the individual courage, martial and civic, of its people. As a national characteristic, that courage was, he thought, a product in part of England's gradual democratic revolution. In 1906, we find him paying tribute to the sacrifices of heroes of England's struggle for religious toleration, parliamentary supremacy, and the rule of law. "The English honor only those who make such sacrifice," he wrote in *Indian Opinion*, a newspaper he founded and ran. "Their shining glory has spread just because great heroes have been and are still among them. Such were Wat Tyler, John Hampden, John Bunyan and others. They laid the foundations of England's supremacy. We shall continue to be in our abject condition till we follow their example." Cultivating a spirit of civic responsibility and courage was a kind of Westernization of which Gandhi approved.

Gandhi's list of English people to admire is pointedly selective. Missing are such names as Isaac Newton, founder of classical physics; James Watt, inventor of the steam engine; Richard Arkwright, inventor of the power-driven loom; the Duke of Wellington, who defeated Napoleon at Waterloo; or any of the other creators of nineteenth-century England's scientific, industrial, and military dominance. Gandhi wanted only one of the two great modern revolutions. He wanted democracy but not science. It's well known that Gandhi, champion of the spinning wheel, rejected Western technological civilization, but less often appreciated is that, even as a young man, he ardently admired the habits of civic virtue that he believed he saw in the West and associated with the democratic revolution. Those virtues were, in fact, more than anything else the foundation of his program and of his hopes for South Africa and then India. Like the ancient Greeks, he regarded courage as the most important virtue, because it was the prerequisite for all the others.

In the first years of the twentieth century, he seems to be ransacking both history and the contemporary world for examples of courage to set before the Indian community of South Africa. He pens eulogies of, among others, George Washington, Giuseppe Mazzini, Socrates, Maxim Gorky, Abraham Lincoln ("the greatest man of the last century"), Tolstoy, and Thoreau.

All were held up as models of the virtue he found wanting in his countrymen. In 1905, when Japan administered its defeat to Russia, Gandhi was overjoyed. "No one ever imagined that Japan was capable of such bravery," the budding pacifist wrote. "But in scouting and watchfulness, Japan surpassed all the others. Admiral Togo's spies were very accurate in their intelligence, and pounced upon the Russian fleet just when it was most vulnerable." As late as 1908 he could still write, "When Japan's brave heroes forced the Russians to bite the dust of the battle-field, the sun rose in the East. And it now shines on all the nations of Asia. The people of Asia will never, never again submit to insult from the insolent whites." Gandhi thought he knew the "secret" of the Japanese success. It was "unity, patriotism and the resolve to do or die," he said, in the tropes of late-Victorian nationalist fervor.

Yet even in these years Gandhi's interest in nonviolence was developing. In 1896 he had read Tolstoy's Christian pacifist manifesto *The Kingdom of God Is Within You* and was "overwhelmed" by it. A few years later, he entered into correspondence with Tolstoy, who celebrated Gandhi's work in *Letter to a Hindu*. As early as 1902, Gandhi gave a speech in Calcutta in which he said that although the "hatred" of the colonials against the Indians was great, what he proposed was "to conquer that hatred by love." His voracious consumption of the news of the day yielded useful examples of nonviolent action. He praised a Chinese boycott of American goods to protest anti-Chinese discrimination in the United States. He saluted a Bengali boycott of British goods to protest the partition of Bengal by the English viceroy, Lord Curzon. He lauded the Irish movement against English rule.

The example that inspired him most, however, was the Russian revolution of 1905, whose first stages were largely nonviolent. For some years, he observed in *Indian Opinion*, the Russian revolutionaries had resorted to terrorist attacks. He admired the courage of the attackers, including "fearless girls, actuated by patriotism and a spirit of self-sacrifice, [who] take the lives of those whom they believe to be the enemies of the country, and themselves meet an agonizing death at the hands of officials." Nevertheless, their method was "a mistake." Now they had discovered a new method:

This time they have found another remedy which, though very simple, is more powerful than rebellion and murder. The Russian workers and all the other servants declared a general strike and stopped all work. They left their jobs and informed the Czar that unless justice was done, they would not resume work. What was there even the Czar could do against this? It was quite impossible to exact work from people by force.

In these years, Gandhi's religious faith was deepening. He did not, however, connect spirituality with any one religion or civilization. In the late 1890s, Anglicized Indian that he was, he had become the South African representative of a group called the Esoteric Christian Union, which taught an eclectic faith.

FINDING GOD IN POLITICAL ACTION

In the first years of the twentieth century, the chief elements that made up Gandhi's outlook on the world hung together uneasily, if they hung together at all. Shortly, under the pressure of events, they were to rearrange themselves convulsively in his mind. The crisis, which spanned three years and amounted to a kind of full-scale revolution in the life of a single man, swept together his social program for his local community, his personal spirituality, his political activity on the South African stage, and his view of the British Empire and the world.

The revolution in Gandhi's local community came with the creation of Phoenix Farm, in November of 1904. Gandhi took nothing in this little community as given, but subjected everything, from the activities of daily life (how to brush your teeth, how to clean the latrine) to the most general and fundamental structures of politics and faith, to scrutiny and revision. Because this scrutiny took the form of experimentation, not obedience to any fixed scripture or dogma, the revision was endless. It included an aspect of his life that has baffled and often repelled many of his admirers—his lifelong tinkering with his austere diet and his Christian Science–like home cures, to both of which he directed great attention.

The turning point in Gandhi's personal life came in 1906, while he was leading his ambulance corps during the Zulu war. It struck him that only someone who was pledged to celibacy and poverty could lead a life of unfettered public service. He "could not live both after the flesh and the spirit," he decided. At the time, he wrote later, he had begun to ask himself some questions: "How was one to divest oneself of all possessions? . . . Was not the body possession enough? . . . Was I to destroy all the cupboards of books I had? Was I to give up all I had and follow Him?" Forthwith, he became celibate—renouncing sex even with his wife, though he remained married—and poor, and remained so for the rest of his life.

Vows of poverty and celibacy were, of course, no novelty. Priests and monks had been taking them throughout history. It was the use to which Gandhi put the life thus disciplined that was new. In the religious traditions of both East and West, holy vows have usually been accompanied by a withdrawal from the world and especially from politics. Gandhi proceeded in exactly the opposite direction. He took his ascetic vows in order to free himself for action.

Significantly, Gandhi likened the common British soldiers— the "Tommies"—he met in the Zulu war to Trappist monks. "Tommy was then altogether lovable," he wrote, and went on to compare them to Arjun, the hero of the Indian epic the Mahabharata. "Like Arjun, they went to the battlefield, because it was their duty. And how many proud, rude, savage spirits has it not broken into gentle creatures of God?" Gandhi's admiration for soldiers was lifelong. Like a monk, he would devote his life to God; but like a soldier he would fight for his beliefs in this world. Of his pursuit of God, he said, "If I could persuade myself that I should find Him in a Himalayan cave, I would proceed there immediately. But I know that I cannot find Him apart from humanity." The aim of his life would be to "see God," but that pursuit would lead him into politics. "For God," he said, reversing centuries of tradition in a short sentence, "appears to you only in action."

To the question of whether political power alone might win out over military power, Gandhi answered without equivocation that it could. His answer, however, raised another question that was of the first importance for the future of nonviolent action. If politics was to be free of violence, must it become religious? The objections to the wedding of secular and spiritual power are of course ancient, dating in the East as far back as Gautama Buddha and in the West as far back as Jesus, another religious activist who lived and taught in a backwater of an empire. Universal Christian love, expressed in the sayings "Love your enemy" and "Forgive those who trespass against you," is the spiritual underpinning of his advice of nonviolence to Simon Peter, "Put up thy sword." Certainly, faith in God and ethical responsibility toward others were inseparable for Jesus. On the other hand, although Jesus was caught up in the politics of his time and place, he conspicuously stopped short of rebellion, nonviolent or otherwise. He steered clear of any claim to political leadership (refusing to accept the title "King of the Jews," which his crucifiers affixed to his cross), and he advised payment of taxes to the Roman authorities, saying, "Render unto Caesar what is Caesar's." In other sayings, too, he seemed to place the realm of faith apart from the realm of politics. When Pilate asked him whether he claimed to be a king—a claim that would have been an offense to Caesar—Jesus answered that he was not "a king of this world." If he had been making a claim of temporal power, he went on, his disciples would have used violence to release him. That they did not showed that his kingship was otherworldly. His prophecy that the world would end soon and the kingdom of heaven come also drew a line of separation between Christian love and politics. What need was there to prescribe a rule for a political realm that was about to be destroyed? It was on the basis of these sayings that the disciple Paul and, much later, St. Augustine founded their far sharper separation of the City of God from the City of Man.

To these Christian ideas we may contrast a few of Gandhi's. As he began a nonviolent campaign in 1930, he declared of the Raj, "I am out to destroy this system of Government. . . . Sedition has become my religion." Gandhi admitted no distinction between the City of God and the City of Man. He installed a political conscience in religion and a religious conscience in politics, and called the two the same.

The objections to such a union have come over the years from both saints and politicians. Faith, saints have said, is a domain of purity that is in its nature unworldly, and will be corrupted and destroyed by association with politics, which is in its nature brutal. Rule, politicians have added, is a rough pursuit that will be enfeebled by any introduction of spiritual rules of conduct. (An object lesson—in the eyes of the eighteenth-century historian

of ancient Rome Edward Gibbon—was the Christianization
and fall of the Roman Empire.) Or else politics, which requires
a spirit of tolerance if its natural, ineradicable violence is at least
to be moderated, may, if inspired by faith, become fanatical,
and even more brutal than it has to be.

To these objections, Gandhi proposed explicit or implicit
answers. The most important was nonviolence itself, which he
called ahimsa—literally, non-harm, or harmlessness—in Hindi.
If the ardor of the spiritual, with its tendency toward absolute
demands, was to be permitted to inspire political action, then
it had to be purged of violence. The spirit must check its guns
at the door, so to speak, before entering the saloon of politics.
Otherwise, saints would prove more murderous than sinners.
He required the intellect, meanwhile, to undergo a parallel
renunciation. It had to rid itself of dogmatic certainty. Shedding dogma was the counterpart in the intellectual world of
nonviolence in the physical world: it was mental disarmament.
Only if the faithful were ready to open their minds to the worth
and validity of other faiths were they likely to be able to hold to
the vow of nonviolence. The test of the "absoluteness" of faith
became not adherence to the exact prescriptions of any sacred
text—what today we call fundamentalism—but the willingness
to make sacrifices, including the sacrifice of one's life, for one's
admittedly fallible beliefs. Sacrifice and suffering without violence ("self-suffering," as Gandhi put it), not doctrinal purity,
was the evidence and "proof" of faith.

These were all ways to permit spiritual love to fuel politics;
but they did not answer the question of whether politics, in
order to be nonviolent, *required* a spiritual basis. The issue is
important, because such a requirement would obviously restrict the appeal of nonviolence. It seems almost in the nature
of things that only a small minority can ever take Gandhi as a
model for their lives—just as only minorities have ever been
drawn to the priestly or monastic life. In particular, Gandhi's
asceticism—and especially his vow of celibacy even within
marriage—which he regarded as essential to the practice of
satyagraha, seems unlikely to serve as a model for very many.
The question is what it is about religious faith that enables it
to serve as a foundation for nonviolence and whether, outside
religion, there may be other foundations.

SOMETHING STRANGE HAPPENS

The transformation in Gandhi's political program in South Africa came just a few months after his vows of celibacy and poverty during the Zulu war. In August of 1906, the Transvaal Legislature announced a so-called Asiatic Law Amendment Ordinance. Its main provision required all Indians above the age of eight to be registered with ten fingerprints and to carry a residency permit thereafter, on pain of fine, prison, or deportation. In combination with other restrictions already in place, the act in effect reduced the Indian community to the status of criminals. Its acceptance, Gandhi believed, "would spell absolute ruin for the Indians in South Africa." In response, Gandhi led the South African Indian community to cross the line from petitioning or otherwise seeking redress within the law to nonviolent lawbreaking.

On September 11, 1906, some three thousand Indian men met at the Empire Theater, in Johannesburg. Gandhi writes, "I could read in every face the expectation of something strange to be done, or to happen." On the agenda was an item resolving that the members of the Indian community would go to jail rather than submit to the Ordinance. One man, Sheth Haji Habib, suggested that the meeting should not only vote for the resolution but publicly vow before God that they would abide by it. Gandhi supported the suggestion in a speech. Such a vow was far different from a mere resolution, he said. It could not be enforced by majority vote; each person had to decide for himself whether to take it and abide by it. But, having once taken the vow, each person was obligated thereafter to keep it, no matter what others did, for "a man who lightly pledges his word and then breaks it becomes a man of straw." All present rose and took the vow.

The "strange" thing had happened. Gandhi knew, he said later, "that some new principle had come into being." Before a year was out, several hundred Indians had gone to jail. This revolution in action, significantly, was born in action. "The foundation of the first civil resistance under the then-known name of passive resistance," he wrote later, "was laid by accident. . . . I had gone to the meeting with no preconceived resolution. It was born at the meeting. The creation is still expanding."

Gandhi was dissatisfied with the term "passive resistance" for what the Indians were doing, and as an alternative came up with the new coinage "satyagraha," which combined the Sanskrit word *sat*, meaning "that which is," or "being," or "truth," with *graha*, meaning "holding firm to" or "remaining steadfast in." It is usually translated as "truth force" or "soul force"—terms that, without further elucidation, are almost as mysterious to the English reader as "satyagraha." Concretely described, satyagraha is direct action without violence in support of the actor's beliefs—the "truth" in the person. The philosophy of satyagraha prescribes nonviolent action in which the actors refuse to cooperate with laws that they regard as unjust or otherwise offensive to their consciences, accompanied by a willingness to suffer the consequences. For the Indian community in Transvaal it meant deliberate violation of the Amendment Ordinance and a commitment to fill the local jails.

SERMON ON THE SEA

The final step in the revolution in Gandhi's life in these years— the reversal of his appraisal of the British Empire—came in 1909, after he had spent several months in England at the head of an Indian delegation fruitlessly pleading with the imperial government for relief from Boer repression in South Africa (which was now about to become the Union of South Africa). Gandhi had already led one delegation to London, right after the passage of the Ordinance, and on that occasion Lord Elgin, the colonial secretary, had played a trick on the Indians. He had informed them that the imperial government would disallow the legislation. Halfway home, they discovered to their joy that it had done so. When they arrived, however, they learned what Elgin had known all along—that the Transvaal would shortly be granted "responsible government," and would then be permitted to adopt the act at will, without imperial challenge, as it soon did.

The second visit was no more productive. The imperial government wished to uphold the appearance of liberalism without paying the price. From the Indian point of view, the problem was not autocratic or arbitrary use of the empire's strength but default and weakness. Notwithstanding the empire's victory in the Boer War, its power in South Africa was waning. Lord Morley, the secretary of state for India, told the Indians that the empire—which, he startlingly said, was "miscalled an imperial system"—could not "dictate to the colonies." The English strategy in South Africa was to shore up overarching imperial power by yielding increased grants of authority to the local whites. For the Cape of Good Hope, like Egypt and the Sudan, was one of those "roads to India" that had to be defended at all costs. Global power politics took precedence over the grievances of the local black majority and the Indian minority, which were hardly a speck on the great imperial horizon. "I have now got fed up," Gandhi wrote home in *Indian Opinion* toward the end of his 1909 visit. "I think the reader, too, must have grown tired of reading uncertain news." At the Empire Theater, Gandhi had broken with the Boers. Now his patience with the British was coming to an end.

The historical predicament faced by Gandhi and other Indian leaders, barred from influence and power in South Africa as well as their own country, was, in its broadest outline, similar to that facing the leadership of all the colonialized countries: how to oppose domination by a foreign state wielding the incomparably superior weapons of the modern West. India's "Omdurman" had been the battle of Plassey, fought in 1757 between English forces under Robert Clive, and those of Siraj-ud-daulah, the nawab of the Mogul Empire. Clive's victory was one of the earliest to show the extreme imbalance that would become such a regular feature of modern imperial war. The nineteenth-century British military historian Colonel Malleson was not exaggerating when he wrote, "The work of Clive was, all things considered, as great as that of Alexander." For after the battle of Plassey, with its loss to England of a handful of soldiers, the power of England over India was not to be seriously challenged again until Gandhi's time.

The power of imperialist Europe presented the Eastern countries with a dilemma that was cultural and psychological as well as military and political. Everywhere in Asia, nascent movements to resist Europe were national, just as, earlier in the century, the European resistance to Napoleon had been national. However much these movements battened on enthusiasm for their own cultures, the most obvious solution to the crisis in which Asia found herself was to abandon her ways and adopt those of the powerful, dangerous West—in short, to "modernize." Nor could this adoption be halfhearted or superficial. The foundations of traditional society, it seemed, had to be uprooted.

In China, the Ottoman Empire, Japan, India, and elsewhere, innumerable variations of this solution to the dilemma were tried out. Science, evidently, was a source of Western power. Why not, then, learn science, and graft it onto Eastern society, combining the strength of the "material" West with the wisdom of the "spiritual" East? Such was the thinking of early Chinese reformers, who, however, soon noted what Clausewitz had discovered—that democracy, too, was a source of Western military power. "Science and democracy" then became the rallying cry of an important school of reformers. Chen Duxiu, a moderate, wrote, "The basic task is to import the foundation of Western society, that is, the new belief in equality and human rights." These Chinese, goaded by their country's humiliation, were perhaps the first anywhere, East or West, to understand and clearly state that at the base of modern power were the scientific and democratic revolutions. But in the early twentieth century it became obvious to them that neither revolution could grow in a vacuum. Both had roots in the emancipation of the individual. In order to be strong, China would have to alter its culture, even its family structure—the very things that, according to earlier reformers, China had been seeking to protect by adopting science. The further one went in Westernizing in order to protect China, it turned out, the less of "China" there was to protect. Not far down this path lay the wholesale condemnation of Chinese tradition that would be expressed by the Chinese Communist Party. The Asian nations, in order to survive in the social Darwinist, adapt-or-die war system that Europe had imposed on the world, seemed to be faced with a choice between watching Europeans destroy their traditional societies and doing the job themselves. It was hard soil in which to grow what later came to be called "national identity."

On a steamer back to South Africa in November of 1909,

Gandhi, writing in his native tongue of Gujarati, poured out the longest and most inflammatory political pamphlet he would ever write, *Hind Swaraj: Indian Home Rule*—also called *Sermon on the Sea*. It dealt head-on with the issue of Westernization. If violence is truly the midwife of revolution, as Marx said, then this pamphlet was the closest Gandhi ever came to preaching it. He portrayed the civilization of England and her empire as an unmitigated evil. Gone now was the praise for Queen Victoria, gone the praise for British justice, gone the vision of a harmonious union of "different sections of ONE mighty empire." The larger villain of the story, however, was not England herself but modern technical civilization, of which England was only one representative. He anathematized it with fundamentalist fury. "This civilization is irreligion," he declared. "According to the teachings of Mahomed this would be considered a Satanic Civilization. Hinduism calls it the Black Age. . . . It must be shunned." To imitate this civilization, as Japan had done and China was trying to do, would be madness. "The condition of England at present is pitiable. I pray to God that India may never be in that plight." He excoriated modern ways. Railways only enabled "bad men [to] fulfil their evil designs with greater rapidity," he said, with primitive logic. English prime ministers had "neither real honesty nor a living conscience." The English Parliament was "a prostitute." The civilization of modern Europe as a whole was a mere "nine-days' wonder" that shortly would destroy itself; one had only to wait.

Indian civilization, he now found, was the opposite of all this. "The tendency of the Indian civilization is to elevate the moral being," he claimed, "that of the Western civilization is to propagate immorality. The latter is godless, the former is based on a belief in God." The foundations of Indian civilization arose, he insisted, from religious roots, when her great religious men had established pilgrimages to holy places, such as the Ganges.

Gandhi's rejection of the West and embrace of his own land was more radical by far than that of other anti-Western leaders of the time. The idea that the East should protect her spiritual treasures by means of a judicious borrowing of Western material techniques had been the stock-in-trade not just of the Chinese and Japanese but of Indians as well. For instance, the religious leader Vivekananda, who in other ways foreshadows

Gandhi, said, "It is . . . fitting that when the Oriental wants to learn about machine-making, he should sit at the feet of the Occidental and learn from him. When the Occident wants to learn about the Spirit, about God, about the Soul, about the meaning and the mystery of this universe, he must sit at the feet of the Orient." Gandhi, by contrast, turns his back entirely on Western material techniques, placing his faith in Eastern spirituality alone.

Gandhi's sweeping rejection of modern technology, let us note, was never put into practice in India, except by himself and a few of his followers. And even Gandhi, though remaining true to his belief, did not propose a wholesale program of deindustrialization, and at times confessed that certain industries might be necessary, as long as they were strictly devoted to the benefit of the people. It is in the arena of nonviolence that Gandhi's repudiation of technology has so far proved historically fruitful. By associating technical progress with violence and both with the West and, on the other hand, technical simplicity with nonviolence and both of these with India, Gandhi and his colleagues forged a nationalistic pride in nonviolence that was to endure from about 1920, when the Congress Party adopted Gandhi's program, until 1948, when India gained independence. Thus was nationalism, which usually feeds on self-aggrandizement and militarism, wedded in India to a principle of self-restraint. (Once independent, the Indian state promptly abandoned nonviolence and immediately went to war with the newly created state of Pakistan over the territory of Kashmir; and it now possesses a large military establishment and a nuclear arsenal.)

Gandhi's embrace of nonviolence provided an escape from the discouraging choice between imitation of the West and defeat by the West. Nonviolence was a method for fighting the West *without* imitating her. As Gandhi put it in *Hind Swaraj*, "My countrymen . . . believe that they should adopt modern civilization and modern methods of violence to drive out the English. *Hind Swaraj* has been written in order to show that they are following a suicidal policy, and that, if they would but revert to their own glorious civilization, either the English would adopt the latter and become Indianized or their occupation in India would be gone."

The idea that India possessed a priceless, spiritually superior civilization was a welcome salve to the injured pride of a people that had been taught for some two hundred years to regard everything English as superior. In the words of India's first prime minister, Jawaharlal Nehru, Gandhi wrought in the consciousness of India "a psychological change, almost as if some expert in psychoanalytic methods had probed deep into the patient's past, found out the origins of his complexes, exposed them to his view, and thus rid him of that burden." In Gandhi's Manichaean celebration in *Hind Swaraj* of one civilization and condemnation of another, there is a note of chauvinism of a kind he later avoided. (Although he never repudiated *Hind Swaraj*, he would declare, "East and West are no more than names . . . there is no people to whom the moral life is a special vocation.") Yet we note at the same time a new clarity and firmness of tone in the pamphlet. Anything of the Uncle Tom that may have clung to the frock-coated, silk-hatted Gandhi as he made the rounds of the ministries of the British Empire has been purged. Soon he would adopt the simplest Indian dress. The disparate elements that composed the worldview of this rootless, much-traveled, English-trained, Esoteric Christian, immigrant to Africa, had fused in a new unity. The verbal "violence" of *Hind Swaraj* was perhaps the violence needed to rend the emotional tie with the empire. Gandhi had discovered a way to serve as a true son of India—at one, he was sure, with the spirit of his forefathers.

THE POWER OF NONVIOLENCE

There was practical as well as moral calculation in Gandhi's satyagraha. The West possessed means of violence that India could not hope to match. Gandhi later said, "Suppose Indians wish to retain by force the fruits of victory won through satyagraha. Even a child can see that if the Indians resort to force they can be crushed in a minute." Sensibly, he did not want to play a losing hand. As he explained, "The Whites were fully armed. It was clear that if the Indians were to come into their own, they must forge a weapon which would be different from and infinitely superior to, the force which the white settlers commanded in such ample measure. It was then that I introduced congregational prayer in Phoenix and Tolstoy Farm as a means for training in the use of the weapon of satyagraha or soul force." In 1909, contemplating the might of the British Empire, he wrote:

> You [British] have great military resources. Your naval power is matchless. If we wanted to fight with you on your own ground, we should be unable to do so, but if the above submissions be not acceptable to you, we cease to play the part of the ruled. You may, if you like, cut us to pieces. You may shatter us at the cannon's mouth. If you act contrary to our will, we shall not help you; and without our help, we know that you cannot move one step forward.

Gandhi's nonviolence, too, is a chapter in the story that began with Clausewitz's Prussia, which, faced with the superiority of the French revolutionary armies, had embarked on its policy of conscious imitation of the French innovations, and continued with the attempts of so many nations to "catch up" with more "modern" powers.

By the time Gandhi wrote *Hind Swaraj*, he had in effect nationalized the principle of nonviolence. He brought it down from the ether of universal beliefs and gave it a terrestrial home—India. Violence, meanwhile, seemed to have taken up residence in the modern West. But where, if anywhere, in Gandhi's newly moralized geography did his *prime* virtue, civil courage, now reside? Previously, he had found it mainly in England, and scolded his countrymen for lacking it. In *Hind Swaraj*, it seems to have been left geographically homeless. Inspiring his countrymen to take active responsibility for their own social and political lives was *the* Gandhian program, yet since India had been defined as the home of the spirit, courage in her case must not take a martial shape (brute force) but must be of a nonviolent kind (soul force). So just when Gandhi's diatribe against the satanic West reaches its highest pitch in *Hind Swaraj*, as if to justify and prepare the way for anti-Western violence, the restraining hand of nonviolence seems to reach in and turn the criticism and toward the passivity of his own countrymen. Psychologically speaking, we can almost watch the anger at the hated "other" being checked and directed back toward the self, which is excoriated with double fury.

Whatever pleasures of national pride Gandhi may have offered his countrymen when he called their ancient civilization the most godly of all he now more than took back. He dashed the sweet cup of national self-congratulation from the thirsting lips of the humiliated Indians. It is in the passages explaining England's domination of India that *Hind Swaraj* began to chart new political territory. Gandhi held Indians, not Englishmen, responsible for India's colonial dependency. "The English have not taken India," he wrote, "we have given it to them." He explained:

> They came to our country originally for purposes of trade. Recall the Company Bahadur. Who made it Bahadur? They had not the slightest intention at the time of establishing a kingdom. Who assisted the Company's officers? Who was tempted at the sight of their silver? Who bought their goods? History testifies that we all did this. In order to become rich all at once we welcomed the Company's officers with open arms. We assisted them.

Gandhi later elucidated his point:

> It is because the rulers, if they are bad, are so not necessarily or wholly by reason of birth, but largely because of their environment, that I have hopes of their altering their course. It is perfectly true . . . that the rulers cannot alter their course themselves. If they are dominated by their environment, they do not surely deserve to be killed, but should be changed by a change of environment. But the environment are we—the people who make the rulers what they are. They are thus an exaggerated edition of what we are in the aggregate. If my argument is sound, any violence done to the rulers would be violence done to ourselves. It would be suicide. And since I do not want to commit suicide, nor encourage my neighbors to do so, I become nonviolent myself and invite my neighbors to do likewise.

Liberal-minded people have often held that society's victims are corrupted by a bad "environment" created by their privileged masters. Gandhi was surely the first to suggest that the victims were creating a bad moral environment for their masters—and to preach reform to the *victims*. Even allowing for a certain raillery and sardonicism in these passages, there can be no doubt that Gandhi is in earnest. Here we touch bedrock in Gandhi's political thinking. All government, he steadily believed, depends for its existence on the cooperation of the governed. If that cooperation is withdrawn, the government will be helpless. Government is composed of civil servants, soldiers, and citizens. Each of these people has a will. If enough of them withdraw their support from the government, it will fall.

This idea had admittedly occurred to political thinkers in the past. For instance, the sixteenth-century French writer Étienne de La Boétie had observed of tyrants, "the more is given them, the more they are obeyed, so much the more do they fortify themselves," and therefore "if nothing be given them, if they be not obeyed, without fighting, without striking a blow, they remain naked, disarmed and are nothing." The philosopher of the English enlightenment David Hume likewise believed that all government, even tyranny, rested on a kind of support. "The soldan of Egypt or the emperor of Rome," he wrote, "might drive his harmless subjects like brute beasts against their sentiments and inclination. But he must, at least, have led his *mameluks* or *praetorian bands*, like men, by their opinion." And James Madison once wrote, "All governments rest on opinion."

Gandhi, however, was the first to found upon this belief a thoroughgoing program of action and a radically new understanding of the relationship of violence to politics. The central role of consent in all government meant that noncooperation—the withdrawal of consent—was something more than a morally satisfying activity; it was a powerful weapon in the real world. He stated and restated the belief in many ways throughout his life:

> I believe and everybody must grant that no Government can exist for a single moment without the cooperation of the people, willing or forced, and if people withdraw their cooperation in every detail, the Government will come to a standstill.

Gandhi's politics was not a politics of the moral gesture. It rested on an interpretation of political power and was an exercise of power. From his surprising premises Gandhi drew a conclusion more surprising still:

> The causes that gave them [the English] India enable them to retain it. Some Englishmen state that they took and they hold India by the sword. Both these statements are wrong. The sword is entirely useless for holding India. We alone keep them.

Gandhi does not merely say that English rule is made possible by Indian acquiescence; he goes a step further and charges that Indians "keep" the English, almost as if the English were struggling to get away and the Indians were pulling them back. Gandhi's claim flies in the face of the one conviction on which everyone else in the imperial scheme, whether ruler or ruled, agreed—that, in the words of the *London Times*, it was "by the sword that we conquered India, and it is by the sword that we hold it." (We cannot prove that Gandhi had read the *Times* editorial, but the similarity in wording of the passage above suggests that he had.) Some enthusiastically approved of this supremacy of the sword, some bowed to it, and some despised it, but only Gandhi denied that it was a fact. Not only was force, in Gandhi's thinking, not the "final arbiter," it was no arbiter at all. What arbitrated was consent, and the cooperation that flowed from it, and these were the foundation of dictatorship as well as of democratic government.

MORE ACTIVE THAN VIOLENCE

Governments do not normally fall simply of their own weight. Action is required. The obligation to act, in Gandhi's view, took precedence over even the obligation to remain nonviolent. "Noncooperation is not a passive state," Gandhi said, "it is an intensely active state—more active than physical resistance or violence." Satyagraha was *soul* force, but equally it was soul *force*.

Asked to choose between violence and passivity, Gandhi always chose violence. "It is better to be violent, if there is violence in our breasts," he said, "than to put on the cloak of nonviolence to cover impotence. Violence is any day preferable to impotence. There is hope for a violent man to become non-violent. There is no such hope for the impotent." "Activist" is a word that fits Gandhi through and through. "I am not built for academic writings," he said. "Action is my domain." Indeed, if he was a genius in any field, that field was action. "Never has anything been done on this earth without direct action."

In 1917, soon after he returned to India, he would say, "There is no love where there is no will. In India there is not only no love but hatred due to emasculation. There is the strongest desire to fight and kill side by side with utter helplessness. This desire must be satisfied by restoring the capacity of fighting. Then comes the choice." In 1918, he would shock his followers by enlisting as a recruiting sergeant for Indian troops to fight for the British in the First World War. How, his colleagues wondered, then and later, could the advocate of nonviolence recruit soldiers for this war—a mechanized slaughter of millions that surely had to rank as the prime exhibit in Gandhi's indictment of modern technical civilization for its "violence of the blackest sort"? His campaign, which proved almost fruitless, can be explained only by his belief that what India needed even more than nonviolence was the will and courage that would propel its people into action—even if this meant serving in war under the British.

Intuitively, nonviolence appears to have a restraining or crippling influence on action. To Gandhi, however, nonviolence appeared in exactly the opposite light. Nonviolent action had nothing to do with quietism or passivity. Noncooperation was, Gandhi believed, supremely energetic. "Another remedy [to injustice] there certainly is, and that is armed revolt," he acknowledged, but "Civil disobedience is a complete, effective and bloodless substitute." If Gandhi embraced nonviolence, it was not because, in the interest of an ideal, he accepted a competitive disadvantage. Satyagraha was not some pale sister of violence, embraced for her virtue alone. For Gandhi such acceptance would have constituted an unacceptable abdication of responsibility.

But how could someone who checked his energy be called more energetic and more powerful than someone who unleashed it without restraint? Weren't Gandhi's two dictates—that one must *act* directly, unhesitatingly, and fearlessly and that one must do so nonviolently—at war with one another? The kinship of action and violence, indeed, seems natural, and it's tempting to see Gandhi's nonviolence only as an attempted remedy for the danger. In this view, nonviolence would be seen as a reduction of freedom in which a certain passivity and loss of energy is the price paid for keeping the peace. And certainly Gandhi did see nonviolence as a cure for the danger inherent in mass action. He often said that in his time the rising tide of action would irresistibly occur whether leaders like him encouraged it or not, and that his job was to help guide it into peaceful channels. "A new order of things is replacing the old," he wrote as he embarked on a campaign of satyagraha on behalf of mill workers in his home city of Ahmedabad. "It can be established peacefully or it must be preceded by some painful disturbances. . . . I presumptuously believe that I can step into the breach and may succeed in stopping harmful disturbances during our passage to the new state of things. . . . I can only do so if I can show the people a better and more expeditious way of righting wrongs." He adamantly denied that the price of restraining violence entailed a reduction of energy and power. On the contrary, he claimed that satyagraha, far from being a restriction on action, was action at last unrestricted and unbound—action grown to the full height of its potential. "Nonviolence," he said, "is without exception superior to violence, i.e., the power at the disposal of a nonviolent person is always greater than he would have if he was violent."

Any action, Gandhi knew, called above all for willpower—for the sort of courage that was especially conspicuous in soldiers. But nonviolent action required even more courage of this sort. Gandhi was fond of a statue of Charles Gordon, a British general of imperial fame, which shows him carrying a mere riding crop instead of a weapon. Gandhi commented:

> The practice of *ahimsa* calls forth the greatest courage. It is the most soldierly of a soldier's virtues. General Gordon has been represented in a famous statue as bearing only a stick. This takes us far on the road to *ahimsa*. But a soldier who needs the protection of even a stick is to that extent so much the less a soldier. He is the true soldier who knows how to die and stand his ground in the midst of a hail of bullets.

Action, moreover, flourishes, Gandhi believed, in freedom; and nonviolent action, precisely because it requires the highest possible degree of courage, exhibits the largest freedom. Violence, although initiated in pursuit of political goals, can take on a life of its own, which distracts from the original goals, and may eventually compete with them or supplant them entirely. On the local scale, this leads to vendetta, which can outlast by generations any political or other purposes that gave rise to a quarrel. On a much wider scale, the logic of war can, as Clause-witz warned with such clarity, entirely supersede the political purposes that lend war whatever sense it may have. On each of these levels, the actors surrender their freedom of action to a process over which they have lost control.

The nonviolent actor exhibits the highest degree of freedom also because his action originates within himself, according to his own judgment, inclination, and conscience, not in helpless, automatic response to something done by someone else. He is thus a creator, not a mere responder. It is not digressive to recall a passage from a writer who might at first appear to be pretty much a polar opposite of Gandhi yet also associated nonviolence not with weakness but with a superabundance of energy and power. Friedrich Nietzsche, asking himself whether such a thing as a Christian turning of the other cheek was really possible, said that, if it were, it would be for only the strongest natures. He wrote:

> To be incapable of taking one enemies, one's accidents, even one's misdeeds seriously for very long—that is the sign of strong, full natures in whom there is an excess of the power to form, to mold, to recuperate and to forget. . . . Such a man shakes off with a *single* shrug many vermin that eat deep into others; here alone genuine "love of one's enemies" is possible—supposing it to be possible at all on earth. How much reverence has a noble man for his enemies!—and such reverence is a bridge to love. . . . In contrast to this, picture "the enemy" as the man of *ressentiment* conceives him—and here precisely is his deed, his creation: he has conceived "the evil enemy," "THE EVIL ONE," and this in fact is his basic concept, from which he then evolves, as an afterthought and pendant, a "good one"—himself!

If such magnanimous characters—free alike of fear and lust for revenge, and braver than soldiers—had not found an appropriate arena for their kind of activity, they might have passed through history without leaving any mark but the admiration of a few people around them. Their arena could not, of course, be war. In fact, it was the arena of nonviolent action, soon to be strewn with the debris of the world's empires and some of its mightiest and most violent regimes.

NONCOOPERATION IN INDIA

In 1915, Gandhi brought his battle-tested instrument of nonviolence from little Natal and Transvaal to great India. In South

Africa, the forty thousand Indians had been a small minority, amounting to less than 10 percent of the total population. In India, they were a huge majority, of more than three hundred million, ruled over by a mere hundred thousand or so English. When forty thousand refused cooperation, it was a serious crisis for the imperial rulers; but if the three hundred million refused cooperation it was the end of the Raj, and probably of the British Empire as well. That, at least, was the view of Winston Churchill, who said in Parliament in 1931, "The loss of India would be final and fatal to us. It would not fail to be part of a process that would reduce us to the scale of a minor power." Gandhi agreed. "Through deliverance of India," he wrote, "I seek to deliver the so-called weaker races of the earth from the crushing heels of Western exploitation in which England is the greatest partner." History proved both men right.

Gandhi began modestly. Following the suggestion of his political mentor in India, the National Congress Party leader Gopal Krishna Gokhale, he maintained a public silence for a year, contenting himself with traveling throughout India in third-class railway compartments, in order to acquaint himself with the state of the country. Beginning in 1917, he engaged in a series of local satyagraha campaigns. One was in opposition to the exploitation of peasants cultivating indigo, out of which dye is made, in Bihar, in the Champaran district; a second was in support of decent wages for the mill workers in his native city of Ahmedabad; a third was in opposition to a British-imposed tax that was ruining the peasants of the Kheda district. Each campaign was a grueling, self-contained, high-stakes drama, pitting the willingness of peasants and workers and of Gandhi himself to suffer for their cause against the will of powerful factory owners and state authorities. "A series of passive resistances is an agonizing effort," he wrote of these campaigns to a friend, Henry Polak. "It is an exalting agony. I suppose the agony of childbirth must be somewhat like it." His modus operandi in these and subsequent campaigns included, as his biographer Judith M. Brown has written, "the search for a peaceful solution at the outset, the sacred pledge as the heart of the struggle, strict discipline and self-improvement among the participants, careful publicity and the generation of an ambience of moral authority and pressure, and finally a compromise solution to save the face and honor of all concerned." In the Ahmedabad strike, he fasted in support of a cause for the first time since arriving in India. His aim was twofold—to bring the pressure of "self-suffering" to bear on his opponent and to purify himself spiritually. A few years later, he explained, "I can as well do without my eyes . . . as I can without fasts. What the eyes are for the outer world, fasts are for the inner." Gandhi's methods and style, which made the privileged, moderate leaders of the Congress Party deeply uncomfortable, appealed strongly to masses of ordinary Indians, and Gandhi became India's first truly national figure.

In 1917, in the most discouraging days of the First World War, England had announced a series of liberal reforms that would increase Indians' participation in the administration of their own country. Yet when the war ended, in November 1918, these hopes were thwarted by the passage of the repressive Anarchical and Revolution Crimes Act, known also as the Rowlatt Act, imposed after an investigation by the British authorities of the possibilities for terrorism and "sedition" in India. In Gandhi's eyes, the Rowlatt bills were for the India of 1918 what the Amendment Ordinance of the Asiatic Act had been for the South Africa of 1906. He called both "black acts," and resisted both with full-scale campaigns of noncooperation. He called the Rowlatt bills evidence of "a determined policy of repression," and announced that henceforth "civil disobedience seems to be a duty imposed on every lover of personal public liberty," declaring that he was ready to fight "the greatest battle of my life."

Noncooperation was to continue in India, on and off, for the next three decades. In February of 1919, Gandhi announced his first nationwide act of resistance—a *hartal*, or strike, against the Rowlatt legislation. The *hartal* was observed throughout the country. This was Gandhi's answer to Omdurman and the weapons of civilization—not India heaping the ground with English corpses but masses of Indians withdrawing cooperation from English rule. A few days after the *hartal*, however, the British arrested him, whereupon riots broke out in Ahmedabad, and Gandhi found himself facing a problem he had not faced in South Africa—violence by his own supporters. An English policeman and others were killed.

Gandhi's response was to launch "*satyagraha* against our-selves," by fasting for three days. "In the place I have made my abode I find utter lawlessness bordering almost on Bolshevism," he now wrote to the viceroy's private secretary. "Englishmen and women have found it necessary to leave their bungalows and to confine themselves to a few well-guarded houses. It is a matter of the deepest humiliation and regret to me. I see that I overcalculated the measure of permeation of satyagraha amongst the people. . . . My satyagraha . . . will, at the present moment, be directed against my own countrymen." In 1922, shortly after launching noncooperation on an even wider scale, he again suspended it, after mobs of protesters burned a police station in the city of Chauri Chaura, and hacked several police-men to pieces. "All of us should be in mourning," he said. "May God save the honor of India." He fasted for five days in penance and the protest never was resumed.

In a campaign of noncooperation against the salt tax in 1930—probably the most renowned of his actions—Gandhi marched with seventy-five or so followers to the sea to make salt, in defiance of an English monopoly on salt making, and then was jailed, after which his followers marched nonviolently upon the saltworks at Dharasana, suffering many dozens of casualties at the hands of police wielding clubs. The upshot was an invitation to meet the viceroy, Lord Reading. The two men agreed that Gandhi would represent India at a constitutional conference in London. The conference failed, and another decade of resistance and repression began. The final nationwide noncooperation campaign—the Quit India campaign—was launched in 1942, in the third year of the Second World War, and was quickly and violently repressed; India did not attain her independence until the war ended, when England's grip on all her imperial possessions was weakening.

It is not certain that it was satyagraha that broke England's grip on India. The great hoped-for day never came on which all India refused cooperation with the English rulers, who therefore, finding themselves barking orders at an indifferent population, had nothing left to do but pull up stakes and leave. The English weathered all the individual satyagraha campaigns. It's also true that many factors other than satyagraha conspired to drive the English out. English trade with India declined in importance. The depression and the two world wars weakened England, forcing her finally to yield her position of global preeminence to the United States.

On the other hand, satyagraha unquestionably succeeded in winning the battle for the hearts and minds of the people of India. When the Second World War ended, although the back of the Quit India campaign had been broken, the viceroy, Lord Wavell, was well aware that "while the British are still legally and morally responsible for what happens in India, we have lost nearly all power to control events; we are simply running on the momentum of our previous prestige." Just as de Gaulle came to understand in Algeria that victories through repression and violence were in the long run as useless as conventional battle-field victories in a people's war, so now Wavell acknowledged that technical victories against nonviolent opponents would in the long run prove equally useless. All these imperial defeats pointed to a lesson, which was spelled out clearly in Gandhi's writings: in a struggle for independence in our democratic age, the decisive contest, whose essence is political and therefore nonviolent, is not for control of any piece of territory but for the loyalty and cooperation of the people. Violence, where it is present, plays only a supporting role. It was Gandhi's discovery that violence did not need to play any role at all.

THE SHADOW

That lesson, however, is in fact a secondary one. When Gandhi arrived back in India in 1915, he knew he faced not only the evil of British rule but also the mountainous social ills of India, most of which had predated the Raj and would outlast it. The most important tasks, he believed, were providing a decent life, including adequate food, shelter, and sanitation, for India's "dumb millions," establishing a system of active self-government in the country's seven hundred thousand villages, ending the Hindu system of untouchability, raising the status of women, and making and keeping peace among Hindus and Muslims. Although *swaraj*—"self-rule"—included ejecting the English, he always believed that addressing these ills was its deeper and more important task.

Noncooperation, taken by itself, was useless for this purpose.

It could do nothing to feed the hungry, to relieve the oppressed, to make peace among India's quarreling ethnic and religious groups. For these purposes, positive action was required. Gandhi gave it the unostentatious name of "the constructive program." Noncooperation embodied the obligation to reject participation in oppression. The constructive program embodied the obligation to actively pursue social betterment—"truth." As such, it was closer than noncooperation to the central meaning of "satyagraha," which is "to hold fast to truth." The story of Gandhi's satyagraha has traditionally concentrated on the three great noncooperation campaigns; but his most persistent efforts were his unceasing work in support of the constructive program. It's notable, for instance, that all of his "fasts unto death" (from each of which he was released by progress in solving the issue about which he was fasting) were launched in the name of one plank or another of the constructive program—of bringing justice to the workers of Ahmedabad, of ending untouchability, of making peace between Hindus and Muslims. "Satyagraha," he said, "is not predominantly civil disobedience, but a quiet and irresistible pursuit of truth. On the rarest occasions it becomes civil disobedience."

A constructive program to address social ills may seem so elementary as scarcely to be an idea; yet few things caused more controversy in the Congress Party than Gandhi's dedication to it. In one of the lulls between noncooperation movements, Gandhi joked that in Congress "I stand thoroughly discredited as a religious maniac and predominantly a social worker." Most of the Congress leaders wanted to concentrate first on winning power and only then on addressing India's social ills. Gandhi reversed this order of business. He wanted Congress to address India's ills immediately and directly without regard to the English and their Raj. (The similarity between this program and the strategy of people's war is clear. In Gandhi's scheme, noncooperation was the nonviolent counterpart of guerrilla war while the constructive program was the counterpart of the Vietnamese *hiérarchies parallèles*.)

His thinking on the relationship of the constructive program to power was revealed in an answer to a letter from a reader of his journal *Indian Opinion* in 1931. The reader had written to protest that his constructive work was getting in the way of the attempt to take political power. "To me," the reader wrote, "political power is the substance, and all the other forms have to wait." Gandhi answered that "political power is not an end but only a means enabling people to better their condition in every department of life." Therefore, "Constructive effort is the substance of political power [while] actual taking over of the government machinery is but a shadow, an emblem." Five years later, at a time when he was devoting himself almost entirely to the constructive program, he wrote:

> One must forget the political goal in order to realize it. To think of the political goal at every step is to raise unnecessary dust. Why worry one's head over a thing that is inevitable? Why die before one's death? . . . That is why I can take the keenest interest in discussing vitamins and leafy vegetables and unpolished rice. That is why it has become a matter of absorbing interest to me to find out how best to clean our latrines.

If the goal was the renovation of India, why not proceed to it directly? Why not pick up a broom and sweep a latrine—as Gandhi in fact did at the first Congress meeting he attended, in 1915. If one concentrated too much on seizing the means of betterment, he feared, one might forget the goal. And in fact when India did achieve independence, this, in Gandhi's view, is exactly what happened. The Congress leaders took power but forgot what power was for. On October 2, 1947, when offered birthday congratulations, he answered, "Where do congratulations come in? It will be more appropriate to say condolences. There is nothing but anguish in my heart."

This is by no means to say, however, that Gandhi did not value political power, or did not believe in winning it or exercising it. He aimed at both throughout his life, though never as a government official. He did not say that the Congress Party should not take power; rather, he said that this was inevitable. Power might be only a "shadow"; on the other hand, there never was a thing that lacked its shadow.

He frequently suggested, indeed, that the constructive program was as effective a path to political power as noncooperation. Political power, he wrote, would in fact increase in "exact proportion" to success in the constructive effort. Whereas noncooperation drained power away from the oppressors, the constructive program generated it in the hands of the resisters. "When a body of men disown the state under which they have hitherto lived," he said in 1921, "they nearly establish their own government. I say nearly, for they do not go to the point of using force when they are resisted by the state."

Gandhi's view that winning state power, though necessary, should not be the supreme goal of India's political activity was also expressed in his arguments against adopting independence from England as the primary aim of Congress. As late as 1928, he opposed—successfully—a Congress independence resolution in response to the appointment by the English of a Statutory Commission for India. He had made his reasons clear as early as the publication of *Hind Swaraj*. Independence meant expelling the English and taking the reins of government. But did India want "English rule without the Englishman"? Gandhi rejected this vision, as was not surprising for someone who at the time regarded the condition of modern England as "pitiable." He explained, "My patriotism does not teach me that I am to allow people to be crushed under the heel of Indian princes if only the English retire."

Independence meant dissociation—a merely negative goal. *Swaraj* meant building up something new. "Not only could *swaraj* not be 'given' to Indians," he said, "but rather it had to be created by them." Gandhi wanted action by Indians to better their own lives, not concessions or grants of authority from foreigners. *Swaraj*, as distinct from independence, must proceed from within each Indian. "Has independence suddenly become a goal in answer to something offensive that some Englishman has done?" he asked. And he went on, in simple words that seem to me to come close to the core of this arch-innovator's view of action and its proper place in the scheme of life, "Do men conceive their goals in order to oblige people or to resent their action? I submit that if it is a goal, it must be declared and pursued irrespective of the acts or threats of others." For Gandhi, ending untouchability, cleaning latrines, improving the diet of Indian villagers, improving the lot of Indian women, making peace between Muslims and Hindus—through all of which he believed he would find God—were such goals.

5

Nonviolent Revolution, Nonviolent Rule

Most of the formative revolutions of modern Western history were violent in one degree or another. They have been consigned—in political theory, if not in historical writing—to the anarchic state in which violence has always been assumed to be the final arbiter of events. The extreme violence of the French Revolution of 1789 and the Russian Revolution of 1917 is in fact probably the chief historical basis for the rarely doubted proposition that in revolution violence rules. We may inquire, though, in light of Gandhi's experience, to what extent the political theorists have been correct. In the chapters that follow, we will reflect upon a pivotal moment in four revolutions—the Glorious Revolution in England in 1689, the American Revolution, the French Revolution, and the Russian Revolution—and then we will turn to the recent Soviet collapse. Our purpose, needless to say, will not be to suggest that these revolutions were lacking in violence. It will be to ask what the roles of violent and nonviolent action were.

One point is clear at the outset: the possibility of nonviolent revolution is rooted in the democratic revolution of modern times. Violence is a method by which the ruthless few can subdue the passive many. Nonviolence is a means by which the active many can overcome the ruthless few. In this respect, it is like people's war. If the people are not politically conscious—if they have not "risen to the height of political being," in the phrase of the German revolutionary Rosa Luxemburg—they can be neither a nourishing sea for the guerrilla fish nor a mighty army of noncooperators. This is not to say that acts of civil disobedience by a few people, or even a single person, are unimportant. "I know this well," the American pioneer of civil disobedience Henry David Thoreau wrote in the 1840s: "If one thousand, if one hundred, if ten men whom I could name—if ten honest men only—ay, if one HONEST man, in this State of Massachusetts, ceasing to hold slaves, were actually to withdraw from this co-partnership, and be locked up in the county jail therefor, it would be the abolition of slavery in America." Yet in the long run the influence of such individuals will depend on the participation of the many. War cannot be waged without guns, tanks, and planes. Nonviolent resistance cannot be waged without active, steadfast, committed masses of unarmed people. The civil-rights movement led by Martin Luther King in the United States provides an illustration. The courageous campaign of a minority, mostly black, touched the conscience of an inactive majority, mostly white, who provided the political support necessary for the movement's historic judicial, legislative, and social victories.

It is also helpful to keep in mind the classic observation that revolutions pass through two distinct stages—overthrow of the ancien régime and foundation of a new one. Political theory as well as common sense suggests that overthrow, an act of destruction, should require violence. It seems equally obvious that the subsequent stage of foundation of the new regime, an act of creation, should be peaceful. However, the historical record shows that the reverse has much more often been the case. The overthrow has often been carried out with little or no bloodshed, while the foundation—and the revolutionary rule that follows it—has been bathed in blood.

THE "BATTLE" OF SALISBURY FIELD

On Sunday, November 5, 1688, when the Dutch stadtholder, William of Orange, landed at the head of fifteen thousand troops at Brixham on Torbay, on the southern coast of England, there was every reason to suppose that the ensuing contest with King James II of England would be a bloody one. Still fresh in everyone's mind was the civil war of the 1640s, in which parliamentary armies had defeated the royal forces of Charles I, and in 1649 beheaded him. William, the head of the Dutch state, was James's nephew and son-in-law, and he had been invited to invade by powerful disaffected British nobles and clergy. The fundamental issues underlying the conflict—whether king or Parliament would be politically supreme and whether Protestantism would prevail in England—had first come to a head in the civil war.

James mustered his troops and sent them to Salisbury field,

where they awaited William's army. The stage was set for a classic decision by arms. But no battle occurred, nor would one during the Glorious Revolution, also known as the Bloodless Revolution. Within a week, James, still in command of numerically superior forces, retreated from the field. A week later he ordered his commander in chief, Lord Feversham, to disband his force, but by then James's army was already dissolving as rapidly as if it had suffered decisive military defeat in classical Clausewitzian combat. James then ordered the destruction of the writs by which parliaments were summoned, threw the Great Seal—emblem of royal authority—into the river Thames, and fled.

What had happened? A contest not of arms but of defection and allegiance had taken place. The tide had run in one direction: the defection was almost all on the side of James, the allegiance on the side of William. The defectors included Colonel Cornbury, the son of Lord Clarendon, one of the king's principal advisers, John Churchill (the future Duke of Marlborough and ancestor of Winston Churchill), and, finally, King James's daughter, Princess Anne. Thomas Macaulay, the nineteenth-century historian and Member of Parliament, wrote in his seminal history of the revolution, "It was true that the direct loss to the crown and the direct gain to the invaders hardly amounted to two hundred men and as many horses. . . . But where could the King henceforth expect to find those sentiments in which consists the strength of states and armies?" He continues, "That prompt obedience without which an army is merely a rabble was necessarily at an end." For, "The material strength of the army were little diminished: but its moral strength had been destroyed." In the first epic battle for hearts and minds of the modern period, the decision had gone, bloodlessly, to the insurrectionary forces.

William did not frame a plan of nonviolent action; but he didn't quite stumble into his nonviolent victory, either. From the beginning, *waiting* had been his calculated strategy. He was an inveterate, zealous soldier—soon he would marshal a coalition of forces that would defeat the expansionist continental plans of Louis XIV, the Sun King of France—but in 1688 he calculated that combat with James would hurt his cause. Actual battle, he feared, would rouse the national spirit of the

English against his mostly foreign troops. James, on the other hand, understood that the mere fact of battle would favor his cause. "The king was eager to fight," Macaulay explains, "and it was obviously in his interest to do so. Every hour took away something from his own strength, and added something to the strength of his enemies. It was important, too, that his troops should be blooded." Win or lose, James knew, a battle in which English soldiers were wounded and killed would stoke the patriotic ire of the English. Unfortunately for James, "All this William perfectly understood, and determined to avoid an action as long as possible."

Commanders in the field naturally weigh the strength of the opposing forces. The two sovereigns who pondered battle at Salisbury, however, had a prior question to consider: *which* forces were the ones that would count, and *where* would the decisive struggle take place? Would it be on the field of combat, where soldiers wounded and killed each other, or would it be on that other, silent "battlefield," the hearts and minds of the people, where allegiance is won or lost? According to Macaulay, James and William somehow understood that the second field was the important one, and so combat played almost no role in the Glorious Revolution. "That great force," Macaulay writes of James's army, "had been absolutely of no account in the late change, had done nothing towards keeping William out, and had nothing towards bringing him in."

Much of what Macaulay—the great purveyor of liberal "Whig history"—wrote in the nineteenth century about the seventeenth has been challenged by historians in the twentieth, but his assessment of the role of violence in the revolution, on the whole, has not. In the 1930s, for example, G. M. Trevelyan wrote, "No encounter of the least military importance took place," and added, "the war was won and lost in the camp at Salisbury, and in the mind and heart of James." And the contemporary historian J. G. A. Pocock has described William's progress as follows: "William of Orange, a powerful European prince, landed in the west of England at the head of an army in campaign order, composed of regiments of long-service professionals in historic transition from the status of *condottieri* [mercenary commanders] to that of a national army. . . . The campaign of 1688 . . . had no military solution, only a political and revolutionary one; by 'revolution' would here be meant the dramatic collapse of a power structure and the overthrow of its head."

Pocock's words suggest that William found himself wrestling with the same distinction between military and political power that arose in people's wars in our century. If the Americans in Vietnam illustrated the negative proposition that military victory can be worthless without political victory, William illustrated the complementary proposition that political victory can be complete without military victory. That is why, whereas no amount of fighting could bring the Americans victory, no fighting at all was necessary to bring victory to William. In both cases, political victory was paramount. (What is perhaps most surprising to modern sensibilities about these pre-national or proto-national events is that William, a foreigner, was the popular, patriotic choice of the English, whereas the native James was spurned.)

William's popularity had not sprung out of nowhere. James's political support had ebbed among the people long before his armies melted away at Salisbury field. Two years earlier, James had sent his army to intimidate London, which was in a state of virtual rebellion against him. "The King . . . had greatly miscalculated," Macaulay tells us. "He had forgotten that vicinity operates in more ways than one. He had hoped that his army would overawe London: but the result of his policy was that the feelings and opinions of London took complete possession of his army." London was in fact the first of many modern capitals whose rebellious spirit was to infect and destroy the allegiance of an army of an ancien régime.

The outcome of this contagion had been prepared by what can aptly be called a protracted, nationwide movement of non-cooperation. The principal issues in the civil struggle between the English Parliament and James II had been in contention throughout his reign: first, whether James, a Catholic, could impose his faith on the largely Protestant English and, second, whether the prerogatives of a king were to be subordinate to the rights and powers of Parliament in particular and of law in general, or whether James was to be an "absolute" monarch, like Louis XIV. The key events in the struggle against James were acts of nonviolent resistance by men ready to pay a high price for their disobedience. Their storied deeds included the refusal of Magdalen College at Oxford to accept the king's arbitrary attempt to impose a Catholic rector on that Protestant institution and the resistance of seven Anglican bishops to his demand that they read a declaration of indulgence, which was offensive to most Anglicans and other Protestants, in their churches. The bishops' resistance was followed by their trial and dramatic acquittal, all leading directly to the decision by the great lords, on the very day of the acquittal, to invite William to invade. When King James, attempting to create a submissive parliament, ordered his lords lieutenant to scour England for subservient electors, Lord Bath was forced to report back, "No one of note will accept." He went on, "Sir, if your Majesty should dismiss these gentlemen [then sitting in Parliament], their successors would give exactly the same answer."

When the king ordered the public reading by the rest of the Anglican clergy of his declaration of indulgence, the result was similar. Macaulay describes what happened in the king's own palace: "The minister who had officiated at the chapel in Saint James's Palace had been turned out of his situation, and a more obsequious divine appeared with the paper in his hand: but his agitation was so great that he could not articulate. In truth the feeling of the whole nation had now become such as none but the very best and noblest, or the very worst and basest, of mankind could without much discomposure encounter." Macaulay's enthusiastic summary is a portrait of the politically engaged portion of the country united in de facto nonviolent resistance to its ruler. "Actuated by these sentiments," Macaulay concludes, "our ancestors arrayed themselves against the government in one huge and compact mass. All ranks, all parties, all Protestant sects, made up that vast phalanx." Here was the victory that put William on the throne, though he was not to arrive in England until a year later. If Macaulay was right, then the face-off at Salisbury was the last act of a long nonviolent struggle that had been waged in civil society. What need was there for a battle if, with the mere passage of time, one side would throw down its arms?

CONQUEST OR CONSENT?

It was one thing for William to defeat James, another to take the English crown. William's approach to foundation was entirely of a piece with his approach to overthrow. In both, he relied for success not on arms but on consent by those Englishmen who had the power to decide the matter. Macaulay explains:

> His only chance of obtaining the splendid prize [the British crown] was not to seize it rudely but to wait till, without any appearance of exertion or stratagem on his part, his secret wish should be accomplished by the force of circumstances, by the blunders of his opponents, and by the free choice of the Estates of the Realm.

William convened a Revolutionary Convention, composed of lords, representatives of the House of Commons, and city magistrates, to deliberate and decide the disposition of the crown and the constitutional shape of the future. The debates revolved around the question of how, in a political system in which most agreed that the throne was and should remain hereditary, an alteration in the line of succession could be justified.

Two factions, already known as Whigs and Tories, put forward their solutions. The Whigs, who had long favored parliamentary power and had led the resistance to James from the beginning, proposed a contract theory of governing, according to which the subject's oath of allegiance to the king must be reciprocated by a royal oath of service to the people and allegiance to the law of the land. A modest, deliberate breach in the succession (William being the son of James's sister), they alleged, would merely bring the underlying contractual character of kingship out into the open—a good thing, in their eyes, for their party and its predecessors had been agitating for a contractual basis for government for more than half a century. The Tories, who denied that there could be any contractual foundation for royal rule or *any* right of resistance to a king's commands by a subject, were in a quandary. They, too, had been driven into opposition to James—by his attack on Anglicanism, among other things. They had done in fact what they had disavowed in theory: they had resisted and then driven out their king. The question was how they could justify this. For some, William's joint investiture with his wife, Mary, James's elder daughter, and the nearest *Protestant* heir to the crown, provided some legitimacy to the deed. Others suggested that they were simply submitting to conquest; for, as Macaulay notes, "No jurist, no divine, had ever denied that a nation, overcome in war, might, without sin, submit to decisions of the God of battles." The advantage to the Tories of claiming that William had conquered England was that it delivered the country from any taint of the hated contract theory. What contract could there be when a people had submitted at swordpoint?

Unfortunately, the claim was clearly contrary to fact. True, armies had marched. True, they had arrayed themselves for battle. But they had never fought. In what sense, then, had the English been conquered? Everything William had won had been delivered to him by willing Englishmen, many of whom were Tories. In effect, the English had chosen a new king. William, ever the realist, declined the temptation to misinterpret his success as a conquest. "For call himself what he might," Macaulay comments, "all the world knew that he was not really a conqueror. It was notoriously a mere fiction to say that this great kingdom, with a mighty fleet on the sea, with a regular army of forty thousand men . . . without one siege or battle, had been reduced to the state of a province by fifteen thousand invaders. Such a fiction . . . could scarcely fail to gall the national pride . . ."

William chose the contractual solution. The choice was anything but arbitrary. More than half a century of struggle between Parliament and the king pointed in that direction. In his announcement of his invasion, he had sworn to defend "a free parliament." Now he would accept the crown only with the agreement of the Revolutionary Convention, on terms that it set forth. They turned out to include a Declaration of Right, later formalized as the Bill of Rights. This decision by William, in turn, laid the foundation for government based on the supremacy of Parliament over the king and of law over both. Overthrow based on consent had made possible foundation based on consent, which in turn made possible government based on consent. Although no balloting had occurred, the English had chosen their political future freely, and they would continue, in greater and greater measure, to do so from then on. The basis for the creation of a government that was to become, after a long development, the liberal democratic rule we know today was, in fact, a nonviolent revolution.

It would be preposterous to present William of Orange—that great warrior-king—as any sort of pacifist. Nevertheless, the revolution he brought about rested not on fear but indeed on a kind of consent. William, who may have merely happened upon the power of nonviolence, was shrewd enough to seize the opportunity. But having seized it, he found himself subject to its laws. William was not a dreamer. His biographers describe him as "cold," "taciturn," "reserved," "gloomy." A Dutchman, he spoke English imperfectly and had little emotional attachment to England. "To him she was always a land of exile, visited with reluctance and quitted with delight." "What the king wanted was power," his recent biographer Stephen B. Baxter writes, "power enough to bring England into an alliance against Louis XIV and to keep her there." But the means to this end, he understood, was not to establish absolute rule in England, even supposing it were possible.

For most of the seventeenth century, William's Stuart predecessors had battled over the power of the purse with Parliament, which had responded at several key junctures by severely curtailing the king's resources for war on the continent. It was their strongest weapon in their fight with the king. William grasped that a free parliament might be willing to loosen its purse strings to an extent that a coerced, manipulated one would not. From his point of view, granting Parliament its freedom was a recipe for more, not less power in pursuit of his aim of fighting Louis on the continent. Thus for a second time William increased his power through an act of restraint. In deciding on both of these policies, he took his bearings from the same underlying fact: his support among the English public. And both policies were richly rewarded in exactly the coin he sought: power. What is more striking still, the system of government thus established proved a fountainhead of new power for the country that established it. England at that moment began the long rise to an international preeminence that lasted through the first several decades of the past century. It is true that England's power was based on other strengths as well, including its central bank and trading system, its technical genius, which placed it in the forefront of the industrial revolution, and its early development of the free-market system, but it may be doubted that any of these would have served England as they did if not reared on the foundation of the unique system of government created in 1689. In the words of Trevelyan, "The Revolution gave to England an ordered and legal freedom, and through that it gave her power."

THE GLORIOUS REVOLUTION
AND POLITICAL THEORY

The nonviolence of the Glorious Revolution, although plainly described and acknowledged in the dominant, Whig school of English history, failed to find reflection in English political theory, in which the conviction persisted that tyrannical rulers could be overthrown only by violence. Pocock has written an essay that bears on the neglect by Whig theorists of the nonviolence of 1689. John Locke's famed *Second Treatise on Government*, which appeared after the revolution, with a dedication to "our great restorer, King William" whose crown was rooted in "the consent of the people," was accepted over time as the classical statement of the principles of the revolution as well as a founding document of liberal thought. However, Pocock notes, the *Treatise* was written before the revolution—probably in the early 1680s. Locke defined conditions under which the "dissolution of government"—i.e., popular rebellion—was justified. The clear reference was to the extremely violent civil war between parliamentary and royal forces that had resulted in the overthrow and beheading of Charles I and the arrival in power of Oliver Cromwell in the 1640s. As Pocock points out, "There is no way of reading Locke's scenario of appeal to heaven [to battle], dissolution of government, and reversion of power to the people except as a scenario of civil war." And yet when revolution came, there was no civil war.

The failure of prophecy was hardly Locke's alone. It was as universal as the failure in our day to predict the nonviolent fall of the Soviet Union. For some, the consequences of the misjudgment were dire. Louis XIV, for one, was badly misled, and at a high cost. "For twenty years," the historian Lord Acton writes, "it had been his desire to neutralize England by internal broils, and he was glad to have the Dutch out of the way [in England] while he dealt a blow at the Emperor Leopold [of Austria]." But as Trevelyan, who quotes this passage, comments, Louis's hopes were "defeated by the unexpected rapidity, peacefulness and solidity of a new type of Revolution." Louis was calculating according to the Realpolitik of his day. How could he guess that a phoenix—the force of modern revolution based on the consent of the governed—would rise up from those obscure and peripheral English quarrels and, in violation of the political principles he and his "realist" advisers knew so well, thwart his continental ambitions? For as Trevelyan has said, "What happened was contrary to all precedent."

The failure of theory to come to grips with the nonviolence of 1689 left both the Whigs and the Tories without adequate terms to account for what had happened. The Whigs and a few moderate Tories, eager to claim the respectability of tradition for their actions, denied that any "dissolution" of the government had in fact occurred. According to them, everything had happened according to fully constitutional processes—in keeping with the "ancient constitution"—which supposedly had been in operation since the Magna Carta. This interpretation enlisted history on the side of contract theory but at the cost of denying that any revolution had occurred. "In 1689, both William's 'conquest' and James' 'treason' could have been read as dissolutions of government," Pocock notes, "but these were unacceptable interpretations, appealing to no more than a handful of radicals, and rejected unceremoniously by the Convention and the political nation at large." The claim that the continuity of royal governance was unbroken would prove especially appealing a hundred years later, when the French launched their bloody revolution, to which the peaceful English "restoration" could be smugly contrasted. As Macaulay boasted, "Because we had a restoration, we did not have to have a revolution."

Some Tories, engaging in an opposite sort of obfuscation, acknowledged that the dethronement of James and his replacement by William were indeed revolutionary but denied, for that very reason, that the events could have been "constitutional" or "bloodless." That is why they revived the idea, rejected by William himself, that the decision by force had in fact taken place. As the conservative Burke wrote later, "The Revolution of 1688 was obtained by a just war, in the only case in which war, and much more, a civil war, can be won." Calling the revolution an outcome of war, Burke could sidestep the detested conclusion that overthrowing kings was in any way provided for in the English constitution.

The idea of nonviolent revolution, although corresponding to the facts of 1689, would have to wait more than two hundred years, until the Indian community in South Africa took its oath in the Empire Theater in 1906. Looking back from the 1850s, Macaulay marveled at the apparent anomaly: "Never, within the memory of man, had there been so near an approach to entire concord among all intelligent Englishmen as at this conjuncture," he wrote, "and never had concord been more needed. Legitimate authority there was none."

"The appeal to heaven meant the drawing of the sword," Pocock aptly comments. "The only alternative for us to imagine is some Tolstoyan or Gandhian process whereby the people dissolve government and revert to natural society by means of purely passive disobedience, and this was not available in an England where subjects who possessed arms were expected to use them." But isn't the history of James II's reign, in which the English stood, as Macaulay says, "in one compact mass" against its king, replete with scenes from just such a process? And didn't this long movement of civil disobedience prepare the way for the defections from James to William at Salisbury? A theory of nonviolent revolution was missing but something close to the fact of it was present.

JOHN ADAMS AND THE JURORS
OF MASSACHUSETTS

Like England's Glorious Revolution, the American Revolution laid the foundation for lasting constitutional government. There could, however, be no Salisbury field in the United States. The surprising turn of events by which the Glorious Revolution was peacefully accomplished—the dissolution of the army of one side—was not possible in America. When the English in 1688 switched their allegiance en masse from one prince to another, they in fact made the nation whole again under a new ruler and a changed system of government. "Treason" turned out to be the path to national unity. It was not likely, however, that the Americans would accomplish a similar miracle among the redcoats, who, in order to defect, would have had to switch national as well as party loyalties. In the United States, a radically new stake was on the table. Not just a new government but a new nation, separated from the old by thousands of miles of ocean and a hundred and fifty years of semiautonomous development, was being born.

Here, at least, battles would be fought; but what would be their role in deciding the outcome of the revolution? George Washington hinted at an answer when, en route to his victory over the English at Yorktown, in September of 1781, he stopped in Philadelphia to report to Congress. "I have been your faithful servant so far as it lay within me to be," he said. "I have endured." A seemingly modest claim—yet to endure had been the heart of Washington's strategy. As long as the army remained in the field, the will of the American people to prevail remained intact; as long as the will of the American people was intact, the British could not militarily defeat the United States; as long as the British could not militarily defeat the United States, the war would go on indefinitely—a burden that the British were not ready to shoulder. Eventually, they had to tire and leave. Washington defined what it meant to endure more precisely in a remark to a crowd of bystanders. "We may be beaten by the English . . . but *here* is an army they will never conquer," he said. Washington's fine but all-important distinction between an army that might be "beaten" and a people that could never be "conquered" expressed the essence of his strategy—a strategy that would have a long and rich history in the people's wars and nonviolent revolutions of the future.

To be sure, General Washington never deprecated victories and, even as he conducted a long series of retreats, won several, including the one at Trenton, New Jersey, following his renowned counterattack across the Delaware River. The war ended, of course, with the triumph at Yorktown, won with the assistance of the French navy. Yet Washington was always aware that his most important task was to insure the survival of his own forces—not strictly for military purposes but to personify the unconquerable will of the American people. The winter at Valley Forge—that epic of endurance, in which the enemy was not the British army but snow, cold, and short rations, and during which Washington invited his troops to read Tom Paine's *American Crisis*, praising these "winter soldiers"—has rightly gone down in American legend as a decisive event in the revolutionary war. Paine stated in clear terms what Washington, as leader of the revolutionary army, could only hint at—that British military victories might be useless to the British cause. In one of the earliest and most succinct formulations of the strategy of nonviolent revolution, he said, "'Tis not in numbers but in unity that our great strength lies; yet our present numbers are sufficient to repel the force of all the world." Therefore, "In the unlikely event that the British conquered the Americans militarily the victory would be utterly fictional." In Paine's view, his biographer John Keane comments, "Rulers can rule only insofar as they have the tacit or active support of the ruled. Without it, they become impotent in the face of citizens acting together in solidarity for the achievement of their own common goals." What is perhaps more surprising is to find the same point being made on the other side of the Atlantic by members of England's antiwar faction, led in Parliament by Edmund Burke. Burke was soon to enter into world-renowned debate with Paine over the nature of the French Revolution, but in the matter of the American Revolution the two men were in substantial agreement. Burke understood early that a policy of force in America was futile. As the British general Howe drove the Continental Army across New Jersey, Burke warned, in words that would be echoed for the next two hundred years by commanders seeking to quell people's war, "Our victories early on in the war can only complete our ruin."

In 1777, after the Americans defeated General Burgoyne at Saratoga, Burke introduced a Bill for Composing the Present Troubles in America. His argument for a quick settlement of the war on terms favorable to the colonies went to the heart of the distinction between power based on force and power based on popular consent, or "love"—a term Burke did not shy from using. The British government, he noted, wanted to obtain revenue from America through taxation. The terms of the tax legislation, however, could be guaranteed only by one of two possible means: "force" or "the honor, sincerity, and good inclination of the people." He argued, "If nothing but force could hold them, and they meant nothing but independency, as the Speech from the throne asserted, then the House was to consider how a standing army of 26,000 men, and 70 ships of war, could be constantly kept up in America. A people meaning independency, will not mean it the less, because they have, to avoid a present inconvenience, submitted to treaty."

There was more. The choice between force and consent was inseparable from the choice that England had made a century earlier for its own government, which, Burke said, was and must continue to be based not on fear but on "the love of the people." He wrote:

> Do you imagine . . . that it is the Land-Tax which raises your revenues? that it is the annual vote in the Committee of Supply which gives you your army? or that it is the Mutiny Bill which inspires it with bravery and discipline? No! Surely, no! It is the love of the people; it is their attachment to their government, from the sense of the deep stake they have in such a glorious institution, which gives you your army and your navy, and infuses into both that liberal obedience without which your army would be a base rabble and your navy nothing but rotten timber.

BEFORE A DROP OF BLOOD WAS SHED

John Adams, who appointed the committee that wrote the Declaration of Independence, served as the first vice president and second president of the United States, and was called "the colossus of independence" by Thomas Jefferson, penned some reflections late in his life that form a perfect complement to those of Washington, Paine, and Burke. If these three had defined negatively what could *not* decide the outcome of the revolution—namely, force—Adams defined positively what it was that *did* decide it: the combination of noncooperation and a constructive program now familiar to us.

Adams, in his late seventies, lacked the time and strength, he said, to write a history of the revolution; and so he offered his reflections only in letters to friends. He was prompted to write by the news that one Major General Wilkinson was penning a "history of the revolution," which was to begin with the battle of Bunker Hill, in 1775. Wilkinson, Adams wrote, would "confine himself to military transactions, with a reference to very few of the civil."

Such an account, Adams protested, would falsify history. "A history of the war of the United States is a very different thing," he claimed, "from a history of the first American revolution." Not only was Wilkinson wrong to concentrate on military affairs; he had located the revolution in the wrong historical period. The revolution, Adams claimed, was over before the war began:

> General Wilkinson may have written the military history of the
> war that followed the Revolution; that was an effect of it, and
> was supported by the American citizens in defence of it against
> an invasion of it by the government of Great Britain and Ireland,
> and all her allies . . . but this will by no means be a history of the
> American Revolution. The revolution was in the minds of the
> people, and in the union of the colonies, both of which were
> accomplished before hostilities commenced.

To his correspondent, Thomas Jefferson, a former political
antagonist, he made the point emphatically: "As to the history
of the revolution, my ideas may be peculiar, perhaps singular.
What do we mean by the revolution? The war? That was no
part of the revolution; it was only an effect and consequence of
it. The revolution was in the minds of the people, and this was
effected from 1760 to 1775, in the course of fifteen years, before
a drop of blood was shed at Lexington."

Adams described an event that for him was a true turning
point in the revolution. The English crown had decided to pay
the judges of the Massachusetts Supreme Court directly. The
colonists were indignant, and, at the suggestion of John Adams,
voted to impeach the judges in the Massachusetts House of
Representatives. The crown ignored the impeachment. Then
came the decisive step. Jurors unanimously refused to serve
under the embattled judges. Adams, who likes to use military
metaphors to describe great deeds of peaceful noncooperation,
remarks, "The cool, calm, sedate intrepidity with which these
honest freeholders went through this fiery trial filled my eyes
and my heart. *That* was the revolution—the decisive blow
against England: In one word, the royal government was that
moment laid prostrate in the dust, and has never since revived
in substance, though a dark shadow of the hobgoblin haunts
me at times to this day."

Adams's gallery of heroes are all civilians, his battles nonviolent ones. When he learns that Congress has appointed a
national painter, he recommends paintings, to be executed in
the grand style, of scenes of protest—a painting, for example,
of Samuel Adams, his cousin and a sparkplug of the revolution,
arguing with Lieutenant Governor Hutchinson against standing armies. "It will be as difficult," he remarks lightly, "to do
justice as to paint an Apollo; and the transaction deserves to be

painted as much as the surrender of Burgoyne. Whether any artist will ever attempt it, I know not."

Acts of noncooperation were one indispensable ingredient of what Adams calls "the real American revolution"; acts of association were another. At their center were the Committees of Correspondence, through which, beginning in the mid-1760s, the revolutionaries in the colonies mutually fostered and coordinated their activities. "What an engine!" Adams wrote of the Committees. "France imitated it, and produced a revolution. England and Scotland were upon the point of imitating it, in order to produce another revolution, and all Europe was inclined to imitate it for the same revolutionary purposes. The history of the world for the last thirty years is a sufficient commentary upon it. That history ought to convince all mankind that committees of secret correspondence are dangerous machines." Here, plainly, is another predecessor of the *hiérarchies parallèles.*

The decisive revolution, according to Adams, was thus the process by which ordinary people withdrew cooperation from the British government and then, well before even the Declaration of Independence, set up their own governments in all the colonies. The war that followed was the *military defense* of these already-existing governments against an attack by what was now a foreign power seeking to force the new country back into its empire. In his view, indeed, independence was nothing that could be *won from* the British; it had to be *forged by* the Americans. "Let me ask you, Mr. Rush," he wrote to his friend Richard Rush in April of 1815, in phrases that startlingly resemble Gandhi's later denial that Indian independence could be "given" her by England, "Is the sovereignty of this nation a gift? a grant? a concession? a conveyance? or a release and acquittance from Great Britain? Pause here and think. No! The people, in 1774, by the right which nature and nature's God had given them, confiding in original right, assumed powers of sovereignty. In 1775, they assumed greater power. In July 4th, 1776, they assumed absolute unlimited sovereignty in relation to other nations, in all cases whatsoever; no longer acknowledging any authority over them but that of God almighty, and the laws of nature and of nations."

In a recent description of the process Adams described, the

historian Gordon Wood has written, "The royal governors stood helpless as they watched para-governments grown up around them, a rapid piecing together from the bottom up of a hierarchy of committees and congresses that reached from the counties and towns through the provincial conventions of the Continental Congress." On May 15, 1776, Adams notes, the Continental Congress declared that "every kind of authority under the . . . Crown should be totally suppressed," and authorized the states to found "government sufficient to the exigencies of their affairs." "For if," Wood comments, "as Jefferson and others agreed, the formation of new governments was the whole object of the Revolution, then the May resolution authorizing the drafting of new constitutions was the most important act of the Continental Congress in its history. There in the May 15 resolution was the real declaration of independence, from which the measures of early July could be but derivations." James Duane, a delegate to the first congress, called this process "a Machine for the fabrication of Independence." Adams responded, "It was independence itself."

It is interesting to observe that another very notable authority on American political history also located the foundation of the Republic before July 4, 1776. "The Union is much older than the Constitution," Abraham Lincoln said in his First Inaugural. "It was formed in fact by the Articles of Association of 1774."

If we accept Adams's view, then both the overthrow of the old regime, laid in the dust (as Adams said) through a series of acts of noncooperation, and the foundation of the new one, accomplished the moment the Americans set up governments to govern themselves, were, like the overthrow and the foundation in 1688–89, nonviolent events, and the war that followed could be seen as a war of self-defense. In that war, Adams wrote to Rush, "Heaven decided in our favor; and Britain was forced not to give, grant, concede, or release our independence, but to acknowledge it, in terms as clear as our language afforded, and under seal and under oath."

6

The Mass Minority in Action: France and Russia

It might seem perverse to mention nonviolence in connection with the French Revolution, a notoriously blood-soaked event that produced, along with much else, the first instance of large-scale, organized revolutionary terror of the modern age. Let us nevertheless consider the best known of all the days of the revolution, July 14, 1789, commemorated in France as Bastille Day.

In June of that year, the Estates-General, an assembly representing the aristocracy, the clergy, and the bourgeoisie, had been summoned, as all French schoolchildren know, by the king to meet for the first time in one hundred and seventy-five years. Louis XVI hoped that if he granted the three "estates" an advisory voice in the country's affairs, their members would agree to raise the new taxes needed to reduce the royal government's perilously high debt, run up during the recent Seven Years' War. Upon meeting, however, the Estates-General immediately passed beyond the issues of taxes and budgets to launch a full-scale challenge to the absolute rule of the king. The representatives of the third estate, the bourgeoisie, declared themselves to be "the nation," and demanded that all three orders vote together, creating a body in which the third estate's large numbers would give it the decisive voice. The king, in alarm, locked the third estate out of its meeting hall, and the body proceeded to the famous tennis court, where it took the solemn Tennis Court Oath, declaring that henceforth they were a National Assembly. Within days, the other two estates yielded to this fait accompli and joined the third, whereupon the king also acceded.

On July 11, however, the king reversed course, firing his minister of finance, Jacques Necker, who was popular in the estates and among the people, and summoning royal troops from the frontier. The stage seemed set for a decision by arms, pitting the royal forces against the Parisian rebels. In fact, however, such a contest would no more occur than had a battle on Salisbury field. Mirabeau, the renowned orator and schemer of the early years of the revolution (and something of a student of the Glorious Revolution), predicted in one of his speeches to the Assembly the course that events actually took. "French soldiers are not just automata," he declared. "They will see in us, their relatives, their friends, and their families. . . . They will never believe it is their duty to strike without asking who are the victims." The French commander in Paris, the Baron de Besenval, apparently was aware of the uncertain loyalty of his troops, because instead of sending them forth to defeat the enemy, he confined them to their barracks. There, some took a secret oath not to act against the Assembly. The king's cavalry briefly got ready to attack a crowd in the Place Vendôme, but Besenval's Gardes Françaises appeared in the crowd's defense and the cavalry fled.

On the fourteenth came the celebrated "storming" by the rebellious Parisians of the infamous royal prison the Bastille. The nineteenth-century French historian of the revolution Jules Michelet describes, with almost a touch of embarrassment, what it actually consisted of: "The bastille was not taken; it surrendered. Troubled by a bad conscience it went mad and lost all presence of mind." After a confused negotiation and a brief skirmish, the governor of the fortress turned it over to the angry crowd. Michelet describes the mood of the prison's French defenders—called *invalides*—among whom were intermixed a few Swiss mercenaries:

> Shame for such cowardly warfare, and the horror of shedding French blood, which but little affected the Swiss, at length caused the *Invalides* to drop their arms.

The Parisian rebels had been ready for a violent showdown but it never materialized; nor did the mighty ancien régime, for all its "absolute" power, ever pull itself together to strike a serious military blow against the revolution. Itself a kind of *invalide*, it in effect dropped its arms without a battle. The nineteenth-century historian of the revolution Thomas Carlyle commented acutely on the reason.

Good is grapeshot, Messeigneurs, on one condition: that the shooter also were made of metal! But unfortunately he is made of flesh; under his buffs and bandoleers, your hired shooter has instincts, feelings, even a kind of thought. It is his kindred, bone of his bone, the same *canaille* that shall be whiffed [fired upon with grapeshot]: he has brothers in it, a father and mother— living on meal husks and boiled grass.

It was with excellent reason that the Romantic poet Cha- teaubriand, in a comment that strongly resembles Adams's observations on the American Revolution, later remarked, "The French revolution was accomplished before it occurred." To the degree that a revolution in hearts and minds had taken place, his comments suggested, violence was unnecessary. Rifles were not fired but thrown down or turned over to the revo- lution. How can there be shooting if no soldiers will defend the old regime? Individual hearts and minds change; those who have changed become aware of one another; still others are emboldened, in a contagion of boldness; the "impossible" becomes possible; immediately it is done, surprising the actors almost as much as their opponents; and suddenly, almost with the swiftness of thought—whose transformation has in fact set the whole process in motion—the old regime, a moment ago so impressive, vanishes like a mirage.

Must we conclude, then, that all revolutions are over before they begin—or, at least, before they are seen to begin? If so, revolutions would all be nonviolent. In France, however, the revolution soon descended into carnage, signaled on the very day of the Bastille's fall by the beheading of two officials and public display of their heads on pikes. Still to come were the massacres in the prisons in September of 1792, the brutal war of repression in the Vendée; the wars against the other European dynastic powers, the execution of the king, the repeated intim- idation of the new legislature by the Paris Commune, and, of course, the Jacobin terror. The revolutionaries would be more violent toward one another than they had been toward the old regime.

In the French Revolution, as in the English and the Ameri- can, the stage of overthrow was nearly bloodless; but the stage of foundation was bloody—establishing a pattern that was to be repeated in more than one revolution thereafter, and never with more fearful consequences than in the Russian Revolution of 1917. (Let us here recall, too, that the foundation of the independent Indian state was violent. It precipitated the partition of India and Pakistan, which cost almost a million lives.)

NONVIOLENT REVOLUTION, VIOLENT RULE

The Bolsheviks seized power in October 1917, through direct action in St. Petersburg, the capital of Russia. Their aim was to relieve the desperate poverty and humiliation of the workers and peasants of Russia by overthrowing the czarist regime and establishing communism—all as a prelude to a wider revolution that would bring communism to the rest of Europe and, in the not-too-distant future, the world. Little, if any, blood was shed in the revolution, although the Bolsheviks were quite prepared to shed it. However, having seized state power without violence, they instantly began, like the French revolutionaries, to defend and consolidate it with extreme violence, directed against not only their adversaries from the overthrown Provisional Government and the former czarist regime but also their fellow socialists. The Jacobin regime of Maximilien Robespierre ruled by terror for a little more than a year, then was overthrown in the reaction of Thermidor, in 1794. The regime founded by Lenin in 1917 did not meet its Thermidor for seventy-four years.

The sequence in which an unexpectedly nonviolent overthrow of Russia's ancien régime produced an unexpectedly violent new regime has given rise to unending interpretive debates, which have been all the more difficult to sort out because the principal actors, including, above all, Lenin, stuck with political theory rather than the facts of the case in their interpretation of their deeds. The Bolsheviks doggedly insisted they had unleashed force to seize power, even sponsoring a movie, the Soviet director Sergei Eisenstein's film *October*, that showed the imaginary battles they believed theoretically necessary. And, to complete the confusion, they falsely denied that, once in power, they ruled by force—a far more sweeping lie.

The regime's legions of subsequent detractors strove to disprove the claim that Bolshevik rule was based on consent but tended, on the whole, to confirm the claim that the takeover had been violent. As happened after the revolution of 1689, historians plainly recorded that the revolution had succeeded almost without bloodshed but theorists insisted that battles had been decisive. Especially problematic has been the assertion, made by many of the Bolsheviks' opponents, that the revolution wasn't a revolution at all but a mere coup d'état—a procedure that by definition is characterized by violence. (According to Webster's, a coup d'état is "a sudden decisive exercise of force in politics; *esp:* the violent overthrow or alteration of an existing government by a small group.")

The issue does not admit of easy resolution. The Bolsheviks, an armed minority party, did indeed unilaterally seize power without seeking permission from anyone. When it was suggested to Lenin that he await the outcome of the forthcoming Russia-wide elections to a Constituent Assembly, his answer was, "No revolution waits for *that*." The Bolsheviks were believers in violent revolution, even in flat opposition to the will of the majority. In July 1917, Lenin wrote, in words that scarcely could have been plainer, "In times of revolution, it is not enough to ascertain the 'will of the majority'—no, one must *be stronger* at the decisive moment in the decisive place and *win. . . .* We see countless instances of how the better-organized, more conscious, better-armed minority imposed its will on the majority and conquered it."

In February 1917, in the fourth year of the First World War, protests against shortages of bread in the capital city of Petersburg led to workers' strikes; the strikes led to demonstrations, and the demonstrations led to mass protest against both the war and the Romanov dynasty. For the second time since the new century began, the Russians were rebelling against the czar's rule. In 1905, after political concessions by the regime had failed to appease the protesters, the government put down an impending revolution by force. In 1917, however, the troops would not fight. They were receptive to the revolutionaries' socialist message of justice for the poor. Like many of James II's troops in 1688 and the Gardes Françaises in Paris in 1789, they went over to the side of the rebels. Once again, the revolutionary spirit of a capital city spread to troops, rendering them useless to the old regime. Once again, defections were pivotal, and Czar Nicholas II abdicated the throne, ending the dynasty.

Leon Trotsky, who had been a leader of the Petersburg soviet, or council, that had sprung up in 1905, had foreseen these defections and the reasons for them. In a speech he gave at his trial for his participation in the events of 1905, he proclaimed:

> No matter how important weapons may be it is not in them, gentlemen the judges, that great power resides. No! Not the ability of the masses to kill others but their great readiness themselves to die—this secures in the last instance the victory of the popular rising.

For:

> Only when the masses show readiness to die on the barricades can they win over the army on which the old regime relies. The barricade does not play in revolution the part which the fortress plays in regular warfare. It is mainly the physical and moral meeting ground between people and army.

These Gandhi-like predictions (let us recall that the revolution of 1905 inspired Gandhi as he forged satyagraha in South Africa just one year later) came true in the revolution of February 1917. The defection of the Petersburg garrison played a decisive role. In its wake, leaders of Russia's consultative congress, the Duma, and the military command joined in counseling the Czar's abdication. From start to finish, the February revolution took less than a week. In the words of the socialist Sukhanov, a firsthand observer of and actor in the revolution, it occurred with "a sort of fabulous ease." The description of these events by Aleksandr Kerensky, the second leader of the government that succeeded the Czar's, shows a remarkable resemblance to descriptions of the more recent collapse of the Soviet regime: "A whole world of national and political relationships sank to the bottom, and at once all existing political and tactical programs, however bold and well conceived, appeared hanging aimlessly and uselessly in space."

The Romanovs were succeeded by a system of "dual power," consisting of two ambiguously connected governing bodies: a Soviet, which was the successor to the Petersburg soviet of 1905, and a Provisional Government, composed chiefly of liberals and socialists, some of them leaders of the old Duma, which had melted away. The Soviet, though already exercising functions of government in the capital (to the extent that anybody did), was unwilling to claim full power, and invited the Provisional Government to share it. Broadly speaking, the Soviet directly represented workers, soldiers, and peasants, and the Provisional Government was the hope of the middle classes. In fact, both bodies were formally provisional, for both had agreed to yield to the Constituent Assembly, which was to be elected by all Russia in the fall and then was to establish a democratic, constitutional government for the nation.

The February revolution had revealed that the allegiance of the military—a largely peasant army, eleven million strong—was indispensable to victory. Other forces in society had, of course, played essential roles: members of the Duma eager to liquidate czarism, a radically disaffected intelligentsia, a peasantry eager and able to seize the land that it tilled, workers in the factories of Petersburg, Moscow, and other cities, and, of course, the radical political parties, including the Bolsheviks, Lenin's centralized "party of a new type." Yet "the decisive revolutionary agent," in the words of the historian Martin Malia, was "the peasant in uniform," for "it was his refusal to obey that neutralized the Imperial government."

THE OVERTHROW

While Russia waited for the election of the Constituent Assembly, the country's politics swung between the extreme right and the extreme left. Although violence constantly threatened in this period, first from one side and then from the other, it never broke out to any great extent. The first and shortest swing was to the left. In late March, the Provisional Government sent its allies in the First World War a note that appeared to support imperialistic and annexationist war aims that were anathema to the left, which was dominant in the Petersburg Soviet, and demanded and obtained the resignation of Minister of War Aleksandr Guchkóv and Foreign Minister Pavel Milyukov. (In the politics of the time, pursuing the war was the position of the right and ending it was the position of the left.) In June, another attempt to revive the war effort was made by the new minister of war, Kerensky (later prime minister of the Provisional Government), who sought to rebuild the prestige of the new revolutionary government by launching an offensive against Austria and Germany. It failed catastrophically, creating conditions for the next swing to the left—the "July days," in which the Bolsheviks led armed demonstrations in the capital that, until the last moment, when the Bolsheviks backed off, gave every appearance of being an attempt to seize power. Now the pendulum swung back with equal force to the right. Lenin went into hiding, while much of the rest of the Bolshevik leadership, including Trotsky, was arrested. A right-wing czarist general, Lavr Kornilov, pursued tangled negotiations with the Provisional Government and then launched an insurrection against it. However, the forces he dispatched suffered a fate familiar to the student of revolutions: they melted away. In Trotsky's words, "After the February days the atmosphere of Petrograd becomes so red hot that every hostile military detachment arriving in that mighty forge, or even coming near to it, scorched by its breath, is transformed, loses confidence, becomes paralyzed, and throws itself upon the mercy of the victor without a struggle."

The way was open for the Bolshevik takeover, and the Party, whose most important leaders were now out of jail, began a debate on how to proceed. Lenin's recommendation was simple and clear. He championed an immediate "armed insurrection"—in other words, a straightforward coup d'état.

> We can (if we do not "await" the Congress of Soviets) strike *suddenly* from three points: Petersburg, Moscow, and the Baltic Fleet . . . we have the technical capability to take power in Moscow . . . we have *thousands* of armed workers and soldiers who can *at once* seize the Winter Palace.

However, Lenin encountered strong opposition, not only from other socialist parties when they got wind of his planned coup but also from other Bolshevik leaders, two of whom, Aleksandr Zinoviev and Lev Kamenev, resigned from the Party in protest. The Bolsheviks had "no right," the pair wrote publicly, "to stake the whole future of the present moment upon the card of armed insurrection." The Party, they observed, faced a basic choice between "the tactic of conspiracy and the tactic of faith in the motive forces of the Russian revolution." The latter path was peaceable; the former led to rule by force, for without a broad coalition, as the Central Committee member Nogin wrote, the regime would "eliminate the mass organizations of the proletariat from leadership in political life . . . and can be kept in power only by means of political terror." At one point, Lenin stood alone in the Central Committee in his championship of an immediate coup.

It was Trotsky who broke the impasse. More mindful of the importance of mass support than Lenin, he proposed an armed insurrection under the auspices of the upcoming second All-Russian Congress of Soviets, in which the political strength of the Bolsheviks was then on the rise. In other words, he proposed that the Provisional Government be overthrown by a Bolshevik armed insurrection legitimated by the Soviet assemblies. (Hence the legendary slogan "All power to the soviets.") But first Trotsky had to take over the Soviets. He promptly launched a successful effort to convene unilaterally an unauthorized, all-Russian Soviet that would be controlled by the Bolsheviks.

Events, however, played havoc with the expectations of all three factions of the Bolshevik Central Committee. Neither Lenin's naked armed coup, nor Kamenev and Zinoviev's peaceful, gradual acquisition of power, nor even Trotsky's subtler, Soviet-sanctioned coup came to pass. Instead, something unplanned by anyone occurred. With Lenin still in hiding, the chief improviser on the spot was Trotsky. In a meeting of the Petersburg Soviet on October 9, a worker affiliated with the Menshevik Party, Mark Broido, proposed the foundation of a Committee of Revolutionary Defense to prepare Petersburg against the advancing German army. The Bolsheviks opposed the plan until it occurred to Trotsky that the committee, which came to be known as the Milrevkom, would, if taken over by the Bolsheviks, be an ideal instrument for overthrowing the Provisional Government. The committee was then established. So important did Trotsky consider the foundation of the committee that he later claimed its creation was in fact a "dry" or "silent" revolution that won "three quarters, if not nine-tenths, of the victory." He meant that, without a shot being fired, the

Bolsheviks now had in their hands a military instrument in the capital with which, as soon as they chose to employ it, they could seize full power.

What happened next lays bare with particular clarity the process by which revolutionaries can neutralize or win over the armed forces of the existing government. (Of the revolutions discussed here, only the American, as noted, had no chance of winning over the opposing army.) The pivotal event—second in importance only to the foundation of the Milrevkom—was a meeting with the regimental committees of the Petersburg garrison, at which a motion by Trotsky was passed assuring the Milrevkom of "full support in all its efforts to bring closer the front and rear in the interest of the Revolution." In the independent socialist Sukhanov's words, "On October 21, the Petersburg garrison *conclusively acknowledged the Soviet as sole power, and the military revolutionary committee as the immediate organ of authority.*"

In Sukhanov's opinion, this decision was more than the prelude to the takeover: "In actual fact, the overturn was accomplished the moment the Petersburg garrison acknowledged the Soviet as its supreme authority." He marveled at the blindness of others to what was happening. An "insurrectionary act" had occurred. The Provisional Government did not respond. It was "busy with something or other in the Winter Palace" (its headquarters) and took no notice. But even the Bolsheviks, Sukhanov thought, were not quite aware of what they had done. "War had been declared," Sukhanov, sounding like Lenin, notes, "but combat activities were not begun." At such a moment, the "correct tactics" in the revolutionary guidebooks were to "destroy, shatter, paralyze" the enemy command, which in this case was the general staff of the army, still following orders from the Provisional Government. A mere "three hundred volunteers" could have carried out the task "without the slightest difficulty," Sukhanov thought. Instead, he observed with a note of scorn, the Bolsheviks merely sent a delegation to the commander, Georgi Polkovnikov, demanding his obedience to the Milrevkom. Polkovnikov refused, but then entered into talks with the Soviet—talks that were still in progress four days later, when the events that have gone down in history as the October 25 Bolshevik takeover occurred.

Of the seeming passivity of the Bolsheviks, Sukhanov rightly comments, "This, to put it mildly, was hardly according to Marx." To that observation, we can add only that it was hardly according to Locke, Hobbes, Rousseau, or almost any other major thinker on revolution, either, since virtually all of them had taught that revolutions had to be decided by the use of force. The whole weight of this tradition bore down on the minds of the actors.

Sukhanov showed greater appreciation of Trotsky's tactics in his report on another important episode in the preparation for the takeover. On October 23, the commander of the Peter-Paul Fortress in the center of Petersburg announced his refusal to obey a commissar sent by the Soviet. Here, surely, a military confrontation was called for, and indeed the Bolshevik Vladimir Antonov-Ovseenko did recommend sending a loyal regiment to disarm their reluctant comrades in arms. Trotsky had another idea. "He, Trotsky," Sukhanov records, would "go to the Fortress, hold a meeting there, and capture not the body but the spirit of the garrison." And he did. He made a speech there that won over the soldiers. Such was the true nature of the "fighting" that occurred in Petersburg in the days leading up to the October revolution.

TROTSKY VS. TROTSKY

In his book *The Russian Revolution*, Trotsky took note of Sukhanov's bafflement regarding the Bolsheviks' failure to unleash force immediately. "The Committee," he explained, "is crowding out the government with the pressure of the masses, with the weight of the garrison. It is taking all that it can without a battle. It is advancing its positions without firing, integrating and reinforcing its army on the march. It is measuring with its own pressure the resisting power of the enemy, not taking its eyes off him for a second. . . . Who is to be the first to issue the call to arms will become known in the course of this offensive, this crowding out." Then, making an addition to our list of observers in various ages who commented that the revolution was over before it seemingly began, he added that the Soviet's "declaration of October 23 had meant the overthrow of the power before the government itself was overthrown."

It was because so much had been accomplished beforehand that the twenty-fifth itself came and went with little violence. Sukhanov reports that on that day Trotsky boasted, "We don't know of a single casualty," and added, "I don't know of any examples in history of a revolutionary movement in which such enormous masses participated and which took place so bloodlessly." Trotsky identified this bloodless activity as the main engine of the revolution. "The unique thing about the October revolution, a thing never before observed in so complete a form, was that, thanks to a happy combination of circumstances, the proletarian vanguard had won over the garrison of the capital before the moment of open insurrection." In point of fact, the garrisons had also been won over before the moment of insurrection in both the Glorious Revolution and the French Revolution. The difference was that Trotsky had deliberately engineered what had happened spontaneously in England and France. Although he didn't put it in so many words, Trotsky had grasped what Mao and Ho would later formulate more explicitly—that even when the readiness and capacity to act violently is present, political action is still the most important factor in a revolutionary struggle.

Quotations from Trotsky attesting to the decisive importance of strictly political action in the revolution could be multiplied many times over. However, he also made statements of exactly the opposite import, claiming that revolutions could succeed only through armed insurrection. For example, after claiming that the main task of the insurrection—winning over the troops—had been accomplished before the twenty-fifth, he went on to add, "This does not mean, however, that insurrection had become superfluous. . . . The last part of the task of the revolution, that which has gone into history under the name of the October insurrection, was therefore purely military in character. At this final stage, rifles, bayonets, machine guns, and perhaps cannon were to decide." Elsewhere, he wrote, "Only an armed insurrection could decide the question." And quotations of this kind, too, could be multiplied many times over. These assertions, however, are unsupported by evidence.

Why, we must ask, would Trotsky wish to contradict his own clearly drawn conclusions as well as the facts of history? One likely reason is that Trotsky wrote his history in the late

1920s, at the end of a decade-long, losing struggle with Stalin to become Lenin's heir, and it was Leninist dogma that the October revolution had been the armed insurrection that Lenin had beforehand asserted it must be. As such it had already gone down in myth and story, including *October*, in which a proper battle is shown. (During the filming, several people were accidentally killed, leading one wit to remark that more people died in the filming of the storming of the Winter Palace than in the actual event.)

A comical episode on the day of the takeover suggests that Lenin, who resumed command of the Party only the day before, never did understand the nature of Trotsky's accomplishment. On the twenty-fourth of October, Bolshevik forces began to move through the capital, taking control of key points, such as the central telephone office. They encountered no resistance, leading one observer to liken the takeover to a mere "changing of the guard." Could this be the "armed insurrection" that revolutionary doctrine called for? Lenin thought not. Where was the gunfire? Where were the bodies in the streets? In his history, Trotsky notes how different from expectation events turned out to be. "The final act of the revolution seems, after all this, too brief, too dry, too businesslike—somehow out of correspondence with the historic scope of the events. . . . Where is the insurrection? . . . There is nothing of all that which imagination brought up upon the facts of history associates with the idea of insurrection."

Although Trotsky doesn't say so, one imagination brought up on these "facts of history" was Lenin's. Emerging from his hiding place in disguise, he could make out nothing that looked to him like the battles he had insisted upon. In despair at what he misjudged to be the irresolution of his colleagues, he harangued them to act. "We are confronting questions that are not solved by consultations, not by congresses (even by congresses of Soviets)," he railed, "but exclusively by the people, by the masses, by the struggle of the armed masses." Failing to see in Trotsky's having captured the spirit rather than the body of the garrison the victory that had been won, he cried out, on the day that the revolution was being accomplished without violence, for the violent revolution he had always believed in.

Trotsky's lip service to Lenin's afactual dogma would have

been reason enough, in the late 1920s in the Soviet Union, for him to contradict his own plainly stated observations and conclusions, but there were other reasons as well. He had not shed blood in 1917, but by the time he wrote his history he had shed it abundantly—as commander and savage disciplinarian of the Red Army, as champion of "war communism," in which workers were subjected to military discipline, as a practitioner of and apologist for the "red terror" that was inaugurated in the first years of Bolshevik rule, and as the pitiless suppressor of the democratic Kronstadt rebellion against the Bolshevik dictatorship, in 1921. The day after the October 1917 overturn, the Bolsheviks carried out a wave of arrests and closed down all the opposition newspapers. The new rulers immediately made known their intention to monopolize power. It was on this occasion that Trotsky made an infamous threat to the non-Bolshevik socialist parties, who asked the Bolsheviks to share power with them. He said:

> And now we are told: renounce your victory, make concessions, compromise. With whom? I ask: with whom ought we to compromise? With those wretched groups who have left us or who are making this proposal? . . . To those who have left and to those who tell us to do this we must say: you are miserable bankrupts, your role is played out; go where you ought to be: into the dustbin of history!

The Menshevik Party and others did in fact walk out of the meeting. Sukhanov, among those who left, later bitterly castigated himself for abandoning the field of the revolution to the Bolsheviks.

In short, while the Bolsheviks did not use violence to win power, they used it, instantly and lavishly, to keep power. Their insistence that they had needed violence to overthrow the Provisional Government provided cover of a sort for their unprovoked use of violence against their former revolutionary comrades who belonged to other parties. The repressive measures of the first days of Bolshevik rule were only the beginning of a wave of repression that almost immediately outdid czarist repression by an order of magnitude. If there was in fact a "coup," it was by the new revolutionary government against the other parties as well as opposition by ordinary citizens. The event was not so much a coup d'état as a *coup par l'état*—or a *coup de societé*—for it consisted not in the violent seizure *of* the state by military forces but in the destruction of society *by* the state once it had been taken over by the Bolshevik Party. Here, truly, were the origins of totalitarianism, to use Hannah Arendt's famous phrase.

The next step was taken in January, when the long-promised Constituent Assembly chosen in Russia's first nationwide election finally met and was promptly dispersed by Bolshevik troops. Eventually, the forcible takeover of society by the state proceeded from mere repression to Stalin's full-fledged totalitarian "war against the nation" (in the words of the Russian poet Osip Mandelstam).

But why would a party that had won power without bloodshed use it violently? The obvious answer is that the Bolsheviks' nonviolence was merely tactical. Indeed, it came as a surprise to them. Unforeseen in advance and forgotten later by Party theorists, the Bolsheviks' capture of the hearts and minds of the Czar's troops was an opportunity latent in events that the agile Trotsky had the wit to see and exploit. The nonviolence of October 25, you might say, belonged to the revolutionary situation, not to the ideology of the Bolsheviks, who believed in violence and used it unstintingly as soon as they deemed it necessary.

The curious record of the Bolsheviks' violence has a bearing on the question of whether October 25 was a mass revolution or merely a coup carried out by a small group of conspirators. Sukhanov, an anti-Bolshevik eyewitness, certainly believed that since the collapse of the Kornilov insurrection the workers of Petersburg had supported the Bolsheviks—"had been *their own people*, because they were always there, taking the lead in details as well as in the important affairs of the factory barracks." True, the Party had won its support because it had been "lavish with promises and sweet though simple fairy tales"; nevertheless, "the mass lived and breathed together with the Bolsheviks." Yet just a few years later the distinguished historian (and first president of Czechoslovakia) Tomáš Masaryk wrote in his work on the revolution, in direct contradiction of Sukhanov, "The October revolution was anything but a popular mass movement. That revolution was the act of leaders working from above and behind the scenes." And many historians have since followed Masaryk in his judgment.

In *The Russian Revolution*, Trotsky quoted and debated Masaryk. He claimed that the lack of street demonstrations and violent mass encounters was proof not of lack of mass support but of near-unanimity. Only because the Bolsheviks won every contest in the bloodless struggle for popular allegiance, he argued, could the takeover occur with so little commotion. All of this sounds very like John Adams describing the revolution in hearts and minds that preceded the Declaration of Independence. Trotsky likened the day of the twenty-fifth to an endgame in chess: "At the end of October the main part of the game was already in the past. And on the day of insurrection it remained to solve only a rather narrow problem: mate in two moves." He concluded, "As a matter of fact, it was the most popular mass-insurrection in all history."

In sorting out these contradictory claims, the most important data are probably the results of the national elections to the Constituent Assembly. They permit two conclusions: first, that in the country at large the Bolsheviks were a minority, commanding only 25 percent of the overall popular vote, and, second, that in Petersburg and Moscow—the two primary scenes of the revolution—they enjoyed a majority. (The Social Revolutionary Party, a rival revolutionary party with a large rural constituency, won 42 percent of the national vote, and the rest was divided among other parties. In the all-important Petersburg garrison, the Bolsheviks won 71 percent of the vote.) As a measure of public opinion, this election might be compared to a single photograph of a wrestling match taken with a flashbulb in a dark room, but its results are consistent with other evidence, such as elections to the Soviets in the period just before the takeover. There was factual support, in other words, both for Trotsky's and Sukhanov's claim that the masses supported the Bolsheviks and for Masaryk's claim that the Bolsheviks were in the minority. The Bolsheviks were, in fact, a *mass minority*. But that mass was concentrated where it most counted in 1917: in the revolutionary cities of Petersburg and Moscow, which were also the seats of government. (Much the same thing had happened in France, where the Parisian radicals assailed and dominated the National Assembly.) Thanks to the

Bolsheviks, who evicted the Constituent Assembly at gunpoint, there are no other reliable election results to examine, but subsequent protests by factory and white-collar workers against the Bolsheviks strongly suggest that even urban support for them declined. Later, the leadership lost support among their own mass organizations, which they soon shut out of political life. What they did not lose—at least until late in the post–Cold War years—was the support of some hundreds of thousands or millions of Communist Party members and of the Red Army.

This pattern of minority mass support amid majority rejection or indifference, I suggest, is an important factor in explaining the paradox that a nonviolent revolutionary overthrow was followed by an act of revolutionary foundation that depended on violence beyond all historical precedent. If we fail to grant the Bolsheviks their measure of mass support, we cannot understand how they came to power in Petersburg *without* violence or why, once they were in power, they were able to impose their rule on almost the whole czarist empire *with* violence. In revolutions (as opposed to coups d'état), success in nonviolence depends on the extent of popular support—on the depth of what John Adams, Chateaubriand, and Trotsky (men so unlike in most respects) identified as the "revolution before the revolution," in hearts and minds. The overthrow in Petersburg could be nonviolent, just as Trotsky said, because the Party enjoyed wide and deep mass support on that particular urban stage. The consolidation of the regime was violent because such support was absent in Russia at large, and therefore could be imposed only by force—force that the Bolsheviks could unleash because of the mass minority support that they *did* possess. In the first case, their support was strong enough that at the crucial moment effective opposition never arose in the locality of the takeover; in the second, it was strong enough to win the civil war and fuel the totalitarian engine of repression nationally—something that a small, isolated band of "conspirators" could not conceivably have done. For it is also true that terror is necessary for rule in the same proportion as support is limited—unless, of course, the party in charge is willing to yield its power to the majority. But this the Bolsheviks were never prepared to do.

Denial that the Bolsheviks enjoyed a degree of mass support may be born, in part, of an understandable wish to deny the last

shred of legitimacy to their brutal rule, but this denial is won
at the cost of historical accuracy. Their message of proletarian
revolution in fact won support in the cities of Russia. Let me
avoid any misunderstanding. Lenin and Trotsky were two of the
most violent men of their supremely violent century. Together
with Stalin, they were in fact the most important figures in the
formation of totalitarian rule, which originates with them and
only then proceeds, whether in imitation (Mussolini, Mao) or
in reaction (Hitler), to spread around the world. Acknowledging all this, however, is no reason to deny the popular character
of the revolution at the time it occurred in the particular cities
in which it took place.

THE MASS MINORITY IN POWER

By way of addendum, let us note that the story of Hitler's
rise to power shows similar features. He first sought to win
power in a violent coup—the Munich beer-hall putsch of 1923.
When it failed, he turned, over time, to a "legal" strategy that
carried him into the chancellorship in 1933. In certain respects,
his strategy was one of building up *hiérarchies parallèles*, or
even, in nightmarish reverse-image, a Gandhian constructive
program. A comparison of these morally opposite characters
of the twentieth century looks less outlandish if we recall that
both Gandhi and Hitler were keen enthusiasts of direct action.
Hitler, too, built up a sort of shadow government outside the
existing regime. "We recognized," he explained in 1936, "that
it is not enough to overthrow the old State, but that the new
State must previously have been built up and be ready to one's
hand. . . . In 1933, it was no longer a question of overthrowing
a State by an act of violence; meanwhile the new State had
been built up and all that remained to do was to destroy the
last remnants of the old State—and that took a few hours."
Grotesque as it might seem, Hitler even bragged about the
nonviolence of his revolution. Sounding eerily like Trotsky on
the day of his triumph, Hitler claimed that it had been "the
least bloody revolution in history." Thereafter, his job was
much easier than that of Lenin, who had to fight a civil war
to consolidate his rule. Nevertheless, the procedures followed
by the two men after arriving in power were of a kind: both

mounted completely successful assaults by the state on the independent institutions of society, political and civil. Society, already partially enlisted in the mass movement, could not or simply did not resist.

Organizationally speaking, a disciplined, aggressive mass minority that had seized state power and was prepared to use any degree of violence to impose its will, in disregard of the will of the majority, was the dangerous new force. If by "democratic" we mean obedient to the will of the majority, then the Bolshevik mass minority was not democratic, and the Nazi movement may or may not have been (Hitler never won a majority in an election, but some historians believe that he gained majority support after coming to power); but if by "democratic" we mean propelled and sustained by the action of large masses of people, then both were democratic. Nevertheless, Trotsky's claim that the Russian Revolution was "the most popular mass-insurrection in all history" is certainly false. If he had been right, the Bolsheviks might well have achieved in all of Russia the bloodless triumph they achieved in Petersburg alone. (This larger miracle of nonviolence in fact had to await the *anti*-Bolshevik forces that in 1991 overthrew the regime Trotsky and Lenin had brought to power.) The English, the American, the French, the German, and the Indian revolutions all demonstrated the power of people to enervate and paralyze a regime by withdrawing support from it while at the same time building up parallel organizations. But unlike the English, the Americans, and the Indians, the French under Robespierre, the Russians under Lenin, and the Germans under Hitler disregarded or rejected the experience of nonviolence that their revolutions had accidentally brought to light, and turned instead—with a vengeance—to force as the method of their rule.

7

Living in Truth

The end of the regime founded by the Bolsheviks in 1917—the collapse, three-quarters of a century later, of the Soviet Union and its satellite regimes in Eastern Europe—presents the most sweeping demonstration so far of the power of "politics" without violence. The story combines many strands—economic, military, political. Among them, the failure of the Soviet economy, especially in comparison to Western economies, was of course especially important. Our subject, however, is chiefly the political processes involved. Two global developments already discussed were powerfully at work in the background. One was the nuclear paralysis of great-power war; the other was the global movement for self-determination. These two factors—one acting from "above," the other from "below," one rooted in the scientific revolution of modern times, the other in the democratic revolution—are basic to understanding the surprising manner in which the Soviet collapse unfolded.

The paralysis of great-power war imposed a stability on international relations that was new. A conviction, unknown perhaps since the days of the Roman Empire or certain dynasties of ancient China, took root that the current shape of things was likely to remain unchanged more or less forever. War itself became "cold." A moment of slightly reduced tension was a "thaw," when in a cooperative frame of mind the two powers aimed at "peaceful coexistence." In one of the acutest crises of the conflict, the Soviet Union's satellite government in East Germany built a wall around Berlin, and the United States acquiesced in the deed. "A wall is a hell of a lot better than a war," President Kennedy remarked to an adviser.

Nuclear strategy reinforced totalitarian strategy in important respects. In both nuclear deterrence and totalitarian rule, terror was used to paralyze. The men in power in Moscow, though putative revolutionaries, dreamed of stasis. In 1965, the Polish Party's first secretary, Wladyslaw Gomulka, asserted that once the Communists arrived in power in a country, they would never give it up. Even after Khrushchev's epochal secret speech denouncing Stalin's rule at the Soviet Party Congress in 1956, when the role of state terror was sharply reduced in the Soviet Union, political paralysis continued. Thereafter, the Soviet ruling class congealed into the privilege- and status-hungry *nomenklatura*, the "new class," or "Red bourgeoisie." The historian Adam Ulam has aptly called their philosophy *immobilisme*, and the state they ran a "bureaucrats' paradise." In 1968, the Soviet government formalized a principle of stasis in what came to be known, in honor of the chairman of the Communist Party of the U.S.S.R., as the Brezhnev Doctrine. On July 18, 1968, at the height of the movement for liberalization in Czechoslovakia called the Prague Spring, an open letter to the Central Committee of the Czechoslovakian Communist Party from a conclave of Communist Parties in Warsaw at which Brezhnev was present stated, "Never will we consent to allow imperialism, whether by peaceful or non-peaceful means, from within or without, to make a breach in the socialist system and change the balance of power in Europe in its favor."

However, it was Nadezhda Mandelstam, the widow of Osip Mandelstam, who penetrated to the heart of the matter. "There was a special form of the sickness—lethargy, plague, hypnotic trance or whatever one calls it," she wrote in the late sixties, in her memoir *Hope Against Hope*, "that affected all those who committed terrible deeds in the name of the 'New Era.' All the murderers, provocateurs, and informers had one feature in common: it never occurred to them that their victims might one day rise up again and speak. They also imagined that time had stopped—this, indeed was the chief symptom of the sickness. We had, you see, been led to believe that in our country nothing would ever change again, and that it was now up to the rest of the world to follow our example and enter the 'New Era.'" George Orwell was another who worried that the new form of rule might be impervious to resistance. "The terrifying thing about the modern dictatorships is that they are something entirely unprecedented," he wrote. ". . . In the past every tyranny was sooner or later overthrown, or at least resisted, because of 'human nature,' which as a matter of course desired liberty. But we cannot be at all certain that 'human nature' is a constant. It may be just as possible to produce a breed of men who do not wish for liberty as to produce a breed of hornless cows."

As Orwell's shaken faith in freedom and loss of confidence in human nature show, the apparent success of totalitarianism in suppressing popular will in the name of that same will produced a crisis of faith in the liberal West. Had the will of the people, nemesis of aristocrats, kings, and emperors in the eighteenth and nineteenth centuries, been nullified in the twentieth by Gauleiters and commissars? Had the totalitarians discovered what had eluded the tyrants of every previous age, a foolproof antidote to human freedom? Had they, with the reinforcement of nuclear terror, wrestled Father Time himself to the ground? Cold indeed was the Cold War, whose dominant note, especially in its first decade, seemed to be this double obedience to terror. No global war, of course, broke out, yet force and the threat of force reigned over the world, all-pervading and ever-present. While the totalitarian leaders were hoping that, metaphorically, time had stopped, they and their Western antagonists were wheeling into place the nuclear machinery that could actually cut short historical time.

And yet the universal conviction proved wrong—stupendously wrong. Human freedom had not died under totalitarian rule. It was about to make a spectacular demonstration of its power. The Cold War, paralyzed at the summit of the world order, was moving along unnoticed, circuitous pathways toward its amazing denouement. Resistance, blocked in the time-tested arteries of military action, was forced into the world's unremarked-on capillary system, where, disregarded, it quietly advanced. And then it gushed forth in mass protest by entire societies. In retrospect, it's apparent that the long series of rebellions against the Soviet empire in Eastern Europe—in East Germany in 1953, in Poland and Hungary in 1956, and in Czechoslovakia in 1968—which at the time looked like exercises in noble futility, were actually stages on the way to the Soviet collapse. The actors were, among others, workers on factory floors, rebellious students, intellectuals talking to one another over kitchen tables or "writing for the drawer," dissidents who were promptly dispatched to concentration camps or psychiatric hospitals, disaffected technocrats, and even bureaucrats in the state apparatus. Every step they took was ventured without a chart or a clear destination. Yet the revolution they made was peaceful, democratic, and thorough.

The nonviolent popular resistance that brought down the Berlin Wall was as historically consequential—as final an arbiter—as either of the two world wars. It ended Soviet communism and its shadow, the specter of "international communism." It finished off an empire whose origins predated the communists. It initiated the creation of more than a dozen new countries. It was the equivalent of a third world war except in one particular—it was not a war.

A BETTER TODAY

It's often said, with good reason, that the Soviet collapse proceeded from the top down. It is no less correct to say that it traveled from the outside in—from the Eastern European periphery to the Soviet center. And in Eastern Europe it decidedly flowed from the bottom up. In the first stage of the collapse, the Solidarity movement of the early 1980s in Poland in effect dissolved the local communist system from within, demonstrating once and for all its previously unsuspected radical weakness of the entire structure of Soviet power. In Czechoslovakia and Hungary, quieter, more gradual movements were under way. It was not the first time that the occupied western territories of the empire proved to be its Achilles' heel. In 1945, in a cable from the American embassy in Moscow to the State Department, George Kennan noted that in the nineteenth century Russian repression had turned Poland into a "hotbed out of which there grew the greater part of the Russian Social Democratic Party which bore Lenin to power." Kennan was one of the few who understood that the Soviet Union's occupation of Eastern European nations after 1945 posed a lethal danger to Moscow. "Successful revolts on their part against Moscow authority," he wrote, "might shake the entire structure of Soviet power." Totalitarian rule, it was turning out, had not endowed the Soviet empire with immunity to the fever for self-determination and freedom that had by then overturned the Western colonial empires. It wasn't until the second stage of the collapse, when Mikhail Gorbachev came to power in Moscow and adopted his radical policies of perestroika and glasnost in the Soviet "center," that change from the top down led to the final dissolution.

Until the late 1970s, the idea that Soviet power might be challenged from within had been largely discarded, and the progress of the revolution from the edges of the empire to its heart caught almost everyone, observers and participators alike, by surprise. Until very late in the day, not even the activists who founded Solidarity imagined that they were inaugurating the collapse of their local, satellite governments, much less the downfall of the whole Soviet system. On the contrary, one of their most original achievements was to discover a way to act and fight for more modest, immediate goals *without* challenging the main structures of totalitarian power head on. Their ambition—itself widely condemned as utopian by Western observers—was merely to create zones of freedom, including free trade unions, within the Soviet framework. And yet once the disintegration at the edges of the empire began, it proved to have no stopping point. The contagion, which combined a longing for national self-determination with a longing for freedom, proceeded, in an unbroken progression from the Eastern European satellites to the peripheral republics of the union (in particular, Lithuania), and from there to Moscow itself, where, to the amazement of all, Russia joined the company of rebels against the Soviet Union, which, lacking now any territory to call its own, melted into thin air.

One of the puzzles of the Soviet downfall is how it happened that a peaceful revolution described by its authors as "self-limiting" (because it did not aim at state power) brought about this unlimited result. As guides to the Eastern European stage of the anti-Soviet revolution, we shall adopt three writer-activists—Adam Michnik, of Poland, Václav Havel, of Czechoslovakia, and Gyorgy Konrád, of Hungary. In the 1970s, the walls of the Kremlin fortress rose impregnable, as it seemed, before their eyes. Fresh in their minds was the succession of defeated rebellions against Soviet domination in East Germany (1953), Poland (1956), Hungary (1956), and Czechoslovakia (1968). From these routs the three writers drew a lesson that might have seemed a counsel of despair but in fact was the basis for a revival of hope and activity. They decided to accept the brute existence of the system as an unchangeable fact of life for the time being. "To believe in overthrowing the dictatorship of the party by revolution and to consciously organize actions in pursuit of this goal is both unrealistic and dangerous," Michnik wrote in 1976, in a pivotal essay called "A New Evolutionism." For "the Soviet military and political presence in Poland is the factor that determines the limits of possible evolution, and this is unlikely to change for some time."

In the mid-1980s, after a declaration of martial law in 1981 had temporarily suppressed Solidarity in Poland, Konrád was still writing, in his book *Anti-Politics*, "It is impossible to alter the . . . system from inside East Europe by means of dynamic, uncontrolled mass movements . . . because the limits of social change are fixed by the military balance, and by a Soviet power elite which labors to preserve the military status quo and has considerable means with which to do it—means that are political as well as military." The division of Europe that had been decided at the summit meeting at the Soviet Black Sea resort of Yalta at the end of the Second World War—an iconic event for Eastern Europeans, known to them simply as "Yalta"—symbolized, Konrád observed, the ancient idea that force has the last word in political affairs:

> The morality of Yalta is simple: those who have the bombs and tanks decide the social and political system. Since the United States and the Soviet Union had the most bombs and tanks, they were called to lead the world. Later—by the fearful light of Hiroshima—their calling was confirmed, for only these two giant nation-states had the resources to build arsenals of nuclear weapons.

Havel, commenting in a similar vein, wrote that what he called the "post-totalitarian" dictatorships of the Soviet empire were "totally controlled by the superpower center and totally subordinated to its interests." He, too, cited the nuclear standoff. "In the stalemated world of nuclear parity, of course," he wrote, "that circumstance endows the system with an unprecedented degree of external stability." Havel, it must be added, was considerably less impressed with the durability of the Soviet edifice than most of his colleagues in resistance. He was one of the very few who suggested that the worldwide self-determination movement, which the Soviets blindly believed to be working in their favor, might undermine the Soviet Union. In an essay in 1978, he took note of the rebellions that in one country after another had rocked the empire, and commented, "If we consider how impossible it is to guess what the future holds, given such opposing trends as, on the one hand, the increasingly profound integration of the [Communist] 'bloc' and the expansion of power within it, and on the other hand the prospects of the USSR disintegrating under pressure from awakening national consciousness in the non-Russian areas (in this regard the Soviet Union cannot expect to remain forever free of the worldwide struggle for national liberation), then we must see the hopelessness of trying to make long-range predictions."

Havel's agnosticism, however, led him to the same practical counsel that Konrád and Michnik were giving: it was a mistake to try to overthrow the system. Activism should be directed at achieving immediate changes in daily life. He proposed unshakable commitment to achieving modest, concrete goals on the local level. "Defending the aims of life, defending humanity," he asserted, "is not only a more realistic approach, since it can begin right now and is potentially more popular because it concerns people's everyday lives; at the same time (and perhaps precisely because of this) it is also an incomparably more consistent approach because it aims at the very essence of things." The three men in effect lowered their field glasses from the remote heights of state power and turned their gazes to the life immediately around them. Gandhi had faced neither totalitarian rule nor nuclear stalemate, yet he, too, had arrived at a decision to aim not at state power directly but at immediate local improvement of life, to be achieved through direct action in the form of the constructive program, which he, too, saw as the essence of things. When Eastern Europeans did this in their own way, a rich field of activity opened up to them, in what they soon began calling civil society.

Neither the term nor the fact of civil society was new. Tom Paine, who so greatly appreciated the power of nonviolent popular resistance during the American Revolution, was, according to his biographer John Keane, the first to fully elucidate the distinction between civil society and civil government. Until

Paine, the terms had been used interchangeably. The key distinction had been the much older one between the wild, contractless, stateless state of nature and the orderly civil state, which was the fruit of the "original contract" among the people. Paine now asserted the existence of two contracts—the original contract, by which the people quit the state of nature and entered *society*, and a second one, by which people in civil society created a *government*. The consequence was the addition of a third state, a purely social state (hence civil "society"), between the traditional state of nature and the civil state. In language that foreshadows the distinctions the Eastern Europeans would draw, Paine praised society at the expense of government:

> Society is produced by our wants, and government by our wickedness; the former promotes our happiness *positively* by uniting our affections, the latter *negatively* by restraining our rule. The one encourages intercourse, the other creates distinctions.

For Paine, the foundation of civil society was an almost entirely benign first step, the foundation of government a regrettably necessary second step.

In the hands of the Eastern European activists, the idea of civil society underwent further development. It was turned into a rival—almost an alternative—to government. Their new rule of thumb was to act not *against* the government but *for* society—and then to defend the accomplishments. In 1976, in "A New Evolutionism," Michnik asserted that the suppression of the Prague Spring and of a Polish student-protest movement in March of 1968 had spelled the end of any hope of reforming the state from within. The new generation must learn to act in a new way: "I believe that what sets today's opposition apart from the proponents of those ideas [of reform in the past] is the belief that a program for evolution ought to be addressed to an independent public, not to totalitarian power. Such a program should give directives to the people on how to behave, not to the powers on how to reform themselves." Michnik later set forth what he called a "philosophy of political activity in a post-totalitarian system." "Why post-totalitarian?" he asked. "Because power is still totalitarian, whereas society isn't any more; it is already anti-totalitarian, it rebels and sets up its own independent institutions, which lead to something we could call civil society, in Tocqueville's sense. That is what we tried to build: civil society."

Michnik's words of 1976 fell on fertile ground. They anticipated (and helped to produce) a blossoming of civic and cultural activity in Poland. An early example was the Worker's Defense Committee. Its purpose was to give concrete assistance to workers in trouble with the authorities—assistance that the organization referred to as "social work." Help was provided to the families of workers jailed by the government. Independent underground publications multiplied. A "flying university," which offered uncensored courses in people's apartments and other informal locations, was founded. Organizations devoted to social aims of all kinds—environmental, educational, artistic, legal—sprouted. In both form and content, these groups were precursors to the ten-million-strong Solidarity movement that arose in 1980.

THE EXPLOSIVE POWER OF LIVING IN TRUTH

What Michnik called a new evolutionism or building civil society Havel called "living in truth"—the title of an essay he published in 1978. Living in truth stood in opposition to "living in the lie," which meant living in obedience to the repressive regime. Havel wrote:

> We introduced a new model of behavior: don't get involved in diffuse general ideological polemics with the center, to whom numerous concrete causes are always being sacrificed; fight "only" for those concrete causes, and fight for them unswervingly to the end.

Why was this living in truth? Havel's explanation constitutes one of the few attempts of this period—or any other—to address the peculiarly ineffable question of what the inspiration of positive, constructive nonviolent action is. By living within the lie—that is, conforming to the system's demands—Havel says, "individuals confirm the system, fulfill the system, make the system, *are* the system." A "line of conflict" is then drawn through each person, who is invited in the countless decisions of daily life to choose between living in truth and living in the lie. Living in truth—directly doing in your immediate surroundings what you think needs doing, saying what you think is true and needs saying, acting the way you think people should act—is a form of protest, Havel admits, against living in the lie, and so those who try to live in truth are indeed an opposition. But that is neither all they are nor the main thing they are. Before living in truth is a protest, it is an affirmation. Havel, who sometimes makes use of philosophical language, explains as follows:

> Individuals can be alienated from themselves only because there is *something* in them to alienate. The terrain of this violation is their essential existence.

That is to say, if the state's commands are a violation deserving of protest, the deepest reason is that they disrupt this *something*—some elemental good thing, here called a person's "essential existence"—that people wish to be or do for its own sake, whether or not it is opposed or favored by the state of anyone else.

This is the point, it seems to me, that John Adams was getting at when he said that the American Revolution was completed before the war, and that Gandhi was making when he suggested that, if independence is a goal, then "it must be declared and pursued irrespective of the acts or threats of others." Like them (and like Nietzsche), Havel rebels against the idea that a negative, merely responding impulse is at the root of his actions. He rejects the labels "opposition" and "dissident" for himself and his fellow activists. Something in *him* craves manifestation.

Of those labels he writes:

> People who so define themselves do so in relation to a prior "position." In other words, they relate themselves specifically to the power that rules society and through it, define themselves, deriving their own "position" from the position of the regime. For people who have simply decided to live within the truth, to say aloud what they think, to express their solidarity with their fellow citizens, to create as they want and simply to live in harmony with their better "self," it is naturally disagreeable to feel required to define their own, original and positive "position" negatively, in terms of something else, and to think of themselves primarily as

people who *are* against something, not simply as people who are what they are.

For Havel, this understanding that action properly begins with a predisposition to truth—often considered a merely private or personal endowment—has practical consequences that are basic to an understanding of political power:

> Under the orderly surface of the life of lies, therefore, there slumbers the hidden sphere of life in its real aims, of its hidden openness to truth. The singular, explosive, incalculable political power of living within the truth resides in the fact that living openly within the truth has an ally, invisible to be sure, but omnipresent: this hidden sphere.

Havel is describing, in words that anticipated the fall of the Soviet Union before that event had occurred, a secular variant of what Gandhi had called "truth force." If Michnik's words anticipated the sudden rise of Solidarity, Havel's bore fruit in the rise of the resistance movement in Czechoslovakia called Charter 77 and in the "velvet revolution" that put an end to communist power in Czechoslovakia.

Konrád offered what might be called a Hungarian version of living in the truth. Having witnessed the slow but surprisingly broad liberalization of the Hungarian system in the 1970s and eighties, he hoped that the changes under way in society would infect the communist functionaries, who would come to see "that their interests were better served by forms of government other than dictatorship." Konrád, who in such passages obliquely debated his Polish and Czech contemporaries on how change might occur, urged "confidence in this growing complexity—in the fact that a society can gradually slough off dictatorship, and that the prime mover in that process is a growing middle class." In his scheme, this liberalization, called "goulash Communism" by some, would gradually turn into goulash decommunization. Konrád wanted society to "absorb" the regime in a "ripening social transformation." He wanted the "iceberg of power . . . melted from within." He cited the historical precedent of the surrender of the dictatorial, right-wing regime of Francisco Franco in Spain to democratic forces in the 1970s. "Proletarian revolution didn't break out in any country of southern Europe," he commented. "If it had, the military dictatorships would only have hardened."

In all three of the Eastern European movements, the strategy was to bypass the government and tackle social problems directly, as Gandhi had done with his constructive program. But whereas "social work" presented no challenge to the Raj, it did challenge the Soviet regime. Within the class of repressive regimes, the Raj was an authoritarian regime, and left vast areas of Indian life untouched. The Raj had no difficulties with Gandhi's constructive program, to which it offered no rival; it was compelled to react only when he practiced noncooperation with the state. To the totalitarian Soviet regime, which sought to control almost every aspect of life, very much including the social, on the other hand, any independent activity looked like the beginnings of a rival governing power. Gandhi had said that once people disown the state under which they live they have "nearly" established their own government. On rare occasions, leaders of totalitarian regimes have also shown that they also understood the danger. In his memoirs, Khrushchev described his fear of the thaw he had started by his secret de-Stalinization speech of 1956. "We were scared—really scared," he wrote. "We were afraid the thaw might unleash a flood, which we wouldn't be able to control and which could drown us. It could have overflowed the banks of the Soviet riverbed and formed a tidal wave which would have washed [away] all the barriers and retaining walls of our society."

We have noted the central role in revolutions of defections among the troops of the old regime. Under a totalitarian regime, which seeks to mobilize the entire population in support of its ideological cause, the people become a sort of army on whose obedience the regime relies. But the very immensity of this army presents a target of opportunity for the opposition. If the essence of totalitarianism is its attempted penetration of the innermost recesses of life, then resistance can begin in those same recesses—in a private conversation, in a letter, in disobedience of a regulation at work, even in the invisible realm of a person's thoughts. Havel gives the example of a brewer he knew who, putting aside official specifications for making beer, set about making the best beer he could. Such was a brewer's living in truth.

Once the unraveling of the single, indivisible fabric of totalitarianism began, the rapidity of the disintegration could be startling. In Havel's prophetic words, "Everything suddenly appears in another light, and the whole crust seems then to be made of a tissue on the point of tearing and disintegrating uncontrollably." Totalitarian rule made constructive work and noncooperation difficult and costly but at the same time was especially vulnerable to those tactics. The pessimistic stock observation that Gandhi could never have succeeded against a totalitarian regime had an optimistic corollary. If such a movement could ever get going, as it did in the Soviet empire, the unraveling would be sudden and irresistible. The "Salisbury field" of a totalitarian regime was its entire society.

The radical potential of constructive work was implicit in a famous saying of Jacek Kuron, an intellectual adviser to Solidarity, who in the late 1970s counseled angry workers, "Don't burn down Party Committee Headquarters, found your own." And that is what they did, in August of 1980, when a spontaneous strike by workers in the Baltic shipyards spread like wildfire through Poland. Soon something like a general strike was under way, and the regime was forced to come to terms by granting, among other concessions, the right to form an independent trade union. The regime would not collapse for another nine years, but its death throes had already begun.

Even before the rise of Solidarity, Havel had reflected on the potential for developing power by founding new associations and organizations. The natural next step for an individual already trying to live in truth in his individual life, he advised in 1978, was to work with others to found what the writer Václav Benda called "parallel structures." These could be expected to arise first, Havel writes, in the realm of culture, where a "second culture," in the phrase he borrows from the rock musician Ivan Jirous, might develop. The step beyond that would be creation of a "parallel polis" (another phrase of Benda's). This was the Czech version of Kuron's advice to the Polish workers to build their own headquarters.

In 1980, when Solidarity sprang into existence, it preferred on the whole to soft-pedal these radical possibilities, which, its leaders believed, might well provoke the Soviet Union to intervene, as it had in the past in Eastern Europe. They proposed instead a novel division of functions. "Society" would run itself democratically, but "power," which is to say the central government (and especially that part of it in charge of foreign affairs), would be left in the hands of the Communist Party dictatorship, whose survival would serve as a guarantee to the Soviet Union that its security interests would not be challenged. Long debates within the Solidarity movement were devoted to negotiating and fixing the boundaries of such a compromise. The debates came to an end only with the imposition of martial law, in December of 1981.

The similarities between the Eastern European movements and Gandhi's movement in India are obvious. If there were evidence that Havel had pored over Gandhi's works, we might suppose that his phrase "living in truth" was an inspired translation of "satyagraha"—a term so difficult to render into other languages. In both movements, we find a conviction that the prime human obligation is to act fearlessly and publicly in accord with one's beliefs; that one should withdraw cooperation from destructive institutions; that this should be done without violence (Gandhi endorses nonviolence without qualifications; each of the Eastern European writers enters some qualifications); that means are more important than ends; that crimes shouldn't be committed today for the sake of a better world tomorrow; that violence brutalizes the user as well as his victim; that the value of action lies in the direct benefit it brings society; that action is usually best aimed first at one's immediate surroundings, and only later at more distant goals; that winning state power, if necessary at all, is a secondary goal; that freedom "begins with myself," as Michnik said, is oriented to love of truth, and only then discovers what it hates and must oppose; and that state power not only should but actually does depend on the consent of the governed.

The differences are also obvious. The Eastern Europeans demonstrated that revolution without violence did not have to depend on religious faith or an abstemious life. Whereas Gandhi's movement was spiritual in inspiration, the Eastern European movements were largely secular (although the Catholic Church played an important role in Poland). Whereas Gandhi called for a strict renunciation of selfish desires in favor of civic obligation, the Eastern Europeans sought to separate the private and other realms of life from political intrusions, of which they were heartily sick after decades of totalitarian rule. (The last thing they would have wanted was a single standard, whether imposed by God, "truth," or anything else, to which people had to subordinate every realm of their existence.) Whereas Gandhi was radically antimaterialistic, the Eastern Europeans were, variously, either only moderately so or hugely interested in material abundance for society. (There can be no such thing as goulash satyagraha.) Whereas Gandhi was an ascetic, the Eastern European leaders tended, in their personal lives, to be *hommes moyens sensuels*. Whereas Gandhi dreamed of a village-based cooperative society unlike any ever seen, then or since, the Eastern Europeans wanted to adopt the kind of parliamentary democracies and free-market economies already functioning in much of the world.

Although nonviolence was not an article of dogma for the Eastern Europeans, it was an essential element of their chosen form of action. "The struggle for state power," Michnik wrote, "must lead to the use of force; yet . . . according to the resolution passed at the memorable Solidarity Congress in Gdansk, the use of force must be renounced." One reason for the choice of nonviolence was pragmatic. The totalitarian state's monopoly on the instruments of violence required a search for some other means. "Why did Solidarity renounce violence?" Michnik asked while in prison after the imposition of martial law. He answered, "People who claim that the use of force in the struggle for freedom is necessary must first prove that, in a given situation, it will be effective, and that force, when it is used, will not transform the idea of liberty into its opposite. No one in Poland is able to prove today that violence will help us to dislodge Soviet troops from Poland and to remove the Communists from power. The USSR has such enormous power that confrontation is simply unthinkable. In other words: we have no guns." But in a comment that adds to our collection of remarks from various times and places claiming that the real revolution has occurred before the fighting (if any) breaks out, Michnik wrote, "Before the violence of rulers clashes with the violence of their subjects, values and systems of ethics clash inside human minds. Only when the old ideas of the rulers lose their moral duel will the subjects reach for force—sometimes."

Also like Gandhi, the Eastern Europeans shunned violence for moral reasons: they did not wish to become like the enemies they despised. The point was not to change rulers; it was to change the system of rule, and the system they opposed had been based on violence. Michnik again: "My reflections on violence and revolution were sparked by my puzzlement about the origins of totalitarianism. I searched for clues in the writings of George Orwell, Hannah Arendt, Osip Mandelstam, and Albert Camus, and I came to the conclusion that the genesis of the totalitarianism system is traceable to the use of revolutionary violence."

Havel concurred. He and his colleagues had "a profound belief that a future secured by violence might actually be worse than what exists now; in other words, the future would be fatally stigmatized by the very means used to secure it." In *Anti-Politics*, Konrád expressed full agreement, and drew an important conclusion. His mention of an active search for an alternative to the traditional ultima ratio is especially noteworthy:

> The political leadership elites of our world don't all subscribe equally to the philosophy of a nuclear *ultima ratio*, but they have no conceptual alternative to it. They have none because they are professionals of power. Why should they choose values that are in direct opposition to physical force? Is there, can there be, a political philosophy—a set of proposals for winning and holding power—that renounces *a priori* any physical guarantees of power? Only antipolitics offers a radical alternative to the philosophy of a nuclear *ultima ratio*. . . . Antipolitics means refusing to consider nuclear war a satisfactory answer in any way. Antipolitics regards it as impossible in principle that any historical misfortune could be worse than the death of one to two billion people.

Violence, the Eastern Europeans found, was to be shunned for another reason: it was useless—more or less beside the point—for the sort of action they had resolved to pursue. Someone once remarked to Napoleon that you can't mine coal with bayonets. Neither are bayonets helpful for writing a book, cleaning a room, designing a microchip, or dressing a wound. Violence might or might not be useful for overthrowing a state, but Solidarity had renounced this ambition.

WHAT IS AND WHAT OUGHT TO BE

The comments of Michnik, Havel, and Konrád bring into the open a question never far from the surface when people choose nonviolent over violent action. Should nonviolence be chosen more for moral and spiritual reasons or more for practical ones? The issue is important because the believer in nonviolent action seems, to an unusual degree, to be ready to suffer defeat rather than abandon his chosen means. For Gandhi, nonviolence was foremost a moral and spiritual requirement. No mere circumstance—least of all the approach of defeat—could justify abandoning it. That is what he meant when he said that nonviolence was for him a creed, not a policy. For Michnik, by contrast, nonviolence was more a policy. He said he wanted the Russians to know that if they used force to put down the Polish movement, they would find themselves "spitting up blood." These are words that Gandhi could never have spoken. On the other hand, as we've seen, Gandhi's nonviolence was founded in part upon the recognition that in a violent fight with the English, the Indians would be "crushed in a minute." In other words, as Michnik said of the Poles, the Indians had no guns. And Gandhi had used language close to Michnik's when he declared that the Indians therefore must create a weapon "which would be different from and infinitely superior to the force which the white settler commanded." In these words, too, there is a kind of ambiguity. Gandhi sought spiritual victory above all else, yet he wanted to win in this world as well.

With Gandhi, we might say, the moral motive is primary, the pragmatic secondary, while with the Eastern Europeans the reverse is true. Either way, it seems to be in the very nature of principled nonviolent action that it tends to combine moral and practical calculation—just as it seems to be in the nature of violent action that, justifying means by ends, it tends to separate the two. That nonviolent action won more and more impressive successes even in the violent twentieth century has, I suggest, a meaning. Isn't it entirely fitting that, in a time when violence has increased its range and power to the point at which the human substance is threatened with annihilation, the most inventive and courageous people would cast about for something better to use? But the wonder of it is not that they have sought but that they have found. Michnik and his colleagues told themselves that they and others had discovered the political equivalent of the "atomic bomb," and they were right—except that their invention in fact accomplished what no actual atomic bomb could accomplish, the defeat of the Soviet Union. When they began their agitation, the iron law of the world dictated that revolution must be violent because violence was the foundation of power, and only power enables you to storm that citadel of violence and power, the state, and so to *take power*. When they were finished, and state after repressive state had been dissolved with little or no use of violence, a new law of the world had been written, and it read: Nonviolent action can be a source of revolutionary power, which erodes the ancien régime from within (even if its practitioners don't aim at this) and lays the foundation for a new state. If totalitarianism is a perversion of the democratic revolution, then the rise of nonviolent revolution is totalitarianism's antidote and cure, pointing the way to a recovery of democracy and, perhaps, to a deeper and truer understanding of democracy's nature, which is bound up with the principle of nonviolence.

Hanging over these political issues are questions of a more philosophical character, having to do with whether or not people are to suppose that the conduct they require of themselves is patterned upon, or takes its cue from, some underlying order of things, natural or divine, or whether, on the contrary, human beings live in an alien, inhuman universe. The tendency of philosophers at least since Nietzsche has been to take this latter view. Neither Gandhi nor Havel considered himself a philosopher, but both plainly thought otherwise. It is striking, for instance, that both chose the word "truth"—perhaps the key word for philosophy—as the touchstone for their actions. Each had very concrete, even mundane, things in mind—for example, the good beer the Czech brewer wanted to brew or the sanitary conditions in India's villages that absorbed Gandhi so much. But each also occasionally touched on metaphysical issues. Describing the illness and death after a jail term in South Africa of a *satyagrahi* called Valliama, Gandhi said, "The world rests upon the bedrock of *satya* or truth. *Asatya*, meaning untruth, also means non-existent, and *satya* or truth also means that which *is*. If untruth does not so much as exist, its victory is out of the question. And truth being that which is can never be destroyed. This is the doctrine of *satyagraha* in a nutshell."

For Gandhi, this "truth" was God. In the essay "Politics and Conscience" Havel, a secular man, wrote in terms that were quite different yet conveyed a similar meaning:

> At the basis of this world are values which are simply there, perennially, before we ever speak of them, before we reflect upon them and inquire about them. It owes its internal coherence to something like a "pre-speculative" assumption that the world functions and is generally possible at all only because there is something beyond its horizon, something beyond or above it that might escape our understanding and our grasp but, for just that reason, firmly grounds this world, bestows upon it its order and measure, and is the hidden source of all the rules, customs, commandments, prohibitions. . . . Any attempt to spurn it, master it, or replace it with something else, appears, within the framework of the natural world, as an expression of *hubris* for which humans must pay a heavy price.

To live in accord with this "something" was to live in truth. A similar confidence was expressed in the saying that, in the Western tradition, must be considered the foundation stone of any philosophy of nonviolence, namely Jesus' "They that live by the sword shall die by the sword." The advice does more than prescribe conduct; it makes a claim about the nature of the human world. We cannot suppose Jesus means that everyone who kills will be killed. But we can suppose he means that violence harms the doer as well as his victims; that violence generates counterviolence; and that the choice of violence starts a chain of events likely to bring general ruin. What Gandhi, Havel, and most of the others who have won nonviolent victories in our time believed and made the starting point of their activity was a conviction—or, to be exact, a faith—that if they acted in obedience to certain demanding principles, which for all of them included in one way or another the principle of nonviolence, there was, somewhere in the order of creation, a fundament, or truth, that would give an answering and sustaining reply.

REVOLUTION FROM THE SIDE

The rise of Solidarity, in which millions of Poles actively and naturally opposed a Soviet-sponsored communist regime,

foreshadowed the collapse of the Soviet Union a decade later.
Solidarity laid bare the previously invisible weakness of Soviet
rule. The trance of totalitarian power of which Nadezhda
Mandelstam had spoken was broken. And yet the collapse of
the Soviet Union itself—"the center," as it was called—proceeded along a different path. Moscow was two steps behind
Poland in 1980. The formative events for Soviet liberals had
been the Prague Spring of 1968, which aroused their hopes
that communism could acquire a "human face," and the intense
disappointment, bordering on despair, they felt when Soviet
tanks rolled into Czechoslovakia. The leaders of the Czech
Party, who were trying to liberalize the Party from within,
had spoken the language of "reform communism," which
Soviet officialdom understood, whereas the Poles in the 1980s
already spoke the language of a post-communist era, which
not even Soviet dissidents could yet imagine. Moscow had not
experienced even Czech-style reformism, much less anything
like Michnik's new evolutionism or Havel's living in truth.
Khrushchev's reformist de-Stalinization of 1956 had been the
limit of their experience of liberalization, and Khrushchev had
been deposed by hard-liners. Such heroic oppositional figures
as the novelist and author of *The Gulag Archipelago* Aleksandr
Solzhenitsyn, the father of the Soviet H-bomb and leader of
the human-rights movement Andrej Sakharov, his wife Yelena
Bonner, and the dissident scientist Yuri Orlov had served as
moral tuning forks for many who shared their beliefs, if not
their almost superhuman courage; but in the face of repression
they had not been able to spark a mass political movement.
The recovery of civil society in the Soviet Union began only in
the late 1980s, after Gorbachev's reforms had been under way
for a few years. Nevertheless, the two processes had something
in common. The nonviolence of the mass movement at the
bottom permitted a largely nonviolent, reformist response.
If Solidarity and Charter 77 had been violent, the nonviolent
Gorbachev reforms would have been unthinkable.

The specific events in the Soviet Union that led directly to
its collapse thus started with drastic reform at the top, not
with a mass movement at the bottom of society. Revolution
from the top, which dates from Peter the Great's attempts at
Westernization, has a long history in Russia. In his memoirs,

Gorbachev explained his thinking. "By the mid-1980s," he said, "our society resembled a steam boiler. There was only one alternative—either the Party itself would lead a process of change that would gradually embrace other strata of society, or it would preserve and protect the former system. In that case an explosion of colossal force would be inevitable." To head off the explosion, he made sure—for much too long, his critics assert—that he remained the leader of the Communist Party, the better to keep it under control. At the same time, he embarked on his programs of glasnost and perestroika—of introducing market reforms, decentralizing the state, liberalizing the press, and gradually democratizing the political process.

In order to understand the importance of the movements in Eastern Europe for the collapse of the Soviet Union, we must recall that the union, like the czarist regime before it, was not only an empire but an empire that ruled an empire. (The Soviet Union proper, that is, was an empire long before it acquired its Eastern European satellites, which were held in subjection by Moscow but never incorporated into the union.) Under the czars, Russia had never experienced a national revolution of the kind that had occurred throughout Western Europe in the late eighteenth and nineteenth centuries. One reason had been precisely that Russia, as an empire, ruled over many nationalities. "For the tsars," the historian Richard Pipes writes, "the imperial principles meant that loyalty to the dynasty, and to the Orthodox faith, took priority over Russian nationalism in the hierarchy of values." Had Russian nationalism become the basis for the state in 1917, it might have caused the breakup of the empire, just as Turkish nationalism under Kemal Ataturk spelled the end of the Ottoman Empire only a few years after the Bolshevik revolution. In 1917, the empire did briefly break up into several independent nations. Its restoration under the Bolsheviks—Stalin's job, accomplished in the civil war and in the years immediately following—was an act of imperial reconquest carried out in the name of revolution. The high tide of this effort was reached in the unsuccessful Bolshevik war against Poland in 1920, which Trotsky, showing a lingering respect for the idea of popular will, opposed, on the ground that revolution cannot be imposed "at the point of a bayonet." Not until the Second World War, when Stalin wished to stir Russian—as distinct from Soviet—patriotism against the German invaders, did the Party explicitly play the national card in Russia, the largest of the union's republics. Even then, it refused to provide Russia with its own "national" communist party.

It would be a mistake, however, to regard the Soviet Union as simply an instrument of Russian domination over imperial colonies—a domination similar, say, to Britain's over its empire. Even though Russians had a preeminent role in governing the union, Russia was to a certain extent one more nation oppressed by a multinational central government, which was at the same time oppressing Ukraine, Armenia, Georgia, and so on. (Stalin, let us recall, was a Georgian.) After the Second World War, when Eastern Europe was incorporated into the socialist "bloc," Russians were often resentful that Russia was subsidizing the Eastern European satellites, many of which did in fact enjoy living standards higher than those in Russia.

Owing to this unique history, there was no clear dividing line in the Soviet Union between "domestic" rule and external conquest, and the methods used in both were extremely similar, if not identical. In *Revolution from Abroad*, the historian Jan Gross observes that the techniques the Soviets used to subjugate Polish society when they invaded Poland in 1939 were the ones they had employed to subjugate their own society in the "war against the nation" in the thirties. The repression that the totalitarian state imposed abroad was a domestic export. The resulting consistency of rule at home and in the satellites meant that a crack in any part of the edifice was more likely to rend the whole. The indivisibility of Soviet rule underlay the indivisibility, from rim to rim of the great empire, of the Soviet collapse.

NONVIOLENCE FROM THE TOP DOWN

When Mikhail Gorbachev came to power in 1985, he embarked on his epic attempt to reform Soviet communism through perestroika and glasnost. He soon realized that reform at home could not succeed if at the same time he was trying to crack down in Eastern Europe. He therefore made a radical decision that few had foreseen, and that even today stands out as remarkable. In a rare act of what we might call nonviolence from the top down, he withdrew the threat of Soviet military invasion that, throughout the Cold War, had been the final guarantee of the survival of the Eastern European communist regimes. In December of 1988, in a speech at the United Nations, he said, "Necessity of the principle of freedom of choice is clear. Denying that right of peoples, no matter what the pretext for doing so, no matter what words are used to conceal it, means infringing even that unstable balance that it has been possible to achieve. Freedom of choice is a universal principle, and there should be no exceptions." His decision marked an acceptance of the new political reality that had been created by Solidarity, Charter 77, and other protest movements in Eastern Europe. (A history of unforced surrender of imperial possessions would make a slender volume. De Gaulle's relinquishment of Algeria even after the military defeat of the F.L.N. would be another of its few chapters.) Military crackdowns in the new conditions might or might not have eventually succeeded. What is certain is that they would have been savage and bloody, and it is for avoiding this that Gorbachev is justly admired. What Gorbachev did not foresee was that by withdrawing the invasion threat, he was pulling the plug on the communist regimes and that their collapse would pull the plug on the Soviet Union itself. Exactly a year after the U.N. speech, the first partially free elections were held in Poland, and the results amounted to a death warrant for communism. Not a single communist running for a contested seat won office. Poland was on its way to full independence and freedom—and after Poland came, in rapid succession, Czechoslovakia, Hungary, East Germany, Bulgaria, and Romania.

Why did the unraveling not stop there? When Britain lost its empire, its domestic system did not collapse. Neither did that of France in the wake of the liquidation of the French empire—although after de Gaulle had announced his readiness to grant Algeria independence he did face a coup attempt by military force stationed in Algeria. Had the Soviet Union been a nation-state, founded, like England and France, upon the consent of its people, it, too, might well have survived. Soviet rule "at home," however, was too much of a piece with Soviet rule "abroad," and the corrosion in the outer empire jumped over into the inner empire. Armenia, Azerbaijan, and Georgia all stirred, but the portal through which the Eastern European sickness (or cure, as we might prefer) entered the union was the Baltic lands, of which the first to rebel was Lithuania.

Having enjoyed semiautonomous status under the czars, the Lithuanians were given their independence after the First World War. In 1939, owing to the Molotov-Ribbentrop pact, in which the U.S.S.R. and Nazi Germany agreed to partition Poland, the Lithuanians were forced to join the Soviet Union. Though living under direct Soviet rule, their memory of an independent national existence was recent and strong. In 1990, they demanded independence. Now the Soviet Union itself was threatened. If the Lithuanian independence movement were crushed, it was unlikely that perestroika could be saved in Russia: the use of the repressive apparatus "abroad" would very likely strengthen it decisively at home. On the other hand, if Lithuania were let go, its release would be a precedent that any or all of the other republics might follow. Now the indivisibility of the choice facing the entire union and empire—a choice, at bottom, between government based on force and government based on consent—became obvious to all. No less clear at that moment was what consent meant: the dissolution of the union. Gorbachev's reforms had activated forces that, if not violently suppressed, were bound to sweep simultaneously from the periphery of the empire into its center and from the bottom of society to the top.

An appeal launched at this hour shed a clear light on the significance of the Lithuanian events for the future. It came from Boris Yeltsin, then president of the Russian Parliament, and it amounted to a call for Russian forces to refuse to participate in a Lithuanian coup. Speaking from the territory of Lithuania's neighbor Estonia, Yeltsin addressed his appeal to the "soldiers, sergeants, and officers of the Soviet Union." He declared, "Today . . . you may be given the order to act against legally created state bodies, against the peaceful civilian population that is defending its democratic achievements. Before you undertake the storming of civilian installations in the Baltic lands, remember your own homes, the present and the future of your own republic, and your own people. Violence against the people of the Baltics will bring new serious crisis phenomena in Russia itself." What gave Yeltsin's words weight was the popular support he had been given in Russia after he had been drummed out of the Party leadership in 1988 and then had quit the Party, paving the way for his election as Russia's president. The last act of the collapse was, naturally, the Russian act.

As the movement spread from the edges into the center, it did not gain in popular intensity and strength. Resistance to Soviet rule was never as strong in the Soviet lands as it was in Eastern Europe. In Poland, there was an explosion; in Russia there was an implosion. Yeltsin, a careful student of the structure of the Soviet Union, had taken note of Stalin's fear of Russia and his refusal to establish a Russian communist party. "God forbid it should rise up and be a counterweight," Yeltsin said in a 1990 interview in the magazine *Soyuz*, elucidating Stalin's thinking. "Understandably, a small republic could not affect the entire Union," he said. "But with giant Russia, if it were to assume its real position, it would be difficult to fight it, or, rather, impossible." Politically, Yeltsin noted, Stalin had made "a precise calculation." Yeltsin made a precise calculation, too. He would use Russia to destroy the Soviet Union. He did not conceal his intention. "It was clear to me," he said, "that the vertical bureaucratic pivot on which the country rested had to be destroyed, and we had to begin a transition to horizontal ties with greater independence of the republic-states. The mood of the people, the democratization of society and the growth of that people's national self-awareness led directly to this."

Yeltsin's opponents, including his rival Gorbachev, have taken him to task for using his support in Russia to break up the union. He used his presidency of Russia, they charge, as a mere instrument for opposing Gorbachev, the union president. And yet the rebellion of Russia against the union—perhaps the least-predicted event in the entire chain of unpredicted events—was of a piece with the story from start to finish. For the last act in Russia, like the first in Poland and most of those in between, was at once democratic, national, and nonviolent. In truth, Russia's self-assertion, putting an end to the Soviet empire, was the final act in the much longer drama of the two-century-long world revolt of nations against the immense empires that ruled over them.

The end came with the failed coup against both Gorbachev and Yeltsin by conservative communist forces, in 1991. While

Gorbachev was held captive by the plotters in his summer retreat in the Crimea, it was left to Yeltsin to win the necessary battle for hearts and minds in Moscow. He had already consolidated his position as the first elected president of Russia in its history. When Gorbachev had sought to bar the election in which he was chosen, tens of thousands of demonstrators had assembled in Moscow in support of Yeltsin, and Gorbachev had backed down. Now, with Gorbachev in captivity and many of his own ministers and aides launching a coup against him, the question was whether the people would obey orders given by the self-appointed coup leadership or those given by Yeltsin. They chose Yeltsin. The decisive factors, it appears, were the crowd that assembled at the risk of its lives in support of democracy in front of the parliament building and the refusal of soldiers and security forces to attack them. As in so many revolutions, including the one in Russia in 1917, the changed mood of the population had spread to the troops, who then went over to the opposition.

When Russia rebelled, "the center" was left suspended in air. Center of what? Where was it? Was it in the Kremlin—a sort of "Kremlinistan"? Or in outer space, where the Soviet Union's manned space station was still orbiting the globe? In Soviet times, Russia, lacking a communist party to call its own, had been called a "ghost state" in the union. Now it was the Soviet Union that would prove the ghost. A few months later, it was gone.

8

Cooperative Power

The professionals of power, in or out of government, were consistently caught off guard by the failures of superior force and the successes of nonviolence. In 1930, when Gandhi was in negotiations with the Raj, Winston Churchill announced that he found it "nauseating and humiliating" that Gandhi, "formerly a Middle Temple lawyer, now posing as a fakir of a type well-known in the East," was to be seen "striding half-naked up the steps of the Viceroy's palace to confer with the representative of the King-Emperor." (Upon hearing of the comment Gandhi wrote, "Dear Prime Minister, You are reported to have the desire to crush the 'naked fakir,' as you are said to have described me. I have been long trying to be a fakir and that naked—a more difficult task. I, therefore, regard the expression as a compliment, though unintended. I approach you, then, as such, and ask you to trust and use me for the sake of your people and mine, and through them those of the world. Your sincere friend, M. K. Gandhi.") Several American administrations were unable to fathom the political power that, in conjunction with inferior instruments of force, was overmatching their military superiority in Vietnam. Soviet leaders soon had a similar experience in Afghanistan. Later, Soviet hard-liners watched in astonishment as state power slipped out of their hands and their empire crumbled with scarcely a shot being fired, and even the nonviolent rebels who brought about this result were startled by their own accomplishment. Most contemporary political theory, wedded to the ageless idea that force was the final arbiter in politics and war, was equally barren of tools for understanding these events, which it could neither foresee nor explain after the fact.

One thinker who did shed light on the new phenomena was Hannah Arendt, whose description and analysis of revolution anticipated the antitotalitarian movements in Eastern Europe with remarkable precision. (Her writing also had a modest influence upon several of the more intellectual-minded Eastern

European activists.) Arendt did not oppose violence on principle, and in her book *Eichmann in Jerusalem* she supported the death penalty for Adolf Eichmann, the Nazi bureaucrat who ran the transportation system for Hitler's program to exterminate the Jews of Europe. Nor was she given to underestimating the role of violence in politics. Born in 1906 into a secular Jewish family in Hanover, Germany, she spent a week in a German prison in 1933 for involvement in a Zionist organization, and shortly fled the country for Prague. She remained stateless for the next eighteen years. In her pioneering work *The Origins of Totalitarianism*, which she wrote in this period, she became one of the first to describe and analyze the full dimensions of the role of terror in totalitarian rule. Nevertheless, in the years that followed she broke decisively with the tradition of political thought that held that the foundation of power is the sword.

VIOLENCE VS. POWER

In approaching the question of power, Arendt followed a procedure characteristic of her thought. Her frequent method was to boldly take sides in debates on the meanings of certain words. Her advocacy of a given meaning might be seen as a bid to push the word in question in one direction or another. The operation proceeded toward both a clarified understanding of the meaning of the word and a new interpretation of historical events. Such was the method she followed when, in the teeth of a tradition as long as history, she asserted that violence, far from being the essence of power, was in fact antithetical to it. It was not enough, she wrote in *On Violence* (1969), to say that "violence and power are not the same." Rather, "Power and violence are opposites; where the one rules absolutely, the other is absent." Therefore, "to speak of nonviolent power is actually redundant." To appreciate just how unorthodox, even shocking, this claim was, we only have to recall A. J. P. Taylor's definition of the great powers of the nineteenth century as "organizations for power, that is, in the last resort, for war." His assumption that an organization for power is "for war" was, of course, perfectly in keeping with the conventional wisdom of his time and ours. Or we can recall the assertion by Max Weber, quoted by Arendt, that the state can be defined as "the rule of men over men based on the means of legitimate, that is allegedly legitimate, violence."

By contrast, Arendt held that power is created not when some people coerce others but when they willingly take action together in support of common purposes. "Power," she wrote, "corresponds to the human ability not just to act but to act in concert." Such action requires "the making and keeping of promises, which in politics may be the highest human faculty." The human endowment Arendt was pointing to was not something mysterious or rare. One of her favorite examples was the Mayflower Compact, in which a small company of people on the high seas swore to "solemnly and mutually in the Presence of God and one another, covenant and combine ourselves together into a civil Body Politic." The idea that power is born out of action in concert had not gone unnoticed in political thought. Burke summed it up in a sentence when he said, "Liberty, when men act in bodies, is power." Tocqueville said much the same in his analysis of the vibrant civil society he witnessed in the United States in the 1830s. "There is no end which the human will despairs of attaining," he asserted, "through the combined power of individuals united into a society." Referring to the "power of meeting," he remarked, "Democracy does not confer the most skillful kind of government upon the people, but it produces that which the most skillful governments are frequently unable to awaken, namely an all-pervading and restless activity, a superabundant force, and an energy which is inseparable from it, and which may, under favorable circumstances, beget the most amazing benefits." We have already noted that Adams's characterization of the peaceful, rebellious civil activity before the revolutionary war—especially in his beloved Committees of Correspondence—is a portrait of the power generated by peaceful association. Gandhi's claim that through acts of noncooperation *satyagrahis* "nearly establish their own government" obviously refers to the same phenomenon, as does his view that political power, though not necessarily a goal of constructive social action, was its inevitable by-product. Havel's "living in truth" and Benda's creation of a "parallel polis" were incarnations of cooperative power. Examples given by Arendt were the "revolutionary councils" that arose, repeatedly and spontaneously, at the beginning of almost all the modern revolutions, including the popular societies of the districts of Paris in the French Revolution, the soviets in the Russian Revolution (in her view, the soviets were promising and positive institutions that were manipulated, abused, and eventually liquidated by the Bolsheviks to win and keep dictatorial power), and the German *Räte* that briefly came into existence in the socialist rebellion of 1918–19. The Interfactory Strike Committees, which coordinated the protests in factories in Poland in 1980 to create the powerful national Solidarity movement, were the very model of the power of concerted action, though Arendt did not live to witness them.

Arendt's conception of power was different in important respects from the liberal conception. The liberal thinkers generally located power in government, and went on to ask what its foundation should be. Some answered with Weber that at bottom it was and had to be fear, inspired by the ever-present threat of violence, while others answered that it should be popular consent. Arendt, by contrast, located power not in government but in societies, whose people generated it by their action in concert, and then might go on to vest it, for a while, in particular government. Like freedom, which was its foundation, power was not to be found in all societies. It existed only latently, until activated by deeds such as the Mayflower Compact and the activities of the revolutionary councils. If citizens became passive, power would evaporate. For, "Where power is not actualized, it passes away, and history is full of examples that the greatest material riches cannot compensate for this loss." When a government was based on the concerted action of its citizens, its power, on the other hand, would be at its maximum. For this to happen, the council system, by which society would organize itself into spontaneous deliberative local bodies, would have to become the foundation of a system of government—something that, to Arendt's regret, had never been accomplished. (An example she cited was Thomas Jefferson's proposal after the American Revolution to divide the counties into town meeting–like "wards.")

In this view, power did not reside, as is usually said, in officials who issue commands but in citizens who follow them. A long tradition had identified the officials as the powerful ones. Arendt quoted her contemporary, the political thinker Bertrand de Jouvenal: "To command and to be obeyed: without that, there is no Power—with it no other attribute is needed for it to be." Or as Weber put it, "Power means every chance within a social relationship to assert one's will even against opposition." Arendt answered, with Hume, Burke, Gandhi, and Havel, that in a deeper sense power is in the hands of those who obey the commands, which is to say with society. Power is indeed "never the property of an individual," she writes; "it belongs to a group and remains in existence only so long as the group keeps together." If society withdrew its obedience, the commander's rule was at an end. Even Clausewitz, let us recall, was of this opinion, for he understood that military victories were useless unless the population of the vanquished army then obeyed the will of the victor. The resolute society that dislikes its ruler can find another ruler; but where would a ruler who had lost the obedience of his society find another society?

If power was the force that is created by action in common and sustained by mutual promises, then it followed that violence, which is the action of one person against another, was in fact destructive of it, inasmuch as violence breaks up the relationships of trust on which power is based. A violent state or group, Arendt well knew, could defeat a more "powerful" rebellion of people acting together peacefully, at least in the short run: "In a head-on clash between violence and power, the outcome was hardly in doubt." What violence could never do was create power: "While violence can destroy power, it can never become a substitute for it. From this results the by no means infrequent political combination of force and powerlessness, an array of impotent forces that spend themselves often spectacularly and vehemently but in utter futility."

Surprisingly, perhaps, Arendt's principal example of the powerlessness of violence was the totalitarianism she had studied so deeply. Precisely its unprecedented dependence on violence, she asserted, deprived it of what she defined as power. "Nowhere is the self-defeating factor in the victory of violence over power more evident," she wrote, "than in the use of terror to maintain domination, about whose weird successes and eventual failures we know perhaps more than any generation before us." Terror, even as it keeps its practitioners in office for a time, destroys the foundation of their power. "The climax of terror is reached when yesterday's executioner becomes today's victim," she observes. "And this is also the moment when power disappears entirely."

Such were the insights that underlay her prophetic comments regarding the long-term fate of Soviet totalitarianism. They permitted her, for example, to perceive that each time the Soviet Union used its tanks to crush a rebellion in Eastern Europe, it was diminishing its power, not increasing it, as most observers thought. In *The Origins of Totalitarianism*, she had taken the full measure of the totalitarian evil, yet she was one of the few writers of the Cold War years to perceive the Soviet Union's underlying weaknesses. It's one thing to grasp in hindsight that the succession of rebellions against Soviet rule in Eastern Europe were shocks portending the fall; it was another to write in 1969, just after the suppression of the Prague Spring, that "the head-on clash between Russian tanks and the entirely nonviolent resistance of the Czechoslovak people is a textbook case of a confrontation between violence and power," and to comment, "To substitute violence for power can bring victory, but the price is very high; for it is not only paid by the vanquished, it is also paid by the victor in terms of his own power." For even as this use of violence restored rule, it destroyed the last reserves of support—even if these amounted only to a minimal, grudging acquiescence or tolerance—that the regime required. The ground was prepared for the later rebellions in Eastern Europe, in which millions of ordinary people, acting together for what they believed in and so creating genuine power in Arendt's sense, precipitated the final convulsion of the Soviet system. Arendt indeed foresaw a more general "reversal in the relationship between power and violence, foreshadowing another reversal in the future relationship between small and great powers."

In a passage that both portrayed the collapses of the anciens régimes that she knew from history and dramatically anticipated the Soviet collapse, she described what happens when, behind the unchanging, impressive facade of violence, the reserves of power run too low. Then, "the situation changes abruptly. Not only is the rebellion not put down but the arms themselves change hands—sometimes, as in the Hungarian revolution, within a few hours. . . . The dramatic sudden breakdown of power that ushers in revolution reveals in a flash how civil obedience—to laws, to rulers, to institutions—is but the outward manifestation of support and consent."

The commonalities between Arendt and Gandhi are obviously many. Her observation that the power of a government depends wholly on civil obedience and evaporates if this is withdrawn is virtually identical to Gandhi's many observations on the subject. Like Gandhi, Arendt also believed not only that revolution can be nonviolent but, among other things, that any politics worth its salt must be rooted in direct action; that the obligation to act is therefore a paramount requirement, after which the mode of action can be considered; that at the heart of action lies freedom, which both inspires action and lends it meaning, and, in fact, lends life meaning; that courage is the sine qua non of freedom and action; that action must proceed by agreement among equals, not through suppression by violence of one party by another; that rule based on violence is in its nature not only destructive but in the long run self-destructive; and that authentic, enduring power must be based on nonviolent action—that, in Arendt's memorable words, "Power is actualized only where word and deed have not parted company, where words are not empty and deeds not brutal, where words are not used to veil intentions but to disclose realities, and deeds are not used to violate and destroy but to establish relations and create new realities."

This closely connected complex of ideas not only is shared by Arendt and Gandhi but is shared, as far as I'm aware, by them alone among twentieth-century analysts of political power. (The nearest exceptions, perhaps, are the Eastern European writers I have cited.) And yet Arendt mentions Gandhi even less often than the Eastern Europeans did. In all of her work, there are only a handful of references to him, and she never quotes him. (All of the mentions, it is true, are admiring. For example, she refers to "Gandhi's enormously powerful and successful strategy of nonviolent resistance"—although she joins those who surmise that it would have failed against a Stalin or a Hitler. Elsewhere, without mentioning Gandhi, she nevertheless seems to refer to him. "Popular revolt against materially strong rulers . . . may engender an almost irresistible power," she writes, "even if it forgoes the use of violence in the face of materially vastly superior forces. To call this 'passive resistance' is certainly an ironic idea; it is one of the most active and efficient ways of action ever devised, because it cannot be countered by fighting, where there may be defeat or victory, but only by mass slaughter in which even the victor is defeated, cheated of his prize, since nobody can rule over dead men.")

On at least one fundamental point, however, Arendt couldn't have differed from Gandhi more sharply. Whereas he turned to spiritual love as the source and inspiration of nonviolent action, Arendt was among those who argued strenuously against introducing such love into the political sphere. Her objections were not those of the realist school, which holds that love is too weak a force to be effective in politics, which is and must be governed by force. Rather, she regarded love as extraordinarily powerful, and expressed intense admiration for those who, like Jesus, she believed were capable of it. It is in part for this reason, she urges, that the wall of separation between the City of God and the City of Man must be left intact.

Politics wrecks love, in her version of the venerable argument, because love's proper domain is the hidden world of the spirit and the heart, and publicity, which is necessary for politics, will coarsen and corrupt it by turning it into a public display, a show. Love wrecks politics also because the demands of the spirit and the heart are peremptory, and cannot endure the legal restraints that must prevail in a sound political order. She cites Robespierre's "terror of virtue" and its Bolshevik epigones. Robespierre's virtue counts for her as "love" because its inspiring motive was "pity" for the suffering of the poor, which she saw as a kind of love. Such pity may be admirable in itself but, if "taken as the spring of virtue, has proved to possess a greater capacity for cruelty than cruelty itself."

Gandhi, the uniter of religion and politics, asserted, "A *satyagrahi* has no other stay but God, and he who has any other stay or depends on any other help cannot offer *satyagraha*." He admitted that a nonbeliever could still be "a passive resister" or a "noncooperator," but "not a true *satyagrahi*." Echoing the liturgy of many faiths over many centuries, he added, "Only in His strength are we strong." The political secularist, however, will answer with Arendt that there is something forbidding, even tyrannical, in the fact of subordinating every sphere of life to the demands of religion. The secularist will be more at home with her careful separation of these spheres and her search within each for virtues proper to each. "Moderation is best in all things," the secularist will say with Montesquieu, "even virtue."

Although Arendt was not as thoroughgoing an opponent of violence as Gandhi, her views were in one respect even more radically subversive than his of any political justification for violence. Gandhi mounted an attack upon violence, so to speak, from outside politics, demanding that politics live up to divine law. Accepting that violence might indeed be a source and instrument of power, he rejected it on moral and spiritual grounds. Arendt, on the other hand, finds all she needs for rescuing politics from violence in politics itself. She calls for no rescue by God. On the contrary, she merely lets the political man know that if he relies on violence he may score successes but in the long run will lose what he most wants, namely power.

Arendt, however, leaves many questions raised by Gandhi unaddressed. Gandhi, we recall, proposed to answer the objections to the spiritualization of politics by placing his *satyagrahis* under two severe restraints as they entered public life: the renunciation, on the physical plane, of violence and, on the intellectual plane, of any claim to absolute truth. Gandhi showed he was in earnest about these restraints by ending satyagraha whenever his followers violated them. Might these two renunciations make "love" safe for political expression? Arendt left us without her reflections on the subject, citing only instances in which the politicization of spiritual love bred fanaticism and violence. What she did leave was her daring bid to redefine politics and, with it, a deeply thought-through approach to nonviolent action that is distinctly un-Gandhian. To the question what the usefulness of violence was and was not, Arendt answered that violence, even when used in the service of goodness, lies outside politics and is destructive of it. And to the question what the role of nonviolent action in politics is, her answer was: politics *is* nonviolent action.

WHAT DO WE LOVE?

Even as Arendt's distinction between power and violence illumines not only the sudden Soviet collapse but aspects of all the revolutions we have discussed, it creates a conceptual problem. It seems to leave dictatorship dangling, linguistically speaking, in midair, without any political properties to call its own. "Tyranny prevents the development of power, not only in a particular segment of the public realm but in its entirety," Arendt wrote. Yet if tyrants—including the totalitarian variety—were not "powerful," what were they? The Bolsheviks' loss of power did not catch up with their dependence on violence for seventy-four long years. What word was appropriate for the sway they exercised in that period?

Gandhi was a more thoroughgoing advocate of nonviolence than Arendt, yet he spoke, as we've seen, of the existence of two kinds of power. "One is obtained by the fear of punishment," he said, "and the other by acts of love." His power based on love closely resembled in practice what Arendt simply called "power." Its methods were noncooperation and constructive action, both of course nonviolent. His power based on fear—what he called *duragraha* (bodily, or coercive, force)—corresponded to what she called violence. But Gandhi's distinction has the advantage over Arendt's of acknowledging the existence of a kind of power based on support without outraging common usage by denying, as Arendt does, the title of "power" to rule by force and fear.

I suggest that the power that is based on support might be called cooperative power and that the power based on force might be called coercive power. Power is cooperative when it springs from action in concert of people who willingly agree with one another and is coercive when it springs from the threat or use of force. Both kinds of power are real. Both make things happen. Both are present, though in radically different proportions, in all political situations. Yet the two are antithetical. To the extent that the one exists, the other is ruled out. To the degree that a people is forced, it is not free. And so when cooperative power declines, coercive power often steps in to fill the vacuum, and vice versa. Society's need for power of one kind or another is so great that in the absence of popular government people will often accept dictatorship, creating a sort of desperate "consent" that is quite different from the "liberal obedience" (in Burke's phrase) that is the bedrock of a system of cooperative power. Likewise, when coercive power weakens, cooperative power may suddenly appear, as it did in the latter days of the Soviet empire.

In this distinction between two kinds of power, love and

fear are functional equivalents (both are sentiments, and both produce obedience, on which, all schools agree, government depends). In a coercive system, fear, of course, is the product of force. But of what, in a cooperative system, is love the product? What summons up the love that produces the consent, the support, the willing agreement on which cooperative power depends?

The answer to this question, obviously of fundamental importance to any politics based on cooperation rather than coercion, is curiously elusive. The things that inspire fear—death, threat of injury—as well as the behavior it prompts have a monotonous uniformity, like the bending of blades of grass in a wind, which is the oldest of metaphors for obedience to oppressive power. But if we ask ourselves what inspires love in the public realm the possible specific answers seem unlimited. For if no one forces us to do his bidding, we are simply free to desire and do anything we may get it into our heads to desire or do, for any reason whatsoever, trivial or grave, wicked or virtuous: build a school, take a bribe, eat an apple, kill a neighbor, save a neighbor's life at the cost of our own. We are left not with a particular goal but with the latitude to choose any goal. In other words, we are left with freedom. According to Tocqueville, a passionate believer in political freedom, it was indeed unworthy of the ideal to identify any particular good as freedom's aim. In his words, "What has made so many men, since untold ages, stake their all on freedom is its intrinsic glamour, a fascination it has in itself, apart from all 'practical' considerations. For only in countries where it reigns can a man speak, live, and breathe freely, owing obedience to no authority save God and the laws of the land. The man who asks of freedom anything other than itself is born to be a slave."

Gandhi, of course, gave a clear and unequivocal answer to the question. The love that should guide political action, he believed, was the love of God, or truth, which for him were the same. "If God who is indefinable can be at all defined," he wrote, "then I should say that God is TRUTH. It is impossible to reach HIM, that is TRUTH, except through LOVE." Havel, too, resorted to the word "truth," but in a secular definition, though now and then he ventured metaphysical explanations. Many other political figures have, without resorting to religion or metaphysics, also drawn a distinction between love, always associated with freedom, and fear. John Adams was drawing it in 1776, when he wrote that in an independent American republic "love and not fear will become the spring of their [the people's] obedience." And Montesquieu stated that "government is like everything else: to preserve it, we must love it." The love he had in mind was "love of the laws and of our country"—a love, he added, "peculiar to democracies." None other than the arch-realist Machiavelli also linked love and freedom. In a passage in *The Prince*, he commented, "Men love at their own free will but fear at the will of the prince." (He therefore recommended *fear* as the basis of government, for "a wise prince must rely on what is in his power and not on what is in the power of others.") Hard as it is to fix any bounds on what people may spontaneously admire, we know how to identify a free person. We call that person free who, in disregard of force and fear, acts in accord with what his soul prompts him to love.

OPINION

One political thinker who reflected on the dual character of political power was the liberal English thinker par excellence of the nineteenth century, John Stuart Mill. In *Representative Government* he put the question, "What is meant by power?" He answered, "Politically speaking, a great part of all power consists in will." "Will" here obviously refers to the capacity for spontaneous, willing allegiance and action that is at the root of cooperative power. Because will was politically important, "opinion," which guides the will, was also important. "Opinion is itself one of the greatest active social forces," he observed, and those who, by teaching or example, could offer people something they admire or believe in therefore may be the most powerful figures on the social landscape. For "They who can succeed in creating a general persuasion that a certain form of government, or social fact of any kind, deserves to be preferred, have made nearly the most important step which can possibly be taken towards ranging the powers of society on its side." He gave two examples. One was the first Christian martyr, St. Stephen, who was "stoned to death in Jerusalem while he who was to be Apostle to the Gentiles [St. Paul] stood by 'consenting unto his death.'" "Would anyone," Mill asked of these first Christians, "have supposed that the party of that stoned man were then and there the strongest power in society? And has not the event proved that they were so? Because theirs was the most *powerful* of then existing beliefs." The other example was Martin Luther at the Diet of Worms, who, because he founded a faith that the people freely chose, was "a more powerful social force than the Emperor Charles the Fifth, and all the princes there assembled."

If, as Mill pointed out, opinion guided the will, and the will moved people to give political support, and political support was the foundation of power, then the most powerful people seemed to be those who, whether in government or out, had the capacity to create or do something that inspired the respect, admiration, loyalty, faith—all of which, again, is to say the love—of others. Power, according to this conception, which dovetails closely with Arendt's, begins with the capacity to create or discover something (including, for example, a republic) that other people cannot help but love—a definition about as far as one can get from A. J. P. Taylor's "organizations for war" or Jouvenel's "to command and be obeyed."

Yet in speaking of someone as more "powerful" than those stoning him to death, or than the princes of his day, because later generations were persuaded by his teaching and example, don't we reach the boundaries of what can be understood by the word "power"? Don't we begin to speak in mere conundrums? If this is the measure of power, then is anyone who catches the attention of the world in one way or another politically "powerful"? The inspiring example of a human being stoned to death is only one ingredient even of cooperative power, which depends on the responding active support of many, and to call such a person powerful is admittedly to flirt with paradox. Why insist on *this* word to describe the phenomenon? Wouldn't it be better to reserve the word, as is so often done, for those who occupy high positions in government or command tank divisions, and leave it at that?

The events of our time, however, rule out this reversion. For in our day the dual aspect of power lies not only in the uses of the word but in the new phenomena it must describe. The power that flows upward from the consent, support, and nonviolent activity of the people is not the same as the power that flows downward from the state by virtue of its command of the instruments of force, and yet the two kinds of power contend in the same world for the upper hand, and the seemingly weaker one can, it turns out, defeat the seemingly stronger, as the downfall of the British Raj and the Soviet Union showed. Therefore, although it may lead to paradox and linguistic tangles to speak of martyrs as being more "powerful" than the authorities who put them to death, the exercise is inescapable. For it is indeed a frequent mistake of the powers that be to imagine that they can accomplish or prevent by force what a Luther, a Gandhi, a Martin Luther King, or a Havel can inspire by example. The prosperous and mighty of our day still live at a dizzying height above the wretched of the earth, yet the latter have made their will felt in ways that have already changed history, and can change it more.

PART THREE

THE CIVIL STATE

9

The Liberal Democratic Revival

Everything we have discussed so far—conventional war, nuclear war, people's war, and revolution—falls under the heading of what the contract theorists of the seventeenth century called the state of nature: their term for conditions, domestic or international, that lie outside the protection of states and their laws. For most of these thinkers, the state of nature was indistinguishable, or scarcely distinguishable, from a state of war, and was the last place they would have gone searching, as we have done, for an escape from political violence. The unexpected appearance in these normally chaotic, blood-spattered precincts of new and historically potent forms of nonviolent action is one measure of the radical difference between their time and ours. Now in the same quest we turn, more conventionally, to the ordered realm of the civil state, and its underpinning, law, to which not only theorists but ordinary people have long looked to give relief from anarchy and violence—to pacify the warring tribes, to prevent the attack of neighbor upon neighbor, to fix the boundaries of states and regulate weights and measures, to mete out justice and provide for the common good. Most visions of world peace, indeed, have traditionally been based on some notion of extending the structures of civil rule to the international realm. The idea that the foundation of a universal state—world government—would put an end to war has been a perennial dream.

One development in the civil sphere that holds promise as a foundation for peace is the liberal democratic revival of the late twentieth century. This revival, however, has been so tightly entangled with contrary forces, including the traditional imperial proclivities of many democratic states, that its potential contributions to peace may be foreclosed before even being offered.

If satyagraha, living in truth, and the spontaneous foundation of institutions of civil society are the forms that cooperative power takes in the state of nature, then liberal democracy is the chief form it takes in the civil state. We have already noted the association of nonviolent revolution and democracy. No less striking is the tendency, noted by recent scholars, of liberal democracies to refrain from war among themselves. This disposition found one of its first articulations in Immanuel Kant's essays "Perpetual Peace" (1795) and "Idea for a Universal History" (1784), in which he called for "a universal civic society," and named the goal "the highest problem Nature assigns to the human race." He advocated a "civic union" of republics that would establish universal and perpetual peace in the world. However, the liberal revival must have a central place in any discussion of nonviolence for a deeper reason: the goal of taming violence is written into liberalism's genetic code.

According to the contract theorists (whose thinking stands behind the rise of liberal government), the choice between force and consent is perennial, because of the ineradicable fact of human existence that human beings are many but inhabit together a world that is one. It was hardly necessary, of course, to postulate an "original" state of nature (which even in Locke's time was proposed more as a thought-experiment than as a description of historical reality) or to travel to a war zone to confirm the truth of this commonsense observation. A visit to any playground, family living room, office, or street corner—not to speak of any company boardroom, university department, or legislature—would do. "The latent causes of action," James Madison wrote, "are . . . sown in the nature of man." Or, in the words of Thomas Hobbes, who, though no liberal, must be classed among the contractarians, "If any two men desire the same thing, which nevertheless they cannot both enjoy, they become enemies; and . . . endeavor to destroy, or subdue one another." Thus arose his "war of all against all."

Broadly speaking, the contractarians identified two possible solutions to the dilemma. The first was that one party imposed its will on the others by force; the second was that the parties found their way to agreement. The first saved the freedom of one party at the expense of the other's; the second saved the freedom of all parties, because all had given their approval—had, though perhaps surrendering a portion of their ambitions, given their consent to the final result. The first was an institutionalization of what we have called coercive power and the foundation of authoritarianism, the second—the liberal program—an institutionalization of cooperative power and the foundation of civil freedom.

Any constitution based on freedom must of course be complex, yet its essential requirements have been defined with remarkable consistency over the more than two thousand years of the democratic tradition. They were summarized in the riposte that, according to Greece's first great historian, Herodotus, the Spartan Demaratus gave to the Persian king Xerxes, who challenged him to explain how Greece, which endowed its citizens with freedom, could produce obedient, steadfast soldiers. "They are free—yes—but not entirely free," Demaratus answered, "for they have a master, and that master is Law, which they fear much more than their subjects fear you." Cicero described the citizen of a free Rome in similar terms. "He obeys the laws not, of course, because of fear," he wrote; "he complies with them and respects them because he judges that such a course is extremely advantageous. He says nothing, does nothing, thinks of nothing except in a free and voluntary manner. All of his plans and all of his acts proceed from himself, and he himself is also the judge of them."

The connection between nonviolence and freedom in a liberal democratic constitution, a moment's thought will show, lies in the nature of both. Freedom is twofold. In the first place, it is a power inherent in the human being to decide to do things and to do them. Shall I eat a pear or a peach? Shall I vote for this candidate or that? Shall I start a school? Yet, having made my decision and embarked on a course of action, I may encounter some obstacle—perhaps prison walls, or a police barricade. If the obstacle is removed, then I am "free" to proceed. And so in the second place freedom is the lack of an external obstacle to my action once I have embarked on it. "Liberty, or freedom," Hobbes wrote, defining this second aspect of freedom, "signifieth, properly, the absence of opposition; by opposition, I mean external impediments of motion."

In the political sphere, the innate human power of doing things is displayed in what has been called positive freedom, which is the capacity to participate in political life, by such acts as voting, demonstrating, even rebelling against the government. Its exercise satisfies the human desire to be an active agent of one's own fate, not just the passive object of the wills of others. The second aspect of freedom—Hobbes's absence of external impediment—has been called negative freedom, which is the citizen's freedom from coercion by the state, typically codified in bills of rights and the like.

The two aspects of freedom are tightly connected in the liberal democratic scheme of government. Negative freedoms such as bills of rights and other legal protections of citizens do not come into existence by themselves; they are creations of those same citizens as exercisers of positive freedom, who either make the laws or choose those who will do so. Negative freedoms represent a collective decision by the citizenry not to use the state's monopoly to coerce themselves as individuals. In a word, negative freedoms are institutional acts of restraint, which is to say acts of nonviolence. By participating in politics, citizens exercise their positive freedom; by institutionally restraining their collective violence, they show respect for the positive freedom of other citizens. But at the same time such restraints on the state's coercive power are precisely what we mean by negative freedom. On the side of the receiver, negative freedom is what Hobbes said it was, absence of impediment. On the side of the bestower, negative freedom is nonviolence.

The nonviolent revolutionary exercises the same restraint, and for the same reason, although in an utterly different context. By declining to coerce his opponent, he grants him a kind of raw negative freedom. Of course, in the midst of a revolutionary contest for power, this freedom cannot take the form of legal guarantees but merely that of leaving the opponent safe from violent harm at one's own hands. Yet nonviolent revolution and liberal government both restrain violence in the name of freedom—the freedom, that is, of *others*, including opponents. Those who "live in truth," and so refrain from violence, even against their oppressors, for fear of reproducing tyranny, are receiving ideal training for office (including the office of citizen) in the liberal state, which must refrain from any violence against the political opposition.

Although Gandhi emphasized love more than freedom—just as he emphasized social service more than politics—he, too, believed that freedom was essential to any healthy political order. "No society can possibly be built on a denial of individual freedom," he said. "It is contrary to the very nature of man. Just as man will not grow horns or a tail so he will not exist as man if he has no mind of his own." The beauty of satyagraha is that it saved the freedom of both the doer and the done to. It is a system of respect for individual freedom without benefit of the civil state. In both satyagraha and liberal democracy, nonviolence reconciles the individual's freedom with his exercise of power. Herein lies the inextricable—indeed the definitional—connection of freedom and nonviolence. These two are inseparable and their union is rooted in the very nature of action and of every scheme so far invented, whether within the civil state or outside it, that seeks to reconcile the exercise of positive freedom with enjoyment of its negative partner.

To the degree that the ideal is realized, a country's constitution and its laws in fact become a hugely ramified road map for the peaceful settlement of disputes, large and small. For if it is true, as the Romans said, that *inter arma silent leges* (when arms speak, the laws fall silent), it is equally true that when the laws speak arms fall silent. Otherwise, who would bother with laws? Every peaceable transfer of power in accord with the decision of an electorate is a coup d'état avoided. Every court case—however acrimonious the lawyers—is a possible vendetta or bloodbath averted. And so the spread of democracy, if it rests on a solid foundation, is an expansion of the zone in which the business of politics is conducted along mainly nonviolent lines. In this basic respect, the long march of liberal democracy is a "peace movement"—possibly the most important and successful of them all.

It is not, of course, liberal government alone that seeks to give society relief from its violent tendencies. Every form of government accepts this responsibility, at least in theory. However, the liberal commitment to nonviolence is deeper than the authoritarian promise to end the war of all against all. Whereas the authoritarian promises only to deliver society from its own "natural" violence, the liberal wants to protect it also from the violence of the state. Beginning by saving human beings from their mutual violence through the establishment of government, it then tries to save them from the savior, by guaranteeing the negative freedoms of the citizen. Why, Locke asked, would men fear violence from one another but not fear the violence of Leviathan? To imagine that, he said, would be to think men are "so foolish that they take care to avoid what mischiefs may be done them by polecats or foxes, but are content, nay, think it safety, to be devoured by lions."

Authoritarian rule is in fact not so much an escape from violence as a rearrangement of it, in which the violence at the disposal of each person is pooled in the hands of the state. Locke took the critical next step. By insisting that government be rooted in the willing support of the people, he sought to change their relationship to it to one of consent—or love, if Montesquieu and Burke speak truly. The fundamental change occurs in what Montesquieu described as "the spirit" of the laws, and what others have called hearts and minds. It is the spirit of consent—this willing disposition of the people, Burke's "liberal obedience"—that is, wherever it exists, the true foundation of the liberal democratic state, just as it is the true foundation of nonviolent direct action. The inner moral change in hearts and minds from fear to consent is the specific genius of liberal democracy, permitting its citizens to remain free even as they obey the commands of the law.

In the teeth of this venerable tradition, many observers have, of course, continued to insist that the foundation of all state power is force. Pointing out that governments claim the power to enforce the laws, they conclude that political power always and everywhere rests on a foundation of violence. Their mistake is to confuse police power with political power—or, in Arendt's terms, violence with power. These two are in fact the same only in a police state. In newly democratic South Africa, for example, the police are called on to enforce the law. Indispensable as enforcement is, its existence doesn't mean that the authority of Parliament, the ministers, and the courts rest on a foundation of police power. On the contrary, their political power obviously depends on the willing support and obedience of the great majority of the public, expressed in free elections. By comparison, the power of the police is a marginal affair. Much less does the domestic power of the government rest on the military, whose abstention from politics is essential to the democratic contract. The instant that the majority of citizens withdrew their support from the system of government, the South African state would cease to be democratic, and revolution or dictatorship would ensue.

AN AMERICAN REFORMATION

In reality, of course, liberal governments live up to their ideals only to a limited extent. Gross, long-lasting, injustices commonly exist alongside real freedoms. The United States—to give one illustration—has been a genuine republic for more than two hundred years, but for its first eighty years it was also a slave power and for a century after that systematically denied fundamental human and democratic rights to its black minority. In the segregated South, blacks were in subjection by an interlocking system involving the states, local government, and economic and social repression. Protest was met with economic sanctions, petty humiliation, beatings, imprisonment, lynching, and other forms of abuse. Not until the civil-rights movement of the 1950s and sixties were legal remedies enacted, and even then social and economic discrimination remained facts of American life. That movement—the most successful expansion of freedom during the past hundred years in the United States (only the labor movement and the women's movement are in the same class)—was nonviolent. It illumines in practice the kinship of democratic government and nonviolent direct action.

In certain respects, the position of blacks in the American constitutional order was like the position of the Indians of South Africa in the English imperial order. Both groups appealed to the highest constituted authority—the federal government of the United States in the first case, the imperial government in London in the second—for relief from local oppression. Both restricted themselves to nonviolence. Neither had any hope of securing its rights through the establishment of an independent nation. (Gandhi's movement in India, on the other hand, aimed at and achieved independence.) The black minority in the United States had suffered far more at the hands of the dominant white majority than that majority had ever suffered at the hands of the English in the years leading up to independence, impelling the Americans "to separation," as the Declaration of Independence says. The Muslim black nationalist Malcolm X, who believed that "there can be no revolution without bloodshed," was certainly correct when he pointed out that the founders of the United States had not hesitated to resort to violence under far milder provocation.

Yet however justified by white precedent, the plan of sep-aration and violence was impractical for the black American minority, if only because it amounted to no more than 15 percent of the population. What Gandhi came to understand in South Africa and Michnik came to understand in Poland—that violence would be self-defeating—was even more obviously true for the black minority in the United States. As Lawrence Guyot of the Student Nonviolent Coordinating Committee put it, "They'll shoot us quicker if we're armed." In these demanding, confining circumstances, an accommodation with the white majority was the only route to equal rights. If blacks could not *separate*, as the white American colonists had done in their revolution, then they must *integrate*.

The strategy of the movement was direct nonviolent action by masses of people in defiance of the Jim Crow laws of the South. The response of the white-run state and local governments and of allied white vigilante groups such as the Ku Klux Klan was ferocious repression. Movement activists asserting their legal rights were hosed, jailed, beaten, bombed, tortured, and murdered. A civil-rights protester in the South of the democratic United States in the early 1960s was almost certainly in more danger of physical violence than an activist in totalitarian Eastern Europe in the 1970s or 1980s. (On the other hand, jail terms were more common and much longer in Eastern Europe, and other basic freedoms, such as freedom of speech, were absent.)

"Unearned suffering is redemptive," said the movement's preeminent leader, Dr. Martin Luther King, Jr. Those to be redeemed by this suffering were, in the first place, the black protesters themselves. One who acts nonviolently in support of justice "lives in the kingdom NOW, and not in some distant day," King declared. And the Birmingham civil-rights leader the Reverend Fred Shuttlesworth asserted that the black preacher was "the freest man on earth." "They can't enjoin us from being free," he pointed out. Those to be redeemed were, in the second place, the white majority, who were challenged to live up to their professed ideals. By bringing the unearned suffering imposed by the system into the light of day, the civil-rights movement forced the white majority to make the choices that it had ducked for a century—either to embrace and fully institutionalize repression or to lift it. Not until public opinion had thus been changed did the national politicians act. It would be wrong, however, to deprive them of credit. On several occasions, they rose above political expediency, and took risks for what they had come to believe in. For example, on June 9, 1963, in the midst of the desegregation crisis in Birmingham, Alabama, President Kennedy decided spontaneously to appear on national television to support an omnibus civil-rights bill. Resisting dismayed advisers who pointed out that he had no carefully prepared text, Kennedy delivered what the *New York Times* called "one of the most emotional speeches yet delivered by a president who has often been criticized as too 'cool and intellectual.'" Kennedy's words "rose from the twin moorings that anchored King's oratory at the junction of religious and democratic sources," Taylor Branch, a chronicler of King and his movement, has written. "We are confronted primarily with a moral issue," Kennedy said. "It is as old as the Scriptures and is as clear as the American Constitution." And President Johnson, whose support for desegregation was stronger than Kennedy's, fought to pass the decisive Civil Rights Act of 1964 in the face of distinct warnings that the political price could be immense for the Democratic Party. "I think we just gave the South to the Republicans," he said prophetically after signing the civil-rights bill.

The civil-rights movement took its stand at the crossroads of democracy and nonviolence. Nonviolence acts upon totalitarianism from without, as a corrosive agent. Under totalitarian rule, the radical suppression of the freedom, or "truth," inhering in each person renders nonviolent action not only exceptionally costly to practice, but, once under way, exceptionally powerful. Precisely because totalitarian control is so thoroughly based on coercive power, nonviolence possesses the capacity, once it appears, to unravel an entire system with breathtaking suddenness. The influence of nonviolent action on democracy is different. Because both are based on cooperative power, nonviolent action can, if successful, strengthen democracy. Under a totalitarian system, nonviolence is revolutionary; under a democratic system it is an agent of reform. For the one it is lethal, for the other curative, as it was for the United States in the time of the civil-rights movement.

King and his colleagues understood the inner unity of democracy and nonviolence more deeply, perhaps, than any earlier leaders of a social movement. They were virtuosos in the art of summoning the American republic to live up to its declared principles. In that sense, they were American conservatives. But because the deepest principles of the American polity—that all men are created equal, that all should live in freedom—are, if taken seriously, radical, the civil-rights leaders were also radicals.

The movement's strategy was to break the law in the name of the law—to practice civil disobedience of the repressive laws of the Southern states in the name of constitutional law. In King's words in his "Letter from a Birmingham Jail," "I submit that an individual who breaks a law that conscience tells him is unjust and who willingly accepts the penalty of imprisonment in order to arouse the conscience of the community over its injustice, is in reality expressing the highest respect for law."

Nonviolence had little to do with moderation. The civil-rights protesters were fearlessly militant. "We mean to kill segregation or be killed by it," said Shuttlesworth. "You know my friends, there comes a time when people get tired of being trampled over by the iron feet of oppression," King told his audience in his first major speech in support of the famed bus boycott against segregation in Montgomery, Alabama. But when the crowd thundered its approval, he immediately went on, "Now let us say that we are not here advocating violence. We have overcome that." And, "There will be no crosses burned at any bus stops in Montgomery. There will be no white persons pulled out of their homes and taken out on some distant road and murdered. There will be nobody among us who stand up and defy the Constitution of this nation." For "If we are wrong—the Supreme Court of this nation is wrong. If we are wrong—God Almighty is wrong! . . . We are determined here in Montgomery—to work and fight until justice runs down like water, and righteousness like a mighty stream!"

King's nonviolence, of course, had foundations deeper than mere legal strategy. It was rooted in the Christian faith of the black churches of the South, which were both a point of origin and a mainstay of the movement, as were Gandhian political methods, which King and a number of other leaders of the movement, including James Lawson, James Bevel, Robert Moses, Bayard Rustin, and Diane Nash, had carefully studied. Gandhi's example was especially important for the youthful Student Nonviolent Coordinating Committee, which was the source of many of the movement's most successful specific techniques of direct action, such as sit-ins and voter-registration drives. King liked to say that Jesus gave him "the message," and Gandhi gave him "the method." King did not distinguish between a City of God and a City of Man any more than Gandhi had, and he moved back and forth between the two realms with singular dexterity. Like Gandhi, he based his political action squarely on love, the polestar of both his faith and his politics. "Standing beside love," he said at twenty-six, "is always justice."

However, the message of Gandhi—a man as little known to the black minority in the United States as to the white majority—was overshadowed by the message of faith, which offered a bond between the two races. Just as King the legal activist called on America to live up to its Constitution, King the preacher called on America to live up to its Christian and Jewish faiths. (The importance of the Old Testament, and especially of the book of Exodus, to the black community created a tie of particular warmth between the civil-rights movement and the American Jewish community.) In any case, King, a Baptist minister, found all that he needed to say about love in the Bible. When his house was bombed during the boycott in Montgomery, and an angry crowd of black supporters assembled, he counseled, "Don't get panicky. Don't get your weapons. If you have weapons, take them home. He who lives by the sword will perish by the sword. Remember that is what Jesus said. We are not advocating violence. We want to love our enemies. I want you to love your enemies. Be good to them. This is what we must live by. We must meet hate with love." Later he said, "Somebody must have sense enough and morality enough to cut off the chain of hate and the chain of evil in the universe. And you do that by love." When an officer who had just called Shuttlesworth a "monkey," then kicked him in the shin and was taking him off to jail, asked him—perhaps in disappointment—"Why don't you hit me?" Shuttlesworth replied, "Because I love you," and smiled.

DEMOCRATIC REVIVAL

The kinship of nonviolence and democracy—and of both with peace among nations—was put on more extensive display in the parade of democratic revolutions of the last quarter of the twentieth century. The threads of liberal development that had been snapped by the global descent into violence in 1914 were picked up in the century's final years. Time after time—as in England in 1689—the power of nonviolent action showed itself, and time after time it led to democratic government. Like the self-determination movement, the liberal revival included defeat of dictatorial governments of every political shape and form—right as well as left, totalitarian as well as authoritarian—and on every continent. Its centerpiece was the democratization of Eastern Europe and, we can still hope, Russia; but it began in southern Europe in the 1970s. In 1974, a junta of Greek colonels, who had overthrown the democratic government of Constantine Karamanlis in a coup in 1967, yielded power to civilians, after the military intervention in Cyprus in support of the Greek community. Next came the overthrow in Portugal of the autocratic regime of Marcello Caetano, successor to the dictator Salazar, by pro-democratic Portuguese military officers abetted by a powerful civil movement. It's a suggestive historical detail that this second in the series of liberal democratic revolutions brought the downfall of the last of the Western European colonial empires in Africa. It might appear a paradox that the feeble, backward, superannuated regime founded by Salazar was able to hold on to its empire longer than the other, more impressive colonial powers. Portugal was hardly mightier than France or England, or more adept at the imperial arts. Rather, its advantage was precisely its backwardness. Its repressive rule abroad was fully consistent with its repressive rule at home. The regime, wedded equally to both, lost both at once. It was a story not to be repeated until the Soviet empire and the Soviet state collapsed in a single cloud of dust. In both Portugal and the Soviet Union, the home population rebelled in the aftermath of colonial revolt as if its country had been just one more colony of the empire.

After Portugal came its neighbor, Spain. In 1975, following Franco's death, the regime, increasingly deserted by important elements in the Catholic Church and by the king, Juan Carlos, yielded without violence to democratic government. Although the liberal revival so far was largely a southern European affair, the fall of Franco foreshadowed the Soviet collapse in certain respects. Among many right-wing dictatorial regimes founded in Europe in the 1930s, only Spain's and Portugal's had survived into the postwar period. Spared the destruction visited by the Allies on Nazi Germany and Fascist Italy in the Second World War, they, like the Soviet Union, were permitted to live out (so to speak) their natural lives. In Spain, the Francoist Cortes, or parliament, helpfully smoothed the path to its own extinction by providing for a free election in which most of its members were defeated. It was not surprising that as the Soviet empire headed toward history's dustbin the Portuguese and Spanish events attracted the attention of Eastern European observers. All three of these violent regimes defied expectation by giving up the ghost with a minimum of violence, or even struggle. By the end of the century, all Europe was under democratic government—the culmination of a remarkable transition on the continent that had given birth to both the right-wing and left-wing versions of totalitarianism and as recently as the late 1930s had been ruled mostly by dictatorships.

Similar events unfolded in Latin America. In 1982, the draconian regime of Argentina's generals surrendered power after suffering defeat by Great Britain in the war over the Falkland Islands, and a year later a civilian president, Raul Alfonsín, came to power in an election. In 1985, a military regime was removed in neighboring Brazil. In 1989, the military dictator of Chile, Augusto Pinochet, also yielded power to an elected government (a successor government later considered prosecuting him). In the same years and in the years following, a profusion of more or less democratic governments replaced outright military dictatorships in most of the other countries of Latin America.

Meanwhile, in Asia several authoritarian governments were giving way to democracies. The dictatorship of Ferdinand Marcos in the Philippines yielded in 1986 to a vigorous, peaceful, popular resistance, led by the Catholic Church and a rebellious faction in the military. Pressure from allies, including the United States, which had previously supported Marcos, played a role. Two years later in South Korea, the autocratic Chun

Doo Hwan agreed to an election that led to his replacement by his rival Roh Tae Woo. In Taiwan, the first multiparty legislative and local elections were held in 1989, after four decades of one-party rule by the Nationalist Party that had once governed mainland China.

In the late 1990s, the autocratic regime of General Suharto fell in Indonesia; free elections were held in Nigeria in 1999; and in Iran a strong opposition challenged the autocratic rule of Islamic mullahs who had installed themselves in power in the revolution of 1978–79, against the regime of Shah Mohammad Reza Pahlavi. In 2001, seventy-one years of unbroken rule by the People's Revolutionary Party in Mexico was ended in a free election won by the presidential candidate of the National Action Party, Vicente Fox. In October of that year, the murderous regime of Slobodan Milosevic in Serbia was overthrown by a nonviolent, democratic movement. In this revolution, the affinity of nonviolence and democracy was demonstrated with particular clarity, for the movement arose in support of election results that had given victory to the democratic forces but had then been falsified by the Milosevic regime. In all previous nonviolent revolutions, the revolt had preceded the elections; in Serbia, the procedure was reversed.

Of all the peaceful transfers of power from tyranny to democracy of the late twentieth century, however, perhaps the most remarkable was the one in South Africa. There, almost every kind of major strife of the twentieth century seemed to be tangled in a single inextricable knot. The conflict was racial: a white minority ran an all-white government along democratic lines but ruled and oppressed a black and "colored" majority under the system of apartheid. (In 1958, Prime Minister Hendrik Verwoerd had announced, "Our motto is to maintain white supremacy for all time to come over our own people and our own country, by force if necessary.") It was national: most whites and more than one group of blacks considered themselves a nation. It was colonial: the whites had installed themselves in Africa in several waves of imperial invasion. It was ideological: the dominant, white government believed in capitalism, but the dominant black organization, the African National Congress (A.N.C.), was socialist, and many of its leaders were communists. As if all this were not enough, the white regime introduced nuclear arms into the picture. In the mid-seventies, South Africa became Africa's sole possessor of nuclear weapons, and this complication, too, required resolution. (Among the deadly poisons of the era, only religious hatred was largely missing.)

The leader of the African National Congress, Nelson Mandela, was not a believer in Gandhian nonviolence; in the early 1950s, in fact, he explicitly rejected it. In 1951, the A.N.C. had declared a defiance campaign that called for nonviolent disobedience of racial laws; in the face of government repression, it faltered, and the A.N.C. embarked on a reappraisal of its tactics. Gandhi's influence was strong, especially among the A.N.C.'s Indian members; the organization's black president, Albert Luthuli, a Christian, was a Gandhi admirer. "The urge and yearning for freedom springs from a sense of DIVINE DISCONTENT," Luthuli wrote, "and so, having a divine origin, can never be permanently humanly gagged." He argued for a continuation of peaceful resistance. But Mandela argued for armed insurrection, and prevailed. He then went underground to create the Umkhonto we Sizwe, Spear of the Nation. "The attacks of the wild beast," he said, quoting an African proverb, "cannot be averted with only bare hands." Later, he explained, "I saw nonviolence on the Gandhian model not as an inviolable principle but as a tactic to be used as the situation demanded."

In South Africa, however, violent rebellion somehow never developed into full-scale people's war. The government was easily able to withstand Umkhonto we Sizwe's attacks, which were few and far between. Mandela was arrested with other leaders of the A.N.C. in July of 1963, sentenced to prison for life, and sent to a jail on Robben Island. The protest of the fifties was followed by what came to be known as "the silent sixties." (South Africa appears to have been one of the few countries on earth that was quiet in that noisy decade.) "Luthuli, Mandela and [the A.N.C. leader Walter] Sisulu were perceived dimly, as if they belonged to another time, long past and long lost," the *Washington Post* writer Jim Hoagland wrote at the time.

Political protest against South Africa's apartheid system revived in the 1970s, and this time it developed, without any particular reference to Gandhi, into something resembling the mass-based civic action that would break out in Eastern Europe a few years later. It engaged mainly in local boycotts and pro-tests in support of concrete causes, such as rent abatement and better sanitation, or in protest against concrete injustices, such as the government's attempt to force all South Africans to learn the white Afrikaners' language, Afrikaans. In 1982, a few years after Havel and Michnik had first argued for resolute activism for limited social objectives, the Soweto Civic Association leader Popo Molefe was urging boycotts and other actions for local objectives that were "essential, real and vital." These, he said, would give people "the confidence that through their united mass action they can intervene and change their lives on no matter how small a scale." Only then could they "start to build progressively more political forms of organization—a process which would culminate in the development of a national democratic struggle." In 1983, this new wave of protest led to the foundation of the United Democratic Front, an umbrella group of more than five hundred civic organizations.

Meanwhile the imprisoned Mandela's influence was growing. By sheer force of courageous and restrained personal example, he established a kind of ascendancy over both his fellow pris-oners and his prison guards. He and the other prisoners held marathon political discussions, read literature (Shakespeare was their favorite), and studied for correspondence degrees. While the Polish activists were establishing a flying university, the A.N.C. prisoners on Robben Island were establishing a captive one. Here the new generation of activists of the seventies and eighties, many of whom knew little of the A.N.C., received an unexpected education from their elders. Mandela's reputation spread and grew. Seemingly powerless in jail, he was on his way to becoming the fulcrum and pivot of South African history.

Behind the myth of the great man—the A.N.C. propaganda, the hero worship—there was in fact a great man. The govern-ment, under pressure from spreading disturbances, and from a growing international movement to impose economic sanctions on the apartheid regime, began to meet with their prisoner Mandela, probably hoping to divide the movement by entering into separate agreements with him. Those hopes foundered on Mandela's unswerving commitment to full majority rule. Nevertheless, Mandela's oppressors found reassurance in the qualities of the person. Instead of finding a broken, pliable man, they encountered the giant who, in spite of them, had grown in stature in their prisons. The first to meet with Mandela, Hendrik Coetsee, the minister of justice, recorded his impressions. "It was quite incredible," he said. "He acted as if we had known one another for years, and this was the umpteenth time we had met. . . . He was like the host." Coetsee continued, "He came across as a man of Old World values. I have studied Latin and Roman culture, and I remember thinking that this is a man to whom I could apply it, an old Roman citizen with *dignitas, gravitas, honestas, simplicitas*." Most surprising was Mandela's lack of bitterness and his capacity for forgiving those who had caused him so much suffering—a capacity that not only was to be writ large in the final settlement of the conflict but perhaps was to make it possible. "Mandela had become famous above all as the man who forgave the enemies who had jailed him," his biographer Anthony Sampson writes. But he goes on to add, "It was not an obvious role for him to play."

The ability to forgive is a spiritual quality, but in Mandela it was not rooted in religion. He was a stoic, as Coetsee's comments suggest, but not an ascetic. "Gandhi took off his clothes," Mandela's friend Fatima Meer has commented. "Nelson *loves* his clothes." Regarding religion, there is no reason to doubt Mandela's assessment of himself—"I'm just a sinner who keeps on trying. I am not particularly religious or spiritual. I am just an ordinary person trying to make sense of the mysteries of life."—or to doubt the assessment of the Nigerian poet Wole Soyinka, who commented that Mandela's character was "the unselfconscious manifestation of uncluttered humanity."

The refusal of bitterness was a matter of both prudence and conviction. "When one is faced with such situations [of provocation and brutality]," Mandela has remarked, "you want to think clearly, and obviously you think more clearly if you are cool, you are steady, you are not rattled. Once you become rattled you can make serious mistakes." He also said, "Bitterness would be in conflict with the whole policy to which I dedicated my life." Of his forgiveness, he once commented, "Courageous people do not fear forgiving, for the sake of peace." Commenting on this stance, Anthony Sampson observes, rightly and factually, "Forgiveness was an aspect of power."

Few countries seemed to have less in common in the late

1980s than South Africa and the Soviet Union, yet the paths to
democracy the two of them took have a surprising resemblance,
as if the world, at certain moments, were indeed guided by
a secret Zeitgeist, just as Hegel said. In both countries, the
leader of the ruling establishment—in the Soviet Union, Gorbachev; in South Africa, President Frederik de Klerk—made an
astonishingly bold commitment to change that led, against his
expectation, to the dissolution of the regime he headed. Both
leaders, it appears, stayed faithful to *principles*, even when it
turned out that in the name of them they had to surrender
cherished *goals*—in the case of Gorbachev, it was a humanistic
communist Soviet Union, and in the case of de Klerk, who
wound up becoming vice president under President Mandela,
it was a regime of power sharing that would have preserved a
white veto over legislation. Of de Klerk after Mandela's release,
Allister Sparks, a chronicler of the A.N.C.-government negotiations, commented, "His own process of change kept pace with
events, which is what has saved him—and South Africa. And so
he remains on the scene, although in a lesser role." De Klerk's
acceptance of the outcome of the process he unleashed, even
more than the original decision to end apartheid, is, as Sparks
wrote, "the real measure of the man's reflective intelligence."

In both countries, violence on the grand scale was averted—
although in South Africa over the four years of negotiation
between the A.N.C. and the regime several thousand people
were killed, most by the government or its agents. In both, the
opposition discovered the virtues of restraint and "self-limiting
revolution." In both, "truth and reconciliation" won out over
revenge. People have often spoken of a "South African miracle."
The government negotiator Albie Sachs has protested the use
of the phrase. The settlement, he accurately claims, was "the
most predicted and consciously and rationally worked-for happening one could ever have imagined, and certainly the most
unmiraculous." But that of course was precisely the miracle.

THE WESTERN SETTLEMENT

The Washington think tank Freedom House keeps a record of
countries it considers to be democracies. In 1971, it counted
thirty; in 2001, after a quarter century of the liberal revival, it

counted one hundred and twenty-one. The question is what such a development portends for peace. Gigantic claims have been made, the most grandiose of which was probably the assertion in 1989 by the American political scientist Francis Fukuyama that the liberal democratic revival heralded the "end of history." He did not mean, naturally, that no new events were to be expected. He was only suggesting that the wide-spread adoption of liberal democracy constituted humanity's final judgment that, among all the forms of government, this one had shown itself to be the best.

A more modest and defensible claim—itself sufficiently sweeping—is that the revival constituted a grand settlement along liberal lines of what might be called the Western civil war of the twentieth century. This civil war began in 1914, with the outbreak of the First World War; paused for two decades after 1918; and resumed with the Second World War, followed of course by the Cold War. At issue was which of the three dominant models of government of the period—fascism (and its various offshoots, such as Japanese militarism and Spanish Falangism), communism, or liberal democracy—would prevail. The first stage of the settlement came when, following their defeat, Germany and Japan enthusiastically took to the dem-ocratic systems imposed on them by the victorious Allies. By making democracy their own, they robbed fascism of almost all of its glamour and appeal for the rest of the century. (What country, upon overthrowing a regime and establishing a new one, has announced that it will model itself on Hitler's Germany or Mussolini's Italy?) The second stage was the overthrow from within of the Soviet Union by the peoples over whom it had ruled, which left liberal democracy standing alone in the Western ring.

In the light of twentieth-century history, the potential im-portance of this settlement for world peace appears great, even if liberal democracy does not continue to spread, and even if it turns out that its existing spread has in many places been superficial and reversible. Since it was the Western world, after all, that thanks to its creation of the global adapt-or-die war system and imperialism, twice turned its local wars into world wars, settlement of the Western civil war at least removes the prime specific cause of the world's most violent wars of the last century. Whatever the cause of war in the future, it is unlikely to be a conflict between Germany and France. The emergence of a political consensus in the West on *any* form of government would have reduced the likelihood of intra-Western war; but a consensus on liberal democracy was especially promising. It laid the basis in Europe for the now-burgeoning European Union, which institutionalizes liberal democratic principles on the regional level.

However, if in the wake of September 11, pacification of the West turns out to set the stage for conflict with an Islamic "East," or a bid for American military hegemony over the entire world, there may be no net gain. The Western settlement also leaves open the question of its relations with the generally poorer, weaker countries of the rest of the world. Once called the Third World, these countries are now more often called the South, while the West, in another shift in quadrant of the world's political compass, has been renamed the North. By the end of the twentieth century, the South had driven back and destroyed the territorial empires that the North had forced upon them. Didn't this reversal deliver the West a blow that undercut its global preeminence? As it turned out, just the opposite has been the case. It is true that the global influence of several European nations—most notably England and France—was reduced (while that of the United States grew). But if we consider the Western world as a whole, it responded to the loss of its territorial empires as if throwing off a burden.

For one thing, territorial imperialism, even as it advanced the market system, had been a source of wars that had impeded that system's smooth spread and weakened democracy at home. (World trade, which had reached a historical high point in the first decade of the twentieth century, steeply declined in the twenties and thirties.) For another, no sooner did the South drive out its imperial oppressors than it found itself reincorporated into the Northern market system, now more pervasive and less escapable than ever. Imperialism had always been economic as well as military. Whether trade was following the flag or vice versa (and the history of imperialism offers abundant examples of both), the two had marched together almost everywhere.

The liquidation of the colonial regimes by no means meant liquidation of economic influence. On the contrary, a united

West—a North—was in certain respects more formidably powerful in the Third World than the old, divided West, whose powers were often played off against one another by the countries they ruled. Nor did those countries manage to confront this united, liberal West with any rival political or economic model that held wide appeal, even to one another, much less to the world. After the Soviet collapse, socialism lost ground almost everywhere. The most prominent new political model, the theocracy of Islamic fundamentalism, first embodied in revolutionary form in the Iranian regime of the Ayatollah Khomeini, could by its nature appeal only to Islamic countries. Even in these it proved more attractive as an inspiration for rebellion than as an actual form of government. (Today, a majority of Iranians regularly vote for moderate candidates who seek to soften the repressive rule of the mullahs.) Of course unliberal governments of all types are still to be found in the Third World, but none of them have been widely imitated. Now that "there is no alternative," as people like to say, the original elements of the West's predominance—its science, its arms, its capitalism, and to some extent its liberal democracy—have become harder than ever to reject.

Precisely because the post–Cold War market system—sometimes called "the Washington consensus," sometimes simply globalization—has become so pervasive, it exerts the sort of irresistible, impersonal, adapt-or-die pressure that the war system exerted in its heyday. The international currency speculators who pulled the rug out from under the Mexican and Argentinean pesos, the Thai baht, the Indonesian rupiah, and the Russian ruble had no interest in humiliating or weakening Mexico, Argentina, Thailand, Indonesia, or Russia; they were seeking only to fatten their bottom lines. The *New York Times* columnist Thomas Friedman has called this system "the golden straitjacket." Golden it may or may not be (Russians, Mexicans, Indonesians, Thailanders, Argentineans, and most Africans, among others, have excellent reasons for finding it less than golden); a straitjacket it certainly is. The paradox of the global market system is that while it offers a wide choice of goods to many consumers within the system, it closes off choice among systems. Countries going shopping for economic systems will find only one product on the shelf. This theoretical enemy of monopoly has itself become a global monopoly. If in the birth canals of the future, some other, better system is getting ready to be born, it is in acute danger of being aborted by the monopolistic pressure of the existing system.

Totalitarianism, in the view of some of its most penetrating analysts, was a monster created from the rib of the predominantly liberal European civilization of the nineteenth century. "If it is true," Hannah Arendt wrote in *The Origins of Totalitarianism*, "that the elements of totalitarianism can be found by retracing the history and analyzing the political implications of what we usually call the crisis of our century, then the conclusion is unavoidable that this crisis is no mere threat from the outside, no mere result of some aggressive foreign policy of either Germany or Russia, and that it will no more disappear with the death of Stalin than it disappeared with the fall of Nazi Germany. It may even be that the true predicaments of our time will assume their authentic form—though not necessarily the cruelest—only when totalitarianism has become a thing of the past."

That day has come. Imperialism, whose tradition is as long in the West as the tradition of democracy, was one of the points of origin of totalitarianism that Arendt identified. Imperialism began not with conquest but with trade, and with corporations licensed by royalty to exploit faraway lands. Economic globalization has so far widened the global gap between rich and poor. "Our British colonizers stepped onto our shores a few centuries ago disguised as traders," the Indian writer Arundhati Roy notes. "Is globalization about 'eradication of world poverty,' or is it a mutant variety of colonialism, remote-controlled and digitally operated?" she asks. On the answers the prosperous countries give to such questions will depend in considerable measure the ability of the liberal nations of the North to make a contribution to the peace of the world.

THE IMPERIAL TEMPTATION

It would be tempting to suppose that imperialism is an alien product imposed upon the liberal democratic political system by the global market system. And it is certainly true that in many places the market system distorts and threatens to overwhelm democracy, which has proved highly vulnerable to the inroads of corporate power. The record suggests, however, that republican political systems have by no means been perverted only by economic pressures. The tendency of republics to engage in imperialism existed before the modern age and the rise of capitalism. Periclean Athens, the birthplace of democracy, was both democratic and energetically imperial. The Roman republic was the only power that has ever conquered almost the whole known Western world. Holland of the seventeenth century had both quasi-republican institutions and a global empire. Not long after France became a republic, Napoleon sent its armies out to conquer Europe. England was both the "mother of parliaments" and the ruler of the most extensive empire the world had ever known. The United States is a republic that now styles itself the "world's only superpower" and increasingly claims the mantle of global hegemony.

There is something in republicanism itself, it appears, that is prone to imperialism. It is equally true, however, that imperialism has been a menace to republican government, destroying the institutions out of which it arose. The conflicts have been persistent and deep. They were described by the historian of the Peloponnesian wars Thucydides, who attributed democratic Athens' downfall to its imperial overreach, which culminated in its disastrous, unsuccessful invasion of the city of Syracuse. The Roman republic fell victim to the Roman Empire—an event symbolized forever by Julius Caesar's decision to send his imperial army across the Rubicon to intervene in the domestic affairs of Rome. The intellectual founders of modern democracy were fully conscious of the lesson. In Jean-Jacques Rousseau's words, "Whoever wants to deprive others of their freedom almost always ends by losing his own; this is true even of kings, and very much more true of peoples." According to Montesquieu, who wrote a book analyzing the downfall of the Roman republic, "If a democratical republic subdues a nation in order to govern them as subjects, it exposes its own liberty, because it entrusts too great a power to its magistrates sent into the conquered provinces." Both opponents and supporters of the European empires also reflected deeply on the contradiction. For example, in his classic *Imperialism* (1902), which had a strong influence on Lenin, J. A. Hobson wrote, "Imperialism and popular government have nothing in common: they differ in spirit, in policy, in method."

As long as colonial peoples remained politically passive, the contradiction could be ignored. But when they began to demand their freedom, a decision was forced. In the 1920s, Leonard Woolf, who had served in the British colonial service in Ceylon, described what this clash of principles led to in practice. "European civilization, with its ideas of economic competition, energy, practical efficiency, exploitation, patriotism, power, and nationalism, descended upon Asia and Africa," he wrote. "But with [nationalism] is also carried, involuntarily perhaps, another set of ideas which it had inherited from the French Revolution and the eighteenth-century forerunners of the French Revolution." These—he meant the ideas of liberty, equality, and fraternity—embodied the principles of democracy. He concluded, "The question imperialism posed was whether or not these [democratic] ideas were really universal. If not, they were discredited at home. If so, imperialism was discredited abroad.

An unusually interesting pro-imperial analyst of the problem, the Frenchman Jules Harmand, who served as the commissioner general in Tonkin (later North Vietnam) in 1884, and in 1910 published *Domination and Colonization*, came to similar conclusions. Imperial conquest, he frankly declared, was based on coercion. "The two ideas of true empire and of force, or at least of constraint," he wrote, "are correlative or complementary. According to the time, circumstance, and procedures, force can be more or less strong or weak, open or hidden, but it can never disappear. On the day when constraint is no longer required, empire will no longer exist. . . . What was taken by force," he went on, "had to be held by force"—indeed, by the "uninterrupted use of force." On the other hand, democracy at home, he well knew, was based on "political liberty" and "equality" of all. Accordingly, imperial conquest was necessarily "disturbing to the conscience of democracies."

Harmand had defined the choices that, over the long run, faced the citizenry of a republic bent on imperialism. They must either reconcile themselves to the uninterrupted use of force, in which case their republic, like that of the Romans, might be lost, or they must "stay at home." Few champions of imperialism have had the frankness to acknowledge this choice.

Most have preferred to bridge the gulf between their principles and their actions with what Hobson called "a sea of vague, shifty, well-sounding phrases, which are seldom tested by close contact with fact," while hoping vainly that some respectable and dignified middle course would present itself.

In the internal politics of dozens of liberal democratic countries, governments really do regularly succeed one another without intervention by armies or secret police; decisions *are* made by elected representatives, freedom of speech and assembly *are* realities, the news media *do* operate with some independence, and most disputes *are* settled by legal means. However, in their foreign dealings many of those same countries have backed dictatorships, supported or sponsored massacres and terrorism, and engaged in imperialism. To the extent that democratic procedure is simply corrupted or overridden by military ambition or economic interest—and no one can doubt that this frequently happens—there is no paradox. However, to the extent that the contradiction emerges from the political system itself, then the question becomes why republics so often generate imperial policies that are destructive of their own domestic institutions. The country that today faces the choice between republic and empire is the United States, of which we will have more to say later.

DEMOCRACY AND MILITARISM

The military historian Victor Hanson has recently argued, in a series of books, that the association of democracy and military aggression predates the modern age. Democratic Athens, he has shown, invented the savage set-piece battles between disciplined infantries that we have come to call conventional war. (Previously, war had been a more disorganized affair, consisting of a series of opportunistic sallies and retreats by cavalry and mounted bowmen, often with little bloodshed.) "Shock battle," as Hanson calls it, gave Western arms a superiority they have never lost. It was not only in modern times that Western armies won lopsided victories. The epochal naval battle at Salamis, at which the Persians lost some forty thousand men, mostly by drowning, and the Greeks probably only a few thousand, revealed a pattern that would often be in evidence from then on.

The decisive advantage, Hanson suggests, was freedom. Because the soldiers of a free state were also citizens and fought for their own freedom as well as that of their city, their morale was high. Because they were leagued with their fellow citizens, they fought with discipline and were ashamed to flee the battlefield. ("Infantrymen of the *polis* think it is a disgraceful thing to run away, and they choose death over safety through flight," Aristotle wrote. "On the other hand, professional soldiers, who rely from the outset on superior strength, flee as soon as they find out they are outnumbered, fearing death more than dishonor.") Because they and their fellow citizens enjoyed free speech, their military campaigns could be discussed and harshly criticized in their assemblies, and so they could learn from their mistakes. Because they could write freely, they could record their own histories. Until recent times, Hanson notes, military history was close to being "an exclusive Western monopoly." (At Omdurman, for example, there was no Sudanese equivalent of Churchill, whose recording eye and hand may have been as important an element of Britain's long-term military superiority as Kitchener's gunboats.) Because their political constitutions were strong, they were able to preserve their communal will and quickly replenish their forces. When the Greek historian Polybius sought the cause of Rome's rise to "universal dominion" in the fifty-two years between 220 B.C. and 167 B.C., he found it in Rome's constitution.

A recurring tragedy of republics has been that freedom, far from enervating the state, as authoritarians have claimed, in fact generates power, which then can be converted into force, which, as in classical tragedies, not only creates nightmares for other nations but recoils upon its possessors, extinguishing the freedom from which it arose. Arendt's precept that violence is inimical to power comes into play, and the empire destroys the republic. James Madison, who was acutely aware of the danger, put it well in a comment on the destruction of the Roman republic that seems pertinent to the United States today: "The veteran legions of Rome were an overmatch for the undisciplined valor of all other nations, and rendered her mistress of the world. Not the less true is it that the liberties of Rome proved the final victim to her military triumphs; and that the liberties of Europe, as far as they ever existed, have, with few exceptions, been the price of her military establishments." The danger, now as in other times, is that democracy's basic nonviolent principles, so promising for the peace of the world, can be undermined by the very power the system generates, bringing itself as well as its neighbors to ruin.

10

Liberal Internationalism

When Caesar crossed the Rubicon, he resolved the contradiction between empire and republic in favor of empire. Others have tried to resolve it the other way around: instead of sending soldiers across the Rubicon into the republic, they have sought, so to speak, to send jurists and citizens from the republic across the Rubicon to tame the savage international arena. The martial tendency of democracy to evolve into empire has its mirror image in the pacific dream that all the world can be turned into a republic. This has been the program of the liberal internationalists. If imperialism and war are lethal to liberalism, they have asked themselves, does not liberalism contain within it a principle that, if extended to international affairs, could be lethal to imperialism and war? For the plan of the liberal democratic state is based on a formula that seems to beg for application in the international sphere. Might not nations enter into a social contract just as individuals supposedly once did? Why should domestic governments alone be founded on nonviolent principles? Why stop at national borders? Shouldn't a system of cooperative power, the key to resolving disputes without violence, be extended to the limits of the earth? Thought glides smoothly and easily to this conclusion. The mechanism is known, its procedures proven within many national states. Liberalism, moreover, lays claim, as science and religion do, to universal principles (that "all men are created equal," that all must enjoy the "rights of man") and feels itself confined and incomplete on a merely national stage. Having asserted the dignity of man against the arrogance of aristocrats and kings, it looks in vain in its stock of principles for any good reason to confine this benefit to just *one* people. (Conservatism, by contrast, looks only to a particular place and circumstance, and proclaims not the rights of man but, with Burke, the "inherited . . . rights of Englishmen.")

Wherever liberalism has flourished domestically, it has been accompanied by visions of liberal internationalism. With few exceptions, the thinkers and statesmen of the liberal tradition have dreamed such dreams or sought to make them a reality. As early as the late seventeenth century, William of Orange was already "busy with a scheme remarkably like the ideal which the League of Nations [attempted] to achieve," in the words of his biographer G. J. Renier. William envisioned a system of collective security that would keep the France of Louis XIV in check. Disputes would be arbitrated by an impartial court, and "recusants would be brought to reason by force of arms."

In the age of revolution, scarcely any of the contract theorists failed to champion some liberal scheme for international harmony. In May 1776, Tom Paine proposed a "European Republic," to be guided by a "General Council," to which nations would submit disputes for arbitration. In *Common Sense*, published in the same year, he recommended, as everyone knows, a union of states to the American colonies—with more telling effect. In his work we find, perhaps for the first time, the belief that republics will be more peaceful abroad than monarchies. But it was in England in the nineteenth century that liberal internationalism took root most deeply. When Jeremy Bentham, the founder of utilitarianism, wrote *The Principles of International Law* (thereby introducing the word "international" into common usage), he included a "Plan for a Universal and Perpetual Peace." To the liberal English mind of the nineteenth century, civil liberties at home, enlargement of the franchise, championship of national movements for independence, like those of Greece, Italy, and the Balkan states, and support for the arbitration of international disputes belonged together, because all were expressions of the fundamental liberal faith in popular self-government under the rule of law. Indeed, a conviction that it is possible to base all policy, foreign and domestic, on the same basic principles, and therefore on a single moral standard, has been one of the enticements of liberal thought since its birth. (This conviction has also been from the beginning a butt of criticism from conservatives, who have regarded it as foolishly idealistic or utopian.)

The statesman with whose name liberal internationalism was most closely associated in the nineteenth century was the Liberal prime minister William Gladstone, who, together with his Tory rival Benjamin Disraeli, dominated British politics in the century's latter half. Gladstone's opposition to Disraeli's policies of imperial expansion and Realpolitik in European affairs had its origins in his belief in the self-determination of nations, which he associated with England's own independence and freedom. His desire for a single standard for judging all conduct was evident in his reaction to news that a British general was carrying out executions of Afghans who resisted British rule. Wasn't it "monstrous," he asked, to "place ourselves in such a position that when the Afghan discharges the first duty of a patriot—namely, to endeavor to bring his countrymen to resist the foreign invader—that is to be treated as a sin?" Each person's right—and patriotic duty—to seek self-government was also the keynote of his epic, unsuccessful campaign to pass a home-rule bill for Ireland. Laws passed in England for Ireland might, he conceded, sometimes be "good laws," but that was beside the point. For "the passing of good laws is not enough in cases where the strong permanent instincts of the people, their distinctive marks of character, the situation and history of their country, require not only that these laws should be good but that they should proceed from a congenial and native source and besides being good laws should be their own laws."

On the moral foundation of self-determination Gladstone built a strategic vision. It emerged most clearly in his response to the crisis in the Balkans in the late 1870s. The strategic problem for Britain in the area was the expansion southward of Russia, which the English regarded as a potential threat to their rule in India. (The Balkans were seen as another of the "roads to India.") At the same time, several Balkan peoples, whose populations were largely Christian, stepped up their resistance to the Ottoman imperial master. The Turks responded with massacres. Russia intervened militarily and, after initial failure, prevailed over the Turks.

Britain's traditional policy, based on keeping the Russians' Balkan road to India shut, had been support for Turkey, a policy that became morally awkward once Turkey, a Muslim power, began butchering Christians. Gladstone's archrival Disraeli nonetheless favored support for Turkey in order to defend the empire. To the intense indignation of Gladstone, he belittled accurate reports of the massacres as "coffee-house babble." "What our duty is at this critical moment," Disraeli said, "is to maintain the Empire of England."

In his election campaign of 1880, Gladstone wove all the strands of liberal internationalism into an appeal that, more than anything else, carried him into office. On the ground of conscience alone, the massacres had to be condemned: "There is not a criminal in a European jail; there is not a cannibal in the South Sea Islands whose indignation would not arise and overboil at the recital of that which has been done." His policy was also strategic. A string of independent Balkan states, Gladstone believed, would form a stronger barrier against Russian expansion than the faltering Ottoman Empire. "Give those people freedom and the benefits of freedom," he said; "that is the way to make a barrier against despotism." Giving voice in familiar terms to the bedrock faith of liberalism that the will of peoples will prevail over tyranny and force, he added, "Fortresses may be levelled to the ground; treaties may be trodden under foot—the true barrier against despotism is in the human heart and the human mind."

At the same time, he championed an extension of the principle of law to the world at large. He proposed a strengthened Concert of Europe, which would be empowered to adjudicate "disturbances, aggrandizements, and selfish schemes." In 1880, he wrote, "Certain it is, that a new law of nations is gradually taking hold of the mind, and coming to sway the practice of the world; a law which aims at permament authority . . . the general judgment of civilized mankind."

Gladstone's liberal internationalism proved easier to preach than to practice. He had excoriated Disraeli's imperialism as "dangerous, ambiguous, impracticable, and impossible." In particular, he called for an "Egypt for the Egyptians." And yet two years later he found himself, to his dismay, ordering military intervention in Egypt (which set the stage for the farce at Fashoda nearly two decades later). He would have been happy to let the Egyptians have Egypt if he had believed that Egypt was the only stake on the table; but Egypt, too, was seen as a station on Britain's road to India—a country to which even Gladstone was unwilling to apply the cherished principle of self-determination. Without dropping out of the Great Game altogether (that is, giving up India), he discovered, he could not indulge his liberalism in Egypt. Whatever its other merits, liberal internationalism made a poor adjunct to the Realpolitik of imperial strategy. Either Egypt was a hitching post on the road to India, or it was a nation, with a right to determine its own affairs. It could not be both.

Not for the first or the last time, the two expansionary tendencies of liberalism—imperialism and liberal internationalism—were in collision. Imperialism extended power by coercive means; liberal internationalism did so by cooperative means. Not for the first or last time, either, empire prevailed.

THE WILSONIAN APOGEE

The fullest expression of liberal internationalism, however, came not in Britain but in the United States, in the statesmanship of President Woodrow Wilson. The political climate of the United States was even more promising than England's for the growth of liberal internationalism. Whereas the English constitution had evolved over hundreds of years, the American constitution had been written at a single convention. Whereas England possessed a global territorial empire, in the 1910s the United States was still mainly a regional power. It was easier for Americans, lacking experience with other countries, to imagine that their constitutional miracle could be repeated on a global scale. The lines of connection between Gladstone's liberalism and Wilson's are nevertheless clear and direct. In September 1915, one year after the outbreak of the First World War, the British foreign secretary, Lord Grey, dispatched a telegram to Wilson. In words that might have been taken directly from Gladstone's speeches in 1880 regarding the Concert of Europe, he inquired, "Would the President propose that there should be a League of Nations biding themselves to side against any Power which broke a treaty . . . or which refused, in case of dispute, to adopt some other method of settlement than that of war?"

The President would. He began a process of reflection that led to his proposal for the League of Nations, which would embody the liberal international program in full. He argued for nothing less than a sudden, complete, systemic change in the international order, which would do for nations in the current anarchic international state of nature what the social contract, according to liberal theory, had done for particular peoples in the primeval state of nature. Wilson intended to revolutionize the international system—to "do away with an old order and to establish a new one," as he said in London as the war was ending. "The question upon which the whole future peace and policy of the world depends," he had declared in January of 1917, "is this: Is the present war a struggle for a just and secure peace, or only for a new balance of power? . . . There must be not a balance of power but a community of power; not organized rivalries, but an organized common peace." The next year, he called for "the destruction of every arbitrary power anywhere that can separately, secretly and of its single choice disturb the peace of the world; or, if it cannot be presently destroyed, at the least its reduction to virtual impotence. . . ." "Trustees of peace," he said not very convincingly, would shoulder this task. In short, Wilson proposed a wholesale liquidation of the war system and its replacement by a structure of cooperative power framed, like the Constitution of the United States, on liberal democratic principles.

THE ALL-OR-NOTHING CHOICE

The watchwords of Wilson's vision were democracy, freedom, self-determination, the rule of law, and peace—principles that still command assent. Yet Wilson of course failed utterly. He failed in his own country, whose Senate rejected the League of Nations, on the ground that Article 10 of its charter, requiring collective action to prevent aggression, would abrogate Congress's constitutional power to declare war. And Wilson failed in the world, which proceeded, as he had warned it would, to a second, even more destructive bout of global war. His scheme foundered upon the huge, interlocking structures of violence—imperialism, totalitarianism, and the war system itself—that were to produce the carnage of the twentieth century. His principle of self-determination would have required dismantling not only the European empires but also the United States' imperial acquisitions of the turn of the century—the Philippines, Hawaii, and Guam. "All the great wrongs of the world," he said, "have their root in the seizure of territory or the control of the political independence of other people." The second of his renowned Four Principles, announced on January 29, 1917, as a basis for settling the war, was "that people and provinces are not to be bartered about from sovereignty to sovereignty as if they were mere chattels and pawns in a game, even the great game, now forever discredited, of the balance of power." Rather, in the words of his fourth principle, "all well-defined national aspirations shall be accorded the utmost satisfaction."

America's allies, England and France, however, had no intention of relinquishing their empires. Neither, for that matter, did the United States propose to give up its new colonies. The victorious powers' chief interest was in parceling out Germany's few colonies among themselves. Western imperialism was at its zenith. The English were still rulers of an empire on which the sun never set. During the war, England, France, and Italy had been secretly and shamelessly bartering peoples from sovereignty to sovereignty. England and France, for example, had signed the secret Sykes-Picot agreement, in which they divided up large chunks of the Middle East between them without consulting either the peoples of the region or their leaders. Japan demanded and received promises of fresh colonial acquisitions in China's Shandong Peninsula in payment for its contributions to the Allied war effort—an outrage that spurred a protest movement in China that turned out to be the precursor to the rise to power of the Communist Party. Italy presented a similar bill for services in the war, in the form of a demand for the Balkan territories of Trieste and Dalmatia. Near the end of the peace conference at Versailles, after Wilson had surrendered ground to his allies on many colonial issues while publicly holding fast to his general principles, the English prime minister, David Lloyd George, remarked with a chuckle to an aide, "He has saved his precious principles, but we got our colonies."

Well might Lloyd George chuckle. Neither Wilson nor the League of Nations that he championed would put the smallest dent in the European colonial empires. The empire that *had* already collapsed in 1918 was the Austro-Hungarian one, in the heart of Europe, and it was here that the Allies could all agree to apply the newly trumpeted principle of self-determination. Unfortunately, this was a part of the world in which such a principle faced immediate, insuperable obstacles. Self-determination calls for each people, or nation, to take sovereign power over the territory in which it lives, but in the lands of the former

Austro-Hungarian Empire national populations were mixed. No matter how the boundaries might be drawn, they divided some people from their national brothers, while intermixing nationalities that did not wish to share a common state. If, in one of these territories, one people claimed national sovereignty, others necessarily were deprived of their rights.

If imperialism was a mature, well-developed structure of violence, totalitarianism, born in and of the late war, was just coming to life. The liberal ideology that had seemed so securely rooted at the turn of the century was about to suffer its worst reversal since the late eighteenth century. Since then, liberal principles had steadily gained ground. In countries with popular suffrage, the franchise was slowly widened and extended, and civil liberties were consolidated. Even in places, including Germany and Russia, in which dynasties remained in power, popular participation in government had steadily increased. The First World War gave birth to an opposite trend. Never had the damage of war to liberalism been more catastrophic. In Russia and Germany, the combination of unprecedented casualties with destruction or defeat created social conditions essential for the rise of totalitarianism. Even in the democracies, the war produced a general disillusionment and bitterness that put democratic institutions on the defensive. In a word, the blow that the war system had already landed on liberalism turned out to have been incomparably more powerful than a staggering liberalism's answering blow. Wilson was in this respect like a man who proposes the construction of additional floors of a building at exactly the moment that the floor he's standing on is collapsing under his feet.

The most intractable of the structures of violence that Wilson faced, however, was the one he had targeted directly, the war system. It was in its prime. The nation in arms, the industrialization of war, and heavy artillery, the tank, the modern battleship, the submarine, the machine gun were already in existence. The full panoply of air war, including the aircraft carrier and strategic bombing, was already under preparation.

Wilson spoke for many in his time when he identified the causes of the First World War as systemic. The origins of the war lay not so much in the ambitions of one actor or another as in the precariousness of an international system that could tip the world into catastrophe if the slightest imbalance of power appeared. In 1898, the imbalance had been at Fashoda, but war had somehow been averted. In 1914, the imbalance had been in the Balkans, and war had come. As Wilson put it, "War had lain at the very heart of every arrangement of Europe—of every arrangement of the world—that preceded the war." But now "Restive peoples . . . knew that no old policy meant anything else but force, force—always force. . . . They knew that it was intolerable."

Sometimes, a revolution can be accomplished in stages. That was not possible with Wilsonism. A fatally flawed global system required a full systemic substitute—a new "constitution for the whole world produced in eight days," as the French Prime Minister Georges Clemenceau, who opposed the plan, described it mockingly. The choice was all or nothing. In the words of the diplomat Harold Nicolson, who attended the Versailles conference as a member of the British delegation and at first was an ardent supporter of Wilson, "Instinctively, and rightly, did we feel that if Wilsonism was to form the charter of the New Europe it must be applied universally, integrally, forcefully, scientifically." If the Wilsonian palace were to be built, the edifice of the war system had to be torn down. If the war system were to survive, it could not be adulterated with Wilsonism. In the Wilsonian system, the sovereignty of nations had to be abandoned, but in the war system sovereignty was inviolable except by force. In the Wilsonian system, the safety of nations required disarmament, but under the war system safety required arms. Wilsonism called for a league of all nations in a system of cooperative security; the balance of power called for specific alliances against specific enemies. Wilsonism hearkened to considerations of equity and justice; the war system attended only to calculations of force.

The best illustration of the stark character of the choice forced upon the conferees at Versailles was the potential threat to victorious but exhausted France from prostrate Germany, whose population and industrial capacity were nevertheless still the greatest in Europe. France wanted guarantees that these strengths would not be brought to bear against it one day in another war. There were two possible solutions to the problem— Wilson's League and a continuation of the balance-of-power policy that belonged to the war system. Each precluded the other. Wilson's plan called for generous treatment of Germany and reconciliation with it. A balance of power required harsh measures—a permanent, enforced second-class status for Germany and ironclad defense guarantees for France by England and the United States. The exorbitant and unrealistic demand for reparations from an impoverished Germany in the Versailles treaty and France's occupation of the German Ruhr in 1923 were elements of such a policy. Ineffective as they were, they nonetheless created a two-tier system of nations based on force, which ruled out Wilson's solution of a concert of equal nations, including Germany, based on a shared conception of international justice. Likewise, the balance-of-power solution would have been ruined by Wilsonian measures—disarmament and conciliation with Germany were hardly compatible with Germany's enduring subjugation.

Wilson's insistence upon a systemic solution may have been hopeless, but it was not gratuitous. He had located the source of the problem at its true depth, and outlined a solution on the scale necessary to solve it. That the cure was beyond the will or capacity of the world of his day does not impeach the accuracy of the diagnosis. Wilson has often been taken to task for the naïveté of his solution, but his analysis of the problem was more realistic—and more prophetic—than that of his detractors. Unfortunately, the flaws in Wilson's system did not mean that the alternative, realist system—the system that had already brought on the First World War and the death of millions—had suddenly become a formula for peace and stability. Clemenceau spoke in Parliament of "an old system which appears to be discredited today, but to which I am not afraid of saying I am still faithful." But his faith, too, was tragically misplaced. The balance of power was never righted. The world was not rescued from another world war by its rejection of Wilsonism.

There is, as George Kennan has remarked, a naïveté of realism as well as a naïvité of idealism. Clemenceau's realist successors fell victim to it. It could, of course, be no comfort to idealists that realism was as unrealistic as their idealism. The interwar period, it appears, was one of those unfortunate times when each school is shrewd in its critique of its rival's plan but credulous regarding its own. There is such a thing as a disease that cannot be cured, and in the first half of the twentieth century the growing cancer of the war system may have been one of them.

In fairness to both the realists and the idealists of the time, however, it must be admitted that neither of their medicines was administered in a full dose. France neither received the real security guarantees that might conceivably have prevented the revival of the German threat nor was given the protection of any genuine system of collective security. What actually happened was that England and the United States offered rhetorical assurances of collective security to France while the League of Nations dissolved. In the 1930s, halfhearted realism vied with quarter-hearted idealism, and the curative effects of neither, even if they were available, were experienced.

In any case, when the participants of Versailles came to understand that Wilson's vision, of which they were already skeptical, might not be backed by the United States, they retreated with alacrity to the known and familiar. "The defensive value of armaments, strategic frontiers, alliances, and neutralization," in Harold Nicolson's words, "could be computed with approximate accuracy: the defensive value of 'virtue all round' could not be thus computed. If in fact Wilsonism could be integrally and universally applied, and if in fact Europe could rely upon America for its execution and enforcement, then indeed an alternative was offered infinitely preferable to the dangerous and provocative balances of the European system."

The puzzle was how, without writing a constitution for the world in eight days, to tackle the war system that had brought disaster. Even Nicolson was impaled on the dilemma. The political credo he offered in *Peacemaking 1919* remained a summation of the liberal internationalist faith.

> In spite of bitter disillusionment, I believe [in the principles of Wilson] today. I believed, with him, that the standard of political and international conduct should be as high, as sensitive, as the standard of personal conduct. I believed, and I still believe, that the only true patriotism is an active desire that one's own tribe or country should in every particular minister to that idea. I shared with him a hatred of violence in any form, and a loathing of despotism in any form. I conceived, as he conceived, that this hatred was common to the great mass of humanity, and that in the new

world this dumb force of popular sentiment could be rendered the controlling power in human destiny. "The new things in the world," proclaimed President Wilson on June 5, 1914, "are the things that are divorced from force. They are the moral compulsions of the human conscience."

Yet having delivered himself of this anathema against force and in favor of the human conscience, Nicolson declared in almost the next breath that force must be the linchpin of the system he had wanted Wilson to build. Asking himself how he had placed his faith in Wilson at the beginning of the conference, he answered unequivocally that it was not the originality of Wilson's ideas, for Wilson "had not . . . discovered any doctrine which had not been dreamed of, and appreciated, for many hundred years." Rather, "The one thing which rendered Wilsonism so passionately interesting at the moment was in fact that this centennial dream was suddenly backed by the overwhelming resources of the strongest Power in the world." For "Here was a man who represented the greatest physical force which had ever existed and who had pledged himself openly to the most ambitious moral theory which any statesman had ever pronounced." Therefore, he possessed "the unquestioned opportunity to enforce these ideas upon the whole world."

Here was a contradiction to contend with. Force was to be expunged from world affairs by the greatest force that had ever been known. Yet if enough force was assembled to overpower the most powerful aggressors, then the question naturally arose what else might be done with that force. The "war to end war" would have to do its job, it seemed, with as much war as it ended. Liberalism called domestically for a limitation on the force in the hands of the state, but here would be force without limit. In reality, the League of Nations never came remotely near to posing such a threat, yet the central quandary had been posed.

On the one hand, there was the likelihood that the League's powers of enforcement would not be strong enough to prevent aggression. On the other hand, there was the danger that if the League did become strong enough, it would have to become something like a world government. Yet a world government based on force would be a global Leviathan. No halfway house, no mere reformist program could resolve this quandary. And given a choice between international anarchy, no matter how bloody, and global Leviathan, how could anyone who loved liberty—that is, how could any *liberal*—choose Leviathan?

The liberal tradition, which had broken the state's reliance on the sword in domestic affairs, seemed full of promise for peace in the world, but Wilsonism was unable to deliver on it. In order to have any part of the Wilsonian program, you had to have all of it, but all of it was too much. This was the unsolved riddle that the liberal internationalist project placed before the world in 1919.

11

Sovereignty

The objections to Wilson's international liberalism had a name, in which the mountainous impediments to its enactment were summed up: national sovereignty. The conflict between Wilsonism and sovereignty was fundamental. No international organization could preserve peace in the world without a grant of immense power, but the principle of sovereignty reserved ultimate power to the national authorities. The American senators who kept the United States out of the League of Nations accordingly asserted that membership in the League would abridge America's sovereign right to decide when to go to war. Would the League or Congress, they demanded to know, make this life-and-death decision? In vain did Wilson argue that the decisions of the League's council would be merely advisory and had to be unanimous in any case, so that the United States could by itself prevent any unwanted outcome. The opposing senators countered that if the United States did not mean to keep its pledge to enforce world peace it should not make it in the first place. "Guarantees must be fulfilled," Senator Henry Cabot Lodge explained. "They are sacred promises—it has been said only morally binding. Why, that is all there is to a treaty between great nations."

The events of the twentieth century that require a rethinking of the sources of political power also require a rethinking of the nature of sovereignty. To this end, we need to return to the intellectual roots of sovereignty, in sixteenth-century Europe. Both the fact and the idea of sovereignty have undergone deep changes. In essence we will see that the idea that power is indivisible, which is at the core of the concept of sovereignty, and has been the greatest of the obstacles to liberal internationalism, turns out to belong to coercive power alone. In the 1920s, the historian E. H. Carr said, "All power is indivisible." He should have said, "All coercive power is indivisible." For cooperative power, the story of democracy shows, can be divided. And this possibility, together with the radical changes in the war system that we have already described, opens up large new possibilities for cooperative action in international politics.

THE SOVEREIGNTY OF KINGS

When the idea of sovereignty arose, it did not create a new political reality; rather, at a particular moment in history it legitimatized a preexisting conception of the state that proved to have remarkable appeal and endurance, not least because the stewards of the state found it to their liking. From the beginning, sovereignty faced in two directions—inward, toward the domestic arena, in which the monarchs of continental Europe were beginning to assert their absolute power, and outward, toward the foreign arena, where, around the time of the Treaty of Westphalia, in 1648, the war system assumed the form of the "Westphalian system" of sovereign states. Since then, sovereignty has, until recently, undergone remarkably little evolution in the foreign sphere; but in the domestic sphere of many countries it has changed a great deal.

The widely acknowledged intellectual father of the concept of sovereignty is Jean Bodin, a French political thinker of the late sixteenth century whose work provided a theoretical basis for the absolute rule of the French monarchs, then in its formative stage. He asserted with unblushing frankness that state power has only one basis: force. "In matters of state the master of brute force," he wrote, "is the master of men, of the laws, and of the entire commonwealth." And so, "An absolute sovereign is one who, under God, holds by the sword alone." In short, according to Bodin, sovereign power was a name given to what we have called coercive power. He knew well that such a thing as cooperative power, based on consent, existed, but he deliberately denied it any role in the state. If cooperation by anyone else were solicited, Bodin asserted, then sovereignty was lost, for if the sovereign "holds of another, he is not sovereign."

What logically followed was the second chief characteristic of sovereignty—that the power of the state must be "indivisible," and must therefore be held entirely in the hands of a single authority, which meant the king. Bodin deduced this aspect of sovereignty from the nature of politics and government, without appealing to any higher authority or sanction. In the words of the scholar Julian H. Franklin, he presented the indivisibility of sovereignty not as an ideal or goal but as "an analytic truth." The indivisibility of sovereignty ruled out consent because consent requires a division of power—between the ruler and those upon whose consent he relies. And so "the principal mark of absolute sovereign majesty, absolute power," is "the right to impose laws regardless of their consent." For, "If the prince can only make law with the consent of a superior he is a subject; if of an equal he shares his sovereignty; if of an inferior, whether it be a council of magnates or the people, it is not he who is sovereign."

Bodin believed his rule was valid for all forms of government, not just monarchy. The sovereign might be a king, a body of aristocrats, or even the people, but it had to be *one* of these. Bodin argued with particular vehemence against the ancient Greek and Roman concept of "mixed" government, in which power was divided among a people, an aristocracy, and a king. In a mixed system Bodin saw only a recipe for civil war. (The civil strife between aristocrats and kings in the France of his time provided a vivid example.) Conflicts between the parties, he wrote, "could only be resolved by an appeal to arms, until by this means it was decided whether final authority remained in the prince, or a ruling class, or in the people." He added a telling analogy: "Just as God, the great Sovereign, cannot make a God equal to Himself because He is infinite and by logical necessity two infinities cannot exist, so we can say that the prince, whom we have taken as the image of God, cannot make a subject equal to himself without annihilation of his power."

The logic at work was simply the logic of force. Every violent conflict must run to extremes, at which point one side wins and the other loses, creating an extreme—an absolute— inequality between the two parties. Here indeed is the root of the all-or-nothing choice imposed by the idea of sovereignty. "All": whatever command I give, the others must obey—or be killed. "Nothing": whatever command I am given, I must obey—or die. In such relationships, there can be no question of consent or of mixed, divided, or balanced powers. It's no surprise, then, that in Bodin's view "Reason and common sense alike point to the conclusion that the origin and foundation of commonwealths was in force and violence."

Having placed all power in a single pair of hands, Bodin went on to identify a single function of government as the heart of sovereignty: the legislative power. The law, he observed, does not appear out of thin air; it requires a lawgiver. But someone who makes the law obviously cannot, like others, be under that same law. Ipso facto, there must be someone who is above the law, and that someone is the sovereign. Bodin's vision of an indivisible monarchical power came to life in seventeenth-century Europe in the growth of absolute rule, based on newly founded standing armies, centralized bureaucracies, and marginalization of the other estates of the realm, including the aristocracy. The absolute monarchs of the age also asserted a new independence from religion—a position captured in the comment by the chief minister of the French state, Cardinal Richelieu: "Man's salvation occurs ultimately in the next world, but States have no being after this world. Their salvation is either in the present or nonexistent."

THE SOVEREIGNTY OF LEGISLATURES

Considering that Bodin's system rested without equivocation on force, it may seem surprising that his central concept of sovereignty would be adopted by the social-contract theorists, whose system was based on consent. Certainly, no self-respecting liberal could embrace the principle that government should rule "by the sword alone." The concept of sovereignty nevertheless survived in liberal thought. For example, Rousseau, who named the people as the new sovereign, placed them as high above the law as Bodin had placed kings, and this understanding of the matter was enshrined in the French Constitution of 1791, which declared that "Sovereignty is one, indivisible, unalienable and imprescriptible; it belongs to the Nation; no group can attribute sovereignty to itself nor can an individual arrogate it to himself." Even the English contractarians, who had defeated absolutism in 1689 and established exactly the sort of mixed, or "balanced," government Bodin had mocked, held fast to the idea of sovereignty, so obviously favorable to the centralized rule that they hated. Locke, for example, called for "one people, one body politic, under one supreme government," and Blackstone, the eminent exegete of English law of the eighteenth century, declared that "an absolute despotic power must reside somewhere." He located it in Parliament. "The power and jurisdiction of Parliament," he wrote, ". . . is so transcendent and absolute that it cannot be confined, either for causes or persons, within any bounds. . . . It hath sovereign and uncontrollable authority. It can change and create afresh even the constitution of the kingdom and of parliaments themselves. . . . True it is that what the parliament doth no authority upon earth can undo." Could Louis XIV have asked for more?

It is *not* surprising, however, that English liberal thinkers, having once decided that they needed an indivisible—even a "despotic"—sovereign in their system, identified it as Parliament, for they, in agreement with Bodin, believed that the essential power of government was the legislative. Here, too, there is unexpected continuity between the absolutists and the liberals. The French revolutionaries were of like mind. "What is a nation?" the French revolutionary constitutional theorist Emmanuel-Joseph Sieyès asked, and answered, "A body of associates living under one common law and represented by the same legislature." The foundation of the legislative power inspired even the normally reserved Locke to raptures. The legislature, he wrote, "is the soul that gives form, life, and unity to the commonwealth," for "from hence the several members have their mutual influence, sympathy, and connection, and, therefore, when the legislative is broken or dissolved dissolution and death follows."

THE SOVEREIGNTY OF PEOPLES

In the light of the agreement among absolutists and liberals that the legislative power is the core of sovereignty, we can ask with greater precision why it is that sovereignty is conceived as supreme and indivisible. The question becomes what it is about the legislative power that, in the opinion of so many thinkers of so many different persuasions, renders it impervious to division. One way to approach the question is by addressing the closely related question of minority rights. According to classical liberal doctrine, the rights of minorities are guaranteed by the protection of individual rights. The members of minority groups can, the liberal argues, fully satisfy their aspirations through the exercise of the same rights of free speech, assembly, and political participation that the majority enjoys. It would therefore in this view be a mistake to offer minorities "collective rights" in addition. Collective rights are ones that, to be realized, must be offered not to an individual but to a group—the right, for example, of an ethnic minority to choose what language will be spoken in the schools its children attend, or of the people of a particular ethnicity or religion to elect a certain proportion of Members of Parliament from their number. Collective rights, the liberal argues, are special privileges that, once granted to a group, will soon lead to a bidding war among all groups for special privileges that has no logical limit and can have no fair or just resolution. In other words, while every individual must have rights, groups must not. In fact, there is only one group that can enjoy rights collectively, and that is the sovereign people.

This solution has left many unsatisfied. One of the earliest and most lucid expositions of its weaknesses was made in 1934 by C. A. Macartney, who was secretary to the Minorities Committee of the League of Nations. In his book *National States and National Minorities*, he described and analyzed the failure of the Minorities Treaties established by the Treaty of Versailles to protect minorities in the states that, thanks to the treaty's sweeping application of the principle of self-determination, were born in Central Europe after the First World War. As he noted, no matter how small one chopped the pieces of the crumbled Hapsburg and Ottoman empires, the resulting units included unhappy national minorities. Macartney quotes Acton: "By making the State and the Nation commensurate with each other in theory, it reduces practically to a subject condition all other nationalities that may be within the boundary."

Strife arises if a minority, seeking more than individual rights, "aspires to political expression," as Macartney put it, or if the dominant nationality tries to make the state "the exclusive instrument of their own national self-expression," in which case "the rule of the majority, exercised, most often, under the title of democracy, is a true tyranny." Such tensions, moreover, had a dangerous tendency to spill across borders and trigger international war of the conventional kind, for the minority in one country "is usually nationally identical with the majority in another, which is often its neighbor." Therein lay the chief concern of the League—charged, above all, with maintaining the peace. It failed in fact either to protect the minorities *or* to prevent war. The ill-treatment of minorities continued and became an important factor in the outbreak of the Second World War.

The roots of the problem lay in the very concept of "self-determination." The "self" in question was, again, a collective self—the particular population that, distinguishing itself from the rest of mankind, announced itself as one of the world's peoples, possessing the right to form a government and so assume the "rightful station" among the peoples of the earth that had been promised so long ago in the American Declaration of Independence. It is this collective self—the nation—that international law endowed with sovereign rights. The formula could not fail to create conflict in those places, such as Central Europe between the world wars and since, in which individual selves in the same locality wished to belong to different collective selves. In our day, for example, when the Bosnian Serbs of the city of Banja Luka "determined" in the early 1990s that their city was to become part of the new collective self of the Republic of Srpska, they proceeded to "ethnically cleanse" their city of those who wished to be part of the collective self of the Bosnian state.

Such clashes are a symptom of a political dilemma of a fundamental character that bedevils sovereignty. It is a basic, structural fact of politics that humankind is divided into a multitude of peoples. The dilemma is how they should be formed. We can call it the separation question. Exactly how should the population of the earth be carved up into political units? First comes the issue of membership. Who shall belong to a given nation? Who's in? Who's out? Who decides? If a nation is to be democratic, the people must decide what their form of government shall be; yet in order to make that decision, they must first choose one another. Before there can be a constitution of the United States, there must be an American people corresponding to the "we the people" that, in the Constitution's preamble, "ordain and establish" the Constitution. What *is* a people, anyway? How can you—or they—tell when a collection of individuals is one? Is it a population that defines itself by preexisting, extrapolitical characteristics, such as race, language, or religion, and then goes on to found a state to protect those characteristics, sometimes called its "identity"? Is it simply any group that decides that it *is* a nation, no matter what the reason? Or is the nation perhaps defined by the state, so that anyone who agrees to the terms of citizenship may belong? But, in that case, what criteria should the state use to choose the population (for instance, when it comes to immigration)? For until the day comes that all humankind lives in a single body politic, every act of foundation—of self-determination—must at the same time be an act of separation, a kind of secession, or perhaps we should say "self-separation." And in this act of separation, dividing Us from the Other, often lie the seeds of murderous hatred and war. For inasmuch as the lines of separation divide one nation from another, the nature and method of this act is obviously of elemental importance for the character and tone of the relations among nations, which thereby become "inter-national" affairs.

In addition to choosing its members, a nation must decide what territory it claims. For just as each body politic lays claim to only a portion of humankind, so those people will occupy only a portion of the earth's surface. Having decided who is a Russian, the Russians must determine where Russians shall live. Where are the borders? Is Chechnya to be part of Russia? Don't the Chechnyans have the same right of self-determination that Russians have? But, if so, then why not any group, of any size or description, living anywhere in Russia?

The final basic issue to be resolved in answering the separation question is how peoples and the territory should match up with states. The preferred solution in modern times has been simple and clear: the people, the territory, and the state should be co-extensive. *One* state should possess exclusive authority over *one* people residing in *one* territory. This is the formula for national sovereignty. For self-determination is nothing but sovereignty under conditions of democracy. "National sovereignty" means that the people, through the agency of their state, justifiably reject any interference in their affairs or on their territory. What the state may do to its own people—or what the majority of its people may do to some minority among them—is solely their own business and no one else's. The solution perfectly fits—and not by accident—the demands of military planning. Only well-consolidated nations living in well-defined territories can have clear, defensible borders. The system so constituted can accept no halfway houses, no dispersed populations, no divided or joint jurisdictions. Under this formula, there cannot be two states with jurisdiction over one territory, or one territory comprising two peoples, or one people on two territories. Under the name of national sovereignty, the absolutism of kings became the absolutism of peoples.

Such was the depth of the issues that Macartney faced when he tackled the minorities question in Central Europe between the wars. The liberal leaders of the victorious powers in the First World War were "guided by their own experience," he wrote. Schooled in "the traditional idealism of Western liberal and humanitarian thought," they naturally turned for models to the efforts of their own countries to provide "full civil and political rights" to Catholics and Jews, among others. Those rights—"liberty, equality, toleration"—were all that these minorities wanted. For example, Jews in the United States requested no special legislation (not to speak of a legislature) to manage Jewish affairs. Nor did Catholics in England demand any "collective rights." Full enjoyment of the individual rights possessed by everyone was all that either group asked for.

It was quite different with minorities in Eastern Europe, who (then and since) found themselves suddenly cut off from a majority of their group in a neighboring country and oppressed by an alien majority in the land and state to which they were assigned. They were not, could not be, satisfied with individual rights. They wanted, at the very least, some collective rights. But collective rights are, in fact, powers—the powers of a group to make decisions about itself. More precisely, they are legislative powers, for a legislative power is nothing but a decision taken by a group and binding upon all its members. A division of legislative powers, however, was exactly the thing that the entire European tradition of national sovereignty, including its liberal branch, ruled out as an abridgment of sovereignty. Liberal theory of the day left the minorities of Central Europe without recourse. They had to either accept repression or seek indivisible legislative rights of their own, which meant that they had to found a nation of their own, through partition, with all its customary bloodshed and horror.

Were these minorities greedy and overambitious? Shouldn't they have contented themselves with individual rights, themselves hard to come by in Central Europe in the 1930s? Weren't "universal" rights enough for them? The problem was that the things they wanted could not be obtained by an exercise of such rights. The right to get an education in a certain language cannot be secured by an individual; a legislature must decide it by majority vote, if the state in question is a democracy. The dilemma of the minorities was that in the states in which they found themselves they could never realistically hope to become a majority, and so could always be outvoted.

The liberals who argued that the minorities of Central Europe should be content with individual rights were in a false position. They had never been prevented from using their own languages or practicing their own customs. For they, *without quite being aware of it*, enjoyed full collective rights—that is to say, full legislative powers. They participated in nation-states in which they were either in the majority or could reasonably expect one day to be in the majority. For what is the democratic state itself but the full—indeed, the *sovereign*—expression of collective rights, in the form of national legislative rights? In other words, they were in full possession of immense powers a mere fraction of which the Central European minorities aspired to enjoy.

The bad faith of the liberal citizen who unconsciously enjoys full sovereign legislative powers but thinks that minorities are seeking special favors when they demand a fragment of these privileges leads into the heart of the whole complex of elemental issues raised by the idea of the indivisibility of sovereign legislative power. For to join a body politic is not merely to acquire rights but to join a body of co-legislators. The right of self-determination begins with the right to decide who those co-legislators, those co-sovereigns, will be. Liberal doctrine specifies that "the people" are to choose their form of government and their governors, but is silent on the matter of who is to choose the choosers, and by what procedure they are to do it. In territories of mixed populations seeking self-determination, people have generally found brutal answers: repression, expulsion, ethnic cleansing, genocide.

Stated theoretically, the idea of collective rights may at first sound either recondite or abstract. In practice, it is neither. It was to get these rights that former Yugoslavs drove each other out of their homes, locked each other up in concentration camps, and cut each other's throats. It was to get these rights, too, that the American colonies, the Irish, and the Indians, among others, battled for independence from the English.

In the nineteenth century, Ireland was represented in the English Parliament (as Northern Ireland still is). In that respect, the Irish enjoyed the rights of the citizens of a democracy. But it was not enough. They wanted also to enjoy the right of choosing their fellow nationals, their co-sovereigns. Americans had the same desire in 1776. They opposed, as every American schoolchild once knew, "taxation without representation." But that slogan did not in fact go to the heart of the matter. In the debates leading up to the Declaration of Independence, the question arose of whether, if the colonies were given due representation in the British Parliament, they might accept the taxation and stay within the British Empire. The answer was no. The Virginia Resolves, authored by Patrick Henry, after stating the principle that "no taxes be imposed" on the people "but with their own consent," added, "the people of these colonies are not, and from their local circumstances cannot be, represented in the House of Commons in Great Britain." To the famous slogan we should therefore add a second one: "And no taxation *with* representation, either"—at least, not if the representation was in England. For it was not merely the issue of representation that was decisive; it was the composition of the population that would send the representatives to the legislature. The critical phrase in Henry's Resolve was the unassuming "from their local circumstances." In that phrase was quietly contained the demand not just for universal "rights and liberties" but for a *nation*—a new body of citizens, on a new territory, assuming the full legislative power themselves. To be ruled by a foreign tyrant was one evil. But to be ruled by a foreign representative government—even *with* representation of one's own—was, in the colonists' opinion, another evil. They rejected both. They wanted "collective rights." They wanted full legislative power. They wanted self-determination. They wanted sovereignty.

As it happened, after independence an instance soon arose—trivial in itself but important for what it revealed—of a claim of a right to separate that the Americans chose *not* to honor. Certain towns in western Connecticut and Massachusetts took the position that each town, regardless of its size, should have one representative in its state legislature. In these towns, which were in a state of virtual insurrection in the years just before and after independence, "it was as if all the imaginings of political philosophers for centuries were being lived out in a matter of years," as the historian Gordon Wood has written. The objective was modest, but the reasoning behind it radical. "Every town government," one William Gordon wrote at the time, "is an entire body politic"—in effect, a nation. Weren't the towns "in the same situation with reference to the state that America is to Britain?" he wanted to know.

Some towns in New Hampshire made similar claims, in language that spelled out the underlying issues with exceptional clarity. The Declaration of Independence, they said, had "nullified all governmental authority." Therefore, their town incorporations were "miniature constitutions that made every one of the towns 'a state by itself,' able to justify binding its minority by the majority." But these claims, too, were rejected. What was a nation? Which bodies of people have the right to separate themselves from all others and lay claim to the sovereign power? No one could say. But somehow almost everyone knew that the United States of America might become a nation while the towns of western Connecticut, Massachusetts, and New Hampshire definitely could not.

National sovereignty can mean many things—the right to speak in one's own tongue, to worship one's own God, to decide to wage war, to be ruled by a native tyrant rather than a foreign one, to invade and occupy a neighbor, to participate in politics as an equal with one's fellow citizens. But in the framework of liberal thought the New Hampshire towns were right: sovereignty was the power to select, and separate from humanity at large, a population among whom a majority binds any minority, thereby exercising the legislative power.

Once we have clearly grasped that this is what sovereignty

meant in a democratic context, we can better understand why the doctrine of sovereignty, which seems to trail so much illiberal, absolutist baggage in its wake, was nevertheless so firmly embraced by liberals in the eighteenth century. For in liberal no less than in absolutist doctrine, sovereignty is the foundation of the legislative power that performs the first and greatest of all political miracles. It lifts unprotected, aggressive, perpetually warring human beings out of the anarchic state of nature and places them under the shelter and protection of the civil state, which is meant, above all else, to provide peace. The virtue of the legislature is that it is the source of law, and the virtue of law is that *all* must obey it, submitting their disputes to its dictates, and so quelling the war of all against all that might otherwise break out. In Locke's words, the "union of the society consisting in having *one will*, the legislative, when once established by the majority, has the declaring and, as it were, keeping of that will." (Emphasis added.) This much Locke and Bodin had in common. If the legislative power is what we essentially mean by sovereignty, then to tamper with sovereignty would be to abort this miracle: to endanger the civil state, destroy the protection it affords the citizen, and consign society to anarchy—a prospect that horrifies the liberal as much as it does the conservative.

To divide the contract was to destroy the contract. To have two judges on earth, Bodin and Locke agreed, was to have no judge. Two judges meant war. One judge—and one alone—meant peace.

The reason neither the minorities of Eastern Europe nor the New Hampshire townships could be permitted to form a body politic within the nation, the reason nations have not been able to find a way to live peacefully together on a single territory in the Balkans, the Middle East, or elsewhere, and the reason neither the League of Nations nor the United Nations could form a supranational body politic was, at least as far as theory goes, the same: sovereignty could not be divided without courting disaster.

SOVEREIGNTY AND CONSENT

One of the first events to open a breach in this remarkably broad embrace of sovereignty was the foundation of the United States of America. During the revolution, however, the American revolutionary leaders joined the consensus. For example, John Adams stated, in words that could have been penned by Bodin, that England and America were debating "the greatest question ever yet agitated," namely the question of sovereignty, which in his opinion dictated that in "all civil states it is necessary there should somewhere be lodged a supreme power over the whole." In the words of Gordon Wood, on whose account of the sovereignty question in the revolution and in the constitutional settlement I draw here, "The doctrine of sovereignty almost by itself compelled the imperial debate to be conducted in the most theoretical terms of political science." Blackstone's conception of the absolute sovereign power of the English Parliament obviously precluded any sharing of the legislative power with an American legislature or American legislatures. And when, in the course of the debate that led to independence, some suggested that America, while forming its own legislative bodies, could still remain in the empire through loyalty to the crown, thus creating a sort of dual, or joint, legislative sovereignty, it turned out that most Americans agreed with their English antagonists that sovereignty was indivisible, and the idea was rejected. All that was left was the all-or-nothing choice between full imperial rule and full independence, which the idea of sovereignty always imposes on international relations. As the republican John Adams wrote, in words that again echoed the absolutist Bodin, two legislatures could not coexist in one body politic "any more than two supreme beings in one universe."

The Latin phrase that referred to the supposed impossibility of dual sovereignty was "*imperium in imperio*"—or "sovereignty within sovereignty"—which was described by Adams as "the height of political absurdity." Benjamin Franklin—who had once sought colonial representation in Parliament—had now drawn the inevitable conclusion when he said that "no middle doctrine can well be maintained" between the proposition "that Parliament has a right to make *all laws* for us, or that it has a power to make *none* for us." (His "no middle" position crystallized in microcosm the dilemma faced by Wilson more than a hundred years later when he faced the decision between the war system and his new constitution for the whole world.) At the beginning of the debate, Americans claimed, with perfect sincerity, that all they demanded was their full "rights as Englishmen." But because those rights included exercise of sovereign legislative power, it turned out that they could enjoy the full rights of Englishmen only by becoming Americans.

One of the few significant voices to dissent from this grand transatlantic consensus among otherwise irreconcilable antagonists was Edmund Burke, champion of reconciliation with the colonies. Just as Burke, lover of the gradual and the organic, would later condemn the doctrine of the rights of man for its abstractness, so now he opposed the abstract character of the doctrine of sovereignty, which in the hands of the English ministers compelled England to make war on the colonies. In 1774, he advised England to keep its mind on concrete colonial issues, and "leave the rest to schools." Assertion of indivisible British sovereignty might provoke the rebellion in the United States that it was meant to suppress. "If, intemperately, unwisely, fatally, you sophisticate and poison the very source of government by urging subtle deductions and consequences odious to those you govern, from the unlimited and illimitable nature of supreme sovereignty," he warned, "you will teach them by these means to call that sovereignty in question." Many observers on both sides of the Atlantic opposed the war between England and America, but Burke was the only important voice, as far as I'm aware, to so much as whisper a word of criticism of the underlying doctrine of sovereignty that forced the two lands toward their irreparable division. Rarely asked—then as now—is whether there could have been another, more flexible conception of state power that would have permitted the American states to govern their own local affairs while remaining conjoined in a voluntary, multinational union.

It was not until the late 1780s, when the Americans turned from their act of separation to their act of consolidation, the framing of the Constitution, that the logic of sovereignty came under serious challenge. The old Latin axioms that had made separation from England seem necessary seemed to make the union of the states impossible. Invocation by the Constitution's opponents of the indivisibility of rule drove the Federalists into genuine political terra incognita. They were now proposing two distinct challenges to the traditional understanding of sovereignty. One was federalism, which divided power between the states and a federal government, and the other was the doctrine of the separation of the federal government's own powers. How, Federalist supporters of the Constitution had to ask themselves, could "sovereign" states combine to form a federal government if sovereignty could not be divided? Wasn't it logically necessary for the national legislature, for example, to make *all* laws or to make *none*? The Anti-Federalists certainly thought so, and did not fail to confront the Federalists with all the familiar arguments. For example, Samuel Adams, an Anti-Federalist, called the Constitution a plan for the absurd "*Imperia in Imperio,* justly deemed a solecism in politics."

James Madison now found his way to the middle ground that theory had so long forbidden as "absurd." He asserted, with uncharacteristic vagueness, that under the Constitution the government would be "not completely consolidated, nor . . . entirely federal." It would be "of a mixed nature," being made up of "many co-equal sovereignties." Alexander Hamilton called a federation "an assemblage of societies." Was there a "sovereign" in the United States? The Constitution remains silent on the point. The word nowhere appears in the document. Strangely, it was not the militant movement for independence of the 1770s but the supposedly "conservative" movement to found the national government in the 1780s that carried the United States into these chartless waters. The Declaration of Independence is the United States' most fiery document but the Constitution is its most radical.

THE DISSOLUTION OF DOMESTIC SOVEREIGNTY

The American formulation marked the beginning of a new chapter in the saga of sovereignty. Sovereignty had proved a pilgrim. Invented for the use of kings, it migrated, in the hands of the English Whigs, to Parliament. Then, in American and French keeping, it descended to the people. In France, at first, sovereignty—*une et indivisible*—remained undividable. In the United States, events took a different turn. Just how, in "the crisis years" between the Declaration of Independence and the ratification of the Constitution, popular sovereignty came to be defined is a marvelous tale of action and thought told in

Gordon Wood's *The Creation of the American Republic*. The important point for our purposes is that the Federalists clinched the argument in favor of their cause when they asserted that sovereignty in a republic resided not in the states or in the federal government—or, for that matter, in any governmental body—but in the people, who were therefore entirely free to add to existing political structures (such as the states) and other structures (such as the federal government) that they might desire. If sovereignty belonged to neither the federal government nor the states, then neither had to possess indivisible power, and a middle ground could be found between them. The institutional innovation that permitted this solution was the state constitutional convention, which, bypassing the state governments, enabled the citizens of each state to ratify or reject the federal constitution directly, in an unmediated exercise of their sovereign power. The constitutional conventions in each state did not so much override the state governments as simply circumvent them through a fresh, direct recourse to the power of the people.

Sovereignty was not like some precious heirloom that could pass unchanged from one pair of hands to another. It was transformed as it made its way from its royal pinnacle to the people. As it descended, it fragmented. The English had resorted to the ungainly phrase "King-in-Parliament" in order to go on imagining that their system, described by themselves as "mixed," nevertheless contained a single, indivisible sovereign. By the time sovereignty was in the people's hands, it had in fact lost its indivisibility. If Bodin had proved that sovereign power—which for him was the same as coercive power—was indivisible, the American Federalists, founders of a national government based on consent, proved that cooperative power was divisible. Far from endowing any single authority with the power to make all decisions, the framers of the Constitution required the concurrence of many authorities in order to make almost any decision. They created a veritable maze through which power had to travel in order to achieve its appointed ends.

But perhaps, someone might argue, the power of the new sovereign, the people, was in fact indivisible. If that were so, however, it was hard to explain why, as Madison commented in *The Federalist Papers*, the "true distinction" of the American

Constitution, "lies in the total exclusion of the people in their collective capacity from any share" in the government. It was a fact that the people, using their powers to amend the Constitution, could, both legally and peacefully, pull down the whole edifice, including their own amending power, and in that sense were supreme. Yet it was no less true that in the ordinary business of government the people were barred from directly making almost any decision. (The exceptions are referenda in certain states.) They could dynamite the whole building but were powerless to so much as change the curtains in any of the rooms. For instance, if the public dislikes a Supreme Court decision, it can try to elect three or four presidents in a row who might appoint a majority of justices who might reverse the decision (as the opponents of abortion have tried to do in recent years), or else the people can convene a constitutional convention and change the document to undo the court's work. But short of these cumbersome or drastic recourses, the people are powerless.

The American Constitution deliberately shuns the establishment of any single, indivisible organ of power. The whole document, one might say, is a device for heading off such a development. Liberal thinkers adopted the doctrine of sovereignty from their absolutist forebears because it embodied what was *the* central requirement of the liberal civil state—namely, procedures for the peaceful arbitration of the disputes that are endemic in human existence. It's evident that the American Constitution provides such procedures. Laws *are* passed; they *are* obeyed; disputes among citizens *are* settled and do *not* lead to the war of all against all. Yet all this happens without concentration of indivisible power anywhere in the system.

Should the word "sovereignty," then, still be applied to name anything in the American system, or were the drafters of the Constitution right to shun the term? Wasn't the doctrine of the indivisibility of sovereignty disproven by the American experience? Hadn't the time come to search for new words? I suggest that the change has been so profound that the word should be dropped. In the United States, sovereignty—if we accept the definition of the word employed for hundreds of years—did not merely change its location or character but disappeared.

This is a linguistic point. The substantive point is that

the claim that the power of the well-ordered state must be indivisible was a deeply entrenched theoretical mistake. The division of sovereignty, in the United States and other liberal democracies all over the world, does not belong merely to the rather large class of events that mainstream theory failed to predict; it belongs to the more select class that mainstream theory had ruled out as impossible but that then happened. The nonviolent collapse of the Soviet Union also belongs to this class. In both cases, an overestimation of the role of force in politics was involved. In fairness to the theorists, though, it has to be admitted that the successful division of state power was a possibility that not even the statesmen accomplishing the feat believed possible. They were almost as surprised by what they had wrought as anyone else.

THE PERSISTENCE OF INTERNATIONAL SOVEREIGNTY

The eclipse of sovereign, coercive power and the rise in our time of divided, cooperative power in the domestic affairs of dozens of governments suggest that a similar eclipse in the international sphere is possible. Isn't it conceivable that states no longer insisting on indivisible, centralized power at home could sooner or later stop insisting on it in their relationships abroad? In that case, might not the international sphere experience growth of the same variety of mixed and federalistic forms of power that the domestic sphere has witnessed in so many countries?

If sovereignty in international affairs were a mere concept, its decline would be a merely intellectual event. In reality it has been much more than that. Above all, it has been an intellectual and juridical crystallization of conduct imposed upon states by the tyranny of the war system. Its first principle—that power was based on force—was the first rule of life under the war system. Its second principle—that power was indivisible—was simply an obvious corollary. As long as the war system remained intact, the new forms of divided power were condemned to remain bottled up within national borders. There was no room in this framework, as Wilson was forced to recognize, for interesting federalistic experiments, or Madisonian "mixed sovereignty." There was room only for the wholesale, go-for-broke replacement of the war system with something like the League of Nations. But in actual practice, of course, it turned out that there was no room for this, either.

The war system, however, has now been revolutionized by the metamorphosis we have chronicled. The age of total wars and world-spanning territorial empires has ended. The implacable pressures of the adapt-or-die system that undid the league and have disabled the U.N. have been lifted. The question arises whether in this new world the new forms of power at home may not be extended to the world at large. There are already promising signs that they might be. The place where the most interesting experiments in divided power are occurring is not, however, the United States but the birthplace of modern sovereignty, Europe, where a quiet but powerful incremental movement is afoot to join the formerly warring lands of that continent into a body politic whose outlines are as unclear as they are unprecedented. But before turning to this matter, we need to discuss the fresh perils, which may prove no less implacable than the old, that have accompanied the new opportunities of our day.

PART FOUR

THE SHAPES OF THINGS TO COME

12

Niagara

Black and hideous to me is the tragedy that gathers, and I'm sick beyond cure to have lived on to see it. You and I . . . should have been spared this wreck of our belief that through the long years we had seen civilization grow and the worst become impossible. The tide that bore us along was then all the while moving to *this* as its grand Niagara—yet what a blessing we didn't know it. It seems to me to *undo* everything, everything that was ours, in the most horrible retroactive way—but I avert my face from the monstrous scene!—

HENRY JAMES, LETTER TO RHODA BROUGHTON,
AUGUST 10, 1914

In these pages so far I have sought to trace, alongside the awful history of modern violence, a less-noticed, parallel history of nonviolent power. The chronicle has been a hopeful one of violence disrupted or in retreat—of great-power war immobilized by the nuclear stalemate, of brutal empires defeated by local peoples fighting for their self-determination, of revolutions succeeding without violence, of democracy supplanting authoritarian or totalitarian repression, of national sovereignty yielding to systems of mixed and balanced powers. These developments, I shall argue, have provided the world with the strongest new foundations for the creation of a durable peace that have ever existed. But first we must turn to the more familiar task of assessing the new violent dangers of our time—most of them present before September 11—that have the potential to make the twenty-first century even bloodier than the twentieth. Many of them are in fact connected with the new opportunities. Even as the self-determination movement was toppling the world's territorial empires, it was fueling a multitude of wars, some of them genocidal, among the successor states and peoples. Even as the Western liberal settlement ended the inter-Western wars that had disrupted the peace of the world for so long, the most prosperous nations were confronting the poorer ones with a new concentration of economic and military power that threatened to create a new line of conflict along a North-South axis. Even as liberal democracy was spreading, the most powerful of the liberal democracies, the United States, was, like ancient Rome, in danger of transforming itself from a republic into a fearsome empire. And, to say what is obvious but too often overlooked, even as nuclear terror paralyzed the old danger of total war, it created a new danger of annihilation—a danger, moreover, that was evolving, for in the post–Cold War period nuclear technology and other technology of mass destruction were rapidly spreading.

WARS OF SELF-DETERMINATION

In the post–Cold War period, the world boiled, as it always has, with local and regional wars, but in at least one respect their general character was different from those of the recent past. They were occurring almost entirely within nations rather than between them. In 2001, according to the Stockholm International Peace Research Institute, twenty-four wars were in progress, of which twenty-one were mainly within nations. Taken by itself, the decline of classic, conventional wars among full-fledged nation-states marks a profound, welcome change. Its causes include the dampening influence of nuclear arsenals; the collapse of the territorial empires, which historically have been a prolific cause of wars; and the absence of any worldwide ideological struggle among states in the post–Cold War world. (The American war on terrorism is so far the nearest thing to a new ideological cause.)

Some of the wars within national borders are turf battles among local warlords, some are civil wars, some are class wars, some are religious wars, some are ethnic wars, and most are a combination of several of the above. One category, however, stands out as prevalent. It is what we can call war of self-determination, in which the issue is the definition, ethnic composition, or birth of a nation. There are several kinds. One is the war of foundation. Historical examples include the three wars that the Prussian Chancellor Otto von Bismarck waged in the 1860s and seventies in order to found the German Reich and the wars waged by Slovenia, Croatia, Bosnia, and Kosovo in the 1990s to extricate themselves from the Yugoslavian federation and establish their independence. The war between Israel and the Palestinians has been a double war of national foundation: first, Zionists fought to found the state of Israel in Palestine; now Palestinians fight to found a Palestinian state in the lands conquered by Israel in 1967. Both parties are, in their own opinion, fighting for their national existence. Another kind is the war of secession—such as the American Civil War or the war of partition that accompanied the withdrawal of Pakistan from India in 1947—in which one part of a nation breaks away from the whole, either to join another or to establish its independence. Still another kind is the territorial war, in which two countries each lay claim to one piece of land that lies between them, as India and Pakistan do with respect to Kashmir. (In Kashmir, there is also an independence movement, adding a third dimension of self-determination to the conflict.)

Because the formula for self-determination—the exact congruity of people, state, and territory—is, in our democratic age, also the formula for national sovereignty, it would be equally appropriate to call wars of self-determination wars of national sovereignty.

The global self-determination movement, which has contributed so much to peace by ridding the world of its colonial empires, has in the postimperial world become a disturber of the peace. Expelling the imperial master turned out to be only the first step in self-determination. The liberated peoples then had to carve up the imperial territories among themselves. In short, imperial withdrawal confronted them with the separation question. In the eighteenth century, when the democratic revolutions occurred in the United States and Europe, many of the peoples involved had the good fortune already to belong to fairly well-defined national populations living within well-defined national borders. The revolutionaries who took to the streets in Paris in 1789 did not have to ask who qualified as a French person or what territory should be their homeland. Those questions had been largely answered by several centuries of dynastic war. The extent of the United Kingdom likewise was quite clear by the middle of the eighteenth century. (The remaining contested zone was Ireland.)

It was different in the lands evacuated in our time by the

European empires, where, as in the Balkans, national populations were often mixed in one territory or dispersed among many territories. Most, as Macartney observed, were unable to find any means but warfare to create nation-states according to the approved formula for self-determination and sovereignty. *People's* wars (wars of the people against imperial overlords), you might say, gave way to *peoples'* wars (wars among newly liberated peoples). The latter have been as sanguinary as the former and certainly less tractable. In people's war against an imperial power, a clean resolution is at least possible. The occupier, once he has decided to leave, can pull up stakes almost overnight. A local people can hardly do the same. People's war ends when the conquerors have had enough and go home. Peoples' wars tend to go on indefinitely, because everyone already is at home.

The end of the British Empire alone touched off a multitude of wars of self-determination. The fall of the Raj led directly to the violent partition of Pakistan and India and set the stage for the three succeeding wars between the two countries. Britain's incomplete withdrawal from Ireland in 1922, which left six mainly Protestant northern counties under British control, created the conditions for the Catholic-Protestant violence that erupted in the late 1960s. Britain's surrender of its mandate over Palestine in 1948 left a political vacuum that was soon filled by Arab-Israeli strife. The British withdrawal from Cyprus prepared the ground, in time, for conflict between its Greek and Turkish communities (backed respectively by Greece and Turkey) and finally the enforced partition of the island. The fall of the Soviet empire also touched off several territorial wars—between Georgia and Abkhazia, between Armenia and Azerbaijan, and between Russia and Chechnya. The disintegration of Yugoslavia led to the multiple, interlocking wars of the 1990s on that territory. The Treaty of Sèvres of 1920, marking the end of the Ottoman Empire, promised the Kurdish people a state of their own but in actuality left them partitioned among and repressed by Iraq, Turkey, Iran, and Syria. Many of the wars now afflicting Africa also have postimperial aspects. Borders established by the imperial powers in the nineteenth century often reflected the outcome of inter-imperial jockeying more than local realities. The imperialists divided tribes by means of "national" boundaries, forced peoples hostile to each other together, and often ran roughshod over distinctions of language, religion, and culture. Often, the movements that won independence had little in common but their hatred for the imperial overlords, and began to fall apart soon after taking power, or even before. Sometimes, the imperial rulers deliberately set one tribe or ethnic group against another, dividing to conquer, and then left the locals to fight it out after they had withdrawn. For example, the Belgian rulers of Rwanda and Burundi fostered divisions between the Hutu and Tutsi tribes that led to the genocidal campaign waged by the Hutu against the Tutsi in Rwanda in 1994.

The anarchy that has often broken out in lands of what some have called "failed states," such as Somalia and Sierra Leone, may be regarded as misbegotten wars of national foundation. In those places of Hobbesian nightmare, no group—be it tribe, clan, religious sect, or political party—generates enough power, whether cooperative or coercive, to found a state, and the country is carved up by chieftains and warlords or simply preyed upon by armed bands or mafias with no clear political loyalties. The people may have had too little in common or too feeble a political will to found a nation. Not abuse of power but default of power is the problem. Whatever may be wrong with the nation-state per se, these cases remind us, its existence is nothing to be taken for granted. Where it does exist, it is an achievement, not a gift.

Inasmuch as the age of the territorial empires has ended, it is possible that the supply of wars of self-determination that often follow in their wake is slowly running out—that these are not the first stage of a new wave of anarchy about to engulf the world, as some have suggested, but rather the last stage of a long wave that will gradually recede. This hope, however, is small comfort for the near future, since wars of self-determination are among the most durable conflicts on record. For example, the conflicts between India and Pakistan and between Israel and the Palestinians, both of which broke out in earnest in the late 1940s, are still continuing a half-century later. And the conflict created by English colonization and domination of Ireland, which may finally be ending, has lasted for almost four hundred years—some would say longer. Shortly after the

First World War, Winston Churchill marveled at its durability. "The integrity of their quarrel is one of the few institutions," he quipped, "that has been unaltered in the cataclysm that has swept the world."

Nations that have solved the separation problem by accomplishing the approved triple overlap of nation, state, and territory have been called "achieved" nations, while those that have fallen short in one way or another have been labeled "unachieved." When we witness the catastrophes that the wars of self-determination have brought to mixed populations, we can well appreciate the value of an achieved nation, such as France or England. Yet this solution to the separation problem has also come with a high price attached. For the homogeneity of peoples that has brought peace *within* state borders has encouraged jingoistic passions that support war *across* state borders. The mutual hatreds removed from the domestic sphere have again and again assumed the familiar form of chauvinistic resentment and hatred of another country, fueling straightforward, old-fashioned conventional war. This is what happened, for example, in South Asia, which has the unfortunate distinction of having run almost the entire gamut of possible forms of violence. Under the Raj, Hindus and Muslims frequently engaged in "communal" violence in their villages; then came "ethnic cleansing" during partition; then the series of conventional wars between the nation-states of Pakistan and India; and now the nuclear buildup and the nuclear confrontation.

It would in truth be hard to decide which was worse in the twentieth century—the killing at close quarters in the post-imperial wars within unachieved nations or the wars fought across national borders by the achieved nations. Either way, the formula that required identity of state, people, and territory has brought catastrophe. The achieved nations of Germany and France, for instance, fell on one another with the utmost savagery in the world wars, bringing to bear all the concentrated violence that technical progress had put in their hands. The riddle is how to avoid both sorts of war, for both are forms of a single dilemma: How can the nation determine its collective self without cultivating murderous hostility toward others? This problem is the unsquared circle of international politics, and, though the frequency of interstate wars has now waned, the internecine variety are rife as the twenty-first century begins.

THE SECOND NUCLEAR AGE AND
THE LAST MAN

The seeds of wars of self-determination are local or regional. The same is true of most revolutions, coups, and ethnic and religious strife, most terrorism and the quarrels of mafias and warlords out for power or lucre. These conflicts need no global war system to keep them going. Their persistent, smoldering flames burn in or under home soil, like peat fires, and can survive the rise and fall of international systems.

Nuclear arsenals, by contrast, are by nature global in their influence and, since the bomb's advent, have continuously been a prime factor shaping the structure of the international political and military systems of the era. It was of course the bomb's arrival that disabled the global war system at its upper levels and replaced it for the duration of the Cold War with the new system of nuclear deterrence. That system, we can see in retrospect, was a strategic adjustment to two dominant historical realities, one political, the other technical. The political reality was the division of the world into two ideologically hostile camps. The technical reality was the restriction of the newborn capacity to build nuclear weapons to just a few nations. (The eventual legal expression of this nuclear oligopoly was the Nuclear Nonproliferation Treaty, which created two classes of powers. One consisted of the five nuclear-weapon states—the United States, the Soviet Union, China, England, and France—who were permitted to retain their nuclear arsenals, on condition that they made good-faith efforts to reduce and then eliminate them, and the other consisted of all the other signatories, who agreed to forgo nuclear arsenals.)

Now both of these realities have been washed away. The world's bipolarity ended with the collapse of the Soviet Union, and the nuclear oligopoly has been steadily yielding to nuclear proliferation. In the late 1980s, Iraq came within perhaps a year of attaining nuclear weapons, but in the aftermath of its defeat in the Gulf War was required to dismantle its bomb-making facilities under the supervision of U.N. inspectors. In 1998, the inspectors were forced out. After September 11, 2001, the United States began to brandish its threats to overthrow the Iraqi government, and the inspectors were readmitted. In May of 1998, India had conducted five nuclear tests, and Pakistan responded with seven, and both nations pronounced themselves nuclear powers, creating the first nuclear confrontation entirely unrelated to the Cold War; in the spring of 2002, after terrorist attacks on the Indian Parliament that India blamed on Pakistan, the two countries went to the brink of nuclear war. North Korea and Iran both have nuclear programs, and in October 2002, North Korea announced that it possessed nuclear weapons. In our day, nuclear danger has been supplemented by the spread of biological and chemical weapons, not only to states but to terrorist groups. If bipolarity shaped the strategy of the first nuclear age, then proliferation, if it is not reversed, is destined to define that of the second.

In assessing nuclear proliferation, it is important to distinguish between the capacity to construct a nuclear arsenal and the deed of actually constructing one. By the count of the State Department, forty-four nations have the capacity, which is to say there are forty-four nations that, if they choose to build nuclear weapons, can be reasonably certain of success. Whereas developing nuclear weapons requires a political decision, acquiring the capacity happens almost of itself. Switzerland, for instance, has never made a decision to acquire the capacity, yet no one can doubt that Switzerland has it. Being a modern, technically competent nation is enough.

This excess of capacity over possession points to the fundamental fact of the nuclear age, known from the beginning to all who have worked on the weapons, that the basic building block of nuclear arms, which is the knowledge required to build them, was destined to spread. In 1945, for example, the physicist Leo Szilard, one of the discoverers of nuclear fission, predicted the terrorist threat that now so deeply worries the United States and other countries. "The position of the United States in the world may be adversely affected by [nuclear weapons'] existence," he wrote. "Clearly if such bombs are available, it will not be necessary to bomb our cities from the air in order to destroy them. All that is necessary is to place a comparatively small number in major cities and detonate them at some later time. . . . The long coastline, the structure of our society, and the heterogeneity of our population may make effective controls of such 'traffic' virtually impossible." In the long run, there can be no "secret" of the bomb. A historical period that, like the nuclear age, is defined by a technology has a natural life cycle. At its birth, the technology may be held by a single pair of hands—in this case, the United States'. In its youth, the technology may be confined to a few nations, as during the Cold War. But in its maturity, which comes with the mere passage of time, it is destined to be available to all. The reason is the innate mobility of scientific knowledge. An era of information and free trade is an especially difficult one in which to keep technical secrets. Like a battery that is slowly charging, the proliferation of nuclear capacity creates a growing potential—a potential that may or may not end in sudden, violent discharge but, as the years go by, *can* be released by an ever-increasing number of states or groups in an ever-increasing number of ways.

The Cold War may have retarded proliferation, but even its continuation probably could not have stopped it. (Would India and Pakistan have been *less* likely to nuclearize their conflict if the Cold War had continued?) The Cold War was in fact a sort of two-power disguise temporarily assumed by the nuclear predicament. This form of the dilemma depended on certain historical conditions that looked highly durable but turned out to be temporary. Its new form will be based on the universal availability of nuclear know-how that is written into the predicament's makeup. To paraphrase Clausewitz, the Cold War was a restricted, "real" form of the nuclear predicament, and now we are on our way to facing it in its unlimited, hydra-headed, "ideal" form. "Ideal," in this context, means that the threat is not only all-embracing but also originates at all points of the compass. And this underlying change will occur irrespective of any military and political decisions. I do not mean that all nations will inevitably build nuclear weapons. I mean that all will be *able* to do so and, in that restricted yet fundamental sense, emanate nuclear danger. The question is to what extent nations will turn capacity into hardware—into nuclear bombs.

Chemical and biological weapons, which are easier to acquire than nuclear weapons, are equally unconfinable. Both are banned by international conventions, although these so far lack adequate provisions for inspection and enforcement. In late September and early October of 2001, three letters containing spores of the lethal virus anthrax were sent to three addresses in the United States, including the office of Senate Majority Leader Tom Daschle. It was the first use in history—however limited—of an acknowledged weapon of mass destruction on American soil. Five people died, Senate buildings were shut down, and the postal service was disrupted for several months. If sophisticated delivery systems had been used, tens of thousands could have died. If the pathogen released had been smallpox, which is contagious, rather than anthrax, which is not, millions of people, experts say, might have died.

During the Cold War, the capacities for violence of the great powers were in effect compressed into a single integrated explosive device, to which a warning sign was affixed that said, "You have the power to set off this device, but if you do, you, too, and perhaps all humankind, are doomed." The doom was real enough, but the compression could not last. As the Cold War ended, and the compression began to weaken, the contents of the device began to seep into the world. During the Cold War, a variety of "thresholds," enforced by strong taboos, confined the danger to a certain extent. One was the clear distinction between the nuclear powers, few in number, and the many nonnuclear powers. Another was the threshold between conventional and nuclear war. Still another was "the brink" between the two superpowers. Today, all these boundaries have been breached or blurred. The line between conventional and nuclear war is being blurred by many developments—by the increasing power of conventional weapons, such as the fifteen-ton American "daisy-cutter" bomb, and by the miniaturization and refinement of American nuclear weapons, including the proposed so-called bunker buster, designed for use against caves deep underground, and by the rise of the chemical and biological threats. The single nuclear abyss on whose dizzying edge the nuclear-armed superpowers stood (and still stand) has, in effect, branched out to form innumerable smaller abysses. They run through Wall Street, where the September 11 attacks occurred; through Kashmir, dividing nuclear-armed India from nuclear-armed Pakistan; through Pyongyang and Beijing;

through Peshawar, Manila, and Mindanao, or wherever Al Qaeda or its like may be preparing weapons of mass destruction for use against the United States or others; and through New Jersey suburbs and Washington post offices and wherever else the anthrax-laden letters may arrive.

Proliferation has still another dimension. Some scientists fear that new, even more deadly and more easily concocted instruments of mass destruction, based on the newly developed techniques of genetic engineering and nanotechnology, may be discovered before long. Bill Joy, a cofounder of Sun Microsystems, has noted that the production of nuclear, and even of today's biological and chemical, weapons of mass destruction requires the resources of states—or, at least, of large teams of scientists. However, the technologies of the future may well lie within the reach of far smaller teams, or even solitary individuals. In Joy's words:

> As this enormous computing power is combined with the manipulative advances of the physical sciences and the new, deep understandings in genetics, enormous transformative power is being unleashed. These combinations open up the opportunity to completely redesign the world, for better or worse: The replicating and evolving processes that have been confined to the natural world are about to become realms of human endeavor. I think it is no exaggeration to say we are on the cusp of the further perfection of extreme evil, an evil whose possibility spreads well beyond that which weapons of mass destruction bequeathed to the nation-states, on to a surprising and terrible empowerment of extreme individuals.

Joy's fears, though fortunately still speculative, help us to understand the novel character of the forces that are defining what we may call the second nuclear age. At the beginning of history, the homicidal "first man," to borrow a term from Nietzsche, confronted his enemy with only his bare hands. Then, at one of history's turning points, or possibly its origin, he availed himself of his first destructive instrument, perhaps a stick or a rock. From that time on, the curve of humanity's technical capacity for violence rose steadily until, in 1945, it invented a device with which it could exterminate itself as a species. Yet that moment, for all its seeming finality, was not the end of the story. Nuclear weapons were hard to make and remained in just a few hands. Since then, the line to watch has been the ascending curve of distribution, which places this apocalyptic power as well as new ones in ever more hands. Its logical end point would be the person—let us borrow another term of Nietzsche's and call him the "last man"—who could concoct and release an unstoppable, contagious bacterium that could end human life.

Nuclear weapons, as all believers in deterrence know, are instruments of *terror*. We should not be surprised to find that they are of particular interest to *terrorists*. Osama bin Laden has sought to acquire nuclear weapons and, soon after the September 11 attack, he announced that he possessed them—but only (shades of the Cold War) for purposes of "deterrence." It's likely that both parts of the statement were false, yet no one can rule out the possibility that Al Qaeda or another group will obtain nuclear weapons. Science is delivering the mass over to the whim of the individual. The bewildering dilemma that the last man—the terrorist with an instrument of annihilation in his or her (as we must add after the suicide bombings by young Palestinian women) hands—presents to the world is the ever-increasing likelihood that a small band of criminals, or even a single evildoer, even today can conceivably cause the death of millions and in a conceivable future could cause the death of all.

"LIBERAL" THREATS TO THE PEACE

Many observers in the prosperous democracies like to imagine that the post–Cold War world's disorder and violence arise only in poor, misgoverned, anarchic lands. Historically, of course, it has been otherwise: the West has been the world's most active military volcano, bringing destruction upon itself through war and on the rest of the world through imperial conquest and exploitation. (The cost of imperialism in human lives rivaled strictly inter-European slaughter. For example, it has been estimated that in the Congo Free State alone, the death toll under the colonial administrations of King Leopold of Belgium and his successors was between ten and twenty million.) Although the Western civil war has been stilled by the liberal settlement, and old-style Western colonial rule has been ended by the world revolt, economic exploitation is alive, active, and rapidly developing new forms, which could prove as destructive—to the natural environment of the earth as well as to its poorer inhabitants—as the old.

The issue of imperial exploitation now arises in the context of economic globalization. According to some, the end of the territorial empires meant the end of imperialism. In Francis Fukuyama's view, for example, imperialism is an anachronism—"an atavism, a holdover from an earlier stage in human social evolution." Others contend that globalization is in fact imperialism in a new guise—"neo-imperialism." An increasingly powerful popular movement has arisen to oppose it. Its members observe that in the era of globalization the gap between the rich and the poor has increased, along with the power of wealthy countries to dictate economic policies to poor ones, that international economic decisions increasingly escape democratic control, and degradation of the environment is proceeding at a gallop. Among the instruments of economic control are the International Monetary Fund, the World Bank, and the World Trade Organization, all of whose decisions are dominated by wealthy countries; but even more powerful pressure is brought to bear by the global market system itself. States that structure their economies along approved lines do so not because they fear that otherwise their capitals will be bombarded and their lands occupied, as in the days of gunboat diplomacy, but because they know that if they do not, international loans and investments will dry up, their currencies will crash, and the living standards of most of their people will nose-dive. A balance sheet of gains and losses to the poorer countries is difficult to draw up, but it's possible that these new strictures, imposing what some call "structural violence" on the poor, may in fact bring more suffering to ordinary people than overt imperial violence once did.

The prosperous nations themselves are, it is true, also subject to market pressures—although generally to a lesser extent, since the system's rules have been written in good measure to advance their interests. The overall health of the global market system depends, as the war system's once did, on a precarious balance that the great powers must exert themselves mightily to preserve. Whereas in 1914 the ministers of foreign affairs flew into a panic when the balance of military power began to tip one way or another, now the ministers of finance scurry to take action when the economic order is threatened by a plunge in the currency in Jakarta, Buenos Aires, or Phnom Penh. These are the Fashodas and Sarajevos of the global market system, which, like the war system, is placed at risk of collapse by local crises that have the potential to start a broader unraveling of the system.

THE WORLD'S ONLY SUPERPOWER

Whether economic globalization will benefit the world or become a new kind of imperialism—a sort of global rule by the rich over the poor—is a question that will be decided by many countries. Whether overt force, as distinct from economic pressure, will be used to renew imperial domination will depend above all on a single country, the United States—the sole power that has military resources on the scale necessary to harbor such an ambition.

In the early years of the Cold War, the United States, born in rebellion against the British Empire, styled itself, as it had for most of its history, an opponent of the European sort of imperialism. But soon in the name of anticommunism the United States was supporting many colonial regimes, including, with notably disastrous results, that of the French in Vietnam. Before long, the United States became the supporter and often the installer of murderous right-wing dictatorships on every continent—a pattern of conduct that, in its brutality and indifference to the will of local peoples, strongly resembled the supposedly rejected European precedent. A short list of such regimes would include those of Shah Reza Pahlavi in Iran, the dictator Saddam Hussein in Iraq (until he invaded Kuwait), the House of Saud in Saudi Arabia, Mobutu Sese Seko in the Congo, Fulgencio Batista in Cuba, Park Chung Hee in South Korea, a succession of civilian and military dictators in South Vietnam, Lon Nol in Cambodia, Suharto in Indonesia, Marcos in the Philippines, the colonels' junta in Greece, Franco in Spain, and a long list of military dictators in Argentina, Chile, Brazil, Uruguay, Guatemala, El Salvador, Nicaragua, and Pakistan. In supporting such governments, the United States was acting in pursuit of both Cold War geopolitical aims and economic advantage: the regimes in question were in general both anticommunist and friendly to American interests.

When the Cold War ended, the United States began to support the revival of democracy, and many of the repressive regimes it had backed, as we've seen, fell from power. At the same time, however, the unexpected collapse of the Soviet Union left the United States standing alone in the world as a military superpower. In economic strength, the United States had peers and near-peers—the European Union, Japan, China—but in military might it was in a class by itself. American military spending equaled that of the next dozen or so countries put together. In the 1990s, as the United States implemented a "revolution in military affairs," which applied information technology to warfare, its lead only increased. Never in history had any single power possessed such military advantage, qualitative as well as quantitative, over any or all other nations, and never had the likelihood of another nation catching up seemed more remote.

The emergence of this freakish imbalance, which came as quickly and unexpectedly as the Soviet collapse that was its proximate cause, posed a fundamental question for both the international order and the United States. The founders of the country had detested "standing armies"—an innovation of the despised absolutist monarchs of Europe. The founders feared that a large army with nothing to do would look for wars to fight. They also feared executive control of the military. In the words of John Jay in *The Federalist Papers*, "absolute monarchs will often make war when their nations are to get nothing by it, but for purposes and objects merely personal, such as a thirst for military glory, revenge for personal affronts, ambition, or private compacts to aggrandize or support their particular families or partisans. These and a variety of other motives, which affect only the mind of the sovereign, often lead him to engage in wars not sanctified by justice or the voice or interests of his people." That is why the constitution they wrote declares, in one of its shortest and least equivocal statements, "The Congress shall have power to declare war."

The United States had often assembled great military forces, but always for a specific war, and had disbanded them when the war was over, as it did, for example, after the First World War. Even after the Second World War, American forces were reduced. (It's also true, however, that the effect of the reduction was more than offset by the creation of a growing arsenal of nuclear weapons—then an American monopoly.) With the end of the Cold War, the situation most feared by the founders came into existence. The nation was, for the first time in its history, in possession of a gigantic military force with no particular enemy to fight. Meanwhile, Congress had in practice yielded its power to declare war to the president.

In the 1990s, the question arose: Would the United States, having lost its global competitor, demobilize (as it had after the two world wars), or would it find some new mission for its military machine? If so, what would that mission be? These questions were especially acute in regard to the nation's thousands of nuclear weapons, whose deployment had been geared almost exclusively to Cold War purposes. Some in power asked (as Secretary of State Madeleine Albright, frustrated by American inaction in the Balkans, once did of Chairman of the Joint Chiefs of Staff Colin Powell), "What's the point of having this superb military that you're always talking about if we can't use it?" Others—distant from power—asked why, if there was little use for such military forces, the United States had to have them.

In the last decade of the twentieth century, the United States arrived at no clear answer: it neither dismantled its military machine nor found a mission for it. Overall military spending briefly dipped, and then resumed an upward curve. In the 1990s, the lone superpower was also a reluctant one. With regard to the two sources of most acute danger—local wars, including wars of self-determination, and weapons of mass destruction—the United States pursued vacillating policies. The American nuclear arsenal, literally deprived of its raison d'être by the disappearance of the Soviet target, fell into a sort of political vacuum. The policies of the United States in regard to nuclear proliferation were equally uncertain. An early decision to preserve the American nuclear arsenal indefinitely and a long hiatus in the START negotiations with Russia (owing in good measure to the decision to expand NATO to include Poland, the Czech Republic, and Hungary) helped prompt other, anxious or ambitious countries to seek or acquire their own arsenals. When the Soviet Union collapsed, the Clinton administration did succeed in brokering the denuclearization of Ukraine, Belorussia, and Kazakhstan, leaving Russia alone as the legatee of the Soviet Union's nuclear arsenal, but the exchange of nuclear tests by India and Pakistan in 1998, in disregard of weak American sanctions, left subsequent American nonproliferation policy in tatters.

A string of local and regional wars provoked American responses with no clear theme. President George H. W. Bush appeared to adopt a strongly interventionist stance when, in the name of a "new world order," he successfully reversed Iraq's annexation of Kuwait; but when violence of near-genocidal proportions broke out in Yugoslavia Secretary of State James Baker declared, "We have no dog in that fight," and the United States stayed out. The lesson seemed to be that the United States intervened only when its interests were at stake. As a presidential candidate, Bill Clinton castigated Bush for his inaction in the Balkans, but as president he, too, was at first inactive there. Only after Serbian forces had laid a long siege to Sarajevo did the United States conduct a bombing campaign under the aegis of NATO to protect the city. In 1999, Clinton ordered American forces to bomb Serbia to obtain its withdrawal from Kosovo. Meanwhile, in 1993, when American soldiers in a force that the United States had sent to stop a famine in Somalia were killed in a battle with a local warlord, Clinton promptly withdrew those troops, creating a strong impression that the United States would use its forces only when it could be sure they would not suffer casualties.

"Humanitarian intervention" was the official description of each of these interventions. Yet the Clinton administration did nothing to stop the worst atrocity of the era, the genocide in Rwanda. Nor did Clinton's Republican opposition—torn between its hawkish wing and its isolationist wing—offer a clear or consistent alternative policy. The reaction of the rest of the world to the uncertain superpower's use of its power was likewise equivocal. On the one hand, many nations—especially European nations—supported the use of American might in the crises in the Gulf, Somalia, and the former Yugoslavia; on the other hand, many nations (including some of the same nations) made clear their alarm that the use of such immense power, even if for ends defined as humanitarian, set a precedent that could soon be abused and was dangerous to the international order.

Then came the attack of September 11. Like the starting gun of a race that no one knew he was to run, this explosion set the pack of nations off in a single direction—toward the trenches. Although the attack was unaccompanied by any claim of authorship or statement of political goals, the evidence almost immediately pointed to Al Qaeda, the radical Islamist, terrorist network, which, though stateless, was headquartered in Afghanistan and enjoyed the protection of its fundamentalist Islamic government. In a tape that was soon shown around the world, the group's leader, Osama bin Laden, was seen at dinner with his confederates in Afghanistan, rejoicing in the slaughter. Historically, nations have responded to terrorist threats and attacks with a combination of police action and political negotiation, while military action has played only a minor role. Voices were raised in the United States calling for a global cooperative effort of this kind to combat Al Qaeda. President Bush opted instead for a policy that the United States alone among nations could have conceivably undertaken: global military action not only against Al Qaeda but against any regime in the world that supported international terrorism. The president announced to Congress that he would "make no distinction between the terrorists who commit these acts and those who harbor them." By calling the campaign a "war," the administration summoned into action the immense, technically revolutionized, post–Cold War American military machine, which had lacked any clear enemy for over a decade. And by identifying the target as generic "terrorism," rather than as Al Qaeda or any other group or list of groups, the administration licensed military operations anywhere in the world.

In the ensuing months, the Bush administration continued to expand the aims and means of the war. The overthrow of governments—"regime change"—was established as a means for advancing the new policies. The president divided regimes into two categories—those "with us" and those "against us." Vice President Cheney estimated that Al Qaeda was active in sixty countries. The first regime to be targeted was of course

Al Qaeda's host, the government of Afghanistan, which was overthrown in a remarkably swift military operation conducted almost entirely from the air and without American casualties.

Next, the administration proclaimed an additional war goal—preventing the proliferation of weapons of mass destruction. In his State of the Union speech in January 2002, the president announced that "the United States of America will not permit the world's most dangerous regimes to threaten us with the world's most destructive weapons." He went on to name as an "axis of evil" Iraq, Iran, and North Korea—three regimes seeking to build or already possessing weapons of mass destruction. To stop them, he stated, the Cold War policy of deterrence would not be enough—"preemptive" military action would be required, and preemption, the administration soon specified, could include the use of nuclear weapons. Beginning in the summer of 2002, the government intensified its preparations for a war to overthrow the regime of Saddam Hussein in Iraq, and in the fall, the president demanded and received a resolution from the Security Council of the United Nations requiring Iraq to accept the return of U.N. inspectors to search for weapons of mass destruction or facilities for building them. Lists of other candidates for "regime change" began to surface in the press.

In this way, the war on terror grew to encompass the most important geopolitical issue facing the world: the disposition of nuclear weapons in the second nuclear age. The Clinton administration had already answered the question regarding American possession of nuclear weapons: even in the absence of the Soviet Union, the United States planned to hold on to its nuclear arsenal indefinitely. In 2002, the Bush administration gave an answer to the question regarding nonproliferation, which throughout the nuclear age had been dealt with exclusively by diplomacy and negotiation, or, on occasion, economic sanctions.

The new answer was force. Nuclear disarmament was to be achieved by war and threats of war, starting with Iraq. One complementary element of the new policy, embraced long before September 11, was the decision to build a national missile defense system to protect the United States against nuclear attack by "rogue nations." But the fundamental element was a policy of preemptive war, or "offensive deterrence." This momentous shift in nuclear policy called, in addition, for programs to build new nuclear weapons and new delivery vehicles; confirmed new missions for nuclear weapons—retaliation for chemical or biological attacks, attacking hardened bunkers unreachable by other weapons—in the post–Cold War world; and listed seven countries (Russia, China, North Korea, Iraq, Iran, Libya, and Syria) for which contingency plans for nuclear attack should be considered. To achieve all these aims, nuclear and conventional, the president asked for an increase in military spending of forty-eight billion dollars—a sum greater than the total military spending of any other nation.

The sharp turn toward force as the mainstay of the policies of the United States was accompanied by a turn away from treaties and other forms of cooperation. Even before September 11, the trend had been clear. Now it accelerated. The Bush administration either refused to ratify or withdrew from most of the principal new international treaties of the post–Cold War era. In the nuclear arena alone, the administration refused to submit to the Senate for ratification the Comprehensive Test Ban Treaty, which would have added a ban on underground tests to the existing bans on testing in the air; withdrew from the A.B.M. Treaty, which had severely limited Russian and American deployment of antinuclear defensive systems; and jettisoned the START negotiations as the framework for nuclear reductions with Russia—replacing them with the Strategic Offensive Reduction Agreement, a three-page document requiring two-thirds of the strategic weapons of both sides to be removed from their delivery vehicles, but then stored rather than dismantled. In addition, the Bush administration withdrew from the Kyoto Protocol of the United Nations Framework Convention on Climate Change, which had become the world's principal forum for making decisions about reducing emissions that cause global warming; refused to ratify the Rome treaty establishing an international criminal court; and declined to agree to an important protocol for inspection and enforcement of a U.N. convention banning biological weapons.

The consequences of this revolution in American policy rippled through the world, where it found ready imitators. On December 12, the Indian Parliament was attacked by terrorists whom India linked to Pakistan. Promptly, nuclear-armed India, citing the American policy of attacking not only terrorists but any state that harbored them, moved half a million men to the border of nuclear-armed Pakistan, which responded in kind, producing the first full-scale nuclear crisis of the twenty-first century. In South Asia, nuclearization did not produce the cautionary effects that the theorists of deterrence expected. High Indian officials openly threatened Pakistan with annihilation. Rajnath Singh, the minister for the state of Uttar Pradesh, declared, "If Pakistan doesn't change its ways, there will be no sign of Pakistan left," and when India's army chief, General S. Padmanabhan, was asked how India would respond if attacked with a nuclear weapon, he answered that "the perpetrator of that particular outrage shall be punished so severely that their continuation thereafter in any form of fray will be doubtful." In Pakistan, the dictator General Pervez Musharraf stated that, in the event of an Indian conventional invasion of Pakistan, "as a last resort, the atom bomb is also possible." In March 2002, Israel, citing the same American precedent and calling for U.S. support for its policy on this basis, responded to Palestinian suicide bombings by launching its own "war on terrorism"—a full-scale attack on the Palestinian Authority on the West Bank.

The revolution in American policy had been precipitated by September 11, but went far beyond any war on terror. It remained to give the policy comprehensive doctrinal expression, which came in an official document, "The National Security Strategy of the United States of America," issued in September 2002. In the world, it stated, only one economic and political system remained "viable": the American one of liberal democracy and free enterprise. The United States would henceforth promote and defend this system by the unilateral use of force—preemptively, if necessary. The United States, the president said, "has, and intends to keep, military strengths beyond challenge, thereby making the destabilizing arms races of other eras pointless, and limiting rivalries to trade and other pursuits of peace." In other words, the United States reserved the entire field of military force to itself, restricting other nations to humbler pursuits. In the words of the "National Security Strategy," "Our forces will be strong enough to dissuade potential adversaries from pursuing a military build-up in hopes

of surpassing, or equaling, the power of the United States." If
the United States was displeased with a regime, it reserved the
right to overthrow it—to carry out "regime change." "In the
world we have entered," President Bush has said, "the only path
to safety is the path of action. And this nation will act."

NIAGARA

A policy of unchallengeable military domination over the earth,
accompanied by a unilateral right to overthrow other governments by military force, is an imperial, an Augustan policy. It
marks a decisive choice of force and coercion over cooperation
and consent as the mainstay of the American response to the dis-
orders of the time. If wars of self-determination and other kinds
of local and regional mayhem multiply and run out of control;
if the wealthy and powerful use globalization to systematize
and exacerbate exploitation of the poor and powerless; if the
poor and the powerless react with terrorism and other forms
of violence; if the nuclear powers insist on holding on to and
threatening to use their chosen weapons of mass destruction;
if more nations then develop nuclear or biological or chemical
arsenals in response and threaten to use them; if these weapons
one day fall, as seems likely, into the hands of terrorists; and if
the United States continues to pursue an Augustan policy, then
the stage will be set for catastrophe. Each of these possibilities
represents a path of least resistance. Local and regional conflicts have been the way of the world since history began. The
spread of nuclear- as well as biological- and chemical-weapon
know-how is an automatic function of technical progress, and
the spread of nuclear arsenals is a self-feeding process of action
and reaction. Continued possession of nuclear weapons by
those who already have them is the path of inertia, of deep
sleep. The imperial temptation for the United States is the path
of arrogance and ignorance.

At the intersection of these tendencies is a Niagara higher
and more violent than the one that a heartbroken Henry James
lived to witness in 1914. It is of course impossible to predict
how and where history might again go over the precipice. It
could be nuclear war in South Asia, bringing the deaths of
tens of millions of people. It could be the annihilation of

one or several cities in the United States in a nuclear terrorist attack, or the loss of millions in a smallpox attack. It could be a war spinning out of control in the Middle East, leading by that route to the use of weapons of mass destruction in the Middle East. It could be war in Korea, or between the United States and China over Taiwan. It could even be—hard as it is to imagine now—intentional or semi-intentional nuclear war between Russia and the United States in some future crisis that we cannot foresee but cannot rule out, either. Or it could be—is even likely to be—some chain of events we are at present incapable of imagining.

After September 11, people rightly said that the world had changed forever. Before that event, who could have predicted the galloping transformation of the politics of the United States and the world, the escalating regional crises, the vistas of perpetual war? Yet the use of just one nuclear weapon could exceed the damage of September 11 ten-thousandfold. Would the global economy plunge into outright depression? Would the people of the world flee their menaced cities? Would anyone know who the attacker was? Would someone retaliate—perhaps on a greater scale? Would the staggering shock bring the world to its senses? Would the world at that moment of unparalleled panic and horror react more wisely and constructively than it has been able to do in a time of peace, in comparative calm, or would it fall victim to an incalculable cycle of fear, confusion, hatred, hostility, and violence, both between nations and within them, as it did after 1914—but this time, in all likelihood, far more swiftly and with incomparably direr consequences? In the face of these questions, predictive powers dim. But attempts at prophecy are in any case the wrong response. Decisions are required.

13

The Logic of Peace

The escalation of violence around the world has been so rapid since September 11, 2001, that this day may appear already to have been the August 1914 of the twenty-first century. The parallels are striking. In 2001 as in 1914 a period of political liberalization, economic globalization, and peace (at least in the privileged zones of the planet) was summarily ended by a violent explosion. The fundamental decision now, as it was then, is between force and peaceful means as the path to safety, and the world has seemed to make a decision for force. Again, observers have been compelled, as Henry James was in 1914, to recognize that the immediate past has been a time of illusion—a time when the world was heading toward a precipice but did not know it, or did not care to know it. Again, an unpredictable chain of violent events has been set in motion—some today have even said that a "third world war" is upon us.

And yet, since history does not repeat itself, the analogy between 1914 and 2001, like all measurements of the present with yardsticks from the past, is useful only for querying events, not for predicting them. There are equally important differences between the two moments, some of them obvious, others less so. In 1914, the great powers' preparations for war were complete. The arms were piled high, the troops massed, the war plans mapped out in detail, the mobilization schedules fixed, the treaties of alliance signed and sealed. Even before the first shot was fired, the whole of the long war to come lay waiting in the file cabinets of the chanceries of Europe, needing only the right incident to spring to life. And when that incident came and the armies were hurled across the borders, no power on earth, including the governments involved, could call them back until the war had run its full bloody course. Our moment, by contrast, is one of exceptional unpredictability and fluidity. No inexorable timetables or web of alliances among great powers threaten to drag everyone together into a new abyss. The unexpected—new crises, abrupt developments, sudden opportunities—is the order of the day. The strength of the forces that attacked on September 11 is unclear, and appears likely to wax or wane in response to events. The Bush administration has announced a series of wars that it may decide to fight, but there will be points of decision at every step along the way. Developments in the field can quickly alter political opinion at home. Resistance, violent and non-violent, in Iraq, has already seriously thrown into question the ability of the United States to attack other countries. The proliferation of weapons of mass destruction can inhibit as well as provoke war. Elections can bring new people to power. Other countries are watching and waiting, uncertain where and how to bring the weight of their influence to bear. The effect of a series of wars, if such occur, on global economic integration is unknown, and huge uncertainties shadow the economic scene.

As shocking as September 11 was, it was not a decisive catastrophe, but rather a warning. No irrevocable decision has in fact been made. The scope for choice remains unusually large, and the new cycle of violence can still be broken or reversed, and new policies adopted. Seen narrowly, September 11 posed the specific question of how the United States and the civilized world should deal with a global terrorist network ready to commit any crime within its power. That question requires all the urgent attention and action that it is receiving. At the same time, I submit, we should be asking what the larger and more fundamental decisions for policy may be. If we take this broader approach, the profound changes that have occurred in the character of violence, politics, and power over the last century will command our attention. In 1918 and 1945, a decision in favor of coercive power clearly meant in practice choosing the old war system, and a decision in favor of cooperative power meant choosing to create ex nihilo a Wilsonian system of global collective security based on international law. Today, neither of these alternatives is open to us. Others are on the table. Let us consider each of the two paths, beginning with the choice of coercive power, then turning to the choice of cooperative power.

VIOLENCE AS THE SOLUTION TO VIOLENCE:
THE END OF BALANCE

Now as in 1918 and 1945, organized violence plays a double role in the decision, for violence is both the problem to be solved and one of the solutions on offer—a solution to itself. This remedy is of course as old as history. When, as we have noted, Clemenceau rejected Wilson's vision in favor of an old system in which he still had "faith," he was referring to definite plans for defending his country within the framework of the global war system. And when the diplomat Harold Nicolson began to lose confidence in Wilsonism and repaired to that old system because the value of "armaments, strategic frontiers, alliances" was already proven, he was reverting to the same faith. Both held to the idea, codified in the realist school of political thought, of creating a balance of power, which had always been the main hope for peace of those who planned to deploy the instruments of violence to prevent violence. When nuclear weapons were invented, war among the great powers became unworkable, yet the idea of balance survived, in the new form of the balance of terror. Some have continued to call the balance of terror a balance of power, but a better term might be a balance of powerlessness, inasmuch as its stability rests on the willingness of the parties to enlist in a community of total jeopardy.

The balance of powerlessness may have been more effective than the balance of power exactly because the penalty for failure, nuclear annihilation, was so much greater. It cannot, of course, be demonstrated conclusively that nuclear terror prevented a third world war. Too many ifs of history are involved to make a firm judgment. (Since we cannot in the present predict what history *will* do, what makes us think that we can say what history *would have done* if such and such an imaginary event had occurred?) For example, we would have to determine that a third world war had been straining to occur—only to be checked by fear of the bomb. We would also have to show that the presence of nuclear weapons did more to prevent world war than to cause it. After all, the most acute crisis of the Cold War, the Cuban missile crisis, was brought about by the deployment of nuclear weapons. If nuclear strategic thinking had anything to do with resolving that crisis (something that is in itself difficult to demonstrate), it was only after causing the crisis in the first place.

Nevertheless, it is as possible as it is necessary, even without resolving these unanswerable questions, to acknowledge that the presence of the bomb weighed heavily in the calculations of the statesmen of the Cold War, inclining them against major war each time a crisis occurred. Their increasing recognition that, as President Ronald Reagan put it, "nuclear war cannot be won and must never be fought" was a central fact, in theory and in practice, of the Cold War.

With these developments, nuclear strategy acquired a Wilsonian dimension. It had evolved into a war stopper. The importance of the role of the balance of terror as a peacekeeper becomes clearer if we consider the varying fates of the century's two major organizations for peacekeeping, the League of Nations and the United Nations. The League was discredited by a series of aggressions and conflicts it was unable to prevent or halt, then swept aside by the Second World War. The Cold War played a similar role in sidelining the United Nations.

President Franklin Roosevelt and Winston Churchill, who first called for such an organization in the Atlantic Charter in 1941, had sought to draw lessons from the fate of the League. Instead of assigning the peacekeeping function to a large council, as the League did, they vested it in an alliance of the prospective victors of the Second World War—the United States, the Soviet Union, China, England, and France—each of whom was given a permanent seat on the Security Council and a veto over its decisions. The hope was that this small, tight-knit group of great powers could guarantee the peace more effectively than the multitude of nations charged with that responsibility under the provisions of the League. But almost immediately after the organization's foundation in 1946, this arrangement was for all intents and purposes nullified by the advent of the Cold War. In 1950, the Korean War, sanctioned by the Security Council after the Soviet Union walked out of its proceedings, confirmed that the breakdown in relations between the United States and the Soviet Union was irreparable.

If this geopolitical split had been the only reason for the U.N.'s failure to perform its central role, the story would be a familiar one, well-known to analysts of the League's collapse: collective security fails to get off the ground because the powers that are supposed to enforce it fall out with one another. The designated peacemakers become the peace-breakers, and no one else is strong enough to bring them into line. In fact, however, the U.N.'s marginalization occurred for another reason as well—the onset of the nuclear age. By an accident of historical timing, the bomb was first tested and dropped in the hiatus between the designing of the United Nations and its founding.

In April of 1945, in San Francisco, the Conference on International Organization formally agreed on the outlines of the U.N. Charter. On October 24, the U.N. came into existence. On August 6, however, the destruction of Hiroshima radically transformed the nature of the main problem, great-power war, that the new organization had been fashioned to solve. Conceived in one age, the U.N. was born in another. Having been designed to cope with a world dominated by the global war system, it came into existence after that system's death knell had been sounded. The central purpose of the U.N. was to prevent a third world war—to, in the words of the Preamble to its Charter, "save succeeding generations from the scourge of war, which twice in our lifetime has brought untold sorrow to mankind." But as the years passed it was not to the U.N., disabled by the Cold War, that the great powers turned to save them from a third world war but to nuclear arsenals. Even as the Cold War was wrecking the U.N. as an instrument for keeping the peace, nuclear deterrence was coopting it. Thus the U.N. was not swept away, as the League had been by approaching world war; it was permitted to live on to perform important, if secondary services—supplying humanitarian relief in disasters of every description, sending peacekeeping forces to calm local conflicts, providing a forum for the expression of international opinion.

With the end of the bipolar Cold War order, and the acceleration of nuclear proliferation, however, the new, nuclearized form of this balance is crumbling. For reasons both political and technical, nuclear terror is rapidly shedding its "Wilsonian" role as a preserver of stability and peace.

Some, it is true, have argued to the contrary that the balance of nuclear terror can actually be extended and strengthened by proliferation. Just as nuclear weapons stopped the two superpowers of the Cold War from fighting a hot war, so, it is suggested, they can immobilize ten or twenty or thirty nuclear powers, in a grand peace based on universal terror. The political scientist Kenneth Waltz, for example, has suggested that "the gradual spread of nuclear weapons is more to be welcomed than feared." He hopes that the Soviet-American stalemate enforced by deterrence during the Cold War might be enlarged to include many more nations. What has not been explained, however, is how a steadily growing number of nuclear powers, each capable of annihilating some or all of the others, can balance their forces in a way that would leave any of them feeling safe. Mutual assured destruction is a policy whose logic fits a bipolar relationship. It defies adjustment to a multi-nuclear-power world.

Proliferation, indeed, undermines stability in every sense of that word. In the first place, it destroys strategic stability. Strategic balance during the Cold War was supposed to depend on the attempt to maintain a rough equality between the forces of the two sides; but in a world of many nuclear powers this goal would be unreachable. If Country A and Country B were to painstakingly craft a stable nuclear balance (something, incidentally, that the Soviet Union and the United States failed to do for as long as the Cold War continued), it could be overthrown instantly by any nuclear-armed Country C that suddenly allied itself with one or the other. The necessary changes in targeting could be accomplished in just a few hours or days. Even in today's world of eight nuclear powers (or perhaps nine, if North Korea's claim to possess nuclear weapons is true), some of the imbalances inherent in nuclear multipolarity are evident. There is little hope of balance, for example, in the quadrilateral relationship of the United States, China, India, and Pakistan. India has stated that it became a nuclear power to balance nuclear-armed China, by whom it was defeated in a conventional border war in 1962. Pakistan became a nuclear power to balance India. If India seeks again to balance China, however, will Pakistan seek to keep up? China, moreover, has supplied nuclear technology to Pakistan. And Pakistan has supplied some to North Korea, receiving missile technology in return. Will India therefore feel compelled to build a nuclear arsenal that equals both China's and Pakistan's? The United States meanwhile has decided to build national missile defenses, which, if they turn out to work, will erode or nullify China's capacity to strike the United States. China has already said that it will respond by building up its still modest nuclear forces. That will put additional pressure on India. Nor can we forget that Russia may, at any point, step into the picture with its still-huge arsenal. The spread of ballistic- and cruise-missile technology, whose proliferation is as predictable as that of nuclear technology, compounds the problem geometrically.

In the second place, proliferation is bound to undermine the foundations of technical stability. During the Cold War, the United States and the Soviet Union sought a kind of safety in the policy of mutual assured destruction. In practice, however, they found that their nuclear command-and-control systems were so vulnerable to a first strike that the retaliation required by the doctrine could not in fact be assured. To cure the problem, the two governments resorted to policies of "launch on warning"—that is, each planned to launch its retaliatory strike after receiving a warning that the other side had launched its first strike but before the missiles had arrived. This system placed severe time pressure on any decision to launch in retaliation, increasing the risks of accidental war. The presidents of the two nations were—and still are—required to make these decisions within five minutes of receiving warning of an incoming strike. The pressures on Russia, which now faces a technically superior American force, have grown especially severe.

If the United States and Russia, with all their resources and an ocean between them, cannot guarantee the survival of their command-and-control systems, is it reasonable to expect that smaller, poorer nations, facing many potential adversaries, with little or no warning time, will accomplish this? The warning time between India and Pakistan, for instance, is effectively zero. For them, not even launch on warning is possible. The requirements for nuclear stability under the doctrine of deterrence are thus altogether lacking.

In the third place, what the experts call arms-control stability—meaning conditions favorable to negotiated limits on or reductions of nuclear arsenals—would be destroyed. During the Cold War, the United States and the Soviet Union, unable to agree on numerical offensive limits, built up their collective arsenals to the preposterous collective level of some seventy-five thousand nuclear warheads. In a multipolar nuclear world, arms-control agreements would become exponentially harder to achieve. How could twenty or thirty nations, few of whom trusted the others or were sure what they were doing, be able to adjust the scores of nuclear balances among them? Containing proliferation (if someone should wish to return to that policy somewhere down the road) would be a pipe dream. How would, say, the twentieth nuclear power persuade the twenty-first that building nuclear weapons is a bad idea?

In the fourth place, multiplying nuclear arsenals would increase the danger of nuclear terrorism. A world of proliferation would be a world awash in nuclear materials. Terrorists who acquired them would be indifferent to nuclear threats from others. The balance of terror depends on fear of retaliatory annihilation, but many terrorists have no country of whose annihilation they are afraid. They are unafraid to lose even their own lives, and blow themselves up with the bombs they aim at others. The terrorist bent on self-immolation with a weapon of mass destruction is the nemesis of balance. Deterrence has no purchase on the dead.

VIOLENCE AS THE SOLUTION TO VIOLENCE: EMPIRE

If the balance of power and the balance of terror are no longer available, does the storehouse of systems of coercive power still offer any resource for keeping peace in the world? One option remains to be considered: universal empire, substantially achieved only once in the history of the Western world, by the Romans. (Even they were unable to conquer certain outlying territories.) The nation now aspiring to a global imperial role is, of course, the United States. Its military dominance is one more reason that a balance of power has become impracticable. Obviously, there can be no balance when one power is mightier than all the others put together. Not a balance of power but a monopoly of power—or, at any rate, of force—is the present American ambition. The new state of affairs is sometimes referred to as "unipolarity," but the term is an oxymoron within a single word, for by definition "polarity" requires two poles. (The Bush administration's official statement of its global policy, the "National Security Strategy," falls into a similar confusion when it speaks of a "balance of power in favor of freedom." A balance that is "in favor of" one side is again by definition not a balance.)

Although both the balance-of-power system and the balance of terror were primarily based on coercion, both contained significant admixtures of cooperation. Both depended on a sort of brute equity among two or more powers. If the balance was to be maintained, neither could claim a right to attack the other: they must coexist. Under the balance of terror, the element of cooperation was even stronger. The two sides were bonded in the common project of avoiding the war that would annihilate both. They were paradoxical partners in survival. A global hegemonic peace, on the other hand, would mark the triumph of coercion. Its foundation would be not equality of any kind but the absolute and unchallengeable superiority of one power and the vassalage of others—not mutual nonaggression but preemption, not coexistence but the right of one, and only one, to execute "regime change."

The idea of American global hegemony thus carries the rule of force to an extreme. And yet, fantastic and unreal as the ambition may be, there is a logic underlying it. Means, this logic runs, must be adequate to ends. Since proliferation is in its nature global so must American domination. The United States will employ its overwhelming military superiority to stop proliferation all around the world. It applies to the world the reasoning that Bodin applied to the state four hundred years ago: the world is now a community; a community needs order; to provide order there must be a sovereign; the sovereign can be none other than the master of the sword; the United States alone can lay a claim to mastering the sword; therefore the United States must be the global sovereign. And so on behalf of its own and the world's safety, the United States will fight a series of what can be called disarmament wars. Under this plan the United States would, indeed, become a "disarmament empire," dedicated to preserving the world from nuclear destruction. (Of course, all empires are in a sense disarmament empires: they rule by defeating—by destroying or disarming—every foe and rival.) It is not going too far to say that *if* the solutions to the danger of nuclear proliferation were restricted to coercive systems, then some form of imperial domination would be the form it would have to take.

To acknowledge the existence of this logic, which lends the American bid for hegemony whatever legitimacy it has, is not to overlook the more mundane and sordid aspects of American imperial ambition. Every empire in history has concealed coarse self-interest behind a veil of noble ideals, and there is no reason to believe that American imperialism would be an exception. The most obvious and the rawest of these motivations is the wish to take control of the oil reserves of Central Asia, the Middle East, and elsewhere. Far more sweeping is the assertion in the "National Security Strategy" that in all the world there is now "a single sustainable model for national success": the American one of "freedom, democracy, and free enterprise." It is a formulation that, when wedded to the assertion of un-challengeable American military superiority and the right to intervene militarily anywhere on earth, plainly sets the stage for attempts to impose America's will on nations in almost any area of their collective existence.

A plan for global hegemony, however, has not suddenly become feasible simply because the balance of power and the balance of terror no longer work. Even if we supposed that the United States were to complete the transition from republic to empire, there are powerful reasons to believe that it would fail to realize its global ambitions, whether idealistic or self-interested. Any imperial plan in the twenty-first century tilts against what have so far proved to be the two most powerful forces of the modern age: the spread of scientific knowledge and the resolve of peoples to reject foreign rule and take charge of their own destinies. If the history of the past two centuries is a guide, neither can be bombed out of existence.

The most persuasive rationale for empire is its promise of deliverance from the threat of weapons of mass destruction. The views of most countries on this subject, however, are far different from those of the United States. The Bush ad-ministration looks out upon the world and sees "evildoers" trying to procure terrible weapons; the world looks back and sees a hypocritical power seeking to deny to others what it possesses in abundance and even plans to use preemptively. Most countries fear those who already have nuclear weapons at least as much as they fear those who are merely trying to get them. In their view, stopping proliferation deals at best with a secondary aspect of the nuclear problem. They still see what has perhaps become invisible to American eyes—that the United States and Russia have thousands of nuclear weapons pointed at one another and at others and have refused to surrender these arsenals. They also see that the club of possessors has grown to include South Asia, where the danger of nuclear war has become acute, and they note that no plan is on the drawing board to denuclearize these powers, either. On the contrary, nuclearization has been a ticket into the good graces of the United States for both countries. Finally, they observe that the Nuclear Nonproliferation Treaty, under which a hundred and eighty-two countries have agreed to forgo nuclear arms, is in jeopardy of breaking down because the five nations that possess nuclear arsenals under the terms of the treaty show no sign of fulfilling their pledge under its Article 6 to eliminate them. (Three other nuclear powers—India, Pakistan, and Israel—are nonmembers of the treaty, and the fourth, North Korea, has announced its intention of withdrawing.) It was in defiance of this nuclear double standard that India set off its nuclear tests in 1998, prompting Pakistan's responding tests. Was "regime change" an option in these cases? Is it in North Korea? Will it be if Iran, Egypt, Syria, or, for that matter, Japan or Germany builds a nuclear arsenal? Does the United States propose to overthrow the government of every country that, rebelling against the attempt to institutionalize the double standard, seeks to acquire weapons of mass destruction? The attempt indeed appears more likely to provoke than prevent proliferation, as has already happened in North Korea. Nations threatened with that nightmare of the ages, a great power seeking global domination, will go to desperate lengths to redress the balance. Weapons of mass destruction are an obvious means.

What is true for proliferation of nuclear weapons is also likely to be true for their use. Force, history teaches, summons counterforce. What goes around comes around. The United States is the only nation on earth that has used these weapons of mass destruction. An American attempt to dominate world affairs is a recipe for provoking their use again, very possibly on American soil.

It's unlikely that the passion for self-determination will be any easier to suppress than the spread of destructive technology. The United States destroyed the incompetent and outmoded Iraqi army and the state of Saddam Hussein with remarkable ease, but the creation of a new state proved another matter. The Pentagon, which had been placed in charge of both the war and its aftermath, appeared to believe that its invasion would be so popular that a new Iraqi government would virtually create itself. More complicated plans embodied in a State Department project called the Future of Iraq were brushed aside. A small Pentagon-sponsored force of Iraqi exiles, led by the businessman Ahmed Chalabi, dissolved on contact with the country. A policy of "regime change" implies that a new regime will replace the old, but the American forces seemed to have forgotten to bring a new regime with them to Baghdad. The stateless nation immediately experienced the wholesale looting by its own people of almost all government buildings and other removable assets. Soon, a guerrilla resistance movement began to operate, and within a few months had caused more casualties to American forces than had the conventional battles. The first American occupation authority was dissolved, and its chief, General Jay Garner, sent home.

Thereafter, plans and organizations to deal with Iraq's political, economic, and social future were announced and discarded every few months. In an act outstanding for its capriciousness even in the improvisatory atmosphere of the occupation, Garner's replacement, J. Paul Bremer, discharged the entire Iraqi army without pay, creating instantly a large body of idle, armed men hostile to the United States. He also appointed a "governing council" that soon turned out to govern little but the fortified villa it was assigned as its headquarters. A plan to write a constitution, with the help of American constitutional experts, was announced—and quickly abandoned, in favor of a plan to create yet another provisional government. Only then would a constitution be written and elections be held. However, that plan, too, soon ran into serious trouble—this time from the first serious, powerful, openly-operating political force to arise in occupied Iraq: the mainstream Shiite clergy, based in the holy city of Najaf and led by the grand Ayatollah Ali Sistani. The new occupation authority had announced a complex scheme in which its national and local appointees would choose the new government. Sistani demanded direct elections. They were elections his supporters could reasonably expect to win, inasmuch as Shiites form sixty percent of the population of Iraq. Sistani was on record calling for a government based on Islamic principles—an eventuality of which the American Secretary of Defense Donald Rumsfeld, no doubt recalling that the attacks of September 11 had been carried out by Islamic extremists, had said, "That's not going to happen."

The United States, in an oversight unusual even in the annals of past imperialism, appeared to believe that its will would simply be unopposed by local people once its armies reached Baghdad. But the people of Iraq, awakening politically from decades of repressive rule, were, like the scores of people before them who wrote the story of the world revolt, turning out to have a will of their own.

Empire, the supreme embodiment of force, is the antithesis of self-determination. It violates equity on a global scale. No lover of freedom can give it support. It is especially contrary to the founding principles of the United States, whose domestic political institutions are incompatible with the maintenance of empire. Historically, imperial rule has rested on three kinds of supremacy—military, economic, and political. The United States enjoys unequivocal superiority in only one of these domains—the military, and here only in the conventional sphere. (Any attempt at regime change in a country equipped with even a modest deliverable nuclear arsenal is out of the question even for the United States.) American economic power is impressive, yet in this domain it has several equals or near equals, including the European Union and Japan, who are not likely to bend easily to American will. In the political arena the United States is weak. "Covenants, without the sword, are but words," Hobbes said in the late seventeenth century. Since then, the world has learned that swords without covenants are but empty bloodshed. In the political arena, the lesson of the world revolt—that winning military victories may sometimes be easy but building political institutions in foreign lands is hard, often impossible—still obtains. The nation so keenly interested in regime change has small interest in nation-building and less capacity to carry it out. The United States, indeed, is especially mistrusted, often hated, around the world. If it embarks on a plan of imperial supremacy, it will be hated still more. Can cruise missiles build nations? Does power still flow from the barrel of a gun—or from a Predator Drone? Can the world in the twenty-first century really be ruled from thirty-five thousand feet? Modern peoples have the will to resist and the means to do so. Imperialism without politics is a naive imperialism. In our time, force can win a battle or two, but politics is destiny.

In the months before and after the invasion of Iraq, the pattern of American military supremacy coupled with political weakness appeared on the global level. On February 15, 2003—one month before the war was launched—unprecedented worldwide demonstrations against any war took place. Polling showed that public opinion in all but a handful of countries agreed with the demonstrators. Even in the countries whose governments supported the war—Britain, Spain, Poland—the public opposed it by large margins. A novel, asymmetrical global tug of war began. On one side was the United States together with its governmental allies. On the other was world opinion. In earlier times, powers seeking hegemony had been opposed by military combinations of their rivals. No such military response now appeared, or seemed likely to appear, to oppose the United States. It remained to be seen what forms of influence and power could be brought to bear by other, non-military means.

Can a nation that began its life in rebellion against the most powerful empire of its time end by trying to become a still more powerful empire? It perhaps can, but not if it wishes to remain a republic. Secretary of State John Quincy Adams defined the choice with precision in 1821. After giving his country the well-known advice that the United States should not go abroad "in search of monsters to destroy" but be "the well-wisher to the freedom and independence of all . . . the champion and vindicator only of her own," he added that if the United States embarked on the path of dominating others, the "fundamental maxims of her policy would insensibly change from liberty to force. . . . She might become the dictatress of the world. She would no longer be the ruler of her own spirit."

A country's violence, Hannah Arendt said, can destroy its power. The United States is moving quickly down this path. Do American leaders imagine that the people of the world, having overthrown the territorial empires of the nineteenth and twentieth centuries, are ready to bend the knee to an American overlord in the twenty-first? Do they imagine that allies are willing to become subordinates? Have they forgotten that people hate to be dominated by force? History is packed with surprises. The leaders of the totalitarian Soviet empire miraculously had the good sense to yield up their power without unleashing the tremendous violence that was at their fingertips. Could it be the destiny of the American republic, unable to resist the allure of an imperial delusion, to flare out in a blaze of pointless mass destruction?

THE COOPERATIVE PATH

In sum, the days when humanity can hope to save itself from force with force are over. None of the structures of violence—not the balance of power, not the balance of terror, not empire—can any longer rescue the world from the use of violence, now grown apocalyptic. Force can lead only to more force, not to peace. Only a turn to structures of cooperative power can offer hope. To choose that path, the United States would, as a first order of business, have to choose the American republic over the American empire, and then, on the basis of the principles that underlie the republic, join with other nations to build cooperative structures as a basis for peace.

For Americans, the choice is at once between two Americas, and between two futures for the international order. In an imperial America, power would be concentrated in the hands of the president, and checks and balances would be at an end; civil liberties would be weakened or lost; military spending would crowd out social spending; the gap between rich and poor would be likely to increase; electoral politics, to the extent that they still mattered, would be increasingly dominated by money, above all corporate money, whose influence would trump the people's interests; the social, economic, and ecological agenda of the country and the world would be increasingly neglected. On the other hand, in a republican America dedicated to the creation of a cooperative world, the immense concentration of power in the executive would be broken up; power would be divided again among the three branches, which would resume their responsibility of checking and balancing one another as the Constitution provides; civil liberties would remain intact or be strengthened; money would be driven out of politics, and the will of the people would be heard again; politics, and with it the power of the people, would revive; the social, economic, and ecological agendas of the country and the world would become the chief concern of the government.

Which path the United States will choose is likely to be decided in a protracted, arduous political struggle in the years ahead. Its outcome cannot be predicted. For the time being, the United States has chosen the coercive, imperial path, but that decision can be reversed. Of course, no American decision alone can secure peace in the world. It is the essence of the task that many nations must cooperate in it. If they do, however, they will find that twentieth-century history has presented them, together with all its violence, an abundance of materials to work with. There are grounds for optimism in the restricted but real sense that if the will to turn away from force and toward cooperation were to develop, history has provided more extensive and solid foundations for accomplishment than have ever existed before. For the anatomy of cooperative power has been transformed by the events of the past century as fully as that of coercive power.

Much that Woodrow Wilson hoped for has in fact come to pass. He wanted a world of popular self-determination. His vision is our reality (to a fault, as the tangled wars of self-determination of recent years demonstrate). He dreamed that the world would be made safe for democracy. We can begin to imagine, in the wake of the liberal democratic revival and the Western liberal settlement, that spreading democracy will help to make the world safe. He hated the territorial empires of his time. Today, they are on history's scrap heap.

Hopeful developments that Wilson could not have foreseen have also occurred. The Wilsonian peace was destroyed in good measure by the rise of totalitarianism. Now totalitarianism, too, lies in the dust. In Wilson's day, revolution was widely thought to be in its nature violent. We have witnessed the power of nonviolent revolution, which was responsible for the downfall of the greatest empires of the previous two centuries, the British and the Soviet. In his day, the global adapt-or-die war system was at the apex of its power. In ours, it is disabled. Each of the aforementioned developments indeed curtailed that system in a different way. The military power deployed at the top of the system ran into the buzz saw of even greater power based on popular will at the bottom. As in Alice in Wonderland's croquet game, in which the mallets were flamingos and the balls were hedgehogs, the pawns in the imperial game, mistaken for inanimate objects by the imperialists, came alive in their hands and began, universally and unstoppably, to pursue their own plans and ambitions. In this new dispensation, which can guarantee against global domination far more reliably than the balance of power ever could, the wills of innumerable local peoples play the role previously played by the resolve of major powers to go to war to stop a global conqueror.

While the self-determination movement was encasing the giant's feet in cement, nuclear weapons were immobilizing his head and limbs. What need was there to obey the dictates of the war system's global logic of force when at the end of every military path was neither victory nor defeat but a common annihilation? Coexistence had always been a wise policy; now it became a necessity. It remains so—American conventional military superiority notwithstanding—for all nuclear-capable powers. Even tiny, impoverished North Korea can deter the United States and all its might if it possesses half a dozen nuclear weapons and the means to deliver them. Of course, it is still quite possible to stumble across the dread threshold, committing genocide and suicide in a single act, but the option is hardly tempting.

Even as self-determination movements and nuclear arsenals were, in their different ways, paralyzing force as the final arbiter in global affairs, nonviolent revolution in the Soviet bloc and elsewhere was proving the existence of a force that now *could* arbitrate. Gyorgy Konrád was right, far-fetched as it may have seemed at the time, to suggest that his "antipolitics" pointed a way out of the Cold War and the nuclear stalemate, and so was Adam Michnik when he said that he and his colleagues had discovered a political equivalent of the atomic bomb. Has the effectiveness of what William James called the moral equivalent of war ever been more effectually demonstrated?

At the same time, the revival of liberal democracy was creating a growing, informal bloc of nations whose members enjoyed peaceful relations not because they bristled with arms or had established a cumbersome structure of collective security but merely because they lacked any reason or inclination for war and possessed cooperative means for resolving such disagreements as did arise.

The success of the self-determination movement, the rise of nuclear capacity, the success of nonviolent revolutions, and the liberal democratic revival are deep-rooted historical realities. Even as (with the exception of nonviolent revolution) they have created new dangers, they have laid down new foundations for a world that can move away from violence as the principal arbiter of its political affairs.

Shall we, then, return to the fray with a third round of Wilsonism? Shall we attempt once more to write a constitution for the whole world? We must answer in the negative. It would not make sense to apply twice-failed solutions to problems that no longer exist. The entrenched war system defeated Wilson, and it is perhaps the most important of our inestimable advantages that we do not face this monster. Its fall has opened up new avenues for action. No longer is it necessary, as it was in his time, to put in place a global system of law as a *precondition* for dismantling the structures of force. The two tasks can proceed along separate tracks, each at its own pace. No longer do we face the impossible task of uprooting the war system in its entirety or leaving it in place. The all-or-nothing dilemma has dissolved. Seeing, just as Wilson did, that by continuing to rely on systems of violence we condemn ourselves to catastrophe and horror, we can adopt his radical goal of creating a peaceful world while remaining at liberty to carry it out step by step. We can borrow a leaf from the Eastern Europeans. Rejecting a choice between accommodation and violent, all-or-nothing revolution, they decided upon the incremental pursuit of revolutionary ends by peaceful, reformist means. Acting on the basis of common principles yet without any blueprint—"in cooperation without unification," in the phrase of the French sociologist Pierre Bourdieu—they pooled the variegated forces of society to achieve a radical renewal of their lives that in the end accomplished everything that was necessary. A revolution against violence in the world at large today would, in imitation of this process, not be the realization of any single plan drawn up by any one person or council but would develop, like open software, as the common creation of any and all comers, acting at every political level, within as well as outside government, on the basis of common principles.

One day, humankind may organize itself into a true body politic. Perhaps this will be some remote variation on the United Nations, whose hand now lies so lightly on the world; perhaps it will be some new organizational form. That day had not come in Wilson's time. It has not come in ours. Even as an ideal, the structure of a global body politic remains uninvented. Such a novel object is unlikely to take a familiar form. The need for global political structures to deal with the globalized economy and the swiftly deteriorating global environment is manifest. Yet it would be premature, for instance, to suppose that they should constitute a "world government" or a "world state." The words "state" and "government" carry too much unwanted baggage from the past. Why should an organization whose purpose and surrounding context would be so different from those of national governments repeat their structures? (The federal tradition is the most promising one perhaps, but no existing federation provides a model.) Nation-states, for example, have been in a condition of unceasing rivalry and conflict with one another and this condition has shaped basic elements of their anatomies. A global body politic, by contrast, would exist alone on earth—a circumstance that must have the profoundest consequences for its character, if only because of the blood-chilling possibility that, if it were endowed with any-thing like the powers to which existing states are accustomed, it might become repressive, leaving no corner of the earth free. There is a raw freedom in the plurality of states that the world should not surrender easily, or without the firmest confidence that a more civilized freedom can be defended and maintained.

In our new circumstances, the starting point of a world poli-tics based in cooperative power would be not a blueprint for an ideal system of law but the reality that has already emerged on the ground. It is a reality for which there is as yet no adequate name. The word, when it appears, will refer to the power of ac-tion without violence, whether in revolution, the civil state, or the international order. I have followed convention in referring to this thing as nonviolence, but the word is highly imperfect for its purpose. "Nonviolence" is a word of negative construction, as if the most important thing that could be said about nonviolent action was that it was *not* something else. Yet that which it negates—violence—is already negative, a subtractor from life. A double negative, in mathematics, gives a positive result. And in fact the thing itself—nonviolence—is entirely positive, as Gandhi said. Yet in English there is no positive word for it. It's as if we were obliged to refer to action as "non-inaction," to hope as "non-hopelessness," or to faith as "non-unbelief." It was in search of a solution to this problem that Gandhi coined his untranslatable "satyagraha." Havel spoke, only somewhat less mysteriously, of "living in truth." Arendt sought to wrest the word "power" from its normal usage and turn it to this end. John Adams and Thomas Jefferson—who differed about many things—spoke of the power of citizens that flowed from the disposition of their hearts and minds, and recognized that such action was the foundation of all systems of political freedom. I have resorted in these pages to the plain phrase "cooperative power," as distinct from "coercive power."

The agenda of a program to build a cooperative world would be to choose and foster cooperative means at every level of political life. At the street level, this would mean choosing satyagraha over violent insurrection—the sit-down or general strike or "social work" over the suicide bombing or the attack on the local broadcasting station. At the level of the state it would mean choosing democracy over authoritarianism or totalitarianism (although some, such as Jefferson, Arendt, and Gandhi, have hoped for the invention of a political system that would provide more participation for citizens than representative democracy does); at the level of international affairs, it would mean choosing negotiation, treaties, and other agreements and institutions over war and, in general, choosing a cooperative, multilateral international system over an imperial one; at the level of biological survival, it would mean choosing nuclear disarmament over the balance of nuclear terror and proliferation. There is no reason to restrict the idea of cooperative power to individuals acting together. We can, to paraphrase Burke, just as well say, "freedom, when nations act in concert, is power." The choice at each level is never merely the rejection of violence; it is always at the same time the embrace of its cooperative equivalent.

Such a program of action, though lacking the explicit, technical coherence of a blueprint, would possess the inherent moral and practical coherence of any set of actions taken on the basis of common principles. History shows that violence incites more violence, without respect for national borders or the boundaries that supposedly divide foreign from domestic affairs. All forms of terror, from the suicide bombing in the pizza parlor to the torture in the basement to the globe-spanning balance of terror, foster one another. Nonviolence is likewise synergistic and contagious. For just as there is a logic of force, there is a logic of peace—a "cycle of nonviolence." Just as violent revolution creates the conditions for dictatorship, nonviolent revolution paves the way for democracy. Just as dictatorships incline toward war, democracies, if they can resist imperial temptations, incline toward peace with one another. Just as war is the natural environment for repression and dominance by the privileged few, peace is the natural environment for human rights and justice for the poor. Consider, for example, the ramifications of the peaceful rebellion against Soviet rule. It was met, as a violent revolution surely would not have been, with Gorbachev's nonviolent, reformist response, which led, however unintentionally, to the end of the Soviet regime, which in turn created the conditions for peace between the Cold War powers. And recall, by contrast, the outbreak of the First World War. It led to the rise of totalitarianism, which led to the Second World War, which led in turn to the advent of the Cold War and the species-threatening nuclear balance of terror. No one planned or could have foreseen these chains of consequences but they were as sure and real as anything anyone did plan.

A revolution against violence—loosely coordinated, multi-form, flexible, based on common principles and a common goal rather than on a common blueprint—would encompass a multitude of specific plans, including ones for disarmament, conventional as well as nuclear; democratization and human rights; advancement of international law; reform of the United Nations; local and regional peacekeeping and peacemaking; and social and ecological programs that form the indispensable content of a program of nonviolent change. To neglect the last of these would be to neglect the lesson that campaigns of non-cooperation are empty without constructive programs. Justice for the poor (victims of "structural violence") and rescue of the abused environment of the earth (victim of human violence done to the other living creatures) are indispensable goals. They are already served by a rich new array of nongovernmental organizations and movements, constituting the beginnings of an international civil society. They range from local protest and rebellion by the poor against their exploitation, through movements of protest in rich countries against undemocratic and anti-environmental trade agreements, through nongovernmental organizations, and philanthropic organizations, both secular and religious, dedicated to human rights, the alleviation of poverty, and other causes, to former statesmen still eager to be of public service in the cause of peace (the former Soviet president Mikhail Gorbachev, the former American president Jimmy Carter, and the former president of Costa Rica, Oscar Arias, are notable examples).

Of equal or greater importance is the feminist revolution, itself a part of the much broader democratic revolution of modern times. The public world has hitherto been run by males, and it is clear that, whatever their virtues and vices, their way of doing things has reached an impasse. Experts can dispute whether the unmistakable male proclivity for war is innate or learned, the product of nature or nurture, but one thing we cannot doubt is that historically organized violence has been bound up with the male way of being human—with men's needs, men's desires, and men's interests. It is no less clear that historically the pursuits of women have been more peaceful. Could it be that nature in her wisdom created two genders in order to have a "second sex" in reserve, so to speak, for just such an emergency as the one we now face? There may be a less violent way of doing things that is rooted in female tradition and now will move to the fore, together with the gender that created it.

Peace begins, someone has said, when the hungry are fed. It is equally true that feeding the hungry begins when peace comes. Global warming cannot be stopped by B-52s any more than nuclear proliferation can; only cooperation in the form of binding treaties can accomplish either task. Peace, social justice, and defense of the environment are a cooperative triad to pit against the coercive, imperial triad of war, economic exploitation, and environmental degradation. Lovers of freedom, lovers of social justice, disarmers, peacekeepers, civil disobeyers, democrats, civil-rights activists, and defenders of the environment are legions in a single multiform cause, and they will gain strength by knowing it, taking encouragement from it, and, when appropriate and opportune, pooling their efforts.

Among the innumerable possible specific plans that such a program could entail, I have picked four to discuss here—not because they are in any way comprehensive, or even, in every case, necessarily the most important ones that can be imagined, but because they all bear directly on the choice between cooperation and coercion, and seem to me to be timely, realistic, and illustrative of the unity in diversity that a broad choice in favor of cooperation would manifest. They are a worldwide treaty to abolish nuclear arms and other weapons of mass destruction; a program of international intervention to ameliorate, contain, or end wars of self-determination on the basis of a reformed conception of national sovereignty; enforcement of a prohibition against crimes against humanity; and the foundation of a democratic league to lend support to democracy worldwide as an underpinning of peace and to restrain existing democracies from betraying their principles in their foreign policies.

A DECISION TO EXIST

In Wilson's day, rejecting violence meant rejecting war—above all, world war. In our time, we must secure not only peace but survival. The menace of annihilation—of cities, of nations, of the species—arguably suppressed the menace of world war, and now we must suppress the menace of annihilation. A decision for nonviolence, in our time, is a decision to exist.

An agreement to abolish nuclear arms and all other weapons of mass destruction is the sine qua non of any sane or workable international system in the twenty-first century. Any other attempted settlement of the issue of weapons of mass destruction will clash with other efforts to bring peace, with common sense, and with elementary decency. No tolerable policy can be founded upon the permanent institutionalization of a capacity and intention to kill millions of innocent people. No humane international order can depend upon a threat to extinguish humanity. Abolition alone provides a sound basis for the continued deepening and spread of liberal democracy, whose founding principles are violated and affronted by the maintenance of nuclear terror: "a democracy based on terror" is, in the long run, a contradiction in terms. And abolition alone can, by ending the nuclear double standard, stop proliferation and make effective the existing bans on other weapons of mass destruction. The logic of abolition is the real alternative to the logic of empire.

In practice, abolition means that the eight or nine nations that now possess nuclear weapons must join the hundred and eighty-two that have renounced them under the terms of the Nuclear Nonproliferation Treaty. (The four nations—Israel, India, Pakistan, and Cuba—that have declined to join the treaty must do so.) The signatories may also wish to convert the treaty into a Nuclear Weapons Convention, which would take its place alongside the existing conventions banning biological weapons and chemical weapons. At that point, the signatories might wish to merge these three conventions into one, banning all weapons of mass destruction, including any that might be invented in the future. The step would be logical and practical, inasmuch as the means of inspection and enforcement would overlap considerably and would gain strength through coordination.

But won't the abolition of nuclear weapons undo one of the very building blocks of peace that I have named? If the ever-present danger of nuclear annihilation has paralyzed great-power war, won't great-power war spring to life once nuclear weapons are removed from the picture? The answer to the question lies at the root of the nuclear predicament. It is a profound misunderstanding of the nuclear age to suppose that its basic features emanate from nuclear hardware. They do not. They emanate, as we have seen, from the knowledge that underlies the hardware. The number of nuclear warheads in the world can fall and the number of fingers on the nuclear button can decrease, even to zero, without subtracting a single digit from the physical equations on which the bomb is based.

It is the spread of this knowledge throughout the world that guarantees that the war system can never operate on a global basis as it did before. The persistence of the knowledge—the inherent capacity to rebuild nuclear arsenals, or to produce other weapons of mass destruction—will stand in the way. Let us imagine that nuclear weapons have been abolished by treaty, and that a nation then violates it by, secretly or openly, building a nuclear arsenal and threatening to use it to bully the world. As soon as the threat has been made, scores of other nations, all nuclear-capable, would be free to build and threaten to use their own nuclear arsenals in response, in effect deterring the violator. Not global hot war but a reflation of cold war would be the result. A crude system of mutual assured destruction would be reestablished, and wider war would be deterred, just as it is in our world of large nuclear arsenals. The important point, as always in matters of deterrence, is not that this would necessarily be done (although the scenario has a credibility that many existing ones lack) but that any government would know in advance that such a response was available, and would have every reason to desist from reckless schemes in the first place. The threat would not constitute nuclear deterrence in the classic sense of threatening instant nuclear retaliation; yet it would still be a kind of deterrence.

Abolition, when seen in this cold light, cannot mean a return to the pre-nuclear age, whether one might wish for such a development or not, nor can it rule out once and for all a resurgence of nuclear armaments in some future dark age, whose coming no one can preclude. It does, however, mean that a return to the global adapt-or-die war system is impossible. Abolition, in view of these circumstances, which as far as we know are unchangeable, would be nothing more—or less—than an indispensable though insufficient recognition by the human species of the terrible, mortal predicament it has got itself into, and a concrete expression of its resolve to find a solution. Abolition should not be undersold but it should not be oversold either.

There is thus more continuity between a policy of nuclear abolition and nuclear deterrence than at first meets the eye. It is as if we were saying, Let us take the deterrence theorists at their word that the goal of deterrence has been to prevent war. Unfortunately, we have to note an obvious fact: if you seek to avoid doing something by threatening to do that same thing, you have, at least to some extent, undermined your own purpose. So let us begin to move to a policy in which the "not using"—called by some "the tradition of nonuse"—gradually predominates, and the "threatening to use" fades away. Abolition then would fulfill the promise that deterrence now makes but cannot keep.

If this happened, the deterrence policy of the Cold War years might appear in history in a more favorable light than is now likely. It might then be seen as a system that in effect *extracted* the violence of the war system of the twentieth century, compacted it into a single world-destroying device, and *shelved* it—declaring to all: "If you want to use violence, then you must use *all* of it, so be wise and use none of it. And, just to make sure that you take us seriously, we are actually going to build and deploy tens of thousands of thermonuclear warheads and place them on rockets on hair-trigger alert." If followed by abolition, this act of extraction and consolidation would be revealed in retrospect as having been a halfway house to the full transformation of the war system into a peace system.

In this sequence, nuclear deterrence replaces the war system with a threat-of-annihilation system; abolition then replaces the threat-of-annihilation system with a peace system—or, at least, with the necessary foundation for a peace system. For abolition would not in itself constitute anything like a full peace system; it would only mark the world's commitment to creating one. The alternative is that Cold War deterrence will prove to have been the training ground for the full nuclearization of international affairs—that is, for nuclear anarchy.

Even after abolition, a critical decision remains to be made: whether or not to continue to rely as a matter of policy on nuclear rearmament in the event that the abolition treaty is violated. The nuts and bolts of any abolition agreement would be highly detailed arrangements for suppressing certain technologies—all, of course, inspected to the hilt. The agreement would specify exactly which nuclear-bomb materials are permitted, in what quantities, and where. There will assuredly be an enforcement provision in any such treaty, specifying what it is that the menaced nations of the world are entitled or obliged to do in the event of the treaty's violation. If nuclear rearmament is specified as a response, and technical arrangements suitable for it are provided, then, to an extent, the world would still be relying on nuclear terror to counter nuclear terror. Such provisions would embody what I have called "weaponless deterrence" and the scholar Michael Mazarr has called "virtual nuclear arsenals." If, on the other hand, the treaty bans nuclear arms absolutely, and forbids nuclear rearmament even in the face of its violation, whose remedy is to be sought by other means, then the world would formally and finally have renounced all dependence on nuclear terror for its safety.

The distinction between abolition, which is achievable, and a return to the pre-nuclear age, which is not, is necessary at the very least in order to understand and appreciate the radical difference between Wilsonism, which proposed to replace war with law, and abolition, which more modestly proposes merely to ratify the abolition of great-power war already imposed by the nuclear age, and to improve on this situation by retiring nuclear terror, which never can be utterly purged from human life, as deep into the background as is humanly possible. In practice, it may well be that if abolition of the hardware takes place, this will be such a momentous event morally, politically, and legally that, once some time has passed, and the world has gained confidence in its new arrangement, the deeper renunciation of nuclear terror will not be a difficult step. It would be deceptive, however, to suggest that a world without nuclear arms would be a world without danger, or even without nuclear danger. The risks, including the risk of nuclear rearmament, would be real. It is, rather, by comparison with the nuclear anarchy or the vain attempts at imperial domination that will otherwise probably be our future that the goal is attractive.

The dangers of abolition stem from potential violators of an abolition agreement. Two concerns have been uppermost— that the agreement could not be adequately inspected and that it could not be adequately enforced. I will confine myself here to a comment on each.

If historical experience is the test, possession of a nuclear monopoly (which a nation would have if it violated an abolition agreement) is much less valuable than nuclear theory predicts. At first glance, it appears that a country possessing a nuclear monopoly would possess an insuperable advantage over any adversary; nuclear-deterrence theory, which teaches that nuclear arsenals can be offset only by other nuclear arsenals, takes this for granted. The matter has already been put to the test several times in the history of the nuclear age, however, and in no case has possession of a nuclear monopoly translated into the foreseen military or political advantage—or, for that matter, into any detectable advantage at all. Nuclear powers have repeatedly fought, and even lost, conventional wars against small, nonnuclear forces, without being able to extract any benefit from their "ultimate" weapons. In the Suez crisis of 1956, nuclear-armed Britain, allied with France and Israel, failed to attain any of its aims against nonnuclear Egypt. France likewise found no utility in its nuclear monopoly in its war against the independence movement in Algeria. Neither did the Americans in Vietnam, or the Soviet Union in its war in Afghanistan, or Israel in its wars in Lebanon and in the West Bank, or China in the border war it fought and lost with Vietnam in 1979. If the only examples were the English, French, American, and Israeli ones, we might wonder whether democracies are constrained from using nuclear bombs by scruples absent in totalitarian regimes. The presence of the Soviet Union and China on the list, however, suggests that other factors are at work. (It's also worth recalling in this connection that the only country ever to use nuclear weapons was a democracy, the United States.)

The question of just why none of these powers used nuclear weapons in these losing wars is not easy to answer. Nevertheless, I would like to suggest a possible reason. Isn't it conceivable that heads of state are reluctant to use nuclear weapons simply because they don't want to kill millions of innocent people in cold blood at a single stroke? This "self-deterrence" may be a more powerful force than theorists have allowed. The moments in which the use of nuclear arms has in fact been seriously threatened have mostly been times when, as in the Cuban missile crisis, two nuclear-armed adversaries were in collision. One-sided threats of use—after the actual use on Hiroshima and Nagasaki—are conspicuous by their rarity. If these reflections have any foundation, then theory has libeled history, and the one clean secret of the nuclear age may be a hidden minimal sanity or humanity in the heads of state who have presided over nuclear arsenals.

However that may be, the relevance to the abolition question of this history is that if six powers, both democratic and totalitarian, in possession of nuclear monopolies, lost six conventional or guerrilla wars against small forces without nuclear arms, then we can hardly suppose that the entire family of nations, having recently staked its security on a nuclear abolition treaty, would stand helpless before a single miscreant regime that, having manufactured a concealed arsenal, stepped forward to give orders to the world. Since a prospective cheater would know that other nations would be fully capable of nuclear rearmament, violation of an abolition agreement could never be a rational plan. Indeed, a policy of one nation bellowing nuclear destruction to the whole world would be plain insanity. To this we can add that if it were done anyway, the world would possess more than adequate means to respond. It is unimaginable that a cowering world would knuckle under to the demands of the cheater. Far more likely, it would react with determination to quell the threat or, at the least, quickly reestablish a balance of terror.

The effectiveness of enforcement is linked to the effectiveness of verification. Verification would include the right of peremptory, unannounced inspection of all suspect facilities. One widely accepted conclusion among experts is that although the discovery of secret facilities for the construction of new nuclear arsenals, which are necessarily extensive, would be comparatively easy under a maximal regime of inspection, the discovery of caches of weapons hidden away before the agreement came into effect—of "bombs in the basement"—would be difficult. Some experts have even suggested that this problem is the fatal flaw in any plan of nuclear abolition. A nontechnical consideration, however, offers reassurance. Any nuclear arsenal, even a hidden one, must not only be maintained and guarded by a large cadre but also supervised by a military and political chain of command leading from the lowest technician up to the head of state. The United States' expenditure of four and a half billion dollars a year on "stockpile stewardship" shows that maintenance of a nuclear arsenal is highly complicated, requiring many hands and minds. There must also be delivery vehicles, plans for mating the warheads to the delivery vehicles, strategies, military and political, for using the weapons, and strategists to draw up the plans. Moreover, changes of regime, whether by violent or peaceful means, will multiply at a stroke the numbers of people privy to the secret. Many of those leaving office, often unwillingly, may be ill-disposed toward those replacing them and inclined to tell what they know; or else the newcomers may disagree with their predecessors' secret treaty violation and fear the wrath of the world. Few undertakings have ever been more secret than the Manhattan Project, yet some of its most highly classified information leaked in profusion to Stalin's spies.

In sum, it is in the nature of things that, over time, a growing body of people will share the secret of a hidden arsenal, and any one of them can reveal its existence to the world. With every year that passes, this body will grow. As in proliferation, the irresistible tendency of knowledge to spread shows itself—in this case to the advantage of disarmament. Time is the friend of inspection and thus of an abolition agreement. In the long run, the secret of a hidden arsenal would be as hard to keep as the secret of the bomb itself.

Like a nuclear monopoly, the bomb in the basement looks much more dangerous in theory than in the context of politics and history. In both circumstances, the natural repugnance that human beings have for nuclear weapons may have real-world consequences unforeseen in the denatured calculations of nuclear strategists—in the first case, inspiring among statesmen who wield monopolies an unexpected reluctance even to consider using their supposed advantage, in the second inspiring whistle-blowers to reveal activities that, under the terms of an abolition agreement, would be named and understood by all to be crimes against humanity.

ALL-OR-NOTHING AGAIN?

Haven't I, though, simply reintroduced the fatal, all-or-nothing Wilsonian dilemma by insisting on the abolition of nuclear weapons rather than, say, their reduction to lower levels, or their reconfiguration in a more stable mode? Could it be that, by demanding abolition, we would be condemning ourselves to the same collapse of an overambitious plan that Wilson suffered? Admittedly, the proposal is ambitious. Yet nuclear abolitionism differs from Wilsonism in critical respects. The war system of Wilson's time was a workable and working machine, tightly integrated into the decision making of global politics, and so able to serve as the "pursuit of politics by other means." This cannot be said of the system of nuclear deterrence that supplanted it. After Nagasaki, no one has figured out how to gain political advantage from using, or even from possessing, nuclear weapons. The nuclear system is far more dangerous and far less useful than the war system was. As such, it should be much easier to clear out of the way.

Another difference is that nuclear arsenals, unlike the old war system, can be eliminated step by step. The first steps have in fact already been taken through arms control agreements. It is the unequivocal commitment to the goal, accompanied by unmistakable steps to achieve it, and not the rapidity of its achievement, that is most important. To be more precise, the period of implementation must be short enough to persuade potential nuclear proliferators that to build a new arsenal would be a worthless and dangerous expense, while being long enough to inspire confidence among the nuclear powers that inspection and enforcement are adequate.

Notwithstanding the absolutist ring of the word, abolition is not "all," even in the context of the nuclear predicament. Thanks to the indelible character of nuclear scientific know-how, the "all" in this matter, however ardently we might desire it, has been moved beyond our reach forever. All we can do in the circumstance is set ourselves against the evil day with the full force of our concerted political will.

It's in the context of a cooperative approach to nuclear nonproliferation that the logic of a cooperative approach to terrorism, nuclear or otherwise, is best understood. Like war, terrorism must now be divided into two categories. Just as we distinguish between conventional war and unconventional war (meaning war with weapons of mass destruction), so we must distinguish between conventional terrorism, using ordinary explosives, and unconventional terrorism, using weapons of mass destruction. Unconventional terrorism—the problem of the small group that wields immense destructive power because it has got hold of one of these weapons—can be addressed only by gaining control over the technology involved. After all, not even the most successful war on terrorism imaginable can reduce the population of terrorists to zero. The rigorous global inspection system of an abolition agreement would be the ideal instrument to choke at its source the danger that terrorists will acquire weapons of mass destruction. Even if such a system were in place, it must be admitted, the problem would not be completely solved. It might still be possible for a group to clandestinely create the needed technology. But the problem might be 98 percent solved, which is perhaps the most that can be hoped for. At each step along the path, the danger of diversion or construction of weapons of mass destruction would decline.

The hope of combating stateless global terrorism of the kind represented by the Al Qaeda network (which must be distinguished from the innumerable local varieties of terrorism around the world) likewise appears destined for disappointment without the creation of cooperative international structures involving the great majority of nations. A global threat requires a global response, and a global response will be possible only if governments work together rather than against one another. Historically, the greatest successes in reducing terrorism have been accomplished by a combination of police action and political attention to underlying causes. There is no reason to suppose that a global version of these largely national efforts would be different.

It is difficult to imagine the United States, acting alone or together with just a few nations, will be able to coerce or overthrow every regime that "supports" terrorism or, for that matter, defeat or destroy every proliferator of weapons of mass destruction. The cooperation of governments, not their antagonism, is the indispensable precondition for a successful policy of opposing and reducing global terrorism of any kind. A cooperative policy alone likewise avoids the danger, posed by the imperial approach, that hostile action, in the Middle East or elsewhere, will widen the pool of recruits for terrorist groups. At the same time, it is the likeliest basis for the political efforts that, over the long run, are the only lasting solution to terrorist threats.

DELAMINATING SOVEREIGNTY

Sovereignty, the conceptual crystallization of the all-or-nothing trap, is, as its first intellectual exegete Jean Bodin knew so well, a bundle of powers forced together under the pressure of military necessity or ambition. That was why at the birth of the concept of sovereignty its two inseparable defining principles were complete reliance upon the sword and indivisibility. That, too, was why, in the later, popular incarnations of sovereignty, the people, their territory, and the land had to be congruent, excluding all overlaps, mixed national populations, collective rights, or divided authorities. Yet long experience with popular government, in the United States and elsewhere, has revealed that when power is cooperative rather than coercive—based on action willingly concerted rather than compelled—then, in the domestic sphere, at least, it does not have to be indivisible. It can be federated; it can be divided among branches of government and localities; it can be delaminated.

It was not clear, on the other hand, whether such division could occur in the international sphere. Certainly, division was out of the question as long as the global adapt-or-die war machine subjected nations to its crushing pressure. However, now that that machine has been paralyzed and the pressure lifted, we can ask the question again. And in fact there are already signs of change. In regions in which coercive power, sovereign and indivisible, has yielded, structures of cooperative power, limited and divisible, have flourished. The most striking example is the European Union. Let us recall that sovereignty was first asserted in Europe by absolutist kings as a scythe to cut down the tangled thickets of medieval political institutions, with their dense, overlapping webs of ecclesiastical as well as secular rights, privileges, and duties. Although sovereignty is now defended as the guarantor of the plurality of states, originally it was diversity's enemy. It was the instrument of a radical simplification of politics, reducing the array of political actors to subjects on the one side and a sovereign on the other. The development of the European Union, however, shows that democratic states at peace with one another are now free to create a rich variety of hybrid arrangements, most of them unimaginable under the terms of the choice between a Wilsonian global constitution and the old war system. The E.U., as the former chancellor of Germany Helmut Schmidt has commented, "marks the first time in the history of mankind that nation-states that differ so much from each other neverthe-less . . . have *voluntarily* decided to throw in their lot together."

The result has not been a simplification of politics. The union's economic and political institutions, which inch forward year by year, are already characterized by a complexity not far from the medieval. They defy analysis on the basis of such simple, clear principles of the recent past as sovereignty, whether of the people, the state, or anyone else.

Formulas for shared or limited sovereignty are also a necessary part of any solution to most wars of national self-determination, in so many of which the requirement of one state for one people on one territory has proved to be a recipe for nightmare. The most ingenious and promising solution is the on-and-off Good Friday accord of 1998, which may one day lead to a resolution of the conflict in Northern Ireland. In the European Union, the absence of conflict made structures of divided power possible; in Ireland, divided structures of power are being used to try to end a conflict—a more difficult challenge.

The Irish conflict, although possessing many singular local and historical features, nevertheless arose out of a dilemma of a kind shared by many other wars of national self-determination. Two neighboring peoples (in this case, the Irish and the English) have a long history of conflict (in this case going back at least four centuries). Between them is a disputed territory, on which their peoples are intermixed. (Northern Ireland, which remained under British rule after Irish independence in 1922, contains a narrow Protestant majority dedicated to preserving the union with Britain and a large Catholic minority of "nationalists" eager to join the Irish Free State.) Similar elements can be found in lands as diverse as Sri Lanka, Kashmir, Crete, Rwanda, several of the former Soviet republics, almost all the former Yugoslavian nations, and Palestine.

The two communities in Northern Ireland appeal to common principles—the right of self-determination and majority rule. The problem is that each has drawn the boundaries of the "self" that is to be "determined" differently. The Protestant unionists draw a line that encompasses Great Britain, then crosses the Irish Sea and runs around the borders of Northern Ireland. Within that circle, which describes an existing institutional reality, the majority is British and Protestant. The Catholic nationalists wish to draw a line that simply circumscribes the Irish island (including, of course, Northern Ireland). Within that circle, representing the dream of a unified Ireland, the majority would be Irish and Catholic. The two circles overlap in Northern Ireland. If the first circle is accepted as "the nation," then majority rule for now dictates that Northern Ireland will remain part of Great Britain; if the second circle is accepted, then Northern Ireland would join Ireland. The problem is the one that lies at the heart of the separation question: Which groups have the right to form themselves into a body politic, in which a vote of the majority binds the minority? This is the question to which liberal democratic thought, from the time of the American Revolution down to our day, has been unable to offer any answer. Indeed, two of its elementary principles, self-determination and majority rule, seem to be part of the problem. An answer can be found only by dividing the supposedly indivisible—by disaggregating the powers fused in national sovereignty. That is what the Good Friday accord does.

The immediate problem was the savage internecine warfare that broke out between nationalist and unionist extremists in Northern Ireland. The path to a solution could not be found in Northern Ireland alone. It lay, as John Hume, the leader of the nationalist Social Democratic and Labour Party, came to understand, also in London, Dublin, Brussels (home of the European Parliament), and even in Washington, where President Bill Clinton played a mediating role. First, the two outside state parties, the United Kingdom and the Irish Republic, had to surrender any claim to a right of sovereignty over Northern Ireland. The Irish Republic did so by amending its constitution, which had claimed sovereignty over the whole island. Great Britain, to which Northern Ireland now belonged, renounced any "selfish, economic" interest in the territory. That is, if Northern Ireland itself wanted to leave the United Kingdom, Great Britain would let it.

The remaining question was how, if the two outside claimants were ready to surrender their claim, the future national status of Northern Ireland was to be determined. The accord's answer was "the principle of consent": the people of Northern Ireland would decide their own future by democratic procedures. In the language of the accord, "It is hereby declared that Northern Ireland in its entirety remains part of the United Kingdom," unless, "voting in a poll," it decides to "form part of a united Ireland."

These provisions ended the tug-of-war between the United Kingdom and the Republic of Ireland for control over Northern Ireland but left intact the tug-of-war—the sanguinary terrorist conflict—between extremists in the two local communities, each longing for union with a different country. The Protestants, still in the majority (though a dwindling one, as the Catholic population is growing faster than the Protestant), would opt for continued union with the United Kingdom, and also might continue to use their majority power to abuse and repress the Catholic minority. Inasmuch as such repression had been a primary cause of the conflict in the first place, it could hardly be taken lightly.

The accord addressed that problem with several further provisions, among them a plan to include a due proportion of nationalists in the Northern Ireland police force and a plan for political power sharing between the two communities. One important feature of the latter was an agreement to apportion ministers of the government of Northern Ireland in accord with party strength in the assembly, rather than adopting a winner-take-all arrangement. This provision was a dramatic grant of exactly the sort of collective minority rights that classical liberal democratic theory was unable to approve. It ordained something that has always been a bête noire of classical liberalism—"concurrent majorities," in which overlapping communities each vote separately for their representatives, who then must share power. In the first government under the accord, half of the ministries went to the minority nationalists.

Still another provision established a North/South Ministerial Council to make decisions on matters of mutual concern, such as agriculture, inland waterways, trade, and tourism. Created by legislation passed both in the British Parliament and in the Irish Republic's Oireachtas, the council includes the Irish Taoiseach and First Minister of Northern Ireland as well as other ministers, and is to arrive at decisions "by agreement of the two sides." A Council of the Isles was also created to deal with matters involving all of Ireland and Britain.

The parties to the Good Friday accord did not set out to dismantle sovereignty, yet that is what the accord does. We will look in vain in this agreement for power that can be called sovereign. The people of Northern Ireland remain citizens of the United Kingdom, yet they have been granted a constitutional right that the citizens of few, if any, other nation-states enjoy—the right to remove themselves and their land and goods to another country upon a majority vote. (It is a right that the Muslims of Kashmir, the Tamils of Sri Lanka, and the Tibetans in China, to give three of many possible examples, would love to acquire.) They have a clear *right* to remain British but no *obligation* to do so. Such a right is, indeed, perhaps the most elementary collective right a people can possess, the right of self-determination, which is the essence of national sovereignty. And yet in Northern Ireland this right, which is in truth a power, is obviously conditioned and limited. It was created by decisions in the United Kingdom, and can be suspended by the United Kingdom, which can restore direct rule over Northern Ireland, as it has done several times in the past three decades. (However, if the people of Northern Ireland once were to exercise their right to join the Irish Republic, England's power to suspend the government would be at an end.) And although it permits the people of Ulster to define themselves politically by a vote, their options are limited. They are not permitted, for example, to establish themselves as an independent state.

As for the Irish Republic, it explicitly renounced its demand for sovereignty over Northern Ireland, yet thereby gained, through the Ministerial Council, more actual influence over the North than ever before. This arrangement has left traditional notions of sovereignty in the dust, clearing the path, as the peoples involved may decide, for all kinds of incremental, mixed institutions and arrangements for shared power that would be far richer and more nuanced than the bare choice between union with Great Britain and union with the Irish Republic. All the while, the Irish Republic can expect a day when Northern Ireland may of its own volition switch allegiance from the United Kingdom to Ireland by a mere majority vote.

At the same time that the United Kingdom was entering into this agreement, it was devolving new powers upon Scotland and Wales, in the most radical constitutional reforms in Britain of the twentieth century. When we consider that both innovations were occurring within the context of the steadily evolving constitutional arrangements of the European Union, we arrive at a picture of fundamental political transformation at every level of European politics, and grasp that national sovereignty is now in the process of giving way to new forms in the very Europe in which the concept was born.

The influence of the Good Friday accord, if it succeeds, may extend far beyond Europe. It would be the first peaceful settlement since the end of the Cold War of a war of national self-determination—the first squaring of the circle. The Irish protagonists admittedly enjoy advantages that the parties in other wars of national self-determination lack. Probably the most important is that all the governments involved—the Irish Republic's, the British, and Northern Ireland's—operate according to democratic principles. Alternatives to the gun—elections, parliamentary debates, free discussion—have always been available for use and have been used. For example, a gradual shift of the Irish Republican Army from violent struggle to electoral struggle has been one of the keys to progress brought by the agreement. In addition, the two governments in the dispute were willing to renounce their claims in favor of a decision by the people of the territory.

Such a combination of advantages is unavailable in almost any of the world's other many wars of national self-determination, in most of which either one or both of the warring parties is authoritarian or is unyielding in its territorial claim. (For example, India, though a democracy, has never been willing to let the people of Kashmir decide their future in a vote.) Nor would a success in Ireland have much value as a model in the lands of failed states, where the problems are more likely to be extreme poverty, lack of civil institutions, and underdevelopment than to be the excessive, murderous strength of political factions. There are parts of the world where neither violent nor nonviolent solutions offer ready answers, where patience is the better part of wisdom, and amelioration of the worst evils, such as famines, or merely heading off further catastrophic deterioration of a situation, may be the best that outside intervention can provide for the calculable future.

Nevertheless, the value of a successful Good Friday accord as a precedent for resolving wars of self-determination could be real, and the idea of delaminating sovereignty has already been proposed as a component of the settlement of other conflicts. In Sri Lanka, any solution to the conflict between the Tamil Tigers, who have been seeking an independent state in the north of the island, and the government that represents the Sinhalese majority will undoubtedly require some kind of power sharing. Some analysts have proposed that if the Israelis and the Palestinians ever return to a peace process, they may want to provide for dual sovereignty over the holy sites of Jerusalem, where not only national populations but religious buildings of high symbolic importance to several faiths are under contention. The Wailing Wall forms one side of a hill on which the Temple, the Jews' most holy site, once stood but on which the Al Aksa mosque, Islam's second-most holy site, now stands. One might suspect that a mischievous God, by permitting this interpenetration of holy objects, had decided to create, in the medium of architecture, a tangible symbol of the riddle of wars of national self-determination. The question He thus put before us was: How, when you cannot physically separate peoples (or their sacred buildings), can you organize the political world so that each people can be true to its deepest beliefs while living in peace with others? The tangible quandary of the holy sites poses an intangible riddle, which, in the words of the Israeli writer Avishai Margalit, is "How does one divide a symbol?" Precisely because a clash of faiths is involved in Jerusalem, which is a holy land for three religions, a settlement there one day would transcend the Good Friday accord in symbolic meaning.

DELAMINATING SELF-DETERMINATION

The possibility of addressing wars of self-determination by delaminating sovereignty could open wider horizons of international reform. The scholar of international law Gidon Gottlieb, for example, has outlined a provocative legal program of surgery upon sovereignty. It would be foolish, he recognizes, to suppose that theoretical breakthroughs can solve real conflicts with long histories. "How 'relevant' are mere ideas and concepts," Gottlieb asks, "when much blood has been shed and where enemies are locked in mortal combat? . . . The setting for peacemaking in ethnic wars is both grim and discouraging. Political efforts are invariably situated in the context of long and complex local histories of strife, of grievances, and of crimes well remembered. Layers upon layers of promises ignored, broken pledges, and treaties violated form the usual background to new promises, new pledges, and new treaties offered."

Yet new ideas have a role to play when they are based on new realities in the situations in question. Gottlieb proposes that the two basic components of sovereignty, the nation and the state, might in some circumstances be separated. The problem of mixed populations, he has suggested, might be easier to solve if the international community created, alongside states but separate from them, a juridical status for nations. The individual person would then have available two internationally recognized statuses—one as a citizen of a state, the other as a member of a nation. In this "deconstruction" of sovereignty, the old unity of state, people, and territory would be dissolved. Each of the two statuses would confer rights and privileges but not the same ones. State rights, for instance, might include all the classical rights of individual liberty, while national rights might include such collective rights as the right to speak one's own language, to control local schools, or to practice one's faith. Special passports to travel between the states that are hosts to one nation might be granted. One nation then could overlap many states, and vice versa.

Among other examples, Gottlieb cites the dilemma of the Kurdish people, now living under the sovereignty of Turkey, Iraq, Iran, and Syria, in all of which they are more or less embattled. The classic solution to the dilemma, establishment of a sovereign Kurdish state according to the traditional rules of self-determination, would solve the problem for the Kurds but at the certain cost of bloody upheaval in four states and the possible creation of the reverse problem of repression of Turks, Iraqis, Iranians, and Syrians within newly drawn Kurdish borders. Instead of heading down this road, something that seems exceedingly unlikely to happen in any case, Gottlieb proposes conferring his formal national status upon the Kurds, guaranteeing them certain cultural and other rights and privileges within the framework of each of the four states. He proposes similar solutions for the struggles of national self-determination in Cyprus, in Canada (over the status of Quebec), and in Armenia and Azerbaijan (over the contested Nagorno-Karabak and Nakhichevan enclaves).

Delaminating sovereignty entails delaminating self-determination, at least as this has traditionally been conceived. Self-determination, one might say, must yield to self-*determinations* and *selves*-determination—that is, to permission for more than one nation to find expression within the border of a single state and to permission for individuals and groups to claim multiple identities—for example, Kurdish and Turkish. As the story of American independence demonstrates, the connection between the concepts of sovereignty and self-determination, otherwise called independence, has been close. Reasoning about the nature of sovereignty compelled the colonists to conclude that the choice they faced belonged in the all-or-nothing category—either full independence or full subordination to Britain. It could not be otherwise in an age when sovereignty was regarded as the prime attribute of a body politic.

Yet even during the age of the colonial empires, some of the best minds cast sidelong glances at middle courses between empire and independence. We have already mentioned the plan that called for replacement of the British Empire by "an association of states endowed with British liberties, and owing allegiance directly to the sovereign head." Similar in character was the "Galloway plan," for a "colonial union under British Authority which included a legislative council made up of representatives from the colonial assemblies and a president general to be appointed by the king." For such plans to have succeeded, either the empire would have had to transform itself into a body based on consent, which is to say into a true federation, or the colony would have had to bow to force. Burke, one of the few Englishmen of his time ready to apply English principles of liberty and consent to the empire as a whole, was also one of the first to glimpse the full difficulty of the task, even in purely intellectual terms. "There is not a more difficult subject for the understanding of men," he commented in words that have held true down to this day, "than to govern a large Empire upon a plan of Freedom."

The difficult subject would arise many more times in the history of modern empires. The French-Algerian crisis of the 1960s inspired the novelist and thinker Albert Camus to tackle another incarnation of it. France had settled a large colony of its citizens—the *pieds-noirs*—in Algeria, whose native population began, in the 1950s, to agitate for independence. Camus, himself a *pied-noir*, devised a confederal plan, in which the fundamental character of the French state would change to incorporate Algeria. An Algerian regional assembly representing Algerian citizens and dealing with Algerian problems would be established under a unicameral federal Senate, which would preside over a Commonwealth consisting of France and Algeria, and elect a confederal government. It would mean, Camus explained, the end of the single nation-state born in 1789, and "the birth of a French federal structure" that would create a "true French Commonwealth." Camus understood, as Burke did, what a profound reconception of the state, called *une et indivisible* in the French Declaration of the Rights of Man and the Citizen, would be entailed in such a plan for a multinational state. "Contrary above all to the deep-rooted prejudices of the French Revolution, we should thus have sanctioned within the Republic two equal but distinct categories of citizens," Camus wrote. "From one point of view, this would mark a sort of revolution against the regime of centralization and abstract individualism resulting from 1789, which, in so many ways, now deserves to be called the *Ancien Régime*." Of particular note in our context is Camus's hope that the new structure might show the way for "the European institutions of the future."

As Jeffrey C. Isaac, a scholar of Camus and of Hannah Arendt, has pointed out, Arendt had been prompted to think along similar lines in the late 1940s in regard to the establishment of Israel. The problem, once again, was two nations—Palestinian and Jewish—on one soil. She, too, believed that the only peaceful solution to dilemmas of this kind was a confederal one. The alternative was imposition of Israeli rule on Arabs and Arab territory by force. "The 'victorious' Jews," she wrote, "would live surrounded by an entirely Arab population, secluded inside ever-threatened borders, absorbed with physical defense to a degree that would submerge all other interests and activities." The accuracy of this prediction does not mean that Arendt's solutions were feasible. (The fact that one solution fails doesn't mean the alternative would have worked.) What is certain is that the hour of the consensual multinational state had no more come in the Middle East in the late 1940s than it had come in England in the 1770s or France in the 1960s. Indivisible national sovereignty remained the rule, and force remained its guiding principle. Not until our day has that hopeful hour perhaps arrived for one or two regions of the world.

ENFORCEMENT

In a program whose overall object is to wean politics from its reliance on force, the question of *enforcement* is obviously vexatious. It's clear, however, that if the international community should ever embark on such a program, enforcement will be a necessary element. The question is what its scope, provenance, and limitations should be. At one extreme is the American imperial plan, which is almost all enforcement—the unilateral right of a single power to attack and overthrow other governments at will. At the other extreme is no enforcement. Somewhere in between is a vision of an international community that fundamentally relies on consent and the cooperative power consent creates, but nevertheless reserves the right to resort to force in certain well-defined, limited circumstances. A nuclear-abolition agreement, for example, would require enforcement in the event of a violation, as would a coordinated international effort to combat global terrorism. Ideally, force would play the restricted policing role it does in a democratic state. I say "ideally," because if an international police force is to be legitimate there must exist an international order whose legitimacy is generally recognized, and this is just what is largely missing in the world today.

In these circumstances—which not even the implementation of every proposal in this book would fundamentally alter, since they do not envision a world state, legitimate or otherwise—there could hardly be a police force acting in the name of such a body to enforce its laws. Yet, as we tackle this question, the advantage of our circumstances over Wilson's are again evident. Because of the war system's demise, we are not in any way required to establish an overwhelming international military force that could impose its will on all miscreants. For excellent reasons, this idea no longer even crosses most people's minds; the only plan remotely like it is the current fantasy of hegemony that tempts American policy makers. And so we are free in the area of enforcement, too, to proceed incrementally. To whatever

extent the international community decides to exist—and no
further—it can seek to enforce a few selected internationally
agreed-upon principles. Such an approach, it is true, would not
end war at one stroke, as the League of Nations was supposed
to do, but it would close the all-too-familiar demoralizing gap
between grandiose rhetoric and trifling deeds—a perennial
consequence of the bad faith of good intentions that was the
curse of attempts at international peacemaking in the twentieth
century.

The immediate need is for a principle defining a task that
is achievable, or may soon be achievable, by the international
community. One such principle has already been identified:
the obligation to prevent and punish crimes against humanity.
The concept of crimes against humanity first gained currency
at the trials at Nuremberg in 1945, in which the victors of
the Second World War held Nazi leaders accountable for the
atrocities of their regime. Recently, it has been applied again in
legal proceedings in special international tribunals against the
former president of Yugoslavia Slobodan Milosevic and against
the perpetrators of genocide against the Tutsis in Rwanda. The
newly constituted International Criminal Court (I.C.C.), making use of the language of the Nuremburg Charter, has defined
crimes against humanity as acts, including murder, torture,
rape, forced disappearance, and persecution, when committed
"as part of a widespread or systematic attack directed against
any civilian population . . ." The key distinction therefore is
between abuses of individuals, which are not crimes against humanity per se, and abuses that occur as part of an assault against
a defined group, whether ethnic, religious, racial, or national.

The most historically important of the crimes against humanity—specifically outlawed by the Convention on the Prevention
and Punishment of the Crime of Genocide, of 1948—is genocide, which may be roughly defined as an assault upon the life of
one of the earth's peoples. There has been debate over whether
the definition should include only ethnic, national, and racial
groups or social classes and political groups, too. If the more
expansive definition is accepted, then the definition of genocide
will be hard to distinguish from the I.C.C.'s definition of crimes
against humanity, and the two concepts would merge.

Why groups, however? Why should the international

community concern itself especially with collectivities rather than individuals as such? An obvious pragmatic reason is that if the international community accepted responsibility for enforcing individual human rights, it would in effect have to constitute itself as a world state. The justifications for collective international intervention would be unlimited, since there is no country on earth in which some human-rights abuses do not occur. There is also a legal reason. All positive law is the law of a community. Whereas each national community is a community of individuals, the international community has, so far, been mainly a community of states, whose sovereignty has been guaranteed by international law (including the U.N. Charter). It therefore makes sense that international law would be especially concerned with states and peoples. When one person kills another, the order of the national community is violated. When a state kills a people, the order of the international community is violated.

Laws mandating international action to set aside sovereignty in the name of stopping crimes against humanity would revise this understanding without throwing it out. The *state* would still be recognized as the prime international actor, but it would no longer necessarily be recognized in every case as the *nation's* legitimate representative. The international community (although not any single power) would assert a sharply limited and exceptional right to judge the fitness of a state to represent its people. Such a recognition would form a natural complement to the revisions of sovereignty needed to settle the wars of national self-determination. In most cases the claims of states, even of repressive states, to represent a nation would be recognized. But when a state perpetrated crimes against humanity upon its own population, it would forfeit its claim to represent them and open itself to international intervention. The right of states to rule in their own territories would cease to be absolute; rather, it would be like a license, valid in almost all circumstances but revocable in limited and extreme cases, to be defined by stringent and well-known principles.

In this shift, the rights of states would not be eliminated in favor of the rights of individuals, thereby opening the floodgates of unlimited intervention; rather, the rights of states would partially yield to the rights of nations—that is, of peoples—whose right of self-determination would remain untouched, and might at times be supported by intervention from without. When Slobodan Milosevic sought to forestall intervention against his genocidal campaign in Kosovo, he invoked sovereignty. In response, the international community could only argue circuitously that his crimes within his own borders were a "threat to peace." A simpler and stronger answer would have been, "In what sense can you call yourself the sovereign representative of a people that you are seeking to destroy? Your genocide nullifies your sovereignty."

Stopping crimes against humanity would be a new vocation for the international community, which has generally looked the other way when such crimes have occurred. Not until very recent times has the concept of collective rights made headway. An enforced prohibition of genocide, based on the conviction that the international community can no more tolerate the murder of one of its peoples than national communities can tolerate the murder of a person, would meet this welcome trend coming the other way. It would be a sheet anchor for the collective rights of peoples. (It is obvious, however, that enforcement even of this limited principle faces large obstacles. It is one thing, for example, to bring the former leader of a small, weak state, such as Serbia, to book for his crimes. It would be quite another to do the same to the leader of a large powerful state, such as Russia or the United States.)

Once established, collective rights might, over the long run, take their place as elements of a grand bargain, a new settlement of the rights, powers, and obligations of the individual, states, nations, and the international community. In such a settlement, the rights of peoples would be increasingly protected by a coherent body of law. Most important, peoples would possess the negative right not to be extinguished. They would possess in addition the positive right to self-determination. This right, while recognized in law, would be guaranteed chiefly by each people's own powers of resistance—powers whose effectiveness were put on such stunning display in the anti-imperial independence movements of the twentieth century—and only secondarily by limited collective assistance from the international community. The right would be understood as belonging, in the last analysis, to nations rather than to their governments.

On the other hand, even when thus properly located, it would not be absolute—not be, that is, sovereign.

A commitment to stop crimes against humanity is a natural corollary to a program that demands nuclear abolition, fosters democracy, and delaminates sovereignty. The required shift in principle would look beyond states to peoples, in whom the roots of political legitimacy would be acknowledged. The principle would also apply to the nuclear threat, whereby not only every people but the human species as a whole has been placed at risk of extinction. The doctrine of deterrence, which "assures" the safety of one people from nuclear attack at the hands of another by menacing both with annihilation, is —described without hyperbole—a policy of retaliatory genocide. Adoption of this policy was the destination to which the great powers, once they had failed to agree on the abolition of nuclear weapons in 1946, were to a certain extent helplessly driven by the logic of the war system in which they were entangled. Nevertheless, it is inescapable that carrying out genocide in the event of nuclear attack is the heart of the policy. One of the deepest and most important consequences of a prohibition of genocide would be a prohibition of the policy of nuclear deterrence.

A DEMOCRATIC LEAGUE

Even as the main structures of coercive power are gradually being retired from use, structures of cooperative power must gradually be built up. One of these would be the foundation of a democratic league, designed to foster and build upon the peaceful proclivities already found in the core of the democratic process. It is true that the power of democratic states to promote democracy outside their own borders is, by the nature of democracy, limited. States cannot create democracies; only peoples can, through their actions and consent. (On the other hand, states are perfectly capable of creating dictatorships, which rule by force over unconsenting peoples.) Nevertheless, democratic states can give assistance to one another or to peoples already seeking to found or preserve democracy. Such assistance would be strengthened by the foundation of an alliance made up of the democratic countries of the world.

The idea first appears in history in the fourth century B.C., when the Athenian statesman Arata, facing a threat to Greece from Philip of Macedon, who was making common cause with autocratic Greek city-states, founded an alliance of the democratic city-states. Whereas Arata's ultimate objective was to win a war, the purpose today would be to preserve and strengthen democracy where it exists, to give it support where it is struggling to come into existence, and, most important, to jointly curb and correct the warlike and imperial tendencies that historically have accompanied the rise of this form of government and forestalled its potential contributions to peace. Such was precisely the purpose of Kant's proposal of a "peaceful union" of republics, which would "gradually spread further and further by a series of alliances."

The main alliances in which the democracies now are involved present an anomalous picture. They are founded on every possible principle but democracy itself. The Clinton administration participated in the establishment of a Community of Democracies devoted to some of these purposes, but, though it now counts 110 nations among its members, it has yet to become a major forum for foreign policy decisions or international policy. NATO is an alliance made up entirely of democracies, but its purpose is strictly military. The central obligation of the treaty—to come to the defense of any member who is attacked—depends in no way on the character of the regimes involved. In the absence of the Soviet Union, whose advance into the center of Europe at the end of the Second World War prompted the alliance's creation, the need even for this pledge of mutual assistance is unclear. The only war in NATO's history—the campaign to drive Serbian forces out of Kosovo—did not involve an attack on a member.

The European Union is another alliance made up of democracies. (It was not until 2001 that the Organization of American States adopted a "democratic charter.") Founded originally to foreclose a military danger—recurrence of war among the nations of Europe—it has evolved over the decades into an organization in which economic concerns predominate. Recently, the European nations have been asking themselves what political and military functions the union might also assume. Although the union has led to many remarkable and hopeful political innovations, including the European Parliament, the European Commission, and the European Court of Human Rights, its boldest initiatives, culminating in the launch of the euro, have so far been commercial. In consequence, when the time came for the West to embrace the newborn democracies in Eastern Europe in the wake of the Soviet collapse, the chief consideration was not the strength of their commitment to democracy but the weakness of their economies. Blocked by this economic hurdle from "joining Europe"—a phrase often used in the broad sense of joining the now-democratic system of the West through joining the E.U.—Poland, Hungary, and the Czech Republic took the easier step of joining NATO. Had a democratic league existed at the time, it would have provided all the Eastern European countries with a way to "join Europe" that was appropriate to the new situation (the end of Soviet rule and the foundation of democracy); that was possible (no economic hurdle would have stood in the way); and that was inoffensive to Russia. Not until 2002 was the decision to invite these countries into the E.U. finally made. A democratic league would also serve to bind the Atlantic community by a tie that really should continue to bind it; namely, a commitment to freedom. The military glue that binds NATO is weakening in the absence of an enemy; and the economic glue of the E.U., although strong, tends in many areas to divide the Europeans from other democracies in the world. A democratic league, on the other hand, would possess a clear, positive, common purpose that NATO lacks—adherence, irrespective of wealth or geographic boundaries, to democracy.

The qualifications for joining the league would of course be observance of exacting standards of democratic governance and human rights. No state that failed to meet the standards could join; any state that departed from them would be subject to sanctions or expulsion. The league's requirements would give expression to the strong interest that every democratic country has in the preservation of democracy elsewhere in the world. The democratic character of all the states involved would also make supranational institutions among them far easier to establish than they are at the United Nations, where dictatorships have equal voice with democracies in votes on human rights. Juridical and legislative institutions of restricted scope could be added to executive ones. The European Convention on Human Rights, which established the European Court of Human Rights, and gives that court jurisdiction over human-rights violations within member states, could be a model—as could the European Parliament, whose members are directly elected, giving limited expression to an all-European public opinion.

The simplest and most obvious direct contribution that such a league could make to international peace would be to pledge to resolve disputes among its members without recourse to war, thus formalizing the historically demonstrated inclination of democracies to remain at peace among themselves. A vow by democratic Finland not to attack democratic India and vice versa would perhaps not be the end of history, yet the creation of a large body of nations in all parts of the earth that, both formally and actually, had renounced war in their mutual relations would provide a powerful example and, over time, perhaps a direction for the world as a whole.

Natural corollaries would be a commitment by the league to support the elimination of weapons of mass destruction, to steadily reduce the sale of conventional arms to other countries, and to devote its resources to restraining or ending wars of self-determination wherever it could.

Far more important and difficult would be a commitment to checking the aggressive tendencies that, in modern as in ancient times, have constituted the brutal, exploitive side of many democracies' relations with the rest of the world. The most serious and lasting contribution of a democratic league would be to choose democracy over imperialism once and for all. In order to be worthy of the name, a democratic league must be an anti-imperial league. Member nations would jointly resolve not to create or support repressive regimes, not to use armed force merely to advance commercial or other national interests, and in general to address international problems on a cooperative basis. A democratic league that sought to keep the peace among its own members even as it fostered aggressive ambitions in the world would destroy its own purpose.

Merely to state such goals, however, is once again to throw into distressing relief the policies of the one democracy in the world that today threatens to make the fearful transition from republic to empire, the United States. It is hard to know which is the greater tragedy—that, as the twenty-first century begins, the United States approaches the world with a drawn imperial sword, or that it discredits and disables its rich and in many ways unique republican traditions, which, especially in their treatment of sovereignty, offer many useful starting points for the new forms of international cooperation, peacemaking, and peacekeeping that the world so badly needs.

THE UNCONQUERABLE WORLD

Fifty-eight years after Hiroshima, the world has to decide whether to continue on the path of cataclysmic violence charted in the twentieth century and now resumed in the twenty-first or whether to embark on a new, cooperative political path. It is a decision composed of innumerable smaller decisions guided by a common theme, which is weaning politics off violence. Some of the needful decisions are already clear; others will present themselves along the way. The steps just outlined are among the most obvious.

I have chosen them not merely because their enactment would be desirable. They represent an attempt to respond to the perils and dangers of this era as it really is, by building on foundations that already exist. For even as nuclear arms and the other weapons of mass destruction have already produced the bankruptcy of violence in its own house, political events both earthshaking and minute have revealed the existence of a force that can substitute for violence throughout the political realm. The cooperative power of nonviolent action is new, yet its roots go deep into history, and it is now tightly woven, as I hope I have shown in these pages, into the life of the world. It has already altered basic realities that everyone must work with, including the nature of sovereignty, force, and political power. In the century ahead it can be our bulwark and shield against the still unmastered peril of total violence.

In our age of sustained democratic revolution, the power that governments inspire through fear remains under constant challenge by the power that flows from people's freedom to act in behalf of their interests and beliefs. Whether one calls this power cooperative power or something else, it has, with the steady widening and deepening of the democratic spirit, over and over bent great powers to its will. Its point of origin is the heart and mind of each ordinary person. It can flare up suddenly and mightily but gutter out with equal speed, unless it is channeled and controlled by acts of restraint. It is generated by social work as well as political activity. In the absence of popular participation, it simply disappears. Its chief instrument is direct action, both noncooperative and constructive, but it is also the wellspring of the people's will in democratic nations. It is not an all-purpose "means" with which any "end" can be pursued. It cannot be "projected," for its strength declines in proportion to its distance from its source; it is a local plant, rooted in home soil. It is therefore mighty on the defensive, feeble on the offensive, and toxic to territorial empires, all of which, in our time, have died. It stands in the way of any future imperial scheme, American or other. This power can be spiritual in inspiration but doesn't have to be. Its watchwords are love and freedom, yet it is not just an ideal but a real force in the world. In revolution it is decisive. Allied with violence, it may accomplish immense things but then overthrow itself; tempered by restraint it can burn indefinitely, like a lamp whose wick is trimmed, with a steady flame. Under the name of the will of the people it has dissolved the foundations first of monarchy and aristocracy and then of totalitarianism; as opinion, it has stood in judgment over democratically elected governments; as rebellious hearts and minds, it has broken the strength of powers engaged in a superannuated imperialism; as love of country, it has fueled the universally successful movement for self-determination but, gone awry, has fueled ethnic and national war and totalitarian rule, which soon suffocate it, though only temporarily. It now must be brought to bear on the choice between survival and annihilation. It is power because it sets people in motion, and fixes before their eyes what they are ready to live and die for. It is dangerous for the same reason. Whether combined with violence, as in people's war, sustained by a constitution, as in democracy, or standing alone, as in satyagraha or living in truth, it is becoming the final arbiter of the public affairs of our time and the political bedrock of our unconquerable world.

Acknowledgments

This book was long in the making, and the list of those to whom I am indebted is long. I want to thank the John D. and Katharine T. MacArthur Foundation's Program on Global Security and Sustainability, the John Simon Guggenheim Foundation, the W. Alton Jones Foundation, and the Samuel Rubin Foundation for their support. The welcome stipend from the Lannan Literary Award for Nonfiction in 1999 was extremely helpful.

Since 1998, I have been the Harold Willens Peace Fellow at the Nation Institute, my indispensable professional home. I want especially to thank Hamilton Fish, the president of the Institute, who has been ingeniously and tirelessly resourceful in making it possible to work on the book and other projects having to do with nuclear disarmament, and Taya Grobow, who with infallible good cheer has kept my working life functional in this period. Elizabeth Macklin's editorial assistance was indispensable. I also wish to thank Matthew Maddy, Kabir Dandona, Jenny Stepp, and Marisa Katz for their long hours of careful research and fact-checking.

I am grateful to Strobe Talbott for holding a seminar at the Brookings Institution, which provided invaluable commentary on the manuscript, and to Paul Kahn who both read the manuscript and organized an equally helpful study session on it at the Yale Law School. I also wish to thank the Joan Shorenstein Center for the Press, Politics, and Public Policy and its wonderful staff, at the John F. Kennedy School of Government at Harvard University, where I was a fellow in the fall of 2002. A number of seminars, at the Center and elsewhere at the University, were sources of very helpful reactions and advice.

With superabundant generosity my friend Wallace Shawn provided detailed comments that became a turning point in the evolution of the book. Robert Del Tredici made wise and useful observations on a late draft. Jerome Kohn and Fred Leventhal made helpful suggestions regarding individual chapters. In the early years of writing the book, my conversations with Niccolo

Tucci were an inspiration, and his memory shines as a model of what the writing life should be.

My agent, Lynn Nesbit, guided the book expertly through innumerable tangles over many years. Sara Bershtel, of Metropolitan Books, has been steadfast in her support, in the face of unmerciful delays. Shara Kay skillfully and tactfully saw me and the book through the ins and outs of the publishing process.

My editor Tom Englehardt has become that rarest of treasures for a writer, a person whose opinions and reactions are as necessary as—going far beyond the call of duty—they are available.

I owe more than I can express to my wife, Elspeth, and my children, Matthew, Phoebe, and Thomas.

Notes

PAGE   INTRODUCTION: THE TOWERS AND THE WALL

373.18–19   *"As for success or":* Thucydides, *The History of the Peloponnesian War*, trans. Rex Warner (New York: Penguin, 1954), p. 116.

378.28   *"The submerged warrior":* John Keegan, *A History of Warfare* (New York: Knopf, 1993), p. 22.

379.2   *"Nothing which was being":* Hannah Arendt, *Imperialism* (New York: Harcourt, Brace & World, 1968), p. 147.

        I. THE RISE AND FALL OF THE WAR SYSTEM

387.16–17   *"War is a true":* Carl von Clausewitz, *On War*, eds. Michael Howard and Peter Paret (Princeton, N.J.: Princeton University Press, 1976), p. 87.

387.22   *"something pointless and":* Ibid., p. 605.

387.35   *"War is an act":* Ibid., p. 77.

388.3   *"The fact that slaughter":* Ibid., p. 260.

388.27–28   *"the loser's scale falls":* Clausewitz, *On War*, p. 604.

389.7–8   *"loss of moral force":* J. F. C. Fuller, *The Conduct of War* (New York: Da Capo Press, 1982), p. 246.

389.25   *"cannot be considered to":* Clausewitz, *On War*, p. 90.

390.7–8   *"Rain can prevent a":* Ibid., p. 120.

390.26   *"a force appeared that":* Ibid., p. 591.

390.33–34   *"slowly, like a faint":* Ibid., p. 589.

391.1   *"tendency toward the extreme":* Ibid., p. 589.

391.5   *"the great democratic revolution":* Alexis de Tocqueville, *Democracy in America*, ed. and trans. Henry Reeve (New York: Schocken Books, 1961), p. lxviii.

391.22–23   *"one fact [of] the":* José Ortega y Gasset, *The Revolt of the Masses* (New York: W. W. Norton, 1932), p. 11.

392.1   *"The various occurrences of":* Tocqueville, *Democracy in America*, p. lxxi.

392.24	*"From this moment on"*: Simon Schama, *Citizens* (New York: Knopf, 1989), p. 762.
392.38	*"War, untrammeled by"*: Clausewitz, *On War*, p. 592.
393.7	*Clausewitz has often been:* For example, the British military historian B. H. Liddell Hart charged in 1931 that Clausewitz "had proclaimed the sovereign virtues of the will to conquer, the unique value of the offensive school carried out with unlimited violence by a nation in arms and the power of military action to override everything."
393.25	*"It is, of course"*: Clausewitz, *On War*, p. 605.
394.21–22	*"Is war not just"*: Ibid., p. 605.
394.37	*"all proportion between"*: Ibid., p. 585.
395.2	*"Were [war] a complete"*: Ibid., p. 87.
395.11	*"the terrible battle-sword"*: Ibid., p. 606.
396.13	*"The natural solution soon"*: Ibid., p. 604.
396.18–19	*"no conflict need arise"*: Ibid., p. 607.
399.13–14	*"The Great Powers were"*: A. J. P. Taylor, *The Struggle for the Mastery of Europe* (New York: Oxford University Press, 1954), p. xxiv.
400.5	*"She [Russia] was beaten"*: Bruce D. Porter, *War and the Rise of the State* (New York: Free Press, 1994), p. 227.
401.15	*Charles Tilly, "War made"*: Ibid., p. xix.
401.19	*"must increase in size"*: Ibid., p. 59.
401.27–28	*"The benefits of [scientific]"*: Francis Bacon, *Novum Organum* (New York: Modern Library, 1930), p. 85.
402.20	*On the bridge of:* Lewis Mumford, *The Pentagon of Power* (New York: Harcourt, Brace, Jovanovich, 1964), p. 119.
402.37	*Tocqueville's word, "irresistible"*: Tocqueville's claim that the democratic revolution is "the most permanent tendency to be found in history" closely parallels Bacon's claim that scientific findings benefit "the whole race of men . . . through all time." When Tocqueville called the democratic revolution a "providential" fact, he was not making a theological point. He was reaching for the strongest possible metaphor to express the inexorability of the social phenomena he wished to describe. (His advice was that since you couldn't stop democracy, the wisest course was to guide and direct it as well as you could.)

403.18–19   *Brissot, who proclaimed:* Albert Mathiez, *The French Revolution* (New York: Knopf, 1928), p. 285.

403.29   *"Tacticians could never":* Jules Michelet, *The French Revolution,* trans. Charles Cooks (Chicago: University of Chicago Press, 1967), p. 328.

404.31   *"had no place for":* E. J. Hobsbawm, *Nations and Nationalism since 1780* (Cambridge: Cambridge University Press, 1990), p. 26.

405.2   *"I see in the":* Richard Cobden, *The Liberal Tradition,* eds. Alan Bullock and Maurice Shock (New York: Oxford University Press, 1956), p. 53.

405.7–8   *Emerson declared that "trade":* Liah Greenfeld, *Nationalism* (Cambridge, Mass.: Harvard University Press, 1992), p. 448.

406.7   *Between 1870 and 1900:* Walter La Feber, *The American Search for Opportunity 1865–1913* (Cambridge: Cambridge University Press, 1993), p. 85.

406.25–26   *As late as 1890:* Ronald Robinson and John Gallagher, *Africa and the Victorians* (New York: Anchor, 1968), p. 78.

407.9   *Lord Curzon spoke for:* Kenneth Rose, *Superior Person* (New York: Weybright & Talley, 1969), p. 229.

407.16   *Lord Haldane, describing his:* Barbara Tuchman, *The Guns of August* (New York: Dell, 1963), p. 72.

408.19   *An expedition of:* David Levering Lewis, *The Race to Fashoda* (New York: Weidenfeld & Nicolson, 1987), p. 3.

409.5   *Queen Victoria, ordinarily:* Thomas Pakenham, *The Scramble for Africa* (New York: Avon, 1991), p. 552.

409.10   *France, lacking comparable naval:* Ibid., p. 549.

409.32   *In a state paper:* George F. Kennan, *The Fateful Alliance* (New York: Pantheon, 1984), p. 268.

410.1   *Therefore, once war had:* Ibid., p. 264.

410.5   *War against "all neighbors":* Ibid., p. 265.

410.12–13   *The Russian foreign minister:* Ibid., p. 105.

410.16   *And when General:* Ibid., p. 95.

410.27   *The war that now:* Ibid., p. 253.

411.7   *"The war's political objects":* John Keegan, *A History of Warfare* (New York: Knopf, 1993), p. 21.

411.31   *"of forgetting that force":* Kennan, *Fateful Alliance,* p. 254.

413.8   *"Through a blur of":* J. B. S. Haldane, as quoted in Freeman Dyson, *Weapons and Hope* (New York: Harper & Row, 1984), p. 122.

2. "Nuclear War"

415.14   *As early as 1952:* McGeorge Bundy, *Danger and Survival* (New York: Random House, 1988), p. 235.

415.16   *At the height of:* Michael Beschloss, *The Crisis Years* (New York: HarperCollins, 1991), p. 87.

418.35–36   *He wrote, "Thus far":* Jonathan Schell, *The Abolition* (New York: Knopf, 1984), p. 42.

419.18   *"The decision by arms":* Carl von Clausewitz, *On War*, eds. Michael Howard and Peter Paret (Princeton, N.J.: Princeton University Press, 1976), p. 97.

420.11   *"The essence of the":* Lawrence Freedman, *The Evolution of Nuclear Strategy* (London: Macmillan, 1981), pp. 397–99.

421.3   *stated, "We will not":* Aleksandr Fursenko and Timothy Naftali, *One Hell of a Gamble* (New York: W. W. Norton, 1997), p. 246.

421.22–23   *In 1960, for example:* Beschloss, *Crisis Years*, p. 65.

421.33   *In August of 1961:* Fursenko and Naftali, *Hell of a Gamble*, p. 138.

421.40   *On one occasion:* Beschloss, *Crisis Years*, p. 244.

422.7   *In a speech delivered:* Ibid., p. 330.

423.13   *He was led to:* Ibid., p. 523.

423.37–38   *Acheson counseled that:* Bundy, *Danger and Survival*, p. 375.

424.4–5   *"The most ardent and":* Ibid., p. 376.

424.28   *But, Kennedy explained:* Ibid., p. 452.

425.36   *We may suspect that:* Beschloss, *Crisis Years*, p. 446.

426.15–16   *When the Soviet ambassador:* Ibid., p. 547.

427.24   *McNamara answered, "I am":* Bundy, *Danger and Survival*, p. 448.

3. People's War

431.29   *Their philosophy in the:* John A. Hobson, *Imperialism* (Ann Arbor: University of Michigan Press, Ann Arbor Paperbacks, 1971), p. 123.

431.38   *Or, as Kipling:* Richard Koebner and Helmut Dan Schmidt, *Imperialism* (Cambridge and London: Cambridge University Press, 1964), p. 216.

434.13   *The rebellion blazed most:* J. Christopher Herold, *The Age of Napoleon* (Boston: Houghton Mifflin, 1963), p. 217.

434.15–16   *"No supreme command had":* Ibid., p. 218.

434.37   *"Clearly, the tremendous":* Carl von Clausewitz, *On War*, eds. Michael Howard and Peter Paret (Princeton, N.J.: Princeton University Press, 1976), p. 609.

435.3   *"The military art on":* Ibid., p. 610.

435.13   *"It follows that the":* Ibid.

435.39–436.1 *The renowned military writer:* Walter Laqueur, *Guerrilla* (New York: Little, Brown, 1976), p. 109.

436.8   *The experience left Jomini:* Ibid., p. 109.

436.24   *"All action is undertaken":* Clausewitz, *On War*, p. 97.

436.26   *Yet a French captain:* Robert B. Asprey, *War in the Shadows* (New York: William Morrow, 1994), p. 97.

436.30   *"a book of wisdom":* Ibid., p. 87.

436.36   *The Spanish guerrilla leader:* Laqueur, *Guerrilla*, p. 40.

436.40   *And a Prussian officer:* Ibid., p. 40.

437.9   *The superior importance:* Harry B. Summers, *On Strategy* (San Francisco, Calif.: Presidio Press, 1982), p. 89.

437.31   *"the days of guerrilla wars":* Laqueur, *Guerrilla*, p. 98.

438.23   *"in no other period":* Leonard Woolf, *Imperialism and Civilization* (New York: Garland Publishing, 1971), p. 12.

440.17   *"Suddenly the whole black":* Winston Churchill, *The River War* (London: New English Library, 1973), pp. 249–50.

440.34   *"about twenty shells":* Ibid., p. 263.

441.4   *"The range was short":* Ibid., p. 268.

441.11   *"They fired steadily and":* Ibid., p. 264.

441.25   *When it was over:* Karl de Schweinitz, Jr., *The Rise and Fall of British India* (London: Methuen, 1983), p. 242.

441.28–29   *"extraordinary miscalculation of":* Churchill, *The River War*, p. 264.

441.32   *"For I hope":* Winston S. Churchill, *The River War: An Historical Account of the Reconquest of Soudan* (London: Longmans, Green & Co., 1899), p. 162.

442.9–10   *In the battle of:* C. E. Carrington, *The British Overseas* (Cambridge: Cambridge University Press, 1968), p. 319.

442.11   *At the battle:* Ibid., p. 165.

442.14   *In 1865, in Tashkent:* V. G. Kiernan, *From Conquest to Collapse* (New York: Pantheon, 1982), p. 63.

442.16–17   *"a Royal Niger Co.":* Daniel R. Headrick, *The Tools of Empire* (Oxford: Oxford University Press, 1981), p. 8.

442.22–23   *"The remnant simply turned":* Kiernan, *Conquest to Collapse*, p. 71.

443.17   *"We are still":* Mao Zedong, *Selected Works*, 2 vols. (London: Lawrence & Wishart, 1954), 2: 168.

443.20   *"a powerful imperialist country":* Ibid., 2: 167.

443.36–37   *Mao never tired of:* Asprey, *War in the Shadows*, p. 255.

444.4   *And the most famous:* Ibid.

445.37   *"the more enduring the":* Mao, *Selected Works*, 2: 177.

446.1–2   *"the whole party must":* Ibid., 2: 270.

446.14   *"It can therefore":* Ibid., 2: 20.

447.13   *"China's weapons are":* Ibid., 2: 159.

447.27   *Mao rejected the idea:* Asprey, *War in the Shadows*, p. 254.

449.28   *"Politics forms the":* quoted in Jonathan Schell, *The Real War* (New York: Pantheon, 1988), p. 16.

449.31   *"Our political struggle":* quoted in Douglas Pike, *Viet Cong* (Cambridge, Mass.: M.I.T. Press, 1966), p. 106.

450.1   *"The purpose of this":* Pike, *Viet Cong*, p. 111.

450.21   *"in the effective control":* Bernard Fall, *The Two Vietnams* (New York: Praeger, 1967), p. 133.

450.28–29   *"the existence of guerrilla":* Ibid.

450.36   *"the 'kill' aspect":* Bernard Fall, *Last Reflections on a War* (New York: Doubleday, 1967), p. 210.

451.15   *"This is where":* Ibid., p. 221.

452.2   *De Gaulle remarked that:* Laqueur, *Guerrilla*, p. 294.

452.24–25   *In the words of:* Neil Sheehan, *A Bright and Shining Lie* (New York: Random House, 1988), p. 631.

453.35   *"Their missile power":* quoted in Lawrence Freedman, *The Evolution of Nuclear Strategy* (London: Macmillan, 1981), p. 230.

454.28   *It would lead to:* A. J. Langguth, *Our Vietnam* (New York: Simon & Schuster, 2000), p. 371.

457.33–34   *When Richard Nixon:* Ibid., p. 514.

458.2–3   *After Tet, in the:* Schell, *The Real War*, p. 30.

4. SATYAGRAHA

463.27   *They believed, with Max:* Gene Sharp, *Gandhi as a Political Strategist* (Boston: Porter-Sargeant Publishers, Extending Horizons Books, 1979), p. 240.

463.32   *"force without right":* John Locke, *The Second Treatise on Government* (New York: Macmillan, 1952), p. 13.

464.1   *"in all states and":* Ibid., p. 88.

464.7   *"becomes a case of":* Edmund Burke, *Reflections on the Revolution in France* (New York: Anchor, 1973), p. 42.

464.15   *At the beginning of:* J. Christopher Herold, *The Age of Napoleon* (Boston: Houghton Mifflin, 1963), p. 37.

464.21   *"Violence is the midwife":* Karl Marx, *Capital* (New York: Modern Library, 1959), p. 824.

464.24   *The leader of the:* Merle Fainsod, *How Russia Is Ruled* (Cambridge, Mass.: Harvard University Press, 1963), p. 135.

464.27   *In a still broader:* Adam Ulam, *The Bolsheviks* (New York: Macmillan, 1992), p. 455.

464.35   *Lenin sneered at:* Martin Green, *The Challenge of the Mahatmas* (New York: Basic Books, 1978), p. 85.

464.36   *And Max Weber:* Bruce D. Porter, *War and the Rise of the State* (New York: Free Press, 1994), p. 303.

464.40   *"All greatness, all power":* quoted in Isaiah Berlin, *The Crooked Timber of Humanity* (New York: Knopf, 1991), p. 117.

466.34   *On a train from:* Stanley Wolpert, *Gandhi's Passion* (New York: Oxford University Press, 2001), p. 35.

467.7–8   *His colleagues at dinner:* Mohandas K. Gandhi, *Essential Writings*, ed. V. V. Ramana Murti (New Delhi: Gandhi Peace Foundation, 1970), p. 39.

467.13   *"I arose with the":* quoted in Joan Bondurant, *The Conquest of Violence* (Princeton, N.J.: Princeton University Press, 1958), p. 155.

468.23   *"I clearly saw that":* Mohandas K. Gandhi, *The Selected Works of*

Mahatma Gandhi, ed. Shriman Narayan, 6 vols. (Ahmedabad, India: Navajivan Publishing House, 1968), 3: 135.

468.27–28   *In 1858, Queen Victoria:* Mohandas K. Gandhi, *The Moral and Political Writings of Mahatma Gandhi*, ed. Raghavan Iyer, 3 vols. (Oxford: Clarendon Press, 1986–87), 3: 278.

468.36   *"The Empire has been":* Mohandas Karamchand Gandhi, *The Collected Works of Mahatma Gandhi*, 100 vols. (New Delhi: Publications Division, Ministry of Information and Broadcasting. Government of India, 1999), 4: 302. The edition of the Collected Works cited here may also be found on the CD "Mahatma Gandhi" produced by the Publications Division, Patiala House, Tilak Marg, New Delhi.

469.5   *"By her large heart":* Ibid., 4: 293.

469.12–13   *"We are all fired":* Ibid., 2: 325.

469.29   *an "empty boast":* Gandhi, *Moral and Political Writings*, 1: 291.

469.30–31   *He denounced "the invention":* Ibid., 1: 288.

470.9   *"The English honor only":* Gandhi, *Collected Works*, 5: 384.

471.3   *"No one ever imagined":* Ibid., 4: 312.

471.9   *"When Japan's brave":* Ibid., 8: 405.

471.14   *"unity, patriotism and":* Ibid., 4: 313.

471.18–19   *"overwhelmed" by it:* Gandhi, *Essential Writings*, p. 55.

471.23–24   *"to conquer that hatred":* Gandhi, *Collected Works*, 2: 433.

471.35–36   *"fearless girls, actuated":* Ibid., 5: 327.

472.1   *"This time they have":* Ibid., 5: 8.

473.1   *"could not live both":* Ibid., 44: 326.

473.3   *"How was one to":* Ibid., 44: 287.

473.21   *"Like Arjun, they":* Ibid.

473.26   *Of his pursuit of:* Judith M. Brown, *Gandhi* (New Haven: Yale University Press, 1989), p. 83.

473.31–32   *"For God appears":* Erik H. Erikson, *Dimensions of a New Identity* (New York: Norton, 1974), p. 44.

474.28   *As he began a:* Sharp, *Gandhi as a Political Strategist*, p. 49.

476.11–12   *"would spell absolute ruin":* Gandhi, *Selected Works*, 3: 135.

476.17–18   *"I could read in":* Ibid., 3: 140.

476.29   *"a man who lightly"*: Ibid., 3: 144.

476.33   *"that some new principle"*: Gandhi, *Collected Works*, 1: xi.

476.35–36   *"The foundation of the"*: Gandhi, *Essential Writings*, p. 440.

478.7   *"dictate to the colonies"*: quoted in Gandhi, *Collected Works*, 4: 208.

478.14–15   *"I have now got"*: Gandhi, Ibid., 10: 184.

478.31   *The nineteenth-century British:* J. F. C. Fuller, *Military History of the Western World*, 3 vols. (New York: Da Capo Press, 1955), 2: 240.

479.18–19   *Chen Duxiu, a moderate:* Jonathan Spence, *The Search for Modern China* (New York: W. W. Norton, 1990), p. 315.

480.10   *"different sections of* ONE*"*: Gandhi, *Collected Works*, 4: 313.

480.14   *"This civilization is"*: Gandhi, *Moral and Political Writings*, 1: 214.

480.18–19   *"The condition of England"*: Ibid., 1: 209.

480.21   *"bad men [to] fulfil"*: Ibid., 1: 220.

480.23   *"neither real honesty nor"*: Ibid., 1: 211.

480.24   *was "a prostitute"*: Gandhi, *Collected Works*, 10: 256.

480.25   *"nine-days' wonder"*: Ibid., 10: 58.

480.28   *"The tendency of the"*: Gandhi, *Moral and Political Writings*, 1: 233.

481.1   *"It is . . . fitting that"*: Vivekananda, *The Yogas and Other Works*, ed. Swami Nikhilananda (New York: Ramakrishna-Vivekananda Center, 1953), p. 698.

481.34   *"My countrymen . . . believe"*: Gandhi, *Essential Writings*, p. 440.

482.4   *In the words of:* Erik H. Erikson, *Gandhi's Truth* (New York: W. W. Norton, 1969), p. 265.

482.13   *"East and West are"*: Gandhi, *Collected Works*, 8: 211.

482.30–31   *"Suppose Indians wish"*: Gandhi, *Essential Writings*, p. 8.

482.34–35   *"The Whites were fully"*: Ibid., p. 49.

483.4   *"You [British] have great"*: Mahatma Gandhi, *Hind Swaraj and Other Writings*, ed. Anthony Parel (Cambridge: Cambridge University Press, 1997), p. 114.

484.9   *"They came to our"*: Gandhi, *Collected Works*, 10: 256.

484.17   *"It is because the":* Gandhi, *Essential Writings*, p. 179.

485.6   *For instance, the:* Peter Duvall Ackerman, *A Force More Powerful* (New York: St. Martin's Press, 2000), p. 11.

485.14   *"The soldan of Egypt":* quoted in Maurizio Passerin d'Entreves, *The Notion of the State* (Oxford: Clarendon Press, 1967), p. 196.

485.18   *"All governments rest":* James Madison, Alexander Hamilton, and John Jay, *The Federalist Papers*, No. 49 (London: Penguin Classics, 1987), p. 314.

485.27   *"I believe and everybody":* quoted in Sharp, *Gandhi as a Political Strategist*, p. 11.

485.35   *"The causes that gave":* Gandhi, *Moral and Political Writings*, 1: 216.

486.7   *it was "by the":* Philip Curtin, *Imperialism* (New York: Harper & Row, 1971), p. 293.

486.22–23   *"it is an intensely":* Gandhi, *Essential Writings*, p. 99.

486.27   *"It is better to":* quoted in Bondurant, *Conquest of Violence*, p. 28.

486.32   *"I am not built":* Raghavan Iyer, *The Moral and Political Thought of Mahatma Gandhi* (New York: Oxford University Press, 1973), p. 10.

486.34–35   *"Never has anything":* Mohandas K. Gandhi, *Non-violent Resistance* (New York: Schocken, 1951), p. 110.

486.36–37   *"There is no love":* quoted in Ved Mehta, *Gandhi and His Disciples* (New York: Viking Press, 1976), p. 183.

487.19–20   *"Another remedy [to injustice]":* Gandhi, *Essential Writings*, p. 99.

488.2   *"A new order of":* quoted in Erikson, *Gandhi's Truth*, p. 338.

488.15   *"Nonviolence is without":* Gandhi, *Essential Writings*, p. 136.

488.24   *"The practice of* ahimsa*":* Ibid., p. 137.

489.16   *"To be incapable of":* Friedrich Nietzsche, *On the Genealogy of Morals*, trans. Walter Kaufmann and R. J. Hollinsdale (New York: Vintage, 1967), p. 39.

490.8   *That, at least, was:* Martin Green, *The Origins of Nonviolence* (State College, Penn.: Pennsylvania State University Press, 1976), p. 35.

490.12   *"Through deliverance of India":* Gandhi, *Essential Writings*, p. 226.

490.31   "A series of passive": quoted in Wolpert, *Gandhi's Passion*, p. 96.

490.36   "the search for a": Brown, *Gandhi*, p. 121.

491.5   "I can as well": quoted in Brown, *Gandhi*, p. 122.

491.27–28 "the greatest battle of": quoted in Wolpert, *Gandhi's Passion*, p. 99.

492.2   "In the place I": quoted in Brown, *Gandhi*, p. 132.

492.14   "All of us should": quoted in Wolpert, *Gandhi's Passion*, p. 114.

492.17   In a campaign of: Wolpert, *Gandhi's Passion*, p. 151.

493.4   On the other hand: Brown, *Gandhi*, p. 359.

494.19   "Satyagraha is not": quoted in Bondurant, *Conquest of Violence*, p. v.

495.1   "To me," the reader: Gandhi, *Essential Writings*, p. 259.

495.5   "Constructive effort is the": Ibid.

495.10   "One must forget the": Ibid., p. 274.

495.25–26 "Where do congratulations come": quoted in Green, *Challenge of the Mahatma*, p. 29.

495.37–38 "exact proportion" to success: Iyer, *Moral and Political Writings*, I: 306.

496.2   "When a body of": Gandhi, *Essential Writings*, p. 33.

496.15   "English rule without": Gandhi, *Hind Swaraj*, p. 205.

496.17   England as "pitiable": Ibid., p. 237.

496.22–23 "Not only could swaraj": quoted in Brown, *Gandhi*, p. 67.

496.31–32 "Do men conceive": Gandhi, *Essential Writings*, p. 254.

5. NONVIOLENT REVOLUTION, NONVIOLENT RULE

497.33   "If one thousand": Henry David Thoreau, *The Annotated Walden; Or Life in the Woods*, ed. Philip Van Dorenstern (New York: Clarkson N. Potter, 1970), p. 465.

499.22–23 "It was true that": Thomas Babington Macaulay, *The History of England* (London: Penguin Classics, 1986), p. 272.

499.27   "That prompt obedience": Ibid.

499.29   "The material strength of": Thomas Babington Macaulay, *The History of England*, 2 vols. (New York: Dutton, 1966), 2: 267.

500.9   Unfortunately for James: Ibid., 2: 263.

500.22   *"That great force"*: Ibid., 2: 384.

500.31   *"No encounter of the"*: George Macaulay Trevelyan, *The English Revolution, 1688–89* (New York: Oxford University Press, 1938), p. 117.

500.35   *"William of Orange"*: J. G. A. Pocock, "The Revolution of 1688–89: Changing Perspectives," in *The Varieties of British Political Thought*, ed. Lois G. Showerer (Cambridge: Cambridge University Press, 1993), p. 55.

501.21   *"The King . . . had greatly"*: Macaulay, *History of England*, 1: 578.

502.11   *"Sir, if your Majesty"*: Ibid., 1: 126.

502.17   *"The minister who had"*: Ibid., 1: 209.

502.26   *"Actuated by these"*: Ibid., 1: 238.

503.3   *"His only chance of"*: Ibid., 2: 284.

503.38–39   *"No jurist, no divine"*: Ibid., 2: 319.

504.12   *"For call himself what"*: Ibid., 2: 320.

505.6   *"To him she was"*: Ibid., 2: 16.

505.9   *"power enough to bring"*: Stephen B. Baxter, *William III, and the Defense of European Liberty* (New York: Harcourt, Brace, 1966), p. 234.

505.38   *"The Revolution gave"*: Trevelyan, *The English Revolution*, p. 240.

506.22   *"There is no way"*: Pocock, "The Revolution of 1688–89," p. 61.

506.30   *"For twenty years"*: quoted in Trevelyan, *The English Revolution*, p. 105.

507.3–4   *"What happened was"*: Trevelyan, *The English Revolution*, p. 106.

507.16   *"In 1689, both"*: Pocock, "The Revolution of 1688–89," p. 202.

507.33   *As the conservative Burke:* Ibid.

508.3–4   *"Never, within the memory"*: Macaulay, *History of England*, p. 279.

508.8   *"The appeal to heaven"*: Pocock, "The Revolution of 1688–89," p. 61.

509.2–3   *George Washington hinted at:* Page Smith, *A New Age Now Begins*, 2 vols. (New York: McGraw Hill, 1976), 2: 1,664.

509.16–17   *"We may be beaten":* quoted in ibid., 2: 1,826.

510.1   *"'Tis not in numbers":* quoted in John Keane, *Tom Paine* (Boston: Little, Brown, 1995), p. 121.

510.4   *"In the unlikely":* Ibid., p. 146.

510.6   *"Rulers can rule":* Ibid., p. 121.

510.17   *As the British general:* Conor Cruise O'Brien, *The Great Melody* (Chicago: University of Chicago Press, 1992), p. 155.

510.32   *"If nothing but force":* quoted in ibid., p. 159.

511.4   *"Do you imagine":* Edmund Burke, *Selected Writings* (New York: Random House, 1960), p. 175.

511.30   *"confine himself to military":* John Adams, *The Works of John Adams*, vol. 10 (Boston: Little, Brown, 1956), p. 85.

511.32–33   *"A history of the":* Ibid., p. 180.

512.1   *"General Wilkinson may":* Ibid.

512.10   *"As to the history":* Ibid., p. 172.

512.26   *"The cool, calm":* Ibid., p. 197.

512.39   *"It will be":* Ibid., p. 253.

513.4   *"the real American revolution":* Ibid., p. 283.

513.8   *"What an engine!":* Ibid., p. 197.

513.27   *"Let me ask you":* Ibid., p. 159.

514.1–2   *"The royal governors stood":* Gordon S. Wood, *The Creation of the American Republic* (New York: W. W. Norton, 1972), p. 314.

514.10   *"For if, as Jefferson":* Ibid., p. 132.

514.22   *"The Union is much":* quoted in Mario M. Cuomo, *Lincoln on Democracy* (New York: HarperCollins, 1990), p. 204.

514.32   *"Heaven decided in our":* Adams, *Works*, p. 159.

6. THE MASS MINORITY IN ACTION: FRANCE AND RUSSIA

516.5–6   *"French soldiers are not":* quoted in Simon Schama, *Citizens* (New York: Vintage, 1990), p. 371.

516.13   *The king's cavalry:* Ibid., p. 380.

516.21   *"The bastille was not":* Jules Michelet, *The French Revolution* (Chicago: University of Chicago Press, 1967), p. 176.

516.28	*"Shame for such cowardly"*: Ibid., p. 177.
517.1	*"Good is grapeshot"*: Thomas Carlyle, *The French Revolution* (New York: Oxford University Press, 1989), p. 179.
517.11	*"The French revolution"*: quoted in Carl Becker, *The Declaration of Independence* (New York: Vintage, 1942), p. 30.
519.14–15	*When it was suggested:* Richard Pipes, *The Russian Revolution* (New York: Vintage, 1991), p. 472.
519.20	*"In times of revolution"*: quoted in ibid., p. 358.
520.7	*"No matter how important"*: quoted in Isaac Deutscher, *The Prophet Armed* (New York: Oxford University Press, 1954), p. 156.
520.27	*"a sort of fabulous"*: N. N. Sukhanov, *The Russian Revolution, 1917* (New York: Oxford University Press, 1955), p. 74.
520.31	*"A whole world of"*: quoted in Pipes, *Russian Revolution*, p. 336.
521.21	*"the decisive revolutionary"*: Martin Malia, *The Soviet Tragedy* (New York: Free Press, 1994), p. 90.
522.17	*"After the February"*: Leon Trotsky, *The History of the Russian Revolution* (Ann Arbor, Mich.: University of Michigan Press, 1957), p. 131.
522.28	*"We can (if we"*: quoted in Pipes, *Russian Revolution*, p. 472.
522.37	*The Bolsheviks had "no"*: Trotsky, *Russian Revolution*, p. 154.
522.39	*The Party, they observed:* Ibid., p. 159.
523.5	*"eliminate the mass"*: quoted in Deutscher, *The Prophet Armed*, p. 334.
523.37	*So important did Trotsky:* Pipes, *Russian Revolution*, p. 479.
524.12	*"full support in all"*: Ibid., p. 487.
524.14	*"On October 21"*: Sukhanov, *Russian Revolution*, p. 583.
524.27	*"War had been declared"*: Ibid., p. 592.
524.33	*"three hundred volunteers"*: Ibid., p. 589.
525.2	*"This, to put it"*: Ibid., p. 592.
525.17	*"He, Trotsky," would:* Ibid., p. 596.
525.37	*"declaration of October 23"*: Trotsky, *Russian Revolution*, p. 118.
526.3–4	*"We don't know of"*: Sukhanov, *Russian Revolution*, p. 627.
526.8	*"The unique thing about"*: Trotsky, *Russian Revolution*, pp. 181–82.

526.29   *"This does not mean"*: Ibid., p. 181.

526.35   *"Only an armed"*: Ibid., p. 87.

527.21   *"The final act of"*: Ibid., p. 232.

527.30–31   *In despair at what*: Pipes, *Russian Revolution*, p. 490.

528.18   *"And now we are"*: quoted in Sukhanov, *Russian Revolution*, p. 639.

529.30   *"had been their own"*: Sukhanov, *Russian Revolution*, p. 529.

529.33–34   *"lavish with promises"*: Ibid.

529.38–39   *"The October revolution"*: quoted in Trotsky, *Russian Revolution*, p. 232.

530.12   *"At the end of"*: Trotsky, *Russian Revolution*, p. 294.

530.15   *"As a matter of"*: Ibid., p. 232.

530.23–24   *The Social Revolutionary Party*: Pipes, *Russian Revolution*, p. 543.

532.34–35   *"the least bloody revolution"*: quoted in Joachim Fest, *Hitler* (New York: Harcourt, Brace & Jovanovich, 1973), p. 447.

7. LIVING IN TRUTH

534.29   *"A wall is a"*: quoted in Michael Beschloss, *The Crisis Years* (New York: HarperCollins, 1991), p. 278.

535.16   *"Never will we consent"*: Adam B. Ulam, *The Communists* (New York: Scribners, 1992), p. 309.

535.22   *"There was a special"*: Nadezhda Mandelstam, *Hope Against Hope* (New York: Athenaeum, 1970), p. 48.

535.34–35   *"The terrifying thing"*: quoted in Jeffrey C. Isaac, *Arendt, Camus, and Modern Rebellion* (New Haven, Conn.: Yale University Press, 1992), p. 43.

537.26–27   *"hotbed out of which"*: George Kennan), *Memoirs* (New York: Pantheon, 1967), p. 534.

537.31   *"Successful revolts on"*: Ibid., p. 533.

539.1   *"To believe in"*: Adam Michnik, *Letters from Prison* (Berkeley: University of California Press, 1985), p. 142.

539.5   *"the Soviet military"*: Ibid., p. 14.

539.10   *"It is impossible to"*: George Konrád, *Anti-Politics* (New York: Harcourt Brace Jovanovich, 1984), p. 70.

NOTES

731

539.22   *"The morality of Yalta"*: Ibid., p. 2.

539.33   *"In the stalemated world"*: Václav Havel, *Living in Truth*, ed. Jan Vladislav (London: Faber & Faber, 1986), p. 37.

540.3–4   *"If we consider how"*: Ibid., p. 111.

540.19   *"Defending the aims"*: Ibid., p. 89.

541.13   *"Society is produced by"*: Thomas Paine, *Common Sense* (New York: Peter Eckler, 1998), p. 1.

541.29   *"I believe that what"*: Michnik, *Letters from Prison*, p. 144.

541.36   *"Why post-totalitarian?"*: Adam Michnik, *Letters from Freedom* (Berkeley: University of California Press, 1998), p. 59.

542.25   *"We introduced a new"*: Václav Havel, *Disturbing the Peace* (New York: Knopf, 1990), p. 83.

542.34–35   *Havel says, "individuals"*: Timothy Garton Ash, *The Uses of Adversity* (New York: Random House, 1989), p. 192.

543.11   *"Individuals can be"*: Havel, *Living in Truth*, p. 57.

543.23   *"it must be declared"*: Mohandas K. Gandhi, *Essential Writings*, ed. V. V. Ramana Murti (New Delhi: Gandhi Peace Foundation, 1970), p. 225.

543.30   *"People who so define"*: Havel, *Living in Truth*, p. 76.

544.7   *"Under the orderly"*: Ibid., p. 57.

544.31   *In his scheme*: Konrád, *Anti-Politics*, p. 73.

544.35   *"iceberg of power"*: Ibid., p. 145.

544.38   *"Proletarian revolution didn't"*: Ibid., p. 73.

545.21   *"We were scared"*: quoted in Ulam, *The Communists*, p. 104.

546.3–4   *"Everything suddenly appears"*: Havel, *Living in Truth*, p. 59.

546.33   *The step beyond that*: Ash, *Uses of Adversity*, p. 195.

548.18   *"The struggle for state"*: Michnik, *Letters from Prison*, p. 89.

548.26   *"People who claim"*: Ibid., p. 86.

548.37   *"Before the violence"*: Ibid., p. 87.

549.5–6   *"My reflections on violence"*: Ibid., p. 106.

549.12–13   *"a profound belief that"*: Havel, *Living in Truth*, p. 93.

549.19   *"The political leadership"*: Konrád, *Anti-Politics*, p. 91.

550.23   *"which would be different"*: Gandhi, *Essential Writings*, p. 49.

551.36–37   *"The world rests upon":* Mohandas K. Gandhi, *The Selected Works of Mahatma Gandhi*, ed. Shriman Narayan, 6 vols. (Ahmedabad, India: Navajivan Publishing House, 1968), 2: 389.

552.4   *"At the basis of ":* Havel, *Living in Truth*, pp. 137–38.

554.1   *"By the mid-1980s":* Mikhail Gorbachev, *Memoirs* (New York: Doubleday, 1996), p. 349.

556.5   *"Necessity of the principle":* quoted in Archie Brown, *The Gorbachev Factor* (New York: Oxford University Press, 1996), p. 225.

557.32–33   *He declared, "Today":* John Morrison, *Boris Yeltsin, from Bolshevik to Democrat* (New York: Dutton, 1991), p. 222.

558.20   *"It was clear":* quoted in ibid., p. 143.

8. COOPERATIVE POWER

560.7   *"nauseating and humiliating":* Martin Green, *Challenge of the Mahatmas* (New York: Basic Books, 1978), p. 122.

560.11–12   *Upon hearing of the:* Ibid.

561.28   *"violence and power are":* Hannah Arendt, *Violence* (New York: Harcourt Brace Jovanovich), p. 56.

561.28–29   *"Power and violence are":* Ibid.

561.38–562.1   *"the rule of men":* quoted in ibid., p. 35.

562.5–6   *"Power corresponds to":* Ibid., p. 44.

562.12   *"solemnly and mutually":* Ibid., p. 172.

562.22   *"Democracy does not":* Alexis de Tocqueville, *Democracy in America* (New York: Schocken, 1961), p. 295.

563.25–26   *"Where power is not":* Hannah Arendt, *The Human Condition* (Chicago: University of Chicago Press, 1958), p. 200.

564.1   *"To command and":* Hannah Arendt, *On Violence* (New York: Harvest, 1970), p. 37.

564.3   *"Power means every":* Max Weber.

564.7–8   *"never the property of ":* Arendt, *On Violence*, p. 44.

564.24   *"In a head-on":* Ibid., p. 37.

564.26   *"While violence can":* Arendt, *The Human Condition*, p. 202.

564.34–35   *"Nowhere is the":* Arendt, *On Violence*, pp. 54–55.

564.40   *"The climax of terror"*: Ibid., p. 55.

565.16   *"the head-on clash"*: Ibid., p. 53.

565.29–30   general *"reversal in the"*: Ibid., p. 11.

565.37   *"the situation changes"*: Ibid., pp. 48–49.

566.21   *"Power is actualized"*: Arendt, *The Human Condition*, p. 200.

566.34   *"Gandhi's enormously powerful"*: Arendt, *On Violence*, p. 53.

566.38   *"Popular revolt against"*: Arendt, *The Human Condition*, p. 200.

567.29   *"taken as the spring"*: Arendt, *On Revolution*, p. 89.

567.36–37   *"Only in His strength"*: Mohandas Karamchand Gandhi, *Nonviolent Resistance*, ed. Bharatan Kumarappa (New York: Schocken, 1951), p. 364.

569.11   *"One is obtained by"*: Raghavan N. Iyer, *The Moral and Political Thought of Mahatma Gandhi* (New York: Oxford University Press, 1986), p. 53.

570.25   *"What has made so"*: Alexis de Tocqueville, *The Old Regime and the French Revolution* (New York: Anchor, 1969), p. 168.

570.35   *"If God who is"*: quoted in Judith M. Brown, *Gandhi* (New Haven, Conn.: Yale University Press, 1989), p. 199.

571.4   *"love and not fear"*: quoted in Gordon S. Wood, *The Creation of the American Republic* (New York: W. W. Norton, 1972), p. 67.

571.7   *"love of the laws"*: Montesquieu, *The Spirit of the Laws* (Berkeley and Los Angeles: University of California Press, 1977), p. 130.

571.10–11   *"Men love at their"*: Niccolò Machiavelli, *The Prince* (New York: Random House, Modern Library, 1950), p. 63.

571.22   *"What is meant"*: John Stuart Mill, "Considerations on Representative Government," in *Utilitarianism*, ed. H. B. Acton (London: J. M. Dent & Sons, 1972), pp. 196–97.

572.7   *"a more powerful social"*: Ibid., p. 197.

572.16   *Power, according to:* A more recent exposition of the power of opinion is the concept of "soft power," introduced by Joseph Nye, Dean of the Kennedy School of Government at Harvard. According to Nye, a nation's soft power, which he distinguishes from its "hard power" (which corresponds to coercive power), is the attractive pull of its best qualities—its culture, its ideology, its prosperity. "This aspect of power—

getting others to want what you want—I call soft power," he writes. "It co-opts people rather than coerces them" (from Joseph Nye, *The Paradox of American Power* [New York: Oxford, 2002], p. 9). A difference between soft power and cooperative power is that whereas the first is generated by a single actor (whether a saint or a country) and belongs to that actor, the second, being a product of action in concert, in its nature can belong only to a group. However, the two are related. Cooperation depends on agreement, and agreement depends on the discovery of common ground. For example, the admiration that one country inspires in another—or that both feel for a common goal or principle—is the sine qua non of common ground. Thus does the "soft power" that countries exert upon one another lay a basis for action in concert, which is the foundation of cooperative power. It follows that it is just as important—though less remarked on—for the United States to find things to admire in other countries as for other countries to admire the United States. Mutual respect creates the opportunity for joint action—for cooperative power.

9. THE LIBERAL DEMOCRATIC REVIVAL

578.9   *He advocated a "civic":* Immanuel Kant, *On History*, ed. Lewis White Beck (Indianapolis, Ind.: Bobbs-Merrill, 1963), pp. 16–17.

578.25   *"The latent causes of":* James Madison, Alexander Hamilton, and John Jay, *The Federalist Papers* (New York: Penguin, 1987), p. 124.

578.28   *"If any two men":* Thomas Hobbes, *Leviathan* (Cambridge: Cambridge University Press, 1996), p. 87.

579.12   *"They are free":* quoted in Orlando Patterson, *Freedom*, vol. 1 (New York: Basic Books, 1991), p. 93.

579.16   *"He obeys the laws":* Cicero, *On the Commonwealth*, trans. George Holland Sabine and Stanley Barney Smith (Columbus, Ohio: Bobbs-Merrill, Library of Liberal Arts, 1960), p. 55.

579.32   *"Liberty, or freedom":* Hobbes, *Leviathan*, p. 145.

580.40   *"No society can":* Raghavan N. Iyer, *The Moral and Political Thought of Mahatma Gandhi*, (New York: Oxford University Press, 1986) p. 351.

582.2   *"so foolish that they":* John Locke, *The Second Treatise on Government* (Indianapolis, Ind.: Hackett Publishing, 1980), p. 53.

584.9	*"They'll shoot us":* quoted in Taylor Branch, *Pillar of Fire* (New York: Simon & Schuster, 1999), p. 331.
584.27	*"Unearned suffering is":* quoted in Diane McWhorter, *Carry Me Home* (New York: Simon & Schuster, 2001), p. 154.
584.34	*"the freest man on":* quoted in ibid., p. 61.
584.34	*"They can't enjoin":* Ibid., p. 109.
585.23	*"I think we just":* quoted in Branch, *Pillar of Fire*, p. 94.
586.7–8	*But because the deepest:* King's radicalism emerged clearly in his opposition to the Vietnam War. Not content to rest on his laurels as an elder statesman of the highly successful civil-rights movement, he felt compelled in the late 1960s to apply his nonviolence in this new area against the very president—Lyndon B. Johnson—who had brought the civil-rights movement to legislative fruition.
586.20	*"We mean to kill":* quoted in McWhorter, *Carry Me Home*, p. 22.
586.21	*"You know my friends":* quoted in Taylor Branch, *Parting the Waters* (New York: Simon & Schuster, 1998), p. 140.
586.32–33	*"If we are wrong":* quoted in ibid.
587.14	*"Standing beside love":* Ibid.
587.34	*Later he said:* Ibid., p. 166.
587.36	*When an officer:* McWhorter, *Carry Me Home*, p. 228.
590.30	*In 1958, Prime Minister:* Bruce Ackerman and Jack Duvall, *A Force More Powerful* (New York: Palgrave, 2000), p. 357.
591.13	*the organization's black:* Anthony Sampson, *Mandela* (New York: Vintage, 1999), p. 89.
591.20–21	*"The attacks of the":* quoted in ibid., p. 149.
591.23	*"I saw nonviolence":* Ibid., p. 68.
591.33–34	*"Luthuli, Mandela and":* Ibid., p. 259.
592.9–10	*These, he said, would:* Ackerman and Duvall, *Force More Powerful*, p. 345.
592.12	*Only then could they:* Ibid., p. 347.
593.2	*The first to meet with:* Allister Sparks, *Tomorrow Is Another Country* (Chicago: University of Chicago Press, 1995), p. 24.
593.14	*"Mandela had become":* Sampson, *Mandela*, p. 512.
593.21	*Mandela's friend Fatima:* Ibid., p. 68.

593.23   *"I'm just a sinner"*: quoted in ibid., p. 415.

593.27–28   *"the unselfconscious manifestation"*: Ibid., p. 546.

593.30   *"When one is faced"*: Ibid., p. 242.

593.34–35   *"Bitterness would be"*: Ibid., p. 406.

593.36–37   *"Courageous people do not"*: Ibid., p. 515.

594.31–32   *"the most predicted"*: Ibid., p. 484.

598.8   *"If it is true"*: Hannah Arendt, *The Origins of Totalitarianism* (New York: Harvest/Harcourt Brace Jovanovich, 1973), p. 460.

598.26   *"Our British colonizers"*: Arundhati Roy, *The Nation*, February 18, 2002.

599.30   *"Whoever wants to deprive"*: Jean-Jacques Rousseau, *Political Writings* (Madison, Wisc.: Wisconsin University Press, 1986), p. 242.

599.34   *"If a democratical"*: Montesquieu, *The Spirit of the Laws* (Berkeley and Los Angeles: University of California Press, 1977), p. 193.

599.40–600.1   *"Imperialism and popular"*: John A. Hobson, *Imperialism* (Ann Arbor: University of Michigan Press, Ann Arbor Paperbacks, 1965), p. 150.

600.8   *"European civilization, with"*: Leonard Woolf, *Imperialism and Civilization* (New York: Garland Publishing, 1971), p. 34.

600.25   *"The two ideas of"*: quoted in Philip D. Curtin, *Imperialism* (New York: Walker, 1971), p. 292.

601.2   *"a sea of vague"*: Hobson, *Imperialism*, p. 206.

602.1   *The decisive advantage*: Victor Davis Hanson, *Carnage and Culture* (New York: Doubleday, 2001), p. 48.

602.16   *"an exclusive Western monopoly"*: Ibid., p. 252.

602.23–24   rise to *"universal dominion"*: Polybius, *The Rise of the Roman Empire*, ed. F. W. Walbank (London: Penguin, 1979), p. 42.

602.36   *"The veteran legions of"*: Madison, Hamilton, and Jay, *The Federalist Papers*, Article 1, Section 8, Clause 12, p. 268.

10. LIBERAL INTERNATIONALISM

605.4   *"busy with a scheme"*: G. J. Renier, *William of Orange* (New York: D. Appleton, 1933), p. 84.

605.20–21   *When Jeremy Bentham*: Carlton J. Hayes, *The Historical*

Evolution of Modern Nationalism (New York: Richard R. Smith, 1931), p. 131.

606.8   *Wasn't it "monstrous":* Alan Bullock and Maurice Shock, *The Liberal Tradition* (Oxford: Oxford University Press, 1956), p. 158.

606.16   *"the passing of good":* quoted in ibid., pp. 175–76.

606.38   *To the intense indignation:* Philip Magnus, *Gladstone* (New York: E. P. Dutton, 1964), p. 240.

606.40   *"What our duty is":* quoted in ibid., p. 241.

607.4–5   *"There is not":* Ibid., p. 242.

607.15   *"Fortresses may be":* quoted in Bullock and Shock, *Liberal Tradition*, p. xxxix.

607.19   *He proposed a strengthened:* Ibid., p. 163.

607.22   *"Certain it is":* quoted in Henry Kissinger, *Diplomacy* (New York: Simon & Schuster, 1994), p. 161.

608.26   *"Would the President propose":* Ibid., p. 223.

608.37   *Wilson intended to:* August Heckscher, *Woodrow Wilson* (New York: Macmillan, 1991), p. 508.

609.2   *"The question upon which":* quoted in Kissinger, *Diplomacy*, p. 51.

609.8   *"the destruction of every":* Ibid., p. 52.

609.33   *"All the great wrongs":* quoted in Robert Tucker, *The New Republic*, February 24,1992, p. 30.

609.36   *The second of his:* Arthur Walworth, *Woodrow Wilson, World Prophet*, vol. 2 (New York: Longmans & Green, 1958), p. 156.

610.29   *"He has saved his":* quoted in Ferdinand Czernin, *Versailles, 1919* (New York: G. P. Putnam & Sons, 1964), p. 430.

612.4–5   *"War had lain at":* Ibid., p. 398.

612.12–13   *"constitution for the whole":* quoted in Heckscher, *Woodrow Wilson*, p. 520.

612.18–19   *"Instinctively, and rightly":* Harold Nicolson, *Peacemaking, 1919* (New York: Harcourt, Brace & World, 1965), p. 70.

613.28–29   *Clemenceau spoke in:* Heckscher, *Woodrow Wilson*, p. 510.

614.18–19   *"The defensive value of":* Nicolson, *Peacemaking, 1919*, p. 192.

614.32   *"In spite of bitter":* Ibid., p. 36.

615.21–22   *"the unquestioned opportunity":* Ibid., p. 191.

11. SOVEREIGNTY

617.20   *"Guarantees must be fulfilled"*: quoted in Ferdinand Czernin, *Versailles, 1919* (New York: G. P. Putnam & Sons, 1964), p. 112.

618.24   *"In matters of state"*: Jean Bodin, *On Sovereignty*, ed. Julian H. Franklin (Cambridge: Cambridge University Press, 1992), p. 108.

618.26–27   *"An absolute sovereign"*: Jean Bodin, *Six Books of the Commonwealth*, trans. M. J. Tooly (Oxford: Basil Blackwell, 1967), p. 36.

618.33   *"holds of another"*: Ibid.

619.4   *"an analytic truth"*: Julian H. Franklin, *Jean Bodin, and the Rise of Absolutist Theory* (Cambridge: Cambridge University Press, 1973), p. 23.

619.7–8   *"the principle mark of"*: Bodin, *Six Books*, p. 32.

619.9   *"If the prince can"*: Ibid., p. 43.

619.26   *"Just as God"*: Bodin, *On Sovereignty*, p. 50.

620.1   *"Reason and common sense"*: Bodin, *Six Books*, p. 19.

620.17–18   *"Man's salvation occurs"*: quoted in Liah Greenfeld, *Nationalism* (Cambridge, Mass.: Harvard University Press, 1992), p. 115.

620.32   *"Sovereignty is one"*: www.Britannica.com.

621.2   *"one people, one body"*: John Locke, *The Second Treatise on Government* (Indianapolis, Ind.: Hackett Publishing, 1980), pp. 47–48.

621.4–5   *"an absolute despotic power"*: quoted in Hannah Arendt, *On Revolution* (New York: Compass, 1967), p. 160.

621.6   *"The power and jurisdiction"*: quoted in R. R. Palmer, *The Age of Democratic Revolution*, vol. 1 (Princeton, N.J.: Princeton University Press, 1959), p. 142.

621.19–20   *"What is a nation?"*: C. A. Macartney, *National States and National Minorities* (London: Oxford University Press, 1934), p. 46.

621.25   *"is the soul that"*: Locke, *The Second Treatise*, p. 108.

622.31   Macartney quotes Acton: Macartney, *National States and National Minorities*, p. 17.

622.36   *"aspires to political expression"*: Ibid., p. 16.

623.3   *"is usually nationally identical"*: Ibid., p. 18.

627.23   *The Virginia Resolves, authored:* Frank Friedel, Richard N. Current, and T. Harry Williams, *A History of the United States,* vol. 1 (New York: Knopf, 1961), p. 120.

628.11   *"it was as if":* Gordon S. Wood, *The Creation of the American Republic* (New York: W. W. Norton, 1972), p. 285.

628.14–15   *"Every town government":* quoted in ibid., pp. 186–87.

628.23   *"miniature constitutions that":* Wood, *American Republic,* p. 288.

629.14   *"union of the society":* Locke, *The Second Treatise,* p. 119.

630.4   *"the greatest question ever":* quoted in ibid., p. 345.

630.9–10   *"The doctrine of sovereignty":* Wood, *American Republic,* p. 345.

630.16   *some suggested that America:* John Keane, *Tom Paine* (Boston: Little, Brown, 1995), p. 100. Cartright's famous letters in favor of American independence were called *American Independence, the Interest and Glory of Great Britain.* They demanded, Keane writes, "the replacement of the British Empire by a free association of states endowed with British liberties and all of them recognizing the king as their sovereign head."

630.29   *was "imperium in imperio":* Wood, *American Republic,* p. 351.

630.30   *described by Adams as:* Ibid.

630.31–32   *Benjamin Franklin—who had:* Ibid.

631.16–17   *"If, intemperately, unwisely":* quoted in Conor Cruise O'Brien, *The Great Melody* (Chicago: University of Chicago Press, 1992), p. 143.

632.9   *For example, Samuel Adams:* Wood, *American Republic,* p. 528. *James Madison now found:* Ibid., p. 559.

632.18   *"an assemblage of societies":* James Madison, Alexander Hamilton, and John Jay, *The Federalist Papers* (London: Penguin, 1987), p. 122.

633.40   *the "true distinction" of:* Alexander Hamilton, James Madison, and John Jay, *Federalist Papers,* ed. Clinton Rossiter (New York: Penguin, 1961), p. 355.

12. NIAGARA

639.3   *"Black and hideous to":* Henry James and Leon Edel, eds., *Henry James Letters* (Cambridge, Mass.: Harvard University Press, 1984), p. 713.

646.35   *"The position of the"*: Leo Szilard and Nina Byers, "Physicists and the Decision to Drop the Bomb," *CERN Courier*, November 2002, p. 270.

649.17   *"As this enormous"*: Bill Joy, "Why the Future Doesn't Need Us," *Wired*, April 2000.

650.4   *Its logical end point:* Francis Fukuyama made use of these terms of Nietzsche's in his book *The End of History and the Last Man*. With all respect to Fukuyama and Nietzsche, my use of the terms seems to me more fitting than theirs. Their first man was an energetic savage, and I follow them in this. Their last man, however, was an enervated, hypercivilized person, who, all savage energy spent, was incapable of almost any feat. It's hard to see how he would be the "last" of anything, unless he expired out of sheer boredom. My last man, on the other hand, would literally and truly be the last, since he would destroy everybody, himself included. It has always struck me likewise that *The End of History* was a perverse term to use in the nuclear age to refer to anything but human extinction by nuclear arms.

651.9   *"an atavism, a holdover"*: Francis Fukuyama, *The End of History and the Last Man* (New York: The Free Press, 1992), p. 265.

653.28–29   *"absolute monarchs will often"*: The Federalist Papers, p. 14.

654.20   *"What's the point"*: Bill Keller, "The World According to Powell," *New York Times*, November 25, 2001.

659.10   *"If Pakistan doesn't change"*: quoted in Rajiv Chandrasekaran, "Terrorism Casts Shadow Over India's Campaign," *Washington Post*, January 27, 2002.

659.13–14   *"the perpetrator of that"*: quoted in Celia Dugger, "Indian General Talks Bluntly of War and a Nuclear Threat," *New York Times*, January 12, 2002.

659.17–18   *"as a last resort"*: quoted in Rory McCarthy and John Hooper, "Musharraf Ready to Use Bomb," *The Guardian*, April 6, 2002.

13. THE LOGIC OF PEACE

667.5–6   *"the gradual spread of"*: Scott Sagan and Kenneth Waltz, *The Spread of Nuclear Weapons* (New York: W. W. Norton, 1997), p. 44.

675.35–36   *"fundamental maxims of her"*: quoted in James Chace, "Imperial America," *World Policy Journal* (spring 2002).

687.24–25   *For abolition would not:* This understanding of abolition as shifting the source of deterrence from hardware to software leaves open an important question. If deterrence survives beyond abolition, aren't we still snared in the riddles and corruption of threatening annihilation to avoid annihilation? Formally speaking, the objection is valid. Abolition so conceived does not purge the "sin" mentioned by Robert Oppenheimer, the scientific leader of the Manhattan Project, in his remark, "In some irredeemable way, the physicists have known sin." What it does do is to back the world across a critical symbolic threshold in the moral and psychological realm (psychology being the whole essence of deterrence in the first place).

688.31   *The dangers of abolition:* For a fuller treatment of my views on these matters, see my books *The Abolition* (New York: Knopf, 1984) and *The Gift of Time* (New York: Metropolitan Books, 1998).

696.3   *If the first circle:* This state of affairs may be changing, for a surprising reason. To the great dismay of the Ulster Protestants, the people of Britain, according to recent polls, are not eager to hold on to the Ulster counties, and would not mind seeing them join the Irish Republic.

700.32   *"How 'relevant' are mere":* Gidon Gottlieb, *Nation Against State* (New York: Council on Foreign Relations, 1993), p. 50.

702.32   *"There is not a":* quoted in Conor Cruise O'Brien, *The Great Melody* (Chicago: University of Chicago Press, 1992), p. 113.

703.31   *"The 'victorious' Jews":* quoted in Jeffrey C. Isaac, *Arendt, Camus, and Modern Rebellion* (New Haven, Conn.: Yale University Press, 1992), p. 214.

709.13   *"gradually spread further":* Immanuel Kant, "Perpetual Peace," in *Political Writings*, ed. Hans Reiss (Cambridge: Cambridge University Press, 1970), p. 105.

Chronology

1943   Born Jonathan Edward Schell in New York City on August 21, the youngest of three children of Marjorie Elizabeth (Bertha) Schell, thirty-one, and Orville Hickock Schell, Jr., thirty-five. Sister Suzanne is five years old; brother Orville III is three. Mother, a graduate of Smith College with a degree in economics who went on to study international affairs at Radcliffe, was born in Chicago, her father a real estate broker and businessman. Father, the son of a New Rochelle obstetrician, is a graduate of Yale and Harvard Law and has worked at Hughes, Hubbard, Blair & Reed, a corporate law firm, since 1937. They married in Winnetka, Illinois, on May 20, 1935, and after a honeymoon in France moved to New Canaan, Connecticut, Orville Jr. commuting to Wall Street.

1944–47   In May 1944, father is commissioned as a lieutenant, junior grade, in the U.S. Navy. The following year he serves as general counsel for the Navy's Bureau of Ordnance and moves the family to Washington, D.C. Back in New York after the war, they take possession of a narrow, four-story brownstone at 520 East 87th Street in Yorkville that will remain the family home for twenty years.

1948–52   In the fall of 1948, at five years old, is sent during the day to The Dalton School, a progressive private institution on New York's Upper East Side. "Jonathan will talk to anyone who will listen," his first teacher reports; "he makes good suggestions and quite often lengthy explanations of why he feels as he does about things." Becomes friendly with future playwright and actor Wallace Shawn, son of *New Yorker* editor in chief William Shawn, also attending Dalton. "Jonathan is as gay as a cricket and as busy as a beaver," a third-grade teacher says on his report card in 1952; "his great trouble is lack of attention which constantly gets him into difficulties."

1953–56   At age ten or eleven, stages plays for the family with Wally Shawn and other friends; they include commercials for an invented cereal brand, "Soggy Ooglies." Teachers praise his intelligence and verbal skill but note deficiencies in his written work. "He is often so careless of the form that it must be rewritten," says one in 1953; "when concentrated effort is required to prepare a paper, organize it, and put it into legible form," says another in 1956, "he falls far short of minimum standards."

1957–60   Father joins board of directors of Merck Pharmaceuticals. In the fall of 1957, at fourteen, begins attending The Putney School, another progressive private school, in Putney, Vermont. Mother persuades the Shawns to send Wally to Putney as well. Learns to play the oboe; a gym teacher describes him as a "very, very rugged lineman." Spends summers with the family in Mattapoisett, Massachusetts. Travels to Mexico in August 1959, visiting the home of classmate Geoffrey Goodridge in the small town of Ajijic, on Lake Chapala. Is encouraged by mother, increasingly involved with the National Committee for a Sane Nuclear Policy (SANE), to write to President Eisenhower to oppose resumption of nuclear testing. Publishes poetry in *Putney Magazine*. Joins the Putney ski team. In 1960, sister graduates from Radcliffe.

1961   Graduates from Putney on June 9 and joins brother Orville at Harvard in the fall. Spends Christmas vacation with family in Paris.

1962   Ends his freshman year with four Bs and four Cs. Returns to Putney for commencement to see friends graduate. Brother enrolls at National Taiwan University; publishes reports on Taiwanese life in *The Boston Globe*. New roommates in the fall include Tom Hayes, Wallace Shawn, Geoffrey Gratwick, Mark Woodcock, and Brian Cooke; they continue to live together for the rest of their college years and remain close thereafter. In October, during the Cuban Missile Crisis, writes to a high school friend: "Excitement has been high over the Cuban situation here at Harvard. This is the only topic of discussion and people feel very personally involved in this crisis. Many fellows are wondering about the possibilities of being drafted, and, of course, about the possibilities of being blown up. Wally has been keeping an unbroken vigil at the radio." The next month, Annie Hennessey, a maid who has worked for the Schell family since Orville Jr. was a boy, returns to her native Ireland: "I feel as if a member of the family has departed," Jonathan writes. She corresponds with the Schell children regularly and they later visit her.

1963   Joins the Harvard ski team. Spends summer as a counselor and oboe apprentice at the Kinhaven Music School in Weston, Vermont; plays the oboe in the Harvard-Radcliffe Orchestra. Brother travels to Laos and South Vietnam, reporting on Communist insurgency and American military involvement.

1964   Paternal grandfather Orville H. Schell dies in New Rochelle on January 10, at eighty-three; maternal grandfather Edward M. Bertha dies in Chicago four days later, at seventy-four. In February, while driving to Williams College for a ski meet, notices a house on fire in Charlemont, Massachusetts, and stops to help; "those people would be corpses today without him," the Charlemont fire chief tells *The North Adams Transcript.* Takes Henry Kissinger's popular Harvard course Principles of International Politics in the spring. Over the summer returns to Vermont to teach at Kinhaven Music School. Plays the oboe in the Bach Society Orchestra at Harvard; sings in the University Chapel Choir and acts in occasional productions at the Loeb Experimental Theatre.

1965   Publishes short pieces in *The Harvard Crimson* on aspects of campus life: the pursuit of good grades, Harvard in the news, the ski team, a Vietnam teach-in. In March, is treated for eye injury at the University Medical Clinic after he and two friends are assaulted by two teenagers in Harvard Square. Facing the draft, begins to make plans for postcollege career; writes to Edwin O. Reischauer, U.S. ambassador to Japan, about possible employment or further education in that country. Writes thesis—"From a New Life to Oblivion: An Analysis of Lu Hsun's Intellectual Development and Personal Crisis between 1918 and 1927"—with East Asian Studies professor Benjamin L. Schwartz. Graduates magna cum laude on June 17. Flies to Ireland in July, visiting Annie Hennessey. Travels to Japan mainly on the Trans-Siberian Railway, stopping in Paris to visit brother Orville and spending a month in East Germany, Poland, and the Soviet Union along the way. Arrives in Tokyo in September and enrolls at the International Christian University, where he takes an intensive Japanese language course: six class hours a day, five days a week. At first finds Japanese "almost depressingly difficult." Mother chairs the New York organizing committee for the November 27 March on Washington for Peace in Vietnam.

1966   Adds private lessons to his study of Japanese, becoming
        increasingly fluent; travels throughout the country. Sister
        receives a master's degree from Columbia Teachers' Col-
        lege; she marries psychiatrist John K. Pearce in New York
        on June 11. Visits Hiroshima, writing to friends: "For the
        first time on my trip I felt a terrible uneasiness bordering
        on shame at being an American. I have heard the reasons
        for dropping the bomb, and am not able to successfully
        argue against them, but I cannot help this uneasiness, and
        no amount of reasoning seems to serve as adequate apology
        to these people who do not even seem to accuse any one in
        particular anyway." Writes to Harvard Graduate School,
        which has admitted him in East Asian Studies for the fall
        with a $2,000 fellowship, postponing his enrollment until
        the spring. Attends more than a dozen meetings of the
        Buddhist sect Soka Gakkai, later completing paper "Orga-
        nization and Ideology in the Soka Gakkai" for a Harvard
        seminar with Robert Bellah.

1967   Arrives in South Vietnam on January 4, hoping to write
        about the war. Calls on François Sully, a French reporter he
        had met at Harvard in 1963, at *Newsweek*'s Saigon bureau.
        Sully introduces him to Bernard Fall, another veteran
        journalist. ("When I greeted Sully," he later recalled, "I had
        Bernard Fall's book under my arm and mentioned that I
        had been reading it. There was another fellow at a desk who
        said 'Could I see the book?' So I went over and gave him
        the book. He opened it up and signed it. It was Bernard
        Fall!") With the pair's help, obtains a press pass as a corre-
        spondent for *The Harvard Crimson* and is alerted to an
        upcoming American offensive, Operation Cedar Falls. On
        January 8, accompanies U.S. troops during a helicopter
        assault against the village of Ben Suc. Witnesses the
        destruction of the village and the subsequent relocation of
        its civilian inhabitants. Returning home, stops in Dhankuta,
        Nepal, to visit Harvard roommate Brian Cooke, then
        serving in the Peace Corps, and at Oxford to see Wallace
        Shawn, studying at Magdalen College. ("After Vietnam,
        where danger is always present, and strange, insane scenes
        of cruelty, suffering, and disruption cannot be escaped,
        Oxford and Wally's dormitory . . . was a scene I could
        hardly believe.") On February 17, back in Cambridge,
        writes to William Shawn to ask for advice about his Ben Suc
        manuscript; calling it a "wonderful piece of writing,"
        Shawn offers to publish it in *The New Yorker*. The following

month, writes to Senator Robert F. Kennedy, praising his recent speech on ending the war and offering his services should Kennedy seek the presidency; Kennedy replies that he intends to remain in the Senate. Returns to Japan in June, finding his alma mater, the International Christian University, in the middle of a student strike; drafts an article on Japanese student protest movements with an eye to publication in *The New Yorker*, but leaves it unfinished. "The Village of Ben Suc" appears in *The New Yorker* on July 15. Returns to South Vietnam as a *New Yorker* correspondent in early August, witnessing U.S. bombing of the provinces of Quang Ngai and Quang Tin. Travels in Vietnam with brother Orville, who is also reporting on the war for *The Atlantic Monthly*; they visit Annie Hennessey in Ireland on the way back to New York. *The Village of Ben Suc* is published in October by Alfred A. Knopf. Speaks with students at Yale's Pierson College at the invitation of college master John Hersey. Meets confidentially with Secretary of Defense Robert McNamara to describe what he has seen in Quang Ngai and Quang Tin, and at McNamara's request spends three days at the Pentagon reading his manuscript into a tape recorder, to be typed by Pentagon staffers. (It is later revealed that McNamara sends the transcript to Ellsworth Bunker, the U.S. ambassador to South Vietnam, who orders a secret inquiry into Schell's findings.) Sends his finished report to William Shawn on November 30. Meets with Senator Edward M. Kennedy in Boston at Kennedy's request; they discuss Kennedy's forthcoming trip to Vietnam.

1968   "Quang Ngai and Quang Tin" appears in *The New Yorker* in two parts, on March 9 and 16. The same month, flies to Wisconsin as a volunteer for the presidential primary campaign of Senator Eugene McCarthy, who opposes the Johnson administration's Vietnam policies. Writes several speeches on Vietnam for McCarthy, and after his April 2 victory in Wisconsin is invited to travel with the campaign as one of two staff speechwriters. Declines because Robert Kennedy has also recently joined the race. *The Military Half: An Account of the Destruction of Quang Ngai and Quang Tin* is published by Alfred A. Knopf on May 29, the firm rushing the book to press. Dedicates the book to his brother Orville, "who, against everyone's better judgment, suddenly dropped out of his junior year in college to set out for the Far East as third cook—or vegetable peeler—on a Norwegian dynamite freighter, and thus set the basic style for the many impulsive, unlikely trips East we have both made since." Leaves the graduate program at Harvard to join the staff of *The New Yorker*. Moves back to New York, renting an apartment at 410 Riverside Drive near Columbia University. Over Labor Day weekend, father announces that he has fallen in love with his former secretary, Ellie Johnson, and intends to begin a separate life; they later have three sons. Visits father in Paris, attempting to persuade him not to leave mother; "dinners are like eating and dealing blows to each other's face between fork falls. We rise bloodied and torn," Schell writes in his journal.

1969   Meets future wife Elspeth Fraser ("Ibs"), twenty-five-year-old sister of *New Yorker* fashion writer Kennedy Fraser, during a stay in England in January; they exchange letters throughout the year. Begins writing for *The New Yorker*'s "Notes and Comment" section, gradually becoming its principal contributor. Mother is profiled and quoted in a November *New York Times* article on middle-aged women against the war: "'We're united,' she says of her family's antiwar sentiments."

1970   Visits England again in January. Mother meets with her lawyer to formalize marital separation. Speaks at Congressional Conference on War and National Responsibility. In May, father organizes a contingent of more than 1,000 lawyers who travel to Washington to lobby against the war in Indochina. Plays oboe for Wallace Shawn's *The Family Play* at Ensemble Studio Theatre. Describes "an emerging strategy of escalation of the war in Indochina" in a November letter to *The New York Times*, written with brother Orville. In December spends time with Elspeth and her family in the West Midlands.

1971   Becomes friendly with Hannah Arendt, whose works deeply impress him; they exchange party and dinner invitations. (After her death, recalls asking Arendt why she had "avoided the nuclear subject" in her works. "*You* do it! You have it in your bones," she replied.)

1972   Works for Democratic presidential nominee George McGovern in August and September, traveling with the campaign and writing speeches including "The Neglect of America," "An Address on Liberty in America," and "A Declaration of Conservative Principles." Though

McGovern "expressed *very* strong enthusiasm" for Schell's drafts—spending several hours editing them with him and scheduling one for a mid-September event at Faneuil Hall in Boston—none was ultimately delivered. Privately complains that McGovern's staff is "completely disorganized" and the candidate himself "not in charge of his campaign"; they "never really knew whether I was coming or going, and I don't think they know whether they're coming or going either."

1973 Receives American Academy of Arts and Letters award in literature for his contributions to *The New Yorker*.

1974 In Paris with Elspeth in November to work on a "Talk of the Town" piece, spends time with Mary McCarthy. "He's such a good and intelligent young man," McCarthy writes her friend Hannah Arendt; "and, by the way, getting better-looking all the time."

1975 Publishes "The Time of Illusion," a six-part series of reflections on the Nixon years, in *The New Yorker* beginning on June 2. In September is asked by William Shawn to edit several *New Yorker* pieces in manuscript. Shawn, now sixty-eight, begins to describe Schell in private as a potential successor.

1976 *The Time of Illusion* is published by Alfred A. Knopf in January.

1977 In February, takes on additional editorial responsibilities at *The New Yorker* in an "experiment" proposed by Shawn, prompting speculation that he has been chosen to succeed Shawn as editor in chief. Unhappiness at this prospect among some of the staff, who feel that Schell lacks editorial experience and is humorlessly political, forces Shawn to deny that any such choice has been made, and in May the experiment is postponed. (In a later-reported joke, one *New Yorker* editor complains to another that Schell would make the magazine "like *Partisan Review* with cartoons." The other replies: "What makes you think there would be cartoons?") Begins reading widely about nuclear issues, researching what will become *The Fate of the Earth*.

1978 Marries Elspeth in New York. Maternal grandmother Agnes Bertha dies in Chicago on November 10.

1979 Son Matthew is born.

1980   Mother dies on May 8 in Cambridge, Massachusetts. Moves
        with family to an apartment at 80 Warren Street, in the
        Tribeca neighborhood of lower Manhattan.

1981   Father becomes chairman of Americas Watch, a nongov-
        ernmental organization tasked with calling attention to
        human rights abuses in the Americas.

1982   "The Fate of the Earth" appears in *The New Yorker* in three
        parts, on February 1, 8, and 15, and is published by Alfred
        A. Knopf in April, the firm rushing the book into print. It
        is widely reviewed and discussed, galvanizing public opin-
        ion and remaining on best-seller lists for the rest of the year;
        the Book of the Month Club offers it at cost to make it
        more widely available. Schell declines interview requests
        and invitations to appear on *60 Minutes, 20/20, Today*, and
        Good Morning America: "I prefer people to concentrate on
        my book rather than me as a person." Phoebe, a daughter,
        is born in May. On June 12, over 500,000 people gather in
        Central Park to call for a nuclear freeze. In the fall, in the
        wake of *The Fate of the Earth*'s success, William Shawn
        again unsuccessfully suggests to some on *The New Yorker*
        staff that Schell might succeed him. German philosopher
        Günther Anders accuses Schell of plagiarism, arguing that
        the phrase "the second death" in *The Fate of the Earth* has
        been taken from his 1956 work *Die Antiquiertheit des
        Menschen* without acknowledgment. Schell travels to West
        Germany in September to contest this accusation in the
        courts; obtains an injunction against Anders, whose work
        he has not read, and retractions of German newspaper
        reports. Anders is ordered to pay his court costs. Wins *The
        Los Angeles Times* Book Prize and is nominated for the
        National Book Critics Circle award for *The Fate of the
        Earth*.

1983   *The Fate of the Earth* is translated into Japanese, German,
        Italian, French, Spanish, Portuguese, Finnish, and other
        languages, and begins to appear on European best-seller
        lists. *The Day After*, a TV movie depicting the effects of
        nuclear war on the city of Lawrence, Kansas, is broadcast
        on ABC on November 20; it is seen by a U.S. audience of
        over 100 million.

1984   Thomas, a son, is born in March. Alfred A. Knopf publishes
        The Abolition in June, a sequel to *The Fate of the Earth*. (It
        had appeared in *The New Yorker* in January). In September

sends a proposal for a speech on nuclear weapons and disarmament to the presidential campaign of Democratic nominee Walter Mondale, hoping unsuccessfully that they will foreground the issue. Visits with Gina and Bill Gapolinsky in Milwaukee over several months (the names changed to protect their privacy), reporting on the 1984 presidential election from the perspective of a single Wisconsin family.

1985   Receives an honorary doctorate of letters from Saint Xavier College in Chicago at its May commencement.

1986   Writes an introduction to *Letters from Prison and Other Essays* by Polish dissident and advisor to the Solidarity movement Adam Michnik, published in August: "it is now a matter of record that by far the most effective resistance movement ever launched against a totalitarian regime was completely nonviolent." *The Fate of the Earth* goes into its ninth printing; 600,000 copies have been sold.

1987   *The New Yorker* owner S. I. Newhouse forces William Shawn to resign as the magazine's editor in chief, hiring Knopf editor Robert Gottlieb as his replacement. Schell joins more than 150 staffers and contributors in a letter asking Gottlieb to decline the position. When this effort fails, he quits in protest. With brother Orville and fellow staff writer Bill McKibben, who also quits, considers starting a new magazine and talks with potential investors. Spends the spring as a fellow at the Kennedy School's Institute of Politics at Harvard. Father dies in Danbury, Connecticut, on June 17. The same month, Knopf publishes Schell's *History in Sherman Park: An American Family and the Reagan-Mondale Election*; "Paradise," an essay on exiled Russian poet Joseph Brodsky, appears in *Granta* on June 25. In the fall, teaches a course on investigative reporting and nuclear weapons at Emory University. Contributes an introduction to Robert Del Tredici's *At Work in the Fields of the Bomb*, a collection of photographs documenting the nuclear industry; corresponds with Del Tredici over subsequent decades.

1988   *The Real War*, published by Pantheon in January, gathers his books *The Village of Ben Suc* and *The Military Half*; contributes an introductory essay that asks in retrospect "why the United States lost in Vietnam." The following month writes a friend: "My head is spinning in eight different directions as I try to figure out what life is going to look like next." Teaches courses in journalism: in the spring at New York University, over the summer at Bard College, and in the fall as Ferris Professor at Princeton. Wife Elspeth obtains New York City teaching license and begins working as a substitute kindergarten teacher. Appears in *To What End?*, a TV documentary on nuclear weapons and national security. Moves with family into a loft apartment at 104–108 Reade Street in Tribeca; schoolmate Turner Brooks, now an architect, designs the space. Is awarded a Guggenheim fellowship to work on *The Unconquerable World*, ultimately published in 2003; Roger Straus at Farrar, Straus and Giroux, with whom he has a book contract, is skeptical about the project, which seems to him "a collection of essays that might or might not work." Concentrates instead on a book about "the rising influence of demographic and survey data throughout American society," interviewing census officials, marketing executives, and political campaign operatives; tentatively titled "The Decision," it is left unfinished.

1989   Joins panel on journalism and the Chernobyl disaster at Princeton in February. *Observing the Nixon Years: "Notes and Comment" from The New Yorker on the Vietnam War and the Watergate Crisis, 1969–1975* is published by Pantheon Books in March; essay "Speak Loudly, Carry a Small Stick" appears in *Harper's* the same month. Is interviewed by Studs Terkel on WFMT radio in Chicago in May. Over the summer, returns to Bard College as part of its "Journalism from the Ground Up" program. Writes on global warming in "Our Fragile Earth," published in *Discover* in October: "the costs of error are so exorbitant that we need to act on theory alone, which is to say on prediction alone." Lectures on "The Nuclear Predicament: The New Context" at the University of Delaware.

1990   In April, travels to Atlanta to speak at a DeKalb College symposium on the environment. Signs a contract with Houghton Mifflin for *The Unconquerable World*, deliverable the following June; receives support from the MacArthur Foundation to work on the book. In September begins writing a regular column for *Newsday*. Along with Anita Brookner, Barbara Ehrenreich, Studs Terkel, his brother Orville, and other writers, ends relationship with publisher Pantheon Books after the resignation of its editorial director André Schiffrin, who refuses to fire staff and to increase profit margins at whatever cost.

1991   Travels in post-Communist Poland in the fall.

1992   William Shawn—"the most astonishing and wonderful man I have ever met"—dies on December 8.

1993   Continues as *Newsday* columnist, writing on U.S. politics and international affairs. Lectures on "Nuclear Weapons in the Post Cold War" at Bennington College.

1994   Visits Hungary in March, Romania in September, and Russia in October, reporting for *Newsday*; also writes columns on North Korea's violation of the Nuclear Non-proliferation Treaty, the Whitewater affair, the war in the former Yugoslavia, the trial of O. J. Simpson, and other subjects.

1995   In May joins Daniel Ellsberg, William Sloane Coffin, Arthur Miller, and others at a rally outside the United Nations in support of extending and strengthening the Nuclear Non-Proliferation Treaty. On August 6, speaks at an event organized by the Coalition for Peace Action at Princeton University, observing the fiftieth anniversary of the bombing of Hiroshima. In the fall, proposes a special issue of *The Nation* exploring the potential abolition of nuclear weapons in the post–Cold War era. Over the next several years interviews dozens of American, former Soviet, and European officials and policy experts for the project.

1996   Attends Republican National Convention in San Diego for *Newsday* in August. Essay "The Uncertain Leviathan" appears in *The Atlantic* the same month; an account of the 1996 presidential race, it argues that both political parties "appear to the public to be an undifferentiated establishment—a new Leviathan—composed of rich, famous, powerful people who are divorced from the lives of ordinary people and indifferent to their concerns." Leaving *Newsday*, begins a yearlong fellowship at the Freedom Forum Media Studies Center.

1997   *Writing in Time: A Political Chronicle* is published by Moyer Bell in January; it gathers his *Newsday* columns on the election, first term, and reelection of Bill Clinton. Interviews former Soviet president Mikhail Gorbachev on April 14 and former West German chancellor Helmut

Schmidt on April 30. Is appointed distinguished visiting writer at Wesleyan University, serving until 2002 and in subsequent years attending the Wesleyan Writers Conference.

1998   Is named Harold Willens Peace Fellow at the Nation Institute and *The Nation*'s peace and disarmament correspondent. On February 2, *The Nation* publishes "The Gift of Time"; along with Gorbachev and Schmidt it includes interviews with Barry Blechman, Bruce G. Blair, General George Lee Butler, Robert S. McNamara, and Alan Cranston. Henry Holt publishes an expanded version in October, *The Gift of Time: The Case for Abolishing Nuclear Weapons Now*. Delivers the Cranbrook Peace Lecture in Detroit.

1999   Speaks at Earlham College on nuclear arms abolition in January. *The Fate of the Earth* is listed among the best 100 works of twentieth-century American journalism by a panel of judges at New York University. In October receives Lannan Literary Award for Nonfiction, and a $75,000 prize. Gives keynote addresses at the annual dinner of Pennsylvania Peace Links in Pittsburgh and at the annual peace and justice convocation of the Christian Conference of Connecticut.

2000   Travels to Kosovo in April, speaking to a packed hall in Prishtina as part of The New School's "Democracy Seminar" program. Presents "The Case for Abolishing Nuclear Weapons Now" at the University of Notre Dame, Goshen College, and Willamette University; gives keynote at New York conference "The Second Nuclear Age and the Academy," organized by Robert Jay Lifton. Is diagnosed with chronic lymphocytic leukemia.

2001   Speaks on "Facing the Challenge of the Nuclear Age" at a dinner of New Jersey Peace Action in May, and at a June rally at the Capitol opposing the Bush administration's plans for national missile defense. Is awarded an honorary Doctor of Laws by the University of Massachusetts. Returns from a trip to London just before the terror attacks of September 11; living only eight blocks from the World Trade Center, is forced to move in with relatives uptown for several weeks. Begins a new column for *The Nation*, "Letter from Ground Zero." ("The strength now needed," he writes in October, "is the strength of restraint. Restraint does not mean inaction; it means patience, discrimination, action in concert with other nations, resolve over the long haul.") In November, Verso publishes *The Unfinished Twentieth Century: The Crisis of Weapons of Mass Destruction*, expanding an essay published in *Harper's* the previous January.

2002   In June, on the twentieth anniversary of the 1982 nuclear freeze protests in New York, issues "End the Nuclear Danger: An Urgent Call" with Randall Caroline Forsberg and David Cortright. Joins Rep. Edward J. Markey at a Washington press conference opposing Bush administration nuclear weapons policies. In the fall, serves as a fellow at the Shorenstein Center for Media, Politics, and Public Policy at Harvard's Kennedy School. Travels in Austria, Slovenia, and Japan over the summer. Lectures at Scripps College, Colgate University, and the University of Notre Dame.

2003   Reports for *The Nation* on the February 15 global demonstrations against the imminent invasion of Iraq. Debates Michael Ignatieff on the *Charlie Rose* show on PBS, opposing the Bush administration's war plans. On March 3, publishes "One Last Time: The Case Against the War" in *The Nation*; joins a teach-in against the war at American University later that month. *The Unconquerable World: Power, Nonviolence, and the Will of the People* is published by Henry Holt in June. *The New York Times* reviewer Richard Falk calls it his "most ambitious" work and one that "over time will be regarded as his most significant." Teaches a course on the nuclear dilemma at Yale Law School. In October, gives keynote address at the University of Wisconsin–Oshkosh's Earth Charter Community Summit.

2004   Lectures on "The United States in the Second Nuclear Age: Republic or Empire" at Gettysburg College in January and at Lake Forest College in March. *A Hole in the World: An Unfolding Story of War, Protest, and the New American Order* is published by Nation Books in June; it gathers his "Letters from Ground Zero" columns for *The Nation*. Contributes essay "Invitation to a Degraded World" to *Final Edition*, a single-issue journal published in the fall by Wallace Shawn. It decries a new "misinformation age," calling "the national capacity . . . to produce and consume illusion" the "specific form of corruption most dangerous to American democracy." In November, Nation Books publishes *The Jonathan Schell Reader*.

2005 Serves as distinguished visiting fellow at the Yale Center for the Study of Globalization; continues teaching at Yale until his death.

2006 Joins Helen Caldicott at the New School in New York and Rebecca Solnit at the Chicago Public Library for discussions of "the dangers of a prospective revival of nuclear power and weapons in the twenty-first century." Contributes an introduction to Hannah Arendt's *On Revolution*.

2007 *The Seventh Decade: The New Shape of Nuclear Danger* is published by Henry Holt in November.

2008 Moves to Brooklyn, New York; spends the last years of his life with Irena Gross.

2009 Travels in Poland in September.

2010 Teaches Strategic, Political, and Moral Dilemmas of the Nuclear Age and Nonviolence and Political Power in the Twentieth Century as a visiting professor at Yale, a position he holds until his death; works with students in nuclear disarmament group Global Zero. Contributes essay "In Search of a Miracle: Hannah Arendt and the Atomic Bomb" to collection *Politics in Dark Times: Encounters with Hannah Arendt*.

2011–14 Reads from his works at an Occupy Wall Street event in February 2011. Dies at home, in Brooklyn, on March 25, 2014, after a long struggle with chronic lymphocytic leukemia; during his final years works on an unfinished book about climate change, *The Human Shadow*. After cremation, he is buried in a family plot on Martha's Vineyard.

Note on the Texts

This volume contains the complete texts of three works by Jonathan Schell: *The Fate of the Earth* (1982), *The Abolition* (1984), and *The Unconquerable World: Power, Nonviolence, and the Will of the People* (2003/4). The texts of *The Fate of the Earth* and *The Abolition* have been taken from first printings, published by Alfred A. Knopf. The text of *The Unconquerable World* has been taken from the first British edition, published by Allen Lane in 2004; Schell revised this edition, updating the first U.S. edition of 2003 with a brief discussion of subsequent events in the Iraq War.

Schell wrote *The Fate of the Earth* and *The Abolition* while working at *The New Yorker*, where both first appeared in print, the former on February 1, 8, and 15, 1982, and the latter on January 2 and 9, 1984. Both were first published in book form by Alfred A. Knopf in New York, the firm accelerating its usual production schedule to make them available as quickly as possible; *The Fate of the Earth* appeared in early April 1982, *The Abolition* in May 1984. ("I immediately wanted the whole world to read it," Schell's editor at Knopf, Robert Gottlieb, later explained of *The Fate of the Earth*.) In the case of both works, the *New Yorker* and Knopf texts differ modestly, those in *The New Yorker* reflecting deliberate condensation and those printed by Knopf prepared with Schell's participation and approval. Drafts, galleys, and page proofs of *The Fate of the Earth*, and drafts of *The Abolition*, are among Schell's papers at the New York Public Library.

Schell is not known to have corrected or revised either work after its initial printing, though both were reprinted on multiple occasions and subsequent editions of each appeared in the U.S. and in Great Britain. The texts of *The Fate of the Earth* and *The Abolition* in the present volume have been taken from the Knopf first printings.

Schell began *The Unconquerable World* in 1988, fifteen years before it was finally published. He received a Guggenheim fellowship that year to work on the book, and he sent an abstract and outline to Roger Straus at Farrar, Straus and Giroux, proposing *The Unconquerable World* as a replacement for another book he had promised the firm—a sequel to *The Fate of the Earth* and *The Abolition*, on the contemporary nuclear dilemma. Straus was unhappy about the proposed substitution, describing *The Unconquerable World* as Schell had outlined it as "a collection of essays that might or might not work." Yet another project began to occupy Schell's attention as well: with

759

the permission of the Guggenheim Foundation, he spent his fellow-ship year instead on *The Decision*, a book not ultimately completed, about the increasing importance of demographic and consumer data in American life.

Schell returned to *The Unconquerable World* in 1990, receiving a second fellowship to support his work, from the MacArthur Foundation, and signing a contract with Houghton Mifflin, his manuscript due in June 1991. Still at work, he signed a new contract with Henry Holt in May 1995, returning his Houghton Mifflin advance. A little more than seven years later, in a letter of August 19, 2002, Sara Bershtel at Henry Holt accepted his completed manuscript, calling it "truly exciting, provocative, original, and unexpectedly—for so theoretical a topic—concrete." She also suggested revisions, listing a number of points at which she thought Schell's prose could be improved and recommending the addition of the subtitle with which the book was ultimately published. Schell accepted her suggestions as he had those of several readers over the course of the book's evolution (see his acknowledgments on page 714 of the present volume). He is not known to have been involved in the preparation of two excerpts from the book that appeared in *Harper's* in April and May 2003, under the title "No More Unto the Breach."

The Unconquerable World: Power, Nonviolence, and the Will of the People was published by Henry Holt in June 2003. While the first edition was at the press, on March 20, 2003, the United States invaded Iraq. Schell took advantage of the subsequent publication of a British edition, by Allen Lane in London on March 25, 2004, to update his text to reflect this fact, adding a few new pages on recent events. Apart from these additions, the first U.S. and first British editions are identical; subsequent American printings follow the first American edition, and subsequent British printings the first British edition. The text included in the present volume is that of the March 2004 first British edition, published by Allen Lane.

This volume presents the texts of the printings chosen as sources but does not attempt to reproduce features of their typographic design. The texts are printed without alteration except for the correction of typographical errors. Spelling, punctuation, and capitalization are often expressive features, and they are not altered, even when inconsistent or irregular. The following is a list of typographical errors corrected, cited by page and line number: 334.15, as least as; 448.30, principle; 473.21, Mahabarata; 496.14, reigns; 547.9, imposition; 641.11, 1948; 649.29, help to; 653.28, the *The Federalist*; 655.10, George H. Bush; 666.32, form the; 675.17, asymetrical; 679.12, principle; 679.17, solution; 700.20, Margolit; 725.4, *sultan*; 728.32, *King's*.

Notes

In the notes below, the reference numbers denote page and line of this volume (the line count includes headings but not blank lines). Biblical quotations are keyed to the King James Version, and quotations from Shakespeare to *The Riverside Shakespeare*, edited by G. Blakemore Evans (Boston: Houghton Mifflin, 1974).

For Schell's original notes to *The Unconquerable World* see pages 716–41 in the present volume.

THE FATE OF THE EARTH

9.39–10.1   Dr. Robert Jay Lifton . . . immersion in death."] See Lipton's *Death in Life: Survivors of Hiroshima* (1968).

11.31–34   Einstein noted . . . energy."] See Einstein's essay "What Is the Theory of Relativity?" first published in the London *Times* on November 28, 1919.

13.36–14.3   Einstein . . . possibilities."] See Einstein's essay "Arms Can Bring No Security" from the *Bulletin of the Atomic Scientists*, March 1950.

36.25–27   "It is no exaggeration . . . ruined instantaneously."] See *Hiroshima and Nagasaki: The Physical, Medical, and Social Effects of the Atomic Bombings* (1979), edited by The Committee for the Compilation of Materials on Damage Caused by the Atomic Bomb in Hiroshima and Nagasaki.

39.9–14   Yoko Ota . . . I had read about as a child] As quoted in Lifton's *Death in Life* (1968).

39.15–17   a history professor . . . disappeared."] As quoted in Lifton's *Death in Life*.

39.23–40.2   Mikio Inoue . . . human beings.] See *Unforgettable Fire: Pictures Drawn by Atomic Bomb Survivors* (1977), edited by the Japanese Broadcasting Corporation.

71.6–11   Dr. Lewis Thomas . . . at all."] See Thomas's essay "Medical Lessons from History," collected in *The Medusa and the Snail: More Notes of a Biology Watcher* (1979).

76.25–27   B. W. Boville . . . on earth."] See Boville's paper "Stratospheric Ozone Layer Research," published in the *Proceedings of the Fourth Conference on the Climatic Impact Assessment Program* (1975), edited by Thomas M. Hard and Anthony J. Broderick.

NOTES

95.5–7   Alfred North Whitehead . . . whole world."] See "The Origins of Modern Science," chapter 1 of *Science and the Modern World* (1925).

96.18–22   Kant . . . advancing one step."] See Kant's 1783 "Prolegomena to Every Future Metaphysics That May Be Presented As a Science."

107.26–27   the remark once made by Kafka . . . us."] As reported by Kafka's friend Max Brod ("Der Dichter Franz Kafka," *Die neue Rundschau*, November 1921).

110.34–36   Hannah Arendt's words . . . realm"] See *The Human Condition* (1958).

114.9–16   Edmund Burke . . . to be born."] See *Reflections on the Revolution in France* (1790).

125.40–126.4   He said . . . thy gift."] Matthew 5:23–24.

129.12   "tomorrow's zero . . . phrase] See *The Diary of a Writer* (1873–81).

130.1–3   Lucretius . . . prostrate?"] As quoted in Michel de Montaigne's essay "That to Philosophize Is to Learn to Die," first published in his 1588 *Essays.*

130.3–6   Freud . . . as spectators."] See Freud's 1915 essay "Thoughts for the Times on War and Death."

133.3–9   Arendt . . . political relevance."] See the preface to Arendt's *Between Past and Future: Eight Exercises in Political Thought* (1961).

135.20–23   Montaigne . . . all torment!"] See "That to Philosophize Is to Learn to Die" (1588).

136.16–17   Jesus . . . into the sea.'] Luke 17:2.

139.23–25   the recent words . . . the sea."] See Kennan's "A Modest Proposal," published in *The New York Review of Books* on July 16, 1981.

142.9–11   T. S. Eliot's . . . whimper"] From Eliot's "The Hollow Men" (1925).

146.1–4   Christ's admonition . . . one of these"] Matthew 6:28–29.

148.16–19   Love's not Time's . . . doom.] Shakespeare, Sonnet 116 (1609).

152.39–153.1   "are able to break . . . Auden).] From Auden's October 1967 lecture "Words and the Word," collected in *Secondary Worlds* (1968).

153.8–9   Camus's lovely remark . . . earth"] From Camus's preface to the 1958 edition of *L'envers et l'endroit* (*The Wrong Side and the Right Side*), subsequently translated as part of his *Lyrical and Critical Essays* (1967).

153.39–40   "onslaught . . . Arendt's phrase] See Arendt's essay "The Crisis in Education," collected in *Between Past and Future: Eight Exercises in Political Thought* (1961): "the world, too, needs protection to keep it from being overrun and destroyed by the onslaught of the new that bursts upon it with each new generation."

154.22–34 Harold Rosenberg . . . spectator-participant."] See section 18 ("Confrontation") of *The De-definition of Art: Action Art to Pop to Earthworks* (1972).

157.6–17 David Rousset . . . absolute solitude.] From Rousset's *Les jours de notre mort* (1947), as translated by Hannah Arendt in *The Origins of Totalitarianism* (1951).

163.7–8 "the summer . . . Herzen).] See Isaiah Berlin's translation of what he calls Herzen's "personal credo" in his 1968 essay "Herzen and His Memoirs": "Art, and the summer lightning of individual happiness: these are the only real goods we have."

163.37–38 "For unto us a child is born."] Isaiah 9:6.

165.1–2 Shakespeare says . . . finds,"] See Shakespeare's Sonnet 116, first published in 1609.

165.37–166.1 Augustine wrote . . . things alone."] From Augustine's *Confessions*, in John Kenneth Ryan's translation of 1960.

170.24–25 "modest hopes of human beings,"] See page 40, lines 1–2 in the present volume.

175.36–39 the words of Clausewitz . . . an extreme."] From the opening chapter of Clausewitz's posthumously published treatise *On War* (1832).

187.12–13 "love the bomb,"] From the subtitle of the film *Dr. Strangelove; or, How I Learned to Stop Worrying and Love the Bomb* (1964).

190.3–5 Herman Kahn . . . inexorable commitment."] See Kahn's *Thinking About the Unthinkable* (1962).

190.16–28 Thomas Schelling . . . adversary with him."] See *The Strategy of Conflict* (1960), chapter III.

212.3–4 as George Kennan suggested] See note 139.23–25.

213.27–31 What Gandhi . . . 'external enemy.'"] From the first volume of Gandhi's *Non-Violence in Peace & War* (1942).

214.25–29 E. M. Forster . . . save the world."] See Forster's novel *Howards End* (1910), Auden's poem "September 1, 1939" (from *Another Time*, 1940), and John 12:47.

THE ABOLITION

223.19–20 William James . . . deterrence.] See "The Moral Equivalent of War," an essay by philosopher William James (1842–1910) first published in *McClure's Magazine* in August 1910.

226.24–26 the breakdown . . . Reduction Talks] The Strategic Arms Limitation Talks (SALT) between the United States and the Soviet Union began in Helsinki in November 1969 and led to the ratification of the Anti-Ballistic Missile Treaty of 1972. Continued as SALT II, these negotiations broke down in the wake of the 1979 Soviet invasion of Afghanistan and were succeeded by a round of Strategic Arms Reduction Talks (START) in 1982; the first START Treaty was signed in 1991, after the publication of *The Abolition* (1984).

240.10   in the Latin . . . ages."] *Novus ordo seclorum*, a Latin motto adapted from Virgil's fourth *Eclogue* for the Great Seal of the United States, by Charles Thomson (1729–1824), secretary of the Continental Congress, in 1782.

242.3–4   war . . . other means."] See the posthumous treatise *On War* (1832) by Prussian general Carl von Clausewitz (1780–1831).

269.38   McGeorge Bundy] See "The Bishops and the Bomb"; Bundy (1919–1996) had previously served as national security advisor to Presidents Kennedy and Johnson.

294.30–295.10   Herman Kahn . . . the next decade.] From Kahn's lecture "The Nature and Feasibility of Thermonuclear War," first collected in *On Thermonuclear War* (1961).

295.26–296.4   George Rathjens . . . seizure at that.] See Rathjens's essay "The Conditions Necessary for Complete Nuclear Disarmament: The Case for Partial Nuclear Disarmament," in *A New Design for Nuclear Disarmament: Pugwash Symposium, Kyoto, Japan* (1977), edited by William Epstein and Toshiyuki Toyoda.

296.36–40   Bertrand Russell . . . bombs as possible.] From a letter Russell wrote to Albert Einstein on February 11, 1955.

304.2–3   Clausewitz's words . . . an extreme"] See note 242.3–4.

305.35–38   Einstein . . . unparalleled catastrophe."] Einstein's remark appears in a telegram he sent to several hundred prominent Americans on May 23, 1946, in support of the Emergency Committee of Atomic Scientists.

310.32   Mandelbaum's . . . possible,"] See *The Nuclear Revolution: International Politics Before and After Hiroshima* (1981) by Michael Mandelbaum (b. 1946).

331.28–29   this year . . . George Orwell] See Orwell's dystopian novel *1984*, first published in 1949.

THE UNCONQUERABLE WORLD

373.34–374.1   Jesus . . . die by the sword."] See Matthew 26:52.

378.14   Vorkuta and Kolyma] Sites of Soviet forced labor camps.

380.35–36   William James called . . . equivalent of war."] See note 223.19–20.

381.19   Jan Palach] Czech student (1948–1969) who set himself on fire on January 16, 1969, in the wake of the Soviet invasion of Czechoslovakia.

391.16–19 Benjamin Constant . . . institutions"] From Constant's 1796 pamphlet *De la force du gouvernement actuel de la France et de la nécessité de s'y rallier.*

391.19–21 Thomas Carlyle . . . Democracy"] From Carlyle's *The French Revolution* (1837), part 1, book 4.

392.18–20 Adolphe Thiers . . . military achievements."] See volume 3 of Thiers's *History of the French Revolution*, originally published as *Histoire de la Révolution Française* (1823–27).

399.13–18 "The Great Powers . . . wage war."] See Taylor's *The Struggle for Mastery in Europe, 1848–1918* (1954).

400.3–12 Joseph Stalin . . . socialist economy."] From a speech Stalin gave at the First All-Union Conference of Leading Personnel of Socialist Industry on February 4, 1931, sometimes translated as "The Tasks of Economic Executives."

401.15–16 Charles Tilly . . . made war."] See *The Formation of National States in Western Europe* (1975).

401.26–30 Francis Bacon . . . all time."] See Bacon's *Novum Organum* (1620), section cxxix.

403.27–30 "Here begins . . . was involved."] From Jules Michelet's 1847 *History of the French Revolution.*

406.12–14 Frederic Seebohm . . . absence of mind,"] See *The Expansion of England* (1883).

418.39–419.1 Winston Churchill . . . annihilation."] From Churchill's last major speech to the House of Commons, delivered on March 1, 1955.

431.22–23 Leonard Woolf . . . world revolt,"] See *Imperialism and Civilization* (1928).

439.30–31 Kipling's . . . the law"] See "Kitchener's School," first published in the London *Times* on December 8, 1898.

440.11 Maxim guns] One of the first fully automatic machine guns, introduced in 1884 and named after its inventor, Hiram Stevens Maxim (1840–1916).

459.10 power . . . a gun"] See *Quotations from Chairman Mao Tse-tung* (1964), which popularized a phrase Mao is reported to have first used in 1927.

466.11 Judith M. Brown titles her chapter] See Brown's 1989 biography *Gandhi: Prisoner of Hope.*

470.12–13 Wat Tyler, John Hampden, John Bunyan] Tyler died in 1381 as a leader of the Great Rising or Peasants' Revolt, which opposed the imposition of a poll tax; Hampden (c. 1594–1643) challenged the authority of Charles I as a member of parliament and died in the succeeding English Civil War; Bunyan (1628–1688), the author of *The Pilgrim's Progress* (1678), spent twelve years in prison for religious nonconformism.

474.2–5   "Love your enemy . . . thy sword."] See Matthew 5:44, 6:14, and 26:52.

474.12–13   "Render . . . Caesar's."] Matthew 22:21.

474.16–17   Jesus answered . . . this world."] John 18:36.

497.26–27   "risen to . . . Rosa Luxemburg] The phrase appears in "The Problem of Nationalities," a chapter of Leon Trotsky's 1930 *History of the Russian Revolution* as translated by Max Eastman in 1932, in which Trotsky addresses Luxemburg's posthumously published essay "The Russian Revolution" (1922).

536.9   Gauleiters] Provincial governors in Nazi Germany.

540.38   his biographer John Keane] See *Tom Paine: A Political Life* (1995).

548.11   *hommes moyens sensuels.*] Men of ordinary appetites.

554.24–27   "For the tsars . . . hierarchy of values."] See *Boris Yeltsin: From Bolshevik to Democrat* (1991) by John Morrison, which paraphrases Pipes.

562.16–17   Burke . . . is power."] See *Reflections on the Revolution in France* (1790).

583.37–38   Malcolm X . . . bloodshed,"] From a speech given on March 8, 1964, as quoted by *The New York Times* the following day.

594.16–19   Allister Sparks . . . lesser role."] See *Tomorrow Is Another Country: The Inside Story of South Africa's Road to Change* (1995).

595.4–6   Francis Fukuyama . . . history."] Fukuyama's essay "The End of History?" first appeared in *The National Interest* in the summer of 1989; he subsequently expanded it as *The End of History and the Last Man* (1992).

597.32–33   Thomas Friedman . . . straitjacket."] See *The Lexus and the Olive Tree* (1999).

617.33–34   historian E. H. Carr . . . indivisible."] See *The Twenty Years' Crisis, 1919–1939: An Introduction to the Study of International Relations* (1946).

639.12   Rhoda Broughton] Broughton (1840–1920) was a Welsh writer of novels and short fiction.

644.1–4   Winston Churchill . . . swept the world."] See Churchill's *The Aftermath: A Sequel to the World Crisis* (1929).

688.5   Michael Mazarr . . . arsenals."] See "Virtual Nuclear Arsenals," *Survival: Global Politics and Strategy*, Autumn 1995.

Index

Huntington, Samuel P., 224
Hutchinson, Thomas, 512
Hutus, 643
Hydrogen bomb, 13, 15–18, 35, 232,
 250, 296, 422, 553

Ideal war, 386–88, 393
Iklé, Fred, 76
Imperialism, 399–400, 405–422,
 430–32, 437–42, 451, 453, 467,
 469, 477–78, 486, 492–93, 535, 537,
 556, 577, 583, 588, 595–96, 598–601,
 604, 606–11, 636, 641–43, 650–52,
 672–78, 711–13
Indenture, 467–78
India, 70, 466, 533, 711; British rule
 of, 379, 409, 438–39, 465, 470–71,
 474, 478–96, 545, 547, 550–51, 560,
 573, 606–8, 642; independence,
 432–33, 442, 465, 496, 513, 518,
 641–44; and Kashmir, 381, 481, 641,
 648, 695, 698–99; nuclear capability,
 351, 377, 644, 646–48, 655, 658–59,
 667–68, 672, 685
Indian Opinion, 470–71, 478, 494
Indians, in South Africa, 466–79,
 489–91, 508, 583–84, 591
Indonesia, 590, 597, 652
Industrialism, 405, 611
Industrial revolution, 239, 399–400,
 404–5, 411, 505
Inner Mongolia, 199
Inoue, Mikio, 39–40
Institute of International Studies, 249
International Criminal Court, 658, 705
International Institute for Strategic
 Studies, 53
Internationalism, liberal, 604–17
International Monetary Fund, 651
Iran, 30, 196–98, 407, 415, 432, 590,
 597, 642, 646, 652, 657–58, 672, 701
Iraq, 415, 642, 645–46, 652, 655,
 657–58, 663, 673–74, 701
Ireland, 471, 606, 627, 641–43,
 695–700
Irish Americans, 627
Irish Republican Army, 699
Isaac, Jeffrey C., 703
Islamists, 597, 656, 674
Israel, 70, 377, 641–43, 659, 672, 685,
 687, 700, 703

Italy, 409, 439, 589, 595, 605, 610

Jacobins, 403, 517–18
James, Henry, 639, 660, 662
James, William, 223, 380, 678
James II, 498–503, 507–8, 519
Japan, 63, 69–70, 149, 166, 479, 595,
 653, 672, 674; atomic bombing of,
 5, 35–44, 339, 418, 448; invasion of
 China, 443–45, 447–48, 450, 458,
 480, 610; opening of, 406, 438–39;
 war with Russia, 431, 442, 471;
 World War II, 339, 416, 418, 430–31,
 455. *See also* Hiroshima, atomic
 bombing of; Nagasaki, atomic
 bombing of
Jarrell, Randall, 110
Jaspers, Karl: *The Future of Mankind*,
 122–23, 126
Jay, John, 653
Jefferson, Thomas, 511–12, 514, 563, 681
Jena, battle of, 386
Jenin, 381
Jerusalem, 374, 381, 572, 700
Jesus, 126–26, 136, 146, 214, 373–75,
 473–74, 552, 567, 587
Jews, 133, 136–37, 156–57, 181, 221, 561,
 587, 625, 700, 703
Jim Crow laws, 584
Jirous, Ivan, 546
Job, 165
Johannesburg, South Africa, 476
John Paul II, 221, 225
Johnson, Lyndon B., 182, 457, 585
Jomini, Henri, 436
Jones, T. K., 226
Jouvenal, Bertrand de, 563–64, 572
Joy, Bill, 649
Juan Carlos, 589
Just war, 282

Kafka, Franz, 107, 153
Kahn, Herman, 190–92, 258–59, 294–
 95; *On Thermonuclear War*, 300;
 Thinking about the Unthinkable, 132
Kamenev, Lev, 522–23
Kant, Immanuel, 96, 117, 709; "Idea
 for a Universal History," 578;
 "Perpetual Peace," 598
Karamanlis, Constantine, 588
Karmal, Babrak, 196

Nitrogen oxides, 21, 72, 78–79, 86, 88–89, 103

Nixon, Richard M., 76, 127, 190, 457–58

Nobel Prize, 152, 156

Nogin, Viktor, 523

Nonaggression, 313–14

Noncooperation, 486–87, 490–95, 497, 511–12, 514, 562

Nonviolence, 379–81, 385, 442, 459, 461–573, 577–80, 582, 584–86, 588, 603–4, 639, 681–82, 712

Nonviolent revolution, 463, 497, 504, 508, 531, 578, 580, 590, 677, 680–81

North American Air Defense Command, 27

North Atlantic Treaty Organization, 178, 198, 226, 263–67, 425, 654–55, 709–10

Northern Ireland, 627, 642, 695–700

North Korea, 69, 646, 648, 657–58, 661, 667, 672, 678

North Vietnam, 196, 198, 349–50, 451–52, 455–57

Nuclear arms control talks, 101, 127, 196, 199, 226, 266, 278, 285, 293, 316, 322, 338, 341, 354, 418

Nuclear arms freeze, 284–85, 287, 307, 338, 355

Nuclear arms race, 258–60, 278, 294, 343, 416–17

Nuclear Nonproliferation Treaty, 101, 322, 645, 672, 685

Nuclear reactors, banning of, 340–41

Nuclear terror, 417–19, 650

Nuclear terrorism, 59, 101, 242, 650, 660–61, 669, 692

Nuclear-war-fighting, 271–77, 279–80, 309–10, 316, 330

Nuclear weapons, 213, 375–77, 379, 385, 413–29, 448, 452–54, 458–60, 481, 534, 539, 550–51, 553, 577, 591, 640, 644–50, 654–55, 657–61, 664–73, 678, 684–92, 708, 711–12

Nuclear winter, 233–35, 237, 261, 292

Nuclear Winter: Global Consequences of Multiple Nuclear Explosions, 234

Nuremberg trials, 705

Nye, Joseph S., Jr., 224

Obruchev, Nikolai, 409–10

Office of Civil Defense, 7–9

Office of Technology Assessment, 6, 19, 57, 71

Ogasawara, Haruko, 37–38

Oil, 32, 196–98, 268, 347

Olympic Games (1980), 196

Omaha, Neb., 18

Omdurman, battle of, 439–42, 478, 491, 602

Opium Wars, 439

Oppenheimer, Robert, 236, 250, 255, 327

Oregon State University, 83

Organization of American States, 709

Orlov, Yuri, 553

Ortega y Gasset, José: *The Revolt of the Masses*, 391

Orwell, George, 331, 535–36, 549

Ota, Yoko, 39

Ottoman Empire, 406, 430, 439, 479, 554, 606–7, 622, 642

Oxford University, 501

Ozone layer, 21, 23, 25, 72, 76–88, 90, 103, 232, 235, 237, 240

Padmanabhan, S., 659

Pahlavi, Mohammad Reza, 590, 652

Paine, Thomas, 511, 540–41; *The American Crisis*, 509–10; *Common Sense*, 605

Pakistan, 377, 481, 518, 641–44, 646–49, 652, 655, 667–68, 672, 685

Palach, Jan, 381

Palestine mandate, 642

Palestinian Authority, 659

Palestinians, 377, 641–43, 650, 659, 689, 695, 700, 703

Palmerston, Viscount (Henry John Temple), 406

Paret, Peter, 393

Paris, France, 348, 515–17, 530, 563, 641

Parity, 263

Park Chung Hee, 652

Parliament, British, 169, 183, 470, 480, 490, 498–99, 501–6, 510, 621–22, 627, 630, 632–33, 697

Parliament, European, 696, 710

Parliament, French, 613

Parliament, Indian, 646, 658

Parliament, South African, 582

Parthia, 433

Pascal, Blaise, 139

318, 334, 350, 379, 534–40, 544–48, 552–54, 710; *glasnost*, 538, 553–55; under Gorbachev, 537, 553–59, 594, 682–83; labor camps, 156, 378, 460, 536; Nazi-Soviet Pact, 557; nuclear capability, 6–8, 28–35, 45, 50, 52–53, 63, 69–70, 100–101, 177–78, 182, 184, 186, 189, 193, 196–99, 206, 212, 223, 226–27, 233, 242, 251, 256–58, 263–68, 271–78, 281, 284, 293–94, 315–16, 323, 336, 338, 346, 351, 364, 415–16, 418, 421–27, 453, 645, 654–55, 657, 667–68; *perestroika*, 537, 553–55; under Stalin, 133, 136, 400, 529, 532, 535, 557, 598; World War II, 241, 376, 445, 448, 665

Soyinka, Wole, 593
Soyuz, 558
Space-based defense, 272, 284–85
Space exploration, 68, 144, 233, 559
Spain, 430–36, 438, 448–49, 544, 588–89, 595, 652
Sparks, Allister, 594
Sparta, ancient, 579
Species loss, 104–11
Speech, freedom of, 584, 601, 622
Spiegel, Der, 266
Sputnik, 450, 453
Sri Lanka, 600, 695, 698–700
SS-4/SS-18/SS-19/SS-20 missiles, 28, 50–51, 265
Stability, 309, 313, 315–17, 325, 327, 351, 355–57, 365
Stalin, Joseph, 133, 136, 400, 527, 529, 532, 535, 545, 553–55, 558, 566, 598, 689
Standing armies, 653
State Department, U.S., 537, 646, 673
State of nature, 304–6, 308, 317, 577–78
State terror, 418, 452, 535, 561, 564
Stephen (saint), 572
Stern, Vernon M., 61
Stimson, Henry, 139
Stockholm International Peace Research Institute, 646
Strategic Air Command, 54
Strategic Arms Limitation Talks, 101, 196, 199, 226, 266, 278, 338, 355
Strategic Arms Reduction Talks, 226, 338, 355, 654, 658

Strategic Offensive Reduction Agreement, 658
Strategic thinking, 181–93, 205, 208, 237, 249–51, 258, 262, 271, 278, 280, 294, 310, 316, 321, 326, 332–33, 346, 365
Strontium-90, 59–60
Stuart dynasty, 505
Student Nonviolent Coordinating Committee, 584, 587
Sudan, 408–10, 439–43, 478, 602
Suez crisis, 689
Suharto, 590, 652
Suicide bombings, 377, 650, 659, 682
Sukhanov, Nikolai, 520, 524–26, 529–30
Sun Microsystems, 649
Supreme Court, U.S., 586, 634
"Survival of Food Crops and Livestock in the Event of Nuclear War," 6–7, 60–61
Switzerland, 343, 646
Sykes-Picot Agreement, 610
Syria, 642, 658, 672, 701
Szilard, Leo, 100, 646–47

Taiwan, 590, 661
Takenaka, Professor, 39
Tamils, 698–700
Tashkent, 442
Tatars, 442
Taylor, A. J. P., 399, 439, 561, 572
Taylor, Theodore, 236
Technological progress, 469–70, 480–81, 487
Technology of war, 405, 412–14, 437, 649, 653
Temple University, 81
Tennessee Valley Authority, 255
Territorial war, 641
Terror: balance of, 417–18, 664–66, 669–71, 676, 681–82, 690; nuclear, 417–19, 650, 658; state, 418, 452, 535, 561, 564
Terrorism, 381, 491, 601, 645–46; nuclear terrorism, 59, 101, 242, 650, 660–61, 669, 692–93; revolutionary, 464, 471, 515; September 11th attacks, 377–79, 596, 639, 646, 648, 656–59, 661–63, 674; solution to, 691–92, 704; suicide bombings, 377,

*This book is set in 10 point ITC Galliard Pro, a face
designed for digital composition by Matthew Carter and based
on the sixteenth-century face Granjon. The paper is acid-free
lightweight opaque that will not turn yellow or brittle with age.
The binding is sewn, which allows the book to open easily and lie flat.
The binding board is covered in Brillianta, a woven rayon cloth
made by Van Heek–Scholco Textielfabrieken, Holland.
Composition by Gopa & Ted2, Inc.
Printing and binding by LSC Communications.
Designed by Bruce Campbell.*